Kitchen & Bath
Source Book

Sweet's Group/McGraw-Hill, Inc.
1221 Avenue of the Americas
New York, New York 10020

GREAT HOMES DEMAND BROAN PRODUCTS

When selecting built-in products for your home, chances are you'll make your decision on the basis of style, convenience and — undoubtedly — quality.

For decades, builders of America's most beautiful homes have turned to Broan — the world leader in home ventilation and specialty products — for those very reasons.

Any one of fourteen product lines will make your home a dramatically more comfortable and pleasing environment. So do your great home justice, and ask for more information on any of the great product lines from Broan.

Just check the appropriate boxes and send your request to Broan, along with your name, address and $2.00 to cover postage and handling.

❏ Range Hoods
❏ Medicine Cabinets & Lights
❏ Bath Fans & Fan/Lights
❏ Door Chimes
❏ Central Vacuum Systems
❏ Music Intercom Systems
❏ Ceiling Fans
❏ Trash Compactors
❏ Whole House Ventilators

❏ Powered Attic Ventilators
❏ Wall Mounted Hair Dryers
❏ Ironing Centers
❏ Vanities
❏ Heaters

BROAN ®

A NORTEK COMPANY

P.O. Box 140 Hartford, WI 53027 **1-800-548-0790**

BR-5-2

Sweet's Group

1221 Avenue of the Americas
New York, New York 10020-1095
Telephone 212/512-3848
FAX 212/512-3441

Stephen B. Bonner
President
Construction Information Group

March 1994

Welcome to the *Kitchen & Bath Source Book*:

If you're like most homeowners today, the very first place you'll look to maximize your investment in your home is the kitchen or the bathroom. It's these two areas that will most readily translate into increased resale value <u>and</u> a more pleasant lifestyle while you own your home.

McGraw-Hill's *Kitchen & Bath Source Book* shows you literally hundreds of products, colors and design ideas **using the manufacturers own catalogs** in an easy-to-use book format. No need to hunt down dozens of brochures only to misplace the one you really wanted at the moment you're ready to move ahead. Everything is right where you left it—between the covers of the *Kitchen & Bath Source Book*.

The Sweet's Group, publishers of the *Kitchen & Bath Source Book*, along with our associates from McGraw-Hill's Construction Information Group at F.W. Dodge, Architectural Record, Engineering News Record, and the Construction News Publications Network, have embarked on a strategic thinking journey to refocus our entire business on you: our *customer*.

While this journey has just begun, I believe that you will see its effect during 1994. For us to succeed in our vision of helping you succeed, we need a candid and interactive relationship with you to guide our actions for the future. To that end, I invite you to share your thoughts, concerns or suggestions as to how Sweet's can become even more valuable to you. My address, telephone and fax numbers appear on this letter, and I look forward to hearing from you.

In the meantime, I hope the *Kitchen & Bath Source Book* provides the products and ideas you need to successfully plan and build a kitchen or bath perfectly designed to suit your family's needs.

Sincerely,

Stephen B. Bonner

Sweet's Group

McGraw-Hill, Inc.
1221 Avenue of the Americas
New York, NY 10020

Regional Offices

Chicago, IL 60601
180 North Stetson Avenue, Suite 700
312-616-3213 • 312-616-3236 – fax
Regional Publisher - Joseph J. Pepitone

Cleveland, OH 44115
1255 Euclid Avenue, 3rd Floor
216-574-2135 • 216-566-1456 – fax
Regional Publisher - Gary E. Darbey

Dallas, TX 75240
14850 Quorum Drive, Suite 380
214-991-4032 • 214-991-8630 – fax
Regional Publisher - Katherine E. Louis

Miami, FL 33174
8700 West Flagler Street, Suite 100
305-223-4470 • 305-220-7444 – fax
Regional Publisher - John A. Fox

New York, NY 10019
1633 Broadway, 13th Floor
212-512-3181 • 212-512-6831 – fax
Vice President/Publisher - Susan F. Leiterstein

San Francisco, CA 94105
221 Main Street, Suite 800
415-882-2885 • 415-882-2824 – fax
Regional Publisher - Nancy E. Harmon

International Offices

Chicago, IL 60601 USA
Two Prudential Plaza
180 North Stetson Avenue, Suite 700
312-616-3230 • 312-616-3236 – fax
International Marketing Specialist,
Steven Gilberg

Montreal, PQ H3G 2A5 Canada
3495 de la Montagne, Suite 11
514-842-9573 • 514-843-3166 – fax
Regional Manager –Pierre Savoie

North York, ON M2J 1R8 Canada
270 Yorkland Boulevard
416-496-3118 • 416-496-3104 – fax
Vice President International – Kenneth D. Hutt

Philadelphia, PA 19107 USA
1234 Market Street, 5th Floor
215-496-4964 • 215- 569-8078 – fax
International Marketing Specialist,
Anthony Mancini

Sweet's Electronic Publishing

99 Monroe Avenue N.W., Suite 400
Grand Rapids, MI 49503
616-732-5500 • 616-454-4150 – fax

President-Sweet's Electronic Publishing
S. Griffin Burgh, AIA

Vice President-Finance
Julie B. Campbell

General Manager-CAP Division
Daniel L. Peak

Vice President-Marketing
Craig B. Soderstrom

SweetSource-Sales Manager
Michael Fowler

President-Construction Information Group
Stephen B. Bonner

Vice President-Construction Information Group
Karl A. Spangenberg

Vice President/Publisher
Susan F. Leiterstein

Vice President-Product Management
Gloria H. Glowacki

Vice President-International
Kenneth D. Hutt

Director-Financial Operations
Scott J. August

Director-Client Service
Jeffrey O. Britt

Director-Systems Development
William E. Keller

Director-Publishing Operations
Thomas H. Koster

Director-Manufacturing Sweet's/Corp. Mfg.
Vicki L. McGehee

Director-Construction Market Services
Jane T. Morrison

Director-Technical Services
Stanley Shapiro

Director-Market Research
Alma L. Weinstein

National Consultant Manager
Martin W. Reinhart, AIA, CSI

Consultant Staff

Anaheim, CA
Albert J. Thomas, AIA, CSI

Chicago, IL
Robert C. Boettcher, AIA, CSI
Daniel C. Colella, AIA
Richard Jamiolkowski, P.E., IES, IEEE
Gary B. Keclik, AIA
Richard J. Mazzuca, AIA, CSI
Wayne W. Puchkors, AIA, CSI
Peter G. Schramm, AIA
G. Robert Steiner, S.E., ASCE, CSI
Paul A. Thogerson, AIA
John S. Vaci, AIA

Miami, FL
Dorothy H. Cox, CSI

Monrovia, CA
William E. White, AIA, CSI

New York, NY
Joseph V. Bower, AIA, CSI
Robert C. Chandler, AIA
John W. Embler, AIA
Raymond M. Hennig, AIA, CSI
E. Michael Hollander, AIA

San Francisco, CA
Cynthia Belisle, AIA, CSI

Cover photo: Celeste Design & Associates

Officers of McGraw-Hill, Inc.

Chairman & Chief Executive Officer
Joseph L. Dionne

President & Chief Operating Officer
Harold W. McGraw III

Executive Vice President - Chief Financial Officer
Robert J. Bahash

Executive Vice President - General Counsel and Secretary
Robert N. Landes

Executive Vice President - Administration
Thomas J. Sullivan

Senior Vice President - Information Management
Edward J. Heresniak

Senior Vice President & Executive Assistant to the Chairman
Barbara A. Munder

Senior Vice President - Treasury Operations
Frank D. Penglase

Chairman Emeritus
Harold W. McGraw, Jr.

The Consumer edition of the Kitchen & Bath Source Book is distributed by Macmillan Publishing Company.

ISBN 0-07-607071-9

Kitchen & Bath
Source Book

Table of Contents

To Find Information Quickly

The *Kitchen & Bath Source Book* is organized in an easy-to-use format. Catalogs are grouped by similar product type to help you quickly locate information on manufacturers and products for your kitchen and bath projects.

Coding System

Catalogs are assigned a four-character code indicating their position in the *Kitchen & Bath Source Book*.

As an example: C123

Refer to the Indexes

The *Kitchen & Bath Source Book* contains complete Firms and Products indexes:

The **Firms** index is an alphabetical list of manufacturers and their catalog codes.

The **Products** index is an alphabetical list of all products within the Book. Manufacturers and their catalog codes appear for each product heading.

The **Trade Names** index contains an alphabetical list of trade names accompanied by a brief product description and the catalog code.

Additional Services Provided by the National Kitchen & Bath Association

The National Kitchen & Bath Association (NKBA), a major industry resource, has provided a valuable reference for your use with Sweet's *Kitchen & Bath Source Book*.

Highlighted in your 1994 edition, you will find a directory of:

- 1,400 Certified Kitchen and Bath Designers.
- 2,000 Kitchen and Bath Dealers.

The NKBA has also furnished important tips, guidelines and rules addressing the latest trends in design and safety—all invaluable tools when planning your kitchen and bath—making the 1994 *Kitchen & Bath Source Book* the complete guide for designing and constructing your kitchen or bathroom.

Conversion Tables

The following tables are furnished to assist you in utilizing the information provided by building product manufacturers.

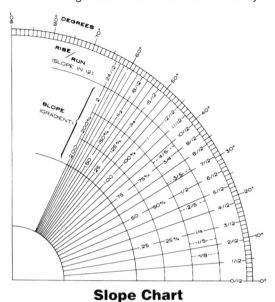

Slope Chart

Basic SI Units (Systéme International d'Unités)

physical quantity	name of unit	symbol for unit
length	metre	m
mass	kilogramme	kg
time	second	s
electric current	ampere	A
thermodynamic temperature	kelvin	K
luminous intensity	candela	cd
area	square metre	m^2
volume	cubic metre	m^3
density	kilogramme per cubic metre	kg/m^3
velocity	metre per second	m/s
angular velocity	radian per second	rad/s
acceleration	metre per second squared	m/s^2
pressure	newton per square metre	N/m^2
kinematic viscosity, diffusion coefficient	square metre per second	m^2/s
dynamic viscosity	newton second per square metre	$N\ s/m^2$
electric field strength	volt per metre	V/m
magnetic field strength	ampere per metre	A/m
luminance	candela per square metre	cd/m^2

Symbols for units do not take a plural form.

Distance

Imperial	Metric		Metric	Imperial
1 inch =	2.540 centimetres		1 centimetre =	0.3937 inch
1 foot =	0.3048 metre		1 decimetre =	0.3281 foot
1 yard =	0.9144 metre		1 metre =	3.281 feet
1 rod =	5.029 metres			= 1.094 yard
1 mile =	1.609 kilometres		1 decametre =	10.94 yards
			1 kilometre =	0.6214 mile

Weight

1 ounce (troy) =	31.103 grams		1 gram =	0.032 ounce (troy)
1 ounce (avoir) =	28.350 grams		1 gram =	0.035 ounce (avoir)
1 pound (troy) =	373.242 grams		1 kilogram =	2.679 pounds (troy)
1 pound (avoir) =	453.592 grams		1 kilogram =	2.205 pounds (avoir)
1 ton (short) =	0.907 tonne*		1 tonne =	1.102 ton (short)

*1 tonne = 1000 kilograms

Capacity

Imperial			U.S.	
1 pint =	0.568 litre		1 pint (U.S.) =	0.473 litre
1 gallon =	4.546 litres		1 quart (U.S.) =	0.946 litre
1 bushel =	36.369 litres		1 gallon (U.S.) =	3.785 litres
1 litre =	0.880 pint		1 barrel (U.S.) =	158.98 litres
1 litre =	0.220 gallon			
1 hectolitre =	2.838 bushels			

Area

1 square inch	= 6.452 square centimetres
1 square foot	= 0.093 square metre
1 square yard	= 0.836 square metre
1 acre	= 0.405 hectare*
1 square mile	= 259.0 hectares
1 square mile	= 2.590 square kilometres
1 square centimetre	= 0.155 square inch
1 square metre	= 10.76 square feet
1 square metre	= 1.196 square yard
1 hectare	= 2.471 acres
1 square kilometre	= 0.386 square mile

***1 hectare = 1 square hectometre**

Volume

1 cubic inch	= 16.387 cubic centimetres
1 cubic foot	= 0.0283 cubic decimetres
1 cubic yard	= 0.765 cubic metre
1 cubic centimetre	= 0.061 cubic inch
1 cubic decimetre	= 35.314 cubic foot
1 cubic metre	= 1.308 cubic yard

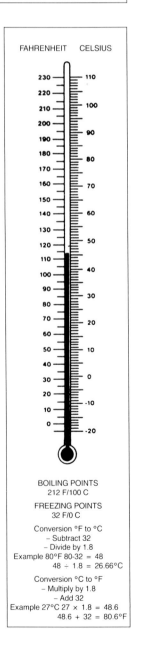

FAHRENHEIT   CELSIUS

BOILING POINTS
212 F/100 C

FREEZING POINTS
32 F/0 C

Conversion °F to °C
– Subtract 32
– Divide by 1.8
Example 80°F 80-32 = 48
48 ÷ 1.8 = 26.66°C

Conversion °C to °F
– Multiply by 1.8
– Add 32
Example 27°C 27 × 1.8 = 48.6
48.6 + 32 = 80.6°F

Conversion Tables

Inches/Feet to Millimetres

inches	millimetres	inches	millimetres	inches	millimetres	inches	millimetres	ft.	in.	millimetres
1/64	0.3969	1 27/32	46.8313	4 21/32	118.269	8 15/16	227.012	3	7	1092.20
1/32	0.7938	1 7/8	47.6250	4 11/16	119.062	9	228.600	3	8	1117.60
3/64	1.1906	1 29/32	48.4188	4 23/32	119.856	9 1/16	230.188	3	9	1143.00
1/16	1.5875	1 15/16	49.2125	4 3/4	120.650	9 1/8	231.775	3	10	1168.40
5/64	1.9844	1 31/32	50.0063	4 25/32	121.444	9 3/16	233.362	3	11	1193.80
3/32	2.3813	2	50.8000	4 13/16	122.238	9 1/4	234.950	4	0	1219.20
7/64	2.7781	2 1/32	51.5938	4 27/32	123.031	9 5/16	236.538	4	1	1244.60
1/8	3.1750	2 1/16	52.3875	4 7/8	123.825	9 3/8	238.125	4	2	1270.00
9/64	3.5719	2 3/32	53.1813	4 29/32	124.619	9 7/16	239.712	4	3	1295.40
5/32	3.9688	2 1/8	53.9750	4 15/16	125.412	9 1/2	241.300	4	4	1320.80
11/64	4.3656	2 5/32	54.7688	4 31/32	126.206	9 9/16	242.888	4	5	1346.20
3/16	4.7625	2 3/16	55.5625	5	127.000	9 5/8	244.475	4	6	1371.60
13/64	5.1594	2 7/32	56.3583	5 1/32	127.794	9 11/16	246.062	4	7	1397.00
7/32	5.5563	2 1/4	57.1500	5 1/16	128.588	9 3/4	247.650	4	8	1422.40
15/64	5.9531	2 9/32	57.9438	5 3/32	129.381	9 13/16	249.238	4	9	1447.80
1/4	6.3500	2 5/16	58.7375	5 1/8	130.175	9 7/8	250.825	4	10	1473.20
17/64	6.7469	2 11/32	59.5313	5 5/32	130.969	9 15/16	252.412	4	11	1498.60
9/32	7.1438	2 3/8	60.3250	5 3/16	131.762	10	254.000	5	0	1524.00
19/64	7.5406	2 13/32	61.1188	5 7/32	132.556	10 1/16	255.588	5	1	1549.40
5/16	7.9375	2 7/16	61.9125	5 1/4	133.350	10 1/8	257.175	5	2	1574.80
21/64	8.3344	2 15/32	62.7063	5 9/32	134.144	10 3/16	258.762	5	3	1600.20
11/32	8.7313	2 1/2	63.5000	5 5/16	134.938	10 1/4	260.350	5	4	1625.60
23/64	9.1281	2 17/32	64.2938	5 11/32	135.731	10 5/16	261.938	5	5	1651.00
3/8	9.5250	2 9/16	65.0875	5 3/8	136.525	10 3/8	263.525	5	6	1676.40
25/64	9.9219	2 19/32	65.8813	5 13/32	137.319	10 7/16	265.112	5	7	1701.80
13/32	10.3188	2 5/8	66.6750	5 7/16	138.112	10 1/2	266.700	5	8	1727.20
27/64	10.7156	2 21/32	67.4688	5 15/32	138.906	10 9/16	268.288	5	9	1752.60
7/16	11.1125	2 11/16	68.2625	5 1/2	139.700	10 5/8	269.875	5	10	1778.00
29/64	11.5094	2 23/32	69.0563	5 17/32	140.494	10 11/16	271.462	5	11	1803.40
15/32	11.9063	2 3/4	69.8500	5 9/16	141.288	10 3/4	273.050	6	0	1828.80
31/64	12.3031	2 25/32	70.6438	5 19/32	142.081	10 13/16	274.638	6	1	1854.20
1/2	12.7000	2 13/16	71.4375	5 5/8	142.875	10 7/8	276.225	6	2	1879.60
33/64	13.0969	2 27/32	72.2313	5 21/32	143.669	10 15/16	277.812	6	3	1905.00
17/32	13.4938	2 7/8	73.0250	5 11/16	144.462	11	279.400	6	4	1930.40
35/64	13.8906	2 29/32	73.8188	5 23/32	145.256	11 1/16	280.988	6	5	1955.80
9/16	14.2875	2 15/16	74.6125	5 3/4	146.050	11 1/8	282.575	6	6	1981.20
37/64	14.6844	2 31/32	75.4063	5 25/32	146.844	11 3/16	284.162	6	7	2006.60
19/32	15.0813	3	76.2000	5 13/16	147.638	11 1/4	285.750	6	8	2032.00
39/64	15.4781	3 1/32	76.9938	5 27/32	148.431	11 5/16	287.338	6	9	2057.40
5/8	15.8750	3 1/16	77.7875	5 7/8	149.225	11 3/8	288.925	6	10	2082.80
41/64	16.2719	3 3/32	78.5813	5 29/32	150.019	11 7/16	290.512	6	11	2108.20
21/32	16.6688	3 1/8	79.3750	5 15/16	150.812	11 1/2	292.100	7	0	2133.60
43/64	17.0656	3 5/32	80.1688	5 31/32	151.606	11 9/16	293.688	7	1	2159.00
11/16	17.4625	3 3/16	80.9625	6	152.400	11 5/8	295.275	7	2	2184.40
45/64	17.8594	3 7/32	81.7563	6 1/16	153.988	11 11/16	296.862	7	3	2209.80
23/32	18.2563	3 1/4	82.5500	6 1/8	155.575	11 3/4	298.450	7	4	2235.20
47/64	18.6531	3 9/32	83.3438	6 3/16	157.162	11 13/16	300.038	7	5	2260.60
3/4	19.0500	3 5/16	84.1375	6 1/4	158.750	11 7/8	301.625	7	6	2286.00
49/64	19.4469	3 11/32	84.9313	6 5/16	160.338	11 15/16	303.212	7	7	2311.40
25/32	19.8438	3 3/8	85.7250	6 3/8	161.925	12	304.800	7	8	2336.80
51/64	20.2406	3 13/32	86.5188	6 7/16	163.512	13	330.200	7	9	2362.20
13/16	20.6375	3 7/16	87.3125	6 1/2	165.100	14	355.600	7	10	2387.60
53/64	21.0344	3 15/32	88.1063	6 9/16	166.688	15	381.000	7	11	2413.00
27/32	21.4313	3 1/2	88.9000	6 5/8	168.275	16	406.400	8	0	2438.40
55/64	21.8281	3 17/32	89.6938	6 11/16	169.862	17	431.800	8	1	2463.80
7/8	22.2250	3 9/16	90.4875	6 3/4	171.450	18	457.200	8	2	2489.20
57/64	22.6219	3 19/32	91.2813	6 13/16	173.038	19	482.600	8	3	2514.60
29/32	23.0188	3 5/8	92.0750	6 7/8	174.625	20	508.000	8	4	2540.00
59/64	23.4156	3 21/32	92.8688	6 15/16	176.212	21	533.400	8	5	2565.40
15/16	23.8125	3 11/16	93.6625	7	177.800	22	558.800	8	6	2590.80
61/64	24.2094	3 23/32	94.4563	7 1/16	179.388	23	584.200	8	7	2616.20
31/32	24.6063	3 3/4	95.2500	7 1/8	180.975	24	609.600	8	8	2641.60
63/64	25.0031	3 25/32	96.0438	7 3/16	182.562	25	635.000	8	9	2667.00
1	25.4000	3 13/16	96.8375	7 1/4	184.150	26	660.400	8	10	2692.40
1 1/32	26.1938	3 27/32	97.6313	7 5/16	185.738	27	685.800	8	11	2717.80
1 1/16	26.9875	3 7/8	98.4250	7 3/8	187.325	28	711.200	9	0	2743.20
1 3/32	27.7813	3 29/32	99.2188	7 7/16	188.912	29	736.600	9	1	2768.60
1 1/8	28.5750	3 15/16	100.012	7 1/2	190.500	30	762.000	9	2	2794.00
1 5/32	29.3688	3 31/32	100.806	7 9/16	192.088	31	787.400	9	3	2819.40
1 3/16	30.1625	4	101.600	7 5/8	193.675	32	812.800	9	4	2844.80
1 7/32	30.9563	4 1/32	102.394	7 11/16	195.262	33	838.200	9	5	2870.20
1 1/4	31.7500	4 1/16	103.188	7 3/4	196.850	34	863.600	9	6	2895.60
1 9/32	32.5438	4 3/32	103.981	7 13/16	198.438	35	889.000	9	7	2921.00
1 5/16	33.3375	4 1/8	104.775	7 7/8	200.025	36	914.400	9	8	2946.40
1 11/32	34.1313	4 5/32	105.569	7 15/16	201.612	37	939.800	9	9	2971.80
1 3/8	34.9250	4 3/16	106.362	8	203.200	38	965.200	9	10	2997.20
1 13/32	35.7188	4 7/32	107.156	8 1/16	204.788	39	990.600	9	11	3022.60
1 7/16	36.5125	4 1/4	107.950	8 1/8	206.375	40	1016.00	10	0	3048.00
1 15/32	37.3063	4 9/32	108.744	8 3/16	207.962	41	1041.40	11	0	3352.80
1 1/2	38.1000	4 5/16	109.538	8 1/4	209.550	42	1066.80	12	0	3657.60
1 17/32	38.8938	4 11/32	110.331	8 5/16	211.138			13	0	3962.40
1 9/16	39.6875	4 3/8	111.125	8 3/8	212.725			14	0	4267.20
1 19/32	40.4813	4 13/32	111.919	8 7/16	214.312			15	0	4572.00
1 5/8	41.2750	4 7/16	112.712	8 1/2	215.900			16	0	4876.80
1 21/32	42.0688	4 15/32	113.506	8 9/16	217.488			17	0	5131.60
1 11/16	42.8625	4 1/2	114.300	8 5/8	219.075			18	0	5486.40
1 23/32	43.6563	4 17/32	115.094	8 11/16	220.662			19	0	5791.20
1 3/4	44.4500	4 9/16	115.888	8 3/4	222.250			20	0	6096.00
1 25/32	45.2438	4 19/32	116.681	8 13/16	223.838			21	0	6400.80
1 13/16	46.0375	4 5/8	117.475	8 7/8	225.425			22	0	6705.60

Millimetres to Inches/Feet

millimetres	inches	millimetres	inches	millimetres	inches	millimetres	inches	millimetres	inches
1	0.0394	91	3.5827	181	7.1260	271	10.6693	361	14.2126
2	0.0787	92	3.6221	182	7.1654	272	10.7087	362	14.2520
3	0.1181	93	3.6614	183	7.2047	273	10.7480	363	14.2913
4	0.1575	94	3.7008	184	7.2441	274	10.7874	364	14.3307
5	0.1969	95	3.7402	185	7.2835	275	10.8268	365	14.3701
6	0.2362	96	3.7795	186	7.3228	276	10.8661	366	14.4094
7	0.2756	97	3.8189	187	7.3622	277	10.9055	367	14.4488
8	0.3150	98	3.8583	188	7.4016	278	10.9449	368	14.4882
9	0.3543	99	3.8976	189	7.4409	279	10.9843	369	14.5276
10	0.3937	100	3.9370	190	7.4803	280	11.0236	370	14.5669
11	0.4331	101	3.9764	191	7.5197	281	11.0630	371	14.6063
12	0.4724	102	4.0158	192	7.5591	282	11.1024	372	14.6457
13	0.5118	103	4.0551	193	7.5984	283	11.1417	373	14.6850
14	0.5512	104	4.0945	194	7.6378	284	11.1811	374	14.7244
15	0.5906	105	4.1339	195	7.6772	285	11.2205	375	14.7638
16	0.6299	106	4.1732	196	7.7165	286	11.2598	376	14.8031
17	0.6693	107	4.2126	197	7.7559	287	11.2992	377	14.8425
18	0.7087	108	4.2520	198	7.7953	288	11.3386	378	14.8819
19	0.7480	109	4.2913	199	7.8347	289	11.3780	379	14.9213
20	0.7874	110	4.3307	200	7.8740	290	11.4173	380	14.9606
21	0.8268	111	4.3701	201	7.9134	291	11.4567	381	15.0000
22	0.8661	112	4.4095	202	7.9528	292	11.4961	382	15.0394
23	0.9055	113	4.4488	203	7.9921	293	11.5354	383	15.0787
24	0.9449	114	4.4882	204	8.0315	294	11.5748	384	15.1181
25	0.9843	115	4.5276	205	8.0709	295	11.6142	385	15.1575
26	1.0236	116	4.5669	206	8.1102	296	11.6535	386	15.1969
27	1.0630	117	4.6063	207	8.1496	297	11.6929	387	15.2362
28	1.1024	118	4.6457	208	8.1890	298	11.7323	388	15.2756
29	1.1417	119	4.6850	209	8.2284	299	11.7717	389	15.3150
30	1.1811	120	4.7244	210	8.2677	300	11.8110	390	15.3543
31	1.2205	121	4.7638	211	8.3071	301	11.8504	391	15.3937
32	1.2598	122	4.8032	212	8.3465	302	11.8898	392	15.4331
33	1.2992	123	4.8425	213	8.3858	303	11.9291	393	15.4724
34	1.3386	124	4.8819	214	8.4252	304	11.9686	394	15.5118
35	1.3780	125	4.9213	215	8.4646	305	12.0079	395	15.5512
36	1.4173	126	4.9606	216	8.5039	306	12.0472	396	15.5906
37	1.4567	127	5.0000	217	8.5433	307	12.0866	397	15.6299
38	1.4961	128	5.0394	218	8.5827	308	12.1260	398	15.6693
39	1.5354	129	5.0787	219	8.6221	309	12.1654	399	15.7087
40	1.5748	130	5.1181	220	8.6614	310	12.2047	400	15.7480
41	1.6142	131	5.1575	221	8.7008	311	12.2441	401	15.7874
42	1.6535	132	5.1969	222	8.7402	312	12.2835	402	15.8268
43	1.6929	133	5.2362	223	8.7795	313	12.3228	403	15.8661
44	1.7323	134	5.2756	224	8.8189	314	12.3622	404	15.9055
45	1.7717	135	5.3150	225	8.8583	315	12.4016	405	15.9449
46	1.8110	136	5.3543	226	8.8976	316	12.4409	406	15.9832
47	1.8504	137	5.3937	227	8.9370	317	12.4803	407	16.0236
48	1.8898	138	5.4331	228	8.9764	318	12.5197	408	16.0630
49	1.9291	139	5.4724	229	9.0158	319	12.5591	409	16.1024
50	1.9685	140	5.5118	230	9.0551	320	12.5984	410	16.1417
51	2.0079	141	5.5512	231	9.0945	321	12.6378	411	16.1811
52	2.0472	142	5.5906	232	9.1339	322	12.6772	412	16.2205
53	2.0866	143	5.6299	233	9.1732	323	12.7165	413	16.2598
54	2.1260	144	5.6693	234	9.2126	324	12.7559	414	16.2992
55	2.1654	145	5.7087	235	9.2520	325	12.7953	415	16.3386
56	2.2047	146	5.7480	236	9.2913	326	12.8346	416	16.3780
57	2.2441	147	5.7874	237	9.3307	327	12.8740	417	16.4173
58	2.2835	148	5.8268	238	9.3701	328	12.9134	418	16.4567
59	2.3228	149	5.8661	239	9.4095	329	12.9528	419	16.4961
60	2.3622	150	5.9055	240	9.4488	330	12.9921	420	16.5354
61	2.4016	151	5.9449	241	9.4882	331	13.0315	421	16.5748
62	2.4409	152	5.9843	242	9.5276	332	13.0709	422	16.6142
63	2.4803	153	6.0236	243	9.5669	333	13.1102	423	16.6535
64	2.5197	154	6.0630	244	9.6063	334	13.1496	424	16.6929
65	2.5591	155	6.1024	245	9.6457	335	13.1890	425	16.7323
66	2.5984	156	6.1417	246	9.6850	336	13.2283	426	16.7716
67	2.6378	157	6.1811	247	9.7244	337	13.2677	427	16.8110
68	2.6772	158	6.2205	248	9.7638	338	13.3071	428	16.8504
69	2.7165	159	6.2599	249	9.8031	339	13.3465	429	16.8898
70	2.7559	160	6.2992	250	9.8425	340	13.3858	430	16.9291
71	2.7953	161	6.3386	251	9.8819	341	13.4252	431	16.9685
72	2.8347	162	6.3780	252	9.9213	342	13.4646	432	17.0079
73	2.8740	163	6.4173	253	9.9606	343	13.5039	433	17.0472
74	2.9134	164	6.4567	254	10.0000	344	13.5433	434	17.0866
75	2.9528	165	6.4961	255	10.0393	345	13.5827	435	17.1260
76	2.9921	166	6.5354	256	10.0787	346	13.6220	436	17.1654
77	3.0315	167	6.5748	257	10.1181	347	13.6614	437	17.2047
78	3.0709	168	6.6142	258	10.1575	348	13.7008	438	17.2441
79	3.1102	169	6.6535	259	10.1969	349	13.7402	439	17.2835
80	3.1496	170	6.6929	260	10.2362	350	13.7795	440	17.3228
81	3.1890	171	6.7323	261	10.2756	351	13.8189	441	17.3622
82	3.2284	172	6.7717	262	10.3150	352	13.8583	442	17.4016
83	3.2677	173	6.8110	263	10.3543	353	13.8976	443	17.4409
84	3.3071	174	6.8504	264	10.3937	354	13.9370	444	17.4803
85	3.3465	175	6.8898	265	10.4331	355	13.9764	445	17.5197
86	3.3858	176	6.9291	266	10.4724	356	14.0157	446	17.5591
87	3.4252	177	6.9685	267	10.5118	357	14.0551	447	17.5984
88	3.4646	178	7.0079	268	10.5512	358	14.0945	448	17.6378
89	3.5039	179	7.0472	269	10.5906	359	14.1339	449	17.6772
90	3.5433	180	7.0866	270	10.6299	360	14.1732	450	17.7165

Catalogs are coded by position within the volume in numerical sequence, e.g., C345.

Products

NOTE: Index headings listed below are based on the manufacturers' descriptions of their products as those descriptions appear in the catalogs distributed by Sweet's. SWEET'S MAKES NO REPRESENTATIONS OR WARRANTIES OF ANY KIND, EXPRESS OR IMPLIED, INCLUDING BUT NOT LIMITED TO IMPLIED WARRANTIES OF MERCHANTABILITY OR FITNESS FOR ANY PARTICULAR PURPOSE AS TO THESE INDEX HEADINGS OR AS TO THE PRODUCTS DESCRIBED BY THESE INDEX HEADINGS. Users of Sweet's Files should not rely on these index headings in connection with selecting products. Users of Sweet's Files should refer to the manufacturers' catalogs for further information regarding characteristics of products indexed below.

a

Accessible products for the disabled
see
  bathroom accessories: —disabled persons' use
  bathroom accessories: —grab bars—specific materials
  cabinets: —bathroom vanity—disabled persons' use
  faucets—types: —sensor-actuated
  mirrors: —tilting
  plumbing fittings and trim
  showers: —seats—wall-mounted
  washroom accessories: —disabled persons' use
  washroom accessories: —grab bars

Acoustic isolation and control
see
  partitions—properties: —sound-insulating or retarding—specific type

Air conditioners
central station units
  Amana Refrigeration, Inc. C481
packaged—unitary
see
  heaters—unit
packaged—window or through-wall
  Amana Refrigeration, Inc. C481

Air conditioning equipment
see
  air conditioners
  dehumidifiers

Air distribution equipment
see
  fans
  ventilators

Air handlers
see
  air conditioners

Air/liquid treatment equipment
see
  air conditioners
  dehumidifiers
  waste handling equipment and systems

Air pollution control
see
  air conditioning equipment
  vacuum cleaning systems

Alarms and alarm systems
horns, sirens, bells and chimes
see
  bells, buzzers, chimes (entrance and alarm)

Appliances—residential—kitchen
see
  ice making machines: —residential
  kitchen appliances—residential

Architectural artwork
moldings and cornices
see
  moldings and cornices
plaques, insignia and tablets
see
  plaques, insignia and tablets

Architectural woodwork
see
  woodwork

Art and decorative objects
see
  plaques, insignia and tablets

Ash handling equipment
see
  vacuum cleaning systems

Association catalogs
see
  product information—associations

Athletic equipment and facilities
see
  bathtubs: —hydro-massage combination
  health club equipment
  saunas and equipment

Audio and visual equipment
see
  intercommunicating systems

b

Bakery equipment
see
  food service equipment—commercial or institutional

Bar furniture and equipment
see also
  ice making machines
elbow rests, tops
  Du Pont Co. C468
sink
  Swan Corp. (The) C563

Barrier-free design products
see
  bathroom accessories: —disabled persons' use
  bathroom accessories: —grab bars—specific materials
  cabinets: —bathroom vanity—disabled persons' use
  faucets—types: —sensor-actuated
  mirrors: —tilting
  plumbing fittings and trim
  showers: —seats—wall-mounted
  washroom accessories: —disabled persons' use
  washroom accessories: —grab bars

Bars
see
  bathroom accessories: —grab bars—specific material
  washroom accessories: —grab bars

Bases
see
  flooring—specific materials
  showers: —stalls and receptors—specific material

Bathroom accessories
see also
  washroom accessories
cabinets and mirrors
see also
  mirrors
  Aristech Chemical Corp. C591
  Basco, Inc. C585
  Broan Mfg. Co., Inc. C587
  Dornbracht, Santile
    International Corp. C568
  NuTone C590
  Wellborn Cabinet, Inc. C536

Cabinets *cont.*

custom-designed
Avonite C465
Broan Mfg. Co., Inc. C587
KraftMaid Cabinetry C526
Wellborn Cabinet, Inc. C536

dispensers—washroom
see
   washroom accessories

doors for
see
   doors—application: —cabinet

**equipment cabinets, racks, consoles—
electrical, electronic**
see
   storage equipment: —cabinets—specific type

filing
see
   office equipment: —filing cabinets—specific type

hutch
Wellborn Cabinet, Inc. C536

kitchen—residential
KraftMaid Cabinetry C526
Wellborn Cabinet, Inc. C536

lavatories
see
   lavatories and accessories: —cabinets for

medicine
see also
   *bathroom accessories: —cabinets and mirrors—
     specific type*
Basco, Inc. C585
Broan Mfg. Co., Inc. . . . . ii; C587
KraftMaid Cabinetry C526
NuTone .C590
Wellborn Cabinet, Inc. C536

product information—associations
see
   *product information—associations: —cabinets—
     kitchen*

residential
KraftMaid Cabinetry C526
Wellborn Cabinet, Inc. C536

shower
see
   *showers: —cabinets and enclosures—specific
     type*

storage
see
   storage equipment: —cabinets—specific type

tops for
Avonite C465
Du Pont Co. C468
Wellborn Cabinet, Inc. C536

washroom vanity
KraftMaid Cabinetry C526

wood
see
   woodwork

Cafeteria equipment
see
   *food service equipment—commercial or
     institutional*

Can openers
see
   kitchen appliances—residential: —can openers

Canopies
inserts for
see
   glass
   plastic

Carvings—wood
see
   woodwork

Casework
see
   cabinets

Castings
see
   specific products

Ceilings—general
fans
see
   fans: —wall, ceiling or pedestal
ventilators
see
   ventilators: —ceiling, wall, window

Ceramic products
see
   sinks—residential: —ceramic, composite

Chimes
see
   bells, buzzers, chimes (entrance and alarm)

Church equipment
windows—inserts for
see
   glass
   plastic

Chutes
rubbish and waste
see
   waste handling equipment and systems

Cleaning systems
see
   vacuum cleaning systems

Closets
accessories for
see
   shelving
water
see
   toilets

Clothes washers
see
   laundry equipment—specific use

Column covers
fire-resistant
Avonite C465
plastic
Avonite C465
stone—simulated
Avonite C465

Columns
covers/enclosures for
see
   column covers

Communicating systems
see
   intercommunicating systems—specific type
   wiring devices—electrical

Compactors—waste
see
   waste handling equipment and systems

Conductors—electrical
see
   *wiring devices—electrical: —cables—specific
     types/application/properties*

Consultants and services
associations
see
   product information—associations
kitchen and bath planning and design
NKBA, National Kitchen &
   Bath Association A105

Controls—lighting
see
   wiring devices—electrical

Conveyors or conveying
systems
pneumatic—tubing or fittings for
see
   piping and tubing accessories

Cooktops
see
   *ranges and ovens—residential: —cooktops:
     —cooktops/grills—convertible*

Cornices
see
   moldings and cornices
   surfacing and paneling—interior

Counters
tops for
Aristech Chemical Corp. C591
Avonite C465
Du Pont Co. C468
Wilson: Ralph Wilson Plastics
   Co. C479

Couplings
piping and tubing
see
   piping and tubing—accessories for

Covers
column
see
   column covers

Covers—with fire-resistant
properties
see
   column covers: —fire-resistant

Curtain walls
see
   panels—building
   store fronts

Curtain walls—window framing
systems
panels for
see
   panels—building

d

Dehumidifiers
Amana Refrigeration, Inc. C481

Dentils
see
moldings and cornices

Desks
residential
Wellborn Cabinet, Inc. C536

Detention equipment
see
glass—properties —burglar-resistant
panels—building—properties: —bullet or
burglar-resistant
partitions—properties: —bullet or burglar-
resistant

Diffusers—air distribution
see
ventilators

Directories/message boards
see
signs

Disabled persons' products
see
bathroom accessories: —disabled persons' use
bathroom accessories: —grab bars—specific
materials
cabinets: —bathroom vanity—disabled persons'
use
faucets—types: —sensor-actuated
mirrors: —tilting
plumbing fittings and trim
showers: —seats—wall-mounted
washroom accessories: —disabled persons' use
washroom accessories: —grab bars

Dishes—soap
see
bathroom accessories: —toilet paper holders,
soap dishes—specific material

Dishwashers—residential
built-in
Amana Refrigeration, Inc. C481
General Electric, Monogram C496
KitchenAid, Inc., Whirlpool
Corp. C503
Viking Range Corp. C517
energy-saving
Viking Range Corp. C517
free-standing or mobile
Amana Refrigeration, Inc. C481
KitchenAid, Inc., Whirlpool
Corp. C503
under-sink
Amana Refrigeration, Inc. C481
KitchenAid, Inc., Whirlpool
Corp. C503

Dispensers
facial tissue, lotion, paper cup, soap
see
washroom accessories: —dispensers—specific
type
hot water
KitchenAid, Inc., Whirlpool
Corp. C503

Disposers—liquid/solid waste
see
food waste disposers
waste handling equipment and systems

Doors
see
doors—application
doors—operation
doors—properties
doors—swinging—by materials/construction

Doors—application
bathtub enclosure
see
bathtubs: —enclosures for—specific type
cabinet
Broan Mfg. Co., Inc. C587
KraftMaid Cabinetry C526
entrance
see
doors—operation
doors—swinging—by materials/construction
inserts for
see
glass
plastic
lights for
see
glass
plastic
sauna
Finlandia Sauna Products,
Inc. .C642
shower
Century Shower Door, Inc. C593
Work Right Products, Inc. C597

Doors—operation
sliding—frame and glass, glass
Century Shower Door, Inc. C593
Work Right Products, Inc. C597
swinging
see
doors—swinging—by materials/construction

Doors—properties
watertight
Century Shower Door, Inc. C593
Work Right Products, Inc. C597

Doors—swinging—by materials/construction
glass—tempered
Century Shower Door, Inc. C593
Work Right Products, Inc. C597
inserts for
see
glass
plastic
lights for
see
glass
plastic

Drainage pipe and fittings
see
piping and tubing—application: —drainage—
specific type
plumbing fittings and trim: —drainage

Drains
plumbing
see
plumbing fittings and trim: —drainage, drains

Drains *cont.*
strainer combination
Geberit Mfg., Inc. C580

Drawers
storage
see
storage equipment: —cabinets with drawers

Dryers
hand or hair
see
washroom accessories: —dryers—specific
type—hand or hair
residential
see
laundry equipment—residential use: —dryers—
specific type

Dust collectors
see
vacuum cleaning systems

e

Ecclesiastical equipment
see
signs

Educational equipment
see
intercommunicating systems

Electrical equipment
see
lighting—application
piping and tubing—application: —gas, water,
electrical or sewer system
wiring devices—electrical

Enclosures
see
bathtubs: —enclosures for—specific type
showers: —cabinets and enclosures—specific
type

Energy conservation
see
specific products

Entrances
doors
see
doors—application
doors—operation
doors—properties
doors—swinging—by materials/construction
store fronts
see
store fronts

Exercise equipment
see
health club equipment

Exhaust systems
air
see
fans
ventilators

f

Facings, refacings or veneers
see
> panels—building
> surfacing and paneling—interior

Fans
see also
> ventilators

fan-light combination
Broan Mfg. Co., Inc. ii
NuTone C590

kitchen or bathroom
Broan Mfg. Co., Inc. C484
NuTone C590

ventilating or exhaust
Broan Mfg. Co., Inc. C484
NuTone C590

wall, ceiling or pedestal
Broan Mfg. Co., Inc. ii
NuTone C590

Fascias
panels—plastic
Avonite C465

panels—stone—simulated
Avonite C465

Faucets
see
> faucets—application
> faucets—types

Faucets—application
bathtub
Grohe America .C564
JADO C588
Jason International, Inc. C574
Strom Plumbing, Sign of the
Crab C584

bidet
Dornbracht, Santile
International Corp. C568

lavatory
Dornbracht, Santile
International Corp. C568
Grohe America .C564
JADO C588
Strom Plumbing, Sign of the
Crab C584

sink—kitchen
Blanco, Inc. A012
Grohe America .C564
JADO C588

sink—service, laundry
Grohe America .C564

Faucets—types
metering, self-closing
Grohe America .C564

**mixing—pressure-balancing,
thermostatic**
Grohe America .C564

pushbutton
Grohe America .C564
JADO C588

sensor-actuated
Grohe America .C564

single supply
Blanco, Inc. A012
Grohe America .C564
JADO C588
Jason International, Inc. C574

Faucets—types cont.
single supply cont.
Strom Plumbing, Sign of the
Crab C584

swivel spout
Blanco, Inc. A012
Grohe America .C564
JADO C588
Jason International, Inc. C574
Strom Plumbing, Sign of the
Crab C584

wall-mounted
Grohe America .C564
JADO C588

water-saving
Blanco, Inc. A012
JADO C588

Fiber glass products
see
> bathtubs: —fiber glass, fiber glass reinforced,
> plastic

Files, filing cabinets
see
> office equipment

Fireproofing
see
> column covers: —fire-resistant

Fire protection equipment and systems
partitions
see
> partitions—properties: —fire-rated: —fire-
> resistant—specific type

Fitness equipment
see
> health club equipment
> saunas and equipment

Fittings
see
> plumbing fittings and trim

Floor cleaning and maintenance equipment
vacuum cleaning systems
see
> vacuum cleaning systems

Flooring
see
> flooring—properties
> flooring—simulated stone

Flooring—properties
acid or alkali-resistant—commercial or institutional use
Avonite C465
fire-resistant
Avonite C465

Flooring—simulated stone
Avonite C465

Food service equipment— commercial or institutional
compactors—waste
see
> waste handling equipment and systems

Food service equipment— commercial or institutional cont.
dispensers
see
> dispensers

ice making machines
see
> ice making machines

menu boards
see
> signs

sinks
Du Pont Co. C468

ventilators
see
> ventilators

waste handling equipment
see
> waste handling equipment and systems

Food waste disposers
see also
> waste handling equipment and systems
residential
KitchenAid, Inc., Whirlpool
Corp. C503

Fountains—soda
beverage dispensers
see
> dispensers

Freezers—residential
see also
> refrigerator-freezer combination: —residential—
> specific type
built-in
Sub-Zero Freezer Co., Inc. C514; C515
free-standing
Amana Refrigeration, Inc. C481
Sub-Zero Freezer Co., Inc. C514; C515
undercounter
Amana Refrigeration, Inc. C481
Sub-Zero Freezer Co., Inc. C514; C515

Fume hoods
see
> ventilators

Furnaces
see
> heaters—unit

Furniture
see
> bar furniture and equipment
> bookcases
> cabinets
> desks
> hospital equipment
> laboratory equipment
> office equipment
> shelving
> tables

g

Garbage disposal equipment
see
> food waste disposers
> waste handling equipment and systems

Gas equipment
see
piping and tubing—application: —gas, water, electrical or sewer system

Generic information
see
specific products/materials

Glass blocks
see
blocks—glass
glass—form: —block
panels—building—materials: —glass, glass block
partitions—materials: —glass block
windows—replacement: —glass blocks for

Glass—film finish for
see
glass—properties

Glass—form
bent, curved
Weck, Glashaus Div. B689
block
see also
blocks—glass
Weck, Glashaus Div. B689
patterned, carved, decorative, etched or textured
Weck, Glashaus Div. B689
structural
see
panels—building—materials: —glass, glass block

Glass—properties
anti-glare/shading
Weck, Glashaus Div. B689
burglar-resistant
Weck, Glashaus Div. B689
diffusing
see
glass—form: —patterned, carved, decorative, etched or textured
fire-resistant
Weck, Glashaus Div. B689
heat-absorbing
Weck, Glashaus Div. B689
insulating panel
Weck, Glashaus Div. B689
security and detention
see
glass—properties
sound-resistant
Weck, Glashaus Div. B689

Glazing
see
glass—form
glass—properties
plastic—form
plastic—properties

Glazing film
see
glass—properties
plastic—properties

Government agency catalogs
see
product information—associations

Grab bars
see
bathroom accessories: —grab bars—specific material
washroom accessories: —grab bars

Graphics
see
plaques, insignia and tablets
signs

Griddles
see
ranges and ovens—residential: —ranges—griddle/broiler/oven combination

Grills—barbecue
see
ranges and ovens—residential: —cooktops/grills—convertible

h

Hangers—clothing
see
bathroom accessories: —hooks—coat or robe—specific type
washroom accessories: —hooks—coat or robe—specific type

Hardware—bathroom, washroom
shower
see
showers: —rods, hardware and tracks

Hardware—shower
see
showers: —rods, hardware and tracks

Healthcare furniture
see
hospital equipment

Health club equipment
see also
saunas and equipment
Finlandia Sauna Products,
Inc. C642

Heaters—general
sauna
see
saunas and equipment

Heaters—unit
electric
Amana Refrigeration, Inc. C481
NuTone C590
electric—with lighting
NuTone C590
steam or hot water
Steamist Co., Inc. C673
steam or hot water—portable
Steamist Co., Inc. C673

Highway drainage
see
piping and tubing—application: —drainage

Holders
washroom, bathroom
see
bathroom accessories: —holders—specific type

Holders cont.
washroom, bathroom cont.
see cont.
washroom accessories: —holders—specific type

Hoods
see
ventilators

Hooks—clothing
see
bathroom accessories: —hooks—coat or robe—specific type
washroom accessories: —hooks—coat or robe—specific type

Hose
connectors
see
piping and tubing—accessories for

Hospital equipment
air conditioning units
see
air conditioners
desks—registration, reservation
see
intercommunicating systems—specific type
grab bars, safety toilet seats, safety towel bars
see
bathroom accessories: —grab bars—specific material
kitchen equipment
see
food service equipment—commercial or institutional
plumbing fittings
see
plumbing fittings and trim
sinks—medical, surgical
Avonite C465

Hotel, motel equipment
bathroom
see
bathroom accessories

Hot water heaters
see
heaters—unit: —steam or hot water—specific type

Hvac terminal units
see
heaters—unit

i

Ice making machines
residential
KitchenAid, Inc., Whirlpool
Corp. C503
Sub-Zero Freezer Co., Inc. C514; C515

Identifying devices
see
plaques, insignia and tablets
signs

Indicators

signs
see
  signs

Insignia

see
  plaques, insignia and tablets

Intercommunicating systems

NuTone .C590

Ironing boards

see also
  laundry equipment—specific type: —iron-ironing
    board—built-in
NuTone .C590

J

Jail equipment

see
  specific products

Janitors' stations

mop sinks, receptors
see
  faucets—applications: —sinks—service, laundry

k

Kitchen appliances—residential

blenders
NuTone .C590
can openers
NuTone .C590
combination food preparation center
NuTone .C590
mixers
NuTone .C590

Kitchen equipment—commercial or institutional

see
  food service equipment—commercial or
    institutional

Kitchen equipment—residential

see
  cabinets: —kitchen—residential—specific type
  consultants and services: —kitchen and bath
    planning and design
  dishwashers—residential
  fans: —kitchen or bathroom
  faucets—application: —sink—kitchen
  food waste disposers: —residential
  freezers—residential
  kitchen appliances—residential
  kitchen planning
  ranges and ovens—residential
  refrigerator-freezer combination: —residential—
    specific type
  refrigerators: —residential—specific type
  sinks—residential
  ventilators: —hoods—residential kitchen—
    specific type

Kitchen planning

see also
  consultants and services: —kitchen and bath
    planning and design
  NKBA, National Kitchen &
    Bath Association A105

L

Laboratory equipment

plumbing fittings
see
  plumbing fittings and trim
work surfaces for
Avonite .C465
Du Pont Co. C468

Laundry equipment—commercial or institutional use

faucets for
see
  faucets—application: —sink—service, laundry
iron-ironing board—built-in
see
  ironing boards

Laundry equipment—residential use

dryers
Amana Refrigeration, Inc. C481
KitchenAid, Inc., Whirlpool
  Corp. .C503
faucets
see
  faucets—application: —sink—service, laundry
iron-ironing board—built-in
see also
  ironing boards
Broan Mfg. Co., Inc. ii
NuTone .C590
washer/dryers—combination
Amana Refrigeration, Inc. C481
KitchenAid, Inc., Whirlpool
  Corp. .C503
washers
Amana Refrigeration, Inc. C481
KitchenAid, Inc., Whirlpool
  Corp. .C503

Lavatories and accessories

cabinets for
Dornbracht, Santile
  International Corp. C568
Wellborn Cabinet, Inc. C536
fittings and trim for
see
  faucets—application: —lavatory
  plumbing fittings and trim
lavatories
Dornbracht, Santile
  International Corp. C568
Du Pont Co. C468
Strom Plumbing, Sign of the
  Crab C584
modular
Dornbracht, Santile
  International Corp. C568
tops for
Avonite .C465
Du Pont Co. C468
Swan Corp. (The) C563
Wilson: Ralph Wilson Plastics
  Co. C479
vanity top and bowl—molded—one piece
Du Pont Co. C468
Swan Corp. (The) C563
wash centers
see
  washroom accessories: —wash centers
    (lavatory with accessories)—specific type

Learning systems

see
  intercommunicating systems—specific type

Letters—architectural

see
  signs

Lift stations

see
  pumps: —sewage ejector or sump—specific
    type

Lighting

see
  fans: —fan-light combination
  heaters—unit: —electric—with lighting
  lighting—application
  luminaires—types
  signs
  wiring devices—electrical

Lighting—application

see also
  luminaires—types
cabinets and mirrors
see also
  bathroom accessories: —cabinets and mirrors—
    with lighting fixtures
Basco, Inc. C585
Broan Mfg. Co., Inc. . . . . ii; C587
NuTone .C590
Wellborn Cabinet, Inc. C536

Lights

window
see
  glass
  plastic

Liquid waste disposal or treatment equipment

see
  waste handling equipment and systems
piping for
see
  piping and tubing—application: —gas, water,
    electrical or sewer system

Louvers

see
  ventilators

Luminaires—types

see also
  lighting—application
fan
see
  fans: —fan-light combination
heater combination
see
  heaters—unit: —electric—with lighting
incandescent
NuTone .C590
signs
see
  signs

m

Marble

counter tops
see
  counters: —tops for

IMPORTANT

The kitchen & bathroom remodeling job is going to bring you and your family a host of decisions. Where should the refrigerator go? How much light will we need? Should we include a bidet, a whirlpool? All these questions should have sound answers which any of the NKBA (National Kitchen & Bath Association) members can provide for you. A complete listing of these individuals can be found in this book.

Please fill out the brief questionnaire below and return it to us. This information is for demographic purposes only. By doing so, we can provide manufacturers with a profile of those involved in the planning, design and selection of products for their upcoming kitchen and bathroom projects.

1. Are you remodeling a kitchen or bathroom?

❏ Kitchen   ❏ Bathroom
❏ Both
❏ Other: _____

2. What is the amount you estimate spending on your remodeling job?

❏ Less than $5,000   ❏ $10,000 - $19,999
❏ $5,000 - $9,999   ❏ $20,000 or More

3. How will the remodeling be completed?

❏ We will purchase the products and complete the remodeling ourselves
❏ We will purchase products, then hire a contractor for installation
❏ We will go to one place for all products and installation

4. How is your remodeling project being designed?

❏ We will design it ourselves
❏ It will be designed by an architect
❏ It will be designed by an interior designer
❏ It will be designed by a Kitchen & Bath specialist
❏ It will be designed by a NKBA member
❏ It will be designed by and built by the remodeling contractor

5. Which product(s) do you plan to replace:

❏ Bath Accessories   ❏ Flooring-Tile/Marble
❏ Refrigerator   ❏ Range
❏ Cabinets   ❏ Flooring-Wood
❏ Countertops   ❏ Freezer
❏ Shower Doors   ❏ Shower Stall
❏ Dishwasher   ❏ Lighting
❏ Disposer   ❏ Medicine Cabinet
❏ Sink   ❏ Toilets
❏ Faucets   ❏ Microwave Oven
❏ Flooring-Resilient   ❏ Oven
❏ Bathtub   ❏ Windows
❏ Vanity   ❏ Vanity Top

6. Which product(s) do you plan to add:

❏ Bidet   ❏ His/Her Sinks
❏ Shower Door   ❏ Skylights
❏ Cooktop   ❏ Hot Tub
❏ Disposer   ❏ Ice Machine
❏ Sound/Intercom System   ❏ Steam Bath
❏ Flooring-Resilient   ❏ Microwave Oven
❏ Flooring-Tile/Marble   ❏ Medicine Cabinet
❏ Sun Room   ❏ Water Purifier
❏ Flooring-Wood   ❏ Sauna
❏ Whirlpool Tub

7. What is the approximate value of your home?

❏ Less than $100,000   ❏ $250,000 - $299,999
❏ $100,000 - $149,999   ❏ $300,000 - $399,999
❏ $150,000 - $199,999   ❏ $400,00 - $499,999
❏ $200,000 - $249,999   ❏ $500,000 or More

8. What is your approximate household income?

❏ Less than $30,000   ❏ $75,000 - $99,999
❏ $30,000 - $49,999   ❏ $100,000 - $149,999
❏ $50,000 - $74,999   ❏ $150,000 or More

9. Are you a double income household?

❏ Yes   ❏ No

10. How long have you lived in your home?

❏ Less than 2 Years   ❏ 11 - 20 Years
❏ 2 - 5 Years   ❏ More than 20 Years
❏ 6 - 10 Years

11. How helpful was this book to you in selecting products?

❏ Very Helpful   ❏ Somewhat Helpful
❏ Not Very Helpful   ❏ Not At All Helpful

12. Where did you buy this book?

Name of store or bookclub:

_____

Location of Store:

City _____

(Please fold and tape this form closed with the return address showing on the outside)

Fold here and seal with tape. Do not staple.

BUSINESS REPLY MAIL

FIRST CLASS MAIL PERMIT NO. 226 NEW YORK NY

POSTAGE WILL BE PAID BY ADDRESSEE

**SWEET'S GROUP
MCGRAW-HILL INC
ATTENTION ALMA L WEINSTEIN
1221 AVENUE OF THE AMERICAS
NEW YORK NY 10124-0026**

Fold here and seal with tape. Do not staple.

Marble products
see
surfacing and paneling—interior—materials:
—marble—specific type

Materials handling equipment
see
storage equipment

Medical equipment
see
hospital equipment
laboratory equipment

Menu boards
see
signs

Merchandising equipment
see
dispensers
storage equipment

Message, announcement boards
see
signs

Metalwork—ornamental
see
plaques, insignia and tablets

Microphones and accessories
see
intercommunicating systems—specific type

Microwave ovens
see
ranges and ovens—residential: —ovens-
microwave—specific type
ranges and ovens—residential: —ranges—
microwave/conventional oven combination

Millwork
wood
see
woodwork

Mirrors
see also
bathroom accessories: —cabinets and mirrors—
specific type
glass
Basco, Inc. C585
Broan Mfg. Co., Inc. C587
Dornbracht, Santile
International Corp. C568
JADO C588
Wellborn Cabinet, Inc. C536
safety
Basco, Inc. C585
tilting
Basco, Inc. C585
with shelf
Basco, Inc. C585

Mixers—food
residential
see
kitchen appliances—residential: —mixers

Moldings and cornices
plastic, composite
see also
surfacing and paneling—interior—materials:
—moldings and trim for—plastic, composite

Moldings and cornices *cont.*
plastic, composite *cont.*
Avonite C465
Du Pont Co. C468
stone—simulated
Du Pont Co. C468

n

Nursing home furniture
see
hospital equipment

o

Office equipment
see also
storage equipment
appliances—compact
see
kitchen appliances—residential
filing cabinets
Wellborn Cabinet, Inc. C536
shelving
see
shelving

Ovens
see
ranges and ovens—specific type

p

Paging or signaling systems
see
intercommunicating systems—specific type

Paneling—prefinished
see
surfacing and paneling—interior

Panels—building
see
panels—building—general
panels—building—materials
panels—building—properties

Panels—building—general
curved
Weck, Glashaus Div. B689

Panels—building—materials
glass, glass block
Weck, Glashaus Div. B689

Panels—building—properties
bullet or burglar-resistant
Weck, Glashaus Div. B689
fire-resistant
Weck, Glashaus Div. B689
insulating
Weck, Glashaus Div. B689

Park equipment
see
consultants and services

Partitions
see
partitions—materials

Partitions *cont.*
see *cont.*
partitions—properties
partitions—shower, toilet, urinal

Partitions—application
shower
see
partitions—shower, toilet, urinal
toilet, urinal
see
partitions—shower, toilet, urinal

Partitions—general
blocks for
see
blocks—specific material
partitions—materials: —glass block

Partitions—materials
glass block
see also
blocks—glass
Weck, Glashaus Div. B689
plastic laminate-faced
Wilson: Ralph Wilson Plastics
Co. C479

Partitions—properties
bullet or burglar-resistant
Weck, Glashaus Div. B689
fire-rated
Du Pont Co. C468
Weck, Glashaus Div. B689
fire-resistant
Weck, Glashaus Div. B689
sound-insulating or retarding—floor-to-
ceiling partitions
Weck, Glashaus Div. B689

Partitions—shower, toilet, urinal
shower—plastic
Swan Corp. (The) C563
toilet, urinal—plastic laminate-faced
Du Pont Co. C468

Physical fitness equipment
see
health club equipment

Piping and tubing
see
piping and tubing—accessories for
piping and tubing—application
piping and tubing—form
piping and tubing—materials
piping and tubing—properties

Piping and tubing—accessories for
see also
plumbing fittings and trim
strainers
Geberit Mfg., Inc. C580
traps
see
plumbing fittings and trim: —drainage

Piping and tubing—application
drainage
Geberit Mfg., Inc. C580
gas, water, electrical or sewer system
Zoeller Co. C576

Piping and tubing—form
prefabricated
Geberit Mfg., Inc. C580

Piping and tubing—materials
plastic
Geberit Mfg., Inc. C580

Piping and tubing—properties
chemical-resistant
Geberit Mfg., Inc. C580

Planning service—manufacturers
see
kitchen planning

Planning services—professional consultants
see
consultants and services

Plaques, insignia and tablets
stone—simulated
Avonite C465

Plastic
see
plastic—form
plastic—properties

Plastic—form
colored
Du Pont Co. C468
corrugated or flat sheet
Aristech Chemical Corp. C591
Avonite C465
Du Pont Co. C468
Wilson: Ralph Wilson Plastics
Co. C479
patterned or textured
Du Pont Co. C468
sheet, coil
Avonite C465
Du Pont Co. C468

Plastic-laminate products
see
partitions—materials: —plastic laminate-faced

Plastic materials—custom-molded
Avonite C465
Du Pont Co. C468

Plastic products
see
column covers: —plastic—specific type
piping and tubing—materials: —plastic—specific type

Plastic—properties
abrasion-resistant
see
plastic—properties: —shock-resistant
chemical-resistant
Avonite C465
Du Pont Co. C468
fire-resistant
Avonite C465
Du Pont Co. C468
heat-absorbing
Du Pont Co. C468

Plastic—properties *cont.*
moldable
Aristech Chemical Corp. C591
Du Pont Co. C468
shock-resistant
Du Pont Co. C468

Plates
wall
see
wiring devices—electrical: —wall plates

Plumbing fittings and trim
see also
piping and tubing accessories
drainage, drains
Geberit Mfg., Inc. C580
faucets/fixture trim
see
faucets
shower or spray
Grohe America C564
JADO C588
Jason International, Inc. C574
Strom Plumbing, Sign of the
Crab C584
shower or spray—automatic-sensing
Grohe America C564
shower or spray—group—column, wall-mounted
Grohe America C564
thermostatic
see
plumbing fittings and trim: —valves—mixing—pressure balancing, thermostatic
traps
Geberit Mfg., Inc. C580
valves—mixing—pressure balancing, thermostatic
Grohe America C564
JADO C588
Jason International, Inc. C574

Plumbing fixtures
see
bar furniture and equipment: —sink
bathtubs
bidets
faucets
food service equipment—commercial or institutional: —sinks
hospital equipment: —sinks—medical, surgical
lavatories and accessories
showers
sinks—commercial or institutional
sinks—residential
toilets

Plywood products
see
shelving: —wood or wood fiber, plywood

Pollution control equipment and systems
see
air conditioners
fans
pumps: —grinder—sewage
vacuum cleaning systems
ventilators
waste handling equipment and systems

Power supplies, protection/conditioning equipment
see
wiring devices—electrical

Prefinished paneling
see
surfacing and paneling—interior

Prison equipment
see
specific products
walls—detention or security
see
partitions—properties: —bullet or burglar-resistant

Product information—associations
see also
specific products
cabinets—kitchen
NKBA, National Kitchen &
Bath Association A105
kitchen and bath/planning and design
NKBA, National Kitchen &
Bath Association A105

Product information—general
see
specific products

Publications
see
product information—associations

Pumps
sewage ejector or sump
Zoeller Co. .C576

r

Ranges and ovens—residential
accessories for
KitchenAid, Inc., Whirlpool
Corp. C503
Viking Range Corp. C517
cooktops
Amana Refrigeration, Inc. C481
General Electric, Monogram C496
KitchenAid, Inc., Whirlpool
Corp. C503
Viking Range Corp. C517
cooktops/grills—convertible
Amana Refrigeration, Inc. C481
General Electric, Monogram C496
KitchenAid, Inc., Whirlpool
Corp. C503
electric
Amana Refrigeration, Inc. C481
General Electric, Monogram C496
KitchenAid, Inc., Whirlpool
Corp. C503
Viking Range Corp. C517
gas
Amana Refrigeration, Inc. C481
General Electric, Monogram C496
KitchenAid, Inc., Whirlpool
Corp. C503
Viking Range Corp. C517
ovens—built-in
Amana Refrigeration, Inc. C481
General Electric, Monogram C496
KitchenAid, Inc., Whirlpool
Corp. C503
Viking Range Corp. C517
ovens—built-in—double
Amana Refrigeration, Inc. C481
General Electric, Monogram C496
KitchenAid, Inc., Whirlpool
Corp. C503

Ranges and ovens—residential
cont.

ovens—built-in—double *cont.*
Viking Range Corp. C517

ovens—energy-saving
Viking Range Corp. C517

ovens—microwave
Amana Refrigeration, Inc. C481
General Electric, Monogram C496
Sharp Electronics Corp. C512

ovens—microwave/conventional combination
Amana Refrigeration, Inc. C481
General Electric, Monogram C496
Sharp Electronics Corp. C512

ovens—microwave—kitchenette units
Amana Refrigeration, Inc. C481
General Electric, Monogram C496

ovens—self-cleaning
Amana Refrigeration, Inc. C481
General Electric, Monogram C496
KitchenAid, Inc., Whirlpool
Corp. C503
Viking Range Corp. C517

ranges—built-in
Amana Refrigeration, Inc. C481
General Electric, Monogram C496
KitchenAid, Inc., Whirlpool
Corp. C503
Viking Range Corp. C517

ranges—energy-saving
Viking Range Corp. C517

ranges—griddle/broiler/oven combination
KitchenAid, Inc., Whirlpool
Corp. C503

ranges—microwave/conventional oven combination
Amana Refrigeration, Inc. C481
General Electric, Monogram C496

ranges—rotisserie combination
KitchenAid, Inc., Whirlpool
Corp. C503

ventilating hoods
see
ventilators: —hoods—residential kitchen—specific type

Receptors—shower
see
showers: —stalls and receptors—specific material

Recreational equipment
see
health club equipment
saunas and equipment

Refacings or facings
see
panels—building
surfacing and paneling—interior

Reference books and publications
see
product information—associations

Refrigerator-freezer combination
residential
Amana Refrigeration, Inc. C481
KitchenAid, Inc., Whirlpool
Corp. C503
Sub-Zero Freezer Co., Inc. C514; C515

residential—built-in
Amana Refrigeration, Inc. C481

Refrigerator-freezer combination
cont.

residential—built-in *cont.*
KitchenAid, Inc., Whirlpool
Corp. C503
Sub-Zero Freezer Co., Inc. C514; C515

Refrigerators
see also
refrigerator-freezer combination

residential
Amana Refrigeration, Inc. C481
General Electric, Monogram C496
KitchenAid, Inc., Whirlpool
Corp. C503
Sub-Zero Freezer Co., Inc. C514; C515

residential—built-in
Amana Refrigeration, Inc. C481
General Electric, Monogram C496
KitchenAid, Inc., Whirlpool
Corp. C503
Sub-Zero Freezer Co., Inc. C514; C515

residential—ice, chilled water dispensers
Amana Refrigeration, Inc. C481
General Electric, Monogram C496
KitchenAid, Inc., Whirlpool
Corp. C503
Sub-Zero Freezer Co., Inc. C514; C515

residential—undercounter
Sub-Zero Freezer Co., Inc. C514; C515

Registers and grilles
see
ventilators

Rehabilitation equipment
see
bathtubs: —hydro-massage combination

Restaurant equipment and furniture
see
food service equipment—commercial or institutional
refrigerator-freezer combination

Rods and bars
see
bathroom accessories: —grab bars—specific material
showers: —rods, hardware and tracks
washroom accessories: —grab bars

Roofing specialties and construction products
fascias
see
fascias

scuppers
see
drains

ventilators
see
ventilators: —roof—specific type

Room assemblies
partitions for
see
partitions

saunas
see
saunas and equipment

Room dividers
see
partitions

Rotisseries
see
ranges and ovens—residential: —ranges—rotisserie combination

s

Safety equipment
mirrors
see
mirrors: —safety

Sandwich panels or walls
see
panels—building

Saunas and equipment
see also
doors—application: —sauna
Finlandia Sauna Products,
Inc. C642

School equipment
intercommunicators
see
intercommunicating systems—specific type

laboratories
see
laboratory equipment

partitions
see
partitions

storage
see
storage equipment

Screens
partitions
see
partitions

space dividers
see
partitions

Scuppers
see
drains

Seats—shower, toilet
see
bathroom accessories: —grab bars—specific material
showers: —seats—specific type

Security and bullet-resistant equipment
see
consultants and services
glass—properties —burglar-resistant
panels—building—properties: —bullet or burglar-resistant
partitions—properties: —bullet or burglar-resistant

Septic tanks and accessories
see
waste handling equipment and systems

Service basins

see
  sinks—commercial or institutional

Sewage treatment equipment and systems

see
  piping and tubing—application: —gas, water,
    electrical or sewer system
  pumps —sewage ejector or pump—specific type
  waste handling equipment and systems

Sheets, strips, plates, coils

glass
see
  glass—form

plastic
see
  plastic—form

Shelving

see also
  storage equipment

bathroom or washroom—glass
  JADO C588
  NuTone C590

bathroom or washroom—metal
  Basco, Inc. .C585

wood or wood fiber, plywood
  Wellborn Cabinet, Inc. C536

Showers

see also
  bathtub/shower—prefabricated unit

cabinets and enclosures
  Aristech Chemical Corp. C591
  Century Shower Door, Inc. C593
  Du Pont Co. .C468
  Jason International, Inc. C574
  Strom Plumbing, Sign of the
    Crab C584
  Wilson: Ralph Wilson Plastics
    Co. C479
  Work Right Products, Inc. C597

doors
see
  doors—application: —shower

fittings, levers, valves
see
  plumbing fittings and trim

group
see
  plumbing fittings and trim: —shower or spray—
    group—column, wall-mounted

partitions
see
  partitions—shower, toilet, urinal

rods, hardware and tracks
  Strom Plumbing, Sign of the
    Crab C584

seats—wall-mounted
  Steamist Co., Inc. C673

stalls and receptors—fiber glass, plastic
  Jason International, Inc. C574

system
  Jason International, Inc. C574

Shutters and louvers—ventilating

see
  ventilators

Siding—general

see
  panels—building

Signs

see also
  plaques, insignia and tablets

engraving stock for
  Avonite C465

Sinks—commercial or institutional

fittings and trim for
see
  plumbing fittings and trim

food service
see
  food service equipment—commercial or
    institutional: —sinks

hospital
see
  hospital equipment: —sinks—medical, surgical

tops for
  Avonite C465
  Du Pont Co. .C468
  Swan Corp. (The) C563

Sinks—residential

bar
see
  bar furniture and equipment: —sink

ceramic, composite
  Avonite C465
  Blanco, Inc. .A012
  Du Pont Co. .C468

faucets
see
  faucets—application: —sink—specific type

fittings for
see
  plumbing fittings and trim

food waste disposers for
see
  food waste disposers

stainless steel
  Blanco, Inc. .A012

tops for
  Avonite C465
  Blanco, Inc. .A012
  Du Pont Co. .C468
  Swan Corp. (The) C563
  Wilson: Ralph Wilson Plastics
    Co. C479

Skirting

see
  fascias

Skylights—operation

ventilators—power-driven
see
  ventilators: —adjustable—manual or power-
    operated

Soap dispensers and holders

see
  bathroom accessories: —toilet paper holders,
    soap dishes—specific materials

Solar energy conversion—components for—passive

glazing—insulating
see
  glass—properties: —insulating—specific type

panels—building
see
  panels—building—properties: —insulating

Space dividers—interior

see
  partitions

Spandrel panels

see
  panels—building—materials

Sports training equipment

see
  bathtubs: —hydro-massage combination
  health club equipment

Stalls—shower

see
  showers

Steam bath rooms and equipment

see
  health club equipment

Steam products

see
  heaters—unit: —steam or hot water—specific
    type

Storage and retrieval systems

see
  shelving
  specific products or applications
  storage equipment

Storage equipment

see also
  office equipment
  shelving

cabinets with doors
  Wellborn Cabinet, Inc. C536

cabinets with drawers
  Wellborn Cabinet, Inc. C536

Store fronts

fire-rated
  Weck, Glashaus Div. B689

fire-resistant
  Weck, Glashaus Div. B689

Strainers

see
  drains
  piping and tubing accessories: —strainers

Sun-bathing equipment

see
  health club equipment

Sun controls

see
  glass
  plastic

Surfacing and paneling—exterior

see
  panels—building

Surfacing and paneling—interior

see
  surfacing and paneling—interior—materials
  surfacing and paneling—interior—properties

Wall coverings—rigid
see
  surfacing and paneling—interior

Washers
clothes
see
  laundry equipment—residential use:
    —washers—specific type

Washroom accessories
see also
  bathroom accessories
disabled persons' use
  Basco, Inc. C585
dispenser cabinets—toilet tissue
  Basco, Inc. C585
dispensers—facial tissue
  Basco, Inc. C585
dryers—electric—hand or hair
  Broan Mfg. Co., Inc. ii
grab bars
  Basco, Inc. C585
holders—toilet paper
  Basco, Inc. C585
  JADO C588
holders—toothbrush and/or tumbler—metal
  Basco, Inc. C585
  JADO C588
hooks—coat or robe
  Basco, Inc. C585
  JADO C588
partitions
see
  partitions—shower, toilet, urinal
shelving
see
  shelving: —bathroom or washroom—specific
    material
wash centers (lavatory with accessories)
  Dornbracht, Santile
    International Corp. C568

Waste handling equipment and systems
see also
  food waste disposers
compactors—residential or institutional
  Broan Mfg. Co., Inc. ii
  General Electric, Monogram C496
  KitchenAid, Inc., Whirlpool
    Corp. C503

Water closets
see
  toilets

Water conditioning equipment
see
  waste handling equipment and systems
piping for
see
  piping and tubing—application: —gas, water,
    electrical or sewer system

Water conservation equipment
see
  plumbing fittings and trim

Water heaters
see
  heaters—unit: —steam or hot water—specific
    type

Whirlpools
see
  bathtubs: —hydro-massage combination

Windows
see
  windows—replacement

Windows—general
church
see
  glass
  plastic
inserts for
see
  glass
  plastic
stained or faceted glass
see
  glass
  plastic
ventilators
see
  ventilators: —ceiling, wall, window

Windows—replacement
glass blocks for
  Weck, Glashaus Div. B689

Wiring devices—electrical
wall plates
  NuTone C590

Wood products
see
  shelving

Woodwork
custom-built
  KraftMaid Cabinetry C526
  Wellborn Cabinet, Inc. C536

Woodwork—simulated
moldings, cornices, door and window trim
see
  moldings and cornices: —plastic, composite

Woven wire mesh
see
  specific products

Catalogs are coded by positions within the volume in numerical sequence, e.g., C345

NOTE: Sweet's has been requested by manufacturers to include the following trade names and trademarks in this index. Sweet's makes no representations or warranties as to the rights of any manufacturer to any trade name or trademark listed in this index.

a

AMANA (furnaces/heat pumps/air
conditioners/appliances) C481
ARISTECH (tub & shower doors/enclosures) C591
AVONITE (solid surface material for
countertops, walls & furniture) C465

b

BASCO (washroom accessories) C585
BLANCO (plumbing fixtures) A012
BRASSTEC (tub, shower & steam
enclosures) C593
BROAN (residential appliances) ....ii ; A003
BROAN (toilet & bath accessories) C587

c

CENTEC (tub, shower & steam enclosures) C593
CENTRAFLOW (steam surface condenser) C585
CENTURY SHOWER (tub & shower
enclosure) C593
CLASSIC (two handle faucets, valves-tub/
shower/diverters) C564
CORIAN (plastic material) C468

d

DURAVIT (plumbing fixtures) C568

e

EUROMIX (single handle faucets, valves-tub
& shower) C564
EUROPA II (stainless steel bath accessories) C585
EUROPLUS (single handle kitchen faucets
ceramic disc) C564
EXQUISIT (two handle faucets, valves-tub/
shower ceramic disc) C564

f

FINLANDIA (heaters/rooms) C642
FINLANDIA (saunas) C642

g

GEBERIT (fittings, trim & accessories) C580
GEBERIT BATH WASTE & OVERFLOW
(whirlpool & tub drain-european styled) C580
GEBERIT REMOTE CONTROL KITCHEN
DRAIN (kitchen sink basket-remote control) C580
GEBERIT SPACE-SAVING KITCHEN
OUTLET W/ TRAP (under sink trap, space-
saving) C580
GENERAL ELECTRIC (appliances) C496

GLASHAUS (glass unit masonry) B689
GLASSTEC (tub, shower & steam
enclosures) C593
GROHMIX (thermostat & thermostat
pressure balance valves) C564

h

HARVIA (heaters/rooms) C642

J

JADO (fittings, trim & accessories) C588
JASON (plumbing fixtures) C574

k

KITCHENAID (residential appliances) C503
KRAFTMAID (kitchen & bath cabinets) C526

L

LADYLUX (single handle kitchen faucets with
pull out spray) C564
LAHR (thermostat mixing valves) C564
LUCETTE (tub, shower & steam enclosures) C593

m

MILAN (cabinets) C536
MODERN MAID (residential appliances) C481
MONOGRAM (appliances) C496
MONTEREY (cabinets) C536

n

NATIONAL KITCHEN & BATH (kitchen &
bath planning & design) A105
NKBA (kitchen & bath planning & design) A105
NUTONE (residential appliances) C590

o

OPTIDESIGN (type of heat exchanger) C585

r

RALPH WILSON (plastic fabrications) C479
RELEXA (handshowers, showerheads, arms,
hoses, unions & bars) C564

s

SANTILE (plumbing fixtures) C568
SHARP ELECTRONICS (appliances,
microwaves) C512
SIGN OF THE CRAB (fittings, trim &
accessories) C584
SLIM LINE (surface-mounted medicine
cabinets) C585
STEAMIST (steam baths & equipment) C673
STROM (fittings, trim & accessories) C584
SUB-ZERO (residential appliances) C514; C515
SWANSTONE (bathtub & shower wall panel
system) C563
SWANSTONE (kitchen & bar sinks) C563
SWANSTONE (vanity tops & bowls) C563

t

TEMPERSAFE (pressure balance valves) C564
TYPE 500 (standard heat exchanger) C585

u

UP-SCALE (lavatory, kitchen faucets & tub/
shower valves) C564

v

VIKING RANGE (residential appliances) C517

w

WECK (glass unit masonry) B689
WELLBORN (kitchen & bath cabinets) C536
WILSON (plastic fabrications) C479
WORK RIGHT (tub & shower doors/
enclosures) C597

z

ZOELLER (toilets) C576

If you don't use one of these...

you better use one of these.

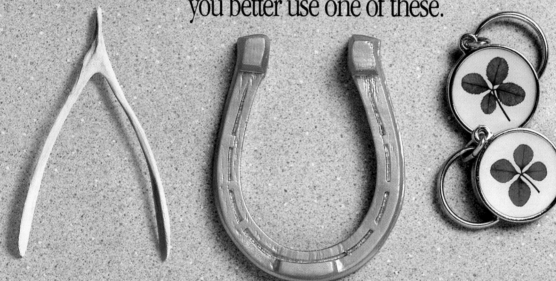

Maybe even all of them, if you're dreaming of a special new kitchen. Because you should ask a lot of the firm you hire to make that dream a reality:

- Will they spend the time to understand what you really want?
- Can they provide new and exciting ideas for making your kitchen look and *work* better?
- Will they do top-quality work at a fair price?
- Do they offer all the services you need?
- Do they have a showroom where you can see the latest trends and products?

Working with a member of the National Kitchen and Bath Association is the only way to be certain you'll get the right answer to each of these questions. So why test your luck?

Go with a sure thing — the total professionalism of every NKBA member. It's the best way to get exactly what you want.

Now that's our idea of a charmed life.

For information on NKBA members in your area, call toll-free: **1-800-FOR-NKBA.**

687 Willow Grove Street, Hackettstown, New Jersey 07840 FAX: (908) 852-1695

Creating Your Dream Kitchen or Bathroom

More than four million kitchens will be built or remodeled in 1994. Some of the projects will be dreams come true. The rest can be nightmares.

When you stop and think about the effects that every alteration has on a room, you realize just how complicated remodeling or building can be. Besides the logistical questions, many decisions must be made in terms of color, hardware, appliances, lighting, plumbing fixtures, countertops, and the overall style of your new room.

"With so many decisions to make and so much to think about, the average consumer needs a professional to organize this project — someone who understands all of the complexities involved," said Donna M. Luzzo, Director of Communications for the National Kitchen & Bath Association (NKBA). "Kitchen and bathroom design is a specialized trade. It requires a good deal of experience and know-how to accomplish successful projects."

The first step in creating a successful new room is a simple one — find an NKBA member to design and coordinate the construction of your room.

"Someone remodeling a kitchen or bathroom wants the project to get off to a good start, and a kitchen and bath professional is definitely the way to go," said Luzzo. "An NKBA member will coordinate every aspect of the design and installation. They are experienced at working with contractors, electricians, plumbers, etc., and can efficiently schedule the jobs involved. And, most important, they are experts at working with the client. They listen to client needs and translate them into the kind of rooms they want."

To help consumers get ready for a remodeling and help them work with a kitchen or bathroom designer, the NKBA offers a 16-page brochure to consumers for $3. NKBA will also send a directory of kitchen/bathroom designers at no charge. Contact NKBA at 687 Willow Grove St., Hackettstown, N.J. 07840, or 1-800-FOR-NKBA.

New Bathroom Guidelines Reflect Safety/Comfort

For much too long, the bathroom has been a miserable space accommodated in the smallest area of the home with the least amount of money. In the past, bathroom planning standards were based on minimum requirements established by the Department of Housing and Urban Development (HUD), which focused solely on the space required for the basic fixtures, and little or no consideration was given to the human anatomy of the user and his/her safe, comfortable movement in the space.

In the years ahead, successful bathroom designers will plan rooms that are designed around the people that will use them, rather than the fixtures that will be installed in them, according to the National Kitchen & Bath Association (NKBA).

"The bathroom is no longer a room reserved for simple personal hygiene," said Annette M. DePaepe, CKD, CBD, NKBA Director of Societies. "Today, people spend more time in the space. Some gather in a family group to enjoy the therapeutic pleasure of a hydromassage bath or sauna; others use the bathroom as a secluded spot away from hectic family and job responsibilities."

In keeping with the changing needs of the American family and issues such as safety and universal design, the NKBA has developed new planning guidelines for bathroom design which are based on the space required for the user(s) to function in the room comfortably and safely. The following is a complete list of these new planning guidelines.

NKBA's 27 Rules of Bathroom Design

1. A clear walkway of at least 32 inches must be provided at all entrances to the bathroom.

2. No doors may interfere with fixtures.

3. Mechanical ventilation system must be included in the plan.

4. Ground fault circuit interrupters specified on all receptacles. No switches within 60 inches of any water source. All light fixtures above tub/shower units are moisture-proof special purpose fixtures.

5. If floor space exists between two fixtures, at least six inches of space should be provided for cleaning.

6. At least 21 inches of clear walkway space exists in front of lavatory.

7. The minimum clearance from the lavatory centerline to any side wall is 12 inches.

8. The minimum clearance between two bowls in the lavatory center is 30 inches, centerline to centerline.

9. The minimum clearance from the center of the toilet to any obstruction, fixture or equipment on either side of toilet is 15 inches.

10. At least 21 inches of clear walkway space exists in front of toilet.

11. Toilet paper holder is installed within reach of person seated on the toilet. Ideal location is slightly in front of the edge of toilet bowl, the center of which is 26 inches above the finished floor.

12. The minimum clearance from the center of the bidet to any obstruction, fixture or equipment on either side of the bidet is 15 inches.

13. At least 21 inches of clear walkway space exists in front of bidet.

14. Storage for soap and towels is installed within reach of person seated on the bidet.

15. No more than one step leads to the tub. Step must be at least 10 inches deep, and must not exceed 7¼ inches in height.

16. Bathtub faucetry is accessible from outside the tub.

17. Whirlpool motor access, if necessary, is included in plan.

18. At least one grab bar is installed to facilitate bathtub or shower entry.

19. Minimum useable shower interior dimension is 32" x 32".

20. Bench or footrest is installed within shower enclosure.

21. Minimum clear walkway of 21 inches exists in front of tub/shower.

22. Shower door swings into bathroom.

23. All shower heads are protected by pressure balance/temperature regulator or temperature-limiting device.

24. All flooring is of slip-resistant material.

25. Adequate storage must be provided in plan, including: counter/shelf space around lavatory, adequate grooming equipment storage, convenient shampoo/soap storage in shower/tub area, and hanging space for bathroom linens.

26. Adequate heating system must be provided.

27. General and task lighting must be provided.

Kitchen Design
Changes with the Times

Home life, as we know it, is a far cry from what went on at the Cleaver residence, or in the Cunningham household, even at the Brady's "hip" pad.

In the past 40 years, lifestyles have undergone a lot of change. And no room in the house exemplifies that change better than the kitchen.

The walls have come down; more appliances have gone in; what we cook, when we cook and who cooks bears little resemblance to what went on two or three generations ago.

Yet, despite the great changes in lifestyle and kitchen use, little attention had been paid to the guidelines followed for kitchen design. Recognizing the need for updated planning standards, the National Kitchen & Bath Association (NKBA) conducted in-depth research into today's kitchens. As a result, today's kitchen planners have a new set of rules to follow in order to meet the needs of their 1990s clients.

"The kitchen did not used to be considered part of the social portion of the home," said NKBA Director of Communications Donna M. Luzzo. "Rather, kitchens were planned as walled-off spaces intended for use by a full-time homemaker who was the primary, from-scratch cook in the household."

Conversely, according to the NKBA, today most families consist of two working parents, creating a need for shared cooking and clean-up responsibilities. The walled-off space of the past has opened into other rooms. And families and guests are gathering in the kitchen to socialize and carry on activities other than cooking.

These changes make an impact on how a kitchen needs to be arranged; as do a host of others, according to Luzzo.

"Microwave ovens, side-by-side refrigerators and dishwashers are commonly found in kitchens," she said. "In addition, our recent research found that more than 700 utensils and food items are kept in the room. That's 400 more items than 40 years ago."

What does it all mean? More cabinet storage is necessary, for one. And the kitchen must become a comfortable setting for today's on-the-go families to gather, unwind, entertain and work in together easily.

The NKBA has established the following 31 rules for planning safe, functional kitchens. Whether remodeling on your own, or working with a professional kitchen planner as recommended by the NKBA, use these rules as guidelines to ensure a functional kitchen plan that will serve the needs of your family.

If you would like a directory of kitchen design firms, contact the NKBA at 1-800-FOR-NKBA and one will be sent to you at no charge.

NKBA's 31 Rules of Kitchen Design

1. A clear walkway at least 32" wide must be provided at all entrances to the kitchen.

2. No entry or appliance door may interfere with work center appliances and/or counter space.

3. Work aisles must be at least 42" wide, and passage ways must be at least 36" wide for a one-cook kitchen.

4. In kitchens 150 square feet or less, at least 144" of wall cabinet frontage, with cabinets at least 12" deep and a minimum of 30" high (or equivalent), must be installed over counter tops. In kitchens over 150 square feet, 186" of wall cabinets must be included. Diagonal or pie-cut wall cabinets count as a total of 24". Difficult to reach cabinets above the hood, oven or refrigerator do not count unless specialized storage devices are installed within the case to improve accessibility.

5. At least 60" of wall cabinet frontage with cabinets which are at least 12" deep and a minimum of 30" high (or equivalent) must be included within 72" of the primary sink centerline.

6. In kitchens 150 square feet or less, at least 156" of base cabinet frontage, with cabinets at least 21" deep (or equivalent) must be part of the plan. In kitchens over 150 square feet, 192" of base cabinets must be included. Pie-cut/lazy Susan cabinets count as a total of 30". The first 24" of a blind corner box do not count.

7. In kitchens 150 square feet or less, at least 120" of drawer frontage or roll-out shelf frontage must be planned. Kitchens over 150 square feet require at least 165" of drawer/shelf frontage. (Measure cabinet width to determine frontage.)

8. At least five storage items must be included in the kitchen to improve the accessibility and functionality of the plan. These items include, but are not limited to: wall cabinets with adjustable shelves, interior vertical dividers, pull out drawers, swing-out pantries, or drawer/roll-out space greater than the minimum 135".

9. At least one functional corner storage unit must be included. (Rule does not apply to a kitchen without corner cabinet arrangements.)

10. Between 15" and 18" of clearance must exist between the countertop and the bottom of wall cabinets.

11. In kitchens 150 square feet or less, at least 132" of usable countertop frontage is required. For kitchens larger than 150 square feet, the countertop requirement increases to 198". Counter must be 16" deep to be counted; corner space does not count.

12. No two primary work centers (the primary sink, refrigerator, preparation center, cooktop/range center), can be separated by a full-height, full-depth tall tower, such as an oven cabinet, pantry cabinet or refrigerator.

13. There must be at least 24" of counter space to one side of the sink, and 18" on the other side. (Measure only countertop frontage, do not count corner space.) The 18" and 24" counter space sections may be a continuous surface, or the total of two angled countertop sections. If a second sink is part of the plan, at least 3" of counterspace must be on one side and 18" on the other side.

14. At least 3" of counter space must be allowed from the edge of the sink to the inside corner of the countertop if more than 21" of counter space is available on the return. Or, at least 18" of counter space from the edge of the sink to the inside corner of the countertop if the return counter space is blocked by a full-height, full-depth cabinet or any appliance which is deeper than the countertop.

15. At least two waste receptacles must be included in the plan, one for garbage and one for recyclables; or other recycling facilities should be planned.

16. The dishwasher must be positioned within 36" of one sink. Sufficient space (21" of standing room) must be allowed between the dishwasher and adjacent counters, other appliances and cabinets.

17. At least 36" of continuous countertop is required for the preparation center, and must be located close to a water source.

18. The plan should allow at least 15" of counter space on the latch side of a refrigerator or on either side of a side-by-side refrigerator. Or, at least 15" of landing space which is no more than 48" across from the refrigerator. (Measure the 48" walkway from the countertop adjacent to the refrigerator to the island countertop directly opposite.)

19. For an open-ended kitchen configuration, at least 9" of counter space is required on one side of the cooktop/range top and 15" on the other. For an enclosed configuration, at least 3" of clearance space must be planned at an end wall protected by flame-retardant surfacing material, and 15" must be allowed on the other side of the appliance.

20. The cooking surface can not be placed below an operable window unless the window is 3" or more behind the appliance, and/or more than 24" above it.

21. There must be at least 15" of landing space next to or above the oven if the appliance door opens into a primary family traffic pattern. 15" of landing space which is no more than 48" across from the oven is acceptable if the appliance does not open into traffic area.

22. At least 15" of landing space must be planned above, below, or adjacent to the microwave oven.

23. The shelf on which the microwave is placed is to be between counter and eye level (36" to 54" off the floor).

24. All cooking surface appliances are required to have a ventilation system, with a fan rated at 150 CFM minimum.

25. At least 24" of clearance is needed between the cooking surface and a protected surface above. Or, at least 30" of clearance is needed between the cooking surface and an unprotected surface above.

26. The work triangle should total less than 26'. The triangle is defined as the shortest walking distance between the refrigerator, primary cooking surface, and primary food preparation sink. It is measured from the center front of each appliance. The work triangle may not intersect an island or peninsula cabinet by more than 12". No single leg of the triangle should be shorter than 4' nor longer than 9'.

27. No major household traffic patterns should cross through the work triangle connecting the three primary centers (the primary sink, refrigerator, preparation center, cooktop/range center).

28. A minimum of 12" x 24" counter/table space should planned for each seated diner.

29. At least 36" of walkway space from a counter/table to any wall or obstacle behind it is required if the area is to be used to pass behind a seated diner. Or, at least 24" of space from the counter/table to any wall or obstacle behind it, is needed if the area will not be used as a walk space.

30. At least 10% of the total square footage of the separate kitchen, or of a total living space which includes a kitchen should be appropriated for windows/skylights.

31. Ground fault circuit interrupters must be specified on all receptacles that are within 6' of a water source in the kitchen. A fire extinguisher should be located near the cooktop. Smoke alarms should be included near the kitchen.

Baths Up, Kitchens Down in Retail Selling Price

Results of the 1992 Kitchen/Bath Industry Trends Survey, released by the National Kitchen & Bath Association (NKBA), indicate that the average bathroom selling price is rising nationally. At the same time, the national average selling price of kitchen projects is down slightly.

The selling price reflects the total cost charged to retail customers or builders for complete kitchen and bathroom projects in newly-constructed or remodeled homes. Included in the selling price are all or most of the following items: labor, cabinets, fixtures/fittings, countertops, flooring, lighting, and appliances. The 1992 Survey tabulated information provided by 300 NKBA-member firms.

According to Paul L. Kelley, NKBA Vice President of Industry Relations and Marketing, the 1992 Trends Survey, which addresses business conducted in 1991, revealed that the average bathroom selling price at this time is $9,215, and the average kitchen selling price $16,491.

The Survey data also indicates that small kitchen jobs (less than 150 square feet) presently represent a larger portion of all kitchen projects installed compared to previous years, perhaps explaining the decrease in average price. Interestingly, small sized (under 35 square feet) bathroom projects now account for 17 percent of the total, up from just one percent of the total reported in the 1990 Survey.

Kitchen Highlights

The gap between the popularity of wood cabinets (75 percent) and laminate cabinets (22 percent) is narrowing. The 1990 figures were 87 and 11.5 percent, respectively. Oak is the most popular wood species for cabinetry (54 percent), but maple (15 percent) is up dramatically since the 1990 Survey. Laminate leads all other countertop materials (54 percent), followed most closely by solid surfacing (30 percent).

Bathroom Highlights

As in the kitchens surveyed, wood cabinets are installed most often (68 percent). Oak (59 percent) leads all other wood species, with cherry (24 percent) and maple (12 percent) in the second and third positions. Both cherry and maple have gained popularity — in the 1990 Survey, the figures tabulated were 11 percent and 3 percent, respectively. Paint (30 percent), wall paper (28 percent) and tile (16 percent) continue as the wall covering materials of choice, although the order of preference has changed since 1990, when wall paper topped the list at 66 percent.

Color

White is still the most important color in both kitchens (48 percent) and bathrooms (62 percent). These figures represent a rise of almost 13 percent in white kitchens installed, when expressed as a portion of total, since the 1990 Survey. White baths have risen a corresponding 19 percent. Wood-toned kitchens and pastel baths are the second most popular choices. Almond is the third most-often chosen color for both kitchens and bathrooms.

How Does Your Kitchen Rate?

How functional and fashionable is your kitchen? Answer these questions from the National Kitchen & Bath Association to find out how the most important room in your home rates.

A. Storage System

1. Do your cabinets feature time-saving accessories such as roll-out shelves, divided drawers and lazy Susans?   YES   NO

2. Is there enough cabinet shelf space?   YES   NO

3. Is the cabinet door style and color up-to-date?   YES   NO

4. Is there a place to sort recyclables?   YES   NO

B. Countertop

1. Is there enough counter space?   YES   NO

2. Is the countertop material undamaged and in good shape? YES   NO

3. Is the counter color/pattern up-to-date?   YES   NO

C. Mechanical Elements

1. Do you have enough electrical outlets?   YES   NO

2. Is there a good ventilation system in the cooking area? YES   NO

D. Appliances/Fixtures

1. Are all of your appliances a pleasant color that looks good? YES   NO

E. Room Orientation

1. Is there a casual dining/conversation area in the room? YES   NO

2. Is the kitchen arranged so that "People Traffic" is directed away from the cook's activities?   YES   NO

If you answered "no" more than "yes," you may need a new room. Take the first step and contact a member of the National Kitchen & Bath Association to ensure a successful project. They are competent to design and install complete kitchens, and subscribe to a strict Code of Conduct. Bring this evaluation with you, and your NKBA Kitchen Dealer or Certified Kitchen Designer will help you use your NO answers to make planning decisions regarding room shape and size, appliance and material selection as well as mechanical specifications. For a complete list of NKBA members contact: NKBA, 687 Willow Grove St., Hackettstown, N.J. 07840 or 1-800-FOR-NKBA.

Does Your Bathroom Pass the Test?

How does your bathroom rate? Is it beautiful...functional...safe? Answer this brief survey from the National Kitchen & Bath Association to find out if your bathroom makes the grade.

A. Fixtures

1. Is the shower safe (non-slip floor, grab bars, bench seat, temperature-controlled faucet)?   YES   NO

2. Is the bathtub safe (easy to get into, faucets within reach, non-slip bottom, grab bars)?   YES   NO

3. Are all the fixtures an attractive color?   YES   NO

B. Storage Systems

1. Is the cabinet door style and color up-to-date?   YES   NO

2. Do cabinets include a well-organized storage system?
YES   NO

3. Is there space for towel storage in or near the bathroom?
YES   NO

C. Mechanical Elements

1. Is there an efficient ventilation system in the room?
YES   NO

2. Is there adequate lighting in the right place(s) for your bathroom activities (shaving, make-up application, reading)?
YES   NO

3. Are all the electrical outlets protected with ground fault circuit interrupters to prevent electrical shock?   YES   NO

D. Major Surfaces

1. Are all the surfaces easy to keep clean?   YES   NO

E. Room Orientation

1. Is the existing bathroom big enough?   YES   NO

2. Can two people use the bathroom comfortably and conveniently at the same time?   YES   NO

More "nos" than "yeses" on your score card may indicate that you need a new bathroom. Take the first step and contact a member of the National Kitchen & Bath Association to ensure a successful project. They are competent to design and install complete bathrooms, and subscribe to a strict Code of Conduct. Bring this evaluation with you, and your NKBA Bathroom Dealer or Certified Bathroom Designer will help you use your NO answers to make planning decisions regarding room shape and size, fixture and material selection as well as mechanical specifications.
For a complete list of NKBA members contact: NKBA, 687 Willow Grove St., Hackettstown, N.J. 07840 or 1-800-FOR-NKBA.

BLANCO SELECT UNDERMOUNT BOWLS INCLUDE A VARIETY OF SIZES IN SILACRON 2000 AND STAINLESS STEEL FOR SOLID SURFACE INSTALLATION. ADD BLANCO'S UNIQUE WASTE CHUTE SYSTEM AND CREATE A DESIGN THAT'S RIGHT FOR YOU!

BLANCO AMERICA: 1001 LOWER LANDING ROAD, SUITE 607, BLACKWOOD, NJ 08012, 609-228-3500.

BLANCO

NATIONAL KITCHEN
NKBA
& BATH ASSOCIATION

FROM INSPIRATION TO SENSATION

Creating Your
Dream Kitchen
Or Bathroom

So, you've decided to create your dream kitchen or bathroom. Great idea. You'll finally be able to apply all of those wishes you've collected on your list over the years, like that kitchen island with a cooktop (and more of that invaluable countertop and cabinet space), or maybe you've always wanted a bathtub-for-two. Whether it's the kitchen or bathroom (or both), you can look forward to an exciting transformation into the room you've always wanted.

But when you stop and think about the effects that every alteration has on a room, you realize just how complicated remodeling or building can be. Take, for instance, the kitchen island with a cooktop. Where there's a cooktop, there's smoke and steam. And where there's smoke and steam, there has to be ventilation. So an overhead hood must be added, unless you have a downventing cooktop. Also, any time you have work space like the added countertop, you need electrical outlets. So wiring will be necessary for the outlets, as well as the cooktop and vent hood. And that's just the beginning.

Besides the logistical questions, many decisions must be made in terms of color, hardware, appliances, lighting, plumbing fixtures, countertops, and the overall style of your new room.

With so many decisions to make and so much to think about, you need a professional to organize this project — someone who understands all of the complexities involved. That's where the National Kitchen and Bath Association (NKBA) comes in.

FINDING THE NKBA MEMBER FOR THE JOB

T he first step in creating your new room is a simple one — find an NKBA member to design and coordinate the construction of your room. You want your project to get off to a good start, and a kitchen and bath professional is definitely the way to go.

WHY?

The National Kitchen & Bath Association is an organization of professionals who focus specifically on kitchens and bathrooms. When you deal with an NKBA member, you'll benefit from specialized expertise, years of experience, a commitment to quality, and a high degree of professionalism. They maintain showrooms with products and complete designs on display so you can get a feel for the type and quality of work they can do.

A kitchen and bath professional can offer sound advice and suggest solutions to any problems that may arise, or, better yet, prevent problems from occurring. They also understand the ways families and individuals relate to their surroundings, and therefore may be able to troubleshoot and meet needs in ways that may not occur to those who don't specialize in kitchens and bathrooms.

An NKBA member will coordinate every aspect of the design and installation. They are experienced at working with contractors — electricians, plumbers, etc. — and can efficiently schedule the jobs involved. And, most important, they are expert at working with you, the client. They listen to your needs and translate them into the kind of room you want.

Don't take chances with your investment. When you make the decision for a new kitchen or bathroom, make the decision to find an NKBA member.

HOW?

NATIONAL KITCHEN NKBA & BATH ASSOCIATION

I t's easy to find an NKBA member, if you know what to look for. And easy identification begins with the NKBA logo, a symbol of quality, dedication and expertise in kitchens and bathrooms.

When visiting kitchen and bath showrooms, look for the logo in windows or on the counter.

If you know anyone who has recently remodeled, talk with them. Ask them who they used and if he or she is associated with the NKBA. Referrals are an excellent source for finding an industry professional, but be sure you're dealing with someone qualified in kitchens and bathrooms specifically — an NKBA member.

You can find all of the NKBA members in your area by contacting the National Kitchen and Bath Association at 687 Willow Grove Street, Hackettstown, New Jersey 07840, **1-800-FOR-NKBA**. They will provide you with a directory of NKBA firms who design, supply and install residential kitchens and bathrooms.

HAVE YOU FINISHED YOUR HOMEWORK?

Now that you have a name in mind (or possibly more than one — you may want to talk with several NKBA professionals to find the one with whom you feel most comfortable), you can go ahead and set up an appointment to discuss your project. But before you actually sit down with the designer, there are several things you should do in preparation. (This is the fun part.)

Chances are you've been thinking about this for a while, but if not, start reading magazines geared toward the home, remodeling, architecture, and especially those that focus on kitchens and bathrooms. Clip out pictures of kitchens or bathrooms that interest you — this will help the designer get a feel for the styles you like. You may even find features that would work in your new room.

Visit kitchen and bath showrooms to see the many options for new countertops and other surfaces, and to collect brochures on fixtures, cabinets, appliances and any other items or materials that interest you.

As you visit different showrooms in your search for ideas and NKBA designers, you should make notes on each one. The best way to find the NKBA member with whom you're most comfortable is to evaluate the designers and their showrooms. Use the following checklist to help you in your decision:

Evaluating the kitchen and bath dealership

	Showrooms				Showrooms		
	#1	#2	#3		#1	#2	#3
Showroom Clean and Neat	___	___	___	Designers Ask Questions About Your Project	___	___	___
Displays Highlight Interesting Design	___	___	___	NKBA Membership Identified	___	___	___
Displays Well-Constructed and Presented	___	___	___	Firm Has Been In Business for at Least Two Years	___	___	___
Broad Range of Styles Offered	___	___	___	Firm Provides Complete Design and Installation Services	___	___	___
Staff Friendly and Helpful	___	___	___				
Staff Knowledgeable About Products and Design	___	___	___	Referrals Provided	___	___	___

As you visit showrooms and gather notes, clippings, photographs, brochures and samples, you may want to organize them into an "idea file." As your file grows, you'll see a definite style emerge from the decorating trends you've chosen — *your* style.

KITCHEN PLANNING WITH YOUR NKBA SPECIALIST

You can save a lot of time and money, and greatly reduce guesswork by first evaluating your needs. Before even your initial consultation, write down some basic lifestyle facts.

Simple facts, like how many hours a week you work, will affect how often you cook and what appliances you use. If you work a lot of hours out of the home, you may cook less often, opting instead for microwave meals, in which case you'd need your microwave in a convenient location and a lot of freezer space.

Who uses your kitchen? Is it a setting for family gatherings, or the private domain of a gourmet chef? Will it function well with two or more cooks? Do you entertain often? All of these answers will affect the size, layout and type of equipment you need for your kitchen.

When preparing your evaluation, first consider your normal cooking habits. For instance, if your family shares in the meal preparation, you may need two sinks and built-in cutting and chopping boards strategically placed throughout the kitchen to maximize food preparation areas.

Will children be active in the kitchen? If so, easy-to-clean surfaces are a must. You may also want to consider a desk or counter setup for homework and after-school snacks.

If you like to entertain, often cooking for large groups of guests, you may need two ovens and a wide-shelved refrigerator.

Do you recycle? You'll need the separating and storage space, depending on your involvement and the requirements in your area.

All of the variables mentioned here (and others your designer will pose) will affect the layout of your kitchen. Each shape — U-shaped, L-shaped, Corridor, Island, One-Wall, or Peninsula — has its own functionality and advantages. Once the NKBA kitchen specialist has laid out your kitchen, he or she will guide you in selecting components. With all of the advances in materials, appliances and designs, this selection process would be overwhelming without the help of a professional.

Your decision-making becomes much easier once you have related your needs to your lifestyle. By providing your NKBA professional with a clear picture of what works best for your family, you'll be off to a head start.

BATHROOM PLANNING WITH YOUR NKBA SPECIALIST

Do you look forward to spending time in your bathroom? Sounds like a strange question to most people. Most bathrooms are cold and claustrophobic, places where comfort is either kept to a bare minimum, or simply not an option. But with the shift in society back toward the home also come changes in the bathroom.

Bathrooms have become more than a necessity. Their role has now expanded to that of "bodyroom," incorporating such amenities as whirlpool tubs, exercise equipment, dual-head showers, heat lamps and entertainment systems.

Before you talk to an NKBA professional about your new bathroom, evaluate your needs by first looking at who will use it, and how. The best way to do that is to examine present bathroom usage. Some NKBA members suggest taking notes as you use the room on a typical weekday and weekend. By mapping out your routine, you and your bath designer will be better-equipped to create a floorplan that is efficient and incorporates the features you need.

For example, you may think the first thing you do when you step out of the shower is to reach for your towel. Keeping a diary, however, might reveal that oftentimes the first move after exiting the shower is to drip, drip, drip across the hall to the linen closet. So, by simply focusing on details and making note of them, you've discovered the need for bathroom towel storage.

If several girls or women use the bathroom, adequate circuits and outlets are necessary for hair dryers and curling irons, as well as appropriate lighting for makeup application.

Special safety and convenience features should be considered for elderly, very young and handicapped family members. High water closet seats, grab bars and locking cabinets are practical options, and your designer will likely have other suggestions.

For family bathrooms which are shared by several people, privacy zones isolating the shower, tub, lavatory and water closet will allow simultaneous use.

Your NKBA bathroom specialist will take into consideration all of these factors and more. They have the experience to anticipate potential problems and point out options that may help you with your choices.

SETTING
PRIORITIES

hen your idea file is overflowing with clippings and photographs, you've thought about style and color, and evaluated your needs, there is one final step that will really help your NKBA professional: your "must-have" and "want" lists. You simply make two lists which include:

1) features you consider essential for your new room, and
2) features you'd like to have, if possible and if budget permits.

It sounds easy, right? Well, this one may force you to make some tough decisions and possibly even some sacrifices, but it is a very valuable step. Just listing and distinguishing the "must-haves" from the "wants" will help you focus on the features most important to you and your family. In fact, you may want to let each member of the family make their own lists. When you can actually see them on paper, it puts your needs into better perspective.

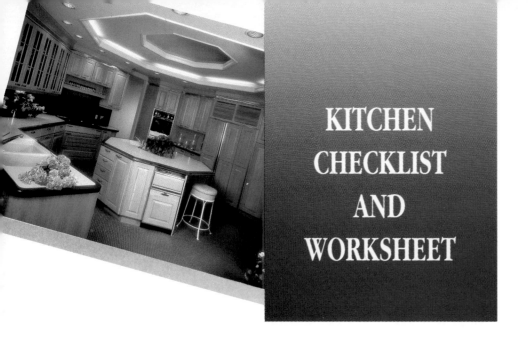

KITCHEN CHECKLIST AND WORKSHEET

Needs and Wants

Check the items you feel your kitchen must have in the "need" column, and the items you would like, if the budget and design allow, in the "want" column. (This should be used as a preliminary guideline; they may change along the way.)

	Need	Want		Need	Want
New cabinets	____	____	Recycling bins	____	____
New countertop	____	____	More workspace	____	____
New floor	____	____	More storage	____	____
New oven(s)	____	____	Pantry	____	____
New refrigerator/freezer	____	____	Wet bar	____	____
New cooktop	____	____	New window(s)	____	____
New microwave	____	____	Desk area	____	____
New dishwasher	____	____	Eating area	____	____
New sink(s)	____	____	Media/TV center	____	____
New light fixtures	____	____	Others _____	____	____
Cutting/chopping surfaces	____	____	_____	____	____
Waste disposal	____	____	_____	____	____
Trash compactor	____	____	_____	____	____

Lifestyle/Room Use

This worksheet will give you some things to think about in your initial planning, but it's only the beginning. Your NKBA kitchen specialist will conduct an in-depth interview with you in order to create a design that suits your lifestyle and satisfies your needs and wants.

Who is the primary cook? _____

How many other household members cook? _____

Do any of these members have physical limitations? _____

What type of cooking do you normally do?
_____ Heat and serve meals
_____ Full-course, "from scratch" meals
_____ Bulk cooking for freezing/leftovers
_____ Other _____

Do you entertain frequently? ____ Formally ____ Informally

Is the kitchen a socializing place? _____

Where do you plan to sort recyclables?
___ Kitchen ___ Laundry ___ Garage ___ Other

What type of feeling would you like your new kitchen space to have?
___ Sleek/Contemporary ___ Warm & Cozy Country
___ Traditional ___ Open & Airy
___ Strictly Functional ___ Formal
___ Family Retreat ___ Personal Design Statement

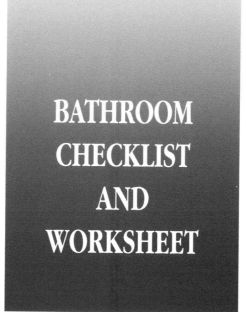

BATHROOM CHECKLIST AND WORKSHEET

Needs and Wants

Check the items you feel your bathroom must have in the "need" column, and the items you would like, if the budget and design allow, in the "want" column. (This should be used as a preliminary guideline; they may change along the way.)

	Need	Want		Need	Want
New vanity	____	____	Heat lamp	____	____
Separate shower	____	____	Bidet	____	____
New lavatory (sink)	____	____	New floor/wall surfaces	____	____
Tub for two	____	____	New countertops	____	____
Whirlpool tub	____	____	Customized storage	____	____
New water closet (toilet)	____	____	Others _____	____	____
Exercise area	____	____	_____	____	____
Entertainment center	____	____	_____	____	____
Linen storage	____	____	_____	____	____
Lighting fixtures	____	____	_____	____	____

Lifestyle/Room Use

This worksheet will give you some things to think about in your initial planning, but it's only the beginning. Your NKBA bathroom specialist will conduct an in-depth interview with you in order to create a design that suits your lifestyle and satisfies your needs and wants.

Who will use this bathroom (i.e., client, spouse, child, guests)?

_____

Type of bathroom?
___ Powder   ___ Children's   ___ Mastersuite   ___ Hall

How many will use it at one time? _____

What activities will take place in the bathroom?
___ Makeup application   ___ Bathing
___ Hair care   ___ Dressing
___ Exercising   ___ Lounging
___ Laundering   ___ Other _____

Would you like his and hers facilities? _____

Do you prefer the water closet and/or bidet to be isolated from the other fixtures? _____

Would you like a closet planned as part of your new bathroom?
          ____ Yes   ____ No

What type of feeling would you like your new bathroom to have?
___ Sleek/Contemporary   ___ Warm/Country
___ Traditional   ___ Open & Airy
___ Personal Design Statement

THE DESIGN CONFERENCE

O.K., you've done your homework — you stand ready with your ideas, lists, samples, photographs, maybe even rough plans. And now it's time to meet with your designer.

You may first meet with the NKBA member at the showroom to look over samples and displays, but then he or she will come out to your house and really get to work. Here's where you'll begin to see what sets NKBA specialists apart from other designers. The NKBA member will take careful and thorough measurements, right down to locating the pipes in the walls (something often overlooked by those who do not specialize in kitchen and bathroom planning).

He or she will look at your idea file and talk with you in depth about your needs. This is an opportunity for both of you to discuss thoughts and opinions, ask questions and determine a direction for your room design. Think of it as an exchange of ideas, a "design conference." This is another advantage of working with an NKBA member. He or she will work *with you* to achieve the best results, instead of simply dictating a design.

One very important determinant for your new room design is your budget. You should have a figure established as you go into this — one that's realistic for your situation. And the initial design conference is the time to talk budgets. Your NKBA specialist will let you know what can be achieved — in the way of materials, construction, appliances, etc. — for what you want to spend. And together, you can set priorities for your design that will allow your new dream room to stay within your budget.

When you both agree on a general direction and a budget, you can make arrangements for payment.

With many firms, payment begins with 50% at the signing of the contract, then 40% when installation begins, and the remaining 10% upon completion of the job. Financing can be arranged through a home improvement loan, or you may be able to negotiate the price into the mortgage when purchasing a home. Remember, your new room is an investment in your home's equity. It increases with the value of your home, and may be recovered when the home is sold.

LET THE TRANS-FORMATION BEGIN

From the first meeting, you'll begin to see how working with an NKBA member will make the project easier, and the results, better. When you've got the knowledge and experience of an NKBA professional on your side, you can rest assured that your new room will be everything you dreamed it would be, and more.

First, your NKBA specialist will design the complete layout, choose the final materials, and begin coordinating the contractors — all with your approval, of course. Then, the construction begins.

Living under construction is never easy, but your NKBA professional will do everything possible to minimize the inconvenience for you. Ask him or her for tips on living under construction. For example, setting up temporary facilities for cooking and cleanup. Your NKBA designer has experience in these matters and will undoubtedly have ideas to make you more comfortable during this phase.

And now it's only a matter of time before you see your dream room become a reality. Exactly how long depends on many variables (whether or not you are having cabinets custom-designed, for example), but in somewhere between two weeks and several months, you'll see the results.

You'll soon see your room taking shape. The ideas you've envisioned, the style you've developed, the colors you've decided upon, you'll see it all materialize at the hands of the craftsmen.

ANOTHER HAPPY ENDING

I t's evening, you're dining in your new kitchen, or soaking in your new whirlpool tub. You proudly gaze around the room. For the next few weeks you'll have to open an extra drawer or two looking for the silverware. Or you may catch yourself walking across the room to where the towels *used to* be. But you'll enjoy getting to know your new room and growing with it. After all, you created it (with a little help from NKBA).

National Kitchen & Bath Association
687 Willow Grove St.
Hackettstown, New Jersey 07840
1-800-FOR-NKBA

GLASS Blocks

 Deliver unexpected drama and your bathroom will never be forgotten. With the widest range of shapes and finishes available, WECK blocks will let you use:

• Soaring walls with no structural gaps, just beautiful glass all the way

• Smooth wall ends with no post construction. Nobody can resist touching the cool sweep and graceful arc of new WeckEnd blocks.

• Dramatic step-downs with new DoublEnd blocks for a feeling of privacy with open space that goes on and on.

• Tight radius turns with AllBend blocks let you use dramatic lighting effects, sunlit columns, or space plan options never before possible. With the WECK touch, you'll have bathrooms that make a statement of elegance!

E

I

J

ALLBend

Smoothly curved 22 1/2° angle blocks combine to make curves and corners, or columns with as small as a 12" radius. May be used with other WECK blocks to give you the look and the angles you choose. Available in Clarity or the distorted Nubio patterns. Compared to blocks with exposed seams, AllBend installs more easily and beautifully.

K

With WECK's new Designer Shapes you can have it your way! The curves, the angles, the circular columns. The beautifully finished wall-ends, smooth corners, whatever your creativity demands for striking drama with light and structure! The most beautiful edges and corners ever known can now accent your designs. New for you from WECK's engineered superiority.

Blocks	AllBend	Outside Radius inches
1 piece 4" x 8" per	4	14.5
1 piece 4" x 8" per	2	16.7
1 piece 8" x 8" per	4	17.5
1 piece 4" x 8" per	1	21.6
1 piece 8" x 8" per	2	21.7
1 piece 8" x 8" per	1	31.9
2 pieces 4" x 8" per	1	32.5

AllBend
DoublEnd
WeckEnd
Corner Block

Specifications

Thickness	Sizes		
AllBend (22 1/2°)	4"	8" high	
WeckEnd	4"	8" x 8"	
DoublEnd	4"	8" x 8"	
Corner (90°)	4"	6" high	
Corner (90°)	4"	8" high	
Corner (90°)	3"	8" high	

Notes:
- All dimensions nominal
- Designer Shapes available in Nubio and Clarity
- 3" thick corner also available in Nubio Goldtone

11 3/4"

AllBend

4 1/8"

3/16"

3"

3/16"

22 1/2°

3 3/8"

1/4"

8"

4 7/8"*

*3" thick version
measures 4 1/8"

GLASS BLOCK *Designs*

Nubio

Nubio Corner Block

WeckEnd

DoublEnd

AllBend

Aktis

Series	Size Nominal	Fire Rating minutes/ max. size sq. ft.	U/R Values	Light Transmission %	Shading Coefficent	Sound Loss Decibels	Compressive Strength psi	Weight per block lbs	Installed Weight Per Sq. Ft.
NUBIO						**CLEAR**			

Intersecting random wave pattern, provides an attractive appearance and excellent privacy. Smooth exterior surface for easy cleaning.

Matching designer shapes provide beauty and flexibility to create angles, curves or finished jambs and/or heads. 45 and 60 minute fire ratings are available.

Series	Size Nominal	Fire Rating	U/R	Light Trans	Shading	Sound	Compressive	Weight	Installed
Standard and Firestop Series (3⅞″ thick)									
	4″ x 8″	45/120	.48/2.08	72-74	.65	41	700	3.6	23.8
	6″ x 6″	45/120	.48/2.08	72-74	.65	41	850	3.5	20.8
	8″ x 8″	45/120	.48/2.08	72-74	.65	42	850	6.4	19.5
	8″ x 8″	60/100	.45/2.22	57	.55	42	1000	7.7	22.7
	12″ x 12″	—	.48/2.08	72-74	.63	42	850	15.3	18.7
Thinline Series (3⅛″ thick)									
	4″ x 8″	45/120	.53/1.89	79	.66	41	700	2.9	18.6
	6″ x 6″	45/120	.53/1.89	79	.66	40	850	3.1	17.2
	6″ x 8″	45/120	.53/1.89	79	.66	41	850	4.5	17.9
	8″ x 8″	45/120	.53/1.89	79	.66	41	850	5.4	15.9
Corner (6″ – 3⅞″ thick) (8″ – 3⅞″ and 3⅛″ thick)									
	6″ High	—	.53/1.89	54	—	39	800	3.4	20.2
	8″ High	—	.53/1.89	50	—	39	750	4.1	18.1
WeckEnd and DoublEnd (3⅞″ thick)									
	8″ x 8″	—	—	70	.65	42	850	6.2	19.1
AllBend (3⅞″ thick)									
	8″ High	—	.48/2.08	68	.65	41	700	3.6	23.8
						GOLDTONE			
Standard Series (3⅞″ thick)									
	8″ x 8″	45/120	.48/2.08	52	.52	42	850	6.4	19.5
Thinline Series (3⅛″ thick)									
	6″ x 6″	45/120	.53/1.89	52	.52	40	850	3.1	17.2
	6″ x 8″	45/120	.53/1.89	52	.52	41	850	4.5	17.9
	8″ x 8″	45/120	.53/1.89	52	.52	41	850	5.4	15.9
Corner (3⅛″ thick)									
	8″ High	—	.53/1.89	32	.52	36	650	3.9	17.7
AKTIS						**CLEAR**			

Elegant crystalline pattern provides privacy and good light transmission, at reasonable cost. Smooth exterior surface.

Series	Size	Fire	U/R	Light	Shading	Sound	Compressive	Weight	Installed
Standard Series (3⅞″ thick)									
	8″ x 8″	45/120	.48/2.08	72-74	.65	42	700	6.4	19.5
Thinline Series (3⅛″ thick)									
	4″ x 8″	45/120	.53/1.89	79	.66	41	700	2.9	18.6
	6″ x 6″	45/120	.53/1.89	79	.66	40	850	3.1	17.2
	6″ x 8″	45/120	.53/1.89	79	.66	41	850	4.5	17.9
	8″ x 8″	45/120	.53/1.89	79	.66	41	850	5.4	15.9

Metric Blocks

Metric blocks are available in three distinctive patterns. Produced to metric dimensions, variable mortar joints will yield 7 3/4″ or 8″ rows. The blocks exterior measurements are 7 1/2″ x 7 1/2″ x 3 1/2″.

Metallic

Welle

Regent

GLASS BLOCK *Designs*

Size Nominal	Fire Rating minutes/ max. size sq. ft.	U/R Values	Light Transmission %	Shading Coefficient	Sound Loss Decibels	Compressive Strength psi	Weight per block lbs	Installed Weight Per Sq. Ft.	Series
CLEAR									**CLARITY**
Standard and Firestop Series (3⅞″ thick)									
4″ x 8″	45/120	.48/2.08	72-74	.65	41	700	3.6	23.8	
6″ x 6″	45/120	.48/2.08	72-74	.65	41	850	3.5	20.8	
6″ x 6″	90/100	.31/3.23	51	.53	43	3000	7.8	37.8	
8″ x 8″	45/120	.48/2.08	72-74	.65	42	850	6.4	19.5	
8″ x 8″	60/100	.45/2.22	57	.55	42	1000	7.7	22.7	
12″ x 12″	—	.48/2.08	72-74	.63	42	850	15.3	18.7	
Thinline Series (3⅛″ thick)									
4″ x 8″	45/120	.53/1.89	79	.66	41	700	2.9	18.6	
6″ x 6″	45/120	.53/1.89	79	.66	40	850	3.1	17.2	
6″ x 8″	45/120	.53/1.89	79	.66	41	850	4.5	17.9	
8″ x 8″	45/120	.53/1.89	79	.66	41	850	5.4	15.9	
Corner (6″ – 3⅞″ thick) (8″ – 3⅛″ and 3⅞″ thick)									
6″ High	—	.53/1.89	54	—	39	800	3.4	20.2	
8″ High	—	.53/1.89	50	—	39	750	4.1	18.1	
WeckEnd and DoublEnd (3⅞″ thick)									
8″ x 8″	—	—	70	.65	42	850	6.2	19.1	
AllBend (3⅞″ thick)									
8″ High	—	.48/2.08	68	.65	41	700	3.6	23.8	
GOLDTONE									
Standard Series (3⅞″ thick)									
8″ x 8″	45/120	.48/2.08	52	.52	42	850	6.4	19.5	
CLEAR									**FORTRESS**
Fire Stop Series (3⅞″ thick)									
8″ x 8″	60/100	.31/3.23	48	.54	48	2850	11.2	30.6	
CLEAR									**X-RIB**
Standard Series (3⅞″ thick)									
6″ x 6″	45/120	.48/2.08	72-74	.65	41	850	3.5	20.8	
8″ x 8″	45/120	.48/2.08	72-74	.65	42	850	6.4	19.5	
12″ x 12″	—	.48/2.08	72-74	.63	42	850	15.3	18.7	
Thinline Series (3⅛″ thick)									
8″ x 8″	45/120	.53/1.89	79	.66	41	850	5.4	15.9	
CLEAR									**SPRAY**
Standard Series (3⅞″ thick)									
8″ x 8″	45/120	.48/2.08	48-55	.41	42	850	6.4	19.5	

CLARITY

This see-through block provides a dramatic grid effect, undistorted vision, and maximum light transmission.

Matching designer shapes provide beauty and flexibility to create angles, curves or finished jambs and/or heads. 45, 60 and 90 minute fire ratings are available.

Clarity

Clarity Corner Block

Clarity WeckEnd

FORTRESS

Extra-heavy block; minimizes vandalism. Available with small line pattern or in Clarity.

Fortress

X-RIB

Vertical ribs on one face and horizontal on the other for privacy.

X-Rib

SPRAY

Grid pattern offers privacy, reduces glare.

Spray

SPECIFICATIONS

PART 1   GENERAL

1.01 WORK INCLUDED
A. WECK GLASS BLOCKS
B. WECK GLASS BLOCKS with (45, 60 or 90) minute listed U.L. fire rating.
C. Integral joint reinforcing.
D. Miscellaneous metal anchors and/or fire rated hollow metal frames.
E. Mortars and sealants.

1.02 RELATED WORK
A. Section (_____-_____) Masonry.
B. Section (_____-_____) Lintels.
C. Section (_____-_____) Sealants.

1.03 REFERENCES
A. ASTM C153B2, Hot Dipped Zinc Coating.
B. ASTM C144, Aggregate for Masonry.
C. ASTM C150, Portland Cement.
D. ASTM C207, Hydrated Lime for Masonry.
E. ASTM C207, Mortar for Unit Masonry.
F. Underwriters Laboratories Building Materials Directory, 1992 Edition.

1.04 SUBMITTALS
A. Submit WECK Catalogue.
B. Submit _____ WECK GLASS BLOCK of each type for approval.

1.05 ENVIRONMENTAL REQUIREMENTS
A. Maintain materials and ambient air temperatures to a minimum of 40°F prior to, during and 48 hours after completion of work.
B. Protect WECK GLASS BLOCK from moisture prior to construction.

Technical drawings have been developed on disks for CAD systems.

WARRANTIES AND REMEDIES - LIMITATIONS

The products shall be free from defects relating to production for a period of 5 years after the date of purchase, but this warranty shall not extend to installation workmanship, accessory materials, or conditions of application, or the performance or results of an installation containing the product. The warranty described in this paragraph shall be IN LIEU OF any other warranty, express or implied, including but not limited to any implied warranty of MERCHANTABILITY OR FITNESS FOR A PARTICULAR PURPOSE. The buyer's sole and exclusive remedy against Glashaus Inc. and/or J. Weck GmbH u. Co. shall be for the replacement, but not installation, of defective products; Glashaus Inc. will also deliver the replacement products to the location where the defective products were originally purchased. The buyer agrees that no other remedy (including, but not limited to, incidental or consequential damages for lost profits, lost sales or injury to person or property) shall be available to the buyer, regardless of the theory of liability upon which any such damages are claimed. This warranty supersedes all prior warranties and representations regarding Weck Glass Block

PART 2   PRODUCTS

2.01 ACCEPTABLE MANUFACTURERS
A. J. WECK GmbH u. Co.

2.02 GLASS UNITS
A. _____ x _____ x _____ Inch.
B. _____ x _____ x _____ Inch with (45, 60 or 90) minute listed U.L. fire rating.
C. Color (Cleartone or Goldtone) _____
D. Pattern _____
E. Edge Coating – White latex based paint.

2.03 ACCESSORIES
A. Joint Reinforcing: Ladder type, hot dipped galvanized, 2-9 gauge parallel longitudinal wire at 2" o.c. for 3⅞" wide block or 1⅝" for 3⅛" wide block and cross rods welded at 8" o.c.
B. Panel Anchors: 20 gauge x 1¾" x 24" hot dipped galvanized steel with staggered perforations as supplied by Glass Masonry, Inc.
C. Perimeter Chase: Masonry recess, aluminum channel or steel channel.
D. Fire rated hollow metal frames as supplied by Glashaus, Inc.
E. Adjustable masonry anchors and wire ties.
F. Asphalt Emulsion: Karnac 100 or equal.
G. Expansion Strips: ⅜" x 3½" polyethylene plastic or glass fiber (for fire rating) as supplied by Glass Masonry, Inc.
H. Sealant: Silicone Type _____ Color.
I. Backer Rod: As recommended by sealant supplier.

2.04 MORTAR MATERIALS
A. Shall be prepared according to ASTM C270 for Type S Mortar. Mortar to have 1 part Portland Cement (Type 1), 1 part lime and 4½ to 6 parts of fine sand passing No. 20 sieve and free of iron compounds to avoid stains. Use white Portland Cement and silica sand for white joints. Mix mortar drier than normal and only an amount that will be used in ½ to 1 hour. Glass block will not absorb water the same as brick. Do not use retempered mortar. Do not use antifreeze compounds or accelerators.
B. Add _____ mortar color per manufacturer's instructions. Side walls of WECK GLASS BLOCK must be same color as mortar. If mortar is not white, strip paint and re-paint with colored latex paint.
C. Add Laticrete 8510 to increase waterproofing qualities of mortar.

PART 3   EXECUTION

3.01 PREPARATION
A. Verify that pocket recesses or chases provided under other sections are accurately located and sized.
B. Establish and protect lines, levels and coursing.

3.02 INSTALLATION
A. Arrange coursing pattern to provide consistent joint work throughout.
B. Locate and secure perimeter metal chase.
C. Coat sill under units with asphalt emulsion as a bond breaker.
D. Mortar joints must be solid. Furrowing not permitted. Neatly tool surface to a concave joint.
E. Place panel reinforcing in horizontal joint above first course of block and not more than 18" o.c. for Standard Series, every other course for Thinline Series and every course for Fire Stop Series. Panel anchors if used shall be installed in the same joints as reinforcing.
F. Isolate panel from adjacent construction on sides and top with expansion strips. Keep expansion joint voids clear of mortar.
G. Maintain uniform joint width of ¼" ± ⅛".
H. Maximum variation from plane of unit to next unit — 1/32".
I. Maximum variation of panel from plane — 1/16".
J. Do not use retempered mortar.
K. Do not tap glass block with steel tools.
L. When mortar has set, pack backer rod in jamb and head channels. Recess to allow for sealant. (Back-up for sealant at fire rated frames is mortar.)
M. Apply sealant.

3.03 CLEANING
A. Remove excess mortar from glass surfaces with a damp cloth before set occurs.
B. Number 4 steel wool can be used to remove remaining mortar.

For technical or installation information request our Design Guide.

Photo Credits:

Cover, **C, D, E, H:** Glass Block Warehouse, Westbury, NY

B,G: Photo: Rob McHugh, Installation: Glass Block Designs, San Francisco, CA

F,L: Orlando Sports Arena, Architect: Lloyd, Jones, Fillpot, Houston, TX Distributor: Glass Masonry Inc.

J: Photo: Terry Farmer, Springfield, IL

I,K: Distributor: Glass Block Source, Auburn, WA

WECK®
Glass Blocks

Glashaus, Inc.
415 West Golf Road
Suite 13
Arlington Heights, IL 60005

TEL: 708/640-6910
FAX: 708/640-6955

AVONITE®

THE
SOLID SURFACE
ADVANTAGE

AVONITE is machined and shaped using conventional wood-working tools much in the same manner as with fine hardwoods. This means greater design flexibility without the limitations associated with other decorative surfacing products. The color and pattern of AVONITE runs throughout its entire thickness. This allows for three-dimensional shaping while eliminating any chance of delamination or irreparable surface damage. Plus, AVONITE is non-porous; providing hygienic and highly stain resistant surfaces suitable for areas subject to repeated moisture or food contact...and our unique system of fabrication eliminates obvious seams or crevices where

The Constitution of the United States of America

1789

AVONITE is a patented, composite material which has the look and feel of natural stone. A designer palette of over thirty colors and textures are available which emulate granite and marble, including solid colors in subtle classic tones. A variety of surface effects can be achieved by specifying finishes ranging from low-maintenance matte, to soft-satin sheen, or high gloss. Consult your AVONITE representative for the finish most appropriate for your project.

AVONITE is limited only by your creative imagination. Combine custom the material is joined. A consistent and uninterrupted surface in any dimension can be easily accomplished.

AVONITE sinks, just like AVONITE countertops are solid through and through... beautiful, durable, and easy to maintain. Select from kitchen sinks in single or double bowl designs, and two distinct lavatory styles.

Our sinks can be flush mounted or undermounted in combination with AVONITE sheet material for an integrated, one piece appearance. Ideal for hospitality applications, medical care, and custom residential.

All AVONITE products are backed with confidence by an exclusive TEN-YEAR LIMITED WARRANTY.

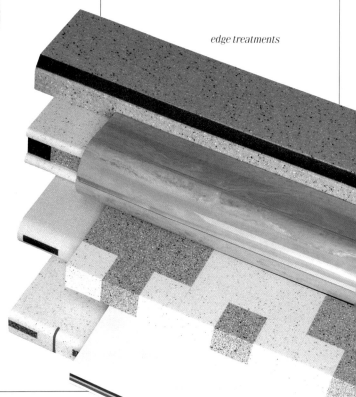

edge treatments

edge facias and splashes in contrasting AVONITE colors for a dramatic effect ... create accents and inlays in AVONITE using wood, metals, acrylic, tinted resins or stone in stone intarsia ... rout and fill corporate logos and graphics into AVONITE's surface, permanently... design unique and functional table-tops for restaurants and food courts... thermoform a sweeping radius front for highly contoured casework. These are only a few of the versatile custom effects possible using AVONITE.

SPECIFICATION INFORMATION

PRODUCT IDENTIFICATION
AVONITE® solid surfacing and shaped products.

MANUFACTURER
AVONITE, INC.
1945 Highway 304
Belen, New Mexico 87002, USA

PRODUCT DESCRIPTION
Composition & Materials: AVONITE is a patented, non-porous homogeneous blend of polyester/acrylic alloys and fillers. This creates a surfacing material that looks like stone but cuts like wood. The grain pattern goes all the way through which allows for three-dimensional shaping.

Basic Uses: Because the material can be worked with conventional woodworking power tools, the design possibilities are unlimited. Countertops, wall cladding, furniture, mouldings, architectural signage and accessories can be beautifully created with a guarantee of durability.

Limitations: Many AVONITE installations are suitable for exterior use. However, contact Technical Services regarding limited approved exterior applications. Do not use in areas exposed to sustained temperatures in excess of 375°F (CI) or 260°F (CIII). Seaming with joint adhesive (fusion material) should not be performed when the ambient temperature of the work area is below 55°F (13°C).

Sizes: Standard polyester AVONITE sheets are available in 36" (915mm) and 30" (762mm) widths by 120" (3050mm) lengths. Formstone® is available in 36" (915mm), 32" (813mm) and 30" (762mm) widths by 96" (2438mm), 120" (3050mm) and 144" (3658mm) lengths. Custom sizes are available on special order.

Thickness: All AVONITE sheets are available in standard thickness of ½" (12.7mm). Class I granites only are also available in ¾" (19mm). Formstone is available in ¾" (19mm), ½" (12.7mm) and ¼" (6.4mm) thicknesses.

Shaped Products: Solid surface sinks in kitchen and lavatory models are available in several standard colors. Combine with AVONITE sheets to create a totally integrated solid surface system. (See brochure #4081 Sinks, for technical data.)

Colors: A complete selection of granite, gemstone, and architectural solids are available. Custom colors can be matched to order for larger projects. Contact local Distributor for samples.

Finish: The factory finish of AVONITE is a matte finish approximating 220 grit sandpaper. A satin sheen or a high polish can be obtained by buffing with prescribed polishing compounds.

Weight: AVONITE sheet stock in ½" thickness weighs approx. 4.0 lbs. per sq. ft. in the Class I rated materials (CI). Class III sheets weigh approx. 3.1 lbs. in ½" thickness (CIII).

MAINTENANCE
AVONITE surfaces may be easily cleaned using conventional cleaning agents such as an ammonia based liquid cleaner (glass cleaner). Dry stains on a matte finish can be removed with Scotch-Brite scouring pad by 3M or a mild abrasive cleanser. Burns or scorches can be removed by sanding with coarse grit sandpaper followed by finer grit sandpaper. Follow sanding with a Scotch-Brite 7447 red pad by 3M (or equivalent) to match finish of sanded area to surrounding area. A final buffing is required on polished surfaces. Accidental nicks or chips can be repaired with special patch kits available in all standard AVONITE colors.

STAIN AND CHEMICAL RESISTANCE
The test method used was NEMA LD 3 –3.9. No lasting effect was noted after the prescribed exposure to 29 common reagents.

SANITARY USE
AVONITE has been tested and approved by the National Sanitation Foundation (NSF). Its inert and non-porous surface will not support the growth of bacteria and is ideal for food service and health-care facilities.

CLASS I FLAMMABILITY RATING
The majority of AVONITE colors have a Class I flammability rating (CI) making it suitable for virtually all horizontal and vertical surfaces in public places. Other AVONITE decorative materials are Class III rated and meet all requirements for residential use and most commercial applications (see Technical Data).

FABRICATION AND INSTALLATION
AVONITE should always be fabricated and installed by accredited fabricators. There are over 8,000 authorized fabricators worldwide. A list of qualified craftspeople is available through your local Authorized Distributor.

WARRANTY
All AVONITE products carry a 10 year written warranty when properly installed by an authorized fabricator. In addition, most AVONITE colors carry a 5 year limited exterior warranty for signage. For copies of AVONITE warranties contact AVONITE, Inc. or an Authorized Distributor.

AVAILABILITY
AVONITE is available through stocking distributors in most major cities throughout the world. Contact AVONITE, Inc. for specific locations.

TECHNICAL SUPPORT AND SERVICES
Contact AVONITE, Inc., in the USA toll-free at (800) 866-8324 or (505) 864-3800, FAX (505) 864-7790. For international inquiries, telephone (213) 299-9900 or FAX (213) 292-1441.

SUGGESTED SHORT FORM SPECIFICATION

Scope of Work
Provide AVONITE surfaces as shown on the drawings and specifications herein:

Materials
AVONITE sheets shall be as supplied by AVONITE, Inc., Belen, New Mexico, and shall be cut to size, seamed and detailed in accordance with approved shop drawings. Color shall be (specify) _____, and surface finish shall be (matte, satin, gloss) _____.

Shop Drawings
Prior to fabrication, the contractor shall furnish and submit detailed shop drawings for the approval of the architect/designer, showing accurate dimensions and details of all AVONITE solid surface work.

Fabrication and Installation
The fabrication and installation of all AVONITE surfaces detailed in this section shall be performed by an Accredited Fabrication shop in accordance with the manufacturer's printed instructions and final shop drawings.

Printed in U.S.A.

TECHNICAL DATA

PROPERTY	TYPICAL VALUES				TEST METHOD
	CLASS I	FORMSTONE	CLASS III	CRYSTELLE	
Specific Gravity	25.5	27.7	19.5	20.5	(grams/cu.in.)
Hardness	60	60	45	50	ASTM D2583
Elongation (percent)	.42	2.2	.55	.34	ASTM D638
Tensile strength (psi)	4,200	4,200	3,000	2,500	ASTM D638
Tensile modulus	11×10^5	11×10^5	5×10^5	8×10^5	ASTM D638
Abrasion resistance @ 1000 cycles, grams	.4	—	.4	.4	ASTM C501
Water absorption after 24 hours, percent	.06	.07	.08	.08	ASTM D570
Izod impact foot pounds per inch	.2	.3	.2	.2	ASTM D256
Impact resistance ½ pound	No fracture	No fracture	No fracture	No fracture	NEMA LD3-3.3
Linear thermal expansion	1.8×10^{-5}	2.0×10^{-5}	3.4×10^{-5}	2.5×10^{-5}	ASTM D696
High temperature resistance	No effect	Slight effect	No effect	Moderate effect	NEMA LD3-3.6
Boiling water resistance	No effect	No effect	No effect	No effect	NEMA LD3-3.5
Stain resistance	No effect	No effect	No effect	No effect	NEMA LD3-3.9
Weight per square foot, ½" thickness, pounds	4	4.4	3.1	3.3	
Flame spread classification	I	I	III	III	ASTM E84

CORIAN®

Corian®. The ultimate surfacing material.

For more than 25 years, DuPont CORIAN has set a standard of beauty, performance and value that no other material can equal. CORIAN is easier to care for than marble or granite, and more durable than any laminate or coating. With all of the elegance of natural stone–and none of the limitations– it truly is the ultimate surfacing material.

DuPont technological innovation combines a patented blend of natural materials and a high-performance acrylic–methyl methacrylate–to create CORIAN. The result is a solid material of lustrous beauty in an endless array of color combinations. Beneath the elegant appearance of CORIAN, however, lies a material whose strength, design flexibility and convenience have made it the leading choice of demanding architects and designers for a quarter century.

An unprecedented, 10-year installed warranty.

DuPont offers the best warranty program in the business—the industry's first installed limited warranty that guarantees the product quality of CORIAN plus its fabrication and installation. The installed limited warranty is available only through DuPont Certified and Approved Fabricators. For details on how your application can be covered by DuPont's installed limited warranty, please see an Authorized CORIAN Distributor or contact DuPont at 1-800-4CORIAN.

Properties.

CORIAN gives architects and designers the freedom to create beautiful interiors plus the confidence that it will stand up to the most demanding applications. The properties of CORIAN include:

- **Impact resistance:** CORIAN resists fracture, chipping and cracking better than marble, stone or polyester products.

- **Stain resistance:** The nonporous surface of CORIAN resists stains. It is unaffected by food stains and common disinfectants, and stubborn stains from cigarette burns, marking pens and hair dyes can be removed easily with routine care.

- **Heat resistance:** While CORIAN withstands heat better than many surface materials, use of a hot pad is recommended before placing hot cookware or electrical cooking appliances on a CORIAN surface.

- **Class I flammability rating:** CORIAN has a Class I flammability rating, making it suitable for virtually any horizontal or vertical application.

- **NSF compliance:** The National Sanitation Foundation has accepted CORIAN under NSF Standard # 51: "Plastic Materials and Components Used in Food Equipment." This sanction means CORIAN is ideal for use in food service, lodging, healthcare and educational institutions.

- **Resistance to germs and mildew:** Independent laboratory tests clearly show that nonporous CORIAN will not support the growth of fungi, mildew, and bacteria such as staph or other germs.

Additional information on radioactive compounds and HIV (AIDS) clean-up is available through a line of bulletins issued by DuPont.

Applications.

No matter what the application–if it calls for durability and beauty–CORIAN is the ideal choice, with over 25 years of proven performance.

- sinks • countertops and work surfaces • vanities • lavatories • tub and shower surrounds • walls and partitions • wainscoting • windowsills • baseboards • molding • thresholds • desk and laboratory tops • furniture

In hotels, restaurants, hospitals, universities and homes, CORIAN is the elegant, durable choice.

Fabrication procedures.

CORIAN products can be fabricated in the shop or on-site. Because CORIAN has working characteristics similar to those of fine hardwood, skilled technicians can form CORIAN to fit your specifications exactly. Installers can cut, drill, sand, rout and form CORIAN, using normal woodworking power tools to create innovative shapes and surface effects. CORIAN can also be thermoformed more readily than other solid materials, creating endless possibilities for flowing forms and rounded edges.

CORIAN may be combined with wood, brass, tile, acrylics and other CORIAN colors for a wide variety of unique designs and edge treatments.

Fabrication and installation information is available from your CORIAN distributor, or you can call DuPont at 1-800-4CORIAN.

Sheet and shape.

CORIAN is readily available from distributors in both sheet and precast shapes. Sheet sizes range up to 760 x 3680mm (30" x 145") in thicknesses of 6mm (¼"), 13mm (½"), and 19mm (¾"). Shaped products include one-piece vanity tops and bowls, kitchen sinks and lavatories.

Easy to care for.
Easy to maintain.

CORIAN is the perfect material for almost any surface because it is so easy to clean and maintain. CORIAN is nonporous, so most stains wipe right off with soap and water. More stubborn stains—even cigarette burns or scratches—can be sanded away with fine sandpaper, or even an abrasive household cleanser. This procedure is not possible with laminates or cultured marble products. Even in cases where damage is severe, CORIAN can be repaired to look like new. For more information, refer to the Care and Maintenance folder (H-47338).

A wealth of beautiful, designer colors.

CORIAN is available in classic and versatile colors to complement any interior.

Genesis Series
Glacier White	Peach
Cameo White	Pearl Gray
Bone	Dusty Rose

Sierra Series
Sierra Midnight	Sierra Evergreen
Sierra Dusk	Sierra Oceanic
Sierra Pink Coral	Sierra Sunset
Sierra Sandstone	Sierra Eclipse
Sierra Burnt Amber	Sierra Aurora

Jewel Series
Garnet	Jade
Black Pearl	Sapphire

Summit Series
Mont-Blanc	Kilimanjaro

Venaro Series
Venaro White	Venaro Gray
Venaro Rose	Dawn Beige

For new color availability, contact your local distributor.

Accessories.

CORIAN Joint Adhesive—for bonding CORIAN to CORIAN.

Silicone Sealant for CORIAN—for installing backsplashes and reveal edges; and for sealing tub and shower seams.

Available in a wide variety of colors, the CORIAN Joint Adhesive can be used to add decorative inlay designs. Rout out the desired design, fill and sand the finished area.

For more details see your local CORIAN distributor.

Corian® Technical Data*

A wide variety of convenient sizes and kits.

Sheet products:
Sheets available in three thicknesses: 6mm (¼"), 13mm (½"), and 19mm (¾").

For vertical applications:
6mm (¼") sheet; 760mm (30") wide; with a length of 2490mm (98").

For horizontal applications:
13mm (½") sheet; 760mm (30") wide; and in lengths of 2490mm (98"), 3070mm (121"), and 3680mm (145"). 19mm (¾") sheet; 760mm (30") x 3680mm (145").

*Metric conversions are approximate.

For color availability, see the CORIAN Product Catalog (H-52597) or your local CORIAN distributor.

New CORIAN Ready-To-Install Tub and Shower Wall Kits and Custom Wall System

Ready-To-Install Kits—Available in 3 versatile styles. Choose from one tub kit and two shower kits: one designed for 3-wall showers and one designed for 2-wall or corner shower installations.

Tub Kit Components
- Package T1–Tub wall panels:
  4 – ¼" x 26¼" x 57⁵⁄₁₆" wall panels
  1 – 57⁵⁄₁₆" "T" molding for the back wall
- Package T2–corners, trim molding and accessories:
  2 – 60" curved corners
  2 – corner filler pieces
  2 – soap/shampoo shelves
  1 – ½" x 3" x 52" trim with radiused edges and ½" rabbet
  2 – ½" x 3" x 28½" trim with radiused edges and ½" rabbet; with left and right miter
  2 – ½" x 3" x 60" trim with radiused edges and ½" rabbet; with left and right miter

Shower Kit Components
- Package S1–wall panels for 3-wall shower:
  3 – ¼" x 30" x 69⁵⁄₁₆" wall panels
- Package S2–wall panels for 2-wall shower:
  2 – ¼" x 30" x 69⁵⁄₁₆" wall panels
- Package S3–corners and accessories:
  1 – 72" curved corners*
  1 – corner filler piece
  1 – soap/shampoo shelves
- Package S4–shower trim molding:
  1 – ½" x 3" x 28" trim with radiused edges and ½" rabbet**
  2 – ½" x 3" x 33" trim with radiused edges and ½" rabbet; with left and right miter
  2 – ½" x 3" x 72" trim with radiused edges and ½" rabbet; with left and right miter

Commercial Tub Kits
4 – ¼" x 30" x 60", 72", 98" wall panels
  with
1 – ¼" x 2" x 98" batten strip
2 – ¼" x 2" x 98" ceiling strips
  and either
2 – ½" x 2" x 98" vertical strips
  or
2 – ¾" x 2" x 98" vertical strips

*1 corner required for 2-wall shower, 2 corners for 3-wall shower

**Trim piece is not required for 2-wall shower

New Custom Tub and Shower Wall System:

Introducing the CORIAN Custom Tub and Shower Wall System only from DuPont. CORIAN tub and shower walls are now available in a convenient, custom system that is quicker and easier to install. This new CORIAN offering from DuPont is comprised of precut, curved corners, and trim molding made to coordinate with the CORIAN tub and shower wall color of your choice. These prefabricated CORIAN components offer remarkable design flexibility, letting you create a beautiful custom shower or tub wall that puts the finishing touches on the fully coordinated CORIAN bath suite.

Because of this combination of easy-care beauty and design versatility, the Ready-To-Install Tub and Shower Kit or the Custom Tub and Shower Wall System is the perfect choice for your next bathroom project. Make your CORIAN bath suite complete, combine it with a CORIAN one-piece vanity top and bowl.

New one-piece vanity tops and bowls:

A variety of new features for easy-care luxury.

- The large, spacious sink is molded into the vanity top for a seamless look.
- A built-in, coved backsplash eliminates crevices and unsightly seams.
- A recessed faucet deck eliminates messy tops.
- An extra thick front edge gives the appearance of a custom design.

Lavatories:

CORIAN lavatories are available in a variety of styles and are an excellent choice in combination with CORIAN sheet vanity tops or conventional vanity top material. Lavatories include topmounted, undermounted, or seamed undermounted models.

Sinks:

Single- or double-bowl units offer complete flexibility of color and placement. Beveled, undermount or seamed undermount installation may be used. Our new Euro-style sinks are the largest sinks in our collection.

How to specify CORIAN.

The following suggested write-up is included to assist you when specifying CORIAN.

- **One-piece CORIAN vanity tops and bowls:** Vanity bowls and tops shall be of a one-piece, monolithic design, made of CORIAN (methyl methacrylate binder) manufactured by DuPont. Color and pattern shall be selected by the architect and physical properties shall conform to the manufacturer's standard specifications. The material shall be homogenous, not coated or laminated. Installation shall be in a workmanlike manner, in accordance with the manufacturer's instructions.
- **Surfaces:** Surfaces shall be CORIAN. Color and pattern shall be selected by the architect. CORIAN sheets shall be ½″ (13mm) or ¾″ (19mm) for countertops. Backsplashes, where specified, ¼″ (6mm), ½″ (13mm), or ¾″ (19mm). Wall coverings shall be ¼″ (6mm) unless otherwise specified. Physical properties shall conform to the manufacturer's standard specifications. The material shall be homogenous, not coated or laminated. Installation shall be in a workmanlike manner, in accordance with the manufacturer's instructions.

When specifying CORIAN for applications that are wider than 30″ (760mm) or require a seam, specify DuPont Joint Adhesive for CORIAN. It can be used to form a smooth, inconspicuous seam for joint applications. Silicone sealant should be used for caulking tub and shower wall seams and edges.

Literature and samples.

A variety of literature and samples, including the CORIAN Product Catalog, are available from your CORIAN distributor, or you can call DuPont toll-free at 1-800-4CORIAN.

Available worldwide.

For more information, write or call:
DuPont Polymers
Wilmington, DE, 19898
1-800-4CORIAN

Table I. Technical Data—CORIAN Solid Surface Products

PROPERTY	TYPICAL RESULT	TEST
Tensile Strength	6000 psi	ASTM-D-638
Tensile Modulus	1.5 x 10^{6} psi	ASTM-D-638
Elongation	0.4% min.	ASTM-D-638
Hardness	94	Rockwell "M" Scale ASTM-D-785
	56	Barcol Impressor ASTM-D-2583
Thermal Expansion	3.02 x 10^{-5} in./in./°C (1.80 x 10^{-5} in./in./°F)	ASTM-D-696
Gloss (60° Gardner)	5-75 (matte—highly polished)	ANSI-Z124 HUD Bulletin UM73
Color Stability	No change—200 hrs.	NEMA-LD-3-3.10
Wear & Cleanability	Passes	ANSI-Z124 HUD Bulletin UM73
Boiling Water Surface Resistance	No visible change	NEMA-LD-3-3.05
High Temperature Resistance (500°F)	No change	NEMA-LD-3-3.06
Izod Impact (Notched Specimen)	0.28 ft.-lbs./in. of notch	ASTM-D-256 (Method A)
Stain Resistance: Sheets	Passes	ANSI-Z124 HUD Bulletin UM73
Impact Resistance: Sheets	No fracture ¼″ slab—36″ drop ½ lb. ball ½″ slab—36″ drop 1 lb. ball ¾″ slab—35″ drop 2 lb. ball	NEMA-LD-3-3.03
Point Impact: Bowls	No cracks or chips	ANSI-Z124 HUD Bulletin UM73
Weatherability	No change—1000 hrs.	ASTM-D-1499
Specific Gravity*	1.8 Standard Color 1.69 Sierra Colors	
Water Absorption	24 hrs. / Long-term 0.04 / 0.4 (¾″) 0.09 / 0.8 (¼″)	ASTM-D-570

Flammability — ASTM-E-84

	STANDARD COLORS				SIERRA COLORS		
Flammability	¼″** Masonry	Gypsum	½″ Sheet	¼″*** Gypsum	¾″ Sheet	½″ Sheet	¾″ Sheet
Flame Spread	15	25	5	20	5	15	15
Smoke Developed	20	25	10	5	15	25	30
Class	1	1	1	1	1	1	1

*Approximate weight per square foot for standard colors: ¼″ (6mm) 2.35 lbs. • ½″ (13mm) 4.7 lbs. • ¾″ (19mm) 7.0 lbs. For Sierra colors: ¼″ (6mm) 2.2 lbs. • ½″ (13mm) 4.4 lbs. • ¾″ (19mm) 6.6 lbs.

**¼″ (6mm) results reflect material adhered to both masonry surfaces and standard grade ½″ (13mm) thick Gypsum Board using Panel Adhesive for DuPont CORIAN® and tested as a composite.

***¼″ (6mm) results reflect material adhered to both masonry surfaces and standard grade ½″ (13mm) thick Gypsum Board using Silicone Adhesive for DuPont CORIAN and tested as a composite.

CORIAN®

DUPONT

Printed in U.S.A.

IT ATTRACTS AND REPELS AT THE SAME TIME.

GIBRALTAR Solid Surfacing is the countertop material sleek and elegant enough to attract plenty of attention. It's available in 32 colors and patterns, with matching kitchen sinks and vanity bowls in select solid colors. But obviously, we didn't name it after the Rock of Gibraltar for its looks.

Like its namesake, GIBRALTAR surfacing is astoundingly durable. When it comes to impact, bruising and fractures, it simply repels the most determined efforts of the typical active American family. In fact, we're so confident of GIBRALTAR's outstanding performance we gave it a ten-year installed limited warranty.

And it's the first solid surfacing to earn Underwriters Laboratory listing, National Association of Home Builders certification, the Good Housekeeping Seal, and the NSF International listing for food contact.

So look no further than GIBRALTAR Solid Surfacing. It's the kind of style you'll never get tired of. (And that's a good thing, because it lasts and lasts.)

This stunning vanity features GIBRALTAR Solid Surfacing in three forms: the vanity top and cabinet handles are Oasis Quarry (D402-QR), the vanity bowl is White Sand (D403-SL), and the backsplash is Oasis (D402-SL).

GIBRALTAR.
S O L I D   S U R F A C I N G

From the Makers of
WILSONART® Brand Decorative Laminate

WHAT IS GIBRALTAR SOLID SURFACING?

This versatile surfacing material is manufactured of polyester and acrylic resins, with fire-retardant fillers and proprietary coloring agents. The patent number is 5,244,941.

The solid color panels and bowls have extraordinarily consistent, uniform color throughout the thickness of each piece.

Stardust, Quarry, and Mirage designs are abstract patterns color-matched to coordinate with selected WILSONART® Brand Decorative Laminate solid colors.

The panels are manufactured with one good face and a sanded back which can be finished.

AVAILABILITY SUMMARY

PANEL WIDTHS:	30″, 36″ (712mm, 914.4mm)
PANEL LENGTHS:	96″, 144″ (2438mm, 3658mm)
THICKNESSES:	Product Type 025: 1/4″ nominal
	Product Type 050: 1/2″ nominal
	Product Type 075: 3/4″ nominal
HALF-INCH STRIPS:	widths — 1 3/4″, 4″, 5 3/4″
(Product Type 050)	lengths — 72″, 96″, 144″
BOWLS:	BV111, BV121 — 12 3/4″ x 15 3/4″ vanity
	BK222 — 16 3/4″ x 16 3/4″ kitchen sink
	BK323 — 10 1/4″ x 16 3/4″ kitchen sink
	BK324 — 21″ x 15 3/4″ kitchen sink
	BK426 — 21″ x 16 3/4″ kitchen sink
	BK327 — 8″ x 15 3/4″ kitchen sink
	BK325 — 9″ x 12″ kitchen sink
	BD321 — 31″ x 18″ double kitchen sink
	BD322 — 30″ x 18″ double kitchen sink
	BK128 — 16 3/4″ x 16 3/4″ round kitchen sink

Minimum quantities may apply to certain sizes and thicknesses. Check with your local distributor for sizes and availability.

WHERE CAN I GET IT?

GIBRALTAR brand products are available from an area distributor. A sales representative at the distribution center near you will be happy to provide any information necessary for any specific project.

MANUFACTURER'S WARRANTY

Call for a copy of the manufacturer's ten-year warranty.

SUGGESTED SHORT SPECIFICATION FORM
FOR GIBRALTAR SOLID SURFACING

Surface shall be GIBRALTAR Solid Surfacing, produced by Ralph Wilson Plastics Co., Temple, Texas 76504.

TYPE:	Fire-Rated Flat Panel(s)
SURFACE:	Color/Design Number: _____
	Color/Design Name: _____
FINISH:	(Specify desired texture of completed application.)
EDGE/APRON	Color/Design Number: _____
TRIM:	Color/Design Name: _____
DECORATIVE/	_____
FUNCTIONAL	_____
TREATMENTS:	_____
ADHESIVE:	GIBRALTAR Seam Kit Adhesive, color-matched to panels to be seamed.
	Color/Design Number: _____
	Color/Design Name: _____
CAULK/	GIBRALTAR Color-Matched Silicone Sealant
SEALANT:	Color/Design Number: _____
	Color/Design Name: _____
FASTENING	
SYSTEM:	_____

CERTIFICATION: Surface shall be UL rated, Class I(A).

Material shall equal or exceed performance standards described in "GIBRALTAR Solid Surfacing Sheet Goods Tech Data." Fabrication and disposal of wastes shall comply with techniques described in "GIBRALTAR Solid Surfacing Fabrication Manual," and with relevant fire codes, and safety and environmental regulations.

MANUFACTURER
Ralph Wilson Plastics Co.
600 South General Bruce Drive
Temple, Texas 76504
Phone: (817) 778-6933
FAX: (817) 778-1822
© 1994 Ralph Wilson Plastics Co.
Printed in U.S.A.

HOTLINE
When you need immediate response to a question, or rapid delivery of product literature (within 24 hours), call toll-free:
                1-800-433-3222
In Texas: 1-800-792-6000

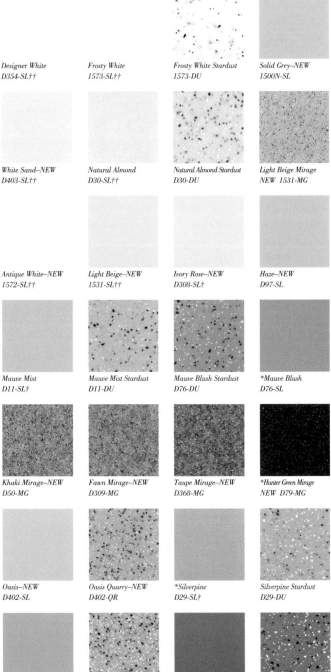

Designer White D354-SL††	Frosty White 1573-SL††	Frosty White Stardust 1573-DU	Solid Grey–NEW 1500N-SL
White Sand–NEW D403-SL††	Natural Almond D30-SL††	Natural Almond Stardust D30-DU	Light Beige Mirage NEW 1531-MG
Antique White–NEW 1572-SL††	Light Beige–NEW 1531-SL††	Ivory Rose–NEW D308-SL†	Haze–NEW D97-SL
Mauve Mist D11-SL†	Mauve Mist Stardust D11-DU	Mauve Blush Stardust D76-DU	*Mauve Blush D76-SL
Khaki Mirage–NEW D50-MG	Fawn Mirage–NEW D309-MG	Taupe Mirage–NEW D368-MG	*Hunter Green Mirage NEW D79-MG
Oasis–NEW D402-SL	Oasis Quarry–NEW D402-QR	*Silverpine D29-SL†	Silverpine Stardust D29-DU
Blue Ice–NEW D319-SL	Blue Ice Quarry–NEW D319-QR	*Larkspur D328-SL Available in decorative strips only.	Larkspur Stardust D328-DU
*Platinum D315-SL†	Platinum Stardust D315-DU	Dove Grey Quarry NEW D92-QR	*Black Stardust 1595-DU

† Matching vanity bowls available
†† Matching kitchen sinks and vanity bowls available
* These colors perform best when used for vertical and fine furniture surfaces, and for decorative accents.

NOTE: Colors and patterns shown are printed reproductions only, at 50% of actual size. Please make decisions based on actual product samples.

GIBRALTAR solid colors are produced to match WILSONART laminates with the same names and numbers. Mirage, Stardust and Quarry particulates are randomly dispersed. Chip location is not predetermined. Some variation may occur. Panels should be pre-assembled for best appearance.

GIBRALTAR®
SOLID SURFACING
From the Makers of WILSONART® Brand Decorative Laminate

LIMITED WARRANTY TO CONSUMER
Good Housekeeping PROMISES
REPLACEMENT OR REFUND IF DEFECTIVE
THIS SEAL APPLIES TO ALL GIBRALTAR® SOLID SURFACING PRODUCTS... NOT INSTALLATION.

Amana
ALL THE RIGHT PIECES

Because you're always looking for an edge in kitchen design, Amana offers you four brand names featuring innovative products that can elevate your latest work from great to spectacular. Amana has all the right pieces for your next project. Let us help you solve the puzzle.

Amana

Modern Maid

Caloric

Speed Queen

1-800-843-0304
FAST FACTS

Call Amana's toll-free number today to promptly receive the most current information on the products you are specifying.

Amana®

Modern Maid®

Caloric®

Speed Queen™

The pieces all fit together when you specify Amana, Modern Maid, Caloric or Speed Queen.

We have the image, products, and sales and service network to support your design specifications.

Look to us for the solution to any of your puzzles, from the casual to the elegant, from the simple to the complex.

■ *Refrigerators:*
  Freezer on the top
  Freezer on the bottom
  Side-by-side
  Freestanding
  Built-in

■ *Microwave Ovens:*
  Over-the-Range
  Full-Size Countertop
  Built-in
  Microwave Convection
  Portable and Compact

■ *Ranges:*
  Freestanding
  Slide-in
  Double Deck
  Electric or Gas

■ *Freezers:*
  Chest
  Upright

■ *Dishwashers*

■ *Dehumidifiers*

1-800-843-0304
FAST FACTS

Call Amana's toll-free number today to promptly receive the most current information on the products you are specifying.

Synergy

- Room Air Conditioners

  Cooktops:
  - Quartz Halogen
  - All Radiant
  - Solid Disk
  - Electric Downdraft
  - Gas Downdraft
  - Gas on Glass

- Central Heating & Cooling Products

- Built-in Toaster/Housing
  Range Hoods

- Wall Ovens:
  - Convection
  - Single Electric
  - Double Electric
  - Combination
  - Single Gas
  - Double Gas

Washers & Dryers

KOHLER COLOR COORDINATES PARTNER

DESIGN BY REFINEMENT

*From traditional to
contemporary design,
Amana has the appliances
for your specific project.*

*Our products are built with
integrity to ensure quality
and your satisfaction.*

Amana
A **Raytheon** Company

© 1992 Amana, Iowa 52204
Form No. 0928R
Printed in U.S.A.

1-800-843-0304
FAST FACTS

*Call Amana's toll-free number today to promptly receive the
most current information on the products you are specifying.*

C484
BuyLine 8612

BROAN
RANGE HOODS

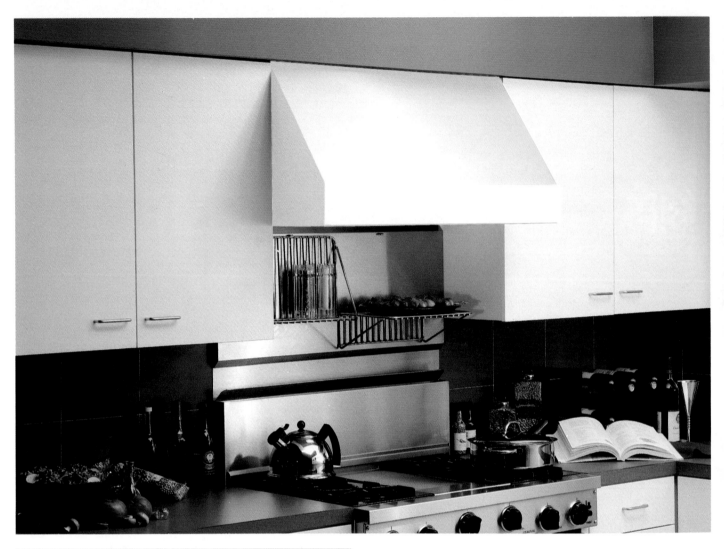

RANGEMASTER™

Powerful, Quiet Ventilation For Professional Style Ranges.

The Broan Rangemaster™ range hood is the perfect answer to the higher ventilation requirements of professional quality home ranges. The Rangemaster's powerful blower systems can deliver up to 1200 CFM of quiet, efficient kitchen ventilation. Its heavy gauge construction and choice of either stainless steel or appliance-matching colors give the Rangemaster durability and a clean, functional appearance that complements all professional ranges.

Professional features — premium performance

■ Infinite solid state speed control with exclusive blower memory.

■ A choice of sizes to match any range — 18" high and 24" deep with widths from 30" to 72" in 6" increments.

■ Exclusive Heat Sentry™ automatically turns blower to high speed when excess heat is detected.

■ Dual warming lamps keep food hot until serving time.

■ Optional stainless steel backsplash with shelves for food warming or condiment storage.

■ Extra large filter area with easy-to-clean, removable aluminum filters that fit in dishwasher.

■ Easy-to-clean stainless steel interior with no sharp edges.

■ Economical dual level fluorescent lighting — select bright cooktop lighting or softer illumination.

■ Optional soffit chimneys are available for installations without soffits.

All controls are mounted for easy operation. Filters are easy to remove and clean.

Optional backsplash with condiment shelves that fold down for food warming.

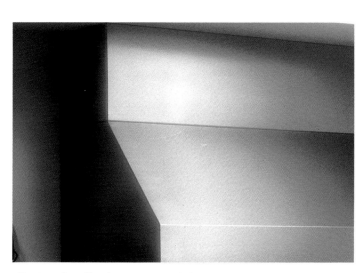

Optional soffit chimney available in a variety of widths and matching colors.

Powerful and quiet ventilation for even the largest range

- Internal-mounted centrifugal blowers are HVI certified at 600 CFM, or 1200 CFM to match range size and cooking needs.
- External roof or wall-mounted 900 CFM fan system also available. (Model 338, See page 15)

Ordering Instructions:

Range hood, blower, backsplash and soffit chimney are ordered separately. Blower includes installation rough-in kit.

Range Hood Selection Table

WIDTH	STAINLESS STEEL	WHITE	BLACK	ALMOND
30"	603004	603001	603023	603008
36"	603604	603601	603623	603608
42"	604204	604201	604223	604208
48"	604804	604801	604823	604808
54"	605404	+	+	+
60"	606004	+	+	+
66"	606604	+	+	+
72"	607204	+	+	+

Options Selection Table

	BACKSPLASH	SOFFIT CHIMNEY			
WIDTH	STAINLESS STEEL	STAINLESS STEEL	WHITE	BLACK	ALMOND
30"	RP3004	RN3004	RN3001	RN3023	RN3008
36"	RP3604	RN3604	RN3601	RN3623	RN3608
42"	RP4204	RN4204	RN4201	RN4223	RN4208
48"	RP4804	RN4804	RN4801	RN4823	RN4808
54"	RP5404	RN5404	+	+	+
60"	RP6004	RN6004	+	+	+
66"	RP6604	RN6604	+	+	+
72"	RP7204	RN7204	+	+	+

+Available as special order

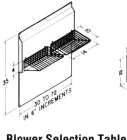

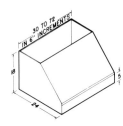

Blower Selection Table and Specifications

MODEL	MOUNTING	CFM	VOLTS	Hz	AMPS*	DUCT SIZE
325	Internal	600	120	60	7.6	7" Round
326	Internal	1200	120	60	8.1	4-1/2" x 18-1/2"**
338++	External	900	120	60	6.0	9" Round

++ Model 338K rough-in kit required for mounting.
   Model no. 99 9" spring loaded in-line damper recommended.
* Includes 4.5 Amps representing all lights.
** Transitions to 10" round available. (see accessory section)

Replacement Bulbs:
Fluorescent: F14T12/SW (Soft White) Any F14T8 or F14T12 15" long preheat fluorescent lamp will fit.
Heat Lamps: 250 Watt, R40 Infrared (Bulbs and lamps not included).

ECLIPSE®

Superior Downdraft Ventilation with New High Styling and Slim-Line Housing

Universal design allows choice of cooktops*

- Thin line styling beautifully complements virtually any cooktop. Ideal for islands & peninsulas.
- Rises to a height of 7" over cooktop surface.
- Vents smoke, vapors or airborne grease without cooling food being cooked or extinguishing a gas burner.
- Quiet, powerful 500 CFM or 900 CFM performance.
- Available with brushed stainless steel (standard) and optional white or black covers.
- 30" and 36" widths fit standard size cabinets.

Space saving design allows maximum storage space in cabinet

- Interior blower housing is only 7" deep (3³/₄" with remote blower) and locates to rear of cabinet to provide maximum storage.
- Connects to standard 3¹/₄" x 10" duct (or 6" round with transition).
- Access panel allows easy cleaning and service.

Easy installation with choice of blower locations

- Anti-vibration neoprene motor mounts provide quiet operation.
- Blower discharges right, left or down; and adjusts side to side to avoid floor joists.
- Interior blower system is rated 500 CFM.
- 900 CFM rated exterior-mounted fan minimizes interior sound. (Model 338. See page 15.)

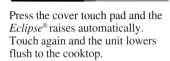

Press the cover touch pad and the *Eclipse®* raises automatically. Touch again and the unit lowers flush to the cooktop.

Infinite speed control with solid state memory is conveniently side-mounted.

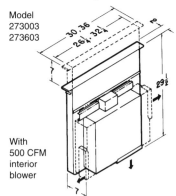

Model 273003 273603

With 500 CFM interior blower

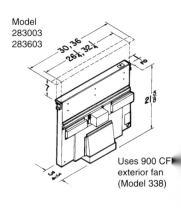

Model 283003 283603

Uses 900 CFM exterior fan (Model 338)

TO FIT NOMINAL COOKTOP SIZE	MODEL	DESCRIPTION	COVER COLOR
30"	273003	Interior Blower Unit	Stainless Steel
36"	273603	Interior Blower Unit	Stainless Steel
30"	283003	Exterior Blower Unit**	Stainless Steel
36"	283603	Exterior Blower Unit**	Stainless Steel
30"	273001C	Optional Cover	White
36"	273601C	Optional Cover	White
30"	273023C	Optional Cover	Black
36"	273623C	Optional Cover	Black

** Exterior unit utilizes Model 338 Exterior-Mounted Fan, ordered separately.

SPECIFICATIONS

MODEL	VOLTS	AMPS	CFM	DUCT
27000	120	4.0	500	3¹/₄" x 10"
28000	120	4.0	900	3¹/₄" x 10"

* Cooktops, countertops and cabinets vary in dimension and support systems depending upon manufacturer. These factors may impact the Eclipse's ability to fit with every worktop/cabinet combination. Specifications subject to change without notice.

4

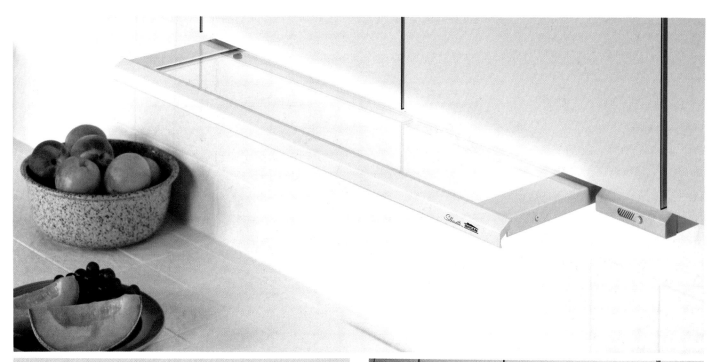

SILHOUETTE™

Dramatic Flair For Today's Euro-Style Kitchens.

Elegant style combines with extraordinary performance

- Contemporary thin-line design unmatched by any other range hood.
- Choice of black or white frame surrounding "see through" glass visor.
- High capacity, dual centrifugal blower system.
- Dual centrifugal blowers deliver superior air movement — HVI certified at 300 CFM.
- Quietest high-performance system available at 4.5 Sones.
- For vented installations only.

Quality and efficiency go hand in hand

- Hood visor easily glides in and out.
- Front-mounted infinite speed control with solid state memory.
- Pull visor out to turn unit on automatically — push in to turn off.
- Exclusive Heat Sentry™ automatically turns blower to high speed when excess cooking heat is detected.
- Exclusive resilient motor mounts isolate blower motor to reduce noise and vibration.

Functional, compact design

- Compact housing leaves ample shelf space behind cabinet doors.
- Installs in standard width cabinets with flush or recessed bottoms.
- 24" fluorescent light (bulb not included) and prismatic glass lens delivers even cooktop lighting.
- Washable foam filter is recessed for greater capture.
- Duct connector with built-in damper included.

Premium features include fluorescent lighting with prismatic glass lens and the exclusive Broan Heat Sentry™.

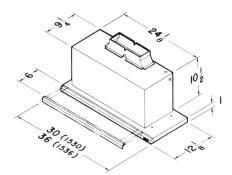

Allow 18 inches minimum from cooking surface to bottom of hood.

Silhouette

WIDTH	WHITE	BLACK
30"	153001	153023
36"	153601	153623

SPECIFICATIONS

VOLTS	AMPS	SONES	CFM	DUCT
120	3.7	4.5	300	3-1/4" X 10" (vertical)

Fluorescent Tube - 24", F20T12 (not included).

90000 SERIES

Precise Electronic Control On Our Highest Performance Range Hood.

State-of-the-art electronic controls combine with distinctive styling and superior performance to make the 90000 the industry's most advanced range hood.

The sleek electronic touchpad controls all hood functions. The advanced temperature monitoring system stays alert to changing ventilation requirements and adjusts blower speeds accordingly.

A high capacity, dual centifugal blower system with electronic solid state circuitry makes the 90000 the quietest high-performance system on the market. Available in ducted or duct-free configuration using our industry leading Microtek® System IV filter.

Advanced temperature monitoring systems

- "AutoTemp" System adjusts blower speeds to match cooking conditions.
- Heat Sentry™ System detects excess heat and automatically turns blower to highest speed.
- High Heat Signal sounds when excessive temperatures are detected.
- Heat Sentry System and High Heat Signal activate whether blower is on or off.
- Test function pad enables user to check temperature monitoring systems.

Electronic control pad

- Fingertip control of seven blower speeds.
- Three light settings including "night light."
- Flush-mounted for easy cleanability.
- Indicator lights signal all hood functions.

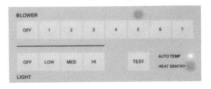

The Broan high capacity, dual centrifugal blower system delivers superior air movement — even in long duct runs. Yet, it's one of the quietest systems on the market.

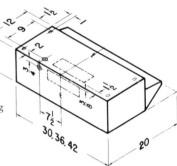

90000 SERIES

WIDTH	WHITE	ALMOND	WHITE ON WHITE	BLACK	STAINLESS
30"	903001	903008	903011	903023	903004
36"	903601	903608	903611	903623	903604
42"	904201	904208	904211	904223	904204

Order Microtek® System IV filter 97007662 for Duct-free operation.

SPECIFICATIONS

VOLTS	AMPS	SONES VER.	SONES HOR.	CFM VER.	CFM HOR.	DUCT-FREE RHP INDEX	DUCT
120	4.5	5.5	6.0	360	350	59.09	3-1/4" x 10"

89000 SERIES

Infinite Speeds —
Powerful, Quiet Performance.

Heavy-duty exhaust capacity ideal for convertible cooktops with barbecue grilles

- Dual centrifugal blowers.
- Vertical discharge HVI certified at 460 CFM, 6.0 Sones.
- Horizontal discharge HVI certified at 440 CFM, 7.0 Sones.
- Use with gas grilles under 14,000 BTU or electric grilles under 4,000 watts (Not for use with charcoal grilles).

Advanced fingertip control

- Infinite speed slide with exclusive solid state memory control.
- Automatic Heat Sentry™ turns blower to high when excess heat detected.
- Two-position light setting for bright cooktop lighting or soft "night light" illumination.

Sleek, contemporary styling with superior features

- Choice of genuine stainless steel or custom finishes.
- Unique motor mounting isolates blower to reduce vibration.
- Safety enhancing mitered sides and hemmed bottom edges.
- Duct connector with built-in damper.
- Twin 9-3/4" x 11-1/2" aluminum filters.

Special Order

Also available in 33" and 39" widths in stainless steel.

Choose 30", 33", 36", 39", 42" and 48" widths in hammered black, white, almond, harvest, avocado, coffee and Silver Lustre.

All finishes are baked enamel except Genuine Stainless Steel.

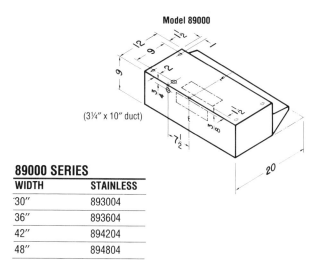

Model 89000

(3¼" x 10" duct)

89000 SERIES

WIDTH	STAINLESS
30"	893004
36"	893604
42"	894204
48"	894804

SPECIFICATIONS

VOLTS	AMPS	SONES		CFM		DUCT
		VER.	HOR.	VER.	HOR.	
120	6.0	6.0	7.0	460	440	3-1/4" x 10"

88000 SERIES

Premium Range Hood With Convertible Microtek® Convenience.

Advanced features and controls

- Infinite speed slide control.
- Exclusive solid state blower memory.
- Two-position light switch for bright working light or softer "night light."
- Broan Heat Sentry™ equipped for automatic high blower speed when excess heat detected.

Ducted or duct-free — engineered for impressive performance and installation flexibility

- Ducted exhaust capacity HVI certified at 360 CFM, 5.5 Sones vertical discharge.
- Horizontal discharge HVI certified at 350 CFM, 6.0 Sones.
- Dual centrifugal blowers for ultra-quiet performance.
- Unique motor mounting isolates blower to reduce vibration.
- Twin 9-3/4" x 11-1/2" aluminum filters.
- Duct connector with built-in damper included.
- Uses Microtek® System Filter No. 97007662 for duct-free installation (available separately).

Superbly crafted

- Mitered sides and hemmed bottom edges for safety and clean styling.

Special Order

88000 also available by special order in 30", 36" and 42" widths, in hammered black and Silver Lustre. 33", 39" and 48" widths available special order in all finishes.

All finishes are baked enamel except Genuine Stainless Steel.

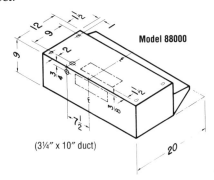

Model 88000

(3¼" x 10" duct)

88000 SERIES (65 *times better than ordinary duct-free range hoods*)

WIDTH	WHITE	ALMOND	WHITE ON WHITE	BLACK	STAINLESS
30"	883001	883008	883011	883023	883004
36"	883601	883608	883611	883623	883604
42"	884201	884208	884211	884223	884204

Also available in Harvest, Avocado and Coffee.

SPECIFICATIONS

VOLTS	AMPS	SONES VER.	SONES HOR.	CFM VER.	CFM HOR.	DUCT-FREE RHP INDEX	DUCT
120	4.5	5.5	6.0	360	350	59.09	3-1/4" x 10"

75000, 76000 & 77000 SERIES

Duct-Free Microtek® Convertibility.

Top-of-the-line features at a moderate price

- Dual centrifugal blowers for top efficiency.
- Infinite speed control for quiet performance.
- Contemporary styling with black matte control panel accenting stainless steel or popular appliance finishes.*
- Safety enhancing mitered sides and hemmed bottom edges contribute to sleeker styling.
- High strength polymeric lens houses 75 watt fixture for bright work area.

*White control panel accents white on white models.

Convertible 76000 Series

- Duct connector with built-in damper included.
- Twin 11-5/8" x 6-5/8" aluminum filters.
- Duct-free convertibility using Microtek® System Filter No. 97007664 (available separately).
- Exhaust capacity HVI certified at 200 CFM, 5.5 Sones vertical discharge; horizontal discharge HVI certified at 200 CFM, 6.0 Sones.

Convertible 75000 Series

- Exhaust capacity HVI certified at 250 CFM, 6.5 Sones vertical discharge; horizontal discharge HVI certified at 250 CFM, 6.0 Sones.
- Other features same as 76000 Series.

Duct-Free 77000 Series

- Shipped ready for duct-free installation with Microtek® System Filter No. 97007664.

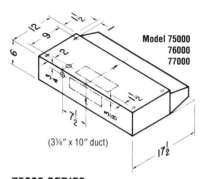

Model 75000
76000
77000

(3¼" x 10" duct)

75000 SERIES *(27 times better than ordinary duct-free range hoods)*

WIDTH	WHITE	ALMOND	WHITE ON WHITE	BLACK	STAINLESS
30"	753001	753008	—	—	753004
36"	753601	753608	—	—	753604
42"	754201	754208	—	—	754204

76000 SERIES *(25 times better than ordinary duct-free range hoods)*

WIDTH	WHITE	ALMOND	WHITE ON WHITE	BLACK	STAINLESS
24"	762401	762408	762411	762423	762404
30"	763001	763008	763011	763023	763004
36"	763601	763608	763611	763623	763604
42"	764201	764208	764211	764223	764204

Also available in Harvest, Avocado and Coffee.

77000 SERIES *(25 times better than ordinary duct-free range hoods)*

WIDTH	WHITE	ALMOND	WHITE ON WHITE	BLACK	STAINLESS
30"	773001	773008	—	—	773004
36"	773601	773608	—	—	773604

Also available in Harvest and Coffee.

SPECIFICATIONS

MODEL NO.	VOLTS	AMPS	SONES VER.	SONES HOR.	CFM	DUCT-FREE RHP INDEX	DUCT
75000	120	3.6	6.5	6.0	250	25.0	3-1/4" x 10"
76000	120	3.0	5.5	6.0	200	22.73	3-1/4" x 10"
77000	120	3.0	—	—	—	22.73	—

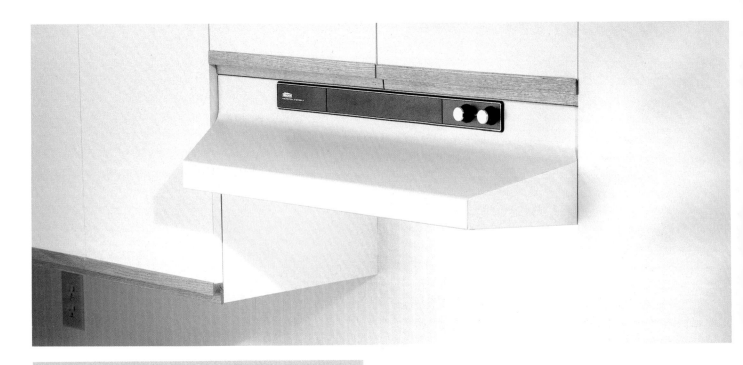

46000 SERIES

Microtek® System II Convertibility. The Most Efficient Duct-Free System In Its Price Range.

Step-up features and impressive performance from our popular economy hood

- Contemporary styling with black matte control panel accenting popular appliance colors or stainless steel.
- Infinite speed control for quiet performance.
- Bright 75 watt light with high strength polymeric lens (bulb not included).
- Safety enhancing mitered sides and hemmed bottom edges contribute to sleeker styling.
- Mixed flow polymeric fan blade.

Ducted

- Exhaust capacity HVI certified at 180 CFM, 7.0 Sones vertical discharge.
- Horizontal discharge HVI certified at 180 CFM, 6.5 Sones.
- Duct connector with built-in damper included.
- 10-1/2" x 8-3/4" aluminum grease filter.

Duct-free

- Easily converted by removing coverplate and installing Microtek® System Filter No. 97007696 (included).

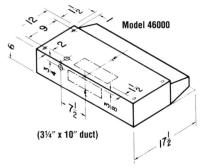

Model 46000

(3¼" x 10" duct)

46000 SERIES (10 times better than ordinary economy duct-free range hoods)

WIDTH	WHITE	ALMOND	STAINLESS
30"	463001	463008	463004
36"	463601	463608	463604
42"	464201	464208	464204

Also available in Harvest, Avocado and Coffee.

SPECIFICATIONS

VOLTS	AMPS	SONES VER.	SONES HOR.	CFM	DUCT-FREE RHP INDEX	DUCT
120	2.5	7.0	6.5	180	9.8	3-1/4" x 10"

40000/41000/42000 SERIES

Two-Speed Economy and Top-Of-The-Line Quality.

The industry's best economy range hood values

- Same shell and durable baked enamel finish as our intermediate models.
- Available in popular appliance colors and genuine stainless steel.
- Safety enhancing mitered sides and hemmed bottom edges contribute to sleek, contemporary styling.
- Two-speed rocker-type fan control.
- 75 watt light with high strength polymeric lens (bulb not included).
- Mixed flow polymeric fan blade.

Ducted 40000 Series

- Exhaust capacity HVI certified at 160 CFM, 5.5 Sones vertical discharge.
- Horizontal discharge HVI certified at 160 CFM, 6.5 Sones.
- Duct connector with built-in damper included.
- 10-1/2" x 8-3/4" aluminum grease filter.

Duct-Free 41000 Series/Microtek® System I

- Includes Microtek® System Filter No. 97007696 for the best duct-free filtration system in its class.
- All other features same as 40000 Series.

7" Round Ducted 42000 Series

- Washable 10-1/2" diameter aluminum filter.
- Use Broan #87 damper (available separately).
- Exhaust capacity HVI certified at 190 CFM, 5.5 Sones (vertical discharge only).
- All other features same as 40000 Series.

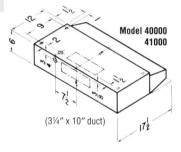

Model 40000 41000

(3¼" x 10" duct)

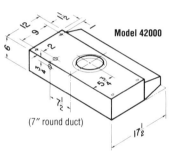

Model 42000

(7" round duct)

40000 SERIES Ducted

WIDTH	WHITE	ALMOND	STAINLESS
24"	402401	402408	402404
30"	403001	403008	403004
36"	403601	403608	403604

Also available in Harvest, Avocado and Coffee.

41000 SERIES Duct-Free *(9 times better than economy duct-free range hoods)*

RHP Index 8.7

WIDTH	WHITE	ALMOND	STAINLESS
24"	412401	412408	412404
30"	413001	413008	413004
36"	413601	413608	413604

Also available in Harvest, Avocado and Coffee.

42000 SERIES 7" Round Ducted

WIDTH	WHITE	ALMOND	STAINLESS
30"	423001	423008	423004
36"	423601	423608	423604

Also available in Harvest, Avocado and Coffee.

SPECIFICATIONS

MODEL NO.	VOLTS	AMPS	SONES VER.	SONES HOR.	CFM	DUCT-FREE RHP INDEX	DUCT
40000	120	2.0	5.5	6.5	160	—	3-1/4" x 10"
41000	120	2.0	—	—	—	8.70	—
42000	120	2.5	5.5	—	190	—	7" Round

Economy hoods are not convertible.

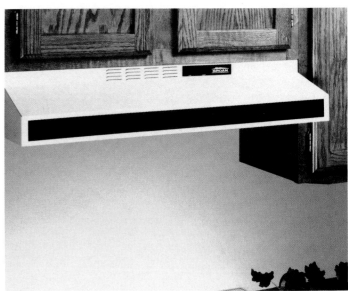

68000/67000 SERIES

48000/47000 SERIES

Sleek White Or Black Glass-Like Styling For Today's Contemporary Kitchens.

Complement Contemporary Kitchen Design With Straight-Side Styling.

7" Round Ducted 68000 Series

- Handsome, easy-to-clean glass-like panel in black or white.
- Built-in, enclosed 75 watt light (bulb not included).
- Washable aluminum filter.
- Damper included.

7" Round Ducted 48000 Series

- Straight-side styling in white, almond or genuine stainless steel.
- Built-in, enclosed 75 watt light (bulb not included).
- Washable aluminum filter.
- Damper included.

Duct-Free 67000 Series

- Includes combination duct-free filter.
- All other features same as 68000 Series.

Duct-Free 47000 Series

- Includes combination duct-free filter.
- All other features same as 48000 Series.

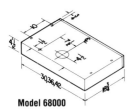

Model 68000

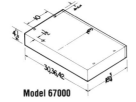

Model 67000

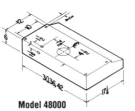

Model 48000

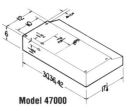

Model 47000

68000 SERIES 7" Round Ducted

WIDTH	WHITE	BLACK
30"	683001	683023
36"	683601	683623
42"	684201	684223

67000 SERIES Duct-Free

WIDTH	WHITE	BLACK
30"	673001	673023
36"	673601	673623
42"	674201	674223

48000 SERIES 7" Round Ducted

WIDTH	WHITE	ALMOND	STAINLESS
30"	483001	483008	483004
36"	483601	483608	483604
42"	484201	484208	484204

47000 SERIES Duct-Free

WIDTH	WHITE	ALMOND	STAINLESS
30"	473001	473008	473004
36"	473601	473608	473604
42"	474201	474208	474204

SPECIFICATIONS

MODEL NO.	VOLTS	AMPS	CFM	SONES
67000	120	2.0	—	—
68000	120	2.5	230	7.0

SPECIFICATIONS

MODEL NO.	VOLTS	AMPS	CFM	SONES
47000	120	2.0	—	—
48000	120	2.5	230	7.0

HIDEAWAY™

Pull-Out Style Disappears Flush To Cabinet Facing When Not In Use.

- Expandable 24"-30" height accommodates 30" cabinet face frame with doors.
- Light and blower turn on automatically when pulled out.
- Exclusive design features built-in storage space.
- Powerful but quiet dual centrifugal blower, HVI certified at 360 CFM horizontal or vertical discharge — 4.5 Sones.
- Exclusive Heat Sentry™ turns blower to high speed automatically when excess cooking heat detected.
- Bright cooktop lighting.
- Install with rough-in kit Model No. 113123.
- For vented installations only.

When not in use, the Hideaway disappears flush to cabinet facing.

The Hideaway provides ample storage space behind cabinet doors.

MODEL 113023 SPECIFICATIONS

VOLTS	AMPS	SONES	CFM	DUCT
120	3.7	4.5	360	3-1/4" x 10"

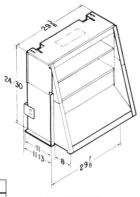

Model 113023

WOOD HOOD

Maintains The Natural Beauty Of All Wood Cabinetry.

- Fits wood hoods with interior width from 28-1/4" to 28-7/8" (can be adapted to hoods up to 42" wide — order kit No. 97009790 available separately).
- Powerful, dual centrifugal blower, HVI certified at 360 CFM, 4.5 Sones horizontal discharge; 360 CFM, 5.0 Sones vertical discharge.
- Exclusive Heat Sentry™ turns blower to high speed when excess cooking heat detected.
- Bright cooktop lighting with 24" fluorescent fixture (bulb not included).
- Built-in duct connector with damper for 3-1/4" x 10" duct.
- Install with rough-in kit Model No. 103123.
- For vented installations only.

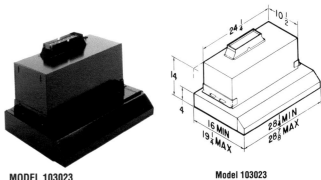

MODEL 103023 SPECIFICATIONS

Model 103023

VOLTS	AMPS	SONES		CFM	DUCT
		VER.	HOR.		
120	3.7	5.0	4.5	360	3-1/4" x 10"

MICROMATE™

Combination Range Hood/Microwave Shelf.

- Accommodates virtually every major brand microwave.
- Installs either ducted or duct-free using Microtek® System Filter No. 97007807 (available separately).
- Exclusive Heat Sentry™ protects microwave from excess heat build-up.
- Bright cooktop lighting.
- Quiet, high performance dual centrifugal blower.

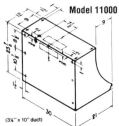

Model 123035

VOLTS	AMPS	SONES	CFM	DUCT-FREE RHP INDEX	DUCT
120	2.7	4.5	300	9.80	3-1/4" x 10"

Special Order
36" available in Hammered White, Hammered Almond, Hammered Harvest, Hammered Avocado and Hammered Coffee.

CANOPY HOOD/11000 SERIES

Infinite Speed, Convertible

- Ducted or Duct-free (Duct-free uses Microtek® Systems Filter No. 97007696).
- Textured hammered finish in popular appliance colors.
- Built-in light accomodates 100 watt bulb or 150 watt flood lamp (bulbs not included).

Model 11000

(3¼" x 10" duct)

11000 SERIES

WIDTH	HAMMERED WHITE	HAMMERED ALMOND	HAMMERED HARVEST	HAMMERED AVOCADO	HAMMERED COFFEE
30"	113036	113042	113047	113048	113049

VOLTS	AMPS	SONES VER.	SONES HOR.	CFM VER.	CFM HOR.	DUCT-FREE RHP INDEX	DUCT
120	3.0	6.0	6.5	190	200	9.80	3-1/4" x 10"

ACCESSORIES

MODEL NO.	DESCRIPTION
634	Roof Cap (includes backdraft damper and birdscreen) 3-1/4" x 10" or up to 8" round
644	Aluminum Roof Cap (includes backdraft damper and birdscreen) 3-1/4" x 10" or up to 8" round
639	Wall Cap 3-1/4" x 10" duct (includes backdraft damper with birdscreen)
641	Aluminum Wall Cap fits 6" round duct (includes backdraft damper with birdscreen)
649	Aluminum Wall Cap fits 3-1/4" x 10" duct (includes damper with birdscreen)
643	Aluminum Wall Cap fits 8" round duct
87	7" Vertical Discharge Damper
97	7" Spring Loaded In-Line Damper
99	9" Spring Loaded In-Line Damper
35	Wall Hanging kit for mounting hoods to wall when cabinets are not used
411	3-1/4" x 10" to 6" Round Transition
412	3-1/4" x 10" to 7" Round Transition
413	3-1/4" x 10" to 8" Round Transition
401	3-1/4" x 10" Duct — 2" section
406	6" Round Duct — 2" section
407	7" Round Duct — 2" section
410	10" Round Duct — 2" section
415	7" Adjustable Elbow (4 per carton)
419	6" Adjustable Elbow
421	Damper Section, 10" round with damper
423	Vertical Transition, 4-1/2" x 18-1/2" to 10" round
424	Rear Transition, 4-1/2" x 18-1/2" to 10" round
425	Horz. Left Transition, 4-1/2" x 18-1/2" to 10" round
426	Horz. Right Transition, 4-1/2" x 18-1/2" to 10" round
428	3-1/4" x 10" Vertical Elbow
429	3-1/4" x 10" Horizontal Elbow
430	Short Eave Elbow for 3-1/4" x 10" duct (includes backdraft damper and grille)
431	Long Eave Elbow for 3-1/4" x 10" duct (includes backdraft damper and grille)
437	High Capacity Roof Cap — up to 1200 CFM
441	Wall Cap with gravity damper — 13-1/8" sq. takes 10" round

EXTERIOR MOUNTED FAN SYSTEMS (Roof and Wall)

Model 338

■ 900 CFM (at 0.1 static pressure)

For indoor barbecues or extra duct runs. All aluminum, weatherproof construction. Thermally protected motor, 120 V. Requires 9" duct. Damper not included.

Model 334

■ 470 CFM (at 0.1 static pressure)

For conventional gas and electric range ventilation. All aluminum weatherproof construction. Thermal protected motor, 120V. Requires 7" round duct. Damper not included. For Roof Mounting use 434 Roof Conversion Kit, includes roof cap and flashing sheet.

SPLASH PLATES

Broan splash plates in appliance matching colors protect your kitchen wall from cooking splatter. Installs easily with four screws. Available in 24 gauge stainless steel or .019 (nominal) aluminum in enamel finishes. For exact sizes, colors and model numbers refer to the Broan Price List.

Specifications represented in this catalog are subject to change without notice.

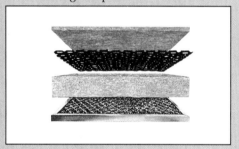
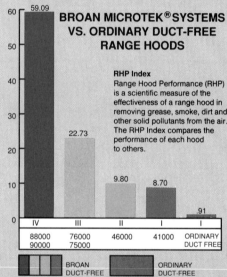

Monogram appliances make a custom kitchen all the

more extraordinary. Integrated with cabinetry, the appliances

define the purpose and reflect the spirit of the kitchen.

Monogram appliances: at home in the finest custom kitchens.

The Monogram line was created for a very good reason: to answer the need for built-in appliances that integrate with the design of the kitchen. Monogram appliances neither intrude or distract. Rather, they seem to meld with their surroundings, graciously contributing to the character of the room.

Monogram built-in appliances are available only from GE, and are supported by the largest service network in the industry. For answers to your questions, call the award-winning GE Answer Center® consumer information service, 800.626.2000, any time of day or night.

Or call your GE Monogram dealer to learn more about how these appliances can make your custom kitchen a truly extraordinary room.

Monogram refrigerators are simply beautiful, inside and out.

ZBD4100SB
Monogram dishwasher,
ZEK756GP
Monogram double convection oven,
ZMC3000B
Monogram built-in microwave/ convection oven,
ZISB48D
Monogram 48" refrigerator. Appliances are also available in white.

Monogram Component Cooktop System:
ZGW125/124EN
gas components,
ZEW175N
downdraft vent,
ZEW165N
downdraft grill.

Monogram built-in refrigerators, in 36", 42" and 48" widths, come ready to accept 1/4" panels and the full-length handles furnished with the appliance. For a more decorative, trimless appearance, the doors can be customized with 3/4" panels and handles. Each refrigerator offers ample storage and amenities such as an automatic icemaker; lighted, full-view drawers; adjustable door bins and interior shelves; and smooth surfaces that are easily wiped clean.

Monogram offers twelve installation options and a choice of custom or standard installation of the ice-and-water dispenser. The vent, at the *top* of the refrigerator (to allow for proper alignment of the toe-kick), may be covered with a height-adjustable decorative panel.

ZISB48D
Monogram 48" refrigerator with black dispenser, 3/4" decorative panels, and custom handles.

ZISB48D
Monogram 48" refrigerator offers a generous expanse of flexible storage space for both fresh and frozen foods.

Monogram refrigerators offer a choice of sizes and models,

a variety of customization options, and one marvelous feature after another.

ZEK757WP
Monogram double convection oven. Also available in black.

Tasteful design and exceptional flexibility. The flush, trimless appearance of Monogram built-in ovens make them compatible with most custom kitchens. Monogram single and double ovens, in conventional and convection models, provide appealing options.

Monogram convection and thermal ovens: valuable assets to the active kitchen.

A most versatile resource, the Monogram convection oven offers four cooking modes: thermal, convection, combination, and convection broiling. The appliance is a true convection oven, equipped with a dedicated heating element and fan that maintain a uniform oven temperature. Because heat is evenly distributed throughout the oven, you can cook foods on two or three shelves at a time with excellent results. Pastries and breads are light-textured and golden brown; meats and poultry are richly browned, moist and delicious.

If you prefer cooking the conventional way, Monogram accommodates your style with single and double thermal ovens. All ovens have electronic controls —so, with just a touch or two, you can select the temperature, pre-set the self-clean cycle, or program the cooking.

ZEK736GP
Monogram single convection oven. Also available in white.

ZBD3300RWB
Monogram dishwashers,
JEM33M
Monogram Spacemaker II™ microwave oven,
ZEK757WP
Monogram double convection oven,
ZISW36D
Monogram 36" refrigerator. Appliances are also available in black.

Monogram Component Cooktop System:
ZGW124/125EN
(3) gas components,
ZEW175N
(2) downdraft vents,
ZEW165N
(2) downdraft grills.

Single and double built-in ovens, conventional and convection models...

Monogram presents an enticing assortment of choices.

Monogram built-in microwave/ convection oven. Also available in black.

Monogram presents its first true built-in microwave oven. The first thing you're likely to notice about the Monogram built-in microwave oven is that it doesn't look like a microwave oven. With a horizontal handle and a door that pulls down to open, it bears a striking resemblance to a conventional oven—a style that is easily integrated with the design of the kitchen. The fresh style and flexibility of the Monogram built-in microwave offer new opportunities for creative kitchen design.

The Monogram line includes microwave ovens as well as microwave/ convection ovens, which cook three ways: microwave only, convection only, and a combination of the two. Each oven has a smooth, understated control panel. By lightly pressing the appropriate touchpads, you can instruct the oven to defrost, cook, roast, extend cooking time by 30 seconds, or prepare microwave popcorn. Automatic cooking processes are monitored by electronic sensors, which signal the oven to shut off when cooking is complete.

Monogram microwave ovens bring new flexibility to the process of creating a custom kitchen.

JEM34M
Monogram Spacemaker II™ microwave oven. Also available in white.

ZBD4300SW
Monogram dishwashers,
ZMC3000W
Monogram built-in microwave/ convection oven,
ZEK757WP
Monogram double convection oven,
ZISW36D
Monogram 36" refrigerator,
ZGU661EM
Monogram downdraft gas cooktop. Appliances are also available in black.

Monogram™

Microwave Ovens

ZMC3000B
Monogram built-in microwave/ convection oven installed above the
ZEK736GP
Monogram single convection oven. Both ovens are available in white.

Monogram microwave ovens: compatible with the finest custom kitchens.

Whether installed alone or paired with a Monogram single wall oven, the Monogram built-in microwave oven is in harmony with its surroundings. But you needn't limit yourself to a single microwave oven.

Consider the addition of a Monogram Spacemaker II™ microwave oven, which can be installed in a wall or beneath a cabinet to conserve counter space. Or a Monogram combination microwave/ convection oven (not shown), which combines the speed of microwave cooking with the gentleness of convection heating.

The variety of Monogram cooking surfaces stirs the imagination...

and satisfies a multitude of cooking requirements.

A handsome,
serviceable cooking
surface, created
with the Monogram
Component
Cooktop System.

ZGW124/125EN
(3) gas components,
ZEW175N
(2) downdraft vents,
ZEW165
downdraft grill.

The Monogram Component Cooktop System lets you design the cooktop.

This innovative system offers you a choice of gas, solid disk and grill components—and lets you create the cooktop. You may mix or match components, which can be installed horizontally or vertically; singly, in pairs, or as a group. The Monogram Component Cooktop system works equally well in traditional and contemporary surroundings. Its modularity makes it adaptable to settings beyond the kitchen, such as the pantry, breakfast room, and entertainment area.

8

Monogram cooktops: refreshing design and exacting performance.

Choose from two styles of Monogram gas cooktops: updraft, for use with a hooded vent above the cooking area, and downdraft, which has an integrated retractable vent. A pilotless electronic ignition system safely drives the cooktop. Each of the five burners is topped with a porcelainized cast-iron grate; sealed burner bowls and a tempered glass surface simplify clean up.

Monogram solid disk cooktops (not shown) further expand your choices. The cooktops feature cast-iron heating units sealed to the glass top, eliminating the need for drip pans. The heating units—an 8" and 9" disk and two 6" disks—are monitored by sensors that maintain the heat level selected. The cooktop, just 3" deep, can be installed in an island or countertop without infringing upon storage space below.

ZGU660EM
Monogram gas downdraft cooktop. Also available in white.

ZBD3300RWB
Monogram dishwasher,
ZEK757WP
Monogram double convection oven,
ZGU661EM
(2) Monogram gas downdraft cooktops,
JEM33M
Monogram Spacemaker II™ microwave oven,
ZISW36D
Monogram 36" refrigerator. Appliances are also available in black.

ZBD4300SW
Monogram
dishwasher with
stainless steel
interior.

**A trio of dishwasher styles,
each designed for the integrated
custom kitchen.** Monogram dishwashers
accept standard panels
or 3/4" custom panels,
flush with surrounding
cabinetry.

And Monogram
offers a choice of three
dishwasher styles:
an electronic model with
an interior of lustrous,
durable stainless steel;
an electronic dishwasher,
and a smartly styled
electromechanical model,
both with PermaTuf®
interior lining. Each
dishwasher is generously
insulated to assure extra-
quiet operation, and
each is covered by a
20-year warranty on the
interior door liner and
tub. Multiple cycles and
options, sophisticated
sensors, and well-
engineered wash and
filter systems work
together to assure
excellent performance.

ZCG3100TBB
Monogram built-in
compactor. Also
available in white.

ZBD4300SW
Monogram
dishwasher with
stainless steel
interior.

With remarkable style and efficiency,

Monogram dishwashers and compactors perform the task at hand.

ZBD3000TBW
Monogram electronic dishwasher. Also available in white.

The Monogram compactor: a sensible addition to the kitchen's recycling center.

ZBD3300RWB
Monogram electromechanical dishwasher. Also available in black.

The Monogram compactor, a mere 12" wide, comes with a reversible black/white drawer panel and accepts a custom panel as well. The toe-kick height is adjustable, allowing alignment of the lower edge of the compactor with that of surrounding cabinetry. Compressing the equivalent of 14 filled kitchen receptacles into a single bag, the Monogram compactor makes a notable contribution to the collective effort.

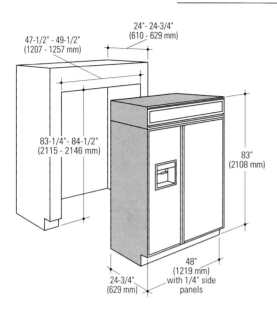

47-1/2" - 49-1/2"
(1207 - 1257 mm)

24"- 24-3/4"
(610 - 629 mm)

83-1/4"- 84-1/2"
(2115 - 2146 mm)

83"
(2108 mm)

24-3/4"
(629 mm)

48"
(1219 mm)
with 1/4" side
panels

ZISW48D

*Built-in side-by-side
refrigerator with
white dispenser*

■
ZISB48D

*Built-in side-by-side
refrigerator with
black dispenser*

Product Dimensions

*H 83" (2108 mm)
Grille panel can be
adjusted to
84-1/2" (2146 mm)
W 48" (1219 mm)
D 24-3/4" (629 mm)
excluding handles*

Cutout Dimensions

*H 83-1/4"– 84-1/2"
(2115–2146 mm)
W 47-1/2"– 49-1/2"
(1207–1257 mm)
D 24"–24-3/4"
(610–629 mm)*

Features
- Total capacity, 29.8 cu. ft.
- Fresh food capacity, 17.8 cu. ft.
- Freezer capacity, 12.0 cu. ft.
- Shelf area, 35.1 sq. ft.
- Lighted through-the-door dispenser delivers ice cubes, crushed ice and chilled water
- Rolls into place on four wheels
- Four-point leveling system, adjustable from front
- Self-closing doors with doorstops
- Separate refrigerator and freezer temperature controls
- 115 Volts/20 Amps
- Approximate shipping weight: 580 pounds

Fresh Food Compartment Features
- Four adjustable glass shelves
- Five adjustable door bins
- Wine holder
- Sealed, self-closing snack pan on roller system
- Two sealed, self-closing vegetable/fruit pans on roller system
- Two unsealed, self-closing storage pans on roller system

Freezer Features
- Automatic icemaker with removable bin that holds up to six pounds of ice
- Three adjustable door bins
- Three adjustable shelves
- Two roll-out utility baskets

1/4" Panel Sizes
- Freezer panels, 18-1/4"H x 19-1/4"W and 36-1/2" H x 19-1/4"W
- Fresh food panel, 67-7/8"H x 27-1/4"W
- Grille panel, 6-7/8"H x 47-1/8"W

Optional Accessory Kits:

ZKWPD48
White Lexan® door panels for dispenser refrigerator model ZISW48D

ZKBPD48
Black Lexan® door panels for dispenser refrigerato model ZISB48D

47-1/2" - 49-1/2"
(1207 - 1257 mm)

24"- 24-3/4"
(610 - 629 mm)

83-1/4"- 84-1/2"
(2115 - 2146 mm)

83"
(2108 mm)

24-3/4"
(629 mm)

48"
(1219 mm)
with 1/4" side
panels

ZIS48N

*Built-in side-by-side
refrigerator*

Product Dimensions

*H 83" (2108 mm)
Grille panel can be
adjusted to
84-1/2" (2146 mm)
W 48" (1219 mm)
D 24-3/4" (629 mm)
excluding handles*

Cutout Dimensions

*H 83-1/4"– 84-1/2"
(2115–2146 mm)
W 47-1/2"– 49-1/2"
(1207–1257 mm)
D 24"–24-3/4"
(610–629 mm)*

Features
- Total capacity, 30.2 cu. ft.
- Fresh food capacity, 17.8 cu. ft.
- Freezer capacity, 12.4 cu. ft.
- Shelf area, 37.1 sq. ft.
- Rolls into place on four wheels
- Four-point leveling system, adjustable from front
- Self-closing doors with doorstops
- Separate refrigerator and freezer temperature controls
- 115 Volts/20 Amps
- Approximate shipping weight: 580 pounds

Fresh Food Compartment Features
- Four adjustable glass shelves
- Five adjustable door bins
- Wine holder
- Sealed, self-closing snack pan on roller system
- Two sealed, self-closing vegetable/fruit pans on roller system
- Two unsealed, self-closing storage pans on roller system

Freezer Features
- Automatic icemaker with removable bin that holds up to six pounds of ice
- Five adjustable door bins
- Four adjustable shelves
- Two roll-out utility baskets

1/4" Panel Sizes
- Freezer panel, 67-7/8"H x 19-1/4"W
- Fresh food panel, 67-7/8"H x 27-1/4"W
- Grille panel, 6-7/8"H x 47-1/8"W

Optional Accessory Kits:

ZKWP48
White Lexan® door panels for non-dispens refrigerator model ZIS48N

ZKBP48
Black Lexan® door pane for non-dispenser refrigerator model ZIS48N

Note
The finished and rough-in dimensions are determined by the type of installation being made and will also be affected by the typ
and thickness of the material being used

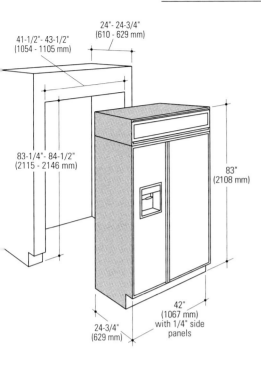

☐
ZISW42D
Built-in side-by-side refrigerator with white dispenser

■
ZISB42D
Built-in side-by-side refrigerator with black dispenser

Product Dimensions
H 83" (2108 mm)
Grille panel can be adjusted to 84-1/2" (2146 mm)
W 42" (1067 mm)
D 24-3/4" (629 mm) excluding handles

Cutout Dimensions
H 83-1/4"– 84-1/2" (2115–2146 mm)
W 41-1/2"– 43-1/2" (1054–1105 mm)
D 24"–24-3/4" (610–629 mm)

Features
- Total capacity, 25.7 cu. ft.
- Fresh food capacity, 16.4 cu. ft.
- Freezer capacity, 9.3 cu. ft.
- Shelf area, 31.0 sq. ft.
- Lighted through-the-door dispenser delivers ice cubes, crushed ice and chilled water
- Rolls into place on four wheels
- Four-point leveling system adjustable from front
- Self-closing doors with doorstops
- Separate refrigerator and freezer temperature controls
- 115 Volts/20 Amps
- Approximate shipping weight: 540 pounds

Fresh Food Compartment Features
- Four adjustable glass shelves
- Five adjustable door bins
- Wine holder
- Sealed, self-closing snack pan on roller system
- Sealed, self-closing vegetable/fruit pan on roller system
- Unsealed, self-closing storage pan on roller system

Freezer Features
- Automatic icemaker with removable bin that holds up to six pounds of ice
- Three adjustable door bins
- Three adjustable shelves
- Two roll-out utility baskets

1/4" Panel Sizes
- Freezer panels, 18-1/4"H x 15-1/4"W and 36-1/2" H x 15-1/4"W
- Fresh food panel, 67-7/8"H x 25-1/4"W
- Grille panel, 6-7/8"H x 41-1/8"W

Optional Accessory Kits:

ZKWPD42
White Lexan® door panels for dispenser refrigerator model ZISW42D

ZKBPD42
Black Lexan® door panels for dispenser refrigerator model ZISB42D

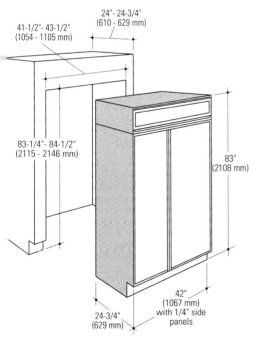

ZIS42N
Built-in side-by-side refrigerator

Product Dimensions
H 83" (2108 mm)
Grille panel can be adjusted to 84-1/2" (2146 mm)
W 42" (1067 mm)
D 24-3/4" (629 mm) excluding handles

Cutout Dimensions
H 83-1/4"– 84-1/2" (2115–2146 mm)
W 41-1/2"– 43-1/2" (1054–1105 mm)
D 24"–24-3/4" (610–629 mm)

Features
- Total capacity, 25.8 cu. ft.
- Fresh food capacity, 16.4 cu. ft.
- Freezer capacity, 9.4 cu. ft.
- Shelf area, 31.7 sq. ft.
- Four-point leveling system, adjustable from front
- Rolls into place on four wheels
- Self-closing doors with doorstops
- Separate refrigerator and freezer temperature controls
- 115 Volts/20 Amps
- Approximate shipping weight: 540 pounds

Fresh Food Compartment Features
- Four adjustable glass shelves
- Five adjustable door bins
- Wine holder
- Sealed, self-closing snack pan on roller system
- Sealed, self-closing vegetable/fruit pan on roller system
- Unsealed, self-closing storage pan on roller system

Freezer Features
- Automatic icemaker with removable bin that holds up to six pounds of ice
- Five adjustable door bins
- Four adjustable shelves
- Two roll-out utility baskets

1/4" Panel Sizes
- Freezer panel, 67-7/8"H x 15-1/4"W
- Fresh food panel, 67-7/8"H x 25-1/4"W
- Grille panel, 6-7/8"H x 41-1/8"W

Optional Accessory Kits:

ZKWP42
White Lexan® door panels for non-dispenser refrigerator model ZIS42N

ZKBP42
Black Lexan® door panels for non-dispenser refrigerator model ZIS42N

Note
The finished and rough-in dimensions are determined by the type of installation being made and will also be affected by the type and thickness of the material being used

Monogram™

Refrigerators

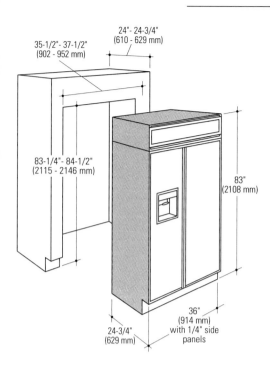

35-1/2"- 37-1/2"
(902 - 952 mm)

24"- 24-3/4"
(610 - 629 mm)

83-1/4"- 84-1/2"
(2115 - 2146 mm)

83"
(2108 mm)

24-3/4"
(629 mm)

36"
(914 mm)
with 1/4" side panels

□
ZISW36D

Built-in side-by-side refrigerator with white dispenser

■
ZISB36D

Built-in side-by-side refrigerator with black dispenser

Product Dimensions

*H 83" (2108 mm)
Grille panel can be adjusted to
84-1/2" (2146 mm)
W 36" (914 mm)
D 24-3/4" (629 mm)
excluding handles*

Cutout Dimensions

*H 83-1/4"–84-1/2"
(2115–2146 mm)
W 35-1/2"–37-1/2"
(902–952 mm)
D 24"–24-3/4"
(610–629 mm)*

Features
- Total capacity, 21.2 cu. ft.
- Fresh food capacity, 12.0 cu. ft.
- Freezer capacity, 9.2 cu. ft.
- Shelf area, 25.7 sq. ft.
- Lighted through-the-door dispenser delivers ice cubes, crushed ice or chilled water
- Rolls into place on four wheels
- Four-point leveling system, adjustable from front
- Self-closing doors with 90° door hold and doorstops
- Separate refrigerator and freezer temperature controls
- 115 Volts/20 Amps
- Approximate shipping weight: 475 pounds

Fresh Food Compartment Features
- Four adjustable glass shelves
- Five adjustable door bins
- Quick Serve™ System. Four dishes held in a tray; go from refrigerator to microwave to dishwasher
- Wine holder
- Sealed, self-closing snack pan on roller system
- Sealed, self-closing vegetable/fruit pan on roller system
- Unsealed, self-closing storage pan on roller system

Freezer Features
- Automatic icemaker with removable bin that holds up to six pounds of ice
- Three adjustable door bins
- Three adjustable shelves
- Two roll-out utility baskets

1/4" Panel Sizes
- Freezer panels, 18-1/4"H x 15-1/4"W and 36-1/2" H x 15-1/4"W
- Fresh food panel, 67-7/8"H x 19-1/4"W
- Grille panel, 6-7/8"H x 35-1/8"W

Optional Accessory Kits:

ZKWPD36
White Lexan® door panels for dispenser refrigerator model ZISW36D

ZKBPD36
Black Lexan® door panels for dispenser refrigerator model ZISB36D

35-1/2"- 37-1/2"
(902 - 952 mm)

24"- 24-3/4"
(610 - 629 mm)

83-1/4"- 84-1/2"
(2115 - 2146 mm)

83"
(2108 mm)

24-3/4"
(629 mm)

36"
(914 mm)
with 1/4" side panels

ZIS36N

Built-in side-by-side refrigerator

Product Dimensions

*H 83" (2108 mm)
Grille panel can be adjusted to
84-1/2" (2146 mm)
W 36" (914 mm)
D 24-3/4 (629 mm)*

Cutout Dimensions

*H 83-1/4"–84-1/2"
(2115–2146 mm)
84-1/2" (2146 mm)
W 35-1/2"–37-1/2"
(902 mm – 952 mm)
D 24"–24-3/4"
(610–629 mm)*

Features
- Total capacity, 21.4 cu. ft.
- Fresh food capacity, 12.0 cu. ft.
- Freezer capacity, 9.4 cu. ft.
- Shelf area, 25.9 sq. ft.
- Rolls into place on four wheels
- Four-point leveling system, adjustable from front
- Self-closing doors with 90° door hold and doorstops
- Separate refrigerator and freezer temperature controls
- 115 Volts/20 Amps
- Approximate shipping weight: 475 pounds

Fresh Food Compartment Features
- Four adjustable glass shelves
- Five adjustable door bins
- Quick Serve™ System. Four dishes held in a tray; go from refrigerator to microwave to dishwasher
- Wine holder
- Sealed, self-closing snack pan on roller system
- Sealed, self-closing vegetable/fruit pan on roller system
- Unsealed, self-closing storage pan on roller system

Freezer Features
- Automatic icemaker with removable bin that holds up to six pounds of ice
- Five adjustable door bins
- Five adjustable shelves
- Two roll-out utility baskets

1/4" Panel Sizes
- Freezer panel, 67-7/8"H x 15-1/4"W
- Fresh food panel, 67-7/8"H x 19-1/4"W
- Grille panel, 6-7/8"H x 35-1/8"W

Optional Accessory Kits:

ZKWP36
White Lexan® door panels for non-dispense refrigerator model ZIS36N

ZKBP36
Black Lexan® door panel for non-dispenser refrigerator model ZIS36N

Note
The finished and rough-in dimensions are determined by the type of installation being made and will also be affected by the t and thickness of the material being used

Optional Trim Kits for Monogram Refrigerators:

ZKH1

Provides for the installation of a custom handle on the standard 1/4" custom panels.

ZKT36, ZKT42, ZKT48

Provides for the installation of 3/4" custom door and grille panels, using the standard full length handle. For 36" models use ZKT36, for 42" models use ZKT42 and for 48" models use ZKT48.

ZKHT1

Provides for the installation of a custom handle using 3/4" door and grille panels. This kit must be used in conjunction with ZKT36, ZKT42 or ZKT48.

ZKCD1

Provides for the installation of a custom collar trim on the dispenser for one continuous custom panel on freezer door. This kit can be used alone, or with others noted.

Model	Panel Thickness		Handle		Dispenser		Trim Kits Required
	1/4"	Trimless 3/4"	Full length Brushed Aluminum	Custom	Standard Full Width	Custom Collar	
Non-Dispenser	●		●				None
Non-Dispenser	●			●			ZKH1
Non-Dispenser		●	●				ZKT36, ZKT42 or ZKT48
Non-Dispenser		●		●			ZKHT1 and ZKT36, ZKT42 or ZKT48
Dispenser	●		●		●		None
Dispenser	●			●	●		ZKH1
Dispenser		●	●		●		ZKT36, ZKT42 or ZKT48
Dispenser		●		●	●		ZKHT1 and ZKT36, ZKT42 or ZKT48
Dispenser	●		●			●	ZKCD1
Dispenser	●			●		●	ZKH1, ZKCD1
Dispenser		●	●			●	ZKCD1 and ZKT36, ZKT42 or ZKT48
Dispenser		●		●		●	ZKHT1, ZKCD1 and ZKT36, ZKT42 or ZKT48

Refrigerator Warranty Information

(Applicable to units manufactured after 12/1/92)

- Full Two-Year Warranty, parts and labor
- Full Five-Year Warranty, parts and labor on the sealed refrigerating system (the compressor, condenser, evaporator and all connecting tubing)
- Additional Limited Seven-Year Warranty on the sealed system parts.

Note

Field-installed custom panels are required for all Monogram refrigerators

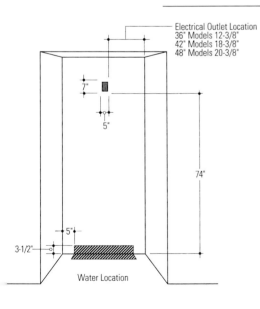

Electrical Outlet Location
36" Models 12-3/8"
42" Models 18-3/8"
48" Models 20-3/8"

7"

5"

74"

5"

3-1/2"

Water Location

Water Location Information

Any location 3-1/2" on back wall or the floor, at least 5" from either side

15

Monogram™

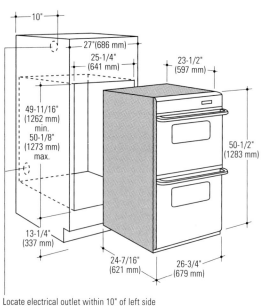

Locate electrical outlet within 10" of left side of opening and 56" above cutout floor or thru the left side of cabinet wall.

☐ **ZEK757WP**

White double convection oven

■ **ZEK756GP**

Black double convection oven

Product Dimensions

H 50-1/2"
(1283 mm)
W 26-3/4" (679 mm)
D 24-7/16"
(621 mm)

Cutout Dimensions

H 49-11/16"
(1262 mm)
W 25-1/4" (641 mm)

Features

- True convection — both ovens
- Solid-state electronic touch controls
- Independent cooking/cleaning controls — cook in one while the other cleans
- Soft touch handles
- White (or black) glass oven doors with window
- Oven interior dimensions — both ovens: 19" W x 15" H x 16" D
- Self-cleaning oven — both ovens
- Motorized self-clean door latches
- Oven interior lights with touch control pad
- Electronic meat thermometer — upper oven
- Dual element bake
- Broiler pan/rack
- 6.8 KW rating at 240V, 5.1 KW at 208 Volts
- Roasting rack
- Full color convection cookbook
- Approximate shipping weight: 175 pounds

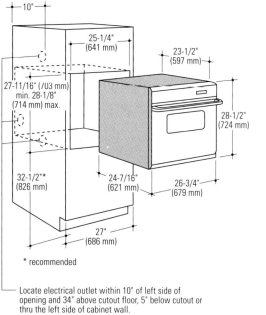

* recommended

Locate electrical outlet within 10" of left side of opening and 34" above cutout floor, 5" below cutout or thru the left side of cabinet wall.

☐ **ZEK737WP**

White single convection oven

■ **ZEK736GP**

Black single convection oven

Product Dimensions

H 28-1/2" (724 mm)
W 26-3/4" (679 mm)
D 24-7/16" (621 mm)

Cutout Dimensions

H 27-11/16"
(703 mm)
W 25-1/4" (641 mm)

Features

- True convection oven
- Solid-state electronic touch controls
- Programmable self-clean cycle
- Two programmable broil selections
- Soft touch handle
- White (or black) glass oven door with window
- Oven interior dimensions: 19" W x 15" H x 16" D
- Self-cleaning oven interior
- Motorized self-clean door latch
- Oven interior light with touch control pad
- Electronic meat thermometer
- Dual element bake
- Broiler pan/rack
- 3.4 KW rating at 240V, 2.6 KW at 208 Volts
- Roasting rack
- Full color convection cookbook
- Approximate shipping weight: 104 pounds

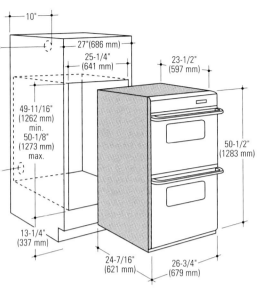

☐
ZEK755WP
White double oven

■
ZEK754GP
Black double oven

Product Dimensions

H 50-1/2"
(1283 mm)
W 26-3/4" *(679 mm)*
D 24-7/16"
(621 mm)

Cutout Dimensions

H 49-11/16"
(1262 mm)
W 25-1/4" *(641 mm)*

Features

- Solid-state electronic touch controls
- Independent cooking/cleaning controls — cook in one while the other cleans
- Soft touch handles
- White (or black) glass oven door with windows
- Oven interior dimensions — both ovens: 19" W x 15" H x 18" D
- Self-cleaning oven — both ovens
- Motorized self-clean door latches
- Oven interior lights with touch control pad
- Electronic clock and reminder timer
- Automatic oven timing
- Electronic meat thermometer — upper oven
- Dual element bake
- Broiler pan/rack
- 6.8 KW rating at 240V, 5.1 KW at 208V
- Approximate shipping weight: 165 pounds

cate electrical outlet within 10" of left side opening and 56" above cutout floor or thru e left side of cabinet wall.

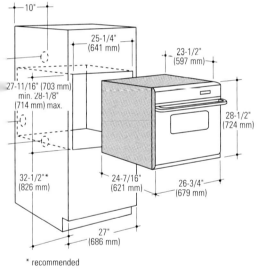

* recommended

— Locate electrical outlet within 10" of left side of opening and 34" above cutout floor, 5" below cutout or thru the left side of cabinet wall.

☐
ZEK735WP
White single oven

■
ZEK734GP
Black single oven

Product Dimensions

H 28-1/2" *(724 mm)*
W 26-3/4" *(679 mm)*
D 24-7/16" *(621 mm)*

Cutout Dimensions

H 27-11/16"
(703 mm)
W 25-1/4" *(641 mm)*

Features

- Solid-state electronic touch controls
- Programmable self-clean cycle
- Two programmable broil selections
- Soft touch handle
- White (or black) glass oven door with window
- Oven interior dimensions: 19" W x 15" H x 18" D
- Self-cleaning oven interior
- Motorized self-clean door latch
- Oven interior light with touch control pad
- Electronic meat thermometer
- Electronic clock and timer
- Dual element bake
- Broiler pan/rack
- 3.4 KW rating at 240V
- Approximate shipping weight: 99 pounds

Oven Warranty Information

Full One-Year Warranty, parts and labor

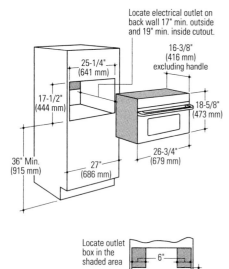

Locate electrical outlet on back wall 17" min. outside and 19" min. inside cutout.

25-1/4" (641 mm)
16-3/8" (416 mm) excluding handle
17-1/2" (444 mm)
18-5/8" (473 mm)
36" Min. (915 mm)
27" (686 mm)
26-3/4" (679 mm)

Locate outlet box in the shaded area
6"
8"

☐ **ZMC3000W**
White built-in microwave/ convection oven

■ **ZMC3000B**
Black built-in microwave/ convection oven

Product Dimensions

H 18-5/8" (473 mm)
W 26-3/4" (679 mm)
D 16-3/8" (416 mm)
cabinet depth

Cutout Dimensions

H 17-1/2" (444 mm)
W 25-1/4" (641 mm)
D 17" min. (432 mm)

Features

- Microwave power output, 800 watts (IEC-705 test procedure)
- Wide, 1.0 cu. ft. capacity
- Electronic touch controls
- Three ways to cook: microwave, convection, and combination
- Ten power levels
- Sensor cooking controls including: Auto Cook Auto Roast (probe), Auto Reheat and Popcorn
- 4-stage programming
- Temp Cook/Hold
- Time Cook I and II
- Add 30 Seconds pad for simple cooking time extension
- Minute/Second timer
- Clock with ON/OFF display switch
- Auto Start
- Auto Defrost
- Express Cook
- Stainless steel oven interior with wire shelf
- 120 Volts/13 Amps
- Deluxe full color cookbook
- Approximate shipping weight: 84 pounds
- Can be installed alone or over Monogram single wall oven

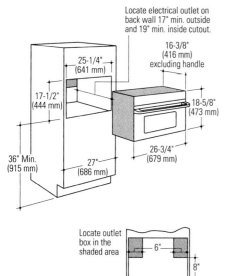

Locate electrical outlet on back wall 17" min. outside and 19" min. inside cutout.

25-1/4" (641 mm)
16-3/8" (416 mm) excluding handle
17-1/2" (444 mm)
18-5/8" (473 mm)
36" Min. (915 mm)
27" (686 mm)
26-3/4" (679 mm)

Locate outlet box in the shaded area
6"
8"

☐ **ZMW2000W**
White built-in microwave oven

■ **ZMW2000B**
Black built-in microwave oven

Product Dimensions

H 18-5/8" (473 mm)
W 26-3/4" (679 mm)
D 16-3/8" (416 mm)
cabinet depth

Cutout Dimensions

H 17-1/2" (444 mm)
W 25-1/4" (641 mm)
D 17" min. (432 mm)

Features

- Microwave power output, 800 watts (IEC-705 test procedure)
- Wide, 1.0 cu. ft. capacity
- Electronic touch controls
- Ten power levels
- Sensor cooking controls including: Auto Cook Auto Roast (probe), Auto Reheat and Popcorn
- 4-stage programming
- Temp Cook/Hold
- Time Cook I and II
- Add 30 Seconds pad for simple cooking time extension
- Minute/Second timer
- Clock with ON/OFF display switch
- Auto Start
- Auto Defrost
- Express Cook
- Stainless steel oven interior with wire shelf
- 120 Volts/13 Amps
- Deluxe full color cookbook
- Approximate shipping weight: 75 pounds
- Can be installed alone or over Monogram single wall oven

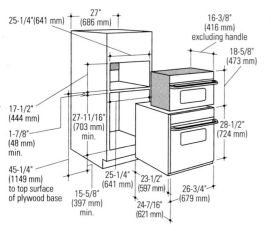

25-1/4"(641 mm)
27" (686 mm)
16-3/8" (416 mm) excluding handle
18-5/8" (473 mm)
17-1/2" (444 mm)
1-7/8" (48 mm) min.
27-11/16" (703 mm) min.
28-1/2" (724 mm)
45-1/4" (1149 mm) to top surface of plywood base
25-1/4" (641 mm)
23-1/2" (597 mm)
26-3/4" (679 mm)
15-5/8" (397 mm) min.
24-7/16" (621 mm)

Installation Option shown at left includes:

ZMC3000W, ZMC3000B, ZMW2000W or ZMW2000B microwave oven installed over a Monogram single wall oven. No trim kits required.

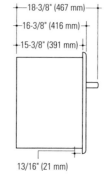

18-3/8" (467 mm)
16-3/8" (416 mm)
15-3/8" (391 mm)
13/16" (21 mm)

Microwave Warranty Information

- Full One-Year Warranty, in-home service, parts and labor
- Additional Limited Nine-Year Warranty, magnetron tube

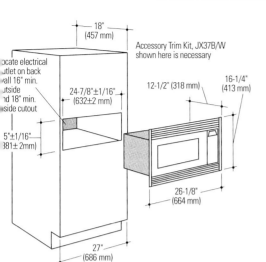

18"
(457 mm)

Accessory Trim Kit, JX37B/W
shown here is necessary

locate electrical
outlet on back
wall 16" min.
outside
and 18" min.
inside cutout

24-7/8"±1/16"
(632±2 mm)

12-1/2" (318 mm)

16-1/4"
(413 mm)

15"±1/16"
(381± 2mm)

26-1/8"
(664 mm)

27"
(686 mm)

☐
JEM33M

*White electronic
Spacemaker II™
microwave oven*

■
JEM34M

*Black electronic
Spacemaker II™
microwave oven*

**Product
Dimensions**

H 11-5/32" (283 mm)
W 23-13/16"
(605 mm)
D 12-1/2" (318 mm)

**Cutout
Dimensions**

H 15" ± 1/16"
(381 mm ± 2 mm)
W 24-7/8" ± 1/16"
(632 mm ± 2 mm)
D 16"–18"
(406 – 457 mm)

Features

- Microwave power output, 800 watts
  (IEC-705 test procedure)
- Oven capacity, .8 cu. ft.
- Electronic touch controls
- Ten power levels
- Removable shelf
- Sensor cooking controls including: Auto Cook, Auto
  Roast (probe), Auto Reheat and Popcorn
- Auto Defrost
- Express Cook
- 5-stage programming
- Temp Cook/Hold
- Time Cook I and II; two timed controlled cooking
  functions within one program
- Add 30 seconds pad for simple cooking time extension
- Minute/second timer
- Clock
- Auto Start
- Cooking complete reminder
- Includes hardware for under-cabinet installation
- 120 Volts/13 Amps
- Approximate shipping weight: 42 pounds

Accessory Kits:

JX37W

Kit is required for
in-cabinet installation
of Model JEM33M

JX37B

Kit is required for
in-cabinet installation
of Model JEM34M

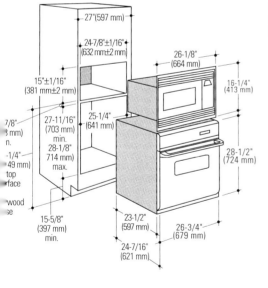

27"(597 mm)

24-7/8"±1/16"
(632 mm±2 mm)

26-1/8"
(664 mm)

15"±1/16"
(381 mm±2 mm)

16-1/4"
(413 mm)

27-11/16"
(703 mm)
min.

25-1/4"
(641 mm)

7/8"
(3 mm)
n.

28-1/8"
714 mm)
max.

-1/4"
(49 mm)
top
surface

28-1/2"
(724 mm)

wood
se

15-5/8"
(397 mm)
min.

23-1/2"
(597 mm)

26-3/4"
(679 mm)

24-7/16"
(621 mm)

**Installation
Option shown at
left includes:**

*JEM33M or
JEM34M
Spacemaker II™
microwave oven
built-in with a
JX37W or JX37B
trim kit above a
Monogram single
wall oven.*

Microwave Warranty Information

- Full One-Year Warranty, in-home service, parts and labor
- Additional Limited Nine-Year Warranty, magnetron tube

19

Monogram™

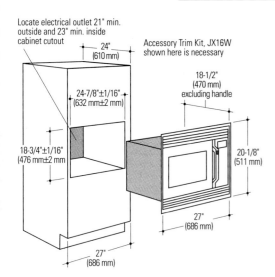

□

JET343G

*White combination
microwave/
convection oven*

Product Dimensions

H 15-1/4" (387 mm)
W 23-13/16"
(605 mm ± 2 mm)
D 18-1/2" (470 mm)
cabinet depth

Cutout Dimensions

H 18-3/4" ± 1/16"
(476 mm ± 22 mm)
W 24-7/8" ± 1/16"
(632 mm ± 2 mm)
D 21"–23"
(533–584 mm)

Features

- Microwave power output, 800 watts (IEC-705 test procedure)
- Four ways to cook: microwave, convection, convection broiling and combination
- Large 1.4 cu. ft. oven capacity
- Electronic touch controls
- Step-by-step word prompting display
- Automatic cooking control—auto cook, combination auto roast and auto defrost
- Auto start for delayed cooking
- Ten microwave power levels
- Minute/second timer and clock
- Removable shelf
- Temp. Cook/Hold
- Full color cookbook
- 120 Volts/13.8 Amps
- Approximate shipping weight: 84 pounds

Accessory Kit:

JX16W

Kit is required for
custom in-wall
installation of model
JET343G

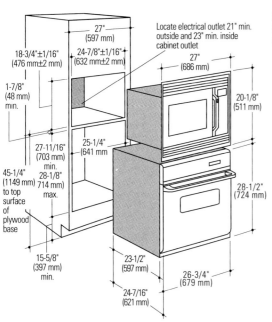

Installation Option shown at left includes:

*JET343G
microwave/convec-
tion oven built-in
with a JX16W trim
kit above a Monogram
single wall oven.*

Microwave Warranty Information

- Full one-year warranty, in-home service, parts and labor
- Additional Limited Four-Year Warranty, magnetron tube

Monogram™

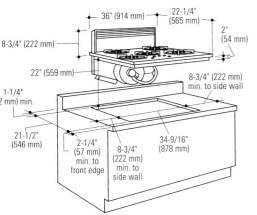

☐
ZGU661EM
White gas downdraft cooktop

■
ZGU660EM
Black gas downdraft cooktop

Product Dimensions
H 22" (559 mm) total height
W 36" (914 mm)
L 22-1/4" (565 mm)

Cutout Dimensions
W 34-9/16" (878 mm)
L 21-1/2" (546 mm)

Features
- Easy-clean tempered glass surface
- Sealed burner bowls for easy cleanup
- High-efficiency burners: two 11,000 BTU and three 6,500 BTU
- Powerful downdraft venting system with variable speed control
- Removable, washable vent filter
- Reliable pilotless, spill proof electronic ignition
- Durable porcelainized cast-iron burner grates
- Front mounted controls
- Convertible to liquid propane gas operation
- 120 Volts
- Approximate shipping weight: 92 pounds

Note
LP conversion orifices packed with both models

Slab Installation
For peninsula or island installation and rear wall ducting, PVC duct should be used if installing under a poured concrete slab

Required Accessory Kits:

JXDV66
Downdraft vent kit required with both models

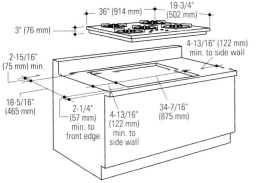

☐
ZGU651EM
White gas updraft cooktop

■
ZGU650EM
Black gas updraft cooktop

Product Dimensions
H 3" (76 mm)
W 36" (914 mm)
L 19-3/4" (502 mm)

Cutout Dimensions
W 34-7/16" (875 mm)
L 18-5/16" (465 mm)

Features
- Easy-clean tempered glass surface
- Sealed burner bowls for easy cleanup
- Only three inches deep to fit over cabinet drawers
- High-efficiency burners: two 11,000 BTU and three 6,500 BTU
- Reliable pilotless, spill proof electronic ignition
- Durable porcelainized cast-iron burner grates
- Front mounted controls
- Convertible to liquid propane gas operation
- 120 Volts
- Approximate shipping weight: 51 pounds

Note
LP conversion orifices packed with both models

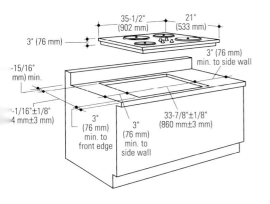

☐
ZEU633L
White solid disk cooktop (Also available in 208 Volts as ZEU634L)

■
ZEU632L
Black solid disk cooktop

Product Dimensions
H 3" (76 mm)
W 35-1/2" (902 mm)
L 21" (533 mm)

Cutout Dimensions
W 33-7/8" ± 1/8" (860 mm ± 3 mm)
L 19-1/16" ± 1/8" (232 mm ± 3 mm)

Features
- Solid cast-iron elements eliminate need for drip pans, make cleaning easy
- 9" rear and 8" front surface heating units with sensors to automatically maintain selected heat
- 6" front and 6" rear surface heating units with automatic temperature limiters
- Only 3" deep
- Easy-care tempered glass surface
- Rated for 240 Volts
- 7.6 KW at 240 Volts (only ZEU634L useable at 208 Volts)
- Approximate shipping weight: 51 pounds

Cooktop Warranty Information
- Full One-Year Warranty, parts and labor
- Additional Limited Four-Year Warranty, solid disk surface heating units

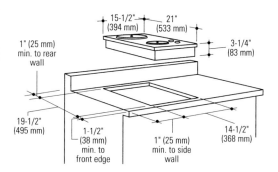

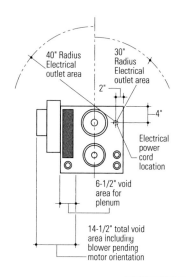

ZEW135N

*Solid disk component
(Available in 208 Volts
as ZEW134N)*

Product
Dimensions

H 3-1/4" (83 mm)
W 15-1/2" (394 mm)
L 21" (533 mm)

Cutout
Dimensions

W 14-1/2" (368 mm)
L 19-1/2" (495 mm)

Features

- Dual cast iron heating units
- One 6" disk and one 8" disk, each equipped with Sensi-Temp™
- Sealed disks eliminate spill-through
- Only 3-1/4" deep, leaving room for a drawer beneath
- ZEW135N – 240 Volts/14.6 Amps
  ZEW134N – 208 Volts/16.8 Amps
- Approximate shipping weight: 26 pounds

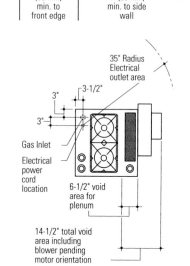

ZGW124EN

*Gas component,
controls on right*

ZGW125EN

*Gas component,
controls on left*

Product
Dimensions

H 3-1/4" (83 mm)
W 15-1/2" (394 mm)
L 21" (533 mm)

Cutout
Dimensions

W 14-1/2" (368 mm)
L 19-1/2" (495 mm)

*Right component shown.
For left component,
dimensions are opposite.*

*Gas inlet pipe extends
1-1/4" from bottom of
component.*

Features

- Available with controls on right or left side for ease of use and added safety
- One large 10,500 BTU burner and one smaller 6,000 BTU burner (lowest setting: 2,000 BTU, large burner; 1,200 BTU, small burner)
- Reliable electronic ignition with automatic reignition
- Durable, porcelainized cast iron grates with dynamic appearance
- 120 Volts/1.0 Amps
- Approximate shipping weight: 28 pounds

Note

Gas components are not convertible to liquid propane gas operation

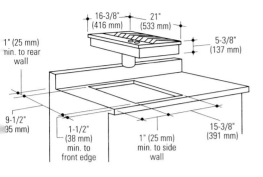

ZEW155N

*Updraft grill component
(Available in 208 Volts
as ZEW154N)*

**Product
Dimensions**

H 15-3/8" (391 mm)
total height
W 16-3/8" (416 mm)
L 21" (533 mm)

**Cutout
Dimensions**

W 15-3/8" (391 mm)
L 19-1/2" (495 mm)

Features

• Rugged, porcelainized cast-iron grate (can be cleaned
  in Monogram dishwasher)
• Separate controls for each half of heating element
• 1,750 watt heating element
• Optional griddle accessory kit available
• ZEW155N–240 Volts/7.3 Amps
  ZEW154N–208 Volts/8.4 Amps
• Approximate shipping weight: 42 pounds

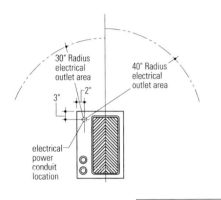

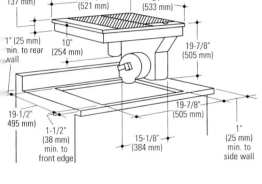

ZEW165N

*Downdraft grill
component (Available in
208 Volts as ZEW164N)*

**Product
Dimensions**

H 19-7/8" (505 mm)
total height
W 20-1/2" (521 mm)
L 21" (533 mm)

**Cutout
Dimensions**

W 19-7/8" (505 mm)
L 19-1/2" (495 mm)

Features

• Outdoor-style cooking in the comfort of your kitchen
• Rugged, porcelainized cast-iron grate (can be cleaned
  in Monogram dishwasher)
• 2,800 watt heating element
• Separate controls for each half of heating element
• Equipped with a downdraft vent which is automatically
  activated when the grill is turned on
• Optional remote control accessory kit available
• Optional griddle accessory kit available
• ZEW165N–240 Volts/13.5 Amps
  ZEW164N–208 Volts/15.3 Amps
• Approximate shipping weight: 82 pounds

**Optional
Accessory Kits:**

JXDD43

Griddle accessory
(240 Volts)

JXDD46

Griddle accessory
(208 Volts)

Pub. No. 3-A010

Remote location of
blower control, for
added convenience
and safety

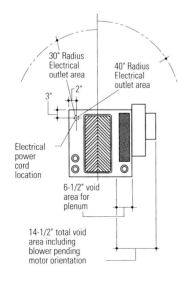

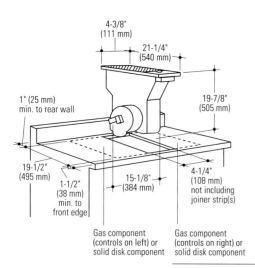

4-3/8" (111 mm)
21-1/4" (540 mm)
19-7/8" (505 mm)
1" (25 mm) min. to rear wall
19-1/2" (495 mm)
1-1/2" (38 mm) min. to front edge
15-1/8" (384 mm)
4-1/4" (108 mm) not including joiner strip(s)

Gas component (controls on left) or solid disk component

Gas component (controls on right) or solid disk component

ZEW175N

Downdraft vent component (For use with Gas or Solid Disk components)

Product Dimensions

H 19-7/8" (505 mm)
W 4-3/8" (111 mm)
L 21-1/4" (540 mm)

Cutout Dimensions

W 4-1/4" (108 mm)
L 19-1/2" (495 mm)

Features

- Rugged, porcelainized cast-iron grate (can be cleaned in Monogram dishwasher)
- Removable, washable filter
- Equipped with variable-speed blower control
- Optional remote control accessory kit available
- 120 Volts/1.8 Amps
- Approximate shipping weight: 45 pounds

Component Warranty Information

- Full One-Year Warranty, parts and labor
- Additional Limited Four-Year Warranty, solid disk surface heating units

Optional Accessory Kit:

Pub. No. 3-A010
Remote location of blower control, for added convenience and safety

Multiple Component Cutout Options

If multiple components will be attached together determine cutout width (dimension A) from the following:

Important Note

Multiple component installations require joiner strips between components. Add 1/4" to total cutout for each downdraft vent-to-cooktop connection; add 3/4" to total cutout for each cooktop-to-cooktop connection. See 1993 Production Planning and Installation Information book Pub. No. 24-M023 for specific installation requirements.

*See "Installation rules" concerning placement of knobs in relation to downdraft vent.

Unit 1	Unit 2	Unit 3	Unit 4	Unit 5	A
Solid Disk / RH Gas / LH Gas	Solid Disk / RH Gas / LH Gas				29-3/4"
Solid Disk / RH Gas / LH Gas	Updraft Grill				30-5/8"
Updraft Grill	Updraft Grill				31-1/2"
Downdraft Vent*	Solid Disk / RH Gas				19"
Downdraft Grill	Solid Disk / RH Gas				34-5/8"
Solid Disk / LH Gas	Downdraft Vent*	Solid Disk / RH Gas			33-3/4"
Downdraft Grill	Solid Disk / RH Gas / LH Gas	Solid Disk			49-7/8"
Solid Disk	Downdraft Vent*	Solid Disk	Downdraft Vent*	Solid Disk	53"
Downdraft Vent*	Solid Disk / RH Gas	LH Gas	Downdraft Vent*	Solid Disk / RH Gas	53-1/2"
Solid Disk / LH Gas	Downdraft Vent*	Downdraft Grill*	Solid Disk / RH Gas		53-7/8"

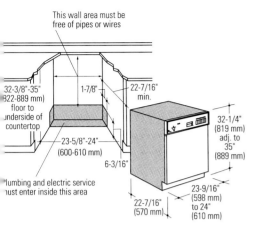

This wall area must be free of pipes or wires

32-3/8"-35" (822-889 mm) floor to underside of countertop

1-7/8"

22-7/16" min.

23-5/8"-24" (600-610 mm)

6-3/16"

32-1/4" (819 mm) adj. to 35" (889 mm)

Plumbing and electric service must enter inside this area

22-7/16" (570 mm)

23-9/16" (598 mm) to 24" (610 mm)

☐ **ZBD4300SW**

White dishwasher with stainless steel interior

■ **ZBD4100SB**

Black dishwasher with stainless steel interior

Product Dimensions

H 32-1/4"–35"
(819–889 mm)
W 23-9/16"–24"
(598–610 mm)
L 22-7/16"
(570 mm)

Cutout Dimensions

H 32-3/8"
(822–889 mm)
W 23-5/8"–24"
(600–610 mm)
L 22-1/2" min.
(572 mm)

Features

- Integrated door comes ready to accept a single 3/4" custom panel
- Stainless steel interior
- Extra-quiet operation
- Six cycles: POTSCRUBBER®, Normal Wash, Rinse & Hold, Light Wash, China/Crystal, Energy Saver
- Pushbutton cycle selector
- Four-level wash system
- Triple filter system
- Temperature sensor system
- Press to close; hidden latch
- Cycle progress indicator
- End-of-cycle indicator
- Rinse-aid dispenser with adjustable flow control
- Nylon-coated upper and lower rack
- Two utility shelves on upper rack
- Deluxe two-position upper rack
- Deluxe silverware basket with handle, designed for easy removal and carrying
- Convection drying
- 120 volts/15 amps,
- Approximate shipping weight: 110 pounds

Note

Field-installed custom panel is required for both models

Dishwasher Warranty Information

- Full One-Year Warranty, parts and labor
- Limited Second-Year Warranty covering replacement parts, but not labor, for any part of the dishwasher that fails because of a manufacturing defect
- Limited Five-Year Warranty covers the new upper and lower racks
- Full Twenty-Year Warranty applies to the stainless steel tub and door liner if it fails to contain water because of a manufacturing defect

Optional Accessory Kits:

GPF61
3/4" Door Panel–Black
GPF62
3/4" Door Panel–White
GPF63
Spacer Kit–Black
GPF64
Spacer Kit–White

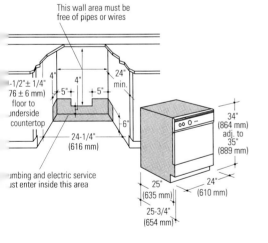

This wall area must be free of pipes or wires

34-1/2"± 1/4" (876 ± 6 mm) floor to underside countertop

4"

4"

5"

5"

24" min.

6"

24-1/4" (616 mm)

34" (864 mm) adj. to 35" (889 mm)

Plumbing and electric service must enter inside this area

25" (635 mm)

25-3/4" (654 mm)

24" (610 mm)

☐ **ZBD3300RWB**

White electromechanical dishwasher

■ **ZBD3100RBW**

Black electromechanical dishwasher

Product Dimensions

H 34" (864 mm)
W 24" (610 mm)
D 25-3/4" (654 mm)

Cutout Dimensions

H 34-1/2" (876 mm)
W 24-1/4" (616 mm)
D 24" min. (610 mm)

Note

- For a flush appearance using models ZBD3300RWB and ZBD3100RBW, countertops will need to be moved forward by use of spacer blocks
- See 1993 Production Planning and Installation Information book, Pub. No. 24-M023 for specific installation requirements

Features

- Cycle selector knob with push-to-start
- New blade-style flat latch knob
- Five cycles, nine options, including: POTSCRUBBER, China/Crystal, and Rinse & Hold
- Exclusive Multi-Orbit® wash arm
- Self-Clean filtering system
- Ultra sound insulation package for quiet operation
- Durable PermaTuf® tub and door liner
- Three-level wash system
- Temperature Sensor System
- Durable super upper and deluxe lower racks
- 120 Volts/8.6 Amps
- Approximate shipping weight: 96 pounds

1/4" Panel Sizes

- Door panel, 19-1/8"H x 23-9/16"W
- Access panel, 3-11/16"H x 23-9/16"W

Dishwasher Warranty Information

- Full One-Year Warranty, parts and labor
- Limited Second-Year Warranty covering replacement parts, but not labor, for any part of the dishwasher that fails because of a manufacturing defect
- Limited Five-Year Warranty covers the new upper and lower racks
- Full Twenty-Year Warranty applies to the PermaTuf® tub and door liner if it fails to contain water because of a manufacturing defect such as cracking, chipping, peeling or rusting

Optional Accessory Kits:

GPF30
Trim strips for 24" deep cabinets
GPF51
Trim strips for 25" cabinets and 6" toekicks
GPF52
Springs for heavy door panels (over 5 pounds)
GPF53
Mounting brackets for countertop of granite or other hard material
GPF54
Trimless door panel kit for two-piece installation

Monogram™

Dishwashers and Compactors

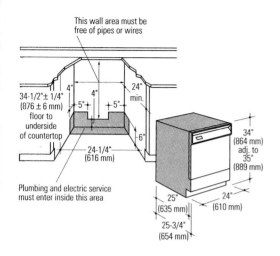

☐
ZBD3000TWB

White electronic dishwasher (Available August/ September, 1993)

■
ZBD3000TBW

Black electronic dishwasher (Available August/ September, 1993)

Product Dimensions

H 34" (864 mm)
W 24" (610 mm)
L 25-3/4" (654 mm)

Cutout Dimensions

H 34-1/2" (876 mm)
W 24-1/4" (616 mm)
D 24" min. (610 mm)

Features

- Solid-state electronic touch controls
- New flat latch knob (matches control panel)
- Five cycles, 37 options, including: POTSCRUBBER, Normal Wash, China/Crystal, Rinse & Hold, Soil Level Selections and 9 Hour Delay Start
- Self-Clean filtering system
- Ultra sound insulation package for quiet operation
- Durable PermaTuf® tub and door liner
- Three-level wash system
- Temperature Sensor System
- Systems monitor includes 11 performance monitoring programs
- Programmable start
- Durable super upper and deluxe lower racks
- 120 Volts/12.5 Amps
- Approximate shipping weight: 96 pounds

1/4" Panel Sizes

- Door panel, 19-1/8"H x 23-9/16"W
- Access panel, 3-11/16"H x 23-9/16"W

Dishwasher Warranty Information

- Full One-Year Warranty, parts and labor
- Limited Second-Year Warranty covering replacement parts, but not labor, for any part of the dishwasher that fails because of a manufacturing defect
- Limited Five-Year Warranty covers the new upper and lower racks
- Limited Five-Year Warranty covers the electronic control module that fails because of a manufacturing defect
- Full Twenty-Year Warranty applies to the PermaTuf® tub and door liner if it fails to contain water because of a manufacturing defect

Note

- For a flush appearance using models ZBD3000TWB and ZBD3000TBW, countertops will need to be moved forward by use of spacer blocks
- See 1993 Production Planning and Installation Information book, Pub. No. 24-M023 for specific installation requirements

Optional Accessory Kits:

GPF30
Trim strips for 24" deep cabinets

GPF51
Trim strips for 25" cabinets and 6" toekicks

GPF52
Springs for heavy door panels (over 5 pounds)

GPF53
Mounting brackets for countertop of granite or other hard material

GPF54
Trimless door panel kit for two-piece installation

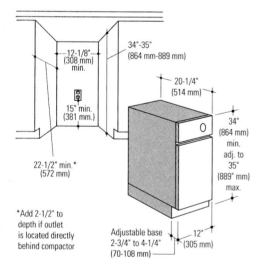

☐
ZCG3300TWW

White built-in compactor

■
ZCG3100TBB

Black built-in compactor

Product Dimensions

H 34"–35" (864–889 mm)
W 12" (305 mm)
D 20-1/4" (514 mm)

Cutout Dimensions

H 34"–35" (864–889 mm)
W 12-1/8" (308 mm)
D 22-1/2" (572)

Features

- Adjustable base allows the toekick depth to be set to match cabinetry
- Drawer type compactor
- Safety lock/start with removable key
- Door latch prevents operation when drawer is open
- Compacts trash volume by 75%
- Full capacity in space saving 12" width
- 1/4" custom panel capability, adaptable to other thicknesses
- White/black reversible drawer panel
- 120 Volts/5 Amps
- Approximate shipping weight: 135 pounds

1/4" Panel Size
24-1/2"H x 11-11/16"W

Compactor Warranty Information
Full One-Year Warranty, parts and labor

26

C496
11452/GEO
BuyLine 9268

All Monogram products are appropriately UL or AGA listed.

Product improvement is a continuing endeavor at General
Electric. Therefore, materials, appearance, and specifications
are subject to change without notice.

For additional copies of this brochure, call 800-848-7722
(800-633-7173 in Kentucky). For more information
about the full line of Monogram products, please order
Pub. No. 24-M053.

For product dimensions and installation information, please
order the 1993 Production Planning and Installation
Information book, Pub. No. 24-M023. Call GE Publications
toll free: 800-848-7722 (800-633-7173 in Kentucky).

To obtain specific information concerning any Monogram
product or service, call GE Answer Center® consumer
information service at 800.626.2000, any time of day or night.

For local service in your area, call 800-GE-CARES
(800-432-2737).

Pub. No. 24-M143
©1993 GE Appliances Printed in U.S.A.

Monogram.™

GE Appliances
Louisville, KY 40225

KitchenAid®

FOR THE WAY IT'S MADE.™

FORM FOLLOWS FUNCTION TO ACHIEVE THE UNDERSTATED ELEGANCE THAT IS THE HALLMARK OF KITCHENAID'S® INTERNATIONAL COLLECTION.

THE RIGHT CHOICE FOR TODAY'S MODERN KITCHENS, KITCHENAID® INTERNATIONAL COLLECTION COOKING PRODUCTS ARE DESIGNED FOR THE TRUE ENJOYMENT OF COOKING. THE SELF-CLEANING 30-INCH OVEN IS AVAILABLE AS A CONVENTIONAL THERMAL OVEN OR AS A VERSATILE THERMAL-CONVECTION™ OVEN. BACKLIT PUSH-PUSH SELECTOR, THERMOSTAT CONTROLS AND AN ELECTRONIC CLOCK ADD CONVENIENCE TO HELP EVEN THE MOST DEMANDING DISHES COME OUT PERFECT.

FOR COMPLETE COOKING FLEXIBILITY, PAIR YOUR BUILT-IN OVEN WITH AN ELECTRIC CERAMIC GLASS COOKTOP. AVAILABLE IN BOTH 30-INCH AND 36-INCH SIZES, AN INTERNATIONAL COLLECTION COOKTOP INSTALLS FLUSH TO COUNTERTOPS FOR A LOOK THAT'S PLEASING TO THE EYE AND EXCEPTIONALLY EASY TO CLEAN. HALOGEN ELEMENTS PROVIDE INSTANT VISUAL RESPONSE WHILE DUAL-CIRCUIT RADIANT ELEMENTS GIVE YOU A CHOICE OF COOKING SPEEDS.

COMPLETE YOUR EUROPEAN-STYLE KITCHEN WITH A KITCHENAID® INTERNATIONAL COLLECTION DISHWASHER WHICH COMBINES A PREMIUM STAINLESS STEEL INTERIOR WITH OUTSTANDING PERFORMANCE AND SLEEK STYLING THAT COMPLEMENTS BOTH AMERICAN AND EUROPEAN-STYLE CABINETRY.

INTERNATIONAL COLLECTION

International Collection KECN567Y 36-inch cooktop provides outstanding performance by combining five radiant/halogen elements. Both 30-inch and 36-inch cooktops come in White or Black.

International Collection Dishwasher Model KUDN230Y shown with optional European Toe-Kick Kit is available in your choice of immaculate All-White or dramatic All-Black styling.

KitchenAid® dishwashers continue the tradition for outstanding attention to detail that has been their trademark since 1949. For example, a six-inch high control panel matches cabinet drawer height, so cabinets and dishwasher flow together in an uninterrupted line. You can take your choice of color-coordinated White, Almond or Black styling. A built-in trim frame accepts custom panels for a truly integrated appearance. Performance is top drawer, too.

Dishes are washed clean without prerinsing and using 25% less water than before, to save water and energy. Water heating is automatic. And the TriDura® porcelain-on-steel tub and inner door are warranted for 25 years!

Model KUDA23SB offers state-of-the art microcomputer controls that let you create the correct washing for every load at a touch. Select White (shown) or Black.

DISHWASHERS

Model KUDS230B gives you easy push-button operation plus Cycle Monitor Lights which show operating status at a glance. Available in Monochromatic Black, White-on-White, Almond-on-Almond.

Behind the handsome paneled doors of this KitchenAid® built-in is home refrigeration that is convenient, functional and eminently stylish as well. Ice and water are dispensed neatly and efficiently through the door. The adjustable temperature-controlled WinterChill™ Meat Locker helps prolong fresh meat storage and the large ClearVue™ Crisper and utility drawers are humidity-controlled to help keep produce fresh. Drawers and baskets move in and out smoothly and easily on the exclusive KitchenAid® RollerTrac™ System. KitchenAid® Built-In refrigerators are 25-inches deep (including doors) to fit flush with cabinets and are shipped ready to accept custom panels, so you can match cabinets, colors or fabrics, even showcase your favorite posters or the kids' artwork, if you like. Choose from 48-, 42- and 36-inch wide models, with or without ice and water dispensers which are available in black or white. Almond, White or Black Glass-Look and Stainless Steel precut panels can be ordered from the factory. 48-inch Model KSSS48DAW, shown here, offers the convenience of ice and water through the door. 28.9 cubic-foot total capacity with a 10.5 cubic-foot freezer is big enough for a very hungry family.

BUILT-IN REFRIGERATORS

42-inch Model KSSS42MAX provides 24.7 cubic-feet of total food storage capacity including a 9.0 cubic-foot freezer. The automatic ice® maker puts a continuous supply of ice crescents at your fingertips.

36-inch Model KSSS36DAW with through-the-door ice and water dispenser offers a 20.4 cubic-foot capacity with a 7.4 cubic-foot freezer.

KitchenAid® built-in ovens are designed for both superlative cooking performance and enduring aesthetic appeal. Two-Element Balanced Baking and Roasting, Variable Temperature Broiling and Variable Self Cleaning all contribute to the quality performance you expect from a KitchenAid® oven.

Choose a Thermal-Convection™ oven for both conventional thermal and even-cooking, even-browning convection operation. In the convection system, heat is generated behind the oven wall and circulated throughout the oven by a fan. Convection baking and roasting temperatures are lower and cooking time shorter than in thermal cooking. Convection Bake uses the rear element and fan, while Convection Roast uses two elements and fan. Convection broiling uses fan-circulated air to cook evenly.

Double your cooking pleasure with a 30-inch Double Thermal-Convection™ Oven. Model KEBS208A, (shown at right) provides Thermal-Convection™ oven cooking capability in both the upper and lower ovens for maximum convenience and versatility. Choose between All-White, Almond or Black styling. Also available in a 27-inch Width, Model KEBS278A (not shown).

BUILT-IN OVENS

Choose Model KEMS378Y 27-inch Superba™ Microwave-Convection/ Thermal-Convection™ oven for microwave speed, convection versatility, and thermal baking and roasting all in one elegant oven. White, Almond, or Black.

The speed of microwave cooking and the flexibility of convection cooking unite in 27-inch Model KEMS377Y Superba™ Microwave/ Thermal-Convection™ combination oven, available in White or Black.

WANT TO STAY ON TOP OF YOUR COOKING? KITCHENAID® GLASS SURFACE COOKTOPS ARE EXCEPTIONALLY PRACTICAL YET DESIGNED TO BLEND SMOOTHLY INTO ALMOST ANY COUNTERTOP SETTING, IN EITHER TRADITIONAL OR MODERN KITCHENS. COMPONENTS ARE SEALED INTO THE COOKTOP SO CLEANUP IS SIMPLE: JUST WIPE THE SURFACE WITH A DAMP CLOTH OR SPONGE. COOKTOPS ARE AVAILABLE IN GAS OR ELECTRIC, 36-INCH OR 30-INCH SIZE, AND IN WHITE, ALMOND OR BLACK. OPTIONAL DOWNDRAFT SYSTEMS MAKE IT POSSIBLE TO CONVERT COOKTOPS TO SELF-VENTILATING OPERATION.

MODEL KGCT365A 36-INCH GAS COOKTOP WITH COLOR-COORDINATED CAST-IRON GRATES, SHOWN AT RIGHT, FITS VIRTUALLY ANY 33-INCH OR 36-INCH CUTOUT.

THE 36-INCH SLIDE-OUT VENT HOOD MODEL KWVU265YBA WITH AUTOMATIC ON/OFF, THREE-SPEED ELECTRONIC CONTROL AND FLUORESCENT COOKING SURFACE WORK LIGHT IS THE ULTIMATE IN EFFICIENT, CONVENIENT VENTING.

BUILT-IN COOKTOPS

Model KECC500W 30-inch electric cooktop has Quick Star Radiant elements and a glass-ceramic surface for fast, even cooking. Infinite-Heat Push-to-Turn controls let you "fine tune" cooking heats.

Model KECC500W 30-inch electric ceramic glass cooktop is also available in Black.

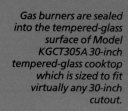

Gas burners are sealed into the tempered-glass surface of Model KGCT305A 30-inch tempered-glass cooktop which is sized to fit virtually any 30-inch cutout.

FREEDOM OF CHOICE TAKES ON A WHOLE NEW MEANING FOR YOUR KITCHEN. NOW YOU CAN DESIGN THE COOKTOP THAT'S RIGHT FOR YOUR KITCHEN AND THE WAY YOU COOK. JUST PUT TOGETHER ANY COMBINATION OF TWO-ELEMENT ELECTRIC OR TWO-BURNER GAS COOKTOP UNITS, ELECTRIC GRILL, AND SIDE-MOUNT DOWNDRAFT SYSTEM. CHOOSE FROM TEMPERED-GLASS CAST-IRON OR GLASS-CERAMIC RADIANT/HALOGEN ELECTRIC OR TEMPERED-GLASS SEALED-BURNER GAS UNITS. ALL ARE AVAILABLE IN WHITE, ALMOND OR BLACK. GRILL AND DOWNDRAFT VENT SYSTEMS COORDINATE WITH COOKTOPS.

SHOWN AT THE REAR: TWO MODEL KGCT025A 12-INCH COOKTOPS, EACH WITH TWO SEALED GAS BURNERS, AND A MODEL KECT025A 12-INCH ELECTRIC TEMPERED-GLASS COOKTOP WITH TWO HIGH-SPEED CAST-IRON ELEMENTS. ALL THREE COOKTOPS HAVE INFINITE-HEAT PUSH-TO-TURN CONTROLS SO YOU CAN "FINE TUNE" COOKING HEATS. MODEL KWVU265YBA 36-INCH SLIDE-OUT VENT HOOD WITH AUTOMATIC ON/OFF, THREE SPEED ELECTRONIC CONTROL AND FLUORESCENT COOKING SURFACE WORK LIGHT PROVIDES AN UPDRAFT VENTILATING SYSTEM.

IN THE ISLAND, MODEL KECG020Y DUAL-ELEMENT ELECTRIC GRILL WITH COLOR-COORDINATED INFINITE-HEAT PUSH-TO-TURN CONTROLS AND MODEL KSVD060Y SIDE-MOUNT DOWNDRAFT VENT SYSTEM WITH EASY-TO-USE FRONT CONTROL.

CREATE-A-COOKTOP SYSTEM

Model KECG020Y electric grill and Model KGCT025A 12-inch sealed burner gas cooktop in White.

Model KECC027Y glass-ceramic cooktop with 6-inch radiant and 8-inch halogen element combines elegance and easy cleanup with fast boiling and uniform cooking.

KITCHENAID® QUALITY GOES ALL THE WAY — ALL THE WAY
TO YOUR LAUNDRY ROOM, THAT IS. WITH KITCHENAID® SUPERBA®
SOLID-STATE ELECTRONIC LAUNDRY APPLIANCES, THE PROOF IS IN THE
PERFORMANCE. MICROCOMPUTER CONTROLS DELIVER THE CORRECT WASHING AND DRYING
FOR ANY LOAD AT A TOUCH. A BROAD SELECTION OF OPTIONS PROVIDES THE FLEXIBILITY
NEEDED TO CUSTOM-TAILOR WASHING AND DRYING FOR SPECIAL LOAD REQUIREMENTS.
SLEEK, MODERN STYLING IS AT HOME IN ANY SETTING.

SUPERBA® SELECTRA MODEL KAWE960W SOLID-STATE
CLOTHES WASHER, SHOWN, OFFERS THREE PRE-WASH
OPTIONS, THREE RINSE OPTIONS, FIVE WASH/RINSE
WATER TEMPERATURE COMBINATIONS, AND A
SELECTABLE CYCLE SENTRY™ SIGNAL WHICH
ALERTS YOU TO THE END OF THE WASHING. THE
MATCHING SUPERBA® SELECTRA MODEL
KGYE960W SOLID-STATE GAS CLOTHES DRYER HAS
FOUR CYCLE SELECTIONS, FIVE CUSTOM DRY
SELECTIONS, AND A QUICK PRESS OPTION FOR
PERMANENT PRESS GARMENTS.

LAUNDRY PRODUCTS

*Choose the Superba®
solid-state laundry pair
with either electric or gas
dryer. Both clothes
washer and clothes dryer
are available in White or
Almond.*

KITCHENAID® TRASH COMPACTORS TAKE THE
UNPLEASANTNESS OUT OF THE JOB NO ONE WANTS TO TAKE ON: TAKING
OUT THE TRASH. COMPACTING ACTION REDUCES A WEEK'S WORTH OF TRASH FOR AN
AVERAGE FAMILY OF FOUR TO A SMALL, EASY-TO-HANDLE PACKAGE. THE ACTIVATED CHARCOAL
FILTER AND ODOR CONTROL FAN EFFECTIVELY DEAL WITH UNPLEASANT TRASH ODORS.
KITCHENAID® TRASH COMPACTORS ARE AVAILABLE IN 15-INCH AND 18-INCH WIDE
MODELS TO SATISFY THE NEEDS OF ALMOST ANY KITCHEN. OPTIONAL
COLOR-COORDINATED CONTROL PANELS AND THE
VARI-FRONT™ PANEL PACKS LET YOU MATCH YOUR
TRASH COMPACTOR TO OTHER APPLIANCES. THE
INSTALLED TRIM KIT CAN ALSO ACCEPT CUSTOM
PANELS. SHOWN ON THE RIGHT IS MODEL
KUCS181B 18-INCH TRASH COMPACTOR WITH
EXCLUSIVE LITTER BIN® DOOR.

TRASH COMPACTORS
ICE CUBE MAKER
INSTANT-HOT®
WATER DISPENSER
FOOD WASTE DISPOSERS

Hands full of trash? Just touch the toe-bar opener on the Model KUCC151B trash compactor and the trash drawer glides open automatically. Rear rollers make installation easy. Also available in White-on-White Styling.

A must in the kitchen, a KitchenAid food waste disposer grinds away even bones and nut shells quickly and quietly. Choose from batch or continuous feed models, with motors up to one HP. Optional flange and stopper kits for continuous-feed models are available in White, Almond or Brass.

The heat's on – at the turn of a tap. The INSTANT-HOT® water dispenser, Model KHWS160V, available in White, Almond or Chrome, delivers up to 60 cups of 190°F water an hour. A great convenience in both kitchen and bathroom.

With the KitchenAid Model KUIS185S automatic ice cube maker, the iceman cometh – and keeps on coming, producing up to 51 pounds of clear ice daily. A lighted bin holds 35 pounds, refills automatically when the ice supply runs low.

KitchenAld
Compactor

Cooktops

Models KECN567Y, KECN560Y, KECN507Y, KECC500W, KGCT365A and KGCT305A

COOKTOP DIMENSIONS All dimensions shown in inches.

Model	Overall			Cutout		
	Width (side to side)	Depth (back to front)	Height	Width (side to side)	Depth (back to front)	Height (min.)
International Collection – Electric KECN567Y – Ceramic Glass Surface, Halogen/Radiant Elements	35½	20	4	34⅞	19¼	—
KECN560Y – Ceramic Glass Surface, Radiant Elements	35½	20	4	34⅞	19¼	—
KECN507Y – Ceramic Glass Surface, Halogen/Radiant Elements	29½	20	4	28⅞	19¼	—
Electric KECC500W – Ceramic Glass Surface, Radiant Elements	30	21	3	29½	20½	3¼
Gas KGCT365A – Glass Surface	36	21¾	4½	33 to 34⅞	18¾ to 20⅝	3¼
KGCT305A – Glass Surface	30¾	21¾	4½	26½ to 29⅝	18¾ to 20⅝	3¼

NOTE: Power/Fuel supply connections extend below Glass Surface Cooktops and are not included in Overall Height dimension.

Electric
ELECTRICAL REQUIREMENTS

240 Volts AC, 60 Hz. Separate 2-wire with ground circuit. 4 ft. flexible steel conduit with product.

Gas
ELECTRICAL REQUIREMENTS

Separate 2-wire with ground circuit. 3½ ft. 120 Volt AC, 60 Hz., 3-wire cord, 3-prong plug with product (for ignition). **Natural Gas** as shipped; converts to LP gas with standard regulator.

Model	Electrical Ratings		Approx. Weights Lbs.	
	KW @ 240V	Circuit Amps (min.)	Net	Shipping
KECN567Y	8.5	40	46	59
KECN560Y	8.5	40	46	59
KECN507Y	7.3	40	37	45
KECC500W	7.6	30	37	45
KGCT365A	—	15*	56	70
KGCT305A	—	15*	50	62

*120 Volt electric service required for ignition.

Create-A-Cooktop System

Models KECC027Y, KECT025A, KECG020Y, KSVD060Y and KGCT025A

COMPONENT DIMENSIONS All dimensions shown in inches.

Model	Overall			Cutout		
	Width (side to side)	Depth (back to front)	Height (top to bottom)	Width (side to side)	Depth (back to front)	Height (top to bottom)
Electric KECC027Y – Glass-Ceramic Cooktop, Radiant/Halogen Elements	11¹⁵⁄₁₆	21¾	4¼	11	20½	4¼
KECT025A – Tempered-Glass Cooktop, Cast Iron Elements	11¹⁵⁄₁₆	21¾	4¼	11	20½	4¼
KECG020Y – Electric Grill	13¹⁵⁄₁₆	21¾	4¼	13	20½	4½
KSVD060Y – Side-Mount Downdraft Vent System	5¹⁵⁄₁₆	21¾	4¼	4½	20½	4½*
Gas KGCT025A – Tempered-Glass Cooktop, Sealed Gas Burners	11¹⁵⁄₁₆	21¾	4¼	11	20½	4½

*Plus Ductwork

DIMENSIONS ARE FOR PLANNING ONLY. FOR COMPLETE DETAILS, SEE INSTALLATION INSTRUCTIONS PACKED WITH PRODUCT. SPECIFICATIONS SUBJECT TO CHANGE WITHOUT NOTICE.

Create-A-Cooktop System

Cutout Dimensions All dimensions shown in inches.

2 Cooktops

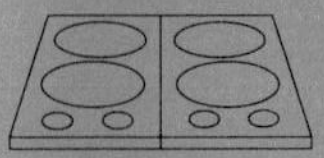

Width (side to side)	23
Depth (front to back)	20½
Height (top to bottom)	4¼

3 Cooktops

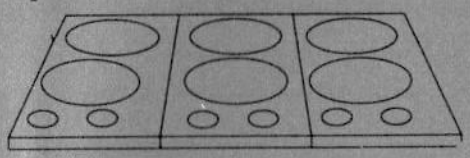

Width (side to side)	35
Depth (front to back)	20½
Height (top to bottom)	4¼

4 Cooktops

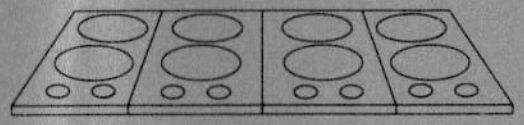

Width (side to side)	47
Depth (front to back)	20½
Height (top to bottom)	4¼

1 Cooktop with Vent

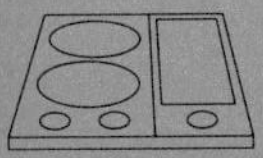

Width (side to side)	16⅞
Depth (front to back)	20½
Height (top to bottom)	4¼*

2 Cooktops with Vent

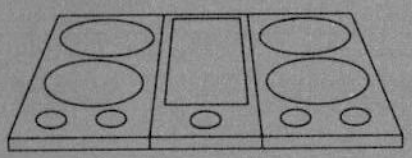

Width (side to side)	29
Depth (front to back)	20½
Height (top to bottom)	4¼*

3 Cooktops with 2 Vents

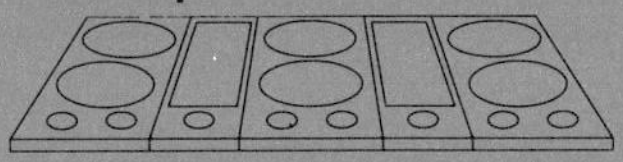

Width (side to side)	47
Depth (front to back)	20½
Height (top to bottom)	4¼*

Cutout Dimensions All dimensions shown in inches.

1 Grill with Vent

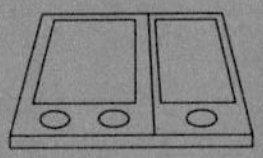

Width (side to side)	18⅞
Depth (front to back)	20½
Height (top to bottom)	4¼*

2 Grills with Vent

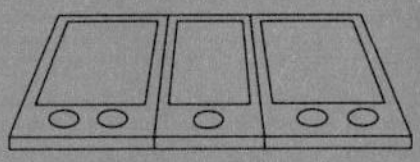

Width (side to side)	33
Depth (front to back)	20½
Height (top to bottom)	4¼*

3 Grills with 2 Vents

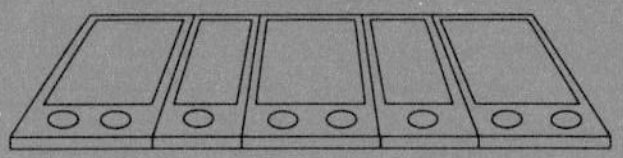

Width (side to side)	53
Depth (front to back)	20½
Height (top to bottom)	4¼*

1 Cooktop, 1 Vent, 1 Grill

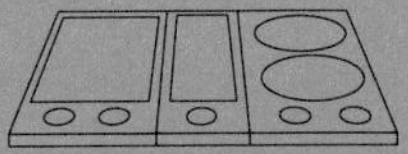

Width (side to side)	31
Depth (front to back)	20½
Height (top to bottom)	4¼*

2 Cooktops, 2 Vents, 1 Grill

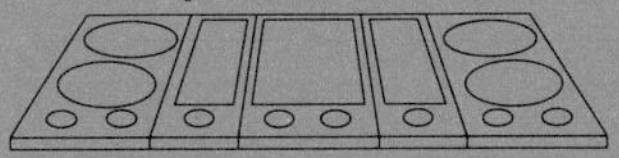

Width (side to side)	49
Depth (front to back)	20½
Height (top to bottom)	4¼*

*Plus Ductwork. Use 6 in. or 3¼ in. x 10 in. duct with a maximum of 26 ft. To calculate length needed, add equivalent feet for each duct piece used in system.

CREATE-A-COOKTOP COMPONENTS

Model	Electrical Ratings		Approx. Weights Lbs.	
	KW @ 240V	Circuit Amps (min.)	Net	Shipping
Electric KECCO27Y – Glass-Ceramic Cooktop, Radiant/Halogen Elements	3.2	20	17	20½
KECTO25A – Tempered-Glass Cooktop, Cast Iron Elements	4.6	20	18½	22
KECGO20Y – Electric Grill	2.2	20	20	23½
KSVDO60Y – Side-Mount Downdraft Vent System	–	15	16	20½
Gas KGCTO25A – Tempered-Glass Cooktop, Sealed Gas Burners	–	15	24½	28

SLIDE-OUT VENTILATION HOODS

Approx. weights shown in pounds.

Model	Net	Shipping
KWVU265Y	34	38
KWVU205Y	32	34

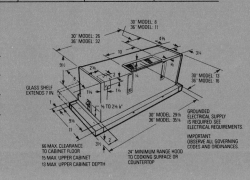

30" MODEL: 8
36" MODEL: 11

30" MODEL 26
36" MODEL 32

30" MODEL 13
36" MODEL 16

30" MODEL: 29⅞
36" MODEL: 35¼

GLASS SHELF
EXTENDS 7 IN.

66 MAX. CLEARANCE
TO CABINET FLOOR
15 MAX UPPER CABINET
13 MAX UPPER CABINET DEPTH

24" MINIMUM RANGE HOOD
TO COOKING SURFACE OR
COUNTERTOP

GROUNDED
ELECTRICAL SUPPLY
IS REQUIRED. SEE
ELECTRICAL REQUIREMENTS.

IMPORTANT:
OBSERVE ALL GOVERNING
CODES AND ORDINANCES.

Dimensions shown in inches.

Built-In Ovens

Models KEBN107Y, KEBS177Y, KEBS277Y, KEMS377X and KEMS378X

ELECTRICAL REQUIREMENTS

Dual rated, 240-208/120 Volts AC, 60 Hz. Separate 3-wire with ground circuit. 4 ft. flexible steel conduit with product. (4½ ft. with KEBN107Y.)

	Electrical Ratings			Approx. Weights Lbs.	
Model	KW @ 240V	KW @ 208V	Circuit Amps (min.)	Net	Shipping
KEBN107Y	3.4	2.6	30	134	154
KEBS177Y	3.1	2.3	30	152	173
KEBS277Y	6.1	4.6	40	260	290
KEMS377Y	5.9	5.1	40	236	266
KEMS378Y	6.3	5.5	40	241	271
KEMS208A	6.3	4.8	40	230	260
KEMS278A	6.3	4.8	40	270	300

OVEN DIMENSIONS All dimensions shown in inches.

	Overall					Cutout		
			Depth (back to front)					
Model	Width (side-to-side)	Height (bottom to top)	Door Closed (to edge of door)	Door Closed (to edge of handle)	Door Open	Width (side to side)	Height (bottom to top)	Depth (min.) (back to front)
International Collection KEBN107Y	29½	23¼	22¼	24	39	27⅞	22¾	24
Thermal-Convection™ KEBS177Y	26	28⅝	26½	28¼	43¾	24½	27⅞	23⅝
KEBS277Y	26	49⅞	26½	28¼	43¾	24½	49	23⅝
Combination KEMS377Y	26	50⅞	26½	28⅝	43¾	24½	49	23⅝
KEMS378Y	26	50⅞	26½	28⅝	43¾	24½	49	23⅝
Double Thermal-Convection™ KEBS208A	29¾	58⅜	25¼	27¾	46½	28½	56 9/16	23
KEBS278A	26	49⅞	26½	28½	43¾	28½	56 9/16	23⅝

Min. distance between cutout and cabinet doors 2½ in.

Dishwashers

Models KUDN230Y, KUDA23SB and KUDS230B

ELECTRICAL REQUIREMENTS

115 Volts, 60 Hz. AC. Max. watts, 1420; max. amps, 12.5. Separate 15-amp, 3-wire grounded circuit required.

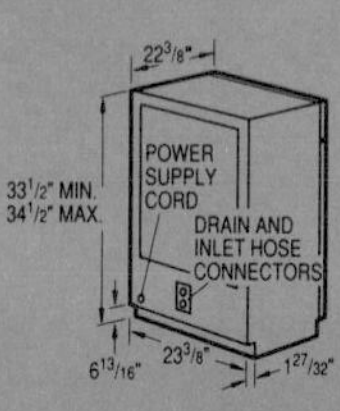

MODEL KUDN230Y

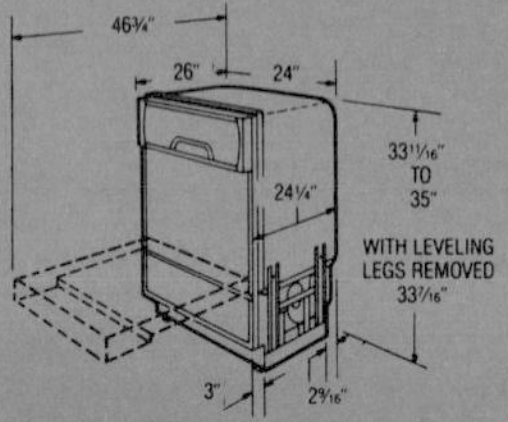

Superba® models require 23⅞" deep cutout; all others, 23½".

"23⅞" DEPTH CUTOUT REQUIRED. IF DRAIN LINE IS FLEXIBLE HOSE, THIS DIMENSION IS 22" ALTERNATE LOCATION.

IF DRAIN LINE IS COPPER, THE COPPER SHOULD BE 12" PLUS A 12" LENGTH OF FLEXIBLE HOSE ATTACHED TO THE END.

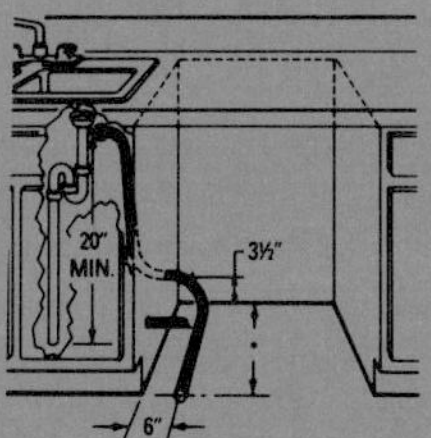

BASIC SIZES FOR CUSTOM FRONT PANELS Shown in inches, weights in pounds.

	Width		Height			
Model	Door	Lower	Door	Lower	Thickness	Max. Weight
KUDN230Y	23 7/32	NA	23 23/32	NA	5/32*	4
KUDA23SB, KUDS230B	23 9/16	23 11/16	17 7/16	6⅝	¼**	7

*If panel is more than 5/32-in. thick, route outer edge; less, install spacer behind panel.
**If panels are more than ¼-in. thick, refer to Installation Instructions for routing information.

PANEL KITS

	Change-Out Control Panel Part Number		Change-Out Door Panel Part Number		
Model	Black	Stainless Steel	Almond/ White	Black/ Harvest Wheat	Stainless Steel
KUDN230Y	NA	NA	*	*	NA
KUDA23SB	NA	NA	4171200	4171201	4171198
KUDS230B	4171736	9741242	4171200	4171201	4171198

*An optional Conversion Kit is available to convert this dishwasher to the flush, built-in look required for installations with European cabinets. White, part number 9741413; Black, 9741416.

DIMENSIONS ARE FOR PLANNING ONLY. FOR COMPLETE DETAILS, SEE INSTALLATION INSTRUCTIONS PACKED WITH PRODUCT. SPECIFICATIONS SUBJECT TO CHANGE WITHOUT NOTICE.

Trash Compactors
Models KUCS181B and KUCC151B

COMPACTOR DIMENSIONS All dimensions shown in inches.

Model	A	B	C	D	E	F	Approx. Weights Lbs. Net	Shipping
KUCS181B	34¹/₈ to 35³/₈*	17³/₄	24⁵/₈ incl. door	34¹/₄ min.	18	24 min.	195	210
KUCC151B	34¹/₁₆ to 34³/₄	14¹⁵/₁₆	24	34¹/₄ min.	15	24 min.	137	150

*Add 1¹/₂ in. when installed freestanding with maple wood optional top.

PANEL KITS

Model	Change-Out Control Panel Part Number Stainless Steel	White	Almond	Change-Out Door Panel Part Number Stainless Steel	Almond Harvest Wheat	Almond/ White	White/ Black	Black/ Harvest Wheat	Fresh Avocado/ Coffee
KUCS181B	–	4178062	4178063	4162888	–	4162889	–	4162890	4162887
KUCC151B	882681	4151847	4151848	882675	4151462	–	4151463	–	–

BASIC SIZES FOR ¼-in. CUSTOM FRONT PANELS All dimensions shown in inches.

Model	Width	Height
KUCS181B LITTER BIN® Door	17⁷/₁₆	7³¹/₃₂
Drawer	17⁷/₁₆	18¹⁵/₁₆
KUCC151B	14⁵/₈	21⁷/₈

ELECTRICAL REQUIREMENTS

	KUCS181B	KUCC151B
Volts (AC)	115	115
Hertz	60	60
Rated Load (Max. Amps)	9	6.5

Special 15 Amp. 3-Wire grounded circuit required.

Food Waste Disposers
Models KBDS250X, KCDS250X, KCDI250X, KCDC250X, KCDC150X, KCDB250S and KCDB150S

DISPOSER DIMENSIONS All dimensions shown in inches.

Model	A	B*	C*	D	E
KBDS250X	16¹/₁₆	9⁷/₁₆	4	10¹/₁₆	7¹/₈
KCDS250X	13¹¹/₁₆	6¹³/₁₆	4	10¹/₁₆	7¹/₈
KCDI250X	13⁷/₁₆	6¹³/₁₆	4	9¹/₁₆	5³/₄
KCDC250X	12³/₄	6¹¹/₁₆	4	7²⁵/₃₂	5³/₄
KCDC150X	12³/₄	6¹¹/₁₆	4	8¹/₁₆	5³/₄
KCDB250S	12⁵/₈	5¹⁵/₁₆	4	6⁵/₁₆	5
KCDB150S	11³/₈	5¹⁵/₁₆	4	6⁵/₁₆	5

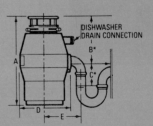

B* – Distance from bottom of sink to center line of disposer outlet. Add ½-in. when stainless steel sink is used.
C* – Length of waste line pipe from center line of disposer outlet to end of waste line pipe.
IMPORTANT: Plumb waste line to prevent standing water in the disposer motor housing.

Built-In Refrigerators
Models KSSS36DAX/DAW, KSSS36MAX, KSSS42DAX/DAW, KSSS42MAX, KSSS48DAX/DAW and KSSS48MAX

ELECTRICAL REQUIREMENTS
115 Volt AC, 60 Hz. Outlet should be positioned approx. 74 in. above floor.

PLUMBING REQUIREMENTS
¼-in. copper water supply line 1 in. above floor or through floor under refrigerator.

REFRIGERATOR DIMENSIONS All dimensions shown in inches.

	KSSS36DAX, DAW, KSSS36MAX	KSSS42DAX, DAW, KSSS42MAX	KSSS48DAX, DAW, KSSS48MAX
A	36	42	48
B	35^5/$_{16}$	41^5/$_{16}$	47^5/$_{16}$
C	35	41	47

Approx. Weights Lbs.

Model	Net	Shipping
KSSS36DAX, DAW	436	522
KSSS36MAX	431	517
KSSS42DAX, DAW	509	577
KSSS42MAX	504	572
KSSS48DAX, DAW	650	677
KSSS48MAX	645	672

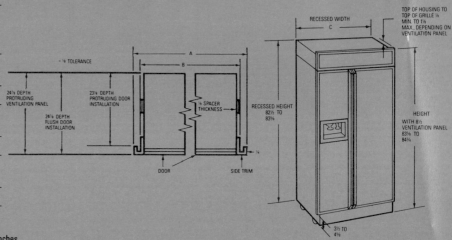

PANEL DIMENSIONS All dimensions shown in inches.

	Height	Width					
		KSSS36DAX, DAW	KSSS36MAX	KSS42DAX, DAW	KSSS42MAX	KSSS48DAX, DAW	KSSS48MAX
8^1/$_2$-in. ventilation panel – std.	6	32^3/$_8$	32^3/$_8$	38^3/$_8$	38^3/$_8$	44^3/$_8$	44^3/$_8$
Freezer door panel	70^7/$_{16}$	–	14^1/$_4$	–	16^3/$_4$	–	19^1/$_4$
Freezer upper door panel	26^1/$_4$	14^1/$_4$	–	16^3/$_4$	–	19^1/$_4$	–
Freezer lower door panel	34^7/$_{16}$	14^1/$_4$	–	16^3/$_4$	–	19^1/$_4$	–
Refrigerator door panel	70^7/$_{16}$	19^1/$_4$	19^1/$_4$	22^3/$_4$	22^3/$_4$	26^1/$_4$	26^1/$_4$

NOTE: Panels should be 1/4 in. thick, with 5/16 in. offset. Tolerance plus or minus 1/16 in.

If custom door panels greater than 1/4 in. thick are used, it may be necessary to rout the handle side of panel a minimum of 3 in. in from the panel edge to provide a 2 in. minimum access to the door handle. Either the full length of the panel or a selected area(s) can be routed. Check with your builder.

FOR MORE INFORMATION ON INSTALLATION AND PANEL DIMENSIONS SEE KITCHENAID PUBLICATION KSR870.

Convertible Ice Cube Maker
Model KUIS185T

APPROX. WEIGHTS
Net, 103 lbs.; shipping, 116 lbs.

WATER SUPPLY
¼-in. O.D. copper tube.

DRAIN
⅝-in. I.D. rubber tube.

ELECTRICAL REQUIREMENTS
115 Volts AC, 60 Hz.

CUSTOM PANEL DIMENSIONS
Dimensions shown in inches.

	Width	Height
Upper	17	11¼
Lower	17	11¹⁵⁄₁₆

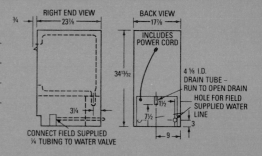

PANEL KITS

Model	Change-Out Control Panel Part Number		Change-Out Door Panel Part Number
	White	Almond	Stainless Steel
KUIS185T	4210583	4210584	819419

Laundry Products
Models KAWE960W/970B and KGYE960W/970B

LAUNDRY PRODUCT DIMENSIONS All dimensions shown in inches.

Model	Height (to top of control panel)	Height (to percelain top/ work surface)	Width	Depth	Approx. Weights Lbs.	
					Net	Shipping
KAWE960W/970B Clothes Washer	42	36	26⁷⁄₈	25¹⁄₂	161	179
KGYE960W/970B Clothes Dryer	42	36	29	27³⁄₄	124	140

KitchenAid® warranty protection
your assurance of long-lasting performance

All KitchenAid® appliances are protected by liberal warranties. All are covered by at least a ONE-YEAR FULL WARRANTY on both parts and labor; most carry extended warranties. Your dealer can give you specific information on KitchenAid® product warranties.

Microwave Ovens

Carousel

R-1440

Now Sharp offers more Over The Range options than ever before. The R-1440 is a streamlined new design that eases both space-planning and budget decisions.

- POPCORN
- COMPU DEFROST ❄
- MINUTE PLUS

BREAKFAST	COMPU COOK	SNACKS & REHEAT
1 Coffee / tea	1 Baked potatoes	1 Dinner plate
2 Roll / muffin, fresh	2 Fresh vegetables	2 Frozen main dish
3 Roll / muffin, frozen	3 Frozen vegetables	3 Pasta / casserole
4 Hot cereal	4 Rice	4 Pizza, slice
5 Scrambled eggs	5 Ground meat	5 Soup

1 2 3 4 5
6 7 8 9 0

POWER LEVEL   TIMER PAUSE   AUTO START CLOCK

TURNTABLE ON/OFF   STOP CLEAR   START

Carousel

- *Styled with new clear view door.*

- *Popcorn key is one-touch easy!*

- *CompuDefrost™ defrosts meats and poultry by weight.*

- *New Breakfast settings plus Snacks & Reheat settings are ultra-easy.*

- *CompuCook™ has 5 settings for automatic cooking.*

- *Programmable for 4-stage cooking.*

- *Advanced electronic controls for hood lamp and powerful fan; built-in exhaust system offers horizontal or vertical discharge or ductless recirculation.*

Engineered with sleek new styling, enhanced flexibility and greater capacity, the R-1440 fits beautifully Over The Range, leaving the counter-top clutter-free. The 12" diameter turntable features On/Off options so the user now can have it both ways! Choose the convenient turntable system or opt for the stirrer system (turntable "Off") for oblong dishes or cooking for a crowd. Details are easy to master with Auto-Touch® controls. Spacious 1.1 cu. ft. interior in a slim new black cabinet design. Output power: 850 watts.

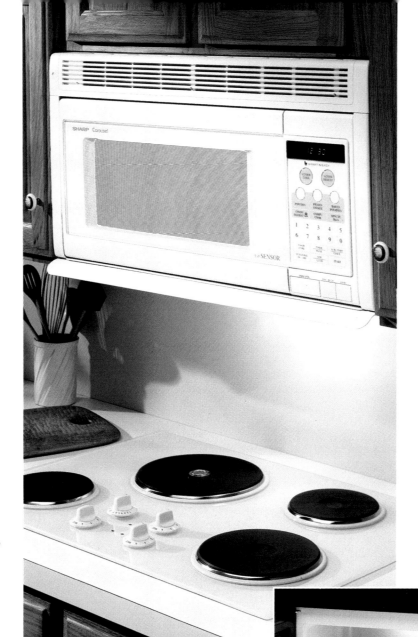

- *Smart & Easy™ Sensor turns a beginner into an expert in no time!*

- *ESP™ Sensor Cook and Sensor Reheat automatically sense when foods are done.*

- *Instant Start Sensor keys for popcorn, frozen entrees and baked potatoes.*

- *CompuCook adds 6 more categories of microwave favorites; CompuDefrost is easy and automatic.*

- *Programmable for 4-stage cooking. Child lock keeps curious fingers away!*

- *Advanced controls for hood lamp and powerful 2-speed fan; built-in exhaust system offers horizontal or vertical discharge or ductless recirculation.*

R-1450
R-1451

The Smart & Easy™ Sensor gives the consumer a choice of two updated designs. Both offer the uncompromising standards of quality and value that have made Sharp the leader in microwaving today.

18⅛"

Spacious 1.1 cu. ft. interior is roomy enough for a party-size 4-quart 15"x10" oblong dish.

Here are two perfect suggestions for reclaiming valuable counter space and gaining flexibility. The R-1450 (black with clear view door) and R-1451 (white-on-white) are smart Over The Range choices. Use the turntable system for 360° cooking; or opt for the stirrer system (turntable "Off") for oblong dishes or large quantities. Advanced technology puts the emphasis on ease throughout an impressive inventory of features. Each design has a generous 1.1 cu. ft. interior with 12" diameter turntable. Output power: 850 watts.

R-1831, R-1830

REHEAT	POPCORN ELEVATE PKG	MINUTE PLUS
BEVERAGE	PIZZA	AUTO START CLOCK
CONVEC	BROIL	SLOW COOK
LOW MIX / BAKE		HIGH MIX / ROAST
1 100°F	2 150°F	3 275°F
4 300°F	5 325°F	6 350°F
7 375°F	8 400°F	9 425°F
TIMER / PAUSE	O 450°F	STOP / CLEAR
POWER LEVEL		START

SENSOR COOK
1 Baked potatoes
2 Fresh vegetables, soft
3 Fresh vegetables, hard
4 Saute
5 Frozen vegetables
6 Soup, clear
7 Soup, cream
8 Hot dogs
9 Bacon
O Fish, seafood

COMPU DEFROST
1 Roast beef, pork
2 Steaks, chops
3 Ground meat
4 Chicken, whole
5 Chicken pieces

COMPU COOK
1 Broiled hamburgers
2 Broiled chicken
3 Roast chicken
4 Roast turkey
5 Layer cakes
6 Bread, loaves

SENSOR TEMP   **TEMP**
1 Roast beef (Rare)
2 Roast beef (Med)
3 Roast beef (Well)
4 Roast pork
5 Turkey breast
6 Casserole
7 Simmer

FAN   **HOOD LAMP**
HIGH/LOW   ON
OFF   OFF

- ESP Sensor Cook automatically cooks favorite foods

- One-touch Pizza, Popcorn, Beverage and Reheat keys

- Auto-Touch controls with 2-color display, clock, 99 minute 99 second timer, Auto Start, Timer/Pause, Minute Plus; also programmable 4-stage cooking; 10 Variable Power levels

- Two combination settings with convection temperature control from 100°F to 450°F; Broil preheats oven, signals when ready

- Slow Cook expands timer up to 4 hours for slow cook recipes such as baked beans, marinated meats, chili and stews

- CompuDefrost is an easy defrost for meat, poultry; visual cues indicate when to turn over, cover or rearrange food

Carousel Over The Range Convection Microwave Ovens are prime examples of space-efficient design, easy-to-understand features and one of the most versatile cooking systems on the market. Designed to install with ease, leaving the counter free and clear for maximum work space.

R-1831 is all white, an important element of style in today's modern or classic kitchens. R-1830 is available in sleek black. Generous 0.9 cu. ft. capacity has a 13" diameter turntable. Each unit features Sharp's advanced electronic controls for the hood lamp and powerful, built-in dual speed exhaust system; 310 cfm horizontal discharge, 300 cfm vertical discharge.

ESP Sensor Cook automatically cooks favorite foods – there's no manual setting of cooking times or power levels. Popcorn, Reheat, Beverage and Pizza keys offer Instant Start ease. Microwave, convection, combination and broil options create an unmatched system that turns out golden brown cakes and breads, plus moist, flavorful meat and poultry. Sensor Temp simplifies automatic temperature probe cooking so food is cooked to the desired degree of doneness. CompuCook computes convection and combination times/temperatures for perfect broiling, roasting and baking. Includes broiling trivet and rack for 2-level baking.

Installs ducted or nonducted without needing recirculating kit and extra space. Optional RK-250 Filler Panel Kit with two 3" black panels for installation in spaces wider than 30". RK-210 Charcoal Filter for nonducted installations. When mounted, oven top must be minimum of 66" from floor, 30" from cooking surface. Output power: 800 watts.

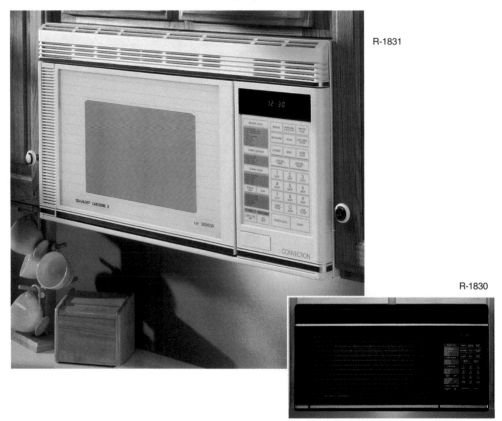

R-1831

R-1830

O V E R   T H E   R A N G E

Smart & Easy™ Sensor Microwave Ovens turn the beginner into an expert in no time at all! **R-5H16** makes news with 1000W high speed for faster cooking. Up-to-the-minute in every way, including style-setting white-on-white with a sleek, rounded new door design. Also available in a stone gray cabinet (R-5H06), with the same new door design. Extra-large 1.6 cu. ft. interior has a 16" diameter turntable. Extra-easy Instant Start Sensor keys eliminate guesswork: Sensor Reheat, Frozen Entree, Popcorn, Baked Potatoes. ESP™ Sensor Cook and CompuCook™ determine best cooking times and power levels for automatic cooking. New "Touch On" feature operates microwave while your finger touches the key. Memory Plus™ stores the most-often-used cooking time for quick recall.

R-4H96 is a white-on-white design featuring 1.2 cu. ft. interior, 14⅛" turntable and 900W output power. Also available in stone gray (R-4H85). Sensor keys for Frozen Entrees, Reheat, Popcorn, Baked Potatoes and Fresh Vegetables make microwaving one-touch easy... for perfect results automatically!

R-5H16 is a white-on-white design with 1000W high speed; also in stone gray (R-5H06)

R-4H96 is a 1.2 cu. ft. white-on-white design with 900W power; also in stone gray (R-4H85)

R-5H16   R-4H96

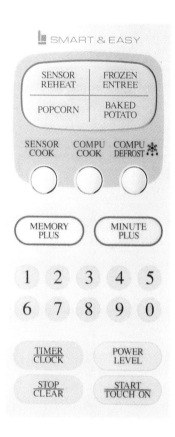

R-5H16, R-5H06, R-4H96 and R-4H85 all feature:

• Auto-Touch control panel for precision and ease of use

• Smart & Easy Sensor keys for easiest-ever microwaving — no guesswork and no mistakes!

• CompuCook™ auto-matically calculates times/ power levels for automatic cooking

• CompuDefrost™ quickly defrosts meats and poultry by weight

• Programmable 4-stage cooking

• Minute Plus™ sets the oven at HIGH for one minute per touch

• 10 Variable Power levels offer great results with many foods

• Kitchen timer provides exact timing for cooking or other household tasks

• Convenient time of day clock

• New child lock safety feature

R-4H96

R-5H16

S E N S O R

R-9H94/B
R-9H84/B

- 4-way cooking team browns, bakes, broils and crisps

- Auto-Touch controls with Auto Start, clock, Timer/Pause key and 99 minute 99 second timer

- Instant Start keys for Reheat, Popcorn, Dinner Plate and Beverage

- Minute Plus sets oven at HIGH with a single touch

- Deluxe ESP Sensor automatically cooks favorite foods

- New Cook & Simmer™ setting for homemade soups and sauces

- Includes broiling trivet and rack for 2-level baking

- Optional Built-in Kit RK-90W (white) or RK-90 (black) for wall oven installation

Carousel Convection Microwave Ovens bring together advanced capabilities with the best ideas in no-guesswork cooking, reheating and defrosting. Both the white and metallic charcoal finish cabinets set the standard for design. The 4-way cooking team browns, bakes, broils and crisps with convection, microwave and broiling options; two combination settings are perfect for roasting and baking.

Heading the impressive lineup of easy-to-use features is ESP Sensor Cook, which automatically determines cooking times and power levels for 8 varieties of microwave favorites. Instant Start keys continue the emphasis on ease, reheating foods, popping popcorn, heating a dinner plate or warming a beverage with one-touch convenience.

CompuDefrost is safe, efficient and always easy. Just touch the key to enter weight of meat or poultry and follow the commands in the display. New Cook & Simmer setting cooks soups and sauces automatically. Simply touch Cook & Simmer and enter the desired simmer time – the oven takes it from there! Memory Plus stores the most often used cooking time.

Convection temperature control ranges from 100°F for proofing bread to 450°F for broiling. Broil key preheats oven, signals when ready. Slow Cook expands timer capacity up to 4 hours. Programmable 4-stage cooking. CompuCook computes times/temperature settings for automatic combination and convection cooking. Features Demonstration Mode and child lock. Large 1.5 cu. ft. capacity; 15³⁄₈" diameter turntable. R-9H94/B is white-on-white; R-9H84/B is metallic charcoal. Output power: 900 watts.

R-9H94/B

R-9H84/B

C O N V E C T I O N

R-9H93
R-9H83

- 4-way cooking team browns, bakes, broils and crisps

- One-touch Popcorn, Pizza, Reheat and Beverage keys

- Deluxe ESP senses when foods are done — no mistakes!

- CompuCook computes times/temperature settings for automatic combination and convection cooking

- CompuDefrost is a safe, efficient defrost based on weight for meat or poultry

- Includes broiling trivet and rack for 2-level baking

- Optional Built-in Kits RK-66A (black) and RK-66W (aluminum) for wall oven installation

Carousel II Convection Microwave Ovens apply the latest technology and timesaving intelligence to everyday cooking, baking, roasting, reheating and defrosting. The 4-way cooking team provides microwave, convection, combination and broil options in a choice of popular cabinets: charcoal pinstripe (R-9H83) or white pinstripe (R-9H93).

Sharp's state-of-the-art convection system circulates super-heated air so meats stay juicy and breads bake golden brown. Two timesaving combination cycles are perfect for roasting or baking. Convection temperature control ranges from 100°F for proofing bread to 450°F for broiling. Broil key preheats oven and signals when ready. Slow Cook expands timer capacity up to 4 hours for baked beans, marinated meats and stews. Programmable for up to 4 cooking stages.

Popcorn, Reheat and new Pizza and Beverage keys are one-touch easy. Deluxe ESP Sensor Cook senses when 8 categories of food are done for automatic cooking. Sensor Temp uses pre-programmed temperature probe settings for combination and microwave cooking— meats are cooked to the desired degree of doneness.

Memory Plus™ stores your most often used cooking time. Auto-Touch controls with 2-color display, Auto Start, clock, 99 minute 99 second timer, Timer/Pause key and Minute Plus. The 10 Variable Power levels provide convenient control over cooking speed. Demonstration Mode permits the demonstration of features without expending microwave energy. Child lock safety feature. Large 1.5 cu. ft. capacity with 15⅜" turntable. Output power: 900 watts.

R-9H83

R-9H93

C O N V E C T I O N

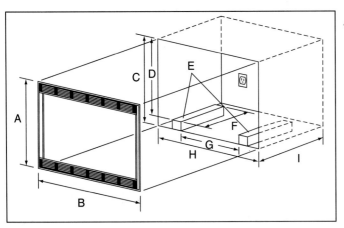

Your Sharp Microwave Oven can be built into your kitchen wall or cabinet using the appropriate Sharp Built-in Kit. Complete hardware and easy-to-follow instructions are included. Prepare cabinet or wall opening according to the illustration at left, providing access to a separate 3-pronged, 115-120V AC outlet, 15 amps or larger.

Each Sharp Over The Range microwave oven can be easily adapted for either outside ventilation (vertical or horizontal) or nonvented, ductless recirculation. Make sure top of oven will be at least 66" from the floor and at least 30" from the cooking surface. A separate 15 amp or greater electrical receptacle must be located in the cabinet directly above the microwave oven.

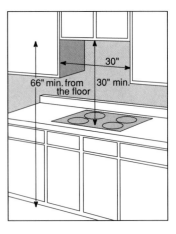

	A	B	C	D	E	F	G	H	I
RK-90, RK-90W	19⁷/₈"	26⁷/₈"	17³/₈" (± height of wood)	17³/₈"	nominal 2" x 2"; actual 1⁵/₈" x 2" x16"	16"	18³/₈"± 1/8"	25¼" ± 1/8"	min. 20½"
RK-81, RK-81W	18¼"	27¼"	16⁷/₈" ±1/8"	–	not used	–	–	24¹³/₁₆" ± ⁷/₁₆"	min. 19⅛"
RK-41, RK-41W	17⅛"	23¼"	15¹³/₁₆" ±1/8"	–	not used	–	–	22³/₁₆" ± 1/8"	min. 18"
RK-66A, RK-66W	19⁷/₈"	26⁷/₈"	17³/₈" (± height of wood)	17⅛"	nominal 2" x 2"; actual 1⁵/₈" x 2" x15"	15"	18³/₈"± 1/8"	25¼" ± 1/8"	min. 19½"

SPECIFICATIONS	R-1831, R-1830	R-1440	R-1451, R-1450	R-9H94/B, R-9H84/B	R-9H93, R-9H83	R-5H16, R-5H06	R-4H96, R-4H85
Oven Capacity:	0.9 cu. ft.	1.1 cu. ft.	1.1 cu. ft.	1.5 cu. ft.	1.5 cu. ft.	1.6 cu. ft.	1.2 cu. ft.
Cooking Uniformity:	Carousel system: 13" diameter porcelain enamel turntable	Carousel system: 12" diameter glass turntable	Carousel system: 12" diameter glass turntable	Carousel system: 15³/₈" diameter porcelain enamel turntable	Carousel system: 15³/₈" diameter porcelain enamel turntable	Carousel system: 16" diameter glass turntable	Carousel system: 14¹/₈" diameter glass turntable
Display:	2-color digital	Lighted digital	Lighted digital	2-color digital	2-color digital	Lighted digital	Lighted digital
Convection Oven Temperature Control:	100˚, 150˚, 275-450˚F in 25˚ increments			100˚, 150˚, 275-450˚F in 25˚ increments	100˚, 150˚, 275-450˚F in 25˚ increments		
Design:	R-1831: White-on-white R-1830: Black-on-black	Black-on-black	R-1451: White-on-white R-1450: Black-on-black	R-9H94/B: White-on-white R-9H84/B: Metallic charcoal	R-9H93: White pinstripe R-9H83: Charcoal pinstripe	R-5H16: White-on-white R-5H06: Stone gray	R-4H96: White-on-white R-4H85: Stone gray
Output Power:	800W	850W	850W	900W	900W	1000W	900W
Outside Dimensions: (WHD)	29⁷/₈" x 16½" x 15"	29⁷/₈" x 15³/₄" x 14"	29⁷/₈" x 15³/₄" x 14"	24⁵/₈" x 14⁷/₈" x 20¹/₄"	24⁵/₈" x 14³/₄" x 18³/₈"	24" x 13¹/₄" x 19"	21⁵/₈" x 12¹/₄" x 17"
Oven Dimensions: (WHD)	13⁵/₈" x 8³/₈" x 13¹/₂"	18¹/₈" x 7³/₄" x 13¹/₄"	18¹/₈" x 7³/₄" x 13¹/₄"	16¹/₈" x 9⁵/₈" x 16¹/₈"	16¹/₈" x 9⁵/₈" x 16¹/₈	16⁷/₈" x 9¹/₄" x 17³/₈"	15" x 8¹/₄" x 16¹/₈
Oven Interior:	Stainless steel with light	Acrylic with light	Acrylic with light	Stainless steel with light	Stainless steel with light	Acrylic with light	Acrylic with light
Approximate Weight:	Net: 74 lbs. Shipping: 87 lbs.	Net: 57 lbs. Shipping: 65 lbs.	Net: 57 lbs. Shipping: 65 lbs.	Net: 60 lbs. Shipping: 66 lbs.	Net: 60 lbs. Shipping: 66 lbs.	Net: 46 lbs. Shipping: 54 lbs.	Net: 37 lbs. Shipping: 42 lbs.
AC Line Voltage:	120V, single phase, 60Hz, AC only	120V, single phase, 60Hz, AC only	120V, single phase, 60Hz, AC only	120V, single phase, 60Hz, AC only	120V, single phase, 60Hz, AC only	120V, single phase, 60Hz, AC only	120V, single phase, 60Hz, AC only
AC Power Required:	1.6kW, 13.0A	1.68kW, 14.0A	1.68kW, 14.0A	1.55kW, 13.0A	1.55kW, 13.0A	1.61kW, 14.0A	1.52kW, 12.8A
Safety Compliance:	FCC, DHHS, UL listed	FCC, DHHS, UL listed	FCC, DHHS, UL listed	FCC, DHHS, UL listed	FCC, DHHS, UL listed	FCC, DHHS, UL listed	FCC, DHHS, UL listed
Supplied Accessories:	Broiling trivet, baking rack, temperature probe			Broiling trivet, baking rack	Broiling trivet, baking rack, temperature probe		
Optional Accessories: (Available at extra cost)	RK-250 Filler Panel Kit (two 3" black panels); RK-210 Charcoal filter for non-ducted installations†	RK-250 Filler Panel Kit (two 3" black panels); RK-220 Charcoal filter for non-ducted installations†	RK-250 Filler Panel Kit (two 3" black panels); RK-220 Charcoal filter for non-ducted installations†	R-9H94/B: Built-in Kit RK-90W (white) R-9H84/B: Built-in Kit RK-90 (black) for in-the-wall installation†	Built-in Kit RK-66A (black) or RK66W (aluminum) for in-the-wall installation†	R-5H16: Built-in Kit RK-81W (white) R-5H06: Built-in Kit RK-81 (black) for in-the-wall installation†	R-4H96: Built-in Kit RK-41W (white) R-4H85: Built-in Kit RK-41 (black) for in-the-wall installation†

Specifications subject to change without notice. †Refer to Operation Manual for installation recommendations. Output wattage based on IEC-705 1988 Test Procedure.

SHARP ELECTRONICS CORPORATION
Corporate Headquarters and Executive Offices
Sharp Plaza, Mahwah, New Jersey 07430-2135
Phone: (201) 529-8703

Regional Sales Offices and Distribution Centers

NORTHEAST
Sharp Plaza, Mahwah, New Jersey 07430-2135
Phone: (201) 529-8703

MIDWEST
1300 Naperville Dr., Romeoville, Illinois 60441
Phone: (708) 759-8555

WESTERN
20600 One Sharp Plaza
South Alameda St., Carson, California 90810
Phone: (310) 637-9488

SOUTHEASTERN
725 Old Norcross Road
Lawrenceville, Georgia 30245
Phone: (404) 995-0717

FROM SHARP MINDS COME SHARP PRODUCTS™

© 1994 Sharp Electronics Corporation
Printed in USA

R-1830, R-1831

R-9H94/B, R-9H84/B, R-9H93, R-9H83, R-5H16, R-5H06, R-4H96, R-4H85

R-1440, R-1450, R-1451

Built~in Home Refrigeration
Designed for Beauty and Performance

The first choice in kitchens of distinction

In remodeling and new construction, the look of distinction in kitchens begins with the beauty of built-in appliances and built-in refrigeration by Sub-Zero. That's why leading custom kitchen designers choose Sub-Zero first. Classic in styling and unequaled for storage, convenience and quality, Sub-Zero true built-ins are the ultimate in elegant home refrigeration.

Enjoy the elegance of built-in refrigeration

Sub-Zero home refrigeration is designed to enhance the beauty of any decor by blending compatibly with other kitchen furnishings. This is possible because of its simple design . . . removable decorative panels and the fact it is the same 24" depth as most base kitchen cabinets. A Sub-Zero is designed with a minimum of external hardware, making it hardly noticeable when built into a kitchen. It also has an exclusive toe-base feature, important in kitchen appliances, which lines up with kitchen cabinets.

All units are constructed with the 24" depth which enables the face to fit flush with most standard base cabinets. A typical free-standing refrigerator protrudes into the room 4 to 6 inches beyond cabinets, creating an unsightly appearance and takes up valuable space in the room.

Sub-Zero built-ins are designed to accept removable exterior panels of any material on the front and sides. In doing so, the unit practically disappears into the overall kitchen, blending completely into the decor instead of dominating the kitchen appearance, as a free-standing unit does. And, because the panels are removable, they can be changed, should the room decor change.

These true built-in features mean your home refrigeration need not be an unattractive standout but can now complement the over-all style of the kitchen and function as an integral part of the total kitchen design. They allow individual styling and expression of your personal taste.

Built-in work savers

Truly an accent to the kitchen of distinction, Sub-Zero built-in refrigeration offers all of the time and work saving features that today's lifestyles require...like convenient usable storage, easy up-keep, simplified cleaning, automatic defrosting and automatic ice maker.

The shallow depth makes it easier to find what you are looking for, eliminating the need to search for items that have found their way to the back shelf area (as in other refrigerators). This, along with the fact that all shelves are fully adjustable, gives even greater flexibility for storage arrangements.

Easy up-keep is achieved because of the quality materials and craftsmanship used in the construction of a Sub-Zero. ...interior, exterior and mechanical.

Cleaning is simplified because of two reasons: First the unit's built-in feature eliminates cracks and crevices that would normally collect dust and also eliminates the chore of pulling the refrigerator out to clean behind it.

Secondly, all shelves in Sub-Zero full-size units are removable to allow for ease of cleaning.

The automatic defrost feature is standard on all full-size models as well as the undercounter models (except

Model 550

249R). This eliminates the need to shut down the refrigerator to defrost and clean the unit.

Another standard feature of the full-size units is the automatic ice maker which produces an adequate supply of ice automatically without the need to handle awkward ice trays.

Many models to choose from

Whatever your space or usage requirements, Sub-Zero offers a selection of over 12 models to fit your needs and specifications. Choose from the popular side-by-side, the over-n-under (freezer on the bottom), the all-freezer and all-refrigerator units, compact undercounter refrigerators and an ice maker. Ranging in width from 18" to 48", Sub-Zero units offer capacities to 30.0 cubic feet. The combination all-refrigerator and all-freezer together provide as much as 40.0 cubic feet of food storage.

Sub-Zero 12-Year Protection Plan

Sub-Zero has always backed what it has manufactured, and offers a warranty package no one can match — the Sub-Zero 12-Year Protection Plan. From the day your Sub-Zero is installed, you have a full five-year (parts and labor) warranty and limited sixth through twelfth-year (parts) warranty on the sealed system, consisting of the compressor, condenser, evaporator, drier and all connecting tubing. You also have a full two-year (parts and labor) warranty on the entire product. (See warranty for non-residential use and other exceptions). Sub-Zero stands behind every refrigerator and freezer they manufacture, ensuring you of the finest in service and trouble-free maintenance.

Outstanding performance and craftsmanship

Sub-Zero is a leader in the industry in engineering functional refrigeration. Because Sub-Zero full-size units use a refrigerant in both the refrigerator and freezer compartments, proper and even temperatures are maintained more consistently throughout. This is the same type system used in some commercial refrigerators and is a standard feature in Sub-Zero home units, to insure top performance and operation. Complete factory testing of every Sub-Zero unit is your assurance of quality workmanship.

More than just refrigeration, Sub-Zero quality craftsmanship is a tradition, custom designed to enhance the value and elegance of your home for years to come.

2

Maximum storage with the
500 SERIES Models 501R and 501F

For large families or those people who need maximum storage, Sub-Zero offers the convenience of its new Eurostyled all-refrigerator (Model 501R) and all-freezer (Model 501F) with a total storage capacity of 40 cubic feet. The "all-refrigerator's" 20 cubic foot capacity makes this exclusive unit the largest built-in all-refrigerator on the market. One of the advantages of these units is the flexibility of planning your kitchen. The units can be installed side-by-side or with a convenient counter between them or at opposite ends of the room, depending on your kitchen layout. Adjustable shelving in both the refrigerator and freezer gives even more storage versatility. The 501F has an automatic ice maker. The "all-refrigerator" Model 501R is also ideal for people who have existing freezer storage. **Separate detailed specification sheets on models 501R and 501F available upon request.**

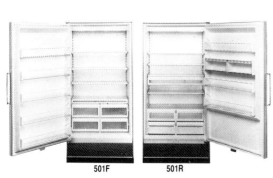

501F   501R

ALL FREEZER
Model 501F—Automatic defrost. Freezer is equipped with automatic ice maker.
ALL REFRIGERATOR
Model 501R—Automatic defrost refrigerator.

Model	501F	501R
Capacity	20.0 cu. ft.	20.0 cu. ft.
Dimensions	Height 73″ Width 36″ Depth 24″	Height 73″ Width 36″ Depth 24″
Finished Roughing-In Dimensions	35½″x72¾″	35½″x72¾″
Weight (lbs.)	363 crated	376 crated

*Additional shelves available at extra cost.

← 23⅞ →
BEHIND FLANGE

← 36 →

PANEL SIZE
34⅛″ W.
x 58¹⁵/₁₆″ H.

73

4

→ 3 ←

Minimum height required (when levelers in) is 72⁷/₁₆″

NOTE: Roughing-in width is 71½″ when these models are installed side by side. If mullion is used to separate cabinets, add mullion width to 71½″ dimension. Filler must be used when installed hinge to hinge.

One 115 volt, 60 cycle single phase, 15 amp. wall outlet must be provided.

Refer to 500 series "Installation Instruction" booklet for detailed installation and panel requirements.

Model 561

Model 561 Interior

Side by Side Combination
Models 561 and 532

The new 500 series incorporates exciting engineering innovations, with built-in beauty and elegant Eurostyled interiors. This series also features the new satin-brushed aluminum exterior trim and simplicity of design. The elegant combination of white and clear interiors, together with the built-in appearance, offers breathtaking beauty.

Sub-Zero's model 561 features an 8.9 cu. ft. freezer and 12.5 cu. ft. refrigeration in convenient top-to-bottom, side-by-side storage. Its two compressors provide independent temperature control of the freezer and refrigerator compartments. The freezer compartment has four pull-out storage baskets, automatic ice maker with removable ice storage drawer and adjustable door storage.

Model 561

COMBINATION REFRIGERATOR-FREEZER
Model 561 — Automatic defrost model. Freezer compartment equipped with automatic ice maker.

Capacity:	12.5 cu. ft. Refrigerator
	8.9 cu. ft. Freezer
Dimensions:	Height 84″
	Width 36″
	Depth 24″
Finished Rough-In Dimensions	35¹⁄₂″ x 83³⁄₄″
Weight (lbs.):	480 lbs. crated

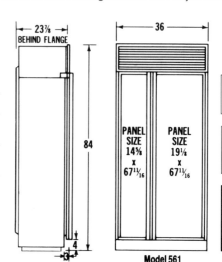

Model 561

One 115 volt, 60 cycle single phase, 15 amp. wall outlet must be provided.

Minimum height required (when levelers in) is 82⁷⁄₈″ (smaller grille recommended).

Refer to 500 series "Installation Instruction" booklet for detailed installation and panel requirements.

4

Model 532   Model 532 Interior

Sub-Zero's huge 30 cu. ft. combination refrigerator/freezer model 532 is one of the largest home built-in units made. It incorporates new engineering innovations and Eurostyled interior. It has an 11.2 cu. ft. freezer and 18.8 cu. ft. refrigerator with convenient top-to-bottom storage.

The freezer compartment has four pull-out storage baskets, an automatic ice maker with roll-out removable ice storage drawer and adjustable door storage. The refrigerator has four self-sealing crispers, each with independent humidity control. It also features an adjustable roll-out utility drawer, adjustable door storage shelves and adjustable glass shelves. This model also has two compressors to provide independent temperature control in both the freezer and refrigerator compartments.

This unit is available in the 48 inch format with water and ice dispensed through the refrigerator door. This is not an option but another addition to our full line called the Model 590.

Detailed specification sheets on model 532, 561 and 590 are available on request.

Optional solid panel grilles that accept matching panels are available for 532 and 561. The panel grille is standard on the 590. Detailed specification sheets on the three units and grilles available upon request.

Model 532

COMBINATION REFRIGERATOR-FREEZER
Model 532—Automatic defrost model Equipped with automatic ice maker.

Capacity:	18.8 cu. ft. Refrigerator 11.2 cu. ft. Freezer
Dimensions:	Height 84" Width 48" Depth 24"
Finished Rough-In Dimensions:	47¹⁄₂" x83³⁄₄"
Weight (lbs.):	563 crated

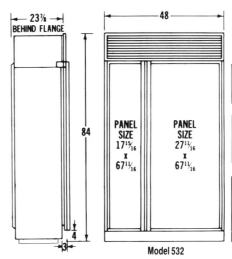

Model 532

One 115 volt, 60 cycle single phase, 15 amp. wall outlet must be provided.

Minimum height required (when levelers in) is 82⁷⁄₈" (smaller grille recommended).

Refer to 500 series "Installation Instruction" booklet for detailed installation and panel requirements.

5

Model 550

Model 550 Interior

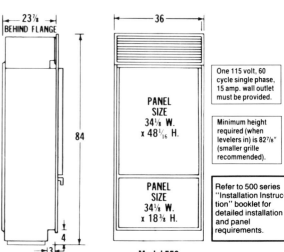

SUB-ZERO ®

Over-N-Under (freezer on bottom)
Models 550 and 511

For those who prefer, Sub-Zero offers a convenient arrangement with freezer on the bottom. This design was prompted by the fact that the refrigerator section is used more often than the freezer, thereby providing the greatest convenience and best accessibility. The refrigerated top half offers full width storage on adjustable shelves while frozen foods below are easily accessible with a pull-out drawer.

The over-n-under units in the 500 series also incorporate exciting engineering innovations with built-in beauty and elegant Eurostyled interiors. These units also feature the new satin-brushed aluminum exterior trim and simplicity of design.

Sub-Zero's 22.1 cu. ft. model 550 over-n-under combination unit has a 6.4 cu. ft. slide-out, double-tier freezer drawer in the

COMBINATION REFRIGERATOR-FREEZER
Model 550 — Automatic defrost model. Freezer compartment equipped with automatic ice maker.

Capacity:	15.7 cu. ft. Refrigerator 6.4 cu. ft. Freezer
Dimensions:	Height 84″ Width 36″ Depth 24″
Finished Rough-In Dimensions	35½″ x 83¾″
Weight (lbs.):	468 crated

Model 550

23⅛ BEHIND FLANGE

84

4
3

36

PANEL SIZE
34⅛ W.
x 48¹⁄₁₆ H.

PANEL SIZE
34⅛ W.
x 18⅜ H.

One 115 volt, 60 cycle single phase, 15 amp. wall outlet must be provided.

Minimum height required (when levelers in) is 82⅞″ (smaller grille recommended).

Refer to 500 series "Installation Instruction" booklet for detailed installation and panel requirements.

Model 550

(Optional panel grille shown)   Model 511

Model 511 Interior

bottom. The freezer has an automatic ice maker with removable ice storage container. The top pull freezer handle and double-tier design provide easy access. The refrigerator has two self-sealing crispers, each with independent humidity control. It has a roll-out utility drawer, adjustable glass shelves and fully adjustable door storage.

The model 511 features a 5.2 cu. ft. slide-out double-tier freezer drawer and a 12.7 cu. ft. refrigerator compartment. Again the freezer has an automatic ice maker with removable ice storage container. Like the model 550, easy freezer access is provided by top pull handle and roll-out double-tier design.

These over-n-under models are extremely versatile for kitchen designs used alone or in various combinations, such as the kitchen shown on the cover of this brochure.

Both units have two compressors which provides independent temperature control in both the refrigerator and freezer compartments. These units are backed by Sub-Zero's exclusive Twelve-Year Protection Plan.

Optional solid panel grilles that accept matching panels also available. Specification sheet available upon request. Detailed specification sheets on models 550 and 511 are available upon request.

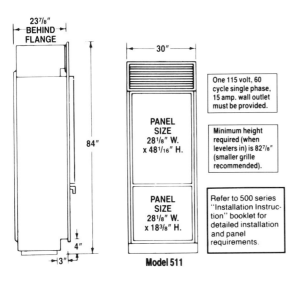

23⁷/₈″ BEHIND FLANGE

30″

84″

4″

3″

One 115 volt, 60 cycle single phase, 15 amp. wall outlet must be provided.

PANEL SIZE 28¹/₈″ W. x 48¹/₁₆″ H.

Minimum height required (when levelers in) is 82⁷/₈″ (smaller grille recommended).

PANEL SIZE 28¹/₈″ W. x 18³/₈″ H.

Refer to 500 series "Installation Instruction" booklet for detailed installation and panel requirements.

Model 511

COMBINATION REFRIGERATOR-FREEZER
Model 511 — Automatic defrost model. Freezer compartment equipped with automatic ice maker.

Capacity:	12.7 cu. ft. Refrigerator 5.2 cu. ft. Freezer
Dimensions:	Height 84″ Width 30″ Depth 24″
Finished Rough-In Dimensions	29¹/₂″ x 83³/₄″
Weight (lbs.):	375 crated

Model 511

Features of full-size, built-in units

1. Convenient Storage

All Sub-Zero units are 24″ in depth to conform to most kitchen base cabinet units. This not only improves appearance of finished installation but provides more accessible storage on interior shelves.

2. Sub-Zero 12-Year Protection Plan

Full five-year (parts and labor) warranty and limited sixth through twelfth-year (parts) warranty on the sealed system, consisting of the compressor, condenser, evaporator, drier and all connecting tubing; and a full two-year (parts and labor) warranty on the entire product from the date of installation. (Does not include installation.) (See warranty for non-residential use and other exceptions.)

3. Automatic Ice Maker

Makes and stores crescent-shaped ice pieces. Although several conditions affect the amount of ice that is produced in a given period of time, an adequate supply is provided. (Model 532 and 561 icemaker shown)

4. Automatic Defrosting

Automatically eliminates frost accumulation in both refrigerator and freezer sections.

5. Accepts Removable Decorative Door Panels

Front panels of virtually any material, not exceeding 1/4″ in thickness are easily installed. Raised panels may also be used when perimeter edge does not exceed 1/4″. **(We recommend routing, recessing or optional extended handles for finger clearance when using raised panels.) Refer to Installation Instruction Guide for detailed information. Only colored and stainless steel panels are available from the factory. (50# per door panel weight limit.)**

6. Side Panels

Unit is made to accept side panels if sides are exposed. Only colored and stainless steel panels are available from the factory.

7. Front-Vented

Allows for true built-in installation and eliminates over heating.

8. Removable and Adjustable Shelves

Cantilever type glass shelves in the refrigerator and wire shelves in the freezer for easy cleaning and flexible storage.

9. Deluxe Crispers

Spacious, self-sealing crispers have easy-glide roller design and adjustable, independent humidity control to assure food freshness.

10. Interiors

Award-winning Eurostyled white and clear interior.

11. Magnetic Door Gasket

Surrounds entire door with a pull that assures a positive seal.
NOTE — Because of a perfect seal, allow a slight delay before reopening door.

12. Right or Left Door Swing

Available, when specified, on all over-n-under and single door units (all side-by-side units are hinged on outside). Doors are not reversible.

13. Portable Egg Trays

Convenient and versatile, they may be carried to the table or preparation area.

14. Adjustable Dairy Compartment

Versatile, positive sealing compartment for dairy items.

15. Adjustable Utility Basket

Adjustable roll-out refrigeration basket offers handy storage for small items.

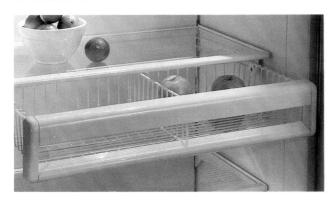

16. Clean Trim

No visible screws.

17. Colored Panels

Decorator front and side steel panels are available from Sub-Zero in the following colors: Harvest Gold, Almond, Avocado, Coffee, Stainless Steel and White.

18. Grilles

Standard grille height is 11″. Other available grille heights range from 10″ to 15″ in 1″ increments. Optional decorative, solid panel grilles that accept matching panels also available in these sizes.

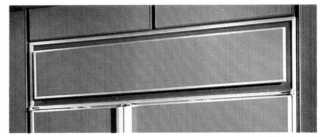

Panel grille

19. Toe Space Base

Integral part of cabinet. Inset is 4″ high by 3″ deep — meeting specifications of American Institute of Architects and conforming with most bases of kitchen cabinets.

20. Door Handles

Standard as shown in photographs throughout this literature.

21. Door Closers

All models equipped with door closers.

22. Door Stops

Although most installations do not require a door stop (door opens to 130°), an optional kit is available if needed. The Door Stop Kit allows the door to open to 90°.

23. Rollers

Unit has rollers and convenient leveling system for ease of installation.

24. Additional Shelves

Available at additional cost.

IMPORTANT: For proper operation and use, the door must open at least a full 90°. A minimum 2″ filler should be used in corner installations to assure a 90° door opening. Remember to allow enough clearance in front of unit for full door swing.

Undercounter models

Sub-Zero undercounter refrigerators, freezers, combinations and ice makers are ideal for the bar, den, family room, yacht or office. They are designed to be installed under a counter. However, some may also be used as free-standing units.

All under-counter models are self-venting, have foamed-in-place insulation, have durable ABS easy to clean interiors and accept front door panels of practically any material to harmonize with cabinets or other equipment. They also have right to left door swings which are interchangeable in the field (kit required except model 245). All of these features and more are backed by Sub-Zero's 12-Year Protection Plan — providing a full five-year (parts and labor) warranty and limited sixth through twelfth year (parts) warranty on the sealed system, consisting of the compressor, condenser, evaporator, drier and all connecting tubing; and a full two year (parts and labor) warranty on the entire product from the date of installation. (Does not include installation.) (See warranty for non-residential use and other exceptions.)

The Sub-Zero combination models 245 and 801 provide automatic defrost, refrigerator storage, freezer storage and automatic ice making.

Sub-Zero also offers "all-refrigerator" and "all-freezer" undercounter units. The model 249RP "all-refrigerator" features automatic defrost, door storage and adjustable compartment shelving. Our model 249FF "all-freezer" features automatic defrost, adjustable compartment shelving and can be equipped with an automatic ice maker, but it must be installed at the factory.

A unit for those who desire primarily refrigerator storage with some freezer storage is the model 249R. This unit is a manual defrost, with a small full-width freezer, door storage and adjustable compartment shelving.

We also offer a built-in ice maker for those who entertain in style. Requirements for clear ice can be satisfied with the model 506, which provides an abundance of crystal-clear cubes in a unit that requires only an 18″ width. Featuring a drop-down hopper-type door, this unit stores up to 35 pounds of 3/4″ cubes. This unit requires a drain or pump.

Separate specification sheet on each undercounter model is available upon request.

Undercounter Model	249R	249RP	249FF	245	801	506
Capacity	4.4 cu. ft. Refrigerator .7 cu. ft. Freezer	4.9 cu. ft. Refrigerator	4.6 cut. ft Freezer	3.0 cu. ft. Refrigerator 1.9 cu. ft. Freezer	2.9 cu. ft. Refrigerator 2.6 cu. ft. Freezer	Stores 35 lbs. of ice
Unit Dimensions [Levelers in] (H × W × D in inches)	33¹³/₁₆ × 23⅞ × 24	33¹³/₁₆ × 23⅞ × 24	33¹³/₁₆ × 23⅞ × 24	34 × 23⅞ × 24	33⅝ × 36 × 23⅞	34¹³/₃₂ × 17⅛ × 23⅞
Weight (lbs.)	120 crated	117 crated	135 crated	139 crated	265 crated	110 crated

Note: Refer to "Installation Instruction" booklet for detailed water, electrical and other installation requirements.

Model 249R

Model 249RP

Model 249FF
(ICEMAKER OPTIONAL)

Model 245

Model 801

Model 506

Installation specifications

Following are the installation specifications for all Sub-Zero full-size and undercounter models. The dimensions shown in the chart correlate with the schematic drawings. For further details refer to the **Installation Instruction Booklet.**

Schematic drawing

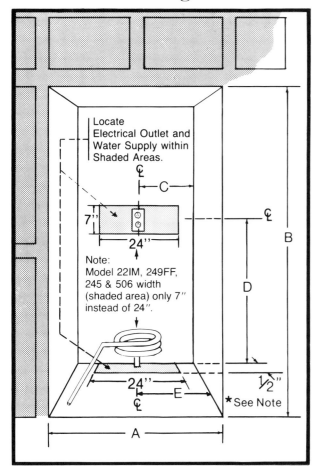

Locate Electrical Outlet and Water Supply within Shaded Areas.

Note:
Model 22IM, 249FF, 245 & 506 width (shaded area) only 7″ instead of 24″.

Door Clearance Schematic Drawing Top View

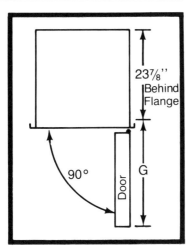

Wood grille not available from Sub Zero.

Model No.	Finished Rough Opening Dimensions		Recommended Electrical Outlet Location		Water Supply Location	Door Panel Dimensions (width x height)	Minimum Door Clearance Requirement at 90°
	A	B	C	D	E	~	G
550	35¹/₂″	83³/₄″	18″	79″	18″	34¹/₈″ x 48¹/₁₆″ & 34¹/₈″ x 18³/₈″	36¹/₁₆″
511	29¹/₂″	83³/₄″	15″	79″	15″	28¹/₈″ x 48¹/₁₆″ & 28¹/₈″ x 18³/₈″	30¹/₈″
561	35¹/₂″	83³/₄″	18″	79″	18″	14⁵/₈″ x 67¹¹/₁₆″ & 19¹/₈″ x 67¹¹/₁₆″	20³/₄″
532	47¹/₂″	83³/₄″	18″	79″	18″	17¹⁵/₁₆″ x 67¹¹/₁₆″ & 27¹¹/₁₆″ x 67¹¹/₁₆″	29¹/₄″
501R	35¹/₂″	72³/₄″	18″	7″		34¹/₈″ x 58¹⁵/₁₆″	36¹/₁₆″
501F	35¹/₂″	72³/₄″	18″	7″	18″	34¹/₈″ x 58¹⁵/₁₆″	36¹/₁₆″
801	35¹/₂″	34¹/₂″	18″	3¹/₂″	18″	16⁷/₈″ x 22⁷/₈″ (both)	18¹/₂″
245	24″	34¹/₂″	5¹/₂″	4¹/₂″	12″	23¹/₂″ x 28¹/₈″	25¹³/₁₆″
249R	24″	34¹/₂″	12″	14″		23⁵/₈″ x 30″	25³/₈″
249RP	24″	34¹/₂″	12″	14″		23⁵/₈″ x 30″	25³/₈″
249FF	24″	34¹/₂″	5″	14″	18″	23⁵/₈″ x 30″	25³/₈″
506	18″	34¹/₂″	6″	6″	11″	17″ x 13³/₁₆″ & 17″ x 11¹⁵/₁₆″	11³/₄″

*NOTE: Water line may come directly thru wall, not higher than 3″ from floor.

11

(Optional panel grille shown)

How to buy

Sub-Zero home refrigeration can be seen and purchased at top custom kitchen dealers and appliance stores in all major cities across the United States and many Canadian cities. If not available in your area, feel free to contact Sub-Zero direct for the distributor nearest you. Call 800-222-7820.

Service

There are hundreds of authorized service centers throughout the country to provide warranty service and perform other service functions. These centers maintain a stock of Sub-Zero approved parts and a staff of qualified repair technicians. The service center nearest you may be found in the yellow pages or by contacting the dealer you purchased the unit from. If service cannot be found, contact Sub-Zero direct: 800-356-5826.

SUB-ZERO FREEZER CO., INC.

Post Office Box 44130
Madison, Wisconsin 53744-4130
608/271-2233

SUB-ZERO

Model 590
Ice & Water Refrigerator-Freezer

Innovative Excellence

SUB-ZERO ®

Sub-Zero has led the built-in home refrigeration industry for years with product enhancements which have set trends. Sub-Zero continues to redefine the art of built-in refrigeration for the 90's with the introduction of the distinctive Model 590 with its innovative version of ice and water through the refrigerator door.

The convenient placement and inconspicuous appearance of the ice and water dispenser and its controls were designed with you in mind.

And the ability to match your kitchen design has been assured with the Model 590. Like all Sub-Zero units, the Model 590 will fit flush with virtually all 24-inch cabinets and accept decorative side and front panels. Another exclusive feature of the Model 590 is the complementary color handle trim panels and glasswells which are offered at no charge.

Craftsmanship, a Sub-Zero trademark, is also built into each of these features:

•**Ice & Water Dispenser**– designed and practically placed for your convenience. A new industry feature, the water is constantly chilled within its huge 51 oz. reservoir.

•**Bulk Ice Dispenser**– conveniently located inside the refrigerator door when larger quantities are needed. This new industry feature is activated at the touch of a button.

•**Two Refrigeration Systems** – ensures independent, accurate freezer and refrigerator temperature control.

•**Decorative Door Panels** – front panels of virtually any material not exceeding 1/4" perimeter thickness are accommodated. Only color and stainless steel panels are available from the factory. (50# per door panel weight limit)

•**Automatic Defrosting** – freezer and refrigerator have own systems.

•**Adjustable Shelves** – cantilever type, easy to move and clean.

•**Spacious Crispers with Humidity Control** – four self-sealing crispers have clear view and individual controls.

•**Adjustable Door Shelves** – easy to adjust shelves provide complete flexibility on both doors.

•**Automatic Ice Maker** – an adequate supply of cresent-shaped ice is ensured.

•**Dairy Module** – a moveable, sealed environment for freshness.

•**Master Switch** – quick practical access is offered to shut unit off.

•**Rollers** – provides easy installation.

•**Positive Sealing Doors** – magnetic gaskets guarantee a tight seal.

•**Brushed Satin Trim** – offers clean design so there's no distraction from the beauty of your kitchen.

•**Portable Egg Containers** – easy access and convenient storage.

•**Panel Grille** – 11" panel grille is standard. Other sizes from 10" to 15" are available in one inch increments.

•**Solid Toe Plate** – allows custom finishing.

Refrigeration System Control and Bulk Ice Dispenser.

Ice & Water Dispenser with Night Light.

Model 590 shown with optional bright white handle trim panel and glasswell.

Sub-Zero 12 Year Protection Plan—full five-year (parts and labor) warranty and limited sixth through twelfth-year (parts) warranty on the sealed system, consisting of the compressor, condenser, evaporator, drier and all connecting tubing; a full two-year (parts and labor) warranty on the entire product from the date of installation. (Does not include installation. See warranty for other exceptions.)

Beauty—our award-winning interior is beautiful to the eye, but more importantly it is spacious with nearly 30 cubic feet of flexible storage for all your needs.
Refrigerator – 18.2 cubic feet.
Freezer – 11.2 cubic feet.

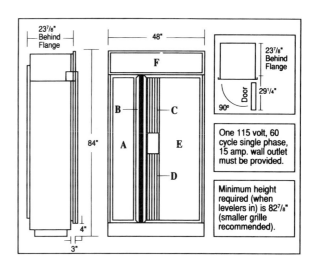

One 115 volt, 60 cycle single phase, 15 amp. wall outlet must be provided.

Minimum height required (when levelers in) is 82⁷/₈" (smaller grille recommended).

Capacity: Refrigerator 18.2 cu. ft. Freezer 11.2 cu. ft.	Dimensions: Height 84" Width 48" Depth 24"
Two Compressors	Finished Roughed-in Dimensions: 47¹/₂ x 83³/₄

Weight: 598 lbs. crated

| Door Panel Dimensions:
A 15 ¹/₈ w x 67 ¹¹/₁₆ h
B 2 ⁹/₁₆ w x 67 ¹¹/₃₂ h
C 6 ⁷/₈ w x 25 ⁷/₃₂ h | **D** 6 ⁷/₈ w x 31 ⁷/₃₂ h
E 20 ⁹/₁₆ w x 67 ¹¹/₁₆ h
Grille Panel Dimension:
F 46 ³/₁₆ w x 9 ³/₁₆ h |

B,C & D may not exceed .050" thickness

Due to our continuous improvement program, models and specifications are subject to change without notice.

Color Selection Guide
for model 590 only

Complete Flexibility

Your Sub-Zero Model 590 will be shipped with handsome pin-striped pewter gray handle trim panels and glasswell. But an exclusive feature from Sub-Zero allows you to change this color scheme to accent your kitchen.

Model 590 shown with standard pin-striped pewter gray handle trim panels and glasswell.

Ask your local dealer about specific color combinations. The eight glasswell and laminate handle trim panel alternatives we offer at no charge are:

P1/G1 Bright White	**P2/G2** Almond Buff
P3/G3 Camel	**P4/G4** Adobe
P5/G5 Pewter Gray	**P6/G6** Smoke Gray
P7/G7 Charcoal	**P8/G8** Port Brown
	P9/G9 Black Slate

The colors illustrated here are only meant to give you an idea of the shades available and you should contact your dealer for more accurate color combinations and shading.

Note: Metal handle trim panels to match Sub-Zero supplied metal door and side panels are also available in white, almond, avocado, coffee, harvest gold and stainless steel at no charge.

Sales

In addition to the Model 590, Sub-Zero features a full line of built-in home refrigeration units with side-by-side, over-and-under and undercounter models which vary in size from 4.5 to 30 cubic feet of storage. For the dealer near you look in the yellow pages or call Sub-Zero at **800/222-7820** for your nearest distributor.

Service

Sub-Zero has an extensive service network throughout the United States and Canada to meet your needs. You can find them in the yellow pages or call us at **800/356-5826.**

SUB-ZERO FREEZER CO., INC.
P.O. Box 44130
Madison ,WI 53744 - 4130
(608) 271- 2233

C517
BuyLine 8643

VIKING

FULL PRODUCT LINE

Professional Performance for the Home

*T*he originator of commercial cooking equipment for the home, Viking Range Corporation offers a complete line of professional-style cooking, ventilation, and kitchen clean-up equipment. Each product in the Viking line represents the finest in heavy-duty, commercial-type construction, performance, and appearance, providing designers, builders, and home-owners with features available only from Viking Range Corporation.

▼ 36" AND 48" WIDE GAS RANGES

The flagship of the Viking Range product line, the ultra-premium VGRC series represents the finest in commercial-type cooking equipment. Available in 36" and 48" widths in a number of versatile surface configurations, the VGRC combines maximum cooking power with the unmistakable appearance of a Viking range.

PROFESSIONAL FEATURES
- Stainless steel, 15,000 BTU surface burners accommodate an infinite range of settings
- Automatic electric spark ignition/re-ignition; surface burners re-light if inadvertently extinguished, even on lowest settings
- 10" by 11", heavy-duty, porcelainized, cast-iron, removable surface burner grates provide virtually continuous front-to-rear, left-to-right surface for easy movement of large pots
- Removable porcelain burner bowls
- Stainless steel drip tray with roller bearing glides
- Large capacity ovens
  - 36" W. range–4.7 cu. ft. bake/broil convection oven
  - 48" W. range–3.8 cu. ft. bake/broil convection oven and 2.3 cu. ft. bake oven
- Convection baking, broiling, dehydrating, and defrosting
- 1,500 degree F., closed-door, smokeless broiling with 18,000 BTU infrared burner
- Large, easy-to-read knobs with childproof, push-to-turn safety feature
- Select models also include a char-grill and/or thermostatically-controlled griddle/simmer plate

MODELS
- VGRC365-6BD–36"wide, six burners, single oven
- VGRC365-4GD–36"wide, four burners, 12"wide griddle/simmer plate, single oven
- VGRC365-4QD–36"wide, four burners, 12"wide char-grill, single oven
- VGRC485-8BD–48"wide, eight burners, double ovens
- VGRC485-6GD–48"wide, six burners, 12"wide griddle/simmer plate, double ovens
- VGRC485-6QD–48"wide, six burners, 12"wide char-grill, double ovens
- VGRC485-4GD–48"wide, four burners, 24"wide griddle/simmer plate, double ovens
- VGRC485-4GQD–48"wide, four burners, 12"wide griddle/simmer plate, 12"wide char-grill, double ovens

▼ 30" WIDE GAS RANGES

Designed to fit the standard cutout space found in conventional kitchen cabinetry, the Viking VGSS300-4BD and VGSC305-4BD allow homeowners to replace their ordinary stoves with the commercial power of a Viking range–without remodeling. Both models feature many of the same professional features found in the VGRC in a 30"wide, 24" deep range.

MODELS
- VGSS300-4BD–four burners, bake/broil oven (4.3 cu. ft.)
- VGSC305-4BD–four burners, bake/broil convection oven (4.0 cu. ft.)

▼ BUILT-IN GAS RANGETOPS

With nine models in three sizes and an extensive array of exclusive features, the Viking VGRT series sets the standard for commercial-type construction, performance, and appearance. From a trim 30" wide model to a 48" wide rangetop with griddle and char-grill, the VGRT series is the most comprehensive line of professional rangetops available for the home.

PROFESSIONAL FEATURES
- Stainless steel, 15,000 BTU surface burners accommodate an infinite range of settings
- Automatic electric spark ignition/re-ignition; surface burners re-light if inadvertently extinguished, even on lowest settings
- 10" by 11", heavy-duty, porcelainized, cast-iron, removable surface burner grates provide virtually continuous front-to-rear, left-to-right surface for easy movement of large pots
- Removable porcelain burner bowls
- Stainless steel drip tray with roller bearing glides
- Large, easy-to-read knobs with childproof, push-to-turn safety feature
- Select models also include a char-grill and/or thermostatically-controlled griddle/simmer plate

MODELS
- VGRT300-4B–30"wide, four burners
- VGRT360-6B–36"wide, six burners
- VGRT360-4G–36"wide, four burners, 12"wide griddle/simmer plate
- VGRT360-4Q–36"wide, four burners, 12"wide char-grill
- VGRT480-8B–48"wide, eight burners
- VGRT480-6G–48"wide, six burners, 12"wide griddle/simmer plate
- VGRT480-6Q–48"wide, six burners, 12"wide char-grill
- VGRT480-4G–48"wide, four burners, 24"wide griddle/simmer plate
- VGRT480-4GQ–48"wide, four burners, 12"wide griddle/simmer plate, 12"wide char-grill

ACCESSORIES–RANGES AND RANGETOPS
- Stainless steel backguard
- Stainless steel high-shelf
- Stainless steel island trim
- Stainless steel countertop side trim
- Curb base front and side in nine finishes (ranges only)
- Custom curb base for locally supplied trim (ranges only)
- Caster/connector kit–agency approved for home use (ranges only)
- Porcelainized, cast-iron "V" grates
- Porcelainized, cast-iron wok grate
- Stainless steel wok ring
- Heavy-duty portable griddle
- Hardwood cover
- Hardwood cutting board

▼ BUILT-IN GAS 36" WIDE THERMAL-CONVECTION OVEN

The Viking built-in gas oven combines commercial-type styling with the precise, even heat of convection baking. The VGSO165 features an infrared broiler and dual bake burners in the largest built-in home convection wall oven available.

PROFESSIONAL FEATURES

- Largest oven cavity available in a built-in convection oven– 3.3 cubic feet
- Conventional baking with dual burners and natural airflow
- Convection baking, broiling, dehydrating, and defrosting
- 1,500° F., closed-door, smokeless broiling with 18,000 BTU infrared burner
- Pilotless electric ignition
- Three heavy-duty, four-position oven racks for maximum baking capacity
- Removable oven doors with see-through windows
- Installs as a single oven, double stacked, or side-by-side in standard depth residential cabinets (for double stacked, order installation kit)

MODEL

- VGSO165–bake/broil convection oven

▼ BUILT-IN GAS AND ELECTRIC 27" WIDE DOUBLE OVENS

Viking built-in double ovens combine commercial-type performance with easy operation and the convenience of self-cleaning. Gas models offer infrared broiling and natural airflow baking in both ovens; electric models feature seven conventional/convection cooking modes.

PROFESSIONAL FEATURES

- Electronic clock/timer with commercial-type, digital L.E.D. display
- Automatic time option for baking/roasting
- 99-minute timer with end-of-timing signal
- Self-cleaning upper and lower ovens
- Automatic self-clean setting with indicator lights
- 12-hour alarm clock
- Removable oven doors with see-through windows
- Porcelain oven interiors

GAS MODEL FEATURES

- 3.0 cubic foot cavity in both ovens
- Conventional baking with natural air flow
- Closed-door, smokeless, infrared broiling
- Pilotless electric ignition

ELECTRIC MODEL FEATURES

- 2.7 cubic foot cavity in both ovens
- Conventional baking and broiling
- Convection baking, broiling, dehydrating, and defrosting
- Convection cooking with single rear element for delicate dishes
- Three heavy-duty racks in both ovens for maximum capacity

MODELS

- VGDO270 (gas)–two bake/broil ovens
- VEDO275 (electric)–two bake/broil convection ovens

▼ VENTILATION SYSTEMS

Designed specifically to complement commercial-type cooking equipment, Viking interior and exterior-powered rangehoods and downdraft systems combine superior ventilating power with quiet operation.

PROFESSIONAL WALL AND ISLAND HOOD FEATURES

- Heavy-gauge steel construction and commercial-type styling
- Precision crafted and designed for super-quiet operation
- Fluorescent lighting for even, shadowless illumination
- Models available in 600 to 1,800 CFM (cubic feet per minute)
- Available in sizes to complement any kitchen

INTERIOR POWER RANGEHOODS

- Filterless CentriVent™ air removal system uses centrifugal action to remove grease from heated vapors
- No hard-to-clean mesh filters
- Eliminates unsightly grease and lint build-up that can pose a fire hazard
- Independent switches for custom ventilation control
- Removable, dishwasher-safe blower housing for quick, easy clean-up

EXTERIOR POWER RANGEHOODS

- Exterior-powered ventilators eliminate motor sounds in the home, combining efficiency with quiet operation
- Infinite settings for precise, variable speed control
- Removable, easy-to-clean, commercial-type, stainless steel baffle filters

INTERIOR POWER REPLACEMENT RANGEHOODS

- 9" high hoods available in standard widths and depths allow replacement of most older, low-performance hoods without cabinet alteration
- Recommended for use over non-griddle and non-grill ranges and rangetops

VERSAVENT™ REAR DOWNDRAFT

- Suitable for both wall and island installations
- Raises and lowers at the touch of a button— when not in use the unit retracts and rests flush with countertop
- Six variable fan speeds ensure efficient ventilation
- Removable, dishwasher-safe, aluminum filters

RANGEHOOD MODELS
18" HIGH INTERIOR POWER

- VRHW300 (24"D.) or VRH30 (27"D.)–30"wide wall hood
- VRHW360 (24"D.) or VRH36 (27"D.)–36"wide wall hood
- VRHW480 (24"D.) or VRH48 (27"D.)–48"wide wall hood
- VRHI360 (27"D.) or VIH36 (30"D.)–36"wide island hood
- VRHI420 (27"D.) or VIH42 (30"D.)–42"wide island hood
- VRHI540 (27"D.) or VIH54 (30"D.)–54"wide island hood

18" HIGH EXTERIOR POWER

- VRHW300-EP (24"D.) or VRH30-EP (27"D.)–30"wide wall hood
- VRHW360-EP (24"D.) or VRH36-EP (27"D.)–36"wide wall hood
- VRHW480-EP (24"D.) or VRH48-EP (27"D.)–48"wide wall hood
- VRHI360-EP (27"D.) or VIH36-EP (30"D.)–36"wide island hood
- VRHI420-EP (27"D.) or VIH42-EP (30"D.)–42"wide island hood
- VRHI540-EP (27"D.) or VIH54-EP (30"D.)–54"wide island hood
- VEPV900-RCK–900 CFM exterior power ventilator

9" HIGH INTERIOR POWER

- VRHW3019–30"wide, 21"deep wall hood
- VRHW3619–36"wide, 21"deep wall hood

VERSAVENT REAR DOWNDRAFT MODELS

- VIPR100–30" wide rear intake
- VIPR160–36" wide rear intake
- VIPR180–48" wide rear intake
- VPIV1600–600 CFM interior power ventilator
- VPEV1900–900 CFM exterior power ventilator

VENTILATION SYSTEMS ACCESSORIES AND OPTIONS

- Duct covers in nine finishes
- Backsplashes (wall hoods)
- Warming shelf panels (wall hoods)
- Heat lamps (wall hoods)
- Rear light option (island hoods)
- Utensil rail/decorative trim
- Intake tops in black or white (downdraft)

▼ UNDERCOUNTER DISHWASHER

A heavy-duty unit with a stainless steel interior, the VUD140 offers sturdy commercial styling, energy-efficient design, and maximum cleaning power in one of the world's quietest dishwashers.

PROFESSIONAL FEATURES

- Sound absorbing double insulation on top, back, and both sides of tank and between inner and outer door panels
- Two motor/pump assemblies for energy-efficient operation
- Normal wash cycle uses only 5.3 gallons of water
- Multi-level wash system
- Choice of five cycles–Pots/Pans, Normal Wash, Light/China, Rinse/Hold, and PlateWarm
- Main wash and rinse cycle heated to 140° F. or Sani Cycle 165° F.
- Random loading in graphite nylon racks with no wasted space
- Two dual-level cup racks
- Large cutlery/silverware basket
- Surgical grade stainless steel tank and inner door

MODEL

- VUD140–undercounter dishwasher

ACCESSORIES

- Formed enamel/steel door and lower front panels in black or white
- 5" high lower panel in nine finishes
- 24" or 60 cm wide kickplates in black or white; 24" wide in black standard with dishwasher
- Tipguard bar for use when screws cannot anchor dishwasher

▼ HEAVY-DUTY FOOD WASTE DISPOSERS

Equipped with exclusive anti-jamming features, sound-absorbing insulation, and the most powerful motor found in a residential model, Viking waste disposers provide the most quiet, efficient operation available.

CHOICE OF BATCH FEED OR CONTINUOUS FEED OPERATION

- Batch feed models
  - Exclusive Reliastart™ Magnetic Start System with cover control; magnets in cover and on disposer repel to start motor
- Continuous feed models
  - Convenient wall switch start

STANDARD FEATURES

- One horsepower, instant start motor–the most powerful available in a residential disposer
- Automatic reversing breaks the jams that stop ordinary disposers
- Fixed, stainless steel blades provide quick, quiet grinding, and eliminate noise generated by ordinary swivel blades
- Approximately eight times the uppercuttings and 15 times the undercuttings of the nearest high-end competitor
- Sound-absorbing, grind area insulation
- Exclusive, virtually indestructible, cast-iron drain chamber

HEAVY-DUTY PLUS MODELS ALSO INCLUDE THE FOLLOWING PREMIUM FEATURES:

- Power Plus Jam-inator™ Button
  - Causes the grind wheel to oscillate 7,000 times per minute, pulverizing even the toughest jams
- Cast stainless steel grind wheel
- Full insulation surrounds unit for super-quiet operation

MODELS

- VCHW1000–continuous feed with grind area insulation
- VBHW1010–batch feed with grind area insulation
- VCFW1020–continuous feed with full insulation
- VBFW1030–batch feed with full insulation

▼ 18" WIDE HEAVY-DUTY TRASH COMPACTOR

The most powerful residential trash compactor available, the VUC180 is a handsome complement to any kitchen or home recycling center.

PROFESSIONAL FEATURES

- Reduces trash to one-fourth its original size in 35 seconds or less
- 1/2 horsepower motor is the most powerful available in a residential compactor
- Built-in small litter area allows loading of small items without opening large trash drawer
- 1.7 cubic foot trash drawer is the largest available; easily holds weekly trash of a family of four
- Break-away trash basket is easy to empty and clean
- Activated charcoal filter and fan eliminate odors

MODEL

- VUC180–undercounter compactor

ACCESSORY

- Undercounter to freestanding hardwood top/conversion kit

▼ FINISHES

- With the exception of the VersaVent Rear Downdraft and disposers, all Viking products are available in Black (BK), White (WH), Almond (AL), Stainless Steel (SS), Viking Blue (VB), Forest Green (FG), Burgundy (BU), Plum (PL), and Teal (TE). All finishes may be ordered with Brass Trim Option.

Viking Range Corporation
111 Front Street   Greenwood, Mississippi 38930 USA (601) 455-1200

 All gas appliances are AGA design-certified for residential installation

Specifications subject to change without notice.

 All electric appliances are UL design-certified for residential installation

© 1993, Viking Range Corporation

F1184B

(1293)

Unmistakably
KraftMaid.

This stunning Country English cabinet style is just one of KraftMaid's more than 50 outstanding door designs. Our rich wood and brilliant laminate cabinets in a distinct array of contemporary and traditional styles will enhance your kitchen beautifully. Optional features such as lazy susans, built-in pantries, mullion doors and classic crown molding add a personal touch. And KraftMaid quality means the assurance of cabinetry you will enjoy for many years to come.

Base Mixer Cabinet A mixer, toaster or any small appliance can be lifted to working height and easily retracted into its hideaway position without handling the appliance. A convenient rollout tray is located below to organize all the attachments.

Vertical Spice Drawers Spices, teas and other small items organize easily in these attractive drawers which require only 6" of width for installation.

Wall Open Easy Reach Display collectibles or often used items on these corner shelves, creating a beautiful accent for your kitchen. Arched fret provides distinctive detailing.

KraftMaid
Cabinetry Inc.

Middlefield, Ohio 44062
216/632-5333

WELLBORN CABINET, INC.

Elite Series

Founded in 1961, Wellborn Cabinet, Inc. produces high quality lines of stock cabinetry in a 750,000 square feet manufacturing facility employing 750 people. Wellborn is fully integrated, operating its own timber processing mill, dry kilns and state-of-the-art production equipment to craft fine kitchen and bath cabinetry. Cabinets are built on four levels of box construction- Elite, Premium, Deluxe and Advantage Series to satisfy every budget. Every facet of building Wellborn cabinets is accomplished in one facility helping to insure the highest quality craftsmanship in the industry.

Monaco
**Elite Series
Wall Cabinet Construction**

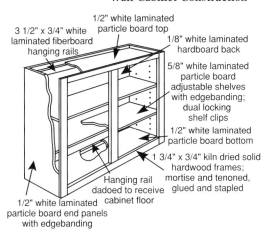

3 1/2" x 3/4" white laminated fiberboard hanging rails

1/2" white laminated particle board top

1/8" white laminated hardboard back

5/8" white laminated particle board adjustable shelves with edgebanding; dual locking shelf clips

1/2" white laminated particle board bottom

1 3/4" x 3/4" kiln dried solid hardwood frames; mortise and tenoned, glued and stapled

Hanging rail dadoed to receive cabinet floor

1/2" white laminated particle board end panels with edgebanding

**Elite Series
Base Cabinet Construction**

3 1/2" x 3/4" white laminated fiberboard hanging rails

Plastic corner braces stapled into sides and frame

1/8" white laminated hardboard back

5/8" white laminated particle board adjustable shelves with edgebanding; dual locking shelf clips

3 1/2" x 3/4" solid hardwood center mullion

1/2" white laminated particle board bottom (solid wood brace on 30" wide and larger cabinets)

Hanging rail dadoed to receive cabinet floor

1/2" white laminated particle board end panels

4 1/2" x 5/8" particle board toe board

1 3/4" x 3/4" kiln dried solid hardwood frames; mortise and tenoned, glued and stapled

Monaco and Sea Spray represent the Elite Series, both with full overlay designs and concealed hinges. Monaco is a white painted door featuring a Roman Arch design on wall cabinets and a square one-piece design on base cabinets. Sea Spray features a white therma foil door with a square profile. Both are made of fiberboard and have an all white interior.

Sea Spray

**Elite Series
Drawer Box
Construction**

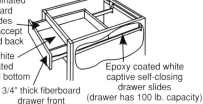

1/2" white laminated particle board drawer sides tenoned to accept sub-front and back

1/8" white laminated hardboard bottom

3/4" thick fiberboard drawer front

Epoxy coated white captive self-closing drawer slides (drawer has 100 lb. capacity)

Premium Series

Capri

OXFORD

Premium Series Wall Cabinet Construction

3 1/2" x 3/4" woodgrain laminated fiberboard hanging rails

1/2" woodgrain laminated particle board top

1/8" woodgrain laminated hardboard back

5/8" woodgrain laminated particle board adjustable shelves with edgebanding Dual locking shelf clips

1/2" woodgrain laminated particle board bottom

1 3/4" x 3/4" kiln dried solid cherry, oak, maple or hickory face frames; mortise and tenoned, glued and stapled

Hanging rail dadoed to receive cabinet floor

1/2" cherry, oak, maple or hickory finished wood veneer end panels

Premium Series Base Cabinet Construction

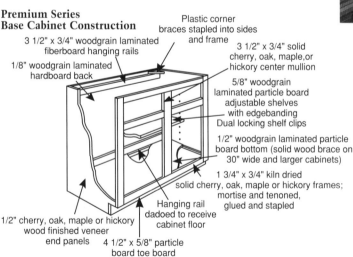

3 1/2" x 3/4" woodgrain laminated fiberboard hanging rails

1/8" woodgrain laminated hardboard back

Plastic corner braces stapled into sides and frame

3 1/2" x 3/4" solid cherry, oak, maple, or hickory center mullion

5/8" woodgrain laminated particle board adjustable shelves with edgebanding Dual locking shelf clips

1/2" woodgrain laminated particle board bottom (solid wood brace on 30" wide and larger cabinets)

1 3/4" x 3/4" kiln dried solid cherry, oak, maple or hickory frames; mortise and tenoned, glued and stapled

Hanging rail dadoed to receive cabinet floor

1/2" cherry, oak, maple or hickory wood finished veneer end panels

4 1/2" x 5/8" particle board toe board

Premium Series Drawer Box Construction

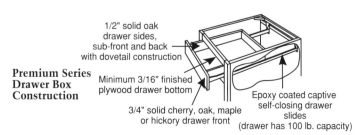

1/2" solid oak drawer sides, sub-front and back with dovetail construction

Minimum 3/16" finished plywood drawer bottom

3/4" solid cherry, oak, maple or hickory drawer front

Epoxy coated captive self-closing drawer slides (drawer has 100 lb. capacity)

Manor House Cherry

Wellborn offers 78 contemporary and traditional door styles in oak, maple, hickory and cherry with finish selections ranging from sparkling white to deep, rich burgundy. Over 70 accessory cabinets are available for modern convenience and efficient space planning. Wellborn has a semi-custom program featuring extended stiles, increased or decreased wall cabinet depths and full height base cabinet doors.

The Premium Series box construction is available on the following door styles:

Oak	Ashley Natural, Light, and Pickle
	Oxford Natural, Light, Medium, and Pickle
	Richland Cathedral Light and Medium
	Richland Square Light and Medium
Hickory	Cheyenne Natural and Medium
Maple	Capri Natural, Light, Pickle, and Burgundy
	Capri Arch Natural, Light, Pickle and Burgundy
Cherry	Manor House Cherry Light
	Mt. Vernon Cherry Dark
	Manor House Cherry Square Light
	Mt. Vernon Cherry Square Dark

Deluxe Series

Wellborn offers our customers Warehouse on Wheels, a quick delivery transportation program designed to meet delivery of 37 inventoried door styles on a 10-day work schedule. A nationwide cycle shipment program provides a tremendous advantage to our customers by eliminating warehousing costs and insuring on-time delivery of orders. Contact your nearest dealer for complete information.

The Deluxe Series box construction is available in these door styles:

Maple	Seville and Seville Arch Light and Pickle
	Essex Natural, Light, Pickle and Burgundy
	Rose Hall Cathedral Natural, Light, Pickle and Burgundy
	Rose Hall Natural, Light, Pickle, and Burgundy
Oak	Highland Natural, Light, Medium and Pickle
	Sierra and Sierra Arch Light and Pickle
	Waverly Cathedral Natural, Light, Medium and Pickle
	Waverly Natural, Light, Medium and Pickle
	Pioneer Cathedral Light, Medium and Pickle
	Pioneer Square Light, Medium and Pickle
	Shady Oak Light, Medium and Pickle
White Laminate	
	Continental with Light or Pickle Oak Pulls

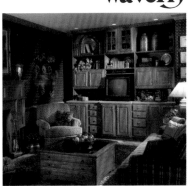

Waverly

Continental

Rose Hall

Sierra Arch

Deluxe Series Wall Cabinet Construction

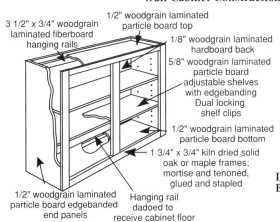

3 1/2" x 3/4" woodgrain laminated fiberboard hanging rails

1/2" woodgrain laminated particle board top

1/8" woodgrain laminated hardboard back

5/8" woodgrain laminated particle board adjustable shelves with edgebanding Dual locking shelf clips

1/2" woodgrain laminated particle board bottom

1 3/4" x 3/4" kiln dried solid oak or maple frames; mortise and tenoned, glued and stapled

1/2" woodgrain laminated particle board edgebanded end panels

Hanging rail dadoed to receive cabinet floor

Deluxe Series Drawer Box Construction

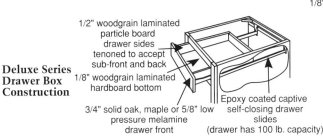

1/2" woodgrain laminated particle board drawer sides tenoned to accept sub-front and back

1/8" woodgrain laminated hardboard bottom

3/4" solid oak, maple or 5/8" low pressure melamine drawer front

Epoxy coated captive self-closing drawer slides (drawer has 100 lb. capacity)

Deluxe Series Base Cabinet Construction

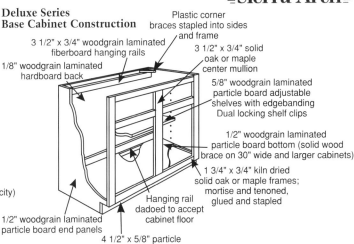

3 1/2" x 3/4" woodgrain laminated fiberboard hanging rails

1/8" woodgrain laminated hardboard back

Plastic corner braces stapled into sides and frame

3 1/2" x 3/4" solid oak or maple center mullion

5/8" woodgrain laminated particle board adjustable shelves with edgebanding Dual locking shelf clips

1/2" woodgrain laminated particle board bottom (solid wood brace on 30" wide and larger cabinets)

1 3/4" x 3/4" kiln dried solid oak or maple frames; mortise and tenoned, glued and stapled

1/2" woodgrain laminated particle board end panels

Hanging rail dadoed to accept cabinet floor

4 1/2" x 5/8" particle board toe board

Advantage Series

Advantage series offers two choices of wood in oak and maple. All doors are made with self-closing, fully adjustable hinges. Sheffield is available in light or medium oak and has a raised panel door. Oak Crest, with its flat panel center comes in light, medium, dark or pickle oak. Silverton and Bellemeade are made of maple and feature a flat center panel. Silverton is exclusively in pickle while Bellemeade is available in our burgundy finish.

With all the many styles and finish choices, Wellborn pleases the most discriminating tastes. Design with Wellborn and be assured of high quality, beautiful cabinetry.

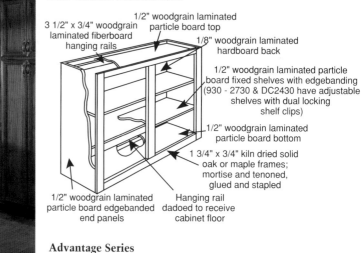

Advantage Series
Wall Cabinet Construction

Sheffield

3 1/2" x 3/4" woodgrain laminated fiberboard hanging rails

1/2" woodgrain laminated particle board top

1/8" woodgrain laminated hardboard back

1/2" woodgrain laminated particle board fixed shelves with edgebanding (930 - 2730 & DC2430 have adjustable shelves with dual locking shelf clips)

1/2" woodgrain laminated particle board bottom

1 3/4" x 3/4" kiln dried solid oak or maple frames; mortise and tenoned, glued and stapled

1/2" woodgrain laminated particle board edgebanded end panels

Hanging rail dadoed to receive cabinet floor

Advantage Series
Base Cabinet Construction

3 1/2" x 3/4" woodgrain laminated fiberboard hanging rails

1/8" woodgrain laminated hardboard back

Plastic corner braces stapled into sides and frame

3 1/2" x 3/4" solid oak or maple center mullion

1/2" woodgrain laminated particle board fixed shelves with edgebanding

1/2" woodgrain laminated particle board bottom (solid wood brace on 30" wide and larger cabinets)

1 3/4" x 3/4" kiln dried solid oak or maple frames; mortise and tenoned, glued and stapled

1/2" woodgrain laminated particle board end panels

Hanging rail dadoed to receive cabinet floor

4 1/2" x 5/8" particle board toe board

Oak Crest

Advantage Series
Drawer Box
Construction

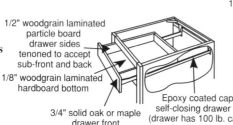

1/2" woodgrain laminated particle board drawer sides tenoned to accept sub-front and back

1/8" woodgrain laminated hardboard bottom

3/4" solid oak or maple drawer front

Epoxy coated captive self-closing drawer slides (drawer has 100 lb. capacity)

WELLBORN
People Who Care

Wellborn Cabinet, Inc.
P.O. Box 1210, Rt. 1, Hwy. 77S
Ashland, AL 36251
(205) 354-7151   Fax (205) 354-7022

It is characteristic of stained wood finishes, especially the pickle white-washed, to age over time when exposed to sunlight and general household chemicals. Due to this aging process, minor differences may develop with color match when replacing doors on existing cabinetry or adding additional cabinetry at a later date. Due to the natural characteristics of wood and the lithographic printing process, slight color variations may occur in the photos reproduced in this brochure. Consult your local Wellborn dealership for actual wood sample color selections.

B8652

SWANSTONE®
Solid Touch of Elegance

Swanstone is a revolutionary and thoroughly proven solid surface material that combines affordable luxury with durability and permanence. Because Swanstone is nonporous and uniformly solid, it is virtually impervious to stains, burns, scratches and gouges.

Kitchen & Bar Sinks

The luxurious appearance, durability, and convenience found in each of these sinks make them a surprisingly economical investment. Swanstone sinks are offered in six bowl styles for the kitchen and two for the bar.

Swanstone sinks are available in solid, aggregate, and galaxy colors. All kitchen and bar sinks are backed with a 10-year limited warranty.

Optional cutting boards, wire baskets, and drain grids are available in a variety of sizes and styles making each a practical and distictive addition to the Swanstone kitchen sink.

Triple Bowl
Model KSTB-4422
22" x 44"

SWANSTONE
**10 YEAR
LIMITED
WARRANTY**

patent pending

Single Bowl
Model KSSB-2522
22" x 25"

Large & Small Bowl
Model KSLS-3322
22" x 33"

Double Bowl
Model KSDB-3322
22" x 33"

**New
Double Bowl**
Model KSDB-3120
20" x 31"

**New
EuroStyle Bowl**
Model KSEU-3020
20" x 39 3/8"

Bar Sink
Model BS-1515
15" x 15"

Bar Sink
Model BS-2525
15" x 25"

SWANSTONE®

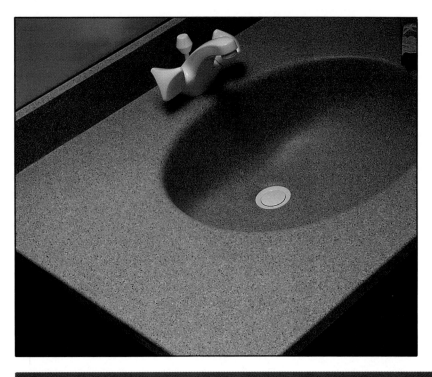

Vanity Tops & Bowls

Exclusively Swanstone, this line of one-piece, solid surface vanity lavatories will highlight any bath. Available in single, double, offset and Neo-Angle bowl models.

SWANSTONE BOWL SELECTIONS
POSITION OF BOWLS

Size	Center	Offset	Double Bowl	Neo Angle
17" x 19"	x	—	—	—
19" x 25"	x	—	—	—
19" x 31"	x	—	—	—
19" x 37"	x	—	—	—
22" x 25"	x	—	—	—
22" x 31"	x	—	—	—
22" x 37"	x	—	—	—
22" x 43"	x	—	—	—
22" x 49"	x	x	—	x
22" x 55"	x	x	—	—
22" x 61'	x	x	x	—
22" x 67"	—	x	—	—
22" x 68"	x	—	—	—
22" x 73"	x	x	—	—
22" x 85"	x	x	—	—

Custom Contrasts Vanity Tops & Bowls

Choose any color top and combine it with any color bowl for a custom look with either a smooth seam or overlap mounting treatment.

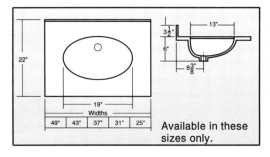

Available in these sizes only.

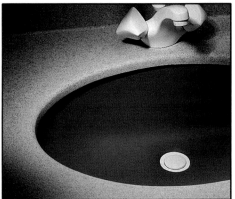

Bathtub & Shower Wall Panel System

The Swanstone bathtub and shower wall panel system allows the opportunity to create a totally luxurious environment. And Swanstone shower floors make an excellent companion to the Swanstone shower wall panels. Sizes are available to accommodate standard shower area applications.

Shower Floors

Designed to be used with Swanstone wall panel systems. Eight sizes are available to accommodate the more popular shower areas.

Color Selection

Solid Colors - White, Bone, Dove Gray, Shell Rose, Blue Mist
Aggregate Colors - Midnight Galaxy, Bermuda Sand, Gray Granite, Rose Granite, Country Blue Granite, Arctic Granite
Galaxy Colors - Mocha Galaxy, Almond Galaxy, Gray Galaxy, Rose Galaxy, Blue Galaxy, Jade Galaxy, Black Galaxy

The Swan Corporation
One City Centre
St. Louis, Missouri 63101
(314) 231-8148

SWANSTONE Patent
25 YEAR Pending
WARRANTY
AGAINST CRACKING Printed in USA

Form #540-12-93-50M

GROHE

for your family safety

Protect your family from accidental scalding in the shower or bath with a Grohmix Thermostat/Pressure Balance Valve...the ultimate in safety, comfort, luxury and quality.

Dial your water temperature just as you would the heat or air conditioning in your home... that simple...that worry-free.

Grohe manufactures an impressive collection of fine products for your kitchen and bath...affordable quality.

GROHE

C564
15445/GRP
BuyLine 7688

for your kitchen

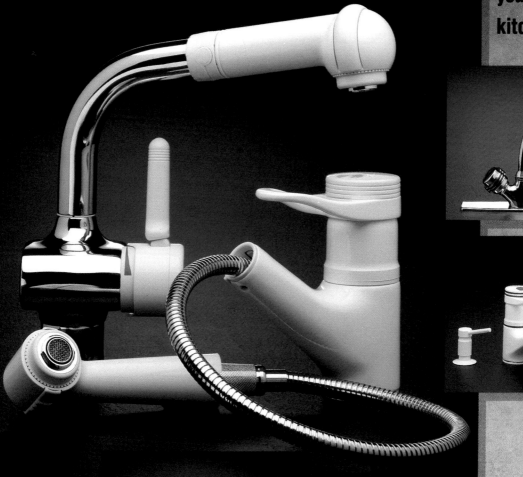

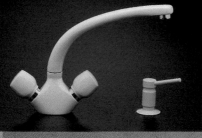

Grohe kitchen faucets... designed to fit your tastes, functional to fit your needs... available in a wide variety of combinations.

Color coordinated soap/lotion dispensers and side sprays are also offered.

Grohe manufactures an impressive collection of fine products for your kitchen and bath...affordable quality.

THE
NOBLESSE COLLECTION™

The Noblesse Collection by Grohe ... for those with
discerning taste who appreciate fine quality, superior
craftsmanship and distinctive design.

Grohe's Noblesse Collection of faucets and matching
accessories is an elegant extension of our European-styled
affordable quality product lines. The Noblesse Collection
is available in chrome, white, polished brass,
chrome/gold and white/gold.

Grohe ... Internationally recognized as the
standard of excellence.

Write or call for Grohe's complete
product literature file.

Grohe America, Inc.
Subsidiary of Friedrich Grohe AG, Germany
241 Covington Drive
Bloomingdale, IL 60108
708-582-7711 Fax: 708-582-7722

© 1993 Grohe America, Inc.

Printed in the U.S.A.

REPRESENTED EXCLUSIVELY BY

6687, JIMMY CARTER BLVD.   NORCROSS, GEORGIA 30071   PHONE 404/416–6224 FAX 404/416–6239

DORN BRACHT

OBINA

SIEGER DESIGN

Design with soul, style avowing individuality.
A total of six different finishes and a choice
of four lever shapes which can be individually
combined. A Sieger Design innovation – for
the installation of the unique bathroom
experience.

TARA

SIEGER DESIGN

Reduction to essentials. Quality of materials
and function of form – measures of the highest
quality. An archetypal design in persuasive
simplicity – yet with a touch of extravagance.
By Sieger Design.

ment through geometry – creative polarity. Harmonious quintessence through perfect design: Edition Fino.

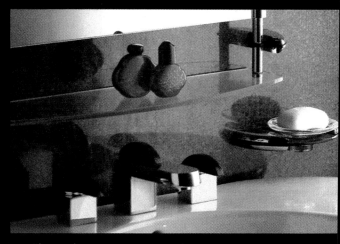

El círculo en oposición a la línea recta: tensión proporcionada por su geometría – polaridad creativa. La quintaesencia armónica de un diseño acabado: Edition Fino.

Il cerchio contro la linea retta: geometrie ricche di tensione, polarità creativa, la quintessenza armoniosa del perfetto design: Edition Fino.

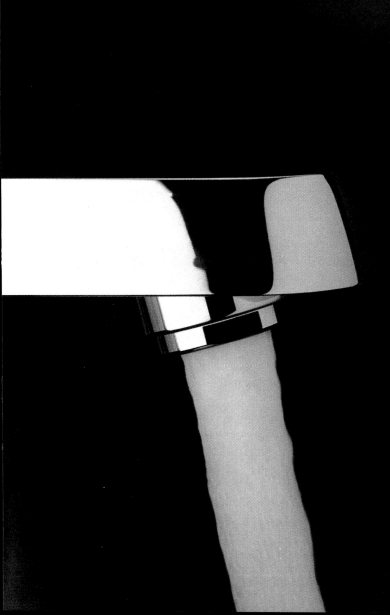

Design: Sieger Design.

Cones and cylinders are the basic elements. The styling is uncompromising and clear, the dialogue between design and function fascinating. Edition Point and its accessories – winner of many awards.

Conos y cilindros como elementos formales. Claridad intransigente del estilo. Fascinante es el diálogo entre el diseño y la función. La Edition Point y sus accesorios: reiteradamente premiado.

Il cono ed il cilindro come forme dominanti, lo styling dalle linee chiare, che non accettano compromessi. Affascinante dialogo tra design e funzionalità. Gli accessori dell'Edition Point: più volte premiate.

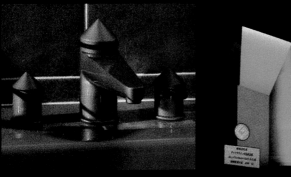

The only universal fitting: "Prize of Good Design", Japan Industrial Design Promotion Association. In the Collection of the Design Museum, London.

Como grifería única universal: «Prize of Good Design», Japan Industrial Design Promotion Asociation. Incluido en el museo de diseño de Londres.

Come unica rubinetteria a livello mondiale: «Prize of Good Design», Japan Industrial Design Promotion Association. Esposta al museo del design di Londra.

Design: Sieger Design.

The Modern Classic. Fittings and accessories in perfect harmony. Excitingly clear styling, made precious by selected high-quality finishes. No other fitting has achieved such wide acclaim, neither nationally nor internationally.

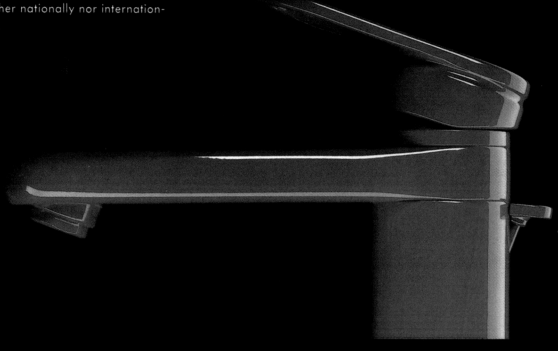

El clásico moderno. Griferías y accesorios en perfecta armonización. Estilo emocionantemente diáfano. Ennoblecido por medio de superficies de una primera calidad exquisita. Ninguna otra grifería fue tan galardonada tanto a nivel nacional como internacional.

Il classico moderno. Le rubinetterie e gli accessori in perfetta sintonia. Lo styling chiaro ed eccitante, impreziosito dalle superfici di alta qualità. Nessun'altra rubinetteria è stata così spesso premiata a livello nazionale ed internazionale.

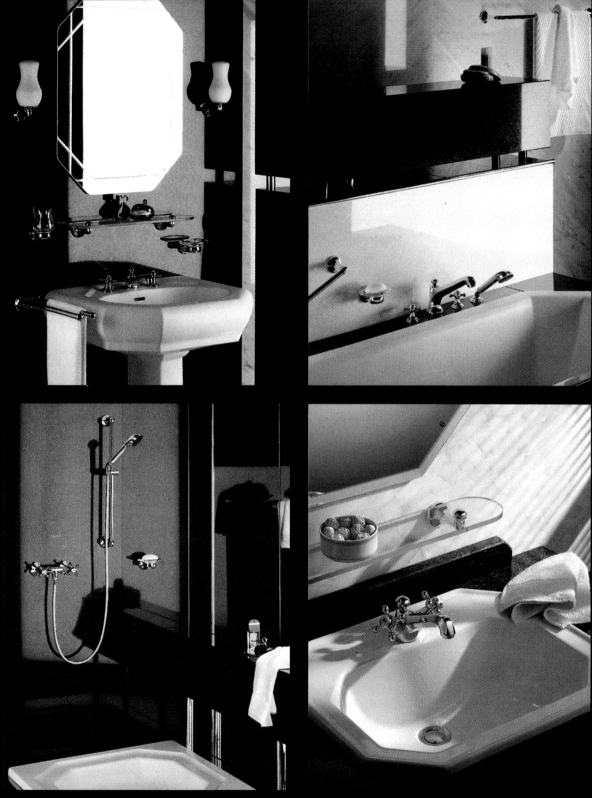

The original set of fittings and its accessories, nostalgic design at the peak of technical perfection. Cross-head handles with porcelain inlays, angular-section outlets, the finest surface finishes. For classical, luxurious bathroom design.

La grifería original y sus accesorios: diseño tradicional en armonía con la más alta perfección técnica. Tiradores en forma de cruz con placas insertadas de porcelana, salidas angulares, las superficies más nobles. Para un diseño del baño clásicamente lujoso.

La rubinetteria originale e i suoi accessori: design nostalgico abbinato a perfezione tecnica di altissimo livello. Le manopole a crociera con le piastrine di porcellana, i rubinetti a sezione angolare e le più pregiate superfici. Per un bagno classico e lussuoso.

The distinctive variant of our great classic. With its stylish lever handles and striking lever inlays, it can be combined in a whole range of beautiful, choice finishes. For the inimitable flair of elegance in your bathroom.

La distintiva variante de nuestro gran clásico. Con tiradores elevables llenos de estilo y relevantes piezas elevables que se combinan diversamente con superficies de una belleza selecta. Para un inimitable instinto de la elegancia en el baño.

La versione elegante del nostro grande classico. Manopole a leva di grande stile, attacchi delle leve dalla forma marcata, abbinabili a combinazioni ricche di contrasti con superfici bellissime. Per un inimitabile tocco d'eleganza nel bagno.

Chic, charming and versatile as no other: six fitting surface finishes of the highest quality, nine types of ring in nine fine finishes. For maximum scope in your individual bathroom design.

Chic, encantadora y variada como ninguna otra: seis superficies de grifería de alta calidad, nueve tipos de anillos en nueve superficies nobles. Para una máxima en cuanto al diseño de un baño individual.

Chic, affascinante e versatile come nessun altro: sei superfici per rubinetterie e nove tipi individuali di anelli con nove superfici diverse in materiale pregiato. Per il massimo d'individualità nel bagno.

Perfectly beautiful bathroom design: graceful the elegance of its lines, exclusive the surface finishes, individual the rings. The fittings and accessories a perfect match.

Diseño de baño de alta perfección y belleza: la elegancia que se desprende sus líneas, exclusivas las superficies, individuales los anillos. Perfecta la armonización de grifería y accessorios.

Creazione di alta perfezione e bellezza: eleganza fluida delle linee, esclusive le superfici con gli individuali tipi di anelli. In splendida armonia le rubinetterie con gli accessori.

EDITION COSMOS

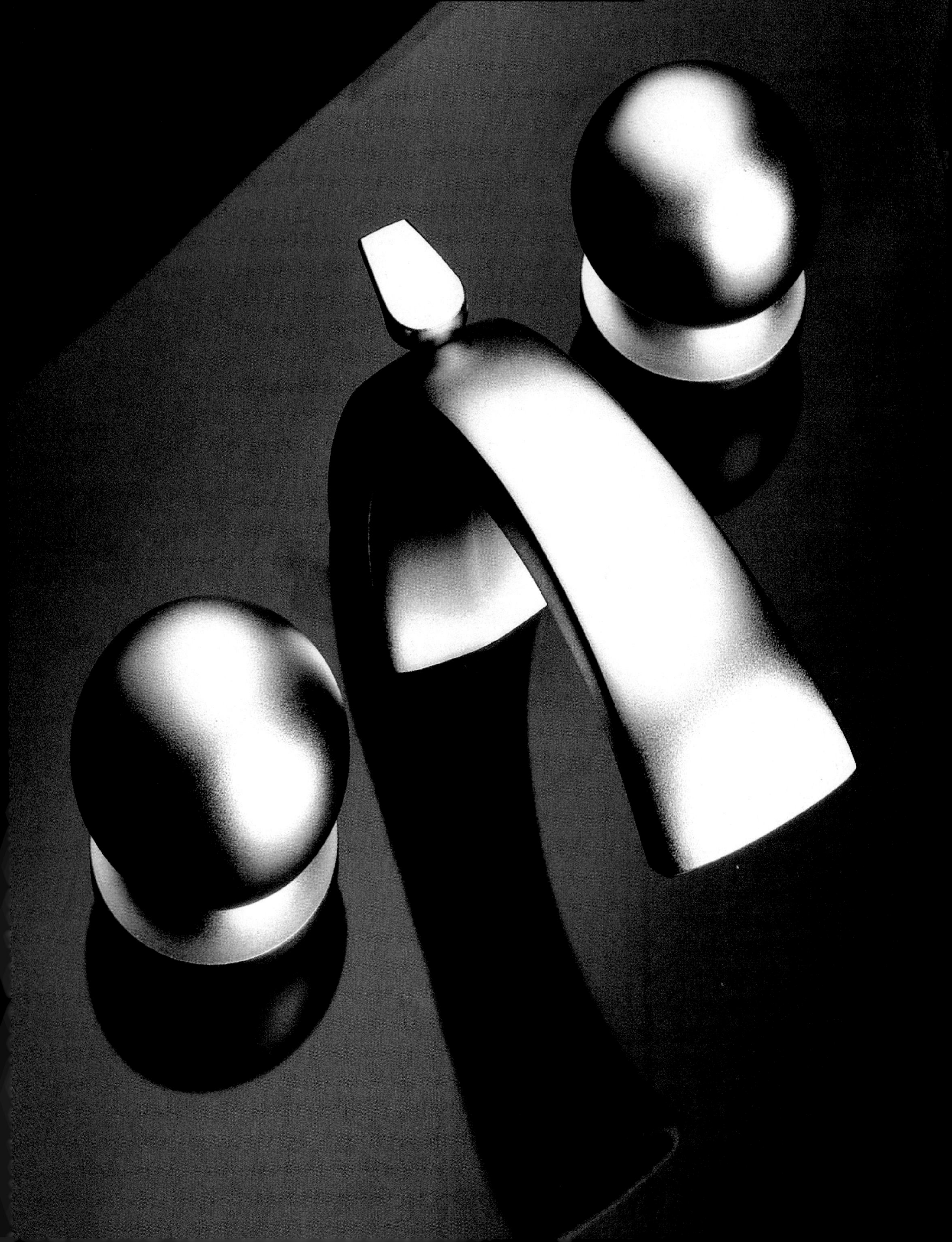

A futuristic, sensuous atmosphere for your bathroom: spherical handles, clear colors, gleaming finishes on the finest materials. Fittings and accessories – for visionary bathroom design.

Atmósfera del baño sensualmente futurista: tiradores de forma esférica, colores claros, superficies resplandecientes llevadas a cabo con materiales de alta calidad. Grifería y accesorios – para un diseño visionario del baño.

Per una atmosfera futuristica e sensuale nel bagno: le manopole sferiche, i colori chiari, le superfici splendenti di materiali pregiati. La rubinetteria e gli accessori per una creazione visionaria del bagno.

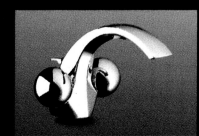

Our classic: dynamic expressiveness of design, appealing contrasts, flowing forms and square handles. Whether gold-plated or chrome, the aristocratic finishes make both fittings and accessories gems of exclusive bathroom furnishing.

Nuestro clásico: expresión de formas dinámicas, contrastes atractivos, formas fluidas y tiradores cuadrangulares. Dorado o cromado – superficies nobles hacen de la grifería y de los accesorios las piezas maestras de un diseño del baño exclusivo.

Il classico: linguaggio dinamico delle forme, contrasti affascinanti, forme fluenti e impugnature rettangolari. Le nobili superfici dorate che chromate fanno delle rubinetterie e degli accessori pezzi pregiati di un bagno dallo stile esclusivo e raffinato.

Classical elegance of timeless beauty. Harmonious lines, stylistic contrasts, exquisit surfaces. Perfekt the matching of fittings and accessories.

Elegancia clásica de una belleza intemporal. Armoniosa la configuración de sus lineas, de un estilo refinado los contrastes, noblemente bellas las superficies. Perfecta la armonización entre la griferia y los accesorios.

Classica eleganza, bellezza senza tempo, armoniose linee, contrasti pieni di stile, finiture scelte. Perfetto abbinamento di rubinetterie e accessori.

Thrilling elegance, daring dynamics: shining dolphin backs that create a lively atmosphere in the bathroom, consistent how the fittings and accessories match, how noble the surfaces are.

Elegancia cargada de tensión, dinámica audaz: los resplandecientes dorsos de los defines aportan al baño un ambiente lleno de vida. Consecuente la armonización entre la grifería y los accesorios, nobles las superficies.

Eleganza ricca di tensione, ardite dinamiche: dorsi scintillanti di delfini donano al bagno un atmosfera di allegra vivacità. Coerente abbinamento di rubinetterie e accessori. Finiture nobili.

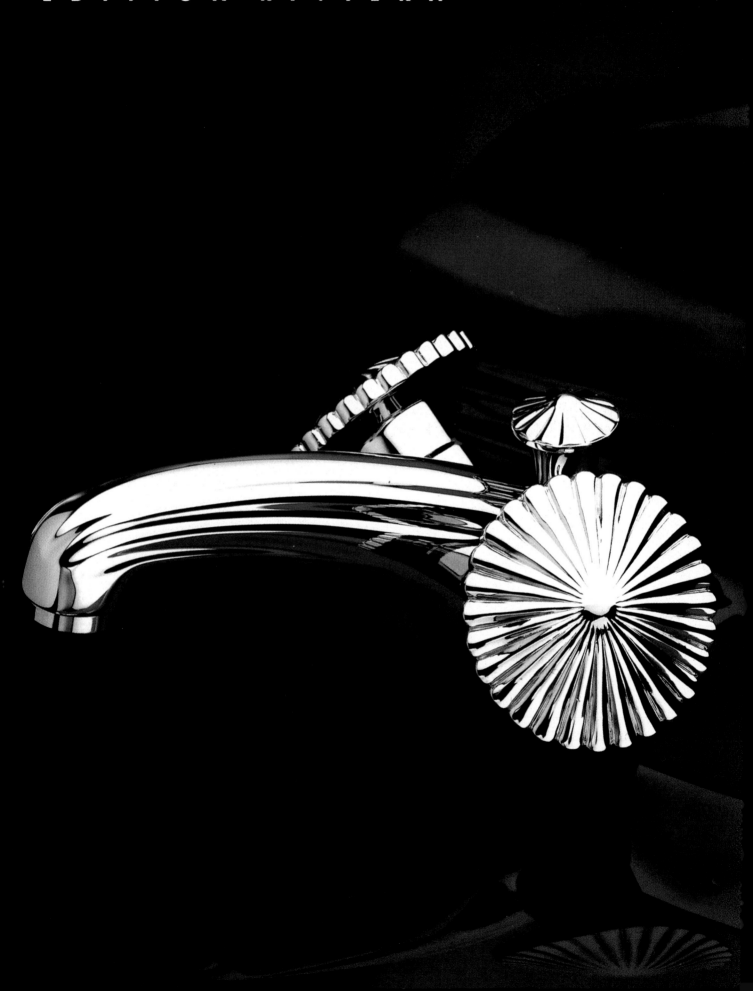

The Mediterranean slant to the bathroom environment. Fittings and accessories in elegant forms, floral design and precious finishes. A sheer delight to the eye.

El ambiente del baño del estilo mediterráneo: grifería y accesorios en formas elegantes, diseño floral y superficies suntuosas. Una delicia óptica.

Un ambiente da bagno mediterraneo: la rubinetteria e gli accessori in eleganti forme dal design floreale e le superfici preziose. Un vero piacere per gli occhi.

EDITION PRINCESSE/ROYAL

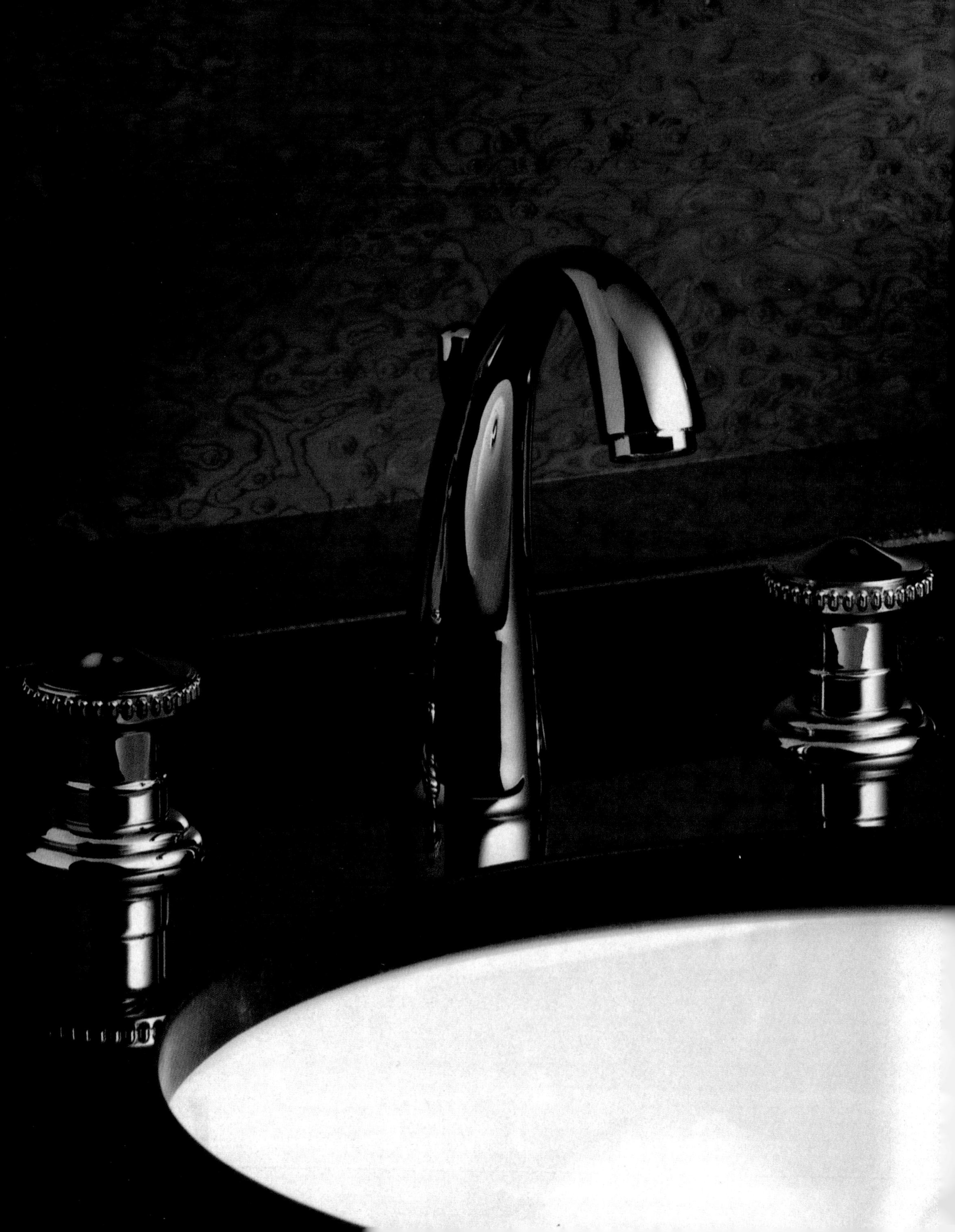

Princely bathroom design down to the finest detail. Whether is be the graceful curves of the outlets, the ring of beading on the handles or the very finest surface finishes, these fittings and accessories make a gem of your bath.

Un diseño de baño principesco hasta en el más refinado de los detalles: Tanto las salidas graciosamente arqueadas, los tiradores embellecidos a modo de corona de guirnaldas como las superficies más nobles – grifería y accesorios transforman el baño en una alhaja.

Un design per il bagno principesco fino nei minimi dettagli: i rubinetti dalle forme morbide ed arcuate, le manopole ornate di una corona di perle oppure le superfici pregiatissime. La rubinetteria e gli accessori fanno del bagno un vero gioiello.

ALOYS F. DORNBRACHT GMBH & CO. KG ARMATURENFABRIK → KÖBBINGSER MÜHLE 6   D-58640 ISERLOHN   ⊠ POSTFACH 14 54   D-58584 ISERLOHN
⊞ AM GROSSEN TEICH 29   D-58640 ISERLOHN   GERMANY   TELEFON 0 23 71- 433-0   TELEX 827780 ADIA D   TELEFAX 0 23 71- 433 132

REPRESENTED EXCLUSIVELY BY

6687, JIMMY CARTER BLVD.   NORCROSS, GEORGIA 30071   PHONE 404/416–6224 FAX 404/416–6239

"Our pride in this collection is passionate. The quality and value have never been higher."

Remo Jacuzzi

THE FIRST FAMILY OF LUXURY BATHING.

Behind Every JASON® Product Stands A Jacuzzi

Foreground: Remo Jacuzzi, President. Standing from left to right: Remo V. Jacuzzi, Vice President of Engineering; Paulo Jacuzzi, Technical Service; Jennifer Jacuzzi Peregrin, Vice President of Finance.

Our family name, Jacuzzi, has come to mean more than kinship. It began in 1915 when my father and his six brothers formed a business called Jacuzzi Brothers, Inc. But in the 1950s my family name became a household word when my uncle, Candido, invented the whirlpool bath.

For many years, I worked for the family business. Then in 1982, after all family members sold their respective interests in the business, I formed Jason International, Inc. Many experienced family members and employees have since joined us.

The first whirlpool baths were effective but primitive devices built solely for therapy.

Today, JASON whirlpool baths combine therapy with luxury and convenience to bring you the absolute state-of-the-art in whirlpool bathing. We've put complete, and incredibly quiet, operation at your fingertips. Our rich acrylic finishes are long lasting and so very easy to clean. Your back, indeed every part of your body, is considered in our designs. Integrated lumbar supports and armrests, recessed therapy jets...everything we do is designed to make your bathing experience more soothing and pleasurable. The new JASON collection within these pages is a testament of how far we've come.

We appreciate this opportunity to tell you about our heritage and our products - and for making us the first family of luxury bathing.

Remo Jacuzzi
President
JASON International, Inc.

2

THE CASARSA™

The Perfect Circle

Our newest bath of the Signature Series - and one of our most exciting. The CASARSA is named after Casarsa, Italy, site of the ancestral home built by Remo Jacuzzi's grandfather, Giovanni Jacuzzi. The circular shape makes this bath ideal for installation in a corner, platform, or island setting. There's ample room for two and a choice of four bathing positions, each with lumbar support. For the greatest relaxation, there are six therapy jets including two recessed Ultrassage™ back jets and two recessed opposing end jets. So a simultaneous back and foot massage can be enjoyed by both you and your bathing partner. As in all Signature Series baths, two silent air controls allow whisper-quiet operation. And the JASON digital control puts complete state-of-the-art whirlpool operation at your fingertips while you bathe in luxury.

CASARSA™

Full selection of colors with complementing fittings. Lumbar supports and armrests. One hp pump (120V, 20A). JASON digital control with programmable timer. Low water level and temperature sensors. Six therapy jets including two recessed Ultrassage™ back jets and two recessed opposing end jets. Two silent air controls. Textured floor. Shown in large photo with optional metal trim kit and two Double Cascade Spout® & faucet sets in bright brass. See page 23 for other options. Individually factory tested, IAPMO and UL listed.

├── 72" (183 cm) diameter ──┤

height: 23" (58 cm)

Roman Goddess of Flowers

We named this bath the FLORA because it is internally shaped like the cup of a flower. And because it exudes a warm and gracious feeling like Remo Jacuzzi's sister, Flora. Designed for corner placement, the dimensions of the FLORA provide generous space for two. To ensure the greatest relaxation, there are six therapy jets including a recessed Ultrassage™ back jet and a recessed opposing end jet. Thus, you can enjoy a soothing lower back and foot massage at the same time. Two silent air controls bring life to a whisper. And, as in all Signature Series baths, the JASON digital control puts complete whirlpool operation at your fingertips. Could life be better?

FLORA™

Full selection of colors with complementing fittings. Lumbar supports. One hp pump (120V, 20A). JASON digital control with programmable timer. Low water level and temperature sensors. Six therapy jets including a recessed Ultrassage™ back jet and a recessed opposing end jet. Two silent air controls. Textured floor. Shown in large photo with optional metal trim kit and Double Cascade Spout® & faucet set in gold. See page 23 for other options. Individually factory tested, IAPMO and UL listed.

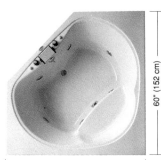

60" (152 cm)

60" (152 cm)

height: 20-1/2" (52 cm)

Ultimate Luxury Resort

Just off the coast of Venice and not far from the Jacuzzi ancestral home, lies la isola Lido, one of Europe's most fashionable and relaxing island resorts. And as one of our most fashionable and relaxing baths, we have named this the LIDO. This bath features five therapy jets including a recessed Ultrassage™ jet to provide you with a most soothing lower back massage. Also for your comfort are raised shoulder supports, armrests, and lumbar support. The JASON digital control puts complete whirlpool operation at your fingertips. Finally, two silent air controls let you calm the roar of the world.

LIDO™

Full selection of colors with complementing fittings. Lumbar support and armrests. One hp pump (120V, 20A). JASON digital control with programmable timer. Low water level and temperature sensors. Five therapy jets including a recessed Ultrassage™ back jet. Two silent air controls. Textured floor. Shown in large photo with optional metal trim kit with grip handles, Double Cascade Spout® & faucet set, and hand held shower in bright brass. See page 23 for other options. Individually factory tested, IAPMO and UL listed.

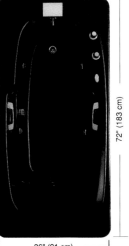

72" (183 cm)

36" (91 cm)

height: 20-1/2" (52 cm)

5

THE BON JOUR™

For A Good Day, Every Day

Here is yet another reason why JASON whirlpool baths are so esteemed. Elegant European styling with raised shoulders and sweeping armrests. The BON JOUR gives you room enough for two. The BON JOUR PETITE™ is a roomy, though more narrow bath, well-suited for remodeling installations. For the greatest relaxation, both baths feature six therapy jets including a recessed Ultrassage™ back jet and a recessed opposing end jet. You can enjoy a soothing lower back and foot massage at the same time. Two silent air controls. JASON digital control puts whirlpool operation at your fingertips. Should you start the day or end the day in the luxury of your JASON BON JOUR? Why not both?

BON JOUR™ & BON JOUR PETITE™

BON JOUR and BON JOUR PETITE are 42" and 36" wide, respectively. Full selection of colors with complementing fittings. Lumbar supports and armrests. One hp pump (120V, 20A). JASON digital control with programmable timer. Low water level and temperature sensors. Six therapy jets including a recessed Ultrassage™ back jet and a recessed opposing end jet. Two silent air controls. Textured floor. Shown in large photo with optional metal trim kit with grip handle, headrests, and Double Cascade Spout® & faucet set in gold. See page 23 for other options. Individually factory tested, IAPMO and UL listed.

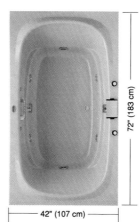

72" (183 cm)

42" (107 cm)

height: 20-1/2" (52 cm)

72" (183 cm)

36" (91 cm)

height: 20-1/2" (52 cm)

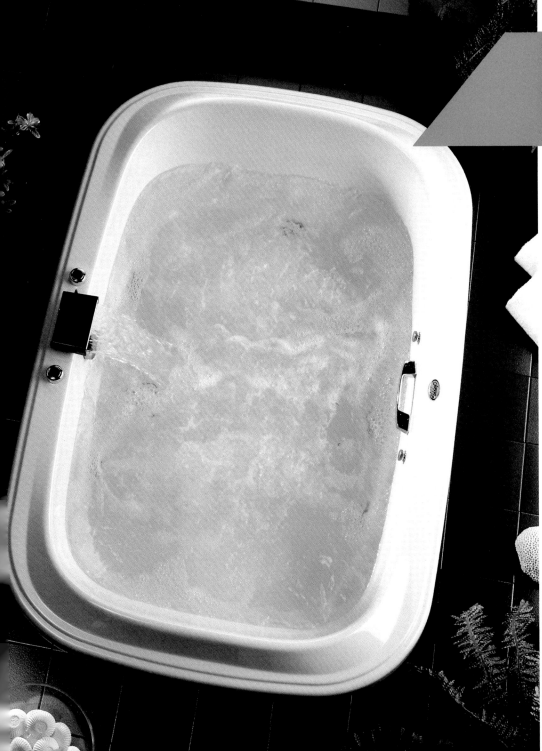

THE MIA™

Two Can Say "It's Mine"

In Italian, mia means "mine." And that might suggest to you that this is a personal-sized bath. But such is not the case, and we can explain. As in other Signature Series baths, the MIA provides you with a recessed Ultrassage™ back jet and a recessed opposing end jet for simultaneous back and foot massage. Yet, in the MIA, these jets are offset from the center so that two of you can relax with a back massage while stretching out in comfort to enjoy the MIA's full length and shoulder room. Not to mention all the Signature Series features. Such as JASON digital control and two silent air controls. So yes, mia means "mine." And in this case, it means "mine" for two.

MIA™

Full selection of colors with complementing fittings. Lumbar supports and armrests. One hp pump (120V, 20A). JASON digital control with programmable timer. Low water level and temperature sensors. Six therapy jets including a recessed Ultrassage™ back jet and a recessed opposing end jet, both offset from center. Two silent air controls. Textured floor. Shown in large photo with optional metal trim kit with grip handle, and Double Cascade Spout® & faucet set in bright brass. See page 23 for other options. Individually factory tested, IAPMO and UL listed.

72" (183 cm)

48" (122 cm)

height: 23" (58 cm)

THE ANGELICA™

As Spacious As The Heavens

One of our most spacious baths, the ANGELICA is as wide as many baths are long. And here is a bath to set your mind free. With two optional Double Cascade Spouts® flowing, it's easy to imagine yourself (and your partner) in a hot spring with twin waterfalls at your feet. Of the six therapy jets, there are two recessed Ultrassage™ back jets so that each of you can enjoy a most therapeutic lower back massage. Each of you can also enjoy a foot massage from the therapy jets at your feet. Shoulder supports, armrests, lumbar supports, silent air controls, and JASON digital control…the ANGELICA gives you all the features that set the standards for luxury bathing.

ANGELICA™

Full selection of colors with complementing fittings. Lumbar supports and armrests. One hp pump (120V, 20A). JASON digital control with programmable timer. Low water level and temperature sensors. Six therapy jets including two recessed Ultrassage™ back jets and two recessed opposing end jets. Two silent air controls. Textured floor. Shown in large photo with optional metal trim kit with grip handles, and two Double Cascade Spout® & faucet sets in gold. See page 23 for other options. Individually factory tested, IAPMO and UL listed.

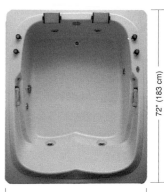

72" (183 cm)

60" (152 cm)

height: 20-1/2" (52 cm)

THE
MADELINE™

An Oval
In An Oval

Designed as an oval within an oval, it is a matter of style that makes the MADELINE so unique. The sculpted design brings comfort to your shoulders while the lumbar support brings relaxation to your back. Six therapy jets surround you with whirlpool action. Opposing, recessed end jets simultaneously provide you with soothing foot and back massage. There's even room for two. Also offered as a soaking bath without whirlpool features (see page 18).

MADELINE™

Full selection of colors with complementing fittings. Lumbar supports and armrests. 3/4 (.75) hp pump (120V, 20A). Variety of control options. Six therapy jets including two opposing recessed end jets. Two silent air controls. Textured floor. Shown in large photo with optional metal trim kit with grip handle, and Double Cascade Spout® & faucet set in bright brass. See page 23 for other options. Individually factory tested, IAPMO and UL listed.

72" (183 cm)

42" (107 cm)

height: 20-1/2" (52 cm)

High Sophistication Without A High Price

Brittany is a region of France and one of the most sophisticated areas of the world. We chose to name this bath the BRITTANY because of its sophisticated (and French influenced) design. We offer the BRITTANY in your choice of two sizes, the BRITTANY V and the BRITTANY VI. Both are spacious enough for two. Both feature a host of standard equipment such as built-in lumbar support and sweeping armrests. And both have recessed therapy jets at your back to comfortably massage you. In addition, the BRITTANY VI provides opposing recessed end jets for a most relaxing massage of your back and feet at the same time. Both baths are also offered as soaking baths without whirlpool features (see page 18).

BRITTANY™ V, VI

Full selection of colors with complementing fittings. Lumbar supports and armrests. 3/4 (.75) hp pump (120V, 20A). BRITTANY V has 60" length, five therapy jets (one recessed back jet). BRITTANY VI has 72" length, six therapy jets (two opposing recessed end jets). Both have two silent air controls, textured floor. Variety of control options. Shown in large photo with optional metal trim kit with grip handle, and Double Cascade Spout® & faucet set in polished chrome. See page 23 for other options. Individually factory tested, IAPMO and UL listed.

42" (107 cm)
height: 20-1/2" (52 cm)
60" (152 cm)

42" (107 cm)
height: 20-1/2" (52 cm)
72" (183 cm)

THE CANTO™

Song Of Joy

In Italy, a canto is a song. And singing is what you'll do when you experience the exceptional value in this fine bath. Because there are so many places to sit in the CANTO, each of the four therapy jets is recessed and located so that they can comfortably massage your back and feet at the same time. There's room for two, of course, and each of you can enjoy your own built-in lumbar support. Also offered as a soaking bath without whirlpool features (see page 18).

CANTO™

Full selection of colors with complementing fittings. Lumbar supports. 3/4 (.75) hp pump (120V, 20A). Four therapy jets, all recessed. Two silent air controls. Textured floor. Variety of control options. Shown in large photo with optional metal trim kit and Double Cascade Spout® & faucet set in bright brass. See page 23 for other options. Individually factory tested, IAPMO and UL listed.

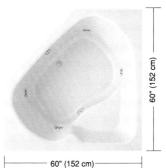

60" (152 cm)

60" (152 cm)

height: 20-1/2" (52 cm)

11

THE ASHLEY™

Extra Shoulder Room

A recent JASON design, the ASHLEY has become one of our most popular baths. It incorporates a bit more width for extra shoulder room. And it offers you recessed therapy jets on each end so you can enjoy simultaneous back and foot massage. Plus, these jets are offset from center so that two can stretch out in comfort and relaxation. Other superb JASON features remain – built-in lumbar supports and sweeping armrests.

ASHLEY™

Full selection of colors with complementing fittings. Lumbar supports and armrests. 3/4 (.75) hp pump (120V, 20A). Six therapy jets including two opposing recessed back jets. Two silent air controls. Textured floor. Variety of control options. Shown in large photo with optional metal trim kit with grip handle, and Double Cascade Spout® & faucet set in bright brass. See page 23 for other options. Individually factory tested, IAPMO and UL listed.

60" (152 cm)

48" (122 cm)

height: 20-1/2" (52 cm)

THE LORELLE™

Understated Spaciousness

The LORELLE is a spacious bath. Yet this quality seems understated in appearance if not in use. Here you'll find room that is sufficient for two. And, of course, JASON features to match. Lumbar support sweeps the entire width. And of the six therapy jets, two are recessed for a very comfortable back massage. Also offered as a soaking bath without whirlpool features (see page 18).

LORELLE™

Full selection of colors with complementing fittings. Lumbar support. 3/4 (.75) hp pump (120V, 20A). Six therapy jets including two recessed back jets. Two silent air controls. Variety of control options. Shown in large photo with optional metal trim kit with grip handles in polished chrome. See page 23 for other options. Individually factory tested, IAPMO and UL listed.

72" (183 cm)

48" (122 cm)

height: 20-1/2" (52 cm)

A Big Idea For Small Space

In Italy, nina means "little girl." Like a little girl, this little bath can bring you great joy. Its small dimensions (and price) make it ideal for replacing a conventional 5' bathtub with the lasting luxury of a JASON whirlpool bath. Yes, this bath is small, but it's hardly short on "big bath" features. Built-in lumbar support and gracefully flowing armrests. Five therapy jets, one of which is recessed for complete massage of your back. Two silent air controls for whisper quiet operation. Also offered as a soaking bath without whirlpool features (see page 18).

NINA™

Full selection of colors with complementing fittings. Lumbar support and armrests. 3/4 (.75) hp pump (120V, 20A). Five therapy jets including one recessed back jet. Two silent air controls. Textured floor. Variety of control options. Shown in large photo with optional metal trim kit with grip handles in polished chrome. See page 23 for other options. Individually factory tested, IAPMO and UL listed.

60" (152 cm)

32" (81 cm)

height: 20-1/2" (52

THE ENCORE™

As Big Or As Small As You Want

With the ENCORE, you can choose from three sizes to fit your needs and space. All are classically designed. All are of the quality you expect from JASON. And all offer you many features you don't expect at this price. Built-in armrests and lower back lumbar support. Five therapy jets for full whirlpool relaxation, one of which is positioned and recessed for soothing massage of your back. Two silent air controls for whisper quiet operation. The ENCORE V and VI are also offered as soaking baths without whirlpool features (see page 18).

ENCORE™ V, V-1/2, VI

ENCORE V, V-1/2, VI have 60", 66", and 72" lengths, respectively. Full selection of colors with complementing fittings. Lumbar support and armrests. 3/4 (.75) hp pump (120V, 20A). Five therapy jets including one recessed back jet. Two silent air controls. Textured floor. Variety of control options. Shown in large photo with optional metal trim kit with grip handles in bright brass. See page 23 for other options. Individually factory tested, IAPMO and UL listed.

60" (152 cm)

36" (91 cm)

height: 20-1/2" (52 cm)

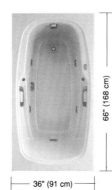

66" (168 cm)

36" (91 cm)

height: 20-1/2" (52 cm)

72" (183 cm)

36" (91 cm)

height: 20-1/2" (52 cm)

15

THE EMILY™

Our Most Adaptable Design

The special design of the EMILY, with its end-drain configuration and reduced length, allows a beautiful installation in a corner, wall, platform, or island setting. Though compact in overall dimensions, this bath will surprise you with its very large bathing well. Of the five therapy jets, one is recessed for a comfortable massage of your back. Two others are positioned for a soothing massage of your feet. One of our most distinctive baths, certainly our most adaptable of the Decorator Series. Also offered as a soaking bath without whirlpool features (see page 18).

EMILY™

Full selection of colors with complementing fittings. Lumbar support and armrests. 3/4 (.75) hp pump (120V, 20A). Variety of control options. Five therapy jets including one recessed back jet. Two silent air controls. Textured floor. Shown in large photo with optional trim kit with grip handle and Double Cascade® Spout in bright brass. See page 23 for other options. Individually factory tested, IAPMO and UL listed.

60" (152 cm)

42" (107 cm)

height: 20-1/2" (52 cm)

A Classic

Designed with a distinctive relief at its border, the LARA is a classic complement to any decor. A bounty of standard equipment includes a built-in lumbar support and two silent air controls. Once you decide this style bath is perfect for you, then your choice is one of two sizes. The LARA V is a personal-sized bath. The LARA VI provides extra length if you need it. Both baths are also offered as soaking baths without whirlpool features (see page 18).

LARA™ V, VI

LARA V and LARA VI are 60" and 72" long respectively. Full selection of colors with complementing fittings. Lumbar support. 3/4 (.75) hp pump (120V, 20A). Four therapy jets. Two silent air controls. Textured floor. Variety of control options. Shown in large photo with optional metal trim kit in polished chrome. See page 23 for other options. Individually factory tested, IAPMO and UL listed.

60" (152 cm)

├── 42" (107 cm) ──┤

height: 20-1/2" (52

SOAKING BATHS

The same construction quality and fine acrylic surfaces found in JASON whirlpool baths are also available in JASON traditional soaking baths without whirlpool features.

	MADELINE™	BRITTANY™ V, VI	CANTO™	LORELLE™	NINA™	ENCORE™ V, VI	EMILY™	LARA™ V, VI
CONSTRUCTION								
High gloss low maintenance fully pigmented acrylic surface.	S	S	S	S	S	S	S	S
Fiberglass reinforced structure.	S	S	S	S	S	S	S	S
Available in full color selection.	S	S	S	S	S	S	S	S
Leveling blocks.	S	S	S	S	S	S	S	S
Built-in lumbar support(s).	S	S	S	-	S	S	S	S
Built-in armrests.	S	S	-	-	S	S	S	-
Textured floor.	S	S	S	-	S	S	S	S
Integral tile-in lip.	-	O	O	-	-	-	-	-
ACCESSORIES								
Plated brass grip handle(s); polished chrome/bright brass/gold.	O	O	-	O	O	O	O	O
Powder coated brass grip handle(s); white/bone/quicksilver.	O	O	-	O	O	O	O	O
Metal overflow drain assembly; polished chrome/bright brass/gold.	O+	O+	O+	O+	O+	O+	O+	O+
Overflow drain kit; polished chrome/bright brass.	O+	O+	O+	O+	O+	O+	O+	O+
Hand held shower kit; polished chrome/bright brass/gold.	O+	O+	O+	O+	O+	O+	O+	O+
Removable headrest; white	O+	O+	O+	O+	O+	O+	O+	O+
Tile flange kit.	-	O	O	O	O	O	-	O
Lateral skirt.	-	O	-	O	O	O	-	O
For additional information, refer to page...	9	10	11	13	14	15	16	17

S = standard   O = optional   O+ = field installable option

NOTE: Soaking bath surfaces may subtly reveal the location where hydrotherapy fittings would be installed if the bath was constructed for whirlpool application. Field plumbing of a soaking bath to convert it to a whirlpool bath will void its warranty.

THE ALEXIA™
Combination Brazilian Shower/Bath

While living in Brazil, Remo Jacuzzi discovered the concept of combining a shower base and small bath into a single unit. Today, JASON offers you the ALEXIA as the embodiment of this concept. In a small space, the stylish ALEXIA provides a shower base, a small bath, and even a seat.

48" (122 cm)

36" (91 cm)

height: 12" (30 cm)

Molded seat. Left or right hand drain. Textured bottom. Tile-in lip on three sides. Shown in large photo with optional tempered glass enclosure. Overlfow drain kit, optional.

SHOWER BASES

Even with all the pleasure that a JASON bath will give you, there are times when there's no time for anything but a quick shower. With a JASON acrylic shower base to complement your JASON acrylic bath, you can enhance the beauty of your bathroom and two can bathe at the same time.

All JASON shower base surfaces are made with thick, quality acrylic. Shower bases of lower quality and price rely on a gel coat surface, which is merely a form of paint. Acrylic looks better and lasts far longer. The finish is more lustrous and easier to clean. And with the wide selection of JASON sizes and configurations — plus, of course, all the rich colors — you're assured of a perfect match to your bath and bathroom alike.

MODEL	DEPTH	WIDTH	HEIGHT
SHOWER BATH...			
ALEXIA	36" (91 cm)	48" (122 cm)	12" (30 cm)
SINGLE THRESHOLD...			
S3232S	32" (81 cm)	32" (81 cm)	6-1/2" (17 cm)
S3448S	34 (86 cm)	48 (122 cm)	5-1/2 (14 cm)
S3636S	36 (91 cm)	36 (91 cm)	6-1/2 (17 cm)
S3648S	36 (91 cm)	48 (122 cm)	6-1/2 (17 cm)
DOUBLE THRESHOLD LEFT OPENING...			
S3232L	32" (81 cm)	33-1/2" (85 cm)	6-1/2" (17 cm)
S3636L	36 (91 cm)	37-1/2 (95 cm)	6-1/2 (17 cm)
S3648L	36 (91 cm)	49-1/2 (126 cm)	6-1/2 (17 cm)
DOUBLE THRESHOLD RIGHT OPENING...			
S3232R	32" (81 cm)	33-1/2" (85 cm)	6-1/2" (17 cm)
S3636R	36 (91 cm)	37-1/2 (95 cm)	6-1/2 (17 cm)
S3648R	36 (91 cm)	49-1/2 (126 cm)	6-1/2 (17 cm)
TRIPLE THRESHOLD CENTER OPENING...			
S3232T	32" (81 cm)	35" (89 cm)	6-1/2" (17 cm)
S3636T	36 (91 cm)	39 (99 cm)	6-1/2 (17 cm)
S3648T	36 (91 cm)	51 (130 cm)	6-1/2 (17 cm)
NEO-ANGLE...			
S3838N	38" (97 cm)	38" (97 cm)	6-1/2" (17 cm)
S4242N	42 (107 cm)	42 (107 cm)	5-1/2 (14 cm)

NEO-ANGLE

With a door opening to the center of the shower, our NEO-ANGLE shower base helps you make any bathroom corner more beautiful, or can even be installed along a straight wall. Tempered glass enclosure is optional.

QUALITY DETAILS

High gloss low maintenance fully pigmented acrylic surface	Standard
Fiberglass reinforced structure	Standard
Available in a full color selection	Standard
Textured bottom (except S3232)	Standard
Integral tile-in lip	Standard
Metal drain assembly; polished chrome.	Standard
Metal drain assembly; bright brass/gold.	Optional
Tempered glass enclosure kits, clear glass doors and panels; with anodized silver or gold finish closely resembling polished chrome or bright brass respectively.	Optional

NOTE: Above options must be field installed

SQUARE CORNERED SHOWER BASES
Single, Double, Or Triple Threshold

The single threshold shower base is designed for wall enclosure on three sides, with a door located on the remaining side.

Triple threshold model with optional shower base drain.

The double threshold shower base is designed for wall enclosure on two adjoining sides. The door opening is normally on the longer of the two remaining sides.

The triple threshold shower base is designed for wall enclosure on one side, with a door located opposite the wall.

Glass enclosure kits are optional. Door openings may be either right or left hand.

A metal drain assembly with polished chrome trim is standard. Bright brass or gold trim is optional.

While some baths are designed to simply look good, JASON baths are designed to feel good as well. JASON combines enduring aesthetics with baths of high therapeutic value. This is a noteworthy distinction between JASON whirlpool baths and competitive products.

Our overall goal is to provide you with a luxurious bath of soothing, therapeutic comfort. Many unique design details* aid us in this goal.

• Built-in lumbar supports and recessed back jets for comfortable support and massage of your lower back.

• Opposing end jets for simultaneous massage of your back and feet.

• Ultrassage™ therapy jets for the deepest, most therapeutic whirlpool massage. This feature is standard in Signature Series baths, optional in most Decorator Series baths.

• Built-in armrests for greater relaxation.

• Bathing wells that are spacious relative to the outside bath perimeter. This allows greater comfort, even in our smaller baths.

Trust The Quality

Besides the details mentioned above, each JASON bath is appointed with other standard features that you'll long appreciate. Rich, deep acrylic colors for lasting beauty. Three layers of fiberglass reinforcement for high strength and rigidity. Self-draining pumps and plumbing for better sanitation. Directionally adjustable jets, specially designed to never freeze in place. Quality fittings and components for years and years of reliable service.

The pump has a run-dry seal for protection if accidentally run without water. Every whirlpool bath is factory tested to assure that everything works exactly as it should. Every whirlpool bath arrives pre-leveled on an exclusive, fully supporting thermoformed base for a simple and solid installation.

The Signature Series

Signature Series designs represent the state-of-the-art in whirlpool bathing. Each Signature Series bath has a more powerful one hp whirlpool pump. Whirlpool operation is programmable and at your fingertips with the JASON digital control. A low water level sensor helps protect your bath and your bathroom. A temperature sensor aids your comfort by monitoring the water temperature of your bath. All are standard Signature Series features.

Many luxury options are available only in our Signature Series baths. A bather-operated heater, for example, can be incorporated into the JASON digital control — allowing you to set and maintain your desired water temperature. The digital control itself is available in six-speed version so you can select your favorite whirlpool action.

Options For All JASON Whirlpool Baths

For both Signature and Decorator Series models, there are many options which help you transform your bath into a very personal luxury.

To determine the standard and optional equipment for each bath, refer to the chart on page 23. Some options are pictured here.

With the help of your JASON dealer, and your imagination, your JASON bath can be equipped just about any way you want.

Programmable JASON Digital Control.
On Signature Series baths, a one-speed digital control is standard and a six-speed digital control is optional. With either, a button at your fingertips lets you set the desired whirlpool time. Then, while you bathe, a digital display informs you of the remaining whirlpool time and the water temperature. With the optional in-line heater, a separate button lets you set and maintain the desired water temperature.

JASON Touch Control.
Optional on all JASON whirlpool baths. The whirlpool "touch" control button is incorporated into the JASON emblem affixed to the bath. Includes a built-in 20-minute timer and protective sensor that shuts off pump if water level is too low. Choose either one-speed or three-speed version.

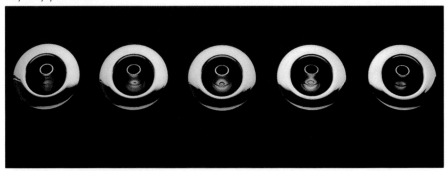

Metal trim package colors
To complement other bathroom fixtures, choose from a variety of metal trim options in either polished chrome, bright brass, or gold finish. Components vary slightly from model to model. Photo shows available escutcheon and jet nozzle combinations. Luxury kits include plated brass jet nozzles to replace standard color-coordinated jet nozzles. Attractive, two-color trim packages are also available. Choose either "polished chrome dominant" or "bright brass dominant" colors. Jet escutcheons and grip handles are provided in the dominant color, with air control knobs and jet nozzles in the highlight color. It is suggested that other bath options be selected in the dominant color.

* Some design details are not available on some models.

& LUXURY

JASON Double Cascade Spout® & faucet set.
Elegantly restyled for 1992, this patented spout is an example of the JASON knack for combining technology and luxury. A beautiful option for most JASON whirlpool baths. Used to fill bath and/or provide aesthetic recirculation of water. Metal finished in polished chrome, bright brass, or gold. Also available in white, bone, and quicksilver powder-coated finishes.

JASON Ultrassage™ Jet.
Standard on Signature Series baths, optional on most others. Jet orifice rotates for deeper, soothing, therapeutic massage over your entire back. Color coordinated assembly. Escutcheon optionally available in polished chrome, bright brass, or gold.

Metal grip handles.
An attractive and useful option. Available for most models. Choose polished chrome, bright brass, or gold plated finish; white, natural bone, or quicksilver powder-coated finishes.

Removable headrests.
Two beautiful models to add comfort on your JASON bath. HR100 raised shoulder contoured model (black only) fits all Signature Series baths except FLORA. HR200 Ultrasoft universal model (white only) fits all JASON baths.

Hand held shower.
A luxury option for all models. Mounts at deck. Provided with extension hose. Facilitates bath cleaning. Choose polished chrome, bright brass, or gold.

Underwater light with mood lenses.
Sets the perfect mood for luxury bathing. Available as an option on all whirlpool models. 12V.

COLORS THAT GLOW WITH QUALITY

With JASON, you're assured of acrylic colors that are rich, deep, and lasting. Care is easy, too. Just wipe with a soft cloth and the finish will return to a high-gloss shine. And just look at the color selection JASON offers you.

Basic Colors

Classic White 001(WT)   **Quicksilver 007(QS)**   **Natural Bone 017(NB)**

Standard Colors

Morning Blue 011(GB)   **Rose 012(RS)**   **Smoke Grey 014(SG)**   **Blush 016(SH)**   **Coral Shell 018(CS)**

Ice Blue 019(IB)   **Rouge 021(RG)**   **Sea Green 022(SN)**   **Peach 027(PH)**   **Rose Bloom 029(RB)**

Classic Beige 031(CB)   **Almond Bone 036(AB)**   **Glacier Grey 038(GG)**   **Bisquite 040(BQ)**

High Fashion Colors

Raspberry 013(RP)   **Black 015(BK)**   **Ruby Red 020(RY)**   **Navy Blue 025(NY)**   **Teal Green 026(TL)**

Style Grey 028(EG)   **Tawny Brown 033(TB)**   **Verde Green 035(VE)**

Unless optional metal fittings are specified, baths are shipped with fittings of complementary color. This color chart should be used as a preliminary reference only. Due to printing process, exact colors may vary from those presented here. To determine exact color, refer to your JASON dealer for an acrylic sample.

BATH FEATURES, OPTIONS & ACCESSORIES

	SIGNATURE SERIES							DECORATOR SERIES								
	CASARSA™	FLORA™	LIDO™	BON JOUR™	BON JOUR PETITE™	MIA™	ANGELICA™	MADELINE™	BRITTANY™ V, VI	CANTO™	ASHLEY™	LORELLE™	NINA™	ENCORE™ V, V-1/2, VI	EMILY™	LARA™ V, VI
CONSTRUCTION:																
High gloss low maintenance fully pigmented acrylic surface.	S	S	S	S	S	S	S	S	S	S	S	S	S	S	S	S
Fiberglass reinforced structure.	S	S	S	S	S	S	S	S	S	S	S	S	S	S	S	S
Pre-leveled thermoformed full-support base.	S	S	S	S	S	S	S	S	S	S	S	S	S	S	S	S
Available in a full color selection.	S	S	S	S	S	S	S	S	S	S	S	S	S	S	S	S
Color coordinated high fashion suction, jet & air fittings.	S	S	S	S	S	S	S	S	S	S	S	S	S	S	S	S
Individually factory assembled & tested to exacting standards.	S	S	S	S	S	S	S	S	S	S	S	S	S	S	S	S
Built-in lower back lumbar support(s).	S	S	S	S	S	S	S	S	S	S	S	S	S	S	S	S
Built-in armrests.	S	—	S	S	S	S	S	S	S	—	S	—	S	S	S	—
Textured floor.	S	S	S	S	S	S	S	S	S	—	S	S	S	S	S	S
Integral tile-in lip.	—	O	—	—	—	—	—	—	O	O	—	—	—	O	—	—
Factory plumbed for Double Cascade Spout® & faucet set.	S	S	S	S	S	S	S	S	S	S	S	—	—	—	S	—
PUMP and BATH CONTROLS:																
3/4 hp single-speed pump and 30-minute wall timer.	—	—	—	—	—	—	—	S	S	S	S	S	S	S	S	S
3/4 hp single-speed pump and air switch with 10-minute timer.	—	—	—	—	—	—	—	O	O	O	O	O	O	O	O	O
3/4 hp single-speed pump and electronic touch control with 20-minute timer & low water level sensor.	—	—	—	—	—	—	—	O	O	O	O	O	O	O	O	O
3/4 hp three-speed pump and electronic touch control with 20-minute timer & low water level sensor.	—	—	—	—	—	—	—	O	O	O	O	O	O	O	O	O
1 hp single-speed pump, digital control with programmable timer, low water level and temperature sensors.	S	S	S	S	S	S	S	—	—	—	—	—	—	—	—	—
1 hp six-speed pump, digital control with programmable timer, low water level and temperature sensors	O	O	O	O	O	O	O	—	—	—	—	—	—	—	—	—
1 hp three-speed pump and electronic touch control with 20-minute timer & low water level sensor.	O	O	O	O	O	O	O	—	—	—	—	—	—	—	—	—
1 hp one-speed pump and electronic touch control with 20-minute timer & low water level sensor.	O	O	O	O	O	O	O	—	—	—	—	—	—	—	—	—
In-line bath heater, 1.5 kw/120V, (temp settings programmable with digital controls above).	O	O	O	O	O	O	O	O	O	O	O	O	O	O	O	O
HYDROTHERAPY SYSTEM:																
Full size JASON directionally adjustable jets for more gentle massage.	S	S	S	S	S	S	S	S	S	S	S	S	S	S	S	S
Super quiet JASON air volume controls for optimal relaxation.	S	S	S	S	S	S	S	S	S	S	S	S	S	S	S	S
IAPMO & UL listed JASON hi-flow suction fitting protects bather.	S	S	S	S	S	S	S	S	S	S	S	S	S	S	S	S
Rigid PVC plumbing to ensure self-draining and hygienic operation.	S	S	S	S	S	S	S	S	S	S	S	S	S	S	S	S
Recessed back jet(s) for more comfortable hydrotherapy.	S	S	S	S	S	S	S	S	S	S	S	S	S	S	S	—
Opposing back and foot jets (except BRITTANY V).	S	S	—	S	S	S	S	S	S	S	S	—	—	—	S	—
ACCESSORIES:																
Metal trim kit; polished chrome/bright brass/gold/two-color. (see page 20).	O	O	O	O	O	O	O	O	O	O	O	O	O	O	O	O
Plated brass grip handle(s); polished chrome/bright brass/gold.	O	—	O	O	O	O	O	O	O	—	O	O	O	O	O	O
Powder-coated brass grip handle(s); white/bone/quicksilver.	O	—	O	O	O	O	O	O	O	—	O	O	O	O	O	O
Overflow drain assembly; metal in polished chrome/bright brass/gold; ABS in white/bone/quicksilver.	O+	O+	O+	O+	O+	O+	O+	O+	O+	O+	O+	O+	O+	O+	O+	O+
Overflow drain kit; polished chrome/bright brass.	O+	O+	O+	O+	O+	O+	O+	O+	O+	O+	O+	O+	O+	O+	O+	O+
Double Cascade Spout® & faucet set; polished chrome/bright brass/gold/white/bone/quicksilver.	O+	O+	O+	O+	O+	O+	O+	O+	O+	O+	O+	—	—	—	O+	—
JASON Ultrassage™ rotating jet for deep, therapeutic back massage, (Ø indicates location on end opposite pump only).	S	S	S	S	S	S	S	Ø	Ø	O	Ø	O	O	O	O	—
Hand held shower kit; polished chrome/bright brass/gold.	O+	O+	O+	O+	O+	O+	O+	O+	O+	O+	O+	O+	O+	O+	O+	O+
Bath light with mood lenses, 12V.	O+	O+	O+	O+	O+	O+	O+	O+	O+	O+	O+	O+	O+	O+	O+	O+
Removable headrests; two styles; white/black (see page 21).	O+	O+	O+	O+	O+	O+	O+	O+	O+	O+	O+	O+	O+	O+	O+	O+
JASON Heat Saver — maintains water temp. non-electrically, (except BRITTANY V and all multi-speed units.)	O	O	O	O	O	O	O	O	O	O	—	O	—	O	—	—
Tile flange kit.	—	O+	—	—	—	—	—	—	O+	O+	—	O+	O+	O+	—	O+
Lateral skirt.	—	—	—	O+	O+	—	—	—	O+	—	O+	O+	O+	O+	—	O+

NOTE: Above options must be factory installed unless otherwise noted and therefore must be specified with bath order.

LEGEND: S = Standard, O = Optional, — = Not available, O+ = Option available for field installation only, Ø = Location on end opposite pump only

Most baths and components are also offered for the electrical requirements of countries other than U.S.A., consult factory.

THE FIRST FAMILY OF LUXURY BATHING.

JASON INTERNATIONAL INC. • 8328 MACARTHUR DRIVE • NORTH LITTLE ROCK, ARKANSAS 72118

1-800-255-5766 (ORDER DESK) / 501-771-4477 / 501-771-2333 (FAX)

A vital contributor to JASON quality is your JASON dealer.
We stake our reputation on these fine people.

MAIL TO: P.O. BOX 16347 • Louisville, KY 40256-0347
SHIP TO: 3280 Old Millers Lane • Louisville, KY 40216
(502) 778-2731 • 1 (800) 928-PUMP • FAX (502) 774-3624

QWIK JON SEWAGE REMOVAL SYSTEMS

SERIES 100/102- Economical sewage systems designed for built in or free standing installation.

MODELS:

Model 100 UL Listed 262 Pump
Model 102 UL Listed 267 Pump
Patent No. 5,038,418

TYPICAL INSTALLATIONS

Versatile installation enables the pump compartment and piping to be concealed by the installation of a wall. **NOTE:** Access must be maintained to the pump compartment. **NOTE:** The Qwik Jon is designed to fit flush with any elevated floor made of standard 2" x 6" material (actual dimensions 1½" x 5½"). And you can add a Lavatory - Bathtub - Shower with the installation of the 2" adapt-a-flex seal (provided). Tub or shower requires built in installation. See Installation Instructions.

INSTALL A QWIK JON
JUST ABOUT ANYWHERE

- Designed to accommodate a toilet, lavatory and a bathtub
- Use with a variety of toilet styles (1.6 Gallon residential flush; other installations should use over 3 gallon flush)
- Perfect for basements, family rooms, warehouse, factories, room additions
- No need to destroy concrete floors
- Reduces construction cost
- Pumps any direction
- Fits just about anywhere

Basic Installation
Toilet, Fixtures and Piping Not Included

Report No. 9348

Built In Installation
Toilet, Fixtures and Piping Not Included

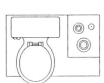
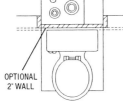
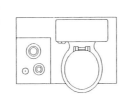

OPTIONAL 2" WALL

Code approved (Consult factory)

TECHNICAL INFORMATION

QWIK JON SYSTEMS INCLUDE:

Sewage Pumps

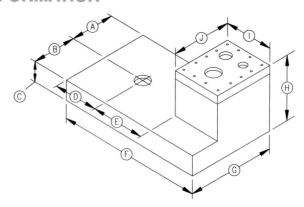

MODEL 100
Pump: Model WM 262
1/2 HP 115V 9.4 amps
P.S.C. Motor
Weight: 33 lbs.
CSA Certified
UL Listed
CSA Certified

Model 102
Model WM 267
1/2 HP 115V 10.4 amps
Split Phase Motor
51 lbs.
UL listed
CSA Certified

NOTE:
Sewage Pumps WM262 & WM267 are designed for use in Qwik Jon units only. They are not designed for use in any other application.

- Automatic level control switch
- Thermal overload protected motor
- Stainless steel screws, bolts & handle
- Non-clogging vortex impeller
- Passes 2" solids (sphere)
- UL listed 3-wire neoprene 10 ft. cord & plug
- Maximum temperature rating - 130° F. (54° C)

Tank
MODEL 100/102 (Patented)
- Polyethylene
- Lt. gray finish
- Lightweight
- Wt. 26 lbs.

2" Back Flow Device and Union
- 2" back flow device (check local codes) required to prevent backflow of water and sewer gas
- No threading of pipe required
- Fits ABS, PVC and steel pipe
- Rated at 25 PSI
- Weight: 2 lbs.

ALL IN ONE CARTON
- Tank, lid & gasket
- ½ HP sewage pump
- Back flow device (check local codes)
- 2" Discharge & 3" Vent with adapt-a-flex seals
- 2" adapt-a-flex seal for additional fixtures
- Floor Flange Extender Kit for ½" & ⅝" thick floors.
- Hardware pack and floor anchor kit
- Installation instructions
- Shipping weight:
  100 System - 85 lbs.
  102 System - 103 lbs.

ITEMS NEEDED BY INSTALLER
- Supply fittings, toilet gasket & waste pipe
- Toilet fixture
- Electrical source with ground fault interrupter protected receptacle
- Water source
- Tools

MODEL NO.	A	B	C	D	E
100/102	12¼	12¼	5¼	12¼	14 ⅛
	F	**G**	**H**	**I**	**J**
100/102	41	25	17	14	17

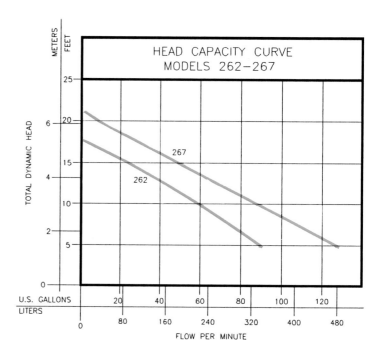

HEAD CAPACITY CURVE
MODELS 262–267

Model		262(100)		267(102)	
Feet	Meters	Gal.	Ltrs.	Gal.	Ltrs.
5	1.52	90	341	128	484
10	3.05	60	227	89	337
15	4.57	22.5	85	50	189
Lock Valve:		18 ft.		21.5 ft.	

NOTE: Recommended for installations up to 16' total dynamic head. Consult factory if installation is above 15' vertical height in 2" pipe.

CAUTION
All installation of controls, protection devices and wiring should be done by a qualified licensed electrician. All electrical and safety codes should be followed including the most recent National Electric Code (NEC) and the Occupational Safety and Health Act (OSHA).

The Geberit ShowerToilet

The Geberit
ShowerToilet —
hygienic, refreshing,
comfortable.
A space-saving
toilet/bidet combination...
and more!

Geberit Remote Control 3½" Kitchen Sink Basket Strainer

The Geberit Remote Control Kitchen Sink Strainer fits into the standard 3-1/2" opening in all stainless steel, cast iron, enameled steel, and composite kitchen sinks. A normal deck hole accommodates the control knob.

Now, there's no need to move dishes, pans, or put hands in the water to lift the basket strainer.

The easy-to-operate kitchen sink strainer is actuated by a rigidly mounted cable which connects the deck-mounted control knob to the basket strainer.

White, almond, and grey finishes are made of solid color GE-Plastics Xenoy, which is guaranteed not to crack, chip, or peel.

Chrome finished strainer and flange are made of 16-gauge stainless steel.

Geberit Decorative 3½" Kitchen Sink Basket Strainer

The Geberit Decorative Kitchen Sink Strainer fits into the standard 3-1/2" opening in all stainless steel, cast iron, enameled steel, and composite kitchen sinks.

Easy to install in new kitchen sink installations, and is ideal as an upgrade to your existing kitchen sink.

Available in Chrome and attractive solid colors of white, almond, and grey to complement today's fashionable kitchen design and decor.

White, almond, and grey finishes are made of GE-Plastics Xenoy, which is known for its durability, and is guaranteed not to crack, chip, or peel.

Chrome finished strainer and flange are manufactured of 16-gauge stainless steel.

Geberit Manufacturing, Inc., P.O. Box 2008, 1100 Boone Drive, Michigan City, Indiana 46360. Phone (219) 879-4466, Toll Free: 1-800-225-7217, Fax (219) 872-8003.

GEBERIT

Advanced plumbing technology

USA 1396 5M / 5682-93

Innovative Drains for Today's Upscale Kitchen and Bathroom

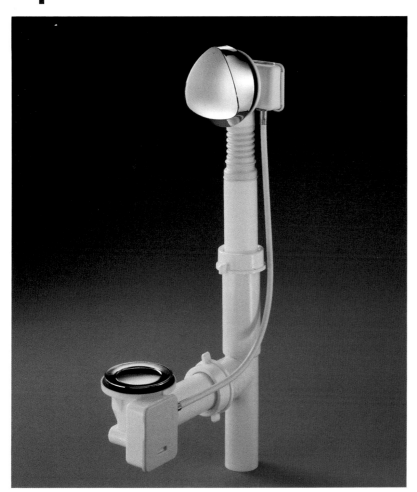

Geberit Remote Control Bath Waste and Overflow

European styling for today's up-graded bath designs. The remote control design puts the critical working parts outside the pipe, away from the water flow. This allows the water to flow freely, prevents clogging, and provides for years of reliable, maintenance-free performance.

A quarter turn of the European style contoured handle provides a smooth, positive drain function that never needs adjustment. Available in various models to fit bathtubs and whirlpools from 12" to 29" deep, whether acrylic, fiberglass, cast iron, stainless steel, or marble composition.

Available in the following popular finishes:
Chrome, Gold, Bright Brass, Antique Brass, Old Silver, Satin Brass, White, Bone, Grey, and Black.

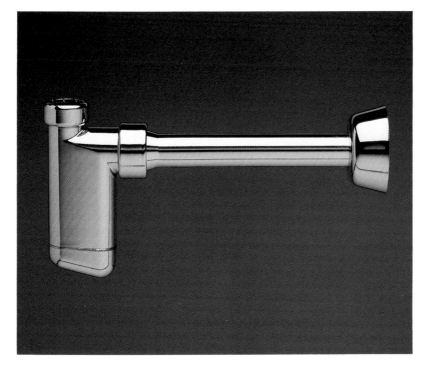

Geberit Decorative Lavatory Trap.

European styling to match the new look of Today's bathroom decor. The GEBERIT Decorative Lavatory Trap fits most wall-hung and pedestal sinks. The unique design allows for straight line connections for easier installation and comes with a 1-1/4" x 10" trap arm and escutcheon. Fabricated from heavy-gauge poly-propylene, the Lavatory Trap is hot water resistant, stands up to caustic household cleaning agents, and, is completely non-corrosive for long, trouble-free service

Available in the following popular finishes:
Chrome, White, Gold, and Bright Brass.

The Geberit ShowerToilet – Swiss quality, function and design brought into perfect harmony

The shower function.

With a push of the button, the spray arm extends from its protected position and a spray of body temperature warm water washes thoroughly, as long as the button is pressed. The intensity of the spray can be regulated with a turn knob.

After the spray button is released, the spray arm retracts into its protected sleeve and is rinsed with fresh water, ensuring that the spray arm and nozzle are cleaned every time.

The drying function.

The wash is automatically followed by a gentle flow of warm drying air. The temperature of the air, supplied by an almost noiseless dryer, can be adjusted to individual preference. When leaving the toilet, the air dryer shuts off by itself.

The air purifier.

The ShowerToilet is also equipped with an automatic air purifier. When the toilet is occupied, seat contact activates a ventilator which extracts the air from the toilet and directs it through an active carbon filter. This extremely effective system eliminates the need for any "masking" air fresheners.

The seat contact.

The seat contact has a multi-purpose function: it activates the air purifier, it prevents the spray unit from operating when the toilet is not occupied, it acts as an off-on switch for the energy saving function of the water heater when continuous heating is not desired, and, it switches off the air dryer when one leaves the toilet.

Models and colors

The Geberit ShowerToilet is available for floor mounting (normal 12″ rough-in), or wall mounting (incl. carrier adjustable for finished height) and comes in a variety of contemporary colors.

Electrical and plumbing connections

110 Volts AC/60 Hertz
Separate 15 Amp. 3-wire grounded circuit required
Water inlet ½″ O.D.
Pressure range: 30 to 80 PSI
Drain: 3″ DWV-PVC pipe

*Flushing performance **1.6 gpf** with a quality china bowl*

The rinsing spray is activated by pressing the spray button

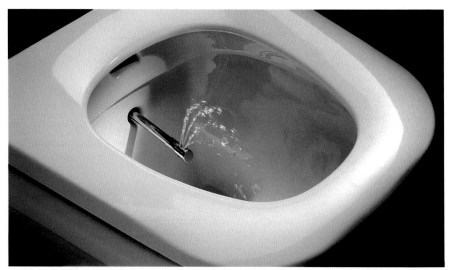

At the push of a button the spray arm extends from its protective sleeve and produces a spray of controlled body temperature warm water. The spray intensity is adjustable.

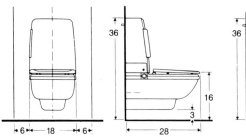

Wall-mounted model

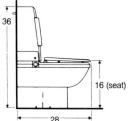

Floor-mounted model

Geberit Manufacturing, Inc., P.O. Box 2008, 1100 Boone Drive, Michigan City, Indiana 46360. Phone (219) 879-4466, Toll Free: 1-800-225-7217, Fax (219) 872-8003.

Advanced plumbing technology

USA/CAN 5331-12-93

Strom Plumbing

BY
Sign of the Crab

C584
BuyLine 8653

No. 9305

$8.00

20th Anniversary Edition

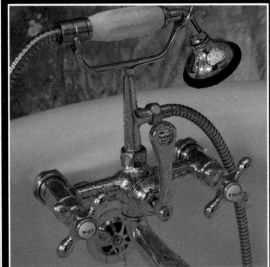

SIGN OF THE CRAB specializes in solid brass plumbing and decorative accessories. Through years of product development, our products include authentic reproduction items and new, designer-oriented products. Also available is the service that is necessary to see your project through to completion. We have custom-made many items to include stainless steel and brass products for the Sheraton Palace Hotel in San Francisco and the Beverly Wilshire Hotel in Beverly Hills.

Enclosed is a sampling of some of our items. Please write to us or call us for our complete catalog available at no charge to the trade. We welcome you to the world of STROM PLUMBING.

SIGN OF THE CRAB, LTD.
3756 OMEC CIRCLE, DEPT. 214
RANCHO CORCOVA
CALIFORNIA 95742

TELEPHONE (916) 638-2722
FAX (916) 638-2725

Plumbing *pages 1-53*

P439

Bath Accessories & Hardware *pages 54-81*

This redesigned P06, the Triumph, is our newest manufacturing breakthrough. It features solid brass components for lasting durability, replaceable seats and the highest quality valve in our industry.

Each of our faucets is solid brass, skillfully manufactured and 100% tested before it leaves our factory. With the optional "supercoat" protected finish, these faucets can be as care-free as any lifestyle, yet have the solid brass durability of the classics.

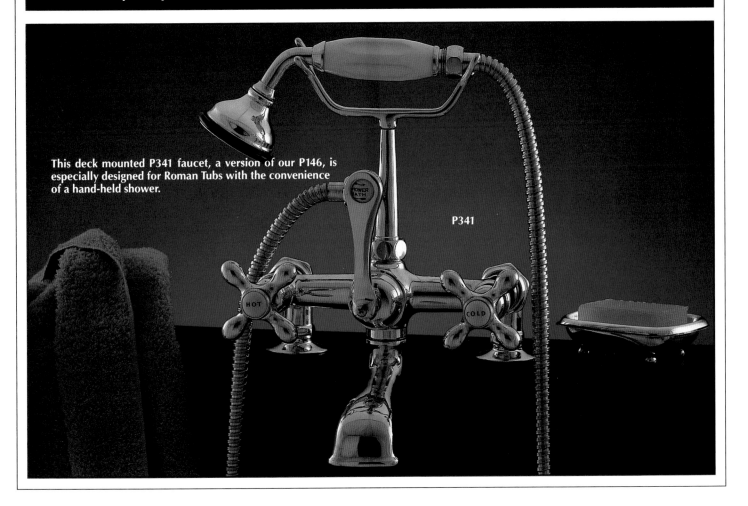

This deck mounted P341 faucet, a version of our P146, is especially designed for Roman Tubs with the convenience of a hand-held shower.

P341

P51

P403
Shower Enclosure
P403 also available in chrome.
Set includes P400 FAUCET, P08
enclosure, P09 RISER, and P10
SHOWER HEAD.

P403P
Shower Enclosure
with Porcelain Showerhead P51

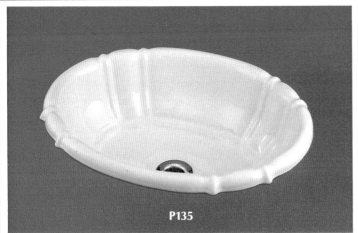

P135

P134-1
Shown With P106
and P98 P Trap

P150
SHOWN WITH P103

P134
Shown With P103

P104
P54
P53
P64
Installed On
Pedestal Sink
P81

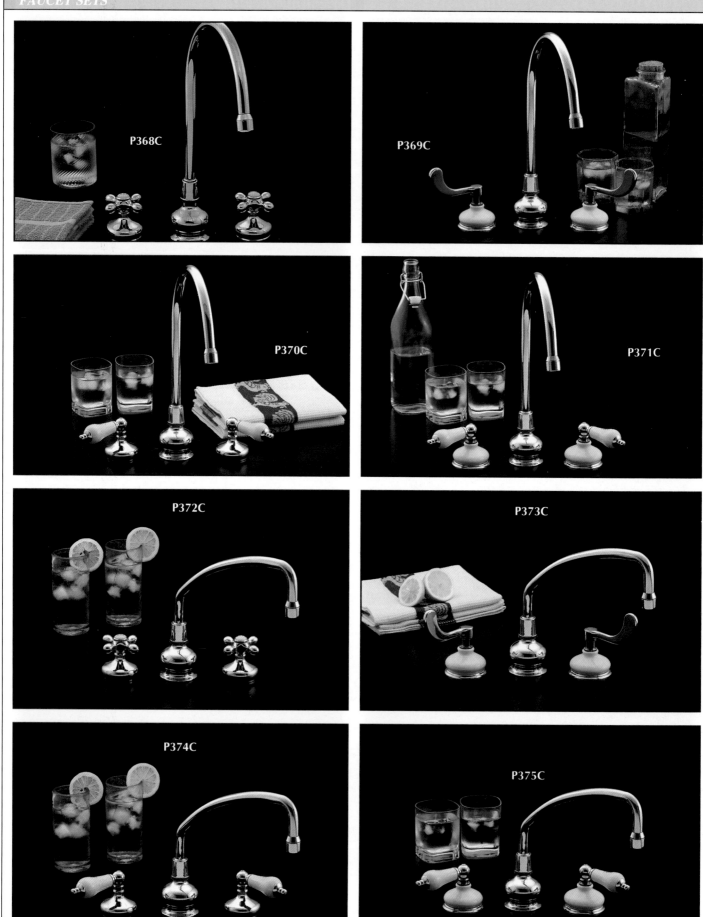

P368C

P369C

P370C

P371C

P372C

P373C

P374C

P375C

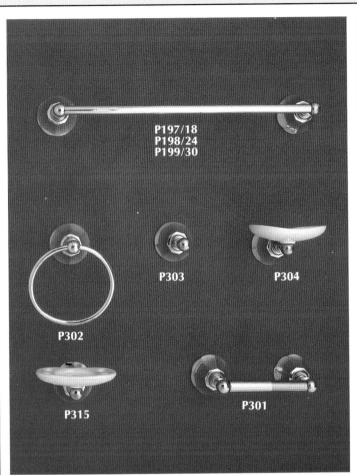

P197/18
P198/24
P199/30

P303

P304

P302

P315

P301

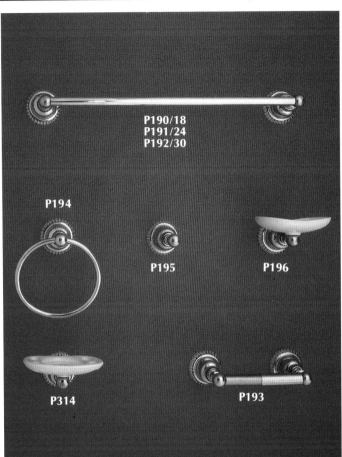

P190/18
P191/24
P192/30

P194

P195

P196

P314

P193

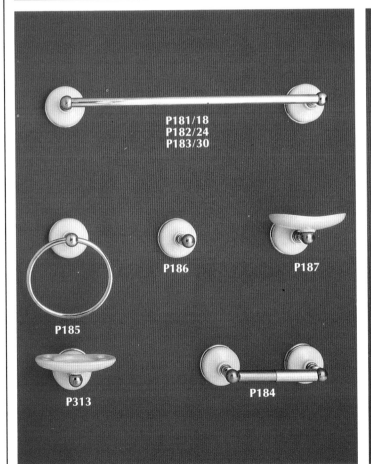

P181/18
P182/24
P183/30

P185

P186

P187

P313

P184

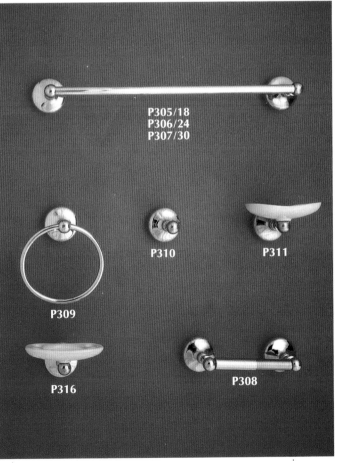

P305/18
P306/24
P307/30

P309

P310

P311

P316

P308

P433

P433C

P434
Roman Spout Only

P435
Roman Tub Set

P434C
Roman Spout Only

P435C
Roman Tub Set

P436 TUB & SHOWER SET
P437 TUB ONLY SET
P438 SHOWER ONLY SET

P436

P439

P440

P441 TUB & SHOWER SET
P442 TUB ONLY SET
P443 SHOWER ONLY SET

P441

Tri-View Medicine Cabinets with Light

MODEL LC-F3630SM-W SHOWN

These superbly crafted medicine cabinets are fabricated of heavy 20 gauge prime cold rolled steel. They are fabricated for SURFACE mounting. The tri-view doors are mounted with completely invisible European-style cabinet hinges. The cabinet body and doors are bonderized after forming to resist rust, spray painted with our special white color enamel paint, then baked at high temperature for durability.

Mirrors are ³⁄₁₆" first quality plate glass and are available in FRAMELESS POLISHED edge or FRAMELESS BEVELED edge. Doors can be completely frameless or have bright stainless steel trim at the top & bottom.

Integral light fixture is bright chrome plated and accepts standard G25 base bulbs. The fixture is four (4") high and one (1") deep and the face of the fixture is flush with the face of the mirrored doors. The chrome light socket base projects and additional one (1") in front of the mirrors. Optional brass light fixture is also available substitute "LB" instead of "LC" at the beginning of the part number.

Overall Size w x h	Mirrored Area Size w x h	Polished Stainless Steel Trim	Frameless Polished Edges	Frameless Beveled Edges	Fixed Metal Shelves	Number Of Bulbs
24" x 28"	24" x 24"	LC-S2424SM-W	LC-F2424SM-W	LC-BV2424SM-W	2	4
24" X 34"	24" x 30"	LC-S2430SM-W	LC-F2430SM-W	LC-BV2430SM-W	3	4
30" X 28"	30" X 24"	LC-S3024SM-W	LC-F3024SM-W	LC-BV3024SM-W	2	5
30" X 34"	30" X 30"	LC-S3030SM-W	LC-F3030SM-W	LC-BV3030SM-W	3	5
36" X 34"	36" X 30"	LC-S3630SM-W	LC-F3630SM-W	LC-BV3630SM-W	3	5
36" X 40"	36" X 36"	LC-S3636SM-W	LC-F3636SM-W	LC-BV3636SM-W	4	5
48" X 34"	48" X 30"	LC-S4830SM-W	LC-F4830SM-W	LC-BV4830SM-W	3	6
48" X 40"	48" X 36"	LC-S4836SM-W	LC-F4836SM-W	LC-BV4836SM-W	4	6
54" X 40"	54" X 36"	LC-S5436SM-W	LC-F5436SM-W	LC-BV5436SM-W	4	6
60" X 40"	60" X 36"	LC-S6036SM-W	LC-F6036SM-W	LC-BV6036SM-W	4	8
72" X 40"*	72" X 36"	LC-S7236SM-W	LC-F7236SM-W	LC-BV7236SM-W	4	9

* STANDARD WITH 4 DOORS, 3 DOOR CABINET OPTIONAL

Bi-View Medicine Cabinets

MODEL BV2030DD SHOWN

These superbly crafted medicine cabinets are fabricated of heavy 20 gauge prime cold rolled steel. They are fabricated for surface mounting.

The bi-view doors are mounted with completely invisible European-style hinges. The cabinet body and doors are bonderized after forming to resist rust, spray painted with our special white enamel paint, then baked at high temperature for durability. Mirrors are ³⁄₁₆" first quality plate glass and are available in FRAMELESS POLISHED edge or FRAMELESS BEVELED edge. Doors can be completely frameless or have bright stainless steel trim at the top & bottom.

Width	Size Height	Depth	Polished Stainless Steel Trim	Frameless Polished Edges	Frameless Beveled Edges	Fixed Metal Shelves
24"	24"	5¼"	S2424DD-W	F2424DD-W	BV2424DD-W	2
20"	30"	5¼"	S2030DD-W	F2030DD-W	BV2030DD-W	3
24"	30"	5¼"	S2430DD-W	F2430DD-W	BV2430DD-W	3
24"	36"	5¼"	S2436DD-W	F2436DD-W	BV2436DD-W	4
24"	42"	5¼"	S2442DD-W	F2442DD-W	BV2442DD-W	4

Custom Sizes Available in Quantity

Corner Medicine Cabinet

MODEL CR1436PE SHOWN

BODY: 20 gauge prime sheets of cold rolled steel.
FINISH: Bonderized after forming to resist rust and sprayed with a special white color enamel, baked on at a high temperature for durability.
MIRRORS: ³⁄₁₆" first quality plate glass
SHELVES: Adjustable glass shelves
DOOR STOP: Stop hinge-reversible swing door.
DOOR STYLES: 1. Polished brass frame
2. Polished stainless steel frame
3. Frameless polished edge mirror
4. Beveled frameless polished edge mirror

Polished Stainless Steel Frame	Polished Brass Frame	Frameless Polished Edge Mirror	Beveled Frameless Polished Edge Mirror	Overall Size W x H	Shelves
CR1430-W	CR1430PB-W	CR1430PE-W	CR1430BV-W	14" X 30"	2
CR1436-W	CR1436PB-W	CR1436PE-W	CR1436BV-W	14" X 36"	3
CR1442-W	CR1442PB-W	CR1442PE-W	CR1442BV-W	14" X 42"	4

SUGGESTED ARRANGEMENT FOR CORNER MEDICINE CABINET

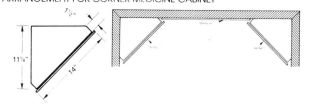

Tri-View Medicine Cabinets

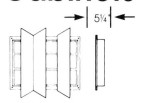

MODEL BV3630SM-W WITH LS-36 LIGHT FIXTURE SHOWN

These superbly crafted medicine cabinets are fabricated of heavy 20 gauge prime cold rolled steel. They can be fabricated for both <u>SURFACE</u> and <u>PARTIALLY RECESSED</u> mounting. The tri-view doors are mounted with completely invisible European-style cabinet hinges. The cabinet body and doors are bonderized after forming to resist rust, spray painted with our special white color enamel paint, then baked at high temperature for durability.

Mirrors are ³⁄₁₆" first quality plate glass and are available in FRAMELESS POLISHED edge or FRAMELESS BEVELED edge. Doors can be completely frameless or have bright stainless steel trim at the top & bottom.

Size w x h	Wall Opening w x h	Polished Stainless Steel Trim	Frameless Polished Edges	Frameless Beveled Edges	Fixed Metal Shelves
24" x 24"	23 ¾" x 23 ½"	S2424XX-W	F2424XX-W	BV2424XX-W	2
24" x 30"	23 ¾" x 29 ½"	S2430XX-W	F2430XX-W	BV2430XX-W	3
30" x 24"	29 ¾" x 23 ½"	S3024XX-W	F3024XX-W	BV3024XX-W	2
32" x 24"	30" x 20"	S3224PR-W	F3224PR-W	BV3224PR-W	2
30" x 30"	29 ¾" x 29 ½"	S3030XX-W	F3030XX-W	BV3030XX-W	3
36" x 30"	35 ¾" x 29 ½"	S3630XX-W	F3630XX-W	BV3630XX-W	3
36" x 36"	35 ¾" x 35 ½"	S3636XX-W	F3636XX-W	BV3636XX-W	4
48" x 30"	47 ¾" x 29 ½"	S4830XX-W	F4830XX-W	BV4830XX-W	3
48" x 36"	47 ¾" x 35 ½"	S4836XX-W	F4836XX-W	BV4836XX-W	4
54" x 36"	53 ¾" x 35 ½"	S5436XX-W	F5436XX-W	BV5436XX-W	4
60" x 36"	59 ¾" x 35 ½"	S6036XX-W	F6036XX-W	BV6036XX-W	4
72" x 36"***	71 ¾" x 35 ½"	S7236XX-W	F7236XX-W	BV7236XX-W	4

"XX" SUBSTITUTE "SM" FOR SURFACE MOUNTED OPTION OR "PR" FOR PARTIALLY RECESSED OPTION. ALL PARTIALLY RECESSED CABINETS REQUIRE A WALL DEPTH OF 3".
**STANDARD WITH 4 DOORS, 3 DOOR CABINET OPTIONAL.

Optional side mirror kits are available for surface mounted tri-views. Mirrors are ⅛" plate mirror, polished on all sides.

TRI-VIEW HEIGHT	MIRROR KIT MODEL NO.
24"	MKTV-24
30"	MKTV-30
36"	MKTV-36

Fully Recessed Tri-View Medicine Cabinets

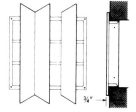

MODEL S3630FR-W WITH G25B436 LIGHT SHOWN

Custom Sizes Available

This tri-view cabinet is a <u>FULLY RECESSED</u> medicine cabinet which when mounted only protrudes from the wall a total of ¾". The doors are mounted with completely invisible European-style hinges which allows the door to sit flush against the wall. The body is heavy 20 gauge prime cold rolled steel bonderized to resist rust, sprayed with a special white color enamel then baked at high temperature for durability. Mirrors are ³⁄₁₆" first quality plate glass and are available in FRAMELESS POLISHED edge or FRAMELESS BEVELED edge. Doors can be completely frameless or have bright stainless steel trim at the top & bottom.

Size w x h	Wall Opening w x h	Polished Stainless Steel Trim	Frameless Polished Edges	Frameless Beveled Edges	Fixed Metal Shelves	Optional Adjustable Glass Shelves
24" x 24"	21 ¾" x 22"	S2424FR-W	F2424FR-W	BV2424FR-W	2	2
24" x 30"	21 ¾" x 28"	S2430FR-W	F2430FR-W	BV2430FR-W	3	3
24" x 36"	21 ¾" x 34"	S2436FR-W	F2436FR-W	BV2436FR-W	4	4
30" x 24"	27 ¾" x 22"	S3024FR-W	F3024FR-W	BV3024FR-W	2	2
30" x 30"	27 ¾" x 28"	S3030FR-W	F3030FR-W	BV3030FR-W	3	3
36" x 30"	33 ¾" x 28"	S3630FR-W	F3630FR-W	BV3630FR-W	3	3
36" x 36"	33 ¾" x 34"	S3636FR-W	F3636FR-W	BV3636FR-W	4	4
48" x 30"	45 ¾" x 28"	S4830FR-W	F4830FR-W	BV4830FR-W	3	N/A
48" x 36"	45 ¾" x 34"	S4836FR-W	F4836FR-W	BV4836FR-W	4	N/A
54" x 36"	51 ¾" x 34"	S5436FR-W	F5436FR-W	BV5436FR-W	4	N/A
60" x 36"	57 ¾" x 34"	S6036FR-W	F6036FR-W	BV6036FR-W	4	N/A
72" x 36"***	69 ¾" x 34"	S7236FR-W	F7236FR-W	BV7236FR-W	4	N/A

ALL CABINETS REQUIRE A WALL DEPTH OF 3 ¼"

**Standard with 4 Doors, 3 Doors Cabinet Optional

Slim Line Surface Mounted With Light

This elegant medicine cabinet is fabricated with a very slim profile and projects only 3-1/2" from the wall. The cabinet is equipped with an integral beveled mirror light fixture with four candelabra base (G16) bulb sockets.

The body is heavy 20 gauge prime cold rolled steel bonderized to resist rust, sprayed with our special white enamel paint then baked at high temperature. Mirrors are first quality 3/16" plate glass with a 1/2" bevel around the perimeter of the mirror. Mirrors on sides of cabinet are 1/8" plate with polished edges on all sides.

The cabinet door is equipped with a spring-loaded touch latch and is hung on completely invisible European-Style hinges.

Model No.	Size
LM423BV-W	16"w x 26⅛"h
LM425BV-W	16"w x 30⅛"h
LM426BV-W	16"w x 34⅛"h
LM427BV-W	18"w x 28⅛"h
LM428BV-W	18"w x 34⅛"h
LM429BV-W	16"w x 40⅛"h
LM431BV-W	18"w x 40⅛"h

Slim Line Surface Mounted Medicine Cabinets

The new Slim Line surface mounted medicine cabinets are a very slim profile wall mounted cabinet that projects <u>only 3 1/2"</u>. The cabinets are available with mirrored sides or with our traditional luxurious painted enamel sides. The cabinet door is equipped with a spring-loaded touch latch and is hung on completely invisible European-Style hinges.
The body is heavy 20 gauge prime cold rolled steel bonderized to resist rust, sprayed with our special white enamel then baked at high temperature for durability. Mirrors are first quality 3/16" plate glass and are available in four different door styles. Mirrors on sides of cabinet are first quality 1/8" plate with polished edges on all sides. See additional door styles on page 7.

Polished Stainless Steel Frame	Polished Brass Frame	Frameless Polished Edge Mirror	Beveled Frameless Polished Edge Mirror	Overall Size w x h	Glass Shelves
WM321-W	WM321PB-W	WM321PE-W	WM321BV-W	13½" X 36"	3
WM323-W	WM323PB-W	WM323PE-W	WM323BV-W	16" X 22"	2
WM325-W	WM325PB-W	WM325PE-W	WM325BV-W	16" X 26"	3
WM326-W	WM326PB-W	WM326PE-W	WM326BV-W	16" X 30"	3
WM327-W	WM327PB-W	WM327PE-W	WM327BV-W	18" X 24"	3
WM329-W	WM329PB-W	WM329PE-W	WM329BV-W	16" X 36"	4
WM331-W	WM331PB-W	WM331PE-W	WM331BV-W	18" X 36"	4
WM333-W	WM333PB-W	WM333PE-W	WM333BV-W	18" X 42"	5

MODEL NUMBERS ABOVE ARE FOR CABINET WITH PAINTED ENAMEL SIDES. ADD "MS" TO THE ABOVE MODEL NUMBERS FOR CABINETS WITH MIRRORED SIDES.

MODEL WM331PE-W-MS SHOWN

AVAILABLE WITHOUT MIRRORED SIDES -
SEE TABLE AT RIGHT

Slim Line Recessed Medicine Cabinets

SLIM LINE medicine cabinets are the ideal cabinets for use in conjunction with wall mirrors or for side wall mounting where the side is exposed on entry to the bathroom. The SLIM LINE cabinet only protrudes from the wall 5/16", eliminating unsightly gaps between cabinet and wall mirror.

The cabinet door is equipped with a spring-loaded magnetic catch. Press gently and the catch releases opening the door. Close the door and the magnet holds it securely. The door is mounted with completely invisible European-style hinges which allow the door to sit flush against the wall.

The body is heavy 20 gauge prime cold rolled steel bonderized to resist rust, sprayed with our special white enamel then baked at high temperature for durability.

Mirrors are 3/16" first quality plate glass. See additional door styles on page 7.

Polished Stainless Steel Frame	Polished Edge Mirror	Beveled Edge Mirror	Wall Opening w x h x d	Overall Size w x h	Glass Shelves
FM321-W	FM321PE-W	FM321BV-W	12⅜ x 34¼ x 3¼	13½ x 36	3
FM323-W	FM323PE-W	FM323BV-W	14⅞ x 20¼ x 3¼	16 x 22	2
FM325-W	FM325PE-W	FM325BV-W	14⅞ x 24¼ x 3¼	16 x 26	3
FM326-W	FM326PE-W	FM326BV-W	14⅞ x 28¼ x 3¼	16 x 30	3
FM327-W	FM327PE-W	FM327BV-W	16⅞ x 22¼ x 3¼	18 x 24	3
FM329-W	FM329PE-W	FM329BV-W	14⅞ x 34¼ x 3¼	16 x 36	4
FM331-W	FM331PE-W	FM331BV-W	16⅞ x 34¼ x 3¼	18 x 36	4
FM333-W	FM333PE-W	FM333BV-W	16⅞ x 40¼ x 3¼	18 x 42	5

Suggested Arrangements for Slim Line Medicine Cabinets

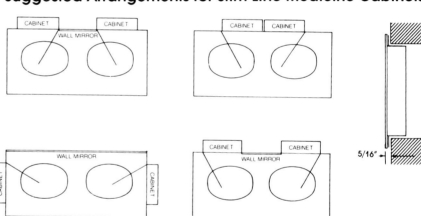

Slim Line Semi-Recessed Series Medicine Cabinets

The SR Series by BASCO is designed for recessing in very shallow walls. The cabinet only recesses into the wall 2" yet provides a fully 3" of storage depth.

The cabinet door is equipped with a magnetic touch latch and invisible European - style hinges. The body is heavy 20 gauge prime cold rolled steel bonderized to resist rust, spray painted with our special white enamel than baked at high temperature.

Mirrors are 3/16" first quality plate glass. See additional door styles on page 7.

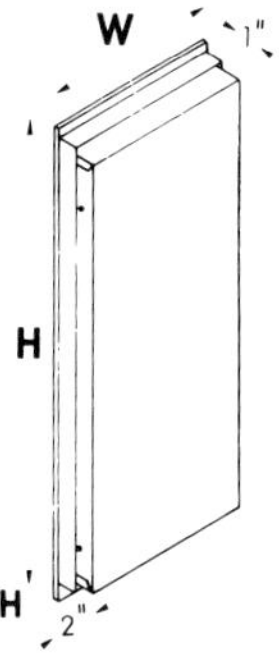

Polished Stainless Steel Frame	Polished Brass Frame	Frameless Polished Edge Mirror	Beveled Frameless Polished Edge Mirror	Wall Opening W x H x D	Overall Size W x H	Glass Shelves
SR321-W	SR321PB-W	SR321PE-W	SR321BV-W	12⅜" x 34¼" x 2	13½" x 36"	3
SR323-W	SR323PB-W	SR323PE-W	SR323BV-W	14⅞" x 20¼" x 2	16" x 22"	2
SR325-W	SR325PB-W	SR325PE-W	SR325BV-W	14⅞" x 24¼" x 2	16" x 26"	3
SR326-W	SR326PB-W	SR326PE-W	SR326BV-W	14⅞" x 28¼" x 2	16" x 30"	3
SR327-W	SR327PB-W	SR327PE-W	SR327BV-W	16⅞" x 22¼" x 2	18" x 24"	3
SR329-W	SR329PB-W	SR329PE-W	SR329BV-W	14⅞" x 34¼" x 2	16" x 36"	4
SR331-W	SR331PB-W	SR331PE-W	SR331BV-W	16⅞" x 34¼" x 2	18" x 36"	4
SR333-W	SR333PB-W	SR333PE-W	SR333BV-W	16⅞" x 40¼" x 2	18" x 42"	5

MODEL SR321PE-W SHOWN   REQUIRES ONLY 2" WALL DEPTH

Stainless Steel Framed Medicine Cabinets

MODEL 378P-W SHOWN

BODY: Heavy 20 gauge prime sheets of cold rolled steel.
FINISH: Bonderized after forming to resist rust and sprayed with a special white color enamel, baked on at a high temperature for durability.
MIRRORS: First quality plate glass, with two coats of silver, then electrolytically copper clad as defined in U.S. Commercial Standard CS-27-36. Warranteed for 5 years against silvering defects.
SHELVES: Glass, adjustable ¼" thick with polished front edge.
DOOR STOP: Stop hinge-reversible swing door.

Recessed Model No.	Surface Model No.	Mirror Type	Wall Opening w x h x d	Overall w x h	Glass Shelves
360-W	SM360-W	⅛" Plate	12" x 18" x 3"	14⅛" x 20¼"	2
370-W	SM370-W	⅛" Plate	10" x 34" x 3"	12⅛" x 36¼"	4
371-W	SM371-W	⅛" Plate	14" x 18" x 3"	16⅛" x 22¼"	2
372P-W	SM372P-W	3⁄16" Plate	14" x 20" x 3"	16⅛" x 22¼"	2
374P-W	SM374P-W	3⁄16" Plate	16" x 22" x 3"	18⅛" x 24¼"	3
375P-W	SM375P-W	3⁄16" Plate	14" x 24" x 3"	16⅛" x 26¼"	3
376P-W	SM376P-W	3⁄16" Plate	18" x 24" x 3"	20⅛" x 26¼"	3
377P-W	SM377P-W	3⁄16" Plate	14" x 34" x 3"	16⅛" x 36¼"	4
378P-W	SM378P-W	3⁄16" Plate	16" x 34" x 3"	18⅛" x 36¼"	4
379P-W	SM379P-W	3⁄16" Plate	16" x 40" x 3"	18⅛" x 42¼"	4
380P-W	SM380P-W	3⁄16" Plate	16" x 58" x 3"	18⅛" x 60¼"	5
390P-W	SM390P-W	3⁄16" Plate	22" x 28" x 3"	24⅛" x 30¼"	4
392P-W	SM392P-W	3⁄16" Plate	22" x 34" x 3"	24⅛" x 36¼"	4

SURFACE CABINETS PROJECT 5" FROM WALL.
Custom Sizes Available in Quantity

**POLISHED BRASS FRAMES ARE AVAILABLE
ADD PREFIX "PB" TO ABOVE MODEL NUMBERS.**

Polished Edge And Beveled Edge Mirror Cabinet

MODEL BV378P-W SHOWN

BODY: Heavy 20 gauge prime sheets of cold rolled steel.
FINISH: Bonderized after forming to resist rust and sprayed with a special white color enamel, baked on at a high temperature for durability.
MIRRORS: First quality 3⁄16" plate glass, with two coats of silver, then electrolytically copper clad as defined in U.S. Commercial Standard CS-27-36. Warranteed for 5 years against silvering defects. Edges polished or polished with ½" bevel.
SHELVES: Glass, adjustable ¼" thick with polished front edge.
DOOR STOP: Stop hinge-reversible swing door.

Beveled Edge Model No.	Polished Edge Model No.	Wall Opening w x h x d	Overall Size w x h	Glass Shelves
BV370P-W	PE370P-W	10" x 34" x 3"	12" x 36"	4
BV371P-W	PE371P-W	14" x 18" X 3"	16" x 22"	2
BV372P-W	PE372P-W	14" X 20" X 3"	16" x 22"	2
BV374P-W	PE374P-W	16" X 22" X 3"	18" X 24"	3
BV375P-W	PE375P-W	14" X 24" X 3"	16" X 26"	3
BV376P-W	PE376P-W	18" X 24" X 3"	20" X 26"	3
BV377P-W	PE377P-W	14" X 34" X 3"	16" X 36"	4
BV378P-W	PE378P-W	16" X 34" X 3"	18" X 36"	4
BV379P-W	PE379P-W	16" X 40" X 3"	18" X 42"	4
BV380P-W	PE380P-W	16" X 58" X 3"	18" X 60"	5
BV390P-W	PE390P-W	22" X 28" X 3"	24" X 30"	4
BV392P-W	PE392P-W	22" X 34" X 3"	24" X 36"	4

ALSO AVAILABLE SURFACE MOUNTED, SPECIFY PREFIX "SM". SURFACE CABINETS PROJECT 5" FROM WALL.
Custom Sizes Available in Quantity

Medi-Lock Box

Securely stores medicines and personal items under lock and key. Installs into any BASCO medicine cabinet 14" or wider.

Fabricated of 20 gauge steel and finished in our special baked white enamel. Equipped with a tumbler lock and furnished with two keys.

MODEL MLB-4 SIZE: 13"w x 5"h x 4"d
MODEL MLB-3 SIZE: 13"w x 5"h x 3"d

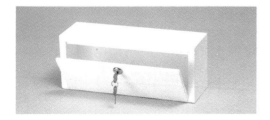

Light Fixture With Bright Chrome or Polished Brass Finish

Basco's lighting fixtures are fabricated entirely of 20 gauge steel, chrome plated steel or brass plated steel. Heavy duty construction ensures durability and safety. All fixtures are U.L. approved. All fixtures use G25 lamps (Not Included). Optional convenience outlets available add suffix - CO to part numbers listed below.

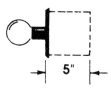

Length	Bright Chrome Model	Polished Brass Model	Size	Number of Bulbs
18"	LS-18	LS-18PB	3½" x 18" x 5" deep	3
24"	LS-24	LS-24PB	3½" x 24" x 5" deep	4
30"	LS-30	LS-30PB	3½" x 30" x 5" deep	5
36"	LS-36	LS-36PB	3½" x 36" x 5" deep	5
48"	LS-48	LS-48PB	3½" x 48" x 5" deep	6
60"	LS-60	LS-60PB	3½" x 60" x 5" deep	8
72"	LS-72	LS-72PB	3½" x 72" x 5" deep	9

Custom Sizes Available

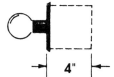

Length	Bright Chrome Model	Polished Brass Model	Size	Number of Bulbs
13"	G25B413	G25B413PB	4" x 13" x 1" deep	2
16"	G25B416	G25B416PB	4" x 16" x 1" deep	3
18"	G25B418	G25B418PB	4" x 18" x 1" deep	3
20"	G25B420	G25B420PB	4" x 20" x 1" deep	4
24"	G25B424	G25B424PB	4" x 24" x 1" deep	4
30"	G25B430	G25B430PB	4" x 30" x 1" deep	5
36"	G25B436	G25B436PB	4" x 36" x 1" deep	5
48"	G25B448	G25B448PB	4" x 48" x 1" deep	6
60"	G25B460	G25B460PB	4" x 60" x 1" deep	8
72"	G25B472	G25B472PB	4" x 72" x 1" deep	9

Custom Sizes Available

Length	White Enamel Model	Size	Number of Bulbs
16"	L4W-16	3½" x 16" x 4" deep	3
18"	L4W-18	3½" x 18" x 4" deep	3
24"	L4W-24	3½" x 24" x 4" deep	4
30"	L4W-30	3½" x 30" x 4" deep	5
36"	L4W-36	3½" x 36" x 4" deep	5
48"	L4W-48	3½" x 48" x 4" deep	6
60"	L4W-60	3½" x 60" x 4" deep	8
72"	L4W-72	3½" x 72" x 4" deep	9

Basco Door Styles

DOOR STYLE #6

The six basic door styles listed are available on all BASCO swing door medicine cabinets.

Many combinations are pictured in our catalog matching various door styles with different size cabinets and body styles.
Since we are a custom medicine cabinet manufacturer we can fabricate any combination of door style with any body style or size.

Your inquiries regarding custom combinations or custom sizes are welcomed.

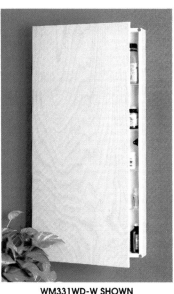

WM331WD-W SHOWN

DOOR STYLES:

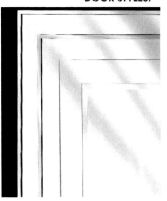

1.
2.
3.
4.

1. Polished brass frame
2. Polished stainless steel frame
3. Frameless polished edge mirror
4. Beveled frameless polished edge mirror
5. Plastic laminated door add "PL" to any Basco part number. PL door is fabricated of ½" thick medium density partical board finished with white melamine on the interior side. The front and edges are finished in Wilsonart Mica.
Standard color is Wilsonart Frosty White Matte #1573. Other Wilsonart colors are available as selected by architect. (not shown)
6. Solid wood door with high quality unfinished birch veneer on the front and edges. Interior side of door is finished in white mica. Add "WD" to any Basco part number.

Fixed Tilting Mirror

FIXED TILTING MIRROR

Basco's new design of fixed tilting mirror attempts to take the institutional look out of accessories for the handicapped. Mirrors are fabricated out of heavy 20 gauge prime cold rolled steel and painted a very appealing white enamel. Mirrors are 3/16" first quality plate mirror and are reinforced with a shock absorbing filler and a 20 gauge steel back. Mirrors project 4" from the wall at the top and 1" at the bottom. Mirrors are mounted on a concealed wall hanger fabricated of 20 gauge galvanized steel. Basco's L4W series light fixtures are especially made 4" deep to compliment the tilting mirrors and are also painted white to match the mirror.

Mirror	Size	Matching Light	Size	Bulbs
HTM-16x30-W	16" x 30"	L4W-16	16"w x 3½"h x 4"d	3
HTM-18x24-W	18" x 24"	L4W-18	18"w x 3½"h x 4"d	3
HTM-18x30-W	18" x 30"	L4W-18	18"w x 3½"h x 4"d	3
HTM-24x30-W	24" x 30"	L4W-24	24"w x 3½"h x 4"d	4
HTM-30x24-W	30" x 24"	L4W-30	30"w x 3½"h x 4"d	5
HTM-36x30-W	36" x 30"	L4W-36	36"w x 3½"h x 4"d	5
HTM-48x24-W	48" x 24"	L4W-48	48"w x 3½"h x 4"d	6
HTM-48x30-W	48" x 30"	L4W-48	48"w x 3½"h x 4"d	6

Other sizes available in quantity.

Medicine Cabinet With Tilting Mirror

This quality medicine cabinet is designed for the use by handicapped persons. The medicine cabinet mirror may be used in the upright position or tilted down to accommodate a seated person. The cabinet door is equipped with a latch to keep the door closed when mirror is tilted down. The tilted mirror is secured by an elbow hinge and a stainless steel piano hinge at the bottom.

BODY: 20 gauge prime sheets of cold rolled steel.
FINISH: Bonderized after forming to resist rust and sprayed with a special white enamel, baked on a high temperature for durability.
MIRRORS: First quality plate glass, with two coats of silver, then electrolytically copper clad as defined in U.S. Commercial Standard CS-27-36. Warranteed for 5 years against silvering defects.
FRAME: Stainless steel.
SHELVES: Glass, adjustable.
DOOR STOP: Stop hinge.

Model No.	Wall Opening	Overall Size	Glass Shelves
372P-ATM - W	14" x 20" x 3"	16⅛" x 22¼"	2
SM372P-ATM - W	SURFACED MTD.	16⅛" X 22¼" X 5¾"	2
374P-ATM - W	16" x 22" x 3"	18⅛" x 24¼"	3
SM374P-ATM - W	SURFACED MTD.	18⅛" X 24¼" X 5¾"	3
375P-ATM - W	14" x 24" x 3"	16⅛" x 26¼"	3
SM375P-ATM - W	SURFACED MTD.	16⅛" X 26¼" X 5¾"	3

Other sizes available in quantity.

Surface Mount/Top Light

BODY: 20 gauge prime sheets of cold rolled steel.
FINISH: Bonderized after forming to resist rust and sprayed with a special white enamel, baked on a high temperature for durability.
MIRRORS: First quality plate glass, with two coats of silver, then electrolytically copper clad as defined in U.S. Commercial Standard CS-27-36. Warranteed for 5 years against silvering defects.
FRAME: Stainless steel.
SHELVES: Glass, adjustable.
DOOR STOP: Stop hinge.

Model No.	Overall Size	Mirror Size	Light
TL-SM-371 - W	16⅛" x 23½" x 7⅜"	16⅛" x 20¼"	(2) 60 watt incandescent bulbs (not included). U.L. approved.

STAINLESS STEEL GRAB BARS

Specifications: All grab bars are fabricated of heavy duty 18 gauge type 304 satin finish stainless steel tubing. Bars are heliarc welded to stainless steel flanges. Bars will withstand a force of 900 lbs. Flanges and cover plates are type 304 stainless steel with a satin finish. All bars have a 1½" wall clearance.

Construction: **CONCEALED WITH SNAP-ON FLANGE**
14 Gauge mounting flange 3" in diameter with 3 mounting holes.
20 Gauge type 304 stainless steel cover

CONCEALED WITH SET SCREWS
10 Gauge 4" deep 3" diameter flange with a minimum of 3 set screws 13 Gauge concealed mounting plate with 3 slotted mounting holes.

EXPOSED SCREW MOUNTING 10 Gauge mounting flange 3" in diameter with 3 mounting holes.

Optional Finishes: PEENED GRIPPING SURFACE:
ADD SUFFIX "P"
KNURLED GRIPPING SURFACE:
ADD SUFFIX "K"
BRIGHT POLISHED FINISH:
ADD SUFFIX "B"
BRASS WITH POLISHED FINISH:
ADD SUFFIX "BB"
BRASS WITH SATIN FINISH:
ADD SUFFIX "SB"

Specifying Instructions: When specifying grab bars insert the model numbers (SHAPES) into the double zeros at the end of the grab bar series number.

EXAMPLE: An exposed fastened 1½" grab bar 24" long is part number 8414H.

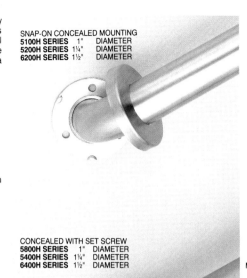

SNAP-ON CONCEALED MOUNTING
5100H SERIES 1" DIAMETER
5200H SERIES 1¼" DIAMETER
6200H SERIES 1½" DIAMETER

CONCEALED WITH SET SCREW
5800H SERIES 1" DIAMETER
5400H SERIES 1¼" DIAMETER
6400H SERIES 1½" DIAMETER

OPTIONAL PEENED FINISH

EXPOSED SCREW MOUNTING
5600H SERIES 1" DIAMETER
5000H SERIES 1¼" DIAMETER
8400H SERIES 1½" DIAMETER

OPTIONAL KNURLED FINISH

STRAIGHT BARS MODEL 11 thru 19 Straight Horizontal

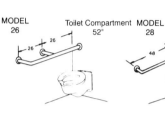

11 Straight horizontal 12"
12 Straight horizontal 16"
13 Straight horizontal 18"
14 Straight horizontal 24"
15 Straight horizontal 30"
16 Straight horizontal 32"
17 Straight horizontal 36"
18 Straight horizontal 42"
19 Straight horizontal 48"

MODEL 21 thru 25 Straight with Centerpost

21 Horizontal 36" with center support
22 Horizontal 42" with center support
23 Horizontal 48" with center support
24 Horizontal 54" with center support
25 Horizontal 60" with center support

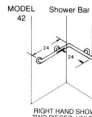

MODEL 26 Toilet Compartment

MODEL 28 Toilet Compartment 52"

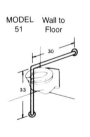

MODEL 51 Wall to Floor

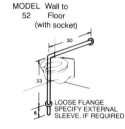

MODEL 52 Wall to Floor (with socket)

LOOSE FLANGE SPECIFY EXTERNAL SLEEVE, IF REQUIRED

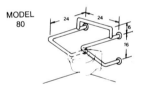

MODEL 80

Toilet Straddle

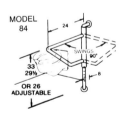

MODEL 84

SWINGS 90°
33
29½
8
OR 26 ADJUSTABLE

MODEL 33 90° Angle 16 x 32

LEFT HAND SHOWN

MODEL 32 90° ANGLE 16 X 32

RIGHT HAND SHOWN

MODEL 42 Shower Bar

RIGHT HAND SHOWN TWO PIECES, UNLESS OTHERWISE SPECIFIED

LEFT HAND SHOWN
MODEL 57

Wall to Floor with Outrigger

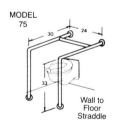

MODEL 75

Wall to Floor Straddle

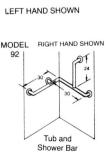

MODEL 92 RIGHT HAND SHOWN

Tub and Shower Bar

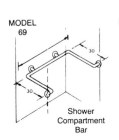

MODEL 69

Shower Compartment Bar

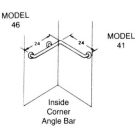

MODEL 46

Inside Corner Angle Bar

MODEL 41 Inside Corner Angle Bar

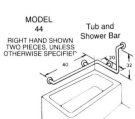

MODEL 44 Tub and Shower Bar

RIGHT HAND SHOWN TWO PIECES, UNLESS OTHERWISE SPECIFIED

9

Europa Hotel Bath Accessories

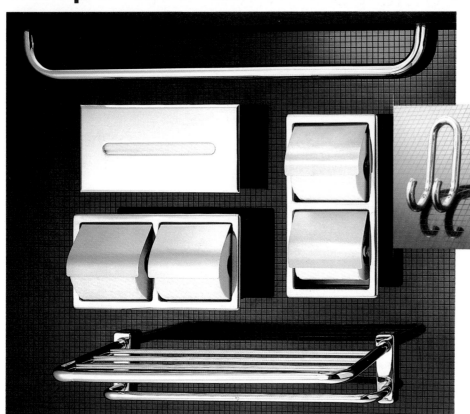

915P Towel Bar
Crafted of 1" diameter seamless 20 gauge type 304 stainless steel tubing polished to a bright finish. Concealed mounting hardware is solid brass. Available in 18", 24", 30", 36", length. (Custom sizes available)

925P Towel Bar
Same as 915P except ¾" diameter.

7925C Recessed Facial Tissue Cabinet
Polished chrome panel with galvanized steel storage box. Overall size: 11¾" x 6". Wall opening required: 10¾" x 5" x 2⅝".

7987P Horizontal Dual Hooded Toilet Paper Holder
Fabricated in one piece of type 304 stainless steel polished to bright finish. Furnished with chrome plated roller. Overall size: 12⅜" x 6½". Wall opening required: 11⅝" x 5¾" x 3".

7988P Vertical Dual Hooded Toilet Paper Holder
Same specifications as Model 7987P. Overall size: 6½" x 12⅜". Wall Opening required: 5¾" x 11⅝" x 3".

1680P Towel Shelf with Towel Bar
Superbly crafted entirely of type 304 stainless steel tubing and then polished to a bright finish. Heavy duty concealed wall brackets are fabricated of 11 gauge (.119) cadmium plated steel. Unique mounting system insures secure attachment to wall.
Sizes: 18" x 9¼" x 4⅞"
             20¾" x 9¼" x 4⅞"
             24" x 9¼" x 4⅞"

1648P Chrome Robe Hook
Size: 2⅛" x 5½" x 2" Projection

All items available in polished brass finish. Add "PB" in front of part number.

Europa II Stainless Steel Bath Accessories

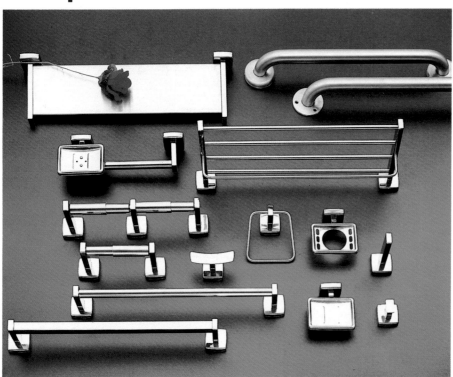

The Europa II series bath accessories are fabricated of type 304 stainless steel and are available in the following finishes:
Bright Polished - add suffix "P" to part number
Satin finish - add suffix "S" to part number
Bronze finish - add suffix "BZ" to part number
Polished Brass - add suffix "PB" to part number

1614*	Soap Dish and Bar with drain holes
1615*	Soap Dish without drain holes
1616*	Soap Dish with drain holes
1618*	Toothbrush Tumbler Holder
1626*	Shelf 6³⁄₁₆" deep - available in 18" and 24" lengths
1630*	Toilet Paper Holder - plastic roller
1631*	Toilet Paper Holder - chrome roller
1630D*	Dual Toilet Paper Holder - plastic roller
1631D*	Dual Toilet Paper Holder - chrome roller
1641*	Square Towel Bar ¾" diameter - available in 18", 24", 30" and 36" lengths
1642*	Round Towel Bar ¾" diameter - available in 18", 24", 30", and 36" lengths
1643*	Double Robe Hook 2" projection
1644*	Single Robe Hook 2" projection
1645*	Towel Pin 4¼" long
1646*	Single Robe Hook 4¼" high
1650*	Towel Ring 5" wide x 4½" high
1651*	Towel shelf 8" deep - available in 18" and 24" lengths
1652*	Towel Shelf w/drying rod 8" deep - available in 18" and 24" lengths

*Add finish code "P", "S", "BZ" or "PB"

THE CONCEALED-MOUNTING SYSTEM
Post is welded to mounting bracket and flange to form an integral unit. Post assembly mounts on stainless steel wall plate and is secured with set screw on bottom.

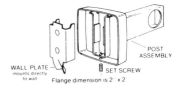

POST ASSEMBLY

WALL PLATE
mounts directly to wall   SET SCREW

Flange dimension is 2" x 2"

Contempo Chrome Bath Accessories

● FUNCTIONAL STYLING   ● DELUXE EXPOSED SCREW DESIGN

The Contempo Series offers easy installation and modern design. BASCO makes these quality fixtures available to you at a price you're sure to enjoy. These triple chrome plated accessories are made of durable Zamac.

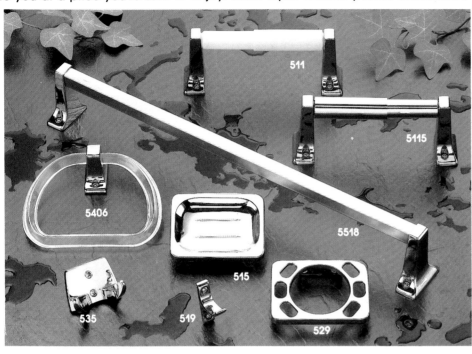

519	Robe Hook
5115	Paper Holder, Chrome Roller
511	Paper Holder, White Roller
535	Double Robe Hook
529	Chrome Toothbrush & Tumbler Holder
515	Chrome Soap Holder
5586	Soap Holder with 8" Grab Bar (not illustrated)
5406	Lucite Towel Ring
5406C	Chrome Towel Ring

⅝" Square Polished Stainless Steel Towel Bar Set

5518	18" Long
5524	24" Long
5530	30" Long
5536	36" Long

⅝" Square Aluminum Bar Towel Bar Set

5518A	18" Long
5524A	24" Long
5530A	30" Long
5536A	36" Long

Basco Shower Rods & Flanges

Shower Rods - Available in 3, 5 & 6 Foot Lengths

MODEL NO.	MATERIAL & FINISH	DIAMETER	WALL THICKNESS
1210	Anodized Aluminum	1"	.022
1210AB	Anodized Alum., Antique Brass	1"	.022
1210PB	Anodized Alum., Polished Brass	1"	.022
1212	Polished Stainless Steel	1"	.015
1213B	Polished Type 304 St. Steel	1"	.035
1213PB	Polished Brass	1"	.042
1214B	Polished Type 304 St. Steel	1"	.049
1215B	Polished Type 304 St. Steel	1¼"	.049
1216B	Polished Type 304 St. Steel	1¼"	.035
1217B	Polished Type 304 St. Steel	1½"	.035
1218B	Polished Type 304 St. Steel	1½"	.049

SHOWER ROD END FLANGES

MODEL NO.	DESCRIPTION	DIAMETER	ILLUSTRATION NO.
1200B	Concealed Screw Stainless Steel	1"	E
1201	Adjustable Chrome Plated Cast Zinc	1"	G
1201AB	Adjustable Antique Brass Cast Zinc	1"	A
1201PB	Adjustable Polished Brass Cast Zinc	1"	(Not Shown)
1202	Extended Exposed Screw Stainless Steel	1"	H
1203	Exposed Screw Chrome Plated Cast Zinc	1"	C
1203PB	Exposed Screw Solid Polished Brass	1"	B
1204B	Exposed Screw Polished Stainless Steel	1"	F
1205B	Exposed Screw Polished Stainless Steel	1¼"	F
1208B	Concealed Screw Chrome Pltd. Brass	1"	I
1209B	Concealed Screw Chrome Pltd. Brass	1¼"	I
1230B	Concealled Screw Stainless Steel	1¼"	E
1235B	Jumbo Exposed Screw Chrome Pltd. Steel	1"	D

Classic Chrome Bath Accessories

Most items available in a polished brass finish. Add prefix "PB" to model number below.

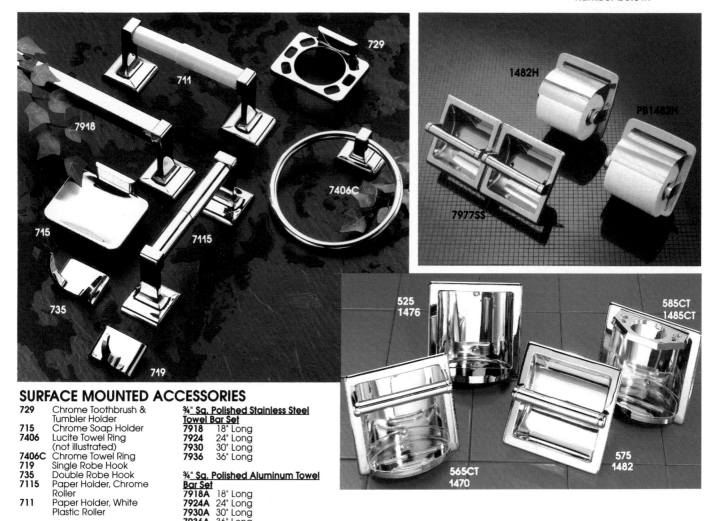

SURFACE MOUNTED ACCESSORIES

729	Chrome Toothbrush & Tumbler Holder	**¾" Sq. Polished Stainless Steel Towel Bar Set**	
715	Chrome Soap Holder	7918	18" Long
7406	Lucite Towel Ring (not illustrated)	7924	24" Long
		7930	30" Long
7406C	Chrome Towel Ring	7936	36" Long
719	Single Robe Hook		
735	Double Robe Hook	**¾" Sq. Polished Aluminum Towel Bar Set**	
7115	Paper Holder, Chrome Roller	7918A	18" Long
711	Paper Holder, White Plastic Roller	7924A	24" Long
		7930A	30" Long
		7936A	36" Long

BASCO'S very finest concealed screw accessories! The classic design of these chrome fixtures will supply you with a complete range of your bathroom needs. Made of durable Zamac, the quality craftsmanship of the Classic Series is unsurpassed. Available with ¾" square towel bars in stainless steel or aluminum. Our easy-to-install concealed screw fixtures are a must for any modern bathroom.

BASCO'S recessed accessories are crafted of solid brass and are luxuriously triple chrome plated, or made of highly polished stainless steel.

RECESSED MOUNTED ACCESSORIES

**Standard Size
Chrome Plated Brass**

Overall dimensions 6¼" x 6¼"
Wall Opening 5¼" x 5¼"
525 Soap Holder
565 Soap Holder & Grab Bar
575 Paper Holder with Chrome Roller
576 Paper Holder with Plastic Roller
525CT Soap Holder with Protective Tray
565CT Soap Holder & Grab Bar with Protective Tray
585CT Toothbrush, Tumbler & Soap Holder with Protective Tray
PB1482 Recessed polished brass toilet paper
Overall Size: 6¼" x 6¼"
Wall Opening: 5¼" x 5¼" x2"
PB1482H Recessed polished brass toilet paper holder with hood.
Overall Size: 6¼" x 6¼"
Wall Opening: 5¼" x 5¼" x2"

**Standard Size
Polished Stainless Steel**

Overall Dimensions 6¼" x 6¼"
Wall Opening 5¼" x 5¼"
1470 Soap Holder and Grab Bar
1476 Soap Holder
1482 Paper Holder with Chrome Roller
1488 Paper Holder with White Plastic Roller
1485CT Toothbrush, Tumbler & Soap Holder with Protective Tray

1482H Recessed Polished stainless steel toilet paper holder with hood.
Overall Size: 6¼" x 6¼"
Wall Opening: 5¼" x 5¼" x 2"

7977SS Recessed polished stainless steel dual toilet paper holder.
Overall Size: 12⅝" x 6¼"
Wall Opening: 11½" x 5¼" x 2"

Installation Clamp

For use with screw type recessed fixtures, this handy device simplifies installation by eliminating framework or setting in cement.
630 Installation Clamp with Retainer Spring
630LS Installation Clamp, less Retainer Spring

Cement and Tile Installation

Add the suffix "L" to any model number. A special lug will be secured to the back of any recessed fixture ordered in this manner, permitting it to be set in cement.

Part No. 630
Optional

BASCO

40 AERO ROAD, P.O. BOX 237, BOHEMIA, N.Y. 11716
(516) 567-4404 • FAX (516) 567-4815

(Printed in USA)

1993

BROAN
MEDICINE CABINETS
& LIGHTING

NINE NEW STYLES
102 NEW MODELS

LE BACCARAT
Expressions

Vive Le Baccarat! The "arch de triumph" — a classic masterpiece of refined grace in the French tradition. An arch-top beveled mirror surrounded in clear or smoked finish frames the clear-mirror swing-door cabinet offered in both recessed and surface mount versions. Matching wall mirrors echo the arched motif and the mosaic beveled glass design.

	Model	Overall Size W H D	Wall Opening W H D
RECESSED CABINET			
Clear	**LBC 10**	24x35³/₈	16¹/₂x25¹/₄x3⁷/₈
Smoked	**LBC 20**	24x35³/₈	16¹/₂x25¹/₄x3⁷/₈
SURFACE MOUNT CABINET			
Clear	**LBC 10SM**	24x35³/₈	None
Smoked	**LBC 20SM**	24x35³/₈	None
WALL MIRROR ONLY			
Clear	**LBM 15**	24x35³/₈	None
Smoked	**LBM 25**	24x35³/₈	None

LBC 10 Cabinet

Expressions OF LUXURY

Like sparkling jewels, our "Expressions" line of luxury cabinets are painstakingly handcrafted of the finest quality materials available, into exquisite designs that set a bold new hallmark of elegance for the bath.

Large, 8" diameter magnifying make-up mirrors may be conveniently mounted at desired height on the inside of any door.

Fully mirrored back walls lend a luxurious touch of elegance to the all stainless steel interiors. 1/4"-thick, smoked glass shelves can be easily adjusted to any desired position.

Fully concealed, 6-way adjustable hinges permit perfect alignment of mirrors and swing open a full 150° on cabinets equipped with magnifying make-up mirrors for convenient viewing. Hinges on models without make-up mirrors open 110° for easy cabinet access.

All edges of the distortion-free plate mirrors are either polished or elegantly beveled to a jewel-like finish. Individual, custom construction of heavy-gauge stainless steel ensures a lifetime of use. Cabinets are hand-crafted one at a time, with custom fitting and assembly that produces unique styling for the most elegant homes.

These outstanding features are included in all the "Expressions" cabinets, pages 2, 3, 4 & 5.

PRC 2160 Cabinet with PRL 2060 Soffit Light

Our leader in luxury options—a polished-edge, clear mirror tri-view cabinet. Available surface mounted, in two widths, framed on the sides and bottom with a classic-patterned beveled mirror trim in clear or smoked finish. Above, an illuminating choice: a matching soffit light mirror trim, completes the framing. Color-correcting, instant-on fluorescent soffit light fixtures provide accurate daytime make-up lighting, while spectacular, parabolic light diffusers soften the light for a decidedly elegant atmosphere.

PRIMEVÉRE
Expressions

	Clear Mirror Model	Smoked Mirror Model No.	Overall Size W H D	Lights
CABINET				
Surface	**PRC 1148SM**	**PRC 2148SM**	48x37^{3}/$_{8}$	
	PRC 1160SM	**PRC 2160SM**	60x37^{3}/$_{8}$	
Matching Soffit Light	**PRL 1148**	**PRL 2048**	48x4^{1}/$_{4}$x5^{3}/$_{8}$	Fluorescent F40C50 or Equivalent
	PRL 1160	**PRL 2060**	60x4^{1}/$_{4}$x5^{3}/$_{8}$	Fluorescent F40C50 or Equivalent

Cabinet 205236

SONATA

These 3-way frameless, beveled-edge plate glass mirror doors are cut in graceful, classic shapes to complement the traditional home. Other features include three family-size storage areas. Heavy gauge steel construction, concealed hinges, two fixed steel shelves, and bright stainless steel side panels. Surface mounted.

	Model	Overall Size W H D	Wall Opening W H D
CABINET	205230	30x32x5 1/4	None
	205236	36x32x5 1/4	None

LYRIC

Unique side light fixtures complement the gentle lines to complete a striking ensemble. Other features: a heavy gauge steel recessed storage cabinet, adjustable shelves, white baked enamel finish and magnetic door catches. Hinged right. Matching side lights feature beveled-edge mirror backplate and distinctive frosted glass shades with grey accent and chrome fittings. Uses standard medium-based bulbs (bulbs not included). Maximum 75W recommended.

	Model	Overall Size W H D	Wall Opening W H D
CABINET	250	16x28	14x18x3 1/2
	258	16x32	14x24x3 1/2
SIDE LIGHT	72052	5x17 1/2x6 1/8	None

Cabinet 258; Light 72052

4

Cabinet 165248; Light HO34890

Cabinet 268; Light 73290

OPUS

Dramatically styled art deco surface mounted cabinet. Beveled-edge plate glass mirrors and mirror appliques for a unique, and very distinctive design. 3-way viewing and a steel cabinet, with white baked enamel finish. 2 fixed steel shelves. Matching top light fixtures use G-45 or G-40 medium-based bulbs (not included).

	Model	Overall Size W H D	Wall Opening W H D	Bulb Capacity
CABINET	165230	30x28 1/4x5 1/4	None	
	165236	36x28 1/4x5 1/4	None	
	165248	48x28 1/4x5 1/4	None	
LIGHT	HO33090	30x4 1/4x5 7/8	None	4
	HO33690	36x4 1/4x5 7/8	None	4
	HO34890	48x4 1/4x5 7/8	None	5

ETERNA

Swing door cabinets feature the same art deco styling of the Opus, and are recess mounted in standard wall openings. Reversible for left or right hand opening. Adjustable shelves. Full piano hinge. Magnetic door catch. Matching top light fixtures use G-45 or G-40 medium-based bulbs (not included).

	Model	Overall Size W H D	Wall Opening W H D	Bulb Capacity
CABINET	260	16x26	14x18x3 1/2	
	268	16x26	14x24x3 1/2	
LIGHT	73290	16x4 1/2x2	None	2

5

Cabinet 151B; Light CL74829

BEL AIRE

Clean contemporary lines make the Bel Aire a big favorite with builders and designers across the nation. Perfect for today's popular, larger bathrooms. Three-way panoramic plate glass mirrors, stainless steel trim top and bottom; polished vertical edges. Two "his-n-hers" storage cabinets. Six adjustable polystyrene shelves in recessed models. Six fixed polystyrene shelves in surface mounted models. Magnetic door catches.

Choice of two matching strip lights: CL Series uses up to 60W G-16$\frac{1}{2}$ candelabra-base bulbs; BA or SB Series uses up to 60W G-25 or G-40 medium-based bulbs (bulbs not included).

	Model	Overall Size (A)	Dist. (B)	Wall Opening (C)x(D)x(E)	Bulb Capacity
CABINET					
Recessed	131D	36x36	18$\frac{1}{4}$	8x33	
	151B	48x36	23$\frac{3}{4}$	11$\frac{1}{4}$x33$\frac{1}{4}$x3$\frac{1}{2}$	
	171B	58x36	33$\frac{3}{4}$	11$\frac{1}{4}$x33$\frac{1}{4}$x3$\frac{1}{2}$	
Surface	136H	36x36x5$\frac{3}{8}$	None	None	
	148G	48x36x5$\frac{3}{8}$	None	None	
TOP LIGHT					
For Recessed	CL73629	36x3$\frac{1}{4}$x1$\frac{3}{4}$	None	None	6
	CL74829	48x3$\frac{1}{4}$x1$\frac{3}{4}$	None	None	8
	BA93629	36x3$\frac{1}{4}$x3	None	None	5
	BA94829	48x3$\frac{1}{4}$x3	None	None	6
For Surface	CL73729	36x3$\frac{1}{4}$x5	None	None	6
	CL74929	48x3$\frac{1}{4}$x5	None	None	8
	SB63629	36x3$\frac{1}{4}$x6$\frac{1}{2}$	None	None	5
	SB64829	48x3$\frac{1}{4}$x6$\frac{1}{2}$	None	None	6

Cabinet 455248

QUANTUM

Smart, frameless, beveled-edge plate glass mirrors softened with radius corners for more elegant appeal. Heavy gauge steel storage cabinet with white baked enamel. Magnetic door catches. Surface mounted. 3 storage areas. Concealed hinges. 2 fixed steel shelves. Built-in top light with matching faceplate. Uses up to 60W G-25 or G-40 bulbs (bulbs not included).

Model	Overall Size W H D	Bulb Capacity
455224	24 1/4x32 1/4x5 1/4	3
455230	30x36 1/2x5 1/4	4
455236	36x36 1/2x5 1/4	5
455248	48x36 1/2x5 1/4	6

Cabinet 1402

RADIUS CORNER   LAFAYETTE

Modern styling with elegant beveled mirror featuring radius corners. Surface mounted with built-in top light for easy, low cost installation. Hinged right. Plate glass mirror door. 3 fixed steel shelves. White baked enamel interior. Full piano hinge. Magnetic door catch. Top light uses G-25 or G-40 bulbs (bulbs not included).

Model	Overall Size W H D	Bulb Capacity
1402	18 1/8x32 3/8x6	3

Cabinet 355236; Light HO33690

AURORA

Beveled-edge plate mirror doors with cut glass design on
left and right doors. 3-way panoramic viewing. Steel
storage cabinet with 2 fixed steel shelves. Recessed or
surface mounted. Magnetic door catches. Concealed hinge
design. White baked enamel interiors. Matching top light
uses G-25 or G-40 bulbs (bulbs not included).

	Model	Overall Size W H D	Wall Opening W H D	Bulb Capacity
CABINET				
Recessed	**355030**	30x28 1/4	27 5/8x24 1/2x3 1/2	
	355036	36x28 1/4	27 5/8x24 1/2x3 1/2	
	355048	48x28 1/4	45 5/8x24 1/2x3 1/2	
Surface	**355230**	30x28 1/4x5 1/4	None	
	355236	36x28 1/4x5 1/4	None	
	355248	48x28 1/4x5 1/4	None	
TOP LIGHT				
For Recessed	**HO43090**	30x4 1/2x2 1/4	None	4
	HO43690	36x4 1/2x2 1/4	None	4
	HO44890	48x4 1/2x2 1/4	None	5
For Surface	**HO33090**	30x4 1/2x5 7/8	None	4
	HO33690	36x4 1/2x5 7/8	None	4
	HO34890	48x4 1/2x5 7/8	None	5

MIRAGE

Swing-door cabinet. Recessed. Reversible for left or right
hand opening. Heavy gauge steel storage cabinet available
in two sizes. Adjustable shelves. Piano hinge. Magnetic
catch.

	Model	Overall Size W H D	Wall Opening W H D
CABINET	1410	16x26	24x18x3 1/2
	1418	16x26	24x24x3 1/2
TOP LIGHT	73290	16x4 1/2x2	None

Cabinet 1410; Light 73290

8

HORIZON

Beveled-edge plate mirror doors. Recessed or surface mounted. Concealed hinge design. Steel storage cabinet with 2 fixed steel shelves. White baked enamel interior. Matching top lights use G-25 or G-40 bulbs (bulbs not included).

Model	Overall Size W H D	Wall Opening W H D	Bulb Capacity
RECESSED CABINET			
255024	24x24	21⁵/₈x30³/₈x3¹/₂	
255030	30x28³/₄	27⁵/₈x24¹/₂x3¹/₂	
255036	36x28¹/₄	33⁵/₈x24¹/₂x3¹/₂	
255048	48x28¹/₄	45⁵/₈x24¹/₂x3¹/₂	
SURFACE CABINET			
255224	24x24x5¹/₄	None	
255230	30x28¹/₄x5¹/₄	None	
255236	36x28¹/₄x5¹/₄	None	
255248	48x28¹/₄x5¹/₄	None	
TOP LIGHT For Recessed Cabinet			
HO42490	24x4¹/₂x2¹/₄	None	3
HO43090	30x4¹/₂x2¹/₄	None	4
HO43690	36x4¹/₂x2¹/₄	None	4
HO44890	48x4¹/₂x2¹/₄	None	5
TOP LIGHT For Surface Cabinet			
HO32490	24x4¹/₂x5⁷/₈	None	3
HO33090	30x4¹/₂x5⁷/₈	None	4
HO33690	36x4¹/₂x5⁷/₈	None	4
HO34890	48x4¹/₂x5⁷/₈	None	5

Cabinet 255236; Light HO33690

SQUARE CORNER LAFAYETTE

Swing-door cabinet. Plate glass mirrors. 3 fixed steel shelves. Surface mounted with built-in top light for easy installation. Piano hinged on right. Magnetic catch. White baked enamel interior. Top light uses up to 60W G-25 or G-40 bulbs (bulbs not included).

Model	Overall Size W H D	Bulb Capacity
1462	18¹/₈x28³/₈x6	3

Cabinet 1462

9

Cabinet 151224; Light SB22429

Cabinet 151230; Light SB23029

BEL AIRE 2

Modern Bel Aire styling for the cost-conscious buyer. Offers easy surface mounting with deluxe features: Silver aluminum frame surrounds 3 plate glass mirror doors; 3-way panoramic viewing; 3 storage areas, 2 fixed steel shelves, magnetic door catches; white interior. Model 151224 has two doors as shown. Matching top light uses up to 60W G-25 or G-40 bulbs (bulbs not included).

	Model	Overall Size W H D	Bulb Capacity
CABINET	151224	23 3/8 x 30 x 5	
	151230	29 x 30 x 5	
	151236	35 x 30 x 5	
TOP LIGHT	SB22429	23 3/8 x 3 x 5 3/4	4
	SB23029	29 x 3 x 5 3/4	4
	SB23629	35 x 3 x 5 3/4	5

STYLELINE 2

Surface mounted with built-in top light for easy, low cost installation. Plate glass mirror door with stainless steel trim top and bottom; polished vertical edges. 3 fixed steel shelves. Hinged right. White baked enamel interior. Full piano hinge. Magnetic door catch. Top light features stainless steel face and uses up to 60W G-25 or G-40 bulbs (bulbs not included).

Swing-Door Model	Overall Size W H D	Bulb Capacity
565	18 x 28 x 6	3

Cabinet 565

10

VIENNA

Contemporary elegance trimmed in polished chrome. Surface mounted tri-view cabinet features 3 storage compartments each with 2 fixed steel shelves. Magnetic door catches. White baked enamel interior. Matching chrome top lights accommodate up to 60W G-25 or G-40 bulbs (bulbs not included).

	Model	Overall Size W H D	Bulb Capacity
CABINET	**155124**	24x26x5 $^1/_2$	
	155130	30x26x5 $^1/_2$	
	155136	36x26x5 $^1/_2$	
TOP LIGHT	**SB22529**	24x4x5 $^1/_2$	3
	SB23129	30x4x5 $^1/_2$	4
	SB23729	36x4x5 $^1/_2$	5

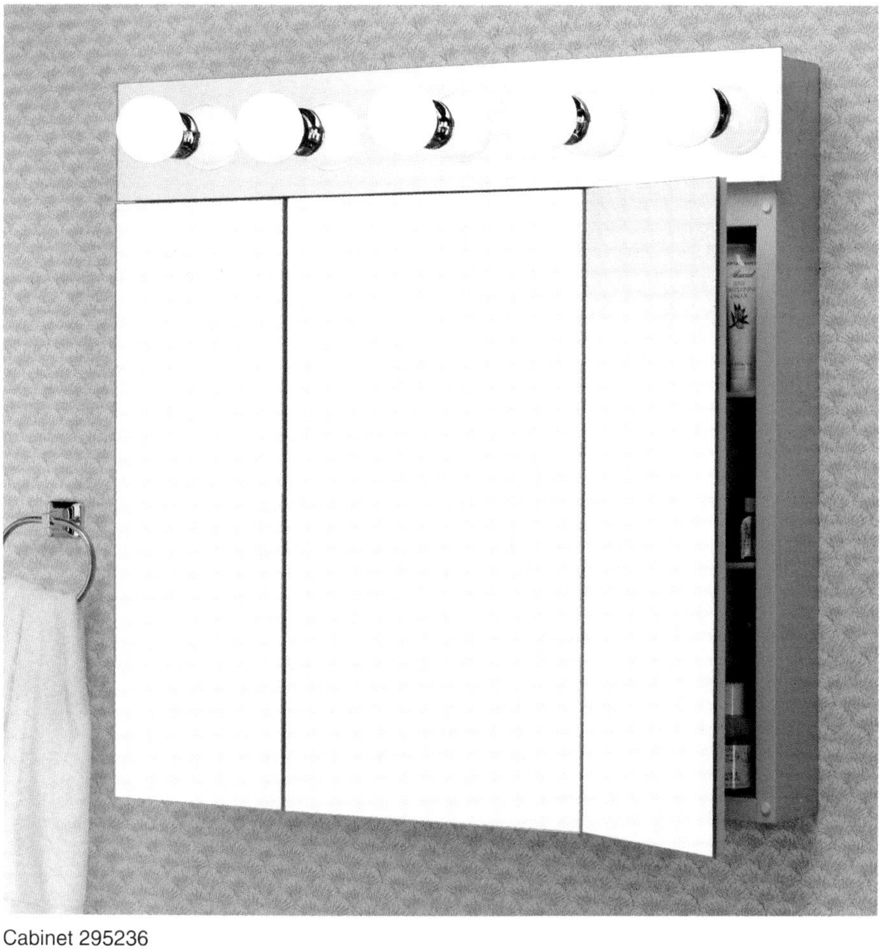

Cabinet 155136; Light SB23729

FOCUS

Simple elegant design. Surface mounted tri-view cabinet with built-in top light. Polished edge plate glass mirrors. 3 doors. 3 storage areas. 2 fixed steel shelves. Concealed hinges. White baked enamel finish. Top light uses up to 60W G-25 or G-40 bulbs (bulbs not included).

Model	Overall Size W H D	Bulb Capacity
295224	24x28 $^5/_8$x5 $^1/_4$	3
295230	30x32 $^3/_4$x5 $^1/_4$	4
295236	36x32 $^3/_4$x5 $^1/_4$	5

Cabinet 295236

TORINO

The timeless beauty of a classic shape. Available in two decorator styles: elegant frosted cut-glass *teardrop* motif and *plain beveled-edge*. Recessed steel storage cabinet features adjustable shelves, magnetic catches, white baked enamel interiors. Hinged right. Matching side light fixtures feature beveled-edge mirror back plate and frosted glass shade. Uses standard medium-based bulbs. Max. 75W recommended (bulbs not included).

	Model	Overall Size W H D	Wall Opening W H D
CABINET			
Teardrop	**5520**	16 1/2x34 1/2	14x18x3 1/2
	5528	16 1/2x34 1/2	14x24x3 1/2
TOP LIGHT	**73591**	5 3/8x13 3/4x6 1/2	None

Cabinet 5520; Lights 73591

Cascading teardrops update a style reminiscent of the art deco era. Frosted cut-glass in clear mirror adds charm to any bathroom decor.

Detail of Cabinet 5520

Cabinet 5518; Lights 73591

	Model	Overall Size W H D	Wall Opening W H D
CABINET			
Beveled Edge	**5510**	16 1/2x34 1/2	14x18x3 1/2
	5518	16 1/2x34 1/2	14x24x3 1/2
SIDE LIGHT	**73591**	5 3/8x13 3/4x6 1/2	None

MIRAGE

Frameless beveled-edged mirrors in elegant styles. Recessed cabinet, with adjustable shelves, magnetic catches and white baked enamel interior. Reversible for left or right hand opening. Matching top lights, or side lights with beveled mirror sconce and tinted glass shade. Uses up to 60W G-25 or G-40 bulbs (bulbs not included).

	Model	Overall Size W H D	Wall Opening W H D
CABINET	1454	18x27	14x18x3 1/2
	1456	17 3/8x32	14x24x3 1/2
MIRROR ONLY	1454WM	18x27	None
SIDE LIGHT	73190	5x12x6 1/2	None

Cabinet 1454; Lights 73190

Cabinet 1450BC; Lights 73190

	Model	Overall Size W H D	Wall Opening W H D
CABINET	1450BC	16x26	14x18x3 1/2
	1458	16x26	14x24x3 1/2
MIRROR ONLY	1450WM	16x26	None
SIDE LIGHT	73190	5x12x6 1/2	None
TOP LIGHT	73290	16x6 1/2x2 1/2	None

Cabinet 1451; Lights 73290

		Model	Overall Size W H D	Wall Opening W H D
CABINET				
Steel		1451	16x26	14x18x3 1/2
	NEW	1448*	16x26	14x24x3 1/2
		1459	16x26	14x24x3 1/2
	NEW	1459 MOD**	16x26	14x18x3 1/2
Molded		1453	16x20	14x18x2 1/2
MIRROR ONLY		1451WM	16x26	None
SIDE LIGHT		73190	5x12x6 1/2	None
TOP LIGHT		73290	16x4 1/2x2	None

*New Stainless Steel Cabinet (See p.16 for details)
**New Modular Shelf Storage (See p.16 for details)

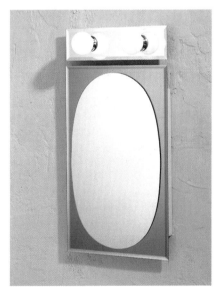

Cabinet 1452; Lights 73290

	Model	Overall Size W H D	Wall Opening W H D
CABINET	1452	16x26	14x18x3 1/2
	1457	16x26	14x24x3 1/2
MIRROR ONLY	1452WM	16x26	None
TOP LIGHT	73290	16x4 1/2x2	None

13

OBSCURA

Auxiliary storage with frameless polished-edge plate glass mirror doors. Special low-profile (1/4" projection from wall) designed to fit flush with adjacent wall mirrors. 3 adjustable shelves. Spring-loaded magnetic door release. Eurostyle concealed hinges.

Model	Overall Size W H D	Wall Opening W H D
629	15x36	14x34x4
639BC	13x36	12x34x4

Large
Hidden
Storage Area

Cabinet 629

AVANTI CORNER CABINET

Triangular-shaped corner cabinet adds storage and 3-way viewing when used in pairs with a simple wall mirror. Ideal for vanity nooks. Or use a single cabinet with wall mirror to make smaller areas look larger while adding storage space. Surface mounted. Reversible. 3 shelves. Stainless steel, gold aluminum or oak trim. Oak version available with white enamel or stainless steel cabinet. Other models with white baked enamel finish cabinet.

7¼"
5¾"
Wall Mirror
12"
13"
1¾"

Triangular Shaped

Model	Trim	Overall Size W H D
631	Stainless Steel	13x36x7¼
632	Gold Aluminum	13x36x7¼
672	Oak	19½x33½x10½
NEW 672SS	Oak (Stainless St. Cab.)	17¼x31x9⅞

Cabinet (2) 631; PEM3636 Mirror; CL73629 Light Strip

Cabinet 672

Cabinet 1420FL; Light 735FL

DECORAH

Elegant floral with soft gold-tone and soft white design. Recessed. Adjustable shelves. Frameless plate glass mirror. Reversible for left or right hand opening. Magnetic catches. White baked enamel interior. Matching top light uses up to 60W G-25 or G-40 bulbs (bulbs not included).

	Model	Overall Size W H D	Wall Opening W H D
CABINET	1420FL	16x26	14x18x3$\frac{1}{2}$
	1428FL	16x26	14x24x3$\frac{1}{2}$
TOP LIGHT	735FL	16x4$\frac{3}{8}$x2	None

Cabinet 5418

ADANTE — Beveled

Arch top shaped beveled-edge mirror is a perfect complement for popular pedestal sinks. Recessed cabinet features white baked enamel interior and adjustable shelves. Unit is reversible for use with optional arch top light for a dazzling 2-piece oval ensemble. Matching top light uses up to 60W G-25 or G-40 bulbs (bulbs not included).

	Model	Overall Size W H D	Wall Opening W H D
CABINET	5410	16$\frac{1}{2}$x26	14x18x3$\frac{1}{2}$
	5418	16$\frac{1}{2}$x31	14x24x3$\frac{1}{2}$
TOP LIGHT	73960	16$\frac{1}{2}$x6$\frac{1}{4}$x2	None

Cabinet 1430

FOCUS

Simple elegance. Swing door cabinet features polished edge plate glass mirror, 2 or 3 adjustable shelves, piano hinge and reversible magnet catch. White baked enamel interior finish.

	Model	Overall Size W H D	Wall Opening W H D
CABINET	1430	16x22	14x18x3$\frac{1}{2}$
	1438	16x26	14x24x3$\frac{1}{2}$

STAINLESS STEEL

Create an exciting bathroom look with either of our new stainless steel models. Both units feature the strikingly clean appearance of high lustre type 304 stainless steel with bright #4 satin finish.

Their sterling finish means these cabinet interiors are easy to clean and rust resistant. They are also ideal for hospitals, nursing homes and settings where extra health protection is desired.

Both models are designed for recessed mounting with door opening either left or right. The model 1448 features a frameless, beveled-edge mirror and three adjustable glass shelves. The 448BC has a classic, stainless steel frame and includes three adjustable stainless steel shelves.

Model	Description	Overall Size W H D	Wall Opening W H D	Refer to Page
1448	Beveled Edge	16x26	14x24x3 1/2	13
448BC	Stainless Steel	16x26	14x24x3 1/2	35

MODULAR SHELF

Our unique cabinet design (patent pending) provides maximum storage capacity. Six modular half-shelves can be positioned in an unlimited number of configurations utilizing four snap-in center posts. This new flexible design means shelves can quickly be adjusted without tools to accommodate various container sizes.

The modular shelf design is available with any of four distinctive frames. Select from solid oak, deluxe bright brass, frameless beveled edge or classic stainless steel. All deliver more storage flexibility with no wasted space!

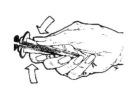 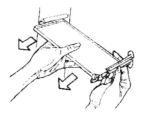

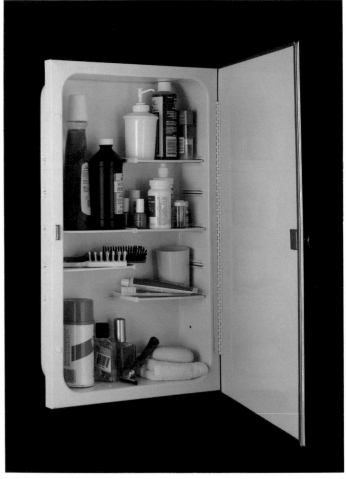

Model	Overall Size W H D	Wall Opening W H D	Refer to Page
8778MOD	16 1/4x26 1/4	14x24x3 1/2	32
318BRMOD	17 1/4x27 1/4	14x24x3 1/2	24
1459MOD	16x26	14x24x3 1/2	13
468MOD	16x26	14x24x3 1/2	35

BEL AIRE AUXILIARY

Designed to meet the variety of needs presented by today's bathroom interiors. Available in either recessed or surface mounted models. Ideal in combination with wall mirror and light strips to provide extra storage and 3-way viewing.

Plate glass mirror, stainless steel trim top and bottom with polished vertical mirror edges. Steel storage cabinet with white baked-on enamel finish. 3 fixed shelves.

Cabinet (two) 626; PEM3630 Mirror, MB63019 Light Strip

	Model	Overall Size W H D	Wall Opening
RECESSED	625	13x36	11^1/$_4$x33^1/$_4$
SURFACE	626	13x36x4^1/$_4$	None

Cabinet 625

HIDEAWAY

Steel swing-door can be wallpapered or painted to blend with wall for hidden storage. Reversible door for left or right hand opening. Rugged piano hinge with magnetic door catch. Adjustable shelves with soft-tone baked enamel interior.

Model	Overall Size W H D	Wall Opening
622	17^1/$_8$x21^1/$_2$	14x18x3^1/$_2$

Cabinet 622

17

Cabinet 473248; Light EA54828

EARLY AMERICAN

Charming, provincial floral pattern creates new decorating possibilities. Warm tone colors can be used to complement or accent your bathroom decor. Bright brass accent trim. White sides. Tri-view cabinet features 3-way viewing, 2 fixed metal shelves, plate glass mirrors, one touch magnetic catch and white baked enamel interiors. Can be recessed or surface mounted. Matching top light features bright brass fittings and face plate insert and uses up to 60W medium-base bulbs (bulbs not included).

	Tri-View Model	Overall Size W H D	Wall Opening W H D	Bulb Capacity
CABINET	473230	30x29 3/4x4	27 1/2x27x3 1/2	
	473236	36x29 3/4x4	33 1/2x27x3 1/2	
	473248	48x29 3/4x4	45 3/8x27x3 1/2	
TOP LIGHT	EA53028	30x8x9 3/4	None	3
	EA53628	36x8x9 3/4	None	4
	EA54828	48x8x9 3/4	None	5

Reversible swing door cabinet. Adjustable shelves on recessed units, fixed shelves on surface mount. Piano hinge. Magnetic catch. Recessed and surface mounted units available. Can be mounted to open left or right. Other features same as tri-view.

	Swing-Door Model	Overall Size W H D	Wall Opening W H D	Bulb Capacity
CABINET				
Recessed	4730	18x27 1/2	14x18x3 1/2	
	4738	18x27 1/2	14x24x3 1/2	
Surface	4732	18x27 1/2x5	None	
TOP LIGHT				
For Recessed	705EA	18x8x7 1/2	None	2
For Surface	706EA	18x8x11	None	2

Cabinet 4738; Light 705EA

Cabinet 471236; Light CT53618

COUNTRY FLORAL

Tri-view cabinet features innovative new design with light, airy floral pattern. Bright brass accent trim. 3-way viewing. Plate glass mirror doors. 2 fixed metal shelves. Recessed or surface mounted. White baked enamel interior. Spring loaded magnetic door catches. Top light features bright brass fitting and clear halothane glass shades. Use 60W medium-based bulbs (bulbs not included).

	Tri-View Model	Overall Size W H D	Wall Opening W H D	Bulb Capacity
CABINET	471230	30x29³/₄x4	27¹/₂x27x3¹/₂	
	471236	36x29³/₄x4	33¹/₂x27x3¹/₂	
TOP LIGHT	CT53018	30x8x9³/₄	None	3
	CT53618	36x8x9³/₄	None	4

Swing door cabinet. Adjustable shelves. Piano hinge. Magnetic catch. Recessed and surface mounted units available. Reversible: can be mounted to open left or right. Other features same as tri-view.

	Swing-Door Model	Overall Size W H D	Wall Opening W H D	Bulb Capacity
CABINET				
Recessed	4710	18x27¹/₂	14x18x3¹/₂	
	4718	18x27¹/₂	14x24x3¹/₂	
Surface	4712	18x27¹/₂x5	None	
TOP LIGHT				
For Recessed	705CT	18x8x7¹/₂	None	2
For Surface	706CT	18x8x11	None	2

Cabinet 4710; Light 705CT

19

Cabinet 350AL (3); Light 745AL (3)

SPECTRUM

With Matching Top Lights

Spectrum bath cabinets are created to match the popular colors of bathroom plumbing fixtures for dramatic colorful bathrooms. "Enduro" frame is designed for long life in high moisture atmosphere. Swing-door cabinets have 2 or 3 adjustable shelves. Full piano hinge. Reversible. Tri-view models feature 3 plate glass mirrors, 3 storage areas and 2 fixed shelves. Matching top light fixtures feature bright chrome panels and trim. Use up to 60W G-25 or G-40 bulbs (not included).

	Swing Door Model	Overall Size W H D	Wall Opening W H D
CABINETS	350 series	18x27 1/2	14x18x3 1/2
	358 series	18x27 1/2	14x24x3 1/2
	313WH Molded*	16x20	14x18x2 1/2
	352 series	18x27 1/2x5	None
MIRROR ONLY	355 series	18x27 1/2	None
TOP LIGHTS			
For Recessed	745 series	18x6 1/2x3	None
For Surface	746 series	18x6 1/2x5 1/2	None
	Tri-View Models		
CABINETS	3230 series	30x30x4 1/4	27 1/2x27x3 1/2
	3236 series	36x30x4 1/4	33 1/2x27x3 1/2
	3248 series	48x30x4 1/4	45 3/8x26 7/8x3 1/2
TOP LIGHTS	SP132 series	30x6 1/2x5 1/4	
For Surface	SP133 series	36x6 1/2x5 1/4	
*White Only	SP134 series	48x6 1/2x5 1/4	

Cabinet 3230WH; Light SP132WH

Cabinet 3336TL

SPECTRUM

With Integral Lights

Spectrum color coordinated bath cabinets with built-in top lights can be recessed or surface mounted. Swing-door cabinets have 2 or 3 adjustable shelves. Full piano hinge. Reversible. Tri-view models feature 3 plate glass mirrors, 3 storage areas and 2 fixed shelves. "Enduro" frame is designed for long life in high moisture atmosphere. Baked enamel white interiors and plate glass mirrors.

Cabinet/Light 2009WR

	Swing-Door Model	Overall Size W H D	Wall Opening W H D
CABINETS w/Built-in Top Lights	**2009 series**	19 1/8x32 1/4x5	16 3/4x28 3/4x3 1/2

	Tri-View Model	Overall Size	Wall Opening
CABINETS w/Built-in Top Lights:	**3330 series**	31x30 3/8x5	28 3/4x27 1/2x3 1/2
	3336 series	37x30 3/8x5	34 3/4x27 1/2x3 1/2

SPECTRUM ORDERING INFORMATION

When ordering Spectrum bath cabinets and top lights, indicate color by including color code after model number. For example, to order a surface mounted 352 series cabinet in Rose (WR), ask for 352WR.

COLORS AVAILABLE

White(WH)   Black(BL)   Almond(AL)   Rose(WR)   Teal(TL)

MAXIM

Classic formal design featuring an inlay of polished black marble-stone with bright brass trim. Tri-view cabinet features 3-way viewing, 2 fixed metal shelves, plate glass mirrors, one-touch magnetic door catches, and white baked enamel interiors. Can be recessed or surface mounted. Brass tone side panels. Matching top lights feature bright brass fittings and clear prismatic glass shades. Uses maximum 60W medium-based bulbs (bulbs not included).

	Tri-View Model	Overall Size W H D	Wall Opening W H D	Bulb Capacity
CABINET	666230	30x29³/₄x5¹/₂	27¹/₂x27x3¹/₂	
	666236	36x29³/₄x5¹/₂	33¹/₂x27x3¹/₂	
TOP LIGHT	BM63018	30x7¹/₄x11¹/₂	None	4
	BM63618	36x7¹/₄x11¹/₂	None	5

Swing-door cabinet. Piano hinge. Magnetic catch. Recessed and surface mounted units available. Reversible: can be mounted to open left or right. Other features same as tri-view.

	Swing-Door Model	Overall Size W H D	Wall Opening W H D	Bulb Capacity
CABINET				
Recessed	**660BC**	18x27¹/₂	14x18x3¹/₂	
	668BC	18x27¹/₂	14x24x3¹/₂	
Surface	**662BC**	18x27¹/₂x5	None	
TOP LIGHT				
For Recessed	**76668**	18x7¹/₄x9¹/₄	None	2
For Surface	**76768**	18x7¹/₄x12¹/₂	None	2

Cabinet 3130BL

TREASURES

Distinctive, Euro-styled cabinet with built-in light. Upscale design features back-to-back mirror doors, with mirrored interior, 3-way viewing from a 2-door cabinet. Can be recessed or surface mounted. White baked enamel interior has 3 adjustable glass shelves. One-touch magnetic door catch. High gloss frame available in White, Black, and Almond with color coordinated side panels, plus striking gold accent stripe and gold faceplate. Built-in light uses up to 60W G-25 or G-40 bulbs (bulbs not included).

	Model	Overall Size W H D	Bulb Capacity
White	3130WH	31x30³/₈x5	4
	3136WH	37x30³/₈x5	5
Almond	3130AL	31x30³/₈x5	4
	3136AL	37x30³/₈x5	5
Black	3130BL	31x30³/₈x5	4
	3136BL	37x30³/₈x5	5

CASPAR

Sculptured contemporary extruded aluminum frame features silver/brass decorator finish. 3-way viewing, plate glass mirror doors. 3 storage areas. 2 fixed metal shelves. Heavy gauge steel storage cabinet can be surface or recessed mounted. Built-in light section features brass faceplate with brass frame; silver faceplate with silver frame. White baked-on enamel interiors. Spring-loaded magnetic door catches. Built-in top light. Uses up to 60W G-25 or G-40 bulbs (bulbs not included).

	Model	Overall Size W H D	Wall Opening W H D
Silver & Brass	113930	30x29³/₈x5¹/₂	28³/₄x27¹/₂x3¹/₂
	113936	36x29³/₈x5¹/₂	34³/₄x27¹/₂x3¹/₂

Cabinet 113930

VICEROY

Bright brass or chrome metallic framing to complement today's bathroom accessories. Plate glass mirror doors feature "one touch" door release. Heavy gauge steel cabinet can be surface or recessed mounted. 2 fixed metal shelves. White baked enamel finish. Built-in top light with matching faceplate. Uses up to 60W G-25 or G-40 bulbs (bulbs not included).

Brass Model	Chrome Model	Overall Size W H D	Wall Opening W H D	Bulb Capacity
171924	172924	23³/₄x29⁵/₈x4¹/₄	22³/₄x27³/₄x3¹/₂	3
171930	172930	30x29⁵/₈x4¹/₄	28³/₄x27³/₄x3¹/₂	4
171936	172936	36x29⁵/₈x4¹/₄	34³/₄x27³/₄x3¹/₂	5
171948	172948	48x29⁵/₈x4¹/₄	46³/₄x27³/₄x3¹/₂	6

Cabinet 171930

CORONA

Bright brass or chrome metallic framing to complement today's bathroom accessories. Plate glass mirror doors feature "one touch" door release. Heavy gauge steel cabinet can be surface or recessed mounted. Hinged right. White baked enamel finish. 3 fixed metal shelves. Built-in top light with matching faceplate. Uses up to 60W G-25 or G-40 bulbs (bulbs not included).

	Brass Model	Chrome Model	Overall Size W H D	Wall Opening W H D	Bulb Capacity
CABINET	2012BR	2022CH	18x31x5	16³/₄x29x3¹/₂	3

Cabinet 2012BR

VERONA

Reflective, glossy metallic-framed cabinet in 2 contemporary finishes. Swing-door cabinet is reversible for right or left hand opening, and features magnetic catch. White baked enamel interior. Available with steel or molded storage cabinet. Reversible: can be mounted to open left or right. Available in brass or chrome. Matching top light uses up to 60W G-25 or G-40 bulbs (bulbs not included).

	Brass Model	Chrome Model	Overall Size W H D	Wall Opening W H D	Bulb Capacity
STEEL CABINET	310BR	310CH	17¹/₄x27¹/₄	14x18x3¹/₂	
	318BR	318CH	17¹/₄x27¹/₄	14x24x3¹/₂	
NEW	318BRMOD*		17¹/₄x27¹/₄	14x24x3¹/₂	
MOLDED CABINET	313BR	313CH	16x20	14x18x2¹/₂	
TOP LIGHT	747BR	747CH	17¹/₄x5¹/₂x3		3

*New Modular Shelf Storage (See p. 16 for details)

Cabinet 318CH; Light 747CH

Cabinet 842236; Light BS84623

BAKER STREET

Cabinet 878; Light 70373

Cabinet 828; Light 70123

Charming Victorian detail lends a distinctive period touch to practical bathroom storage. Choose from classic Colonial White or Warm Honey Oak solid wood frames. Plate glass mirror doors. Steel construction assures a lifetime of family use. White baked enamel interiors. Magnet door catches. Matching light fixtures feature frosted glass shades and bright brass fittings. Uses medium-base bulbs (not included).

Tri-View Cabinets include 3-way viewing, 3 storage areas, two fixed shelves. Surface mounted with matching woodtone sides.

	Colonial White	Honey Oak	Overall Size W H D	Wall Opening W H D	Bulb Capacity
CABINET					
	842230	847230	30x28¹/₂x5¹/₂	None	
	842236	847236	36x28¹/₂x5¹/₂	None	
TOP LIGHT					
	BS84023	BS84073	30x6x6¹/₂	None	3
	BS84623	BS84673	36x6x6¹/₂	None	4

Swing-Door Cabinets include adjustable shelves in recessed models (2 or 3). Fixed shelves in surface model. Full piano hinge. Reversible. Matching sidelight fixtures feature unique brass towel rings.

	Colonial White	Honey Oak	Overall Size W H D	Wall Opening W H D	Bulb Capacity
CABINET					
Recessed	820	870	18x27	14x18x3¹/₂	
	828	878	18x27	14x24x3¹/₂	
Surface	822	872	18x27x5	None	
SIDE LIGHT	70123	70173	6¹/₂x13¹/₂x9¹/₂	None	1
TOP LIGHT					
For Recessed	70223	70273	18x6¹/₂x3	None	2
For Surface	70323	70373	18x6¹/₂x5¹/₂	None	2

Cabinet 567248; Light GS54873

GOLDEN SAND

Natural honey oak frames complementary brown-toned inlay of "touchstone" simulating warm granite texture. Tri-view cabinets features 3-way viewing, 2 fixed metal steel shelves, plate glass mirrors, one-touch magnetic door catches, and white baked enamel interiors. Surface mounted. Matching wood-tone sides. Matching top lights feature bright brass fittings and clear-ribbed prismatic glass shades. Uses maximum 60W medium-based bulbs (bulbs not included).

	Tri-View Model	Overall Size W H D	Bulb Capacity
CABINET	567230	30x28 1/2x5 1/4	
	567236	36x28 1/2x5 1/4	
	567248	48x28 1/2x5 1/4	
TOP LIGHT	GS53073	30x7 1/4x12 1/4	3
	GS53673	36x7 1/4x12 1/4	4
	GS54873	48x7 1/4x12 1/4	5

Reversible swing door cabinet. Adjustable shelves. Piano hinge. Magnetic catch. Recessed and surface mounted units available. Can be mounted to open left or right. Other features same as tri-view.

	Swing-Door Model	Overall Size W H D	Wall Opening W H D	Bulb Capacity
CABINET				
Recessed	5670	17 1/8x27 1/8x2	14x18x3 1/2	
	5678	17 1/8x27 1/8x2	14x24x3 1/2	
Surface	5672	17 1/8x27 1/8x5 1/2	None	
TOP LIGHT				
For Surface	707GS	17 1/8x7 1/4x6 3/4	None	2
For Recessed	708GS	17 1/8x7 1/4x10 1/8	None	2

Cabinet 5670; Light 707GS

Cabinet 562248; Light WH54873

Cabinet 5620; Light 707WH

WHITE MARBLE

Natural honey oak frames complements white marble inlay of "touchstone" simulating high gloss marble finish. Tri-view cabinets features 3-way viewing, 2 fixed metal shelves, plate glass mirrors, one-touch magnetic door catches, and white baked enamel interiors. Surface mounted. Matching wood-tone sides. Matching top lights feature bright brass fittings and clear-ribbed prismatic glass shades. Uses maximum 60W medium-based bulbs (bulbs not included).

	Tri-View Model	Overall Size W H D	Bulb Capacity
CABINET	562230	30x28^1/2x5^1/4	
	562236	36x28^1/2x5^1/4	
	562248	48x28^1/2x5^1/4	
TOP LIGHT	WH53073	30x7^1/4x12^1/4	3
	WH53673	36x7^1/4x12^1/4	4
	WH54873	48x7^1/4x12^1/4	5

Swing door cabinet. Adjustable shelves. Piano hinge. Magnetic catch. Recessed and surface mounted units available. Reversible: can be mounted to open left or right. Other features same as tri-view.

	Swing-Door Model	Overall Size W H D	Wall Opening W H D	Bulb Capacity
CABINET				
Recessed	5620	17^1/8x27^1/8x2	14x18x3^1/2	
	5628	17^1/8x27^1/8x2	14x24x3^1/2	
Surface	5622	17^1/8x27^1/8x5^1/2	None	
TOP LIGHT				
For Recessed	707WH	17^1/8x7^1/4x6^3/4	None	2
For Surface	708WH	17^1/8x7^1/4x10^1/8	None	2

27

Cabinet 182248; Light SE24828

CANTERBURY

Surface mounted tri-view cabinet in traditional cathedral arch design features, 3-way viewing and 3 separate storage areas. 2 fixed metal shelves. Choose natural light honey oak or traditional colonial white frame with matching sides. Plate glass mirrors. Magnetic door catches. white baked enamel interior. Matching top lights with clear ribbed prismatic glass shades and bright brass fittings. Maximum 60 watt bulbs recommended (bulbs not included).

	Honey Oak Model	White Model	Overall Size W H D	Bulb Capacity
CABINET	187230	182230	30x28^1/$_2$x5^1/$_2$	
	187236	182236	36x28^1/$_2$x5^1/$_2$	
	187248	182248	48x28^1/$_2$x5^1/$_2$	
TOP LIGHT	SE23078	SE23028	30x8x11	3
	SE23678	SE23628	36x8x11	4
	SE24878	SE24828	48x8x11	5

HENLEY

Swing-door cabinet features adjustable shelves on recessed models, fixed shelves on surface models, piano hinge, magnetic door catch. Hinged right.

	Honey Oak Model	White Model	Overall Size W H D	Wall Opening W H D	Bulb Capacity
CABINET					
Recessed	8570	8520	18^1/$_4$x27^1/$_4$	14x18x3^1/$_2$	
	8578	8528	18^1/$_4$x27^1/$_4$	14x24x3^1/$_2$	
Surface	8572	8522	18^1/$_4$x27^1/$_4$x5^1/$_2$	None	
TOP LIGHT					
For Recessed	76378	76328	18x8x8	None	2
For Surface	76478	76428	18x8x11^1/$_2$	None	2

Cabinet 8578; Light 76378

Cabinet 177930

OAKHILL

Popular honey oak framed tri-view cabinet with built-in top light. One-touch spring-loaded magnetic door releases. Can be surface mounted or recessed. 3-way viewing plate glass mirrors. 3 storage areas. 2 fixed shelves. White baked-on enamel finish, steel storage cabinet. Built-in top light features chrome faceplate and uses G-25 or G-40 bulbs (bulbs not included).

Model	Overall Size W H D	Wall Opening W H D	Bulb Capacity
177924	23 1/4x29 5/8x4 1/4	22 3/4x27 1/2x3 1/2	4
177930	30x29 5/8x4 1/4	28 3/4x27 1/2x3 1/2	4
177936	36x29 5/8x4 1/4	34 3/4x27 1/2x3 1/2	5
177948	48x29 5/8x4 1/4	46 3/4x27 1/2x3 1/2	5

OAKDALE

Swing-door cabinet with built-in top light features 3 fixed shelves and can also be recessed or surface mounted. Hinged right. White baked-on enamel finish, steel storage cabinet. Built-in top light features chrome faceplate and uses G-25 or G-40 bulbs (bulbs not included).

Model	Overall Size W H D	Wall Opening W H D	Bulb Capacity
2072	18x31x5 1/2	16 3/4x28 3/4x3 1/2	3

Cabinet 2072

29

Cabinet 816236; Light OK81668

PRAIRIE

Genuine 3/4" hardwood frames with traditional detailing and matching woodtone sides. Choose from the graceful warmth of honey oak or blonde oak or the splash of a colonial white. All are equipped with plate glass mirror doors and heavy duty steel storage cabinets engineered for strenuous family use. Matching toplight fixtures feature clear prismatic glass shades and bright brass fittings. Use medium-base bulbs — 60W maximum recommended.

Cabinet 8170; Light 70978

Cabinet 8120; Light 71928

	Colonial White	Blonde Oak	Honey Oak	Overall Size W H D	Wall Opening W H D	Bulb Capacity
SWING DOOR CABINET						
Recessed	8120	8160	8170	18x27$^{1}/_{2}$	14x18x3$^{1}/_{2}$	-
	8128	8168	8178	18x27$^{1}/_{2}$	14x24x3$^{1}/_{2}$	-
Surface	8122	8162	8172	18x27$^{1}/_{2}$	None	-
TOP LIGHT						
For Recessed	70928	70968	70978	18x8x8	None	2
For Surface	71028	71068	71078	18x11$^{1}/_{2}$x8	None	2
TRIVIEW CABINET						
Surface	812230	816230	817230	30x28$^{1}/_{2}$x5$^{1}/_{2}$	None	-
	812236	816236	817236	36x28$^{1}/_{2}$x5$^{1}/_{2}$	None	-
TOP LIGHT						
For Surface	OK81028	OK81068	OK81078	30x8x11	None	3
	OK81628	OK81668	OK81678	36x8x11	None	4

Cabinet 197236

AUTUMN

The warmth of honey oak enhanced by a new canopy design shields bulbs and delivers plenty of subdued lighting. Can be recessed or surface mounted. 2 fixed metal shelves. Plate glass mirrors. Matching oak frame and wood-tone sides completes this practical tri-view cabinet. Uses maximum 60W standard medium-based bulbs (not included).

Model	Overall Size W H D	Wall Opening W H D	Bulb Capacity
197230	30x29x5 $^1/2$	28 $^3/4$x27 $^1/2$x3 $^1/2$	4
197236	36x29x5 $^1/2$	34 $^3/4$x27 $^1/2$x3 $^1/2$	5
197248	48x29x5 $^1/2$	46 $^3/4$x27 $^1/2$x3 $^1/2$	5

Cabinet 807236; Light PL3677

SHENENDOAH

An elegant and spacious honey oak surface mounted cabinet that complements traditional oak vanity bases. Sturdily constructed with a solid oak frame and plywood interior. 2 fixed metal shelves Plate glass mirrors. Etched glass shades and bright brass trim provide the finishing touch. Uses maximum 60W standard medium-based bulbs (not included).

	Model	Overall Size W H D	Bulb Capacity
CABINET	807230	30x32x5	
	807236	36x32x5	
	807248	48x32x5	
LIGHT	PL3077	30x7 $^1/2$x11 $^1/2$	4
	PL3677	36x7 $^1/2$x11 $^1/2$	4
	PL4877	48x7 $^1/2$x11 $^1/2$	5

GRAND OAK II

Can be recessed or surface mounted.
3 storage areas. Light honey oak
framed plate glass mirrors, 2 fixed
shelves, magnetic door catches. White
baked enamel finish. Surface mounted
top lights use up to 60W G-25 or G-40
bulbs (bulbs not included).

Tri-View Model	Overall Size W H D	Wall Opening W H D	Bulb Capacity
CABINET			
277924	24x25	22 1/4x23x3 1/2	
277930	29x28 7/8	27 1/2x27x3 1/2	
277936	35x28 7/8	33 1/2x27x3 1/2	
277948	47x28 7/8	45 1/2x27x3 1/2	
TOP LIGHT			
SG32479	24x5 5/8x5 1/4	None	3
SG33079	29x5 5/8x5 1/4	None	4
SG33679	35x5 5/8x5 1/4	None	4
SG34879	47x5 5/8x5 1/4	None	4

Cabinet 277930; Light SG33079

GRANT

Light honey oak frame available with steel or molded polystyrene storage cabinets in recessed and surface mounted
styles. Reversible for left or right hand opening. Matching
top light uses two G-25 or G-40 bulbs (bulbs not included).

	Swing-Door Model	Overall Size W H D	Wall Opening W H D
CABINET			
Recessed Steel	8770	16 1/4x24 1/4	14x18x3 1/2
	8778	16 1/4x26 1/4	14x24x3 1/2
NEW	8778MOD*	16 1/4x26 1/4	14x24x3 1/2
Recessed Molded	8773	16 1/4x22	14x18x2 1/2
Surface Steel	8772	16 1/4x24 1/4x5 1/2	None
TOP LIGHT			
For Recessed Cabinet	74279	16 1/4x5 1/2x3	None
For Surface Cabinet	74379	16 1/4x5 1/2x6 1/2	None

*New modular shelf storage (See p. 16 for details)

Cabinet 8778; Lights 74279

CHAPEL HILL

The warmth of natural light honey oak frames. Reversible units can be mounted to open left or right. Matching top light features gold-tone accent panel and uses up to 60W G-25 or G-40 bulbs (bulbs not included).

Cabinet 8278; Light 75719

	Model	Overall Size W H D	Wall Opening W H D
CABINET Recessed	8278	17¹/₄x27¹/₄	14x24x3¹/₂
TOP LIGHT (3 bulbs) For Recessed	75719	17¹/₄x5¹/₂x3	None

DUNHILL

Classic cameo oval with the warmth of natural honey oak. Recessed storage with adjustable shelves. Plate glass mirrors. Magnetic door catch. Reversible for left or right hand opening. Matching oak side light fixtures. Smoked glass shade. Clear 60 watt bulb maximum recommended (bulb not included).

Cabinet 1370; Light 72676

	Model	Overall Size W H D	Wall Opening W H D
CABINET	1370	21x31	14x18
	1378	24x35³/₄	14x24
WALL MIRROR ONLY	1375	21x31	None
SIDE LIGHT	72676	6¹/₂x6x8	None

KINGSTON

Contemporary honey oak frames and beveled-edge plate glass mirrors. Adjustable shelves, magnetic door catches and white baked enamel finish. Reversible swing-door. Matching top light has chrome centerplate and uses up to 60W G-25 or G-40 bulbs (bulbs not included).

Cabinet 318CH; Light 747CH

	Model	Overall Size W H D	Wall Opening W H D	Bulb Capacity
CABINET Recessed	8370	16¹/₂x26¹/₂	14x18x3¹/₂	
	8378	16¹/₂x26¹/₂	14x24x3¹/₂	
TOP LIGHT	71829	16¹/₂x5¹/₂x2¹/₄	None	3

ADANTE

Graceful arched oak framed cabinet features beveled plate glass mirror. Recessed cabinet with adjustable shelves, magnetic door catches and white baked enamel interior. Hinged right. Matching side lights feature oak sconce and frosted glass shades. Uses standard medium-based bulbs. Maximum 60W recommended (bulbs not included).

Cabinet 5470; Light 73679

	Model	Overall Size W H D	Wall Opening W H D
CABINET	5470	18³/₄x33¹/₈	14x18x3¹/₂
	5478	18³/₄x33¹/₈	14x24x3¹/₂
SIDE LIGHT	73679	5³/₈x13¹/₄x7¹/₄	None

33

Cabinet WF4070; Light 72876

OAK CHELSEA

Stylish replacement cabinet for standard wall openings. Features solid oak frame, ceramic door pulls and adjustable shelves. Recessed. Available with 3 bulb top light (bulbs not included).

	Model	Overall Size	Wall Opening
CABINET	WF4070	29 1/2x21x3	26 1/4x17 1/2
TOP LIGHT	72876	24 3/4x6x9	None

Cabinet 2471IL

OAK HOLLYWOOD

Surface mounted cabinet features honey oak frame and matching wood-tone sides. Other features include built-in top light (bulbs not included), grounded outlet, on-off switch and gold-tone door pulls.

	Model	Overall Size
CABINET	2471IL	24 3/4x24 1/2x9
	2871IL	28 3/4x24 1/2x9

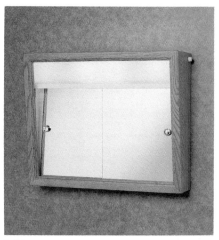

Cabinet 2472

HOLLYWOOD STANDARD

Oak-look, vinyl wrap frame and chrome door pulls. Surface mounted. Other features include built-in top light (bulbs not included) and on-off switch.

	Model	Overall Size
CABINET	2472	24 3/4x20 1/2x9
	2872	28 3/4x20 1/2x9

Cabinet SDL25

BEAUTY GLIDE

Stainless steel shadow box frame with adjustable shelves and chrome door pulls. Attached fluorescent light includes tubes. Grounded outlet and on-off switch.

Model	Overall Size	Wall Opening	Lamp (Watts)
CABINET			
Unlighted			
SD15	24x18 3/4	21 1/2x17x3 1/2	None
SD41	27 1/2x19 1/4	26 1/4x17 1/4x3 1/2	None
Fluorescent Top Lighted			
SDL25	24x21 1/4	21 1/2x16 1/2x3 1/2	1 (20)
SDL82	27 1/2x22	26 1/4x18 1/4x3 1/2	1 (20)

Cabinet 128LP

ENSIGN

Stainless steel trim with built-in light (bulbs not included). Surface mounted with fixed shelves. Includes convenient grounded outlet and on-off switch.

Model	Overall Size	Mirror Size
CABINET		
124LP	24x23 1/2x8 1/4	(2) 12x18
128LP	28x23 1/2x8 1/4	(2) 14x18

Cabinet 323LP

FLAIR

Our economy leader includes fixed shelves, stainless steel trim, built-in light (bulbs not included) and on-off switch.

Model	Overall Size	Mirror Size
CABINET		
323LP	24x19 1/2x8	(2) 12x14
327LP	28x19 1/2x8	(2) 14x14

Cabinet 407BC

Recessed, white molded polystyrene storage cabinet with two fixed shelves. Stainless steel frame. Magnetic catch.

Model	Mirror	Overall Size	Wall Opening
401BC	**WINDOW**	16x20	14x18x2 $^1/_2$
407BC	**WINDOW**	16x22	14x18x2 $^1/_2$
449BC	**PLATE**	16x22	14x18x2 $^1/_2$

Cabinet 452SM

Surface mounted steel storage cabinet with fixed shelves. Reversible for left or right door opening. White baked enamel interior. Stainless steel frame. Magnetic catch.

Model	Mirror	Overall Size	Wall Opening
412SM	**WINDOW**	16x22x4 $^3/_4$	None
422SM	**WINDOW**	14x20x5	None
452SM	**PLATE**	16x22x4 $^3/_4$	None

Cabinet 455FL

Recessed, one-piece steel storage cabinet with two adjustable shelves. Stainless steel frame. Attached fluorescent side lights (tubes included). Grounded outlet and on-off switch.

Model	Overall Size	Wall Opening	Bulbs
455FL	21 $^1/_2$x22 $^1/_4$x3 $^1/_2$	14x18x3 $^1/_2$	2

Cabinet 555IL

Surface mounted steel storage cabinet with two fixed shelves. Attached 2-bulb top light fixture (bulbs not included). Stainless steel frame and trim. White baked enamel interior. Grounded outlet and on-off switch.

Model	Mirror	Overall Size	Bulbs
555IL	**PLATE**	16x24X8	2

Cabinet 410BC

Recessed, one-piece steel storage cabinets with adjustable shelves. Classic stainless steel frames and easy installation make this series a builder's favorite. Full piano hinge. White baked enamel finish. Reversible for right or left door opening. Magnetic catch.

Model	Mirror	Overall Size	Wall Opening
410BC	**WINDOW**	16x22	14x18x3 $^1/_2$
420BC	**WINDOW**	16x22	14x20x3 $^1/_2$
421BC	**PLATE**	16x22	14x20x3 $^1/_2$
NEW **448BC***	**PLATE**	16x26	14x24x3 $^1/_2$
451	**PLATE**	16x22	14x18x3 $^1/_2$
458	**PLATE**	16x26	14x24x3 $^1/_2$
468	**WINDOW**	16x26	14x24x3 $^1/_2$
NEW **468MOD****	**WINDOW**	16x26	14x24x3 $^1/_2$
490	**PLATE**	18x24	16x21 $^1/_2$x3 $^1/_2$
471FS*	**PLATE**	16x22	14x18x3 $^1/_2$
478FS*	**PLATE**	16x26	14x24x3 $^1/_2$
495	**PLATE**	20x30	16 $^1/_4$x26 $^1/_4$x3 $^1/_2$

* New stainless steel cabinet (See p. 16 for details)
**New modular shelf storage (See p. 16 for details)
***Meets or exceeds all government specifications as published in Federal Spec #WW-P-541/8B.

COMMODORE

Combination VM230M

Light IL36; Mirror PEM3624; Cabinet V36

Match and install individual components to create a custom ensemble that precisely matches your lighting and storage needs. Components are channeled for easy installation. Light fixture includes grounded switch and outlet. Quality plate glass mirrors feature polished edges and copper backing. Stainless steel trim.

COMBINATION MIRROR & CABINET

Mirror Door	Styrene Door	Overall Size
	VM218P	$18^1/4$x32x$4^1/8$
VM224M	VM224P	$24^1/4$x32x$4^1/8$
VM230M	VM230P	$30^1/4$x32x$4^1/8$
VM236M	VM236P	$36^1/4$x32x$4^1/8$

STORAGE CABINETS

Model	Overall Size
V24	$24^1/4$x$8^3/4$x$4^1/4$
V30	$30^1/4$x$8^3/4$x$4^1/4$
V36	$36^1/4$x$8^3/4$x$4^1/4$
V48	$48^1/4$x$8^3/4$x$4^1/4$

INCANDESCENT LIGHT FIXTURES

Model	Overall Size	(Lamp) Watts
IL24	24x4x$7^1/2$	(4) 60
IL30	30x4x$7^1/2$	(4) 60
IL36	36x4x$7^1/2$	(4) 60
IL48	48x4x$7^1/2$	(6) 60

WALL MIRRORS

Model	Overall Size
PEM2424	24x24
PEM3024	30x24
PEM3624	36x24
PEM4824	48x24
PEM3036	30x36
PEM3636	36x36
PEM4836	48x36
PEM6036	60x36

Cabinet 602, 605, 608 Pine Louver
UNFINISHED PINE - ARCH TOP

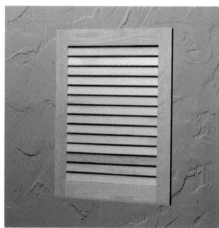

Cabinet 606, 607, 609 Pine Louver
UNFINISHED PINE - FLAT TOP

Cabinet 603 White Louver
WHITE MOLDED - ARCH TOP

LOUVER DOOR

This versatile auxiliary cabinet series offers added storage to mirrored walls. Rugged piano hinged doors and reversible for left or right hand opening. Steel cabinets feature adjustable shelves. Molded cabinets feature fixed shelves. Also feature soft--tone baked enamel interior and magnetic door catch.

Model	Cabinet	Overall Size	Wall Opening	Model	Cabinet	Overall Size	Wall Opening	Model	Cabinet	Overall Size	Wall Opening
602	Steel	16x24	14x18x$3^1/2$	606	Steel	16x22	14x18x$3^1/2$	603	Molded	16x$22^1/4$	14x18x$2^1/2$
605	Molded	16x24	14x18x$2^1/2$	607	Molded	16x22	14x18x$2^1/2$				
608	Steel	16x28	14x24x$3^1/2$	609	Steel	16x28	14x24x$3^1/2$				

DELUXE OAK FRAMED CABINET

NEW

Prestique *Bathroom Cabinets*

Handsome surface mounted cabinet features a deluxe solid oak frame with beveled plate glass mirrors. All wood constructed cabinet has 2 fixed shelves, 3 doors, 3 storage areas and 3-way viewing. Matching top lights are UL approved and use G-25 or G-40 bulbs, up to 60 watts (bulbs not included).

	Model	Overall Size W H D	Bulb Capacity
CABINET	917224	24x26x3³/₄	
	917230	30x26x3³/₄	
	917236	36x26x3³/₄	
	917248	48x26x3³/₄	
TOP LIGHT	CF92479	24x7x5¹/₂	3
	CF93079	30x7x5¹/₂	4
	CF93679	36x7x5¹/₂	5
	CF94879	48x7x5¹/₂	6

Cabinet 917236; Top Light CF93679

OAK FRAMED CABINETS

NEW

Prestique *Bathroom Cabinets*

Tri-view or swing door cabinets feature solid oak frame. Surface mounted. All wood constructed cabinet with finished interiors, plate glass mirrors. The Tri-views have 2 fixed shelves, 3 storage areas and 3-way viewing. 24", 30" or 36". Large swing-door models have 2 fixed shelves. Available individual, or pallet packs for easy merchandising. Matching top lights are UL approved and use G-25 or G-40 bulbs, up to 60 watts (bulbs not included).

	Tri-View Model	Overall Size W H D	Bulb Capacity
TRI-VIEW CABINET	907224	24x26x4³/₄	
	907230	30x30x4³/₄	
	907236	36x30x4³/₄	
	907248	48x30x4³/₄	
TRI-VIEW TOP LIGHT	CR92479	24x5⁷/₈x5¹/₂	3
	CR93079	30x5⁷/₈x5¹/₂	4
	CR93679	36x5⁷/₈x5¹/₂	5
	CR94879	48x5⁷/₈x5¹/₂	6
SWING DOOR CABINET	902	16x20x4³/₄	
	982	16x26x4³/₄	

Available in Pallet Packs

	Model	Overall Size W H D	Bulk Pack
PALLET PACK - TRI-VIEW CAB.	907224BP	24x26x4³/₄	24
	907230BP	30x30x4³/₄	20
	907236BP	36x30x4³/₄	18
PALLET PACK - SWING-DOOR CAB.	902BP	16x20x4³/₄	38
	982BP	16x26x4³/₄	38

Cabinet 902

Cabinet 907236; Top Light CR93679

OAK FRAME
WITH DECORATIVE WHITE INLAY

Genuine oak frame with white laminate inlay and plate glass mirrors. All wood constructed cabinet has 2 fixed shelves, 3 doors, 3 storage areas and 3-way viewing. Surface mounted. Matching top lights are UL approved and use G-25 or G-40 bulbs, up to 60 watts (bulbs not included).

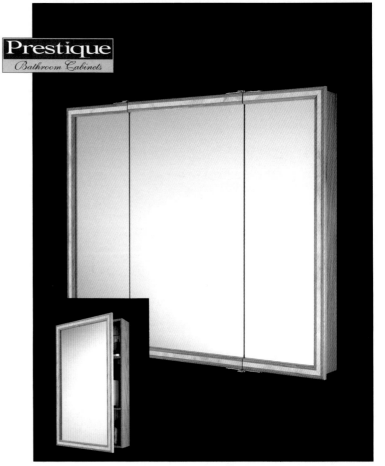

	Tri-View Model	Overall Size W H D	Bulb Capacity
CABINET	927230	30x30x4 3/4	
	927236	36x30x4 3/4	
	927248	48x30x4 3/4	
TOP LIGHT	CW93079	30x5 7/8x5 1/2	4
	CW93679	36x5 7/8x5 1/2	5
	CW94879	48x5 7/8x5 1/2	6

Swing-door cabinets are surface mounted. Model 928 features two fixed shelves, model 922 has one fixed shelf.

	Swing-Door Model	Overall Size W H D
CABINET	922	16x20x4 3/4
	928	16x26x4 3/4

Cabinet 928   Cabinet 927236

BRIGHT BRASS FRAME
WITH DECORATIVE BLACK INLAY

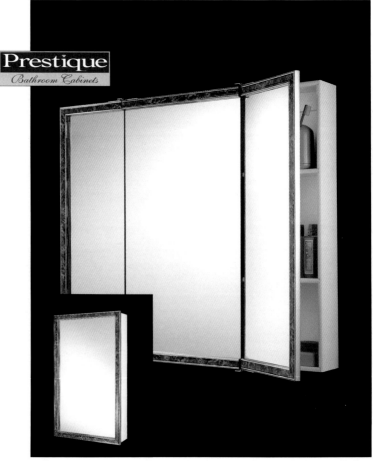

Handsome surface mounted cabinet features a brass like frame with black laminate inlay and plate glass mirrors. White, all wood constructed cabinet has 2 fixed shelves, 3 doors, 3 storage areas and 3-way viewing. Matching top lights are UL approved and use G-25 or G-40 bulbs, up to 60 watts (bulbs not included.)

	Tri-View Model	Overall Size W H D	Bulb Capacity
CABINET	931230	30x30x4 3/4	
	931236	36x30x4 3/4	
TOP LIGHT	CB93019	30x5 7/8x5 1/2	4
	CB93619	36x5 7/8x5 1/2	5

Swing-door cabinets are surface mounted. Model 938 features two fixed shelves, model 932 has one fixed shelf.

	Swing-Door Model	Overall Size W H D
CABINET	932	16x20x4 3/4
	938	16x26x4 3/4

Cabinet 938   Cabinet 931236

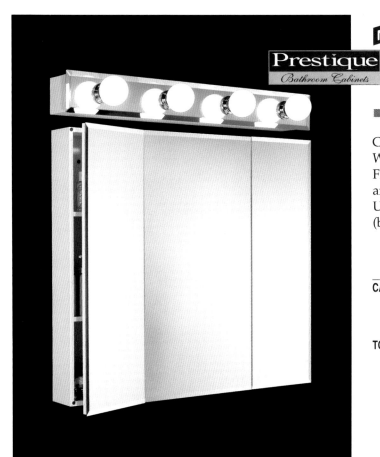

FRAMELESS BEVELED EDGE MIRROR CABINET

NEW

Classic frameless styling with beveled plate glass mirrors. White surface mounted cabinet is all wood construction. Finished interior with 2 fixed shelves, 3 doors, 3 storage areas and 3-way mirror viewing. Matching top lights are UL approved and use G-25 or G-40 bulbs, up to 60 watts (bulbs not included).

	Tri-View Model	Overall Size W H D	Bulb Capacity
CABINET	905224	24x26x4^3/$_4$	
	905230	30x30x4^3/$_4$	
	905236	36x30x4^3/$_4$	
	905248	48x30x4^3/$_4$	
TOP LIGHT	CR92490	24x5^7/$_8$x5^1/$_2$	3
	CR93090	30x5^7/$_8$x5^1/$_2$	4
	CR93690	36x5^7/$_8$x5^1/$_2$	4
	CR94890	48x5^7/$_8$x5^1/$_2$	5

Cabinet 905236; Top Light CR93690

WHITE FRAMED CABINETS

NEW

Attractive white wood frame with white, all wood cabinet body. Surface mounted, finished interiors. All plate glass mirrors, 2 fixed shelves. 3 doors, 3 storage areas and 3-way mirror viewing. Matching top lights are UL approved and use G-25 or G-40 bulbs, up to 60 watts (bulbs not included).

	Tri-View Model	Overall Size W H D	Bulb Capacity
CABINET	902224	24x26x4^3/$_4$	
	902230	30x30x4^3/$_4$	
	902236	36x30x4^3/$_4$	
	902248	48x30x4^3/$_4$	
TOP LIGHT	CR92429	24x5^7/$_8$x5^1/$_2$	3
	CR93029	30x5^7/$_8$x5^1/$_2$	4
	CR93629	36x5^7/$_8$x5^1/$_2$	5
	CR94829	48x5^7/$_8$x5^1/$_2$	6

White framed swing-door models also feature all wood construction. Surface mounted, finished interiors. Plate glass mirrors. Model 982WH swing-door has 2 fixed shelves.

	Swing-Door Model	Overall Size W H D
CABINET	902WH	16x20x4^3/$_4$
	982WH	16x26x4^3/$_4$

Cabinet 902236; Top Light CR93629   Cabinet 982WH

Broan Quality Assurances

Steel construction for lifelong service and value. Most cabinets have heavy gauge steel cabinet storage, either deep-draw (recessed) or formed and welded (surface mounted). They are treated with a phosphate bath to inhibit rust and final finished with acid-resistant Hi-temp baked enamel. Cabinets with built-in or attached lighting are pre-wired at the factory and are listed by Underwriters' Laboratories, Inc. All mirrors are made from the finest silvering glass obtainable. Silvering is protected by electroplated copper backing. All products are shipped in specially engineered Hi-impact packaging able to withstand extra heavy duty handling to assure safe delivery.

Specifications represented in this catalog are subject to change without notice.

A NORTEK COMPANY

BROAN MFG. CO., INC. HARTFORD, WISCONSIN 53027

ALL THE COMFORTS OF HOME™

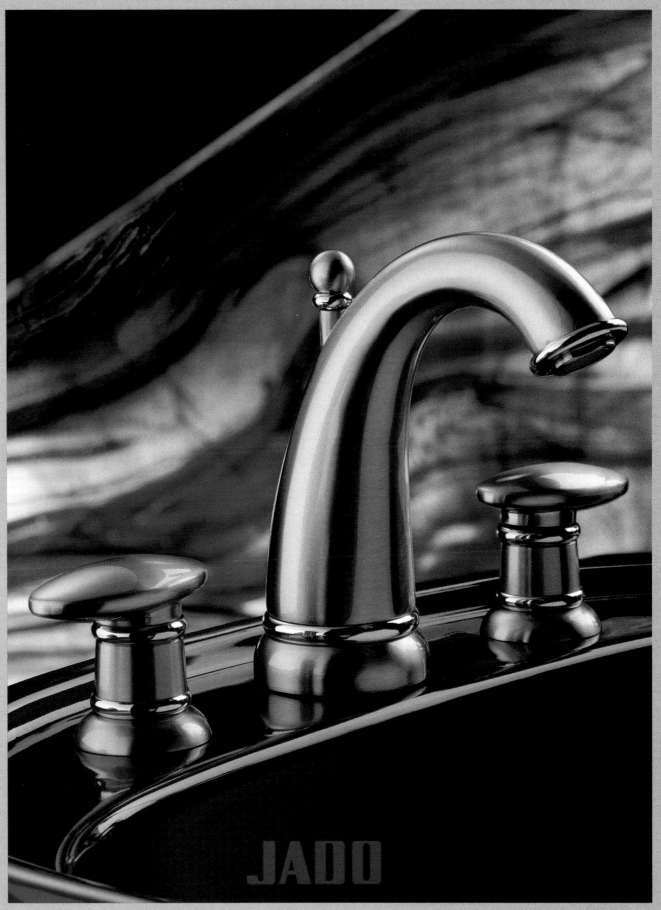

JADO

Faucets and Accessories
COORDINATED DESIGN

Dear JADO friend,

For years we have offered the finest quality and innovation in our industry. Now JADO moves lengths ahead of even its closest competition. I've never been so pleased to introduce a product brochure and to present new lines that reflect JADO's unmatched technology and superb design.

The beauty of JADO fittings combines elegant design with the assurance of proven performance. It is quality without question in luxury faucets and bath accessories. JADO has led the way in the development of coordinated design with series after series hailed as the finest in our field. Designs by such notables as Kevin Walz, Frogdesign and De lapine to name a few, assure you that you've purchased the best.

That's why we believe nothing this exquisite lasts as long. We've continued the tradition with Amadea and the Santa Fe collection. Whether it is classic elegance you need or the most contemporary design, you'll find it with JADO. Examine our craftsmanship. Just holding it in your hands is remarkable. The weight, finish and precision engineering confirm our commitment to excellence.

When you look for quality in automobiles, you turn to German excellence and luxury. When you seek that same distinctive style and longevity of investment in luxury plumbing and hardware, the only parallel is JADO.

Our products are available only through designer showrooms and authorized dealers who carry the full line of coordinated design series and accessories. JADO is the choice of discriminating buyers worldwide. It just may be the most enduring investment of elegance you'll ever purchase for your home.

Dennis D. Dickover
President
JADO, U.S.A.

TABLE OF CONTENTS

JADO *coordinated accessories 1994*

A M A D E A

J A D O P R O U D L Y P R E S E N T S
T H E A M A D E A C O L L E C T I O N

The graceful sweep of this Amadea faucet characterizes a line of outstanding elegance.

Made from solid brass in the JADO tradition, Amadea fixtures are hand-finished in Silver Nickel/Gold or Brushed Nickel/Gold.

The Amadea line includes lavatory sets, a Roman tub set, pressure balanced tub and shower combination, bidet set and more. As with all JADO products, Amadea is manufactured to exacting standards.

JADO…generations of excellence without measure.

K E V I N   W A L Z

838/001
Classic single
lever lavatory set

838/600
Pressure balanced
tub and shower
combination

838/007
Roman tub set
with hand shower

038/145
Tissue holder
with cover

038/150
Towel ring 6"

038/141
Tumbler clear

Available in Polished Chrome/Ultrabrass or
Ultrabrass

*What you see below is
the most expensive way
to manufacture a
valve. JADO starts
with the best material
available and forges a
valve with a brass body
throughout. This is the
only way JADO
can feel confident of
smooth operation in the
critical area where
water enters the
faucet. And they back
this confidence in
precision manufactur-
ing with a lifetime
mechanical warranty.
If a JADO valve
should ever prove
faulty, it would be
replaced immediately;
there is no time limit
and never a charge.*

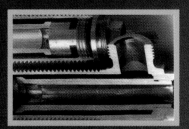

Handle selection

**014/145
Tissue holder
with cover**

**853/997
Widespread
lavatory set**

**014/600
Towel bar**

**875/907
Single control
thermostatic
shower set**

**855/927
Roman tub set with
hand shower**

Available in SiNi/Gold or Brushed Nickel/Gold

J E T L I N E

Handle
selection

512/145
Tissue holder
with cover

512/150
Towel ring 6"

512/010
Robe hook

859/912
Complete personal
hand shower set

512/460
Towel bar 18"

Available in Polished Chrome or SiNi/Gold

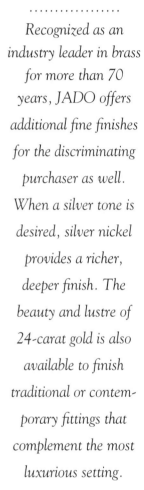

....
*Recognized as an
industry leader in brass
for more than 70
years, JADO offers
additional fine finishes
for the discriminating
purchaser as well.
When a silver tone is
desired, silver nickel
provides a richer,
deeper finish. The
beauty and lustre of
24-carat gold is also
available to finish
traditional or contem-
porary fittings that
complement the most
luxurious setting.*
....

**Handle
selection**

**843/912
Widespread lavatory set -
flat spout**

**031/150
Towel ring 6"**

**031/010
Robe hook**

**031/145
Tissue holder
with cover**

**031/460
Towel bar 18"**

**Available in Black Chrome/Gold, SiNi/Gold
or Brushed Nickel/Gold**

T I O R A

036/150
Towel ring 6"

036/800
Towel bar 30"

036/131
Soap dish
clear

036/145
Tissue holder
with cover

806/008
Roman tub set
with hand shower

806/650
Pressure balanced
shower set

Available in Polished Chrome/Ultrabrass

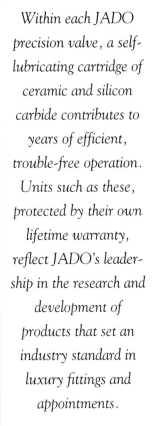

Within each JADO precision valve, a self-lubricating cartridge of ceramic and silicon carbide contributes to years of efficient, trouble-free operation. Units such as these, protected by their own lifetime warranty, reflect JADO's leadership in the research and development of products that set an industry standard in luxury fittings and appointments.

C L A S S I C

Handle
selection

Handle
selection

Handle
selection

508/010
Robe hook

508/146
Tissue holder

820/751
Mirror

**Available in Polished Chrome, Polished Brass,
Ultrabrass, Polished Chrome/Ultrabrass,
Porcelain or Brushed Nickel**

V O G U E

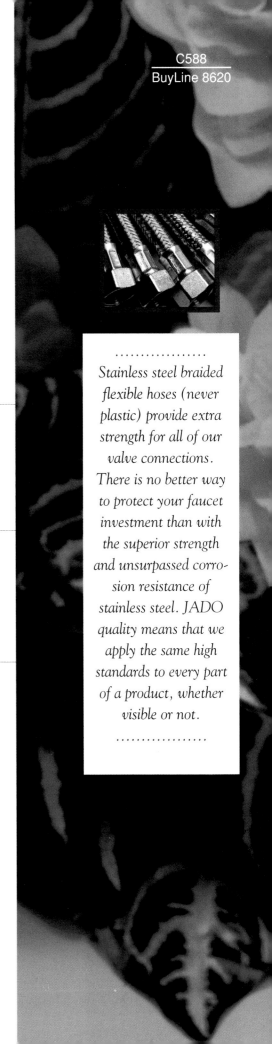

837/011
Widespread
lavatory set

837/015
Roman tub set
with hand shower

037/460
Towel bar 18"

037/150
Towel ring 6"

037/010
Robe hook

037/145
Tissue holder
with cover

Available in Polished Chrome, White/Polished
Chrome or Polished Chrome/Gold

. . . .
*Stainless steel braided
flexible hoses (never
plastic) provide extra
strength for all of our
valve connections.
There is no better way
to protect your faucet
investment than with
the superior strength
and unsurpassed corro-
sion resistance of
stainless steel. JADO
quality means that we
apply the same high
standards to every part
of a product, whether
visible or not.*
. . . .

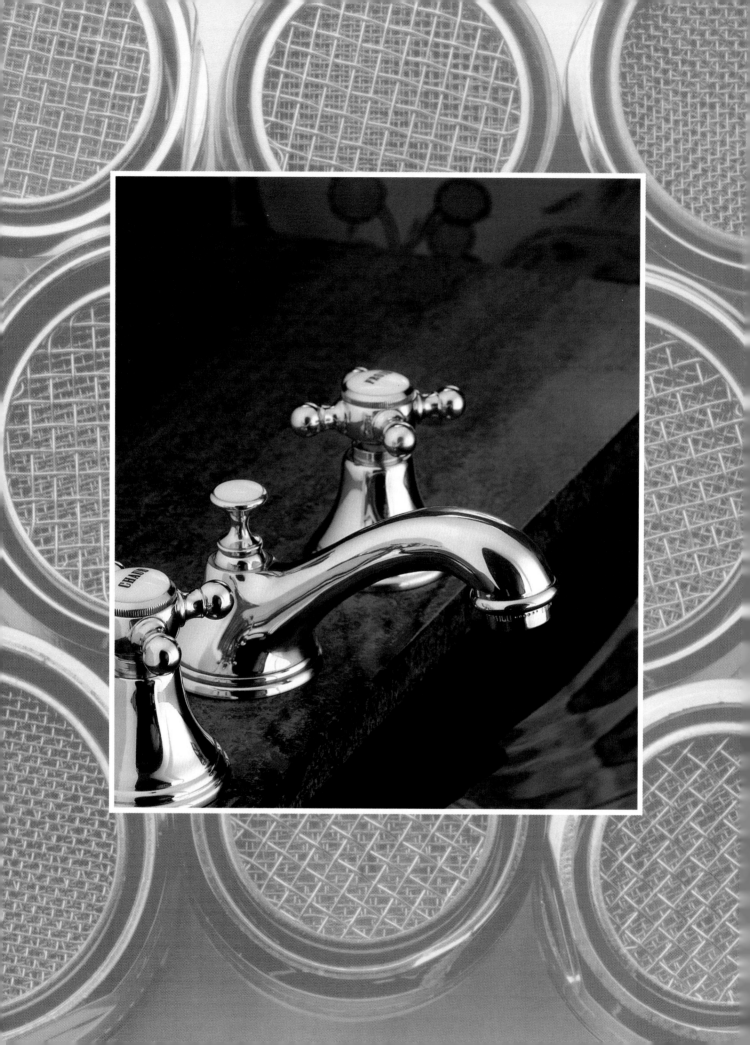

C O L O N I A L

033/010
Robe hook

033/460
Towel bar 18"

033/140
Tissue holder

033/141
Tumbler clear

033/612
Clear shelf 24"

875/908
Single control thermostatic
shower set

Available in Polished Chrome, Polished Brass,
Ultrabrass or Porcelain
For handle selection, see Classic series-page nineteen

P E R L R A N D

Handle
selection

Handle
selection

862/102
Bar faucet

501/150
Towel ring 6"

501/185
Shaving mirror

501/145
Tissue holder with
cover

Available in Polished Brass, Ultrabrass or Gold

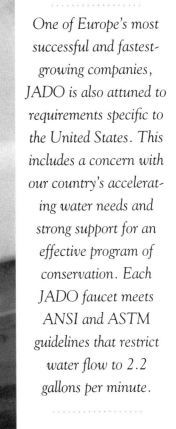

One of Europe's most successful and fastest-growing companies, JADO is also attuned to requirements specific to the United States. This includes a concern with our country's accelerating water needs and strong support for an effective program of conservation. Each JADO faucet meets ANSI and ASTM guidelines that restrict water flow to 2.2 gallons per minute.

Handle
selection

Handle
selection

030/612
Clear shelf 24"

030/150
Towel ring 6"

030/010
Robe hook

859/925
Complete personal
hand shower set

Available in SiNi/Gold or White/Gold

O R I E N T A L

Handle selection

891/903
Single hole lavatory set

894/933
Roman tub set with hand shower

891/650
Pressure balanced shower set

033/145
Tissue holder with cover

033/150
Towel ring 6"

Available in Polished Brass, Ultrabrass, SiNi/Gold or Gold

....
JADO's beauty is not just skin deep—it goes all the way through. This cutaway of a solid brass handle shows the quality typical of all of our luxury fittings. The high density of the material, forged under 800 tons of pressure, provides strength and durability and is essential in achieving our exceptional finishes which include rich silver nickel and lustrous 24-carat gold as well as brass.
....

S W A N

Available in Gold only

897/002
6" Wall spout

896/502
Roman tub set with hand shower -
crystal knobs

896/303
Widespread lavatory set -
crystal knobs

895/002
Widespread lavatory set-
crystal knobs

Available in Brushed Nickel only

508/600
Towel bar
853/948
Spread set

181 series-cabinet knob
611 series-ball cabinet knob
754 series-cabinet knob

508/150
Towel ring 6"

508/010
Robe hook
508/145
Hooded tissue holder

Luxury Forged Brass from Germany

Products Available

Single Hole LAV Sets
Widespread LAV Sets
Wet Bar Faucets
Single Hole Bidet Sets
3-Hole Bidet Sets
Roman Tub Sets
Roman Tub with Hand Shower
Pressure Balanced Tub and Shower Sets
Pressure Balanced Shower Sets
3 Valve Tub and Shower Sets
2 Valve Shower Sets
Single Control Thermostatic Shower Sets
3/4" Thermostatic Mixing Valve Sets
5-Port Diverters
4-Port Diverters
1/2" and 3/4" Wall Valves
Body Sprays
Wall Angle Stops

Hand Shower Systems
Robe Hooks
6" Towel Rings
18" Towel Bars
24" Towel Bars
30" Towel Bars
Tissue Holders
Tumbler Holders
Soap Dish Holders
24" Shelves
Mirrors
Facial Tissue Box
Waste Paper Baskets
Wire Soap Trays

1/4 Turn Ceramic Disc Cartridge-LIFETIME WARRANTY

THE MUSGROVE GROUP

For further information call:
805 482 2666
800 227 2734
FAX 800 552 5236

P.O. BOX 1329 CAMARILLO, CA 93011

NuTone

KITCHEN & BATH GUIDE

The NuTone Food Center: One powerful built-in motor operates 9 appliances...makes cooking and storage easier!

The powerful, yet compact Food Center Power Unit installs easily *beneath* your countertop ... operates 9 of your most-used kitchen appliances!

You see only the flush Surface-Plate in Decorator White or Classic Stainless Steel. It's always conveniently there when you need it, but you have complete use of your counter when not using it.

Solid-State Infinite Speed Control assures the correct speed

Blender – 272, shown on Power Unit 251SS with classic stainless steel surface-plate.

Food Processor – 256N, shown on Power Unit 251WH with handsome Decorator White finish surface-plate.

for each lightweight, full size appliance – every one beautifully designed to handle food prep jobs with ease.

With no heavy, bulky motors, they're easy to put away in a cabinet when you are not using them. And instead of 9 cords to plug in and get tangled up, you have none!

For complete information on the NuTone Food Center, see Catalog MP-800.

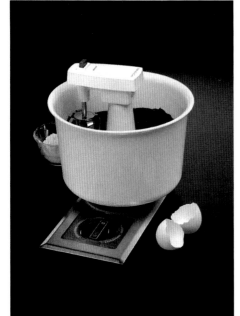

Mixer – 271

Fruit Juicer – 173N

Coffee Grinder – 276

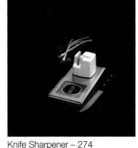

Knife Sharpener – 274

Can Opener – 279

Ice Crusher – 281

Shredder-Slicer – 278N

NuTone Decorator Range Hoods help keep kitchens fresh, clean and beautiful!

Mounted directly above your cooking surface, a NuTone Range Hood collects and filters out lingering cooking odors, smoke, heat, humidity or excessive grease in your kitchen.

NuTone offers styling to match or complement any kitchen decor. Both ducted and non-ducted models are available, providing powerful air movement. And all NuTone Hoods are UL listed.

NuTone Range Hoods. Designer styling plus proven power and performance – *guaranteed!*

Sleek new styling. 400 CFM. 5.5 sones.

New V-91 Range Hood has automatic shut off, electronic speed bar, plus night light
Just touch the `speed bar' anywhere, or slide your fingertip across it to vary fan speed to the prescise setting you want. Touching `Auto Off' continues fan for two minutes, then gradually shuts down within five minutes. Night light wattage is variable. Powerful 400 CFM at 5.5 sones vented horizontally, 420 CFM at 6.0 sones vertically. 30" and 36" widths. White, Almond or Stainless Steel finish. **VS-92 Range Hood** has similar features, but uses Exterior Power Units shown on page 3 for maximum air movement.

New V-91 and VS-92 Range Hoods offer finger touch control of variable fan speed and convenience features, including automatic shut down and variable intensity lighting.

NN8300 Convertible Twin Blower Hood with night light.
Right up to the time of installation you can decide to use it with 3 ¼" x 10" ducting ...or as a Non-Duct. *And no special kit is needed!*

Powerful, but quiet. Solid-state controls. Activated charcoal filters combined with grease filters included. 30" and 36" sizes in four enamel finishes plus stainless steel.

NuTone   SOLID STATE

SH-1000WH Series Slide-Away Range Hood

SH-1000WH Slide-Away Range Hoods Easily install in a standard cabinet above range or cooktop. Ideal for remodeling an existing kitchen, as well as for new homes. Only the slim, squared-off Hood 'visor' is visible – a thin line underscoring your beautiful cabinetry.

To remove smoke, steam or cooking odors, just pull out the tempered glass visor. This turns on an exceptionally efficient dual-centrifugal blower to keep your kitchen fresh.

Easily accessible sliding controls operate variable speed fan, bright cooking light or night light. 30", 36". 320 CFM, 5.0 sones.
SH-1030WH 30", White.
SH-1036WH 36", White.

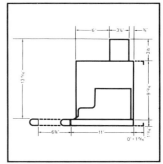

SH-1000 is easily installed in a standard cabinet above the range or cooktop

Slim, sliding visor of the SH-1000WH is virtually invisible ... until things get cooking!

MM Series Decorator Range Hood

MM6500 Convertible Decorator Hood with night light One beautiful hood – three ducting options! Infinite speed control for quiet, efficient operation. Right up to the time of installation, you can decide to use it with 3 1/4" x 10" duct horizontally or vertically...7" round duct...or as a non-duct. 30", 36", 42" sizes. Four enamel finishes plus stainless steel.

Choose a super quiet exterior mounted Power Unit for your VS-92 Range Hood ... any fan noise is outside the home!

RF-35 Roof Fan
Strong centrifugal blower, 270 CFM. Uses 7" round duct. Aluminum damper opens and closes automatically.

WF-1N Wall Fan
All aluminum housing with stainless steel fittings, rainshield included. 650 CFM.

RF-1N Roof Fan
1/8 HP motor, 620 CFM. Aluminum housing with 24" sq. self-flashing flange.

WF-35 Wall Fan Housing is baked enamel on zinc-coated steel. Similar to RF-35.

RF-35 Roof Fan

WF-35 Wall Fan

WF-1N Wall Fan

RF-1N Roof Fan

For complete information on the full line of NuTone Range Hoods, see Catalog V-300.

NuTone Ironing Center 'hides' in the wall until you need it!

NUTONE BUILT-IN IRONING CENTERS
Great idea — an ironing board that hides in the wall 'til you need it. Simply reach into the cabinet, pull down the board and you're ready to iron.

AVC-40NDR Deluxe Ironing Center Cabinet Board swivels a full 180° and adjusts up or down to just the right height. Features include: automatic safety timer, a safety shut-off switch, a convenient electric outlet for your iron, adjustable work light, garment hook, and a sturdy steel cabinet.

Recesses between 16" O.C. studs for a built-in look. Optional Surface Mount Frame available.

AVC-41NDR Economy Ironing Center Cabinet The built-in convenience you want in a non-electric model. Steel cabinet features board that adjusts up and down, storage shelf, and garment hook.

Customize your NuTone Ironing Center with your choice of three door styles. Order cabinet and door separately. All doors can be hinged for right or left opening.

AVC-M Attractive mirror door with pencil edge.

AVC-RP Traditional genuine oak raised panel door can be painted or stained.

AVC-W Smooth unfinished wood door – paint, paper or stain to match decor.

Board folds up into cabinet for storage

Board swivels 180° to face any direction

For complete information on the full line of NuTone Ironing Centers, see Catalog MP-800.

Specialty Heaters add comfort in those special areas

'Kickspace' Heater 9515 (120 Volts) – 9515X (240 Volts)
Fits under bathroom vanity ... kitchen cabinet ... many other areas where vertical space is limited. Quiet tangential blower wheel distributes heat evenly. Black louvered grille.

Two models give you a choice of volts – you select 750W or 1500W at installation with simple 'plug-in' of either one or two heating elements. Grille is 18 1/4" wide x 3 5/8" high.

'Register' Heater with Thermostat 9315T (120 Volts) 9315XT (240 Volts) Compact fan-forced

heater styled like conventional forced-air 'register'. Built-in rotary thermostat On/Off switch.

Select 750W or 1500W at installation with simple 'plug-in' of either one or two heating elements. Easily installed. Grille is 12" wide x 9 3/8" high.

9840 Hi-Wattage Wall Heater (240 Volts) Fan-forced. Handy built-in switch lets you choose 2000W or 4000W as needed. Built-in rotary thermostat lets you dial the comfort level you want – or turn Heater Off. One-piece grille is 15 1/2" wide x 20" high.

4

For complete information on the full line of NuTone Heaters, see Catalog V-300.

With a Built-In NuTone Pants Presser you can have professionally pressed pants any time!

NUTONE BUILT-IN PANTS PRESSER EPP-30 mpp

Effectively eliminates wrinkles and restores a sharp crease to pants in just 30 minutes.* Works great on neckties, scarves and handkerchiefs too. An excellent way to save on dry cleaning bills. Ideal for master bedroom, dressing room or guest room.

Reversible front panel is set in a chrome frame...light oak-finished woodgrain look on one side, unfin-

ished genuine oak veneer on the other. Unfinished side can be painted, stained or wallpapered. Panel may also be replaced with a mirror or color-coordinated laminate panel (purchase separately).

*Additional time may be required if pants are extremely wrinkled.

Easy to install. Recesses between 16" o.c. studs for a built-in look.

Thinline design blends with any decor. Black top panel with silver trim opens to reveal 30 minute timer, on/off indicator light plus a compartment for your watch, wallet, coins and keys.

Place pants in the NuTone Presser while you take a shower or before you go to bed. Set the timer for 30 minutes and forget it. Timer automatically shuts off unit when time has elapsed. Pants may be safely left in unit overnight.

(UL)

For complete information on the NuTone Pants Presser, see Catalog MP-800.

NuTone Radio-Intercom works for you in every room!

Located in the kitchen, the Master Station becomes the communication and entertainment center of your home

NuTone Radio-Intercoms mpp

You can be in two places at once! NuTone Radio-Intercom gives you room-to-room intercom ... the security of answering your front door without opening it ... lets you listen in on the baby or to a sick room ... enjoy FM/AM radio in any room, poolside or on the patio!

Plus – now you can see, hear and talk to whoever's at the door with optional Video Door-Answering and Surveillance. A valuable security feature!

Imagine seeing, hearing and talking to callers at the front door from your bathroom, bedroom or anywhere you have a remote speaker in your home

NuTone offers a complete line of Radio-Intercom systems to meet every home or budget requirement.

IMA-4006

Door Speakers IS-58V, IS-69PB, ISB-64

VALUABLE HOMEOWNER'S WARRANTY

NUTONE PRODUCTS GUARANTEED FOR AS LONG AS YOU OWN YOUR HOME

mpp

For complete information on NuTone Radio-Intercoms, see Catalog MP-800.

NuTone Bath Cabinets add sparkle, elegance and convenient storage to today's larger, more luxurious baths and powder rooms

NuTone lets you put an end to the "lookalike" bathroom! Classic designs are combined with useful features in a vast selection of quality Bath Cabinets.

Select from stunning all-glass mirrored styles ... wood or metal framed cabinets, some with built-in lights, matching toplights or sidelights ... or a magnificent TriVista with all-around viewing.

Today there's no need to choose between a spacious all-glass look or convenient storage. Because all NuTone Bath Cabinets include the wonderful *bonus* of right-there storage ... the most appreciated luxury of all!

The Radiance Collection's modular design lets you create an infinite variety of custom combinations.

Turn your bath from ordinary to *extraordinary!* The NuTone Radiance series includes dazzling clear glass cabinets, mirrors, toplights and coordinating shelves. The mirrored glass is richly detailed with striking polished v-grooves and beveled edges. The cabinets can be recessed or surface mounted. Pair several modular pieces for a breathtaking ensemble for the master bath. Or, use a single cabinet and matching toplight for a smaller bath or powder room.

For example, in the elegant grouping shown on the facing page, two Radiance cabinets are surface mounted, separated by a matching mirror. The Radiance toplights and shelf unite the three units into a single, coordinated ensemble – to make any bath more luxurious, more spacious looking.

D-2000 Radiance Cabinet D-2000-LK-4 Radiance Toplight Beveled mirrors with striking v-grooves surround a double-sided mirror door. Inside ... a spacious cabinet with full mirror behind 3 adjustable glass shelves. A magnifying cosmetic mirror is also included. Add a coordinated toplight and the look is complete. Cabinet recesses. Overall dimensions: 24" x 33". Can be surface mounted with kit D-2000-SM.

D-2000-LK4 Radiance Toplight Handsome coordinating glass light for use with D-2000 recessed cabinet or D-2000-M mirror. Overall dimensions: 24" x 4" x 4".

Radiance models available:
D-2000 Cabinet
D-2000-SM Surface-Mounting Kit
D-2000-M Mirror
D-2000-LK4 Toplight
D-2000-LK8 Toplight
D-2000-S48 Shelf
D-2000-S72 Shelf

New! 4230-FO Ridgewood Cabinet DL4230-FO Ridgewood Toplight Magnificent TriVista cabinet accented with Forest Oak, crowned by a toplight combining the same Oak with inlaid mirrors, creates a striking new look. Recessed cabinet with ample storage, three metal shelves. Cabinet is $31^{7}/_{32}$" x $28^{13}/_{16}$", Toplight is $33^{3}/_{32}$" x $7^{1}/_{4}$". Also available in White finish (4230-W Cabinet and DL4230-W Toplight).

D-71 Viewpoint Brilliant, uncommonly elegant round mirrored cabinet is highlighted with polished v-grooves and a 1/2" beveled edge. Recessed cabinet with two adjustable glass shelves. Overall size: 28" diameter.

D-2000 Radiance Cabinet
D-2000-LK-4 Radiance Toplight

D-2000-LK4 Radiance Toplight

NuTone Radiance cabinets feature all the "extras" you want. Double-sided beveled mirror door, full mirror on back of cabinet, glass shelves, magnifying cosmetic mirror (6¾" round), specially designed European hinges that allow cabinet door to open a full 135° and push-to-release magnetic catches.

For complete information on the full line of NuTone Bath Cabinets, see Catalog BC-900.

Radiance D-2000 (two)/D-2000-SM (two)/D-2000-M, D-2000-LK8 (two)/D-2000-LK4 Valance Lights and D-2000-S72 Mirrored Shelf.
Put together a custom look for your bath with unique Radiance cabinets, mirrors, top lights and shelves. Components can be combined in an almost infinite number of ways.

D-71 Viewpoint

New! 4230-FO Ridgewood Cabinet, DL4230-FO Ridgewood Toplight

7

NuTone offers functional Bath Cabinet design options with enduring beauty, for every decor

3130L Imperial TriVista

D-146 Reflections Distinctive octagonal beveled mirror-on-beveled-mirror creates three-tiered illusion. Overall size: 18" x 28".

D-169N Deauville Polished brass finish seamless aluminum tubing outlines graceful arched beveled mirror. Size: 17¾" x 29¾".

D-171 Continental Cabinet DL-171 Continental Top Light Polished Brass half-round frame adds rich detail to rectangular mirror door. Matching Toplight features mirror-chrome backplate. Cabinet 16" x 26", Toplight 16" x 5".

D-370L Bright Lights TriVista All-in-one cabinet with center beveled mirror door and mirrored toplight, two beveled-edge wing mirrors. Surface-mount steel cabinet has two adjustable shelves, convenience outlet and switch. Overall size: 35" x 26".

D-530LPC Beacon Handsome polished chrome finish frame outlines this surface-mount slider. Built-in light strip. Sturdy enameled steel cabinet with two adjustable shelves. Two sizes: 23¾" x 25" and 29¾" x 25".

2130BE Aurora All-glass bi-view cabinet. Sturdy, enameled steel surface-mount cabinet. Two shelves and magnifying mirror. Overall size: 30" x 30¾".

3130L Imperial TriVista Goldtone frame with dramatic black marble-look insert. Trio of 1/2" beveled mirror doors. Inside, there's storage plus two adjustable glass shelves, convenience outlet and switch. Two sizes: 30¼" x 30⅞" and 36¼" x 30⅞".

3333-36HO Richwood TriVista Solid oak framed TriVista. Trio of mirrored doors for all-round viewing. Easy-to-open, push-to-release catches. Inside, there's generous storage with two adjustable shelves. Four sizes: 25¼" x 32", 31¼" x 32", 37¼" x 32", 49¼" x 32".

3530BE Minuet TriVista Beveled-edge mirror doors open for ample storage and all-round viewing. Sturdy steel cabinet with two shelves. Surface-mounted. Overall size: 30" x 34½".

3736LBE Hollywood TriVista Radius corner bevel-edge mirror doors, toplights for extra dramatic impact. European hinges. Steel cabinet surface mounts. Two shelves and convenience outlet. Two sizes: 30" x 33⅛" and 36" x 33⅛".

3930LPB Park Avenue TriVista Polished Brass half-round frame surrounds three hinged mirror doors for all-round viewing. Built-in lights have reflective backplate for added brilliance. No visible hardware. Steel surface-mount cabinet. Two sizes: 29¾" x 30½", 35¾" x 30½".

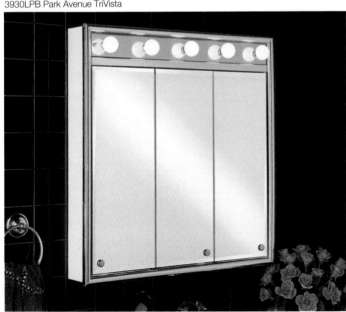

3930LPB Park Avenue TriVista

3530BE Minuet TriVista

For complete information on the full line of NuTone Bath Cabinets, see Catalog BC-900.

2130BE Aurora

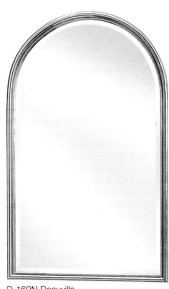

D-169N Deauville

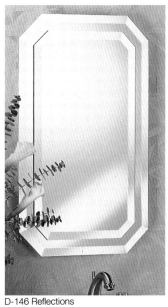

D-146 Reflections

D-530LPC Beacon

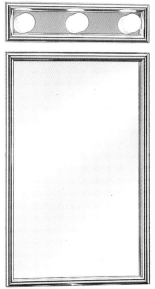

D-171 Continental Cabinet
DL-171 Continental Top Light

D-370L Bright Lights TriVista

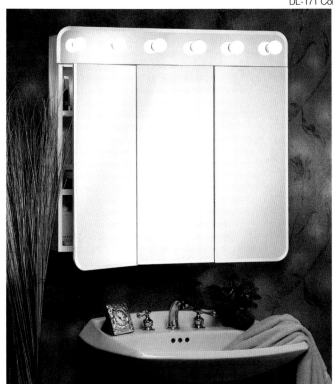

3736LBE Hollywood TriVista

3333-36HO Richwood TriVista

9

NuTone HallMack Bath Accessories are styled to perfectly complement luxury bathroom decors

Everything you need to help create a stunning traditional or contemporary bath environment can be yours with HallMack by NuTone Bath Accessories.

The Sovereign Collection: superb quality, hot forged solid brass accessories, crafted in two distinctive finishes ... plus exquisite sidelights.

AristoChrome: fine-forged solid brass in Polished Brass or Polished Chrome finish.

Select from an array of beautiful, functional HallMack by NuTone accessories for luxurious convenience.

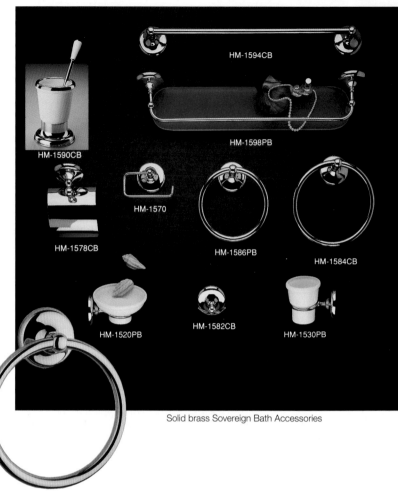

Solid brass Sovereign Bath Accessories

Sovereign Bath Accessories and Sidelights.

Choose your Sovereign accessories in classic Polished Brass or the contemporary look of Polished Chrome touched with Brass. Both styles are protected with clear lacquer that will stand up to years of use. Creamy white ceramic pieces and frosted glass add a distinctive touch. Concealed-screw surface mountings enhance Sovereign's flowing lines.

Stunning sidelights of frosted or white glass with either solid brass wall mounts or arched mirror back plates add the perfect illumination.

No matter which NuTone Sovereign pieces you choose, the results will be simply elegant!

Sovereign

DL-615	Sovereign Sidelight 5" wide x 12" high; extends 7⅝" (Polished Brass only) Lamp wattage: 60W*
DL-1505	Sovereign Sidelight 6½" W x 8¾" H extends 8½" (Polished brass only) Lamp wattage: 60W*
HM-1502	Mirror Support Brackets. Set of 4. (Polished Brass only).
HM-1520	Soap Holder with ceramic soap dish
HM-1530	Tumbler Holder with ceramic tumbler
HM-1570	Paper Holder
HM-1578	Paper Holder with Hood
HM-1582	Double Robe Hook
HM-1584	Towel Ring 9" dia.
HM-1586	Towel Ring 7¾" dia.
HM-1590	Urn and Brush Ceramic urn 7½" tall Brush 12⅞" long with ceramic handle
HM-1594	Towel Bar - ⅝" round Lengths: 24" or 30"
HM-1598	Glass Shelf, frosted 24¾" long

*Lamps not included

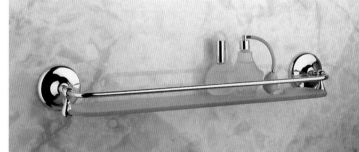

HM-1598 Glass Shelf

DL-1505 Sidelight

DL-615 Sovereign Sidelight shown with NuTone 790N Elegance Mirror (available separately) and HM-1502 Sovereign Mirror Support Brackets.

For complete information on the full line of NuTone HallMack Bath Accessories, see Catalog BC-900.

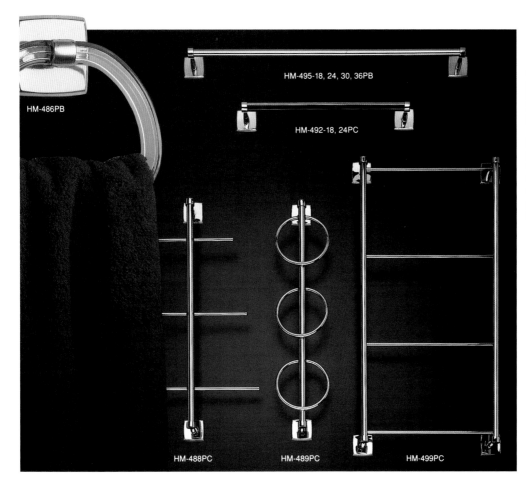

HM-486PB

HM-495-18, 24, 30, 36PB

HM-492-18, 24PC

HM-488PC   HM-489PC   HM-499PC

AristoChrome Bath Accessories in two beautiful finishes – Polished Brass and Polished Chrome.

HallMack by NuTone meets the demands of the most discriminating with the splendid craftsmanship of AristoChrome in fine-forged solid brass!

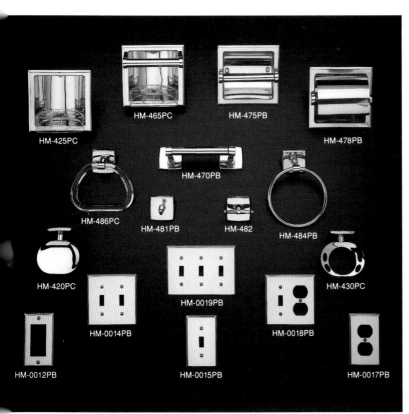

HM-425PC

HM-465PC

HM-475PB

HM-478PB

HM-470PB

HM-486PC   HM-481PB   HM-482   HM-484PB

HM-420PC

HM-0019PB

HM-430PC

HM-0014PB   HM-0015PB

HM-0012PB

HM-0018PB   HM-0017PB

AristoChrome

HM-420	Soap Holder
HM-425	Recessed Soap/ Tumbler Holder with removable polystyrene tray
HM-430	Toothbrush & Tumbler Holder
HM-465	Recessed Soap and Bar with removable polystyrene tray
HM-470	Surface-Mounted Paper Holder
HM-475	Recessed Paper Holder
HM-478	Recessed Paper Holder with Hood
HM-481	Single Hook
HM-482	Double Hook
HM-484	Towel Ring
HM-486	Towel Ring (clear lucite ring)
HM-488	Towel Tree* 15 1/2"W x 24"H
HM-489	Triple Towel Ring* 24" high
HM-492	Towel Bar* 3/4" hexagonal stainless steel bar Lengths: 18" & 24"

HM-495	Towel Bar 3/4" round bar Lengths: 18", 24", 30" & 36"
HM-499	Towel Ladder* 16 3/4" x 32"

Solid Brass Switchplates

Polished Brass finish

HM-0012PB	GFI Switch Plate (not shown)
HM-0014PB	Double Switch Plate
HM-0015PB	Single Switch Plate
HM-0017PB	Duplex Receptacle Plate
HM-0018PB	Duplex Receptacle and Switch Plate
HM-0019PB	Triple Switch Plate

*Available in Polished Chrome only

For complete information on the full line of NuTone HallMack Bath Accessories, see Catalog BC-900.

11

NuTone Exhaust Fans and Fan-Lights provide quiet, efficient ventilation to help make today's homes more comfortable

Powerful yet quiet! NuTone ventilation can rid your home of airborne contaminants, heat, smoke, humidity and stale odors from cooking, cleaning and showering.

NuTone's great selection of designs and decorator finishes please the most discriminating homeowner. And all models shown are guaranteed for as long as you own your home. *mpp*

New! QT100L QuieTTest® Fan-Light with Night Light 100 CFM at 1.5 sones. For baths up to 95 sq.ft., other rooms to 125 sq. ft. 100W ceiling light, 7W night light**. White Moonstone Lens.

QT140L Fan-Light 150 CFM at 2.0 sones. 100W ceiling light, 7W night light.** For baths to 140 sq. ft., other rooms to 185 sq. ft. White polymeric grille.

New rounded grilles for QT80/90/110

QT80 For baths up to 75 sq. ft., other rooms to 100 sq. ft. 80 CFM at 1.5 sones.

QT90 90 CFM at 1.5 sones. Meets Washington State code for houses 1300-1800 sq. ft. For baths up to 85 sq.ft., other rooms to 115 sq. ft.

QT110 For bathrooms up to 105 sq. ft., other rooms to 135 sq. ft. 110 CFM at 2.0 sones. 4" duct.

QT130 Twin blowers deliver 130 CFM at a mere 1.0 sones! For baths up to 120 sq.ft., other rooms to 160 sq.ft.*

QT150 For baths up to 150 sq. ft., other rooms to 200 sq. ft. Powerful – 160 CFM at 2.5 sones!

QT200 Ventilates rooms up to 250 sq. ft. 200 CFM at 2.0 sones. Horizontal or vertical ducting.

QT300 For rooms up to 375 sq. ft., 300 CFM at 4.5 sones.

8663/8673 Series Fan-Lights

100 CFM at 3.5 sones. For baths to 95 sq.ft., other rooms to 125 sq.ft.
Genuine Wood Fan-Lights – 8663LG Round 8673LG Square Oak-stained frames, brass finish grilles. Glass lens.
Decorator Metal Fan-Lights 8663MAB – Antique Brass 8663MBR – Polished Brass 8663MSA – Satin Aluminum Can be used in shower or tub enclosure.** Uses 100W lamp.
Polymeric Fan-Lights – 8663P Round 8673P Square White polymeric grille. 100W lamp. 7W night light. Can be used in shower or tub enclosure.**
8663F Fluorescent Fan-Light Combines energy-saving fluorescent lamps with high performance. White polymeric grille.

8814 Exhaust Fan for large baths. Polymeric grille in white pebble finish. Can be used in shower or tub enclosure.** 110 CFM for baths up to 105 sq. ft.

8833 Concealed-Intake Bath Fan Brushed aluminum center panel can be painted or papered. For baths up to 75 sq. ft., other rooms to 100 sq. ft. 80 CFM, 3.5 sones.

New! 8832WH Bath Fan Rounded grille, lower sones. 80 CFM, 2.5 sones. For baths up to 75 sq. ft., other rooms to 100 sq. ft.

8145 Room-to-Room Fan Moves 220 cu. ft. of air every minute at peak setting. Solid-state speed control. Adobe white textured grille.

8070WH/8070SA 8" Automatic Fan 160 CFM. No duct Thru-the-Wall-Fan. Choose white or silver anodized aluminum grille.
8170WH/8170SA 10" 270 CFM.

8010WH/8010SA 8" Pull-Chain Fan 250 CFM. No duct Thru-the-Wall-Fan. Choose white or silver anodized aluminum grille.
8110WH/8110SA 10" 550 CFM.

8220 8" Round Vertical Discharge Fan 170 CFM, 4.0 sones.

8210 7" Round Vertical Discharge Fan 210 CFM, 6.5 sones.

8490 10" Round Vertical Discharge Fan 260 CFM, 5.5 sones.

8510 10" Round Fan For Walls or Ceilings 300 CFM, 7.5 sones.

8310 8" Round Fan 180 CFM, 5.5 sones.

Exterior-Mounted Fans

RF/WF-35 Roof/Wall Fans Strong centrifugal blower, 270 CFM. Uses 7" round duct. Aluminum damper opens and closes automatically.

WF-1N Wall Fan All aluminum housing with stainless steel fittings, rainshield included. 650 CFM.

RF-1N Roof Fan 1/8 HP motor, 620 CFM. Aluminum housing with 24" sq. self-flashing flange.

*Meets Northwest Energy Ventilation Code.
**UL Listed for use in a tub or shower enclosure when used with GFI branch circuit.

RF-40 Heavy Duty Roof Fan 1000 CFM. 1/8 HP motor. All-aluminum housing.

Deluxe Attic Cooling Fans

RF-69N Aluminum Attic Fan 1250 CFM. 22" dia. Automatic thermostat. Ball-bearing motor. Bird guard.

RF-59N Enameled Attic Fan Same as RF-69N, but with zinc-coated steel housing finished in baked enamel.

RF-68H Attic Fan 1530 CFM. Ball-bearing motor. Heavy-gauge aluminum housing. Bird guard. Automatic thermostat.

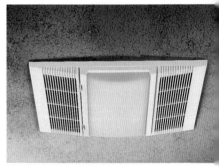

QT140L QuieTTest Fan-Light

New! QT100L QuieTTest Fan-Light

8673LG Wood Fan-Light

8673P Polymeric Fan-Light

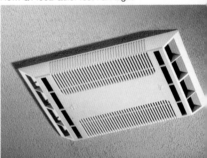

QT130, QT150, QT200, QT300 QuieTTest Twin Blower Fans

8814 Bath Fan

New! QT80, QT90, QT110 QuieTTest Fans

8663LG Wood Fan Light

8663MBR Polished Brass Fan-Light

8663P Polymeric Fan-Light

8663F Fluorescent Fan-Light

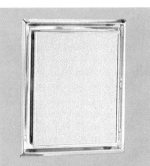

8833 Concealed-Intake Bath Fan

8663MAB Antique Brass Fan-Light

8663MSA Satin Aluminum Fan-Light

New! 8832WH Bath Fan

8145 Room-to-Room Fan

8070SA, 8170SA Thru-the-Wall Automatic Fans

8010WH, 8110WH Thru-the-Wall Pull-Chain Fans

8210, 8220, 8490 Exhaust Fans

8310, 8510 Ceiling Exhaust Fans

RF35 Roof Fan

WF35 Wall Fan

RF-1N Roof Fan

WF-1N Wall Fan

RF40 Heavy Duty Roof Fan

RF68H Roof Fan

RF69N Roof Fan

RF59N Roof Fan

VALUABLE HOMEOWNER'S WARRANTY

NUTONE PRODUCTS GUARANTEED FOR AS LONG AS YOU OWN YOUR HOME

mpp

For complete information on the full line of NuTone Exhaust Fans, see Catalog V-300.

13

NuTone Built-in Electric Heaters...turn the cold spots in your home into cozy warm...save heating the whole house

A NuTone auxiliary heater can make any room – the bath, nursery, den, family room – more pleasant in any season.

NuTone heaters save energy too! They make the room you're in warm and cozy, without turning up your whole-house thermostat.

Just look at the selection of models and finishes! Deluxe fan-forced multi-function units provide heat, light, ventilation – even a night light – singly, or in combination. There are silent radiant ceiling heaters, plus handsome wall heaters!

Build-in beauty, comfort and *quality* with NuTone Electric Heaters. *Guaranteed!* m̂ρρ▌

QT-9093BR and
9093BR Heat-A-Ventlites®

**QT-9093 QuieTTest®
Heat-A-Ventlite®**
Enjoy NuTone QuieTTest performance in this classic Heater, Fan, Light and Night Light combination fixture! 1500W heating element with blower evenly distributes heat. 110CFM at a quiet 2.5 sones. Bright 100W ceiling light, 7W night light. Includes Switch.
**QT-9093BR Polished Brass
QT-9093CH Chrome
QT-9093WH White**

9093 Deluxe Heat-A-Ventlite® This combination Heater, Ventilator and Ceiling Light has been an industry standard for years. Now a handy Night Light makes it even better! 1500W heating element, aluminum blower, glass lens. Uses 100W lamp. Four function Switch included.
**9093AB Antique Brass
9093BR Polished Brass
9093CH Chrome
9093WH White**

9013NL Heat-A-Lite® Heat, bright light – and now a convenient Night Light, plus Switch to control all functions separately! Ideal for rooms with a separate ventilating fan. Chrome grill.

9965 Heat-A-Ventlite® Performance plus great contemporary styling! 1500W Heat, 100W Light, 70 CFM Ventilation and Night Light operate singly or in combination. White polymeric grille. Switch included.

9960 Heat-A-Lite® with Night Light. Same as 9965, but without vent fan.

9905 Heat-A-Vent® Same as 9965, but without lights. Switch included.

9427 Two-Bulb Heat-A-Vent®
Silent, instant warmth and ventilation ... together or separately. White Noryl® ceiling plate. Automatic reset thermal protection.

9417D One-Bulb Heat-A-Vent®
has same features as 9427, above.

9422 Two-Bulb Heat-A-Lamp®
Instant radiant heat with two 250W infrared lamps. Compact design for medium size bathrooms. White Noryl® ceiling plate. Automatic reset thermal protection.

9412D One-Bulb Heat-A-Lamp®
for smaller bathrooms. Uses 250W infrared lamp. White Noryl® ceiling plate.

9840 Deluxe Hi-Wattage Wall Heater Powerful 240 Volt Heater is perfect for larger rooms – offices, family rooms, vestibules! Handy built-in switch lets you choose 2000W or 4000W of cozy warmth. Built-in rotary thermostat. Light almond steel grille accented with black chrome louvers, bright chrome anodized aluminum frame.

**Fan-Forced Wall Heaters
9810BWN Brown Wood-grain
9810WH White** Strong, even heat from a 1000W instant heating element to warm an entire room. Handsome, heat-resistant Noryl® grille in choice of brown wood-grain or Bright White finish.

9815BWN, 9815WH 1500W Fan-Forced Wall Heater. Same features as 9810. **9819BWN, 9819WH** 1920W Fan-Forced Wall Heater. Same features as 9810.

9965 Heat-A-Ventlite®

9960 Heat-A-Lite®

9905 Heat-A-Vent®

9840 Hi-Wattage Wall Heater

9810WH, 9815WH, 9819WH
Wall Heaters

For complete information on the full line of NuTone Electric Heaters, see Catalog V-300.

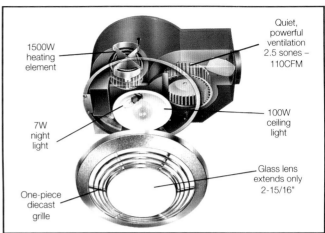

1500W heating element

Quiet, powerful ventilation 2.5 sones – 110CFM

7W night light

100W ceiling light

One-piece diecast grille

Glass lens extends only 2-15/16"

Cutaway view QT-9093CH

9417D One-Bulb Heat-A-Vent®

9427 Two-Bulb Heat-A-Ventlite®

9422 Two-Bulb Heat-A-Lamp®

9412D One-Bulb Heat-A-Lamp®

QT-9093BR, 9093BR

QT-9093CH, 9093CH, 9013NL

QT-9093WH, 9093WH Heat-A-Ventlite®

VALUABLE HOMEOWNER'S WARRANTY

NUTONE PRODUCTS GUARANTEED FOR AS LONG AS YOU OWN YOUR HOME

mpp

NuTone products add comfort, convenience, security and entertainment to your home

Central Vacs

Imagine vacuum cleaning so thorough you have to dust less often! So quiet you can vacuum while baby naps or the family watches TV. So convenient you don't have to lug around a heavy motor. All you carry is a lightweight hose and cleaning tool. Cleaning room-to-room, up and down stairs, basement, garage is easier. No wonder NuTone Central Vac is one of today's most-wanted features.

The power unit is built-in. NuTone offers *five* different systems – sanitary, fully disposable soil bag models, and a bagless unit with the revolutionary NuTone Drawdown™ Cyclonic patented technology. Easy to install, they add value to any home.

On/Off inlets come in colors to blend with your home decor. Simply plug in the cleaning hose and the powerful motor is on – ready to wisk away dirt and dust.

Door Chimes

Express your personal decorating touch with a traditional or contemporary NuTone Chime. Chime tones range from two-note to chordtone to the beloved Westminster chime sequence ... or even one you can program to play any tune you can whistle, sing or hum! There are even wireless chimes and a visual door signal for the hearing impaired!

Paddle Fans
Add comfort and energy efficiency with an elegant NuTone contemporary or traditional fan. Light Kits are also available.

mpp This symbol identifies NuTone Maximum Performance Products – *guaranteed for as long as you own your home.*

For the name of your nearby NuTone sales outlet, **DIAL FREE 1-800-543-8687** in the contiguous U.S.

Send for FREE Full Line catalog

NuTone Inc., Dept. KBS-94
P.O. Box 1580, Cincinnati, Ohio 45201

Name _____ Title _____

Company _____

Address _____

City _____ State _____ Zip _____

Phone _____ 9946

Product specifications subject to change without notice.   Form 9946, Printed in U.S.A.

NuTone

Quality, durability and color versatility in tub, shower and whirlpool surfacing.

ARISTECH ACRYLIC SHEET

The plumbingware surface material of the future is available today...Altair® I-300 Acrylic Sheet, manufactured by Aristech Chemical Corporation.

Today all of the major plumbingware manufacturers have chosen Altair I-300 acrylic surfaces for their premier whirlpool, tub and shower units.

Designers, builders and remodelers are also discovering that when given a choice, more and more home buyers and remodeling customers are choosing Altair I-300 acrylic surfaces for their plumbingware products.

WHAT ARE THE ADVANTAGES OF ACRYLIC PLUMBINGWARE SURFACES?

Fact: Tubs, showers and whirlpools with Altair I-300 acrylic surfaces look better and last longer than units made from competitive materials. And when you get right down to the bottom line (and what customer doesn't), the long-term durability of acrylic translates into economic savings. Economics also play a leading role for builders since installation times are minimized.

■ *Altair I-300 is the most attractive plumbingware surface material available anywhere.*

That's a pretty bold statement, but it's a fact. Altair I-300 comes in a vast array of glossy colors. Other surface materials don't. Consumers can now choose from over thirty solid colors and soft marbles for any specific decor.

■ *Altair I-300 is easily maintained.*

Consumers will especially appreciate that the vibrant, high-gloss features of Altair I-300 are retained for years with minimal care using mild household cleaning materials. No back-breaking scrubbing is required to clean Altair I-300 because it's not a porous material. Dirt and grime can't penetrate the surface and cause discoloring. With just a few wipes, Altair I-300 looks brand new again...and stays that way year after year.

■ *Altair I-300...a very durable plumbingware surface material.*

Altair I-300 has earned a reputation as a tough and durable acrylic surface. It has proven impact resistance. Tests and field experience have shown that under normal use and conditions, it will not chip, crack or craze...and the colors won't fade over the years.

■ *Altair I-300 is economical, too.*

When you consider that Altair I-300 acrylic retains its appearance and physical properties years longer than other materials, it truly is the economical choice.

And Altair I-300 acrylic plumbingware surfaces have a "warm" feel. Unlike the cold sensation you get from contact with steel or cast iron, Altair I-300 retains heat

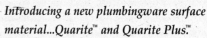

naturally...making it an energy-efficient material.

So when you're specifying tubs, showers, modular tub/showers and whirlpools, choose the surface material of the future... today. Aristech's Altair I-300.

Introducing a new plumbingware surface material...Quarite™ and Quarite Plus.™

Quarite and Quarite Plus, new acrylic sheet products recently added to our product line, have surfaces with the appearance and texture of granite. Their patented formulation results in a cross-linked acrylic sheet suitable for whirlpools, tubs, spas, pool steps, signage and many architectural uses.

Pigmented acrylic chips dispersed randomly in the matrix produce the unique granite surface look. Once thermoformed, our Quarite products develop a textured or pebbled non-skid surface while retaining all of the outstanding characteristics associated with our standard opaque I-300 sheet products described in this brochure.

For more information about where plumbingware products with Altair® I-300 surfaces are available near you, contact a manufacturer listed below.

SPA CUSTOMERS

Blue Pacific
7630 South Union Ave.
Bakersfield, CA 93307
805-836-2779

California Acrylic Industries
1462 E. 9th St.
Pomona, CA 91766
714-623-8781

Clearwater Spas
P.O. Box 2140
Woodinville, WA 98072
206-483-1877

Colorado Made Spas
389 Wadsworth
Lakewood, CO 80226
303-233-7103

DFA
205 S. 28th St.
Phoenix, AZ 85034
602-225-0101

Delair Group
I Delair Plaza
Delair, NJ 08110
609-663-2901

Dolphin Spas
717 N. McKeever Ave.
Azusa, CA 91702
818-334-0099

Gold Country Spas
3899 Security Park Dr.
Rancho Cordova, CA 95742
916-351-0721

Grecian Spas
7200 Hazard Ave.
Westminster, CA 92683
714-891-6641

Jacuzzi Spas
2121 N. California Blvd.
#475
P.O. Drawer J
Walnut Creek, CA 94596
510-938-7070

Leisure Bay Spas
P.O. Box 607366
Orlando, FL 32860-7366
407-297-0141

Marquis Corp.
596 Hoffman Rd.
Independence, OR 97351
503-838-0888

Quality Acrylic Spas
8993 Tara Blvd.
Jonesboro, GA 30236
404-603-0058

SSI/Alternate Eng.
2593 South Raritan St.
Englewood, CO 80110
303-936-1828

Saratoga Spa and Bath
33 Wade Rd.
Latham, NY 12110
206-383-1727

Spa-N-Save
1474 Grass Valley
Auburn, CA 95603
916-888-6077

Sundance Spas Inc.
13951 Monte Vista St.
Chino, CA 91710
714-627-7670

Tadd Manufacturing
P.O. Box 1186
Poplar Bluff, MO 63901
314-686-7266

In Canada

City Fiberglass Co. Ltd.
c/o Triac Industries
40 Minuk Acres
West Hill, Ontario, Canada
M1E 4Y6
416-281-9475

Donner Plastic Products
5721 Production Way
Langley, B.C., Canada
V3A 4N5
604-530-2684

Leisure Mfg./Sunrise
417 Read Rd.
St. Catherines, Ontario,
Canada L1R 7K6
416-646-7727

Pacific Pool Water Products
6315 202nd St.
Langley, B.C., Canada
V3A 4P7
604-533-4771

Technican Industries
383 Elgin St., Box 1870
Brantford, Ontario, Canada
N3T 5W4
519-756-3442

Waterworks
2351 Simpson Rd.
Richmond, B.C., Canada
V6X 2R2
604-270-0485

PLUMBINGWARE CUSTOMERS

Aker Plastics Co. Inc.
1001 N. Oak Rd.
P.O. Box 484
Plymouth, IN 46563
219-936-3838

American Molds Dist.
900 Kirby
Wylie, TX 75098
214-442-6116

American Standard
605 S. Ellsworth Ave.
Salem, OH 44460
216-332-9954

American Whirlpool Products
3050 N. 29th Ct.
Hollywood, FL 33022
305-921-4400

Aqua Glass
P.O. Box 412
Industrial Rd.
Adamsville, TN 31310
901-632-0911

Bath-Tec Corporation
P.O. Box 1118
Ennis, TX 75120
214-299-5625

Bremen Glass Company
1010 W. Dewey St.
Bremen, IN 46506
219-546-3298

Crane Plumbing
8290 South Central Exp.
Dallas, TX 75239
214-371-8700

Four Flags Bath Factory
5 Greenwood Ave.
Romeoville, IL 60441-1398
815-886-5900

Hamilton Plastics
P.O. Box 31, Hwy. 78 So.
Hamilton, AL 35570
205-921-7858

Hessco
160 E. Foundation
La Habra, CA 90631
213-691-6478

Hydro Swirl
2150 Division St.
Bellingham, WA 98225
206-734-0616

Jacuzzi
2121 N. California Blvd.
#475
P.O. Drawer J
Walnut Creek, CA 94596
510-938-7070

Jetta Products Inc.
500-A Centennial Blvd.
Edmond, OK 73013
405-340-6661

Kohler Company
444 Highland Dr.
Kohler, WI 53044
414-459-1671

Kohler Company
P.O. Box 1987
Spartanburg, SC 29301
803-582-3401

Lifestyles
6100 237th Place S.E.
Woodinville, WA 98072
206-481-9000

National Fiberglass
5 Greenwood Ave.
Romeoville, IL 60441
708-257-3300

Novi American Inc.
P.O. Box 44649
Atlanta, GA 30336
404-344-5600

Pearl Bath Inc.
9224 73rd Ave. No.
Minneapolis, MN 55428
612-424-3335

Premier Plastics
P.O. Box 359
Pontotoc, MS 38863
601-489-2007

Swirl-way
P.O. Box 210
1505 Industrial Dr.
Henderson, TX 75252
903-657-1436

Trajet Whirlpool Baths
7025 Sarpy Ave.
Omaha, NB 68147
402-734-2268

Universal Rundle Corp.
P.O. Box 960
New Castle, PA 16103
800-955-0316

In Canada

Acryli Plastique J.R. Inc.
118 St. Pierre
Quebec, Canada G0S 1V0
819-389-5818

Fiberez Canada
235 Saunders Dr.
P.O. Box 1057
Cornwall, Ontario, Canada
K6H 5V2
613-933-3525

Kohler Company
RR #3 Spallumcheen Dr.
Armstrong, B.C., Canada
V0E 1B0
604-546-3196

Maax Inc./Acrylica
600 Rue Cameron
St. Marie Beauce, Quebec,
Canada G6E 3C2
418-387-4155

Mirolin Industries
60 Shorncliffe Rd.
Toronto, Ontario, Canada
M8Z 5K1
416-231-9030

Sherlic
2755 Boudreau St.
Fleurimont, Quebec,
Canada J1J 3N1
819-562-3500

TCRV, Inc.
64 Grandes Fourches Nord
Sherbrook, Quebec,
Canada J1H 5G2
819-563-4030

V & R Sensational Marble
Fiberglass Products
29 Torbarrie Rd.
Downsview, Ontario,
Canada K3L 1G5
416-241-4441

ARISTECH
ACRYLIC SHEET
Quality that comes to the surface.

Altair I-300 is a registered trademark of Aristech Chemical Corporation, Acrylic Sheet Unit, 7350 Empire Drive, Florence, KY 41042. Phone (800) 354-9858.

C593
10820/CEN
BuyLine 7554

Century

Century Shower Door

CENTURY

Century Brasstec & Glasstec lines are available in the following finishes:

Century glass options include: clear safety glass, obscure, mirror, striped grey, striped bronze, grey tint, bronze tint, v-groove, beveled or custom.

Polished Brass

Satin Brass

Antique Brass

Polished Chrome

Satin Chrome

Polished Nickel

Satin Nickel

Polished Copper

24K Gold

Century has these distinct advantages that make it the clear leader in the industry:

Variety in design and formats including: sliding, hinged, framed & frameless.

Design dedicated assistance is available to answer questions and solve problems.

Quality and satisfaction is guaranteed with the unmatched Century Guarantee.

Delivery is the best in the business due to our multi-million dollar inventory.

Century aluminum finishes include: polished aluminum, gold anodized, fifteen standard paint colors or custom matching to your specifications.

Charcoal Granite	
Grey Stone	
Desert Stone	
Dusty Rose	
Teal Green	
BronzeTone	
Cobalt Blue	
Royal Red	
AlmondTone	
Cameo Cream	
Caramel	
Linen White	
Platinum Grey	
Powder Grey	
Black Onyx	

Custom applications are a specialty at Century. We are the only manufacturer with full-time product designers to answer questions and solve problems, guaranteeing the best possible service and fit. We stock the widest possible selection of aluminum extrusions and glass options for immediate delivery to meet virtually any need. In addition, our brass line includes over 30 designer channels to fit any configuration.

Century Guarantee We at Century Shower Door guarantee your complete satisfaction with our products. We stand by our enclosures and our customers.

Brasstec enclosures are heavy gauge solid brass, in 1" or 1¼" frame
■ Four different designs are available: sliding, hinged, framed & frameless
■ Nine different finish options are available including polished, satin, or antique brass, polished or satin chrome, polished or satin nickel, copper & 24K gold.

Glasstec frameless enclosures are constructed of ⅜" or ½" tempered glass with a beveled glass design that seals tight to eliminate the need for channels.
■ Patented hinge, header and hardware is available in solid brass and the full Century range of finishes, each individually crafted to customer specifications.
■ Glasstec handles are available in standard and "Highline" styles as shown.

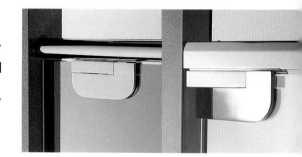

Centec frameless sliding enclosures feature a unique rounded header design constructed of heavy gauge anodized aluminum with ¼" tempered glass doors.
■ Finishes include: polished aluminum, gold anodized, twelve standard painted finishes, custom-matched colors, and Stonetec painted granite finish.
■ Centec features pass-through towel bars and low-maintenance bottom track.

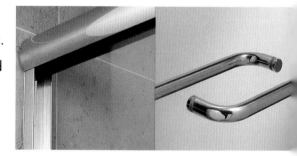

Lucette framed aluminum enclosures have been designed as a system to fit all standard formats and virtually any custom configuration you can dream up.
■ Finishes include: polished aluminum, gold anodized, twelve standard painted finishes or custom colors, and the widest range of glass and sizes available.
■ A system of over 72 extrusions provides angles & sizes to meet any need.

Crest framed aluminum enclosures are a low cost option for standard formats.
■ Available in chrome anodized aluminum finish with a range of glass options.
■ Crest is available in hinged & sliding door styles in standard configurations.

Century design options are endless. With Brasstec you can choose from four styles, four handle designs and nine finishes, all in solid brass. Create beautifully clear barriers with Glasstec enclosures in solid brass or aluminum and two handle styles. Century also offers three lines of aluminum framed and frameless enclosures to match any color scheme or budget.

CENTURY

Brasstec enclosures are heavy gauge solid brass, in 1" or 1¼" frame

■ Four different designs are available including: sliding, hinged, framed & frameless

■ Nine different finish options are available including polished, satin, and antique brass, polished and satin chrome, polished and satin nickel, copper & 24K gold.

■ Century offers the most extensive brass line available and the Century Guarantee.

Bras

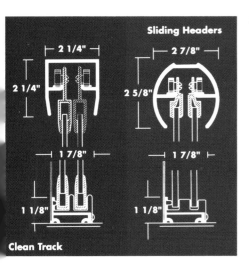

Sliding Headers

2 1/4"
2 7/8"
2 1/4"
2 5/8"
1 7/8"
1 7/8"
1 1/8"
1 1/8"

Clean Track

Hinged Headers

1"
1 1/4"
1 1/4"
1 1/4"
1 3/8"

Door to panel connection

1 1/4"
1 1/4"
3/4"

Specifications

PART 1 – GENERAL

1.1 SUMMARY
    A. This Section consists of standard and custom fabricated framed solid brass shower and tub enclosures.

1.2 SUBMITTALS
    A. Literature: Manufacturer's catalog cuts, detail sectional drawings and installation instructions.
    B. Shop drawings: Plan and elevations, bearing dimensions of actual measurements taken at the project.
    C. Selection samples: Sample card indicating Manufacturer's full range of finishes available for selection by Architect
    D. Verification samples:
        1. Samples of special order glass type.
        2. Sectional samples, illustrating brass finish.

1.3 DELIVERY, STORAGE AND HANDLING
    A. Deliver, store, and handle enclosure components following manufacturer's recommended procedures.

1.4 FIELD MEASUREMENTS
    A. Take field measurements before preparation of shop drawings and fabrication, to ensure proper fit.

PART 2 – PRODUCTS

2.1 MANUFACTURER
    A. Manufacture: To establish a standard of quality, design and function desired, Drawings and specifications have been based on Century Shower Door Inc., 250 Lackawanna Avenue, West Paterson, NJ 07424, (201)-785-4290, Product: "Brasstec", no substitution will be accepted.

2.2 COMPONENTS
    A. Frame and hardware: Extruded Architectural Bronze, copper alloy number 385.
    B. Glass: [*select one of the following*]
        1. Clear safety glass, conforming to ANSI Z97.1 and certified by Safety Glazing Certification Council.
        2. Custom glazing: [*Optional glass types, include obscure glass, mirror glass, striped grey, striped bronze, grey tint, bronze tint, "v-groove" and other custom glass types are available, contact Century Shower Door for more information.*]
    C. Hinge: Adjustable continuous piano hinge or pivot, as required.

2.3 FACTORY FINISH
    A. Frame and hardware: [*select one of the following*]
        1. Polished Brass, US 3 finish (Bright brass, clear coated).
        2. Satin Brass, US 4 finish (Satin brass, clear coating).
        3. Antique Brass, US 5 finish (Satin brass blackened).
        4. Polished Chrome plate, US 26 finish (Bright chromium plated).
        5. Satin Chrome plate, US 26D finish (Satin chromium plated).
        6. Polished Nickel plate, US 14 finish (Bright nickel plated).
        7. Satin Nickel plate, US 15 finish (Satin nickel plated).
        8. Bright Copper finish.
        9. Custom 24 K gold plate.

PART 3 – EXECUTION

3.1 INSTALLATION
    A. Install shower and tub enclosures in accordance with manufacturer's instructions. Install plumb and level, securely and rigidly anchored, with doors operating freely and smoothly.

stec

CENTURY

Glasstec frameless enclosures are constructed of $\frac{3}{8}$" or $\frac{1}{2}$" tempered glass with a beveled glass design that seals tight to eliminate the need for channels. ■ Patented hinge, header and hardware is available in solid brass and the full Century range of finishes, each individually crafted to customer specifications. ■ Glasstec handles are available in standard and "Highline" styles as shown.

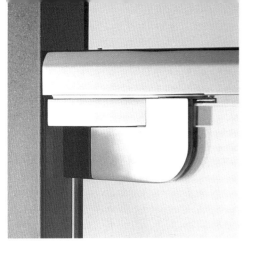

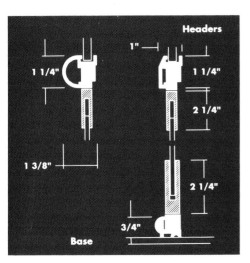

Headers

1 1/4"

1"

1 1/4"

2 1/4"

1 3/8"

2 1/4"

3/4"

Base

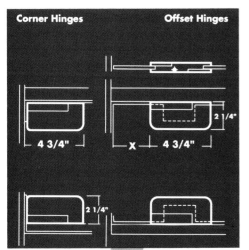

Corner Hinges   **Offset Hinges**

2 1/4"

4 3/4"   X   4 3/4"

2 1/4"

Specifications

PART 1 – GENERAL

1.1 SUMMARY
   A. This Section consists of standard and custom fabricated 'heavy glass' shower and tub enclosures.

1.2 SUBMITTALS
   A. Literature: Manufacturer's catalog cuts, detail sectional drawings and installation instructions.
   B. Shop drawings: Plan and elevations, bearing dimensions of actual measurements taken at the project.
   C. Selection samples: Sample card indicating Manufacturer's full range of finishes available for selection by Architect
   D. Verification samples:
      1. Samples of special order glass type.
      2. Sectional samples, illustrating metal finish.

1.3 DELIVERY, STORAGE AND HANDLING
   A. Deliver, store, and handle enclosure components following manufacturer's recommended procedures.

1.4 FIELD MEASUREMENTS
   A. Take field measurements before preparation of shop drawings and fabrication, to ensure proper fit.

PART 2 – PRODUCTS

2.1 MANUFACTURER
   A. Manufacture: To establish a standard of quality, design and function desired, Drawings and specifications have been based on Century Shower Door Inc., 250 Lackawanna Avenue, West Paterson, NJ 07424, (201)-785-4290, Product: "Glasstec", no substitution will be accepted.

2.2 COMPONENTS
   A. Header, trim and hardware: Extruded Architectural Bronze, copper alloy number 385.
   B. Glass: [*select one of the following*]
      1. Clear tempered glass: 3/8 or 1/2 inch thick safety glass, ASTM C 1048 FT, complying with Class 1 clear, quality q3 glazing select, conforming to ANSI Z97.1.
      2. Custom glazing: [*Optional grey tinted, bronze tinted, sandblasted, or etched glass is available, contact Century Shower Door for more information.*]
   C. Hinge: Adjustable pivot hinge, solid brass matching selected frame finish. Hinge shall allow glass to come within 1/32 inch from sidewall, and be capable of 1/4 inch side to side adjustment and 3/16 inch front to back adjustment.

2.3 FACTORY FINISH
   A. Header, trim and hardware:
      1. Polished Brass, US 3 finish (Bright brass, clear coated).
      2. Satin Brass, US 4 finish (Satin brass, clear coating).
      3. Antique Brass, US 5 finish (Satin brass blackened).
      4. Polished Chrome plate, US 26 finish (Bright chromium plated).
      5. Satin Chrome plate, US 26D finish (Satin chromium plated).
      6. Polished Nickel plate, US 14 finish (Bright nickel plated).
      7. Satin Nickel plate, US 15 finish (Satin nickel plated).
      8. Bright Copper finish.
      9. Custom 24 K gold plate.

PART 3 – EXECUTION

3.1 INSTALLATION
   A. Install shower and tub enclosures in accordance with shop drawings and manufacturer's instructions. Install plumb and level, securely and rigidly anchored, with doors operating freely and smoothly.

Centec frameless sliding enclosures feature a unique rounded header design constructed of heavy gauge anodized aluminum with ¼" tempered glass doors.

■ Finishes include: polished aluminum, gold anodized, twelve standard painted finishes, custom-matched colors, and Stonetec painted granite finish.

■ Centec features pass-through towel bars and low-maintenance bottom track.

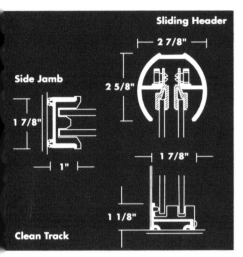

Sliding Header

2 7/8"

Side Jamb

2 5/8"

1 7/8"

1"

1 7/8"

1 1/8"

Clean Track

Specifications

PART 1 – GENERAL

1.1   SUMMARY
     A.   This Section consists of standard and custom fabricated shower and tub enclosures, with frameless sliding glass doors.

1.2   SUBMITTALS
     A.   Literature: Manufacturer's catalog cuts, detail sectional drawings and installation instructions.
     B.   Shop drawings: Plan and elevations, bearing dimensions of actual measurements taken at the project.
     C.   Selection samples: Sample card indicating Manufacturer's full range of colors available for selection by Architect
     D.   Verification samples:
         1.   Samples of special order glass type.
         2.   Sectional samples of perimeter frame, illustrating custom finish.

1.3   DELIVERY, STORAGE AND HANDLING
     A.   Deliver, store, and handle enclosure components following manufacturer's recommended procedures.

1.4   FIELD MEASUREMENTS
     A.   Take field measurements before preparation of shop drawings and fabrication, to ensure proper fit.

PART 2 – PRODUCTS

2.1   MANUFACTURER
     A.   Manufacture: To establish a standard of quality, design and function desired, Drawings and specifications have been based on Century Shower Door Inc., 250 Lackawanna Avenue, West Paterson, NJ 07424, (201)-785-4290, Product: "Centec", no substitution will be accepted.

2.2   COMPONENTS
     A.   Perimeter frame: Extruded aluminum, alloy 6463-T5. [*Optional Brass-Centec is available with solid brass perimeter framing, contact Century Shower Door for more information.*]
     B.   Glass: [*select one of the following*]
         1.   Clear tempered glass: 1/4 inch thick safety glass, ASTM C 1048 FT, fully tempered, complying with Class 1 clear, quality q3 glazing select, conforming to ANSI Z97.1. [*Brass Centec is available with 1/4, 3/8 or 1/2 inch thick tempered glass*]
         2.   Special order glazing: [*Optional "v-groove", grey tinted or bronze tinted glass is available, additionally, sandblasted glass or etched glass is available with Brass Centec.*]

2.3   Factory Finishes
     A.   Frame and hardware: [*select one of the following*]
         1.   Bright aluminum finish: Highly specular bright finish, clear anodized; Aluminum Association AAC31A21.
         2.   Bright gold finish: Highly specular bright finish, colored anodized; Aluminum Association AAC31A21.
         3.   Colored finish: Sprayed-applied thermo-set colored finish in manufacturers standard or custom color as directed by the Architect.
         4.   Stonetec finish: Sprayed-applied thermo-set multi-colored 'granite pattern' finish in color selected by Architect from manufacturer's available range.
         5.   Brass Finishes [Same finishes are available as *Brasstec* enclosures, *with optional solid brass framing.*]

PART 3 – EXECUTION

3.1   INSTALLATION
     A.   Install shower and tub enclosures in accordance with manufacturer's instructions. Install plumb and level, securely and rigidly anchored, with doors operating freely and smoothly.

CENTURY

Lucette framed aluminum enclosures have been designed as a system to fit all standard formats and virtually any custom configuration you can dream up.

■ Finishes include: polished aluminum, gold anodized, twelve standard painted finishes or custom colors, and the widest range of glass and sizes available.

■ A system of over 72 extrusions provides special angles & sizes to meet any need.

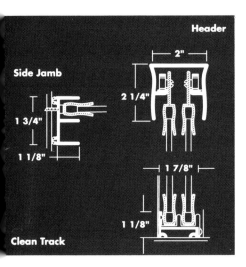

Side Jamb

Header

2"

2 1/4"

1 3/4"

1 1/8"

1 7/8"

1 1/8"

Clean Track

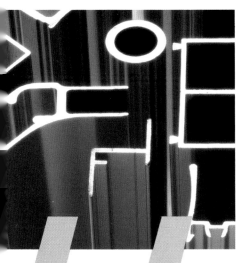

Over 72 different profiles guarantee that we can create the right enclosure for any need.

Specifications

PART 1 – GENERAL

1.1 SUMMARY
   A. This Section consists of standard and custom fabricated shower and tub enclosures, with aluminum framed glass doors, both hinged and sliding types.

1.2 SUBMITTALS
   A. Literature: Manufacturer's catalog cuts, detail sectional drawings and installation instructions.
   B. Shop drawings: Plan and elevations, bearing dimensions of actual measurements taken at the project.
   C. Selection samples: Sample card indicating Manufacturer's full range of colors available for selection by Architect.
   D. Verification samples:
      1. Samples of special order glass type.
      2. Sectional samples of shower door frame, illustrating custom colored finish.

1.3 DELIVERY, STORAGE AND HANDLING
   A. Deliver, store, and handle enclosure components following manufacturer's recommended procedures.

1.4 FIELD MEASUREMENTS
   A. Take field measurements before preparation of shop drawings and fabrication, to ensure proper fit.

PART 2 – PRODUCTS

2.1 MANUFACTURER
   A. Manufacture: To establish a standard of quality, design and function desired, Drawings and specifications have been based on Century Shower Door Inc., 250 Lackawanna Avenue, West Paterson, NJ 07424, (201)-785-4290, Product: "Lucette", no substitution will be accepted.

2.2 COMPONENTS
   A. Frame: Extruded aluminum, alloy 6463-T5.
   B. Glass: [*select one of the following*]
      1. Obscure glass: Patterned safety glass, nominal 5/32 inch thick, conforming to ANSI Z97.1.
      2. Clear safety glass, conforming to ANSI Z97.1 and certified by Safety Glazing Certification Council.
      3. Custom glazing: [*Optional glass types, include mirror glass, striped grey, striped bronze, grey tint, bronze tint, "v-groove" and other custom glass types are available, contact Century Shower Door for more information.*]
   C. Hinge [*with hinged doors*]: Continuous aluminum piano hinge, matching selected frame finish.
   D. Track [*with sliding doors*]: Extruded aluminum, matching frame finish. Provide doors with adjustable rollers with ball bearings and nylon tires.

2.3 FACTORY FINISH
   A. Frame: [*select one of the following*]
      1. Bright aluminum finish: Highly specular bright finish, clear anodized; Aluminum Association AAC31A21.
      2. Bright gold finish: Highly specular bright finish, colored anodized; Aluminum Association AAC31A23.
      3. Colored finish: Sprayed-applied thermo-set colored finish in manufacturers standard or custom color as directed by the Architect.

PART 3 – EXECUTION

3.1 INSTALLATION
   A. Install shower and tub enclosures in accordance with manufacturer's instructions. Install plumb and level, securely and rigidly anchored, with doors operating freely and smoothly.

CENTURY

Crest framed aluminum enclosures are a low cost alternative for all standard formats.

■ Available in chrome anodized aluminum finish with a full range of glass options.

■ Crest is available in hinged and sliding door styles in all standard configurations.

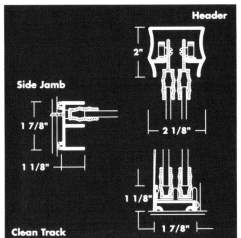

Header

Side Jamb

2"

2 1/8"

1 7/8"

1 1/8"

1 1/8"

1 7/8"

Clean Track

Specifications

PART 1 – GENERAL

1.1 SUMMARY
    A. This Section consists of shower and tub enclosures in manufacturer's standard sizes, with aluminum framed glass doors, both hinged and sliding types.

1.2 SUBMITTALS
    A. Literature: Manufacturer's catalog cuts, detail sectional drawings and installation instructions.

1.3 DELIVERY, STORAGE AND HANDLING
    A. Deliver, store, and handle enclosure units following manufacturer's recommended procedures.

1.4 FIELD MEASUREMENTS
    A. Take field measurements, to ensure openings fit manufacturer's unit sizes.

PART 2 – PRODUCTS

2.1 MANUFACTURER
    A. Manufacture: To establish a standard of quality, design and function desired, Drawings and specifications have been based on Century Shower Door Inc., 250 Lackawanna Avenue, West Paterson, NJ 07424, (201)-785-4290, Product: "Crest", no substitution will be accepted.

2.2 COMPONENTS
    A. Frame: Extruded aluminum, alloy 6463-T5, having diffuse bright finish, clear anodized; Aluminum Association AAC32A21.
    B. Glass: [*select one of the following*]
        1. Obscure glass: Patterned safety glass, nominal 5/32 inch thick, conforming to ANSI Z97.1.
        2. Clear safety glass, conforming to ANSI Z97.1 and certified by Safety Glazing Certification Council.
    C. Hinge [*with hinged doors*]: Continuous aluminum piano hinge, matching frame finish.
    D. Track [*with sliding doors*]: Extruded aluminum, matching frame finish. Provide doors are adjustable rollers with ball bearings and nylon tires.

PART 3 – EXECUTION

3.1 INSTALLATION
    A. Install shower and tub enclosures in accordance with manufacturer's instructions. Install plumb and level, securely and rigidly anchored, with doors operating freely and smoothly.

Options	Brasstec	Glasstec	Centec	Lucette	Crest
Sliding	■	■	■	■	■
Hinged	■	■		■	■
Standard Sizes	■	■	■	■	■
Custom Sizes	■	■	■	■	
Finishes					
Bright Aluminum		■	■	■	■
Anodized Gold		■	■	■	
Century Colors	■	■	■	■	
Stonetec			■		
Brass Finishes (8)	■	■	■		
24K Gold	■	■	■		
Glass					
$3/16''$ $5/32''$ Tempered	■		■	■	■
$3/8''$ $1/2''$ Tempered		■			
$1/4''$ Laminated	■			■	■
Obscure	■			■	■
Mirror	■			■	■
Bronze Tint	■	■	■	■	■
Grey Tint	■	■	■	■	■
Bronze Striped	■			■	■
Grey Striped	■			■	■
V-groove	■		■		
Custom Glass	■	■	■	■	
Transoms					
Steam Vent	■	■		■	
Grille	■			■	■

...ower Door, Inc. ■ 250 Lackawanna Avenue ■ West Paterson, NJ 07424 ■ 201 785 4290 ■ 800 524 257...

SS1190

Master Designed Shower Environments

WORK RIGHT

If you can imagine it, Work Right creates it. In just about any size or shape you dream up. Enclose a tub for a peaceful hide-away. Transform a shower into an invigorating steam room. And place your shower center stage as the star of the master bath.

SS1190

SS11135 with in-line panels

Open the door to beauty, luxury & ease

*L*eave it to the master designers at Work Right to offer the finest in modern shower environments. Like frameless doors that open the space visually like never before. Butted-glass corners for seamless transparency. And a modular framing system that can be used for either standard applications or custom enclosures.

From traditional to contemporary, large or small—Work Right shower environments are featured in over one million of the finest hotels and homes throughout the world.

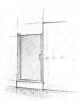

Full Height Shower Door Model D-1000

FOR OPENINGS	HEIGHT	USE MODEL
20" to 21"	66 5/8"	D-1000-20
21" to 22"	66 5/8"	D-1000-21
.... Through		
34" to 35"	66 5/8"	D-1000-34

1" adjustable jambs,
header and curb available as option

Pivot Door Model D-2000

FOR OPENINGS	HEIGHT	USE MODEL
24 1/2" to 26 1/2"	67 15/16"	D-2000-24 to 26
26 1/2" to 28 1/2"	67 15/16"	D-2000-26 to 28
28 1/2" to 30 1/2"	67 15/16"	D-2000-28 to 30
30 1/2" to 32 1/2"	67 15/16"	D-2000-30 to 32
32 1/2" to 34 1/2"	67 15/16"	D-2000-32 to 34
34 1/2" to 36 1/2"	67 15/16"	D-2000-34 to 36

2" adjustable jambs, no header, with full curb

Stall Shower Model SS-11180

FOR OPENINGS	HEIGHT	USE MODEL
34" to 42"	69"	SS-11180-42
42" to 48"	69"	SS-11180-48
48" to 60"	69"	SS-11180-60
60" to 72"	69"	SS-11180-72*

panel and full height door in line or
*door centered between two side panels

Stall Shower Model SS-1190-34

FOR OPENINGS	HEIGHT	USE MODEL
Up to 34" x 34"	69"	SS-1190-34

panel and full height door at 90°

Stall Shower Model SS-1190-38/48

FOR OPENINGS	HEIGHT	USE MODEL
Up to 38" x 38"	69"	SS-1190-38
Up to 48" x 48"	69"	SS-1190-48

two panels and full height door at 90°

Stall Shower Model SS-11135-38

FOR OPENINGS	HEIGHT	USE MODEL
Up to 24" x 27" x 24"	69"	SS-11135-38

two panels at 135° neo-angle to full height door

Tempered glass is strong for added family safety.

Quality craftsmanship

Work Right shower environments are as beautiful inside as they are outside. We use only the best and most durable materials. Heavy extruded aluminum frames. Tempered safety glass. Vinyl seals. And nylon latches and rollers.

Then we add precision-engineered details developed over 20 years. Finally, we make Work Right showers a breeze to keep clean. Our frameless doors—swinging, sliding and pivot—eliminate grooves and corners that can gather dirt. And Work Right's unique open-track design lets you clean the base of sliding doors in just one wipe.

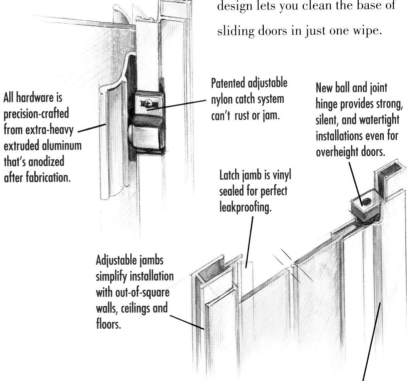

All hardware is precision-crafted from extra-heavy extruded aluminum that's anodized after fabrication.

Patented adjustable nylon catch system can't rust or jam.

New ball and joint hinge provides strong, silent, and watertight installations even for overheight doors.

Latch jamb is vinyl sealed for perfect leakproofing.

Adjustable jambs simplify installation with out-of-square walls, ceilings and floors.

Nylon and aluminum hinge assemblies provide strong, smooth, and quiet operation.

Not shown: Sloping drain bar sends excess water back into the shower, keeping floors dry.

SE1400

Since the glass door won't be hanging open in a bathroom walkway, sliding doors are ideal for young families, the senior set and hotels where guests come and go.

Best of all, sliders blend safety *and* style. You can design an enclosure wall up to 84". And you won't have those bulky frames at the hinge. So you can enjoy an uninterrupted feeling of airiness and spaciousness that only a continuous expanse of glass can provide.

All sliding models can be ordered as tub or shower enclosures.

Step into a world of indulgence

*N*ow bathrooms short on space can be long on style with a Work Right sliding shower enclosure. If you're working with cramped quarters and don't have the room for a swinging door, consider a slider.

TE1600

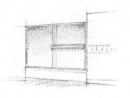

Sliding Tub/Shower Enclosure 1400 Series

FOR OPENINGS	USE MODEL	
Sliders	Tub 57 3/8" HT	Shower 70 3/8" HT
Up to 48"		SE-1400-48
48" to 60"	TE-1400-60	SE-1400-60
60" to 66"	TE-1400-66	

Sliding Tub/Shower Enclosure 1400 Series

FOR OPENINGS	USE MODEL	
Sliders up to 60" with 12" in-line panel	Tub 57 3/8" HT TE-1400-1-72	Shower 70 3/8" HT SE-1400-1-72
Sliders Up to 60" with 24" in-line panel	Tub 57 3/8" HT TE-1400-1-84	Shower 70 3/8" HT SE-1400-1-84

Sliding Tub/Shower Enclosure 1400 Series

FOR OPENINGS	USE MODEL	
Sliders up to 60" with two 12" in-line panels	Tub 57 3/8" HT TE-1400-2-84	Shower 70 3/8" HT SE-1400-2-84

Sliding Tub/Shower Enclosure 1400 Series

FOR OPENINGS	USE MODEL	
Sliders up to 60" with 36" end panel at 90°	Tub 57 3/8" HT TE-1400-3	Shower 70 3/8" HT SE-1400-3

Sliding Tub/Shower Enclosure 1400 Series

FOR OPENINGS	USE MODEL	
Sliders up to 60" with 12" & 24" end panels at 135° neo-angle	Tub 57 3/8" HT TE-1400-4	Shower 70 3/8" HT SE-1400-4

Tracks: 1400 Series ships with open track. To order a "W" shaped track use a 1200 Series designation. All resulting heights will be 3/8" less than the 1400 Series listings.

Glass: 1400 Series and 1200 Series use minimum 3/16" glass.

Custom color and glass etching are available from many local Work Right dealers.

Design and color options

High Light™ finished frames color-coordinate with today's bright and beautiful fixtures. Opt for buffed and bright dipped metals or powder-coated paints. In glass, choose from obscure to sparkling clear or warm bronzes to cool frosts. Plus, any model can be fitted with bars that accommodate the thirstiest towels. Ask your local dealer to help you customize your bathroom right down to the last detail.

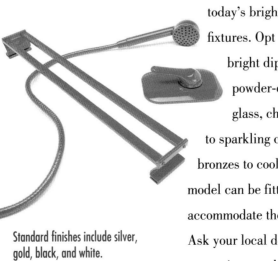

Standard finishes include silver, gold, black, and white.

PRESTIGE DOORS

All the luxury at half the cost

Only Work Right gives you a master-designed shower environment with sophisticated elegance—at an affordable price!

Shop and compare. Then come back to Work Right. Because you can get the upscale look and feel of heavy glass and chrome on brass at a fraction of the cost charged by other shower companies.

At Work Right, we believe your shower can add value and pleasure to your day—and to your home. That's why we use sturdy materials and employ talented craftsmen. The result is a shower environment that's master designed for the ultimate in beauty and functionality.

SE1600

Prestige® sliding door headers offer twice the framing options in just one piece. Use the rounded side to enhance curvacious porcelain. Or flip it to flat for a mirror-bright complement to the crispness of contemporary fixtures.

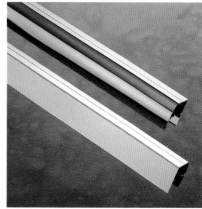

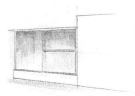

The Euro design Prestige frames are engineered to accommodate heavier glass and operate with an unmistakable feel of quality.

Prestige showers have no interior towel racks that can be mistakenly used for grab bars. Plus, tubular towel bars complement the soft curve of the frame.

Prestige Tub/Shower Enclosure 1600 Series

FOR OPENINGS	USE MODEL	
Sliders	Tub 57 3/8" HT	Shower 70 3/8" HT
Up to 48"		SE-1600-48
48" to 60"	TE-1600-60	SE-1600-60
60" to 66"	TE-1600-66	

Prestige Tub/Shower Enclosure 1600 Series

FOR OPENINGS	USE MODEL	
Sliders up to 60" with 12" in-line panel	Tub 57 3/8" HT TE-1600-1-72	Shower 70 3/8" HT SE-1600-1-72
Sliders Up to 60" with 24" in-line panel	Tub 57 3/8" HT TE-1600-1-84	Shower 70 3/8" HT SE-1600-1-84

Prestige Tub/Shower Enclosure 1600 Series

FOR OPENINGS	USE MODEL	
Sliders up to 60" with two 12" in-line panels	Tub 57 3/8" HT TE-1600-2-84	Shower 70 3/8" HT SE-1600-2-84

Prestige Tub/Shower Enclosure 1600 Series

FOR OPENINGS	USE MODEL	
Sliders up to 60" with 36" end panel at 90°	Tub 57 3/8" HT TE-1600-3	Shower 70 3/8" HT SE-1600-3

Prestige Tub/Shower Enclosure 1600 Series

FOR OPENINGS	USE MODEL	
Sliders up to 60" with 12" & 24" end panels at 135° neo-angle	Tub 57 3/8" HT TE-1600-4	Shower 70 3/8" HT SE-1600-4

Tracks: 1600 Series ships with open track.

Glass: 1600 Series use minimum 1/4" glass.

Work Right provides your builder—and you—with color chips, specification sheets, line drawings, installation and maintenance instructions, and design suggestions.

For smooth installation, each model is precut, predrilled and prepackaged with all parts. What's more, our qualified dealer/installers—over 200 nationwide—are trained and backed by comprehensive technical support. The result for you is product performance that's equal to your bath's unique and stunning style.

For complete design information, or the location of your nearest Work Right dealer/installer, call 800/358-9064 (800/862-4995 from California).

Guide Specifications

Part 1 General

1.1 Work included: Provide shower doors as needed for a complete and proper installation

1.2 Related work by others

  a. Shower receptor base (specify one — tile shower pan, pre-fab shower pan, bathtub)

  b. Wall surface (specify one — tile, marble, cultured marble, fiberglass/plastic, non-porous watertight material

  c. Sealants and caulking (specify a compatible sealant for aluminum and glass)

1.3 Quality assurance

  a. Mock up/sample installation Factory approved mock up sample will represent minimum quality for the work

  b. Source quality control Factory tests for metal hardness, finish and dimensional tolerance

  c. Code compliance
  ANSI Z.97.1
  CPSC 16CFR1201 II
  ASTM C1048-85
  USFS DD-G-1403B

1.4 Delivery, storage and handling by others

  a. Deliver to job site door(s) assembled and ready for installation

  b. Store off ground, under cover, protected from weather and construction activities

  c. Do not lay glass flat either in transport or storage

1.5 Sequencing/Scheduling
Shower door(s) are to be installed only after related work 1.2a and 1.2b is completed

Part 2 Systems

2.1 Specified system or equal
Work Right Products, Inc.
Lakeport, CA
(specify one: D-1000, D-2000, TE-1200, TE-1400, TE-1600, SE-1200, SE-1400, SE-1600, SS-11180, SS-1190, SS-11135)

2.2 Materials

  a. Shower door(s) shall be constructed of (specify clear, obscure, bronzed or custom etched) 3/16" or 1/4" tempered safety glass with all exposed edges polished and rounded

  b. Aluminum sections shall be 6463 T5 aluminum alloy with a minimum thickness of .062"

  c. Aluminum sections shall be buffed and bright dipped anodized or powder coat painted (specify finish or color)

  d. Swinging shower door(s) shall have vinyl seal at both the latch jamb and hinge jamb side of door

  e. Sliding shower enclosures shall have patented roller brackets at the top of each sliding panel

2.3 Fabrication

  a. Shop assembly of doors and sliding panels shall be completed prior to delivery to job site

  b. Fabrication of metal for out-of-plumb or out-of-level

conditions exceeding normal adjustments shall be done prior to installation

  c. Roller brackets for clear glass sliding panels shall be bonded to glass with silicone sealant 24 hours prior to installation, with screws torqued to 28 inchpounds

  d. Handles shall be secured by means of pressure fitting

  e. Sliding shower enclosures shall have one piece, pressure fitted handles and roller brackets

Part 3 Execution

3.1 Surface preparation
Prior to installation of unit, installer shall be sure that surface is free from foreign matter that could compromise the watertight bond of unit to surface (e.g., rust, dirt, grease, paint, mastic, taping compound, etc.)

3.2 Installation
Unit(s) shall be installed consistent with current manufacturer's guidelines and instructions

3.3 Field quality control
Installer shall be responsible to test that door operates smoothly and that at no time does the glass come into contact with metal during normal operation

3.4 Adjusting and cleaning
Installer shall be responsible for adjusting door operation and for securing the owner care and maintenance card to unit

---

WORK RIGHT

MASTER DESIGNED SHOWER ENVIRONMENTS

Lakeport, CA
Call (800) 358-9064
California (800) 862-4995
Intl. (707) 263-0290
FAX (707) 263-4048

U.S. Pat. No. 3,827,737; 3,796,405; 3,787,936; 4,484,411

POP DG 002   1/92/150K

FINLANDIA Sauna The Pacesetter

We have built our reputation as "old country" Sauna builders since 1964, by believing that it takes individual attention to provide each customer with a quality piece of workmanship. Our FINLANDIA Sauna packages are custom cut with special care and experienced craftsmanship. It's the little extras that count—so we take the extra effort—such as nailing our benches from the bottom to make sure that our customers will have no worries (or burns) from protruding nails. We bevel our wall and ceiling boards for the tightest fit, to eliminate unsightly corner moldings. We countersink any surface nails, and we fill any visible nail holes.

FPC Packages Include

PRECUT WALL & CEILING BOARDS
1" x 6" (redwood) or 1" x 4" (cedar), full ¾" thickness, certified, kiln-dried T&G, cut to size with 2% bevel for tight fit.

BOARDS ARE CUT FOR HORIZONTAL INSTALLATION.

ASSEMBLED BENCHES of clear V.G. S4S kiln-dried 2" x 2" tops with ½" spacing, and 2" x 4" facing (much superior to standard 1" x 3" lightweight benches, in design and strength).

PREHUNG GLASS DOOR (FGD) 2'0"x 6'8" as per specs page 12.

ASSEMBLED HEATER FENCE

ASSEMBLED HEADREST/BACKREST for upper bench(es).

TRIM AND BASE

SUPER DEK as per specs page 12 (enough for walking area of floor).

FINLANDIA SAUNA HEATER

PERIDOTITE STONES

CONTROL/CONTACTOR PANEL (if required by heater).

LIGHT wall mounted, vapor-proof.

VENTS (two sets) for installation in upper and lower wall areas.

ACCESSORIES thermometer #3444, wooden bucket #100, wooden dipper #106/40, bathing sign.

INSTRUCTIONS for building.

NAILS hot dipped, galvanized.

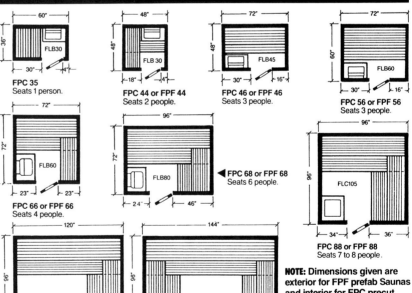

FPC 35
Seats 1 person.

FPC 44 or FPF 44
Seats 2 people.

FPC 46 or FPF 46
Seats 3 people.

FPC 56 or FPF 56
Seats 3 people.

FPC 66 or FPF 66
Seats 4 people.

FPC 68 or FPF 68
Seats 6 people.

FPC 88 or FPF 88
Seats 7 to 8 people.

FPC 810 or FPF 810
Seats 8 to 9 people.

FPC 812 or FPF 812
Seats 12 people.

NOTE: Dimensions given are exterior for FPF prefab Saunas and interior for FPC precut packages. Specify right or left door hinge when ordering. We precut to size, you install on your framed, insulated wall and ceiling surfaces.

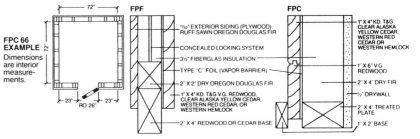

FPC 66 EXAMPLE
Dimensions are interior measurements.

FPF

- ¹¹/₃₂" EXTERIOR SIDING (PLYWOOD) RUFF SAWN OREGON DOUGLAS FIR
- CONCEALED LOCKING SYSTEM
- 3½" FIBERGLAS INSULATION
- TYPE "C" FOIL (VAPOR BARRIER)
- 2" X 2" DRY OREGON DOUGLAS FIR
- 1" X 4" KD. T&G V.G. REDWOOD, CLEAR ALASKA YELLOW CEDAR, WESTERN RED CEDAR, OR WESTERN HEMLOCK
- 2" X 4" REDWOOD OR CEDAR BASE

FPC

- 1" X 4" KD. T&G CLEAR ALASKA YELLOW CEDAR, WESTERN RED CEDAR OR WESTERN HEMLOCK
- 1" X 6" V.G REDWOOD
- 2" X 4" DRY FIR
- ½" DRYWALL
- 2" X 4" TREATED PLATE
- 1" X 2" BASE

FINLANDIA SPECIFICATIONS FOR ARCHITECTS/CONTRACTORS

GENERAL CONTRACTOR SPECIFICATIONS:

Framing of walls and ceiling shall be of dry Douglas Fir, construction grade no. 1 or 2, 16″ center. Use pressure treated plates (against concrete)

Ceiling shall be 7′0″ from finished floor to ceiling joists (16″ center)

Door shall be roughed in at 26″x82″ and must open out

Insulation of walls and ceiling shall be of R11 foil faced fiberglas batts (R19 if Sauna has exterior location)

Drywall shall be ⅝″ firewall (only if required by local building codes)

Added Vapor Barrier shall be of Type C (Reynolds) Construction foil over insulation or drywall—walls and ceiling (recommended as second vapor barrier)

Flooring shall be of hard surfaced, waterproof type—concrete, ceramic tile, heavy-duty seamless vinyl

Floor Drain is recommended for new construction and is essential for commercial and public Saunas

Exterior Walls shall be of drywall, paneling, tile, etc. and exterior painting, door finishing, etc. shall be included

ELECTRICAL CONTRACTOR SPECIFICATIONS:

(Must be licensed and bonded)

Roughin for Sauna controls, heater, room light shall be as per Finlandia wiring diagram (provided with control box or in heater box)

Hookup of controls, heater, light shall be as per Finlandia wiring diagram (see pgs. 8–9 for wire size, amperage, etc.) USE COPPER WIRE ONLY

FINLANDIA SAUNA CONTRACTOR SPECIFICATIONS:

Walls and Ceiling shall be 1″x4″ or 1″x6″ select, certified, kiln-dried (moisture content not exceeding 11%) T&G, v joint, clear, vertical grain Redwood, clear Western Red Cedar, clear Alaska Yellow Cedar, or clear Western Hemlock. All boards shall be blind nailed with 7p galvanized, hot dipped nails, or power stapled with galvanized staples.

The following specs shall include and match one of the four woods chosen above:

Benches shall be clear S4S kiln-dried 2″x2″ tops with ½″ spacing and 2″x4″ facing; glued and fastened with exposed nails countersunk. Bench tops shall be fastened from bottom to eliminate exposed metal)

Door shall be FGD 2′0″x6′8″ of vertical grain Douglas Fir rails and clear hermetically sealed, double glass, tempered (15¾″x60″) with casing, jamb, and threshold of Redwood.

Door Hardware shall be (3) 4″x4″ butt hinges, Ives ball catch MP347B3. (2) wooden door pulls 3431

Vents shall be (2) 4″x10″ louvered V10 for upper wall placement and lower wall placement

Removable Flooring shall be Super Dek interlocking 12″ squares—sanitary, non-skid surface in terra cotta color—over walking area of base floor

Light shall be wall-mounted, vapor-proof Progress P5511, satin finish cast aluminum, rated for 75 watts

Sauna Heater shall be FINLANDIA model … as per room cubic footage and voltage requirements (see chart pgs. 8–9)

Heater Fence shall be of 2″x2″ & 1″x2″ and shall be placed 2½″ away from Sauna heater

Temperature Control/Contactor panel shall be model … from pg. 9

Accessories shall be … from pg. 10

Stones shall be a peridotite, heat tested, igneous type from Finland

Precut and Prefab Saunas shall be as per specifications pgs. 4–5

Warranty shall be 1 yr. on room materials and workmanship and 5 yr. limited warranty on Sauna heaters when installed according to Finlandia specifications and wiring information

Maintenance

Finlandia Sauna heaters and rooms require minimum care and maintenance. Basic household methods, including cleaning of Sauna room floor with a product such as Pine Sol, and occasional scrubbing of benches with a mild soap, is necessary for sanitary and odor-free atmosphere. When wood becomes dark or stained from perspiration, a light sanding will help to restore its beautiful appearance. Do not use sealers, paint, or varnish on interior wood, as toxic vapors could be dangerous in the high temperatures of a Sauna.

Note: When figuring room capacities for number of bathers, allow 2′ of bench space per person.

FINLANDIA SAUNA IS THE ONLY U.S. COMPANY WHICH OFFERS A CHOICE OF THE WORLD'S BEST SAUNA WOODS:

100% vertical grain California Redwood, clear Western Red Cedar, clear Alaska Yellow Cedar, and clear Western Hemlock. All are a full 3/4″ thickness (others use 1/2″ to 5/8″ thickness).

Our CALIFORNIA REDWOOD is 100% vertical grain (tight grain to prevent raising and slivering in the high heat), is the most fire resistant, most dry-rot resistant, most termite resistant, and does not warp. Redwood, however, does darken with age.

The best-known and most widely used of the West Coast cedars is WESTERN RED CEDAR. It has the most beautiful color variation, has a refreshing aroma, and is dry-rot resistant. Because it's the softest wood, it is least hot to sit on or lean against.

ALASKA YELLOW CEDAR is a beautiful white variety of cedar which does not dry-rot or warp. It has a silky smooth finish and a wonderful, refreshing aroma.

Our clear WESTERN HEMLOCK is an excellent wood for people who have wood allergies—it has no aroma and no resins.

Finlandia Sauna does not use inexpensive woods such as thin knotty spruce which has a tendency to cup, shrink, warp, and crack; (and some knots come loose when the pitch and resin around them dries in the high heat of the Sauna). Many European Saunas, however, are built from knotty spruce as it has been the available wood for centuries. Knotty spruce cannot be used for benches as it gets too hot, and the knots and pitch can burn the bather; so African Abachi is imported for benches. Abachi is a clear wood and it's comfortable for sitting; but, it has a peculiar, unpleasant odor. Finlandia uses only clear Western softwoods which have the proper matching wood for benches.

NOTE! Page numbers referenced on this page are from the complete 12 pg. brochure available from Finlandia Sauna.

Transform yourself with a luxurious spa.

The pleasures of steambathing appreciated for centuries, have never been easier to enjoy in your own home.

Having your own personal steambath can help you sleep better and work better. Because above all, you'll feel better.

Entering this warm, moisturizing enclave will relax you before retiring. Linger and let stiffness and fatigue melt away under the soft fingers of soothing steam. After your steambath a shower will give you new life.

Steambathing contributes to a brighter, healthier outlook, increases blood circulation and metabolism, provides a haven from mental and physical stress.

Steamist will enhance the quality of life for both you and your family each and every day.

Steamist transforms your bath area as well

By adding a new level of convenience, beauty and practicality, your Steamist steambath will let you enjoy its pleasures without distractions.

Steamist controls are simple and unobtrusive. In a choice of polished chrome, brass or white finish, they complement the appearance of any bath decor.

And the easy-to-reach controls are just as simple to operate — At the press of a button, your steambath is ready. The controls regulate the time cycle and temperature automatically, holding the temperature precisely at your pre-set comfort level — allowing you to lose yourself completely and confidently, in your period of relaxation.

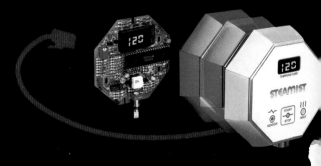

TC-130

Plug-in connections make it easy to install...

Our telephone type connectors make it a snap to install the Steamist generator. The plumbing hookup and electric lines are similar to that of your existing hot water heater, and the unit can be installed as far as 25 feet from the bath area.

The compact steam generator hides quietly in the vanity, closet, or even an insulated attic or basement. In addition, low voltage controls are safe and easy to operate and the system is maintenance free.

A Relaxing Steambath with the Push of a Button

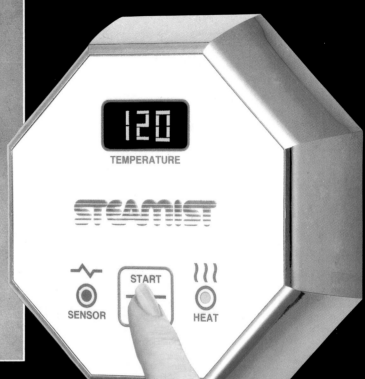

120
TEMPERATURE

Steamist

SENSOR START HEAT

TC-130

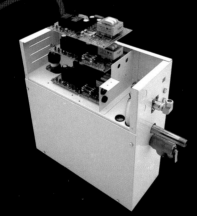

Steamist has been the leading manufacturer of personal steambaths for over 25 years, using our expertise to design convenience and reliability into a choice of contemporary systems. Steamist adds value to both your home and your well-being.

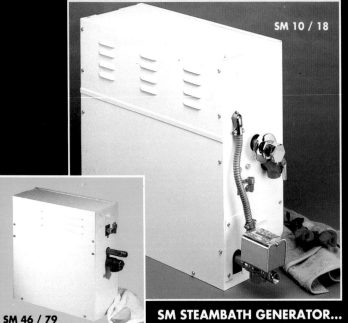

SM 10 / 18

SM 46 / 79

TC-130 DIGITAL TIMER AND TEMPERATURE CONTROL

This control operates on a pre-set time cycle and the start/stop feature allows complete control of your steambath from within. Located inside the steamroom, it is perfect for bathers who require an exact temperature.

TC-120 TIMER AND TEMPERATURE CONTROL

This control is pre-set for your steambath duration and maintains exact temperature. A simple control adjustment by you will change the temperature and keep it within 11/2°F. A start/stop keypad is located inside the steamroom.

SM STEAMBATH GENERATOR...
The Industry Standard for over 30 Years

The model # SM - 46 and SM - 79 offer exceptional flexibility of design by providing an adjustable kilowatt level to better size the unit to your bath area. The larger STEAMIST generators can be equipped with an optional auto drain to enhance the performance. All SM units feature Stainless Steel construction and Solid State circuitry and are designed to last for years of maintainance free operation. Conservative on water and electricity, STEAMIST generators are UL Listed and include a Five Year Limited Warranty.

STEAMIST • SM SERIES • RESIDENTIAL

Model No.	Maximum Cu. Ft. Range	KW Rating	Volt	Phase	Maximum AMPS	Wire Size 90 C Copper AWG	Line Fuse Req'd	Cabinet Dimensions H x W x L
SM-46	60 -130	4.5/6	208	1	29	8	40	15.5" x 6" x 15"
			240	1	25			
SM-79	135-300	7.5/9	208	1	44	8	50	15.5" x 6" x 15"
			240	1	38			
*SM-10	375	10.5	208	1	50	6	60	20.5" x 8" x 20"
			208	3	29	8	40	
			240	1	44	6	60	
			240	3	25	8	40	
*SM-12	410	12	208	1	58	6	70	20.5" x 8" x 20"
			208	3	33	8	40	
			240	1	50	6	60	
			240	3	29	8	40	
*SM-15	475	15	208	1	72	4	90	20.5" x 8" x 20"
			208	3	42	8	50	
			240	1	63	6	70	
			240	3	36	8	50	
*SM-18†	575	18	208	1	87	3	100	20.5" x 8" x 20"
			208	3	50	6	60	
			240	1	75	4	90	
			240	3	44	6	60	
*SM-24†	800	24	208	1	115	CONTACT MANUFACTURER		
			208	3	67			
			240	1	100			
			240	3	58			
*SM-30†	1000	30	208	1	144	CONTACT MANUFACTURER		
			208	3	84			
			240	1	126			
			240	3	72			

* Optional auto drain available for SM-10 thru SM 30
† UL Pending

Distributed by:

3/93

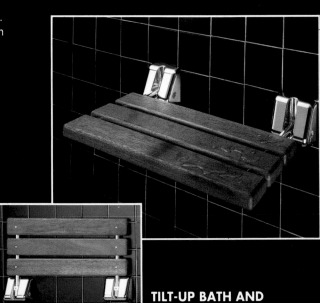

TILT-UP BATH AND SHOWER SEAT

The STEAMIST tilt-up bath and shower seat is designed to make your bathing as practical and comfortable as possible. This attractive seat combines natural hand rubbed exotic European wood on your choice of chrome, white or brass frame. It matches perfectly to any designer bathroom decor.
Dimensions: 19 1/4" x 13" D

STEAMIST®
a new dimension in bathing

East Coast Office:
One Altman Drive • Rutherford, NJ 07070
Telephone: (201) 933-0700 • Fax: (201) 933-0746

West Coast Office:
Telephone: (714) 533-6033 • Fax: (714) 533-8357

For further information about Steamist Heavy Commercial Steambath Generators, Steambath Enclosures, and other accessories, write for a full product line brochure.

APPROVED NKBA KITCHEN
and BATHROOM DEALER
MEMBERS

ALABAMA

Alabaster

COUNTER DIMENSIONS
PO Box 220
Alabaster, AL 35007

Birmingham

BREWER CABINETS INC
One West Park Drive
Birmingham, AL 35211

CABINET SYSTEMS SOUTH
INC
410 Lorna Square
Birmingham, AL 35216

Decatur

CLASSIC CABINETS INC
1415 Kathy Lane SW
Decatur, AL 35601

Hartselle

THE CABINET STORE INC
1902 Highway 31 SW
Hartselle, AL 35640

Homewood

KATHY'S DESIGNER
KITCHENS, INC
1826 29th Avenue South
Homewood, AL 35209

Montgomery

REDLAND DESIGN
1067 B-1 Woodley Road
Montgomery, AL 36106

Oxford

THE KERR COMPANY
2009 Barry Street
Oxford, AL 36203

Tuscaloosa

COOPER CABINETS
PO Box 2757
813 31st Avenue
Tuscaloosa, AL 35403

Montgomery Woodworks, Inc.
1705 44th Avenue NE
Tuscaloosa, AL 35404

ARIZONA

Mesa

KITCHENS UNLIMITED INC
105 W Hoover Avenue #2
Mesa, AZ 85210

Phoenix

COPPERSTATE CABINET
COMPANY
1932 W N Lane
Phoenix, AZ 85021

DESIGNER CABINETRY
4350 E Camelback Road
Suite 110-C
Phoenix, AZ 85018

FINCH ASSOCIATES
2524 E Washington Street
Phoenix, AZ 85034

QUALITY KITCHENS
817 W Indian School Road
Phoenix, AZ 85013-3103

Scottsdale

SUNVEK
8361 E Gelding Drive
Scottsdale, AZ 85257

Tucson

ALBRITE BATH & KITCHEN
3640 E. Ft. Lowell
Tucson, AZ 85716

ARIZONA DESIGNS
KITCHENS & BATHS
3444 N. Dodge Blvd.
Tucson, AZ 85716

DAVIS KITCHENS INC
3391 E Hemisphere Loop
Tucson, AZ 85706

DORADO DESIGNS INC
4640 E Sunrise Drive
Tucson, AZ 85718

TUCSON OUTSTANDING
PRODUCTS
3820 S Palo Verde
Suite 105
Tucson, AZ 85714

ARKANSAS

Jonesboro

BARTON'S OF JONESBORO
3023 Brown's Lane
Jonesboro, AR 72401

Little Rock

BATH AND KITCHEN
GALLERY
921 Rushing Circle
Little Rock, AR 72205

LAING SALES & SERVICE INC.
200 West Roosevelt Road
Little Rock, AR 72206

CALIFORNIA

Alameda

INTERNATIONAL KITCHENS
ALAMEDA INC
2319 Lincoln Avenue
Alameda, CA 94501

R.L. ENTERPRISES
2425 Clement Avenue
Alameda, CA 94501

Albany

HOUSE OF KITCHENS INC
1325 Solano Avenue
Albany, CA 94706

Anaheim

REBORN CABINETS INC
2821 E White Star Avenue
Suite K
Anaheim, CA 92806

Apple Valley

HITT PLUMBING COMPANY
INC
13608 Hitt Road
PO Box 638
Apple Valley, CA 92037

Arcata

ARCATA CABINET & DESIGN
COMPANY
5000 W End Road
Arcata, CA 95521

Auburn

CABINETICS
4465 Granite Drive #540
PO Box 4831
Auburn, CA 95604-4831

Azusa

D-DESIGNS & ASSOCIATES
623 N Azusa Avenue
Azusa, CA 91702

Belmont

THE COUNTERTOP STORE
1475 Old County Road
Belmont, CA 94065

Berkeley

TRUITT & WHITE LUMBER
COMPANY
642 Hearst Avenue
Berkeley, CA 94710

Big Bear Lake

PINNACLE DOOR & FINISH
42106 Big Bear Boulevard
PO Box 536
Big Bear Lake, CA 92315

Burbank

CALIFORNIA KITCHENS
2305 W Alameda Avenue
Burbank, CA 91506

Burlingame

SIGNATURE KITCHENS
344 Lorton Avenue
Burlingame, CA 94010

Camarillo

SHOWCASE KITCHENS &
BATHS
2650 Ventura Blvd
Suite 101
Camarillo, CA 93010

Carmel

SEGER'S KITCHENS & BATHS
OF CARMEL
26386 Carmel Rancho Lane
Carmel, CA 93923

Cathedral City

MASTERCRAFT
68-444 Perez Road #G
Cathedral City, CA 92234

Cerritos

EVANS ENTERPRISES INC
11304 South Street
Cerritos, CA 90701

Chico

GINNO'S KITCHEN &
APPLIANCES SYSTEMS INC.
2505 A Zanella Way
Chico, CA 95928

Chula Vista

BAY KITCHEN & BATH
REMODELERS
669 Palomar Street
Suite A
Chula Vista, CA 91911

City of Industry

BACCARO KITCHEN & BATH
CENTRE
18605 East Gale Avenue
Suite 110
City of Industry, CA 91748

Concord

CREATIVE KITCHEN CENTER
1325 Galindo Street
Concord, CA 94520

EL MONTE KITCHEN
DESIGNS
1476 Wharton Way
Concord, CA 94521

THE CABINET SHOP
288 Buchanan Field Road
Concord, CA 94520

Corona Del Mar

KITCHENS DEL MAR
3536 E Coast Highway
Corona Del Mar, CA 92625

Costa Mesa

EUROBATH & TILE
2915 Red Hill Avenue
Suite F102
Costa Mesa, CA 92626

KITCHEN SPACES
2915 Redhill Avenue
Ste B105
Costa Mesa, CA 92626

Covina

ARTISTIC KITCHENS &
BATHS INC
310 E Rowland Street
Covina, CA 91723

Downey

ALL AMERICAN HOME
CENTER
7201 E Firestone Boulevard
Downey, CA 90241

Dublin

RENOVATIONS DESIGN/BUILD
CENTER
7127 Amador Plaza Road
Dublin, CA 94568

THE PLUMBERY
11825 Dublin Boulevard
Dublin, CA 94568

El Toro

VALLEY CONCEPTS &
DESIGN
22541 Aspan
Suite A
El Toro, CA 92630

Fortuna

OESTER CABINETS
600 L. Street Suite B
PO Box 673
Fortuna, CA 95540-0673

Fountain Valley

KITCHENS BY JONI
18384 Brookhurst
Fountain Valley, CA 92708

Fremont

CUSTOM KITCHEN BATH
CENTER
40900 Fremont Boulevard
Fremont, CA 94538

Fresno

KITCHENS ETC
1441 N Thesta
Fresno, CA 93703

NELSON DYE REMODELING
SPECIALISTS
4937 E Dakota Avenue
Fresno, CA 93727

Gardena

ALEXANDER CABINET
CENTER
17209-A S Figueroa Street
Gardena, CA 90248

Glendale

H & S CABINETS &
CONSTRUCTION
3609 N Verdugo Road
Glendale, CA 91208

Glendora

JB KITCHENS BATHS &
DESIGN
631 E Arrow Highway
Suite Q
Glendora, CA 91740

Goleta

INTERIOR CABINET
CORPORATION
7330 Hollister Avenue
Goleta, CA 93117

Grand Terrace

SOUTHERN CALIFORNIA
KITCHENS
12036 La Cross Avenue
Grand Terrace, CA 92324

Greenbrae

BYGG INC
2100 Redwood Highway
Greenbrae, CA 94904

Hanford

PIEROTTE'S PLUMBING INC
602 E. 6th Street
Hanford, CA 93230

Irvine

THE J M COMPANY KITCHEN
& BATH SHOWROOM INC
15333 Culver Drive
Suite 220
Irvine, CA 92714

La Jolla

DESIGN STUDIO WEST
7422-24 Girard Avenue
La Jolla, CA 92037

KITCHEN EXPO
7458 La Jolla Boulevard
La Jolla, CA 92037

La Mesa

KITCHENS PLUS
7953 University Avenue
La Mesa, CA 91941

LaMesa

KITCHENS BY DELUCA
7872 LaMesa Boulevard
LaMesa, CA 91941

Lafayette

AUTOMATIC APPLIANCE &
KITCHEN CABINETRY
3458 Mount Diablo Boulevard
Lafayette, CA 94549

Long Beach

KITCHENS BY THE SEA
4403 Los Coyotes Diagonal
Long Beach, CA 90815

MR Z'S SPECIALTIES
KITCHENS BATHS & BARS
1819 Redondo Avenue
Long Beach, CA 90804

PLUMBING WORLD
6152 Cherry Avenue
Long Beach, CA 90805

Los Altos

KITCHENS OF LOS ALTOS
155 Main Street
P.O. Box
Los Altos, CA 94023

Los Angeles

BULTHAUP
153 S Robertson Boulevard
Los Angeles, CA 90048

C & H KITCHEN CABINETS
1016 S Wilton Place
Los Angeles, CA 90019

CLEVELAND WRECKING
COMPANY
3170 E Washington Boulevard
PO Box 23427
Los Angeles, CA 90023

COOPER-PACIFIC KITCHENS
INC
8687 Melrose Avenue
Suite G #776
Los Angeles, CA 90069-5701

KITCHEN GALLERY
8687 Melrose Avenue
Suite G686
Los Angeles, CA 90069

MAR VISTA LUMBER
COMPANY THE KITCHEN
CENTER
3860 Grandview Blvd PO Box
661007
Los Angeles, CA 90066

MODERN CONCEPT KITCHEN
& BATH SHOWROOM
3403 W 43rd Street
Los Angeles, CA 90008

SNYDER DIAMOND
DISCOUNT PLUMBING &
APPLIANCES
100 S Robertson
Los Angeles, CA 90048

THE KITCHEN WAREHOUSE
2149 W Washington Boulevard
Los Angeles, CA 90018

Menlo Park

GREAT KITCHENS
842 Santa Cruz Avenue
Menlo Park, CA 94025

Millbrae

KITCHENS BATHS &
CABINETS
1795 El Camino Real
Millbrae, CA 94030

Mission Viejo

LIFETIME KITCHENS
23332-F Modero Road
Mission Viejo, CA 92691

Monterey

G O REMODEL STORE
1105 Del Monte Avenue
Monterey, CA 93940

M & S BUILDING SUPPLY
2456 Del Monte Avenue
Monterey, CA 93940

Mountain View

KITCHENS BY MEYER, INC
278 Castro Street
Mountain View, CA 94041

N Hollywood

FAMILIAN PIPE & SUPPLY
MAJOR APPLIANCE DIVISION
12556 Saticoy Street S
N Hollywood, CA 91605

Napa

DESIGN SHOWCASE
686 Soscol Avenue
Napa, CA 94559

Newhall

KITCHENS ETC
23119 W Lyons Avenue
Newhall, CA 91321

Newport Beach

KITCHEN & BATH DESIGNS
1000 Bristol Street N 21
Newport Beach, CA 92660

North Hollywood

SNYDER DIAMOND
DISCOUNT PLUMBING &
APPLIANCES
12725 Vanowen Street
North Hollywood, CA 91605

Novato

MARIN KITCHEN WORKS INC
401 D Bel Marin Keys Boulevard
Novato, CA 94949

NOVATO KITCHENS AND
BATHS
PO Box 1133
Novato, CA 94948

Oakland

CUSTOM KITCHENS BY JOHN
WILKINS INC
6624 Telegraph
Oakland, CA 94609

FEDERAL BUILDING
COMPANY A DESIGN-BUILD
GENERAL CONTRACTOR
3630 Park Boulevard
Oakland, CA 94610

ROCKRIDGE COMPANY
1865 Pleasant Valley Avenue
Oakland, CA 94611

SUPERIOR HOME REMODELING
4700 Telegraph Avenue
Oakland, CA 94609

Orange

CAREFREE KITCHENS INC
453 North Anaheim Boulevard
Orange, CA 92668

KITCHENEERING INC
514 W Katella Avenue
Orange, CA 92667

Orinda

PREMIER KITCHENS
2 Theater Square 140
Orinda, CA 94563

Oxnard

KITCHEN QUEEN
CORPORATION
138 South
Oxnard, CA 93030

Pacific Grove

KITCHEN & BATH DESIGN
SHOWROOM
158 Fountain Avenue
Pacific Grove, CA 93950

Palm Desert

KITCHENS OF THE DESERT
73405 El Paseo Drive
Palm Desert, CA 92260

Palm Springs

LUMBERMEN'S BUILDING
CENTER
3455 N Indian Avenue
PO Box 2008
Palm Springs, CA 92263

Palo Alto

BENCHMARK
781 High Street
Palo Alto, CA 94301-2447

Pasadena

KOKKEN-SCANDINAVIAN
KITCHEN DESIGN
54 W Green Street
Pasadena, CA 91105

SNYDER DIAMOND
DISCOUNT PLUMBING &
APPLIANCES
3660 E Colorado Boulevard
Pasadena, CA 91107

Pleasanton

CANAC KITCHENS OF NO.
CALIFORNIA
6654 Koll Center Parkway
Suite 333
Pleasanton, CA 94566

Redding

KITCHENS & BATHS BY
SHIRLEY
1301 Court Street
Suite B
Redding, CA 96001

Redondo Beach

SOUTH BAY KITCHEN &
BATH STUDIO
312 S. Catalina Avenue
Redondo Beach, CA 90277

THE KITCHEN COLLECTION
241 Avenida Del Norte
Redondo Beach, CA 90277

Roseville

INNOVATIVE KITCHENS INC
1125 Orlando Avenue #C
Roseville, CA 95661

Sacramento

KUSTOM KITCHENS DESIGN
CONSULTANT
1220
Sacramento, CA 95818

THE PLUMBERY
9778 Business Park Drive
Sacramento, CA 95827

Salinas

TYNAN'S CUSTOM HOUSE
325 Front Street
Salinas, CA 93901

San Bruno

SAN BRUNO LUMBER
COMPANY
101 San Bruno Avenue
San Bruno, CA 94066

San Carlos

CABINET WORLD INC
1501 Laurel Street
San Carlos, CA 94070

San Clemente

KITCHEN & BATH DESIGN
CENTER ORANGE COAST
PLUMBING
1108 N El Camino Real
San Clemente, CA 92672

San Diego

DA VINCI CABINETS
1241 Morena Boulevard
San Diego, CA 92110

KITCHENS PLUS
7160 Miramar Road
San Diego, CA 92121

KOVACH KITCHEN &
REMODELING
10382 Carioca Court
San Diego, CA 92124

MIRAMAR KITCHEN & BATH
6904 Miramar Road #205
San Diego, CA 92121

San Francisco

BK DESIGN CENTER
2741 16th Street
San Francisco, CA 94103-4215

CONTINENTAL KITCHENS &
BATHS
151 Vermont Street
Suite 8
San Francisco, CA 94103

DELUXE KITCHEN AND
BATH
2234 Taraval Street
San Francisco, CA 94116

FLOORCRAFT
470 Bay Shore
San Francisco, CA 94124

GILMAN SCREENS &
KITCHENS
228 Bay Shore Boulevard
San Francisco, CA 94124

KEN TOPPING HOME
IMPROVEMENTS
3101 Vicente Street
San Francisco, CA 94116

MAJOR LINES OF CALIFORNIA
235 Bay Shore Boulevard
San Francisco, CA 94124

NOVA DESIGNS
300 DeHaro Street at 16th Street
San Francisco, CA 94103

STUDIO BECKER KITCHENS
1355 Market
Suite 239
San Francisco, CA 94103

San Gabriel

L & W HOME CENTER
8812 Las Tunas Drive
San Gabriel, CA 91776

San Jose

CONCEPTS KITCHENS &
BATHS PLUS
466 Meridan Avenue
San Jose, CA 95126

M.A.M. DESIGN CENTER
1676 Monterey Highway
San Jose, CA 95112

WILLOW GLEN KITCHEN &
BATH
351 Willow Street
San Jose, CA 95110-3223

San Marcos

DISTINCTIVE KITCHEN &
BATH DESIGN INC
730 Nordahl Road Suite 109
San Marcos, CA 92069

San Rafael

CTW DESIGNS
610 C Dubois Street
San Rafael, CA 94901

CULINARY DESIGNS
15 Dodie Court #M
San Rafael, CA 94901

LAMPERTI ASSOCIATES
1241 Andersen Drive
San Rafael, CA 94901

SUNWORKS
425 Irwin Street
San Rafael, CA 94901

Santa Barbara

SANTA BARBARA KITCHENS
710 N Milpas
PO Box 21656
Santa Barbara, CA 93121

SANTA BARBARA PLUMBING
SUPPLIES
621 N. Milpas Street
Santa Barbara, CA 93103

THE KITCHEN COMPANY
1717 State Street
Santa Barbara, CA 93101-2521

THIELMANN'S KITCHENS
AND BATHS
208 Cottage Grove Avenue
Santa Barbara, CA 93101

Santa Monica

BAY CITIES KITCHENS/BATHS/
APPLIANCES
1412 14th Street
Santa Monica, CA 90404

SNYDER DIAMOND
DISCOUNT PLUMBING &
APPLIANCES
1399 Olympic Boulevard
Santa Monica, CA 90404

Santa Rosa

DESIGN HOUSE KITCHEN &
BATH
3504 Industrial Drive
Santa Rosa, CA 95403

FRIEDMAN BROS. KITCHEN
CENTER
4055 Santa Rosa Avenue
Santa Rosa, CA 95407

WESTERN CABINETS
1845 Piner Road
Santa Rosa, CA 95403

YAEGER & KIRK
PO Box 1919
Santa Rosa, CA 95402

Scotts Valley

SCARBOROUGH LUMBER &
BUILDING SUPPLY INC
20 El Pueblo Road
Scotts Valley, CA 95066

Seaside

KITCHEN STUDIO OF
MONTEREY PENINSULA
INCORPORATED
1096 Canyon Del Rey Boulevard
Seaside, CA 93955

South San Francisco

QUALITY KITCHEN
CABINETS
161 El Camino Real
South San Francisco, CA 94080

Spreckels

WESTERN CABINET &
COUNTER
PO Box 7188
Spreckels, CA 93962

Stockton

MAZZERA'S INC
501 N Baker Street
Stockton, CA 95203

Sunnyvale

CUSTOM REMODEL SUPPLY
548 S Murphy Avenue
Sunnyvale, CA 94086

INTERNATIONAL KITCHEN
EXCHANGE
1175 E Homestead Road
Sunnyvale, CA 94087

KITCHENLAND INC OF
SUNNYVALE
984 W El Camino Real
Sunnyvale, CA 94087

THE BATH ROOM INC
1291 W El Camino Real
Sunnyvale, CA 94087

Truckee

TRUCKEE-TAHOE LUMBER
COMPANY
PO Box 369
Truckee, CA 96160

Upland

CLASSIC KITCHENS & BATHS
669 E Foothill Boulevard
Upland, CA 91786

Van Nuys

I.C.C. KITCHEN DESIGN
CENTER
16142 Wyandotte Street
Van Nuys, CA 91406

KITCHEN & BATH
SPECIALIST INC
7820 Balboa Boulevard
Van Nuys, CA 91406

Ventura

BETTER KITCHENS & BATHS
1884 Eastman Avenue
Suite 106
Ventura, CA 93003

KITCHEN PLACES & OTHER
SPACES
1076 B Front Street
Ventura, CA 93001

Walnut Creek

KITCHENS ETC
1501 N California Boulevard
Walnut Creek, CA 94596

SIMON STORES
1500 Botelho Drive
Walnut Creek, CA 94596

THE KITCHEN CENTER
1100 Boulevard Way
Walnut Creek, CA 94595

Westlake Village

BETTER HOMES AND
KITCHENS
31121 Via Colinas #1004
Westlake Village, CA 91362

Woodland

FISHER DESIGN & BUILDING
427 Main Street
Woodland, CA 95695

COLORADO

Boulder

KITCHEN CONNECTION
4619 Field Court
Boulder, CO 80301

KITCHEN PLANNERS
1627 28th Street
Boulder, CO 80301

Colorado Spring

KITCHEN'S AT THE DEPOT
76 S Sierra Madre St #B
PO Box 489
Colorado Spring, CO 80903-0489

Denver

CASEY'S DESIGN CENTER
2055 S Raritan Street
Denver, CO 80223

ECONOMY BUILDING
MATERIALS
957 W Mississippi Avenue
Denver, CO 80223

EDWARD HANLEY &
COMPANY
1448 Oneida Street
Denver, CO 80220

KITCHEN CONNECTION
1331 E. 7th Avenue
Denver, CO 80218-3420

KITCHEN GALLERY LTD
66 S Logan Street
Denver, CO 80209

KITCHEN MASTERS INC
5280 W 38th Avenue
Denver, CO 80212

THE COMPLEAT KITCHEN
INC
1039 S Gaylord Street
Denver, CO 80209

THURSTON INC
2920 E 6th Avenue
Denver, CO 80206

TIMBERLINE KITCHEN AND
BATH INC
1842 South Broadway
Denver, CO 80210

WILLIAM OHS SHOWROOMS
INC
2900 E 6th Avenue
Denver, CO 80206

Edwards

KITCHENS BY DESIGN
40784 Hwy 6 & 24
P.O. Box 1775
Edwards, CO 81632

Englewood

THE KITCHEN SHOWCASE
INC
6555 South Kenton Street
Suite 3309
Englewood, CO 80111

Evergreen

KITCHEN CENTERS OF
COLORADO INC
3755 Evergreen Parkway
PO Box 4299
Evergreen, CO 80439

Fort Collins

AAAH! THE KITCHEN PLACE
INC
226 South College Avenue
Fort Collins, CO 80524

ALLEN PLUMBING &
HEATING INC
101 South Link Lane
PO Box 567
Fort Collins, CO 80522

Glenwood Springs

MODERN KITCHEN CENTER
5050 Road 154
Glenwood Springs, CO 81602

Greeley

KITCHEN & BATH
REVELATIONS INC
2126 W 9th Street
Greeley, CO 80631

Lafayette

TECHNI-KITCHEN & BATH
DESIGN
613 E Emma Street
Lafayette, CO 80026

Lakewood

BATH BEAUTIFUL ENT INC
65 Sheridan Boulevard
Lakewood, CO 80226

Littleton

KITCHEN DISTRIBUTORS INC
1309 W Littleton Boulevard
Littleton, CO 80120

Pueblo

KITCHEN'S DESIGN
1416 East 4th Street
Pueblo, CO 81001

Steamboat Spring

SKI COUNTRY KITCHENS
PO Box 770060
1475 S Lincoln
Steamboat Spring, CO 80477

CONNECTICUT

Avon

DESIGNER KITCHENS
HOLLAND CARPENTERS
195 W Main Street
Avon, CT 06001

Bethel

RING'S END INC
Taylor Avenue
Bethel, CT 06801

SECURED KITCHEN
INVESTMENTS
219 Greenwood Avenue
Bethel, CT 06801-2113

Bristol

DOUGLAS KITCHENS INC
270 Riverside Avenue
Bristol, CT 06010

Centerbrook

DISTINCTIVE KITCHEN
DESIGNS
24 Main Street
PO Box 297
Centerbrook, CT 06409

Cornwall Bridge

NORTHWEST LUMBER &
HARDWARE INC
26 Kent Road
Cornwall Bridge, CT 06754

Cos Cob

PUTNAM KITCHENS INC
406 E Putnam Avenue
Cos Cob, CT 06807

Danbury

KITCHEN BROKERS INC
132 Main Street
Danbury, CT 06810

Darien

BLACK FOREST KITCHENS
1472 Post Road
Darien, CT 06820

RING'S END INC
181 West Avenue
PO Box 1066
Darien, CT 06820

Derby

HOUSATONIC LUMBER
COMPANY
23 Factory Street
Derby, CT 06418

East Woodstock

BRUNARHANS DESIGN
Woodstock Road
PO Box 208
East Woodstock, CT 06244

Fairfield

DOMESTIC KITCHENS INC
553 Commerce Drive
Fairfield, CT 06430

FAIRFIELD LUMBER &
SUPPLY
185 Thorpe Street
PO Box 400
Fairfield, CT 06430

Glastonbury

EHL EURO CONCEPTS
110 Commerce Street
Glastonbury, CT 06033

NICK NAPLES REMODELING
SHOWCASE
141 Hebron Avenue
Glastonbury, CT 06033

Greenwich

CERAMIC DESIGN LTD
26 Bruce Park Avenue
Greenwich, CT 06830

FORM LTD
32 West Putman Avenue
Greenwich, CT 06830

Groton

KITCHEN BEAUTIFUL
79 Gold Star Highway
Route 184
Groton, CT 06340

Guilford

EMERSON SUPPLY INC
PO Box 1468
640 Boston Road
Guilford, CT 06437

Hamden

THE KITCHEN BARRON INC
1700 Dixwell Avenue
Hamden, CT 06514

Jewett City

A.D. TRIPP CO.
6 Mathewson Street
Jewett City, CT 06351

Madison

KITCHENS BY GEDNEY INC
84 Bradley Road
Madison, CT 06443

Manchester

MASTERPIECE CABINETRY/A
DIV OF MANCHESTER
LUMBER
401 New State Road
Manchester, CT 06040

Meriden

CLASSIC KITCHEN & BATH
INC
464 Pratt Street Ext
Meriden, CT 06450

S.J. PAPPAS INC
718 Old Colony Road
Meriden, CT 06450

Middlebury

KITCHEN ELEGANCE INC
Route 64 Middlebury Hamlet
PO Box 809
Middlebury, CT 06762

Middlefield

NORTON KITCHEN & BATH
480 Meriden Road
PO Box 32
Middlefield, CT 06455

Monroe

NEW ENGLAND KITCHEN
DESIGN CENTER INC
Village Square Shopping Ctr Rte
111
Monroe, CT 06468

New Britain

SANSON, INC.
1340 East Street
New Britain, CT 06053-2524

New Canaan

KITCHEN DESIGN STUDIO OF
NEW CANAAN
21 South Avenue
New Canaan, CT 06840

New London

GENERAL WOODCRAFT
531 Broad Street
New London, CT 06320

New Milford

RINGS' END INC
140 Danbury Road
New Milford, CT 06776

Newington

ROGERS SASH & DOOR
COMPANY
385 Stamm Road
PO Box 310816
Newington, CT 06131-0816

North Franklin

UNIQUE KITCHENS & BATHS
574 Route Thirty Two
North Franklin, CT 06254

North Haven

THE KITCHEN COMPANY INC
370 Sackett Point Road
North Haven, CT 06473

North Stonington

CREATIVE KITCHEN DESIGN
391 Norwich Westerly Road
PO Box 175
North Stonington, CT 06359

Norwalk

FRONT ROW KITCHENS INC.
73 Main Street
Norwalk, CT 06851

Norwich

DAVID HECHT CUSTOM
KITCHEN CENTRE
675 W Thames Street
Norwich, CT 06360

Old Lyme

PAUL DOLAN COMPANY INC
Halls Road
Old Lyme Shopping Center
Old Lyme, CT 06371

Quaker Hill

SCRIBNER'S KITCHEN &
BATH DESIGNS
44 Route 32
Quaker Hill, CT 06375

Ridgefield

ALTIMA INC KITCHENS
BATHS & MORE
722 Danbury Road
Ridgefield, CT 06877

Seymour

L & M CUSTOM KITCHENS &
BATHS
151 Main Street
Seymour, CT 06483

South Windsor

GENERAL BUILDING SUPPLY
KITCHEN & BATH CENTER
75 Johnfitch Blvd Route 5
South Windsor, CT 06074

Stamford

KITCHENS BY DEANE INC
1267 E Main Street
Stamford, CT 06902

MOHAWK KITCHENS INC.
48 Union Street
Stamford, CT 06906

TODAY'S KITCHENS LTD
111 High Ridge Road
Stamford, CT 06905

Stratford

ENER-G TECH
400 Surf Avenue
Stratford, CT 06497

Torrington

DUCCI KITCHENS
379 Goshen Road
Torrington, CT 06790

Waterbury

GIORDANO CABINETS INC
560 Chase Avenue
Waterbury, CT 06704

LEWIS KITCHEN & BATH
CENTER, INC.
130 Scott Road
Waterbury, CT 06705

Watertown

CABINET GALLERY
WATERTOWN BUILDING
SUPPLY
PO Box 299
Watertown, CT 06795

West Hartford

WHAMSCO KITCHENS &
BATHS
1048 New Britain Avenue
West Hartford, CT 06110

West Haven

THE KITCHEN STUDIO
DIVISION WEST HAVEN
LUMBER
741 Washington Avenue
West Haven, CT 06516

Westbrook

COVENANT KITCHENS &
BATHS
1871 Boston Post Road
Westbrook, CT 06498

Westport

GALLERY OF KITCHENS &
BATHS
1027 Post Road East
Westport, CT 06880

KITCHEN SYSTEMS INC
56 Post Road West
Westport, CT 06880

Wilton

KITCHENS BY BENSON INC
297 Danbury Road
Wilton, CT 06897

DELAWARE

Marydel

U.L. HARMAN INC
PO Box 56
Marydel, DE 19964

Millsboro

THE HOWLETT COMPANY
280 Old Landing Road
Millsboro, DE 19966

Newark

INNOVATIVE KITCHENS
DESIGN CENTER INC
33 Possum Park Mall
Newark, DE 19711

Seaford

CREATIVE KITCHENS AND
FLOORS INC
8 N Arch Street
Seaford, DE 19973

Wilmington

A H ANGERSTEIN INC
315 New Road
Wilmington, DE 19805

CRAFT-WAY KITCHENS INC.
3913 Evelyn Drive
Wilmington, DE 19808

ESPRIT DESIGN LTD
4001 Kennett Pike #134
Wilmington, DE 19807-2000

GIORGI KITCHENS INC
218 Philadelphia Pike
Penny Hill
Wilmington, DE 19809

KITCHENS INC
2411 Lancaster Avenue
Wilmington, DE 19805

THE KITCHEN & BATH
STORE INC
502 Rockwood Road
Wilmington, DE 19802-1119

Yorklyn

SNUFF MILLS KITCHENS/
INTERIORS
2892 Creek Road
PO Box 404
Yorklyn, DE 19736

DISTRICT OF COLUMBIA

Washington

CHESAPEAKE KITCHENS INC
4620 Wisconsin Avenue N W
Washington, DC 20016

THE KITCHEN GUILD
5027 Connecticut Avenue NW
Washington, DC 20008

W.T. WEAVER & SONS INC.
1208 Wisconsin Avenue NW
Washington, DC 20007

FLORIDA

Alachua

DESIGN CABINETS &
FURNITURE INC
PO Box 1108
Alachua, FL 32615

Alva

MONTGOMERY CABINETRY
COMPANY INC
2191 Dixie Lane
Alva, FL 33916

Boca Raton

INNOVATIVE CABINETRY
COMPANY
6590 W Rogers Circle
Studio #7
Boca Raton, FL 33487

ULTIMATE KITCHEN AND
BATH INC.
1000 Clint Moore Road Suite 105
Boca Raton, FL 33487

Bonita Springs

GULFSHORE KITCHENS
8951 Bonita Beach Road SE Ste
660
PO Box 2201
Bonita Springs, FL 33959

Bradenton

MANATEE CABINETS INC
8700 Cortez Road W
Bradenton, FL 34210

Bunnell

COASTAL CABINETS INC
519 N State Road
PO Box 535
Bunnell, FL 32110

Cape Coral

PARKWAY DESIGNS CORP.
4409 S E 16th Place
Suite 10
Cape Coral, FL 33904

Charlotte Harbor

KITCHEN CLASSICS INC.
4265 K Tamiami Trail
Charlotte Harbor, FL 33980

Clearwater

DEEM CABINETS INC
2114 Drew Street
Clearwater, FL 34625

Coral Gables

LA ASSOCIATES
4200 Aurora Street
Suite B
Coral Gables, FL 33146

Coral Springs

PRINCETON CUSTOM
CABINETRY
11336 Wiles Road
Coral Springs, FL 33076

Dania

SAM JOLLEY'S PLUMBING
INC
55 N W 1 Avenue
Dania, FL 33004

Deerfield Beach

DEERFIELD BUILDERS
SUPPLY
77 SE 2nd Avenue
Deerfield Beach, FL 33441

Fort Lauderdale

ALLIED KITCHENS & BATHS
616 W Oakland Park Boulevard
Fort Lauderdale, FL 33311

BATHS & KITCHENS BY
LUCCI
4363 N Andrews Avenue
Fort Lauderdale, FL 33309

DESIGNER KITCHENS &
BATHS INC
2500 Wilton Drive
Fort Lauderdale, FL 33305

LIFESTYLE CABINETRY INC
2303 N E 26th Street
Fort Lauderdale, FL 33305

THE KITCHENWORKS
117 NW 2nd Avenue
Fort Lauderdale, FL 33311

Fort Myers

KITCHEN CABARET INC
16295 S Tamiami Trail
Fort Myers, FL 33908

KITCHENS & BATHS BY
AMBIANCE INC
16520-9 South Tamiami Trail
Fort Myers, FL 33908

SAHARA CABINETS INC
2171 Flint Drive
Fort Myers, FL 33916

Fort Walton

CABINET CREATIONS OF
THE GULF COAST, INC.
15 Shell Avenue South East
Fort Walton, FL 32548

Fort Walton Beach

LINN'S PRESTIGE KITCHEN'S
INC
218 Greenacres Road
Suite 100
Fort Walton Beach, FL 32547

MARBLE WORKS - KITCHEN
AND BATH CENTER
20 Ready Avenue
Fort Walton Beach, FL 32548

Jacksonville

KITCHENS ETC BY REGENCY
8321 Atlantic Boulevard
Jacksonville, FL 32211

Lakeland

FLORIDA KITCHEN DESIGNS
608 N Ingraham Avenue
Lakeland, FL 33801

Largo

A & B KITCHEN DESIGN, INC.
12517 Ulmerton Road
Largo, FL 34644

KITCHEN & BATH CONCEPTS
1642 N Missouri Avenue
Largo, FL 34640

THE CABINET CORNER INC
426 W Bay Drive
Largo, FL 34640

Maitland

CLASSIC KITCHENS AND
BATHS INC
1455 S Orlando Avenue
Maitland, FL 32751

Miami

DETAILS
7404 SW 48th Street
Miami, FL 33155

TRIM LINE KITCHENS &
BATHS
10001 S Dixie Highway
Miami, FL 33156

Miami Springs

KITCHEN CENTER INC
3968 Curtiss Parkway
Miami Springs, FL 33166

Naples

DESIGN KITCHENS & BATHS
1673 Pine Ridge Road
Naples, FL 33942

KITCHEN KABINETS &
KOUNTERS INC
1460 Golden Gate Parkway
108
Naples, FL 33942

KITCHEN KONCEPTS INC
3906 Exchange Avenue
Naples, FL 33942

Ocala

CLASSIC KITCHENS INC
3100 NE 70th Street
Ocala, FL 32670

FERGUSON LUMBER
COMPANY
948 North West 30th Avenue
Ocala, FL 32678

Pensacola

KAY'S KITCHEN & BATH
DESIGNS
2901 N
Pensacola, FL 32501

Port Charlotte

STOTTLEMYER &
SHOEMAKER LUMBER
COMPANY
1615 Market Circle
Port Charlotte, FL 33953

Saint Petersburg

COX LUMBER COMPANY
3300 Fairfield Avenue South
Saint Petersburg, FL 33712

KITCHEN CENTER PLUS INC
2900 4th Street North
Saint Petersburg, FL 33704

Sarasota

AQUI KITCHEN & BATH
613 North Washington Blvd
Sarasota, FL 34236

ASGARD KITCHENS & BATHS
437 Burns Court
Sarasota, FL 34236

COOK'S CUSTOM CABINETRY
INC
1191 Palmer Wood Court
Sarasota, FL 34236

EUROTECH CABINETRY INC
1609 DeSoto Road
Sarasota, FL 34234

KITCHENS BY DESIGN OF
SARASOTA INC
4233 Clark Road #4
Sarasota, FL 34233

LAWRENCE CABINETS
215 Interstate Boulevard
Sarasota, FL 34240

RAY ROUTH INC
1502 N Lime Avenue
Sarasota, FL 34237

STOTTLEMYER &
SHOEMAKER LUMBER
COMPANY
2211 Fruitville Road
Sarasota, FL 34237

TOTAL BATH & KITCHEN
DESIGN INC
1760 East Avenue N
Suite B
Sarasota, FL 34234

Stuart

STYLECRAFT FINE
CABINETRY
712 S Dixie Way
Stuart, FL 34994

Sunrise

KITCHENS UNIQUE INC
10795 N W 53 Street
Sunrise, FL 33351

Tallahassee

MAYCO KITCHEN & BATH
2184 West Tennessee Street
Tallahassee, FL 32304

TALLAHASSEE KITCHEN
CENTER, INC.
634 E. Park Avenue
Tallahassee, FL 32301-2527

Tampa

EUROPEAN KITCHEN
CENTRE
4218 4220 W Kennedy Boulevard
Tampa, FL 33609

HOUSE OF CABINETS INC
3401 W Kennedy Boulevard
Tampa, FL 33609

Vero Beach

DESIGN FIRST KITCHENS &
BATHS INC
951 Old Dixie Highway
SUITE A 1&2
Vero Beach, FL 32960

FANTASY KITCHENS &
BATHS INC
943 20th Place
Vero Beach, FL 32960

MR. KITCHEN
1400 26th Street
Vero Beach, FL 32960

THE KITCHEN SCENE
89 Royal Palm Boulevard
Vero Beach, FL 32960

Winter Park

ARCHITECTURAL
ARTWORKS, INC.
163 East Morse Boulevard
Winter Park, FL 32789

GEORGIA

Atlanta

BROOKWOOD KITCHENS
2140 Peachtree Road NW
Suite 310
Atlanta, GA 30309

CANAC KITCHENS OF
GEORGIA
666 Miami Circle NE
Atlanta, GA 30324

DESIGN GALLERIA LTD/FINE
CABINETRY
351 Peachtree Hills Avenue NE
Suite 234
Atlanta, GA 30305

KITCHENSMITH INC
1198 N Highland Avenue NE
Atlanta, GA 30306

MASTER BATH & KITCHEN
3872 Roswell Road
Suite A-2
Atlanta, GA 30342-4400

ST. CHARLES OF ATLANTA
3487 Northside Parkway NW
Atlanta, GA 30327

THE APEX SHOWROOM
DIVISION APEX SUPPLY
COMPANY INC
2500 Button Gwinnett Drive
Atlanta, GA 30340

THELEN KITCHEN & BATH
STUDIOS
5566 Chamblee Dunwoody Road
Atlanta, GA 30338

Martinez

MARTINEZ CABINET &
MILLWORKS INC
3825 Martinez Boulevard
Martinez, GA 30907

Newnan

CLASSIC KITCHENS INC
PO Box 963
Newnan, GA 30264

Norcross

BERKELEY WOODWORKING
4600 Berkeley Lake Road
Norcross, GA 30071

DIVERSIFIED CABINET
DISTRIBUTOR
6292 Dawson Boulevard
Norcross, GA 30093

Roswell

KITCHEN AND BATH
CONCEPTS
11444 Alpharetta Highway
Roswell, GA 30076

Saint Simons Island

BMW DESIGNER KITCHENS
INC
508 E. Island Square Drive
Saint Simons Island, GA 31522-
1640

KITCHEN & BATH CONCEPTS
OF ST SIMONS SIMONS INC.
1627 Frederica Road
Suite 16
Saint Simons Island, GA 31522

Savannah

CUSTOM CABINETS BY
RIVERSTREET MILL
7601 Waters Avenue
Suite H
Savannah, GA 31406

Toccoa

COPE INCORPORATED
CABINETRY
1139 West Currahee Street
Toccoa, GA 30577

Tucker

PLUMBING CENTER
3771 Lawrenceville Highway
Tucker, GA 30084

Tyrone

H A SANAK INC CABINET &
DESIGN
119 Palmetto Road
Tyrone, GA 30290

HAWAII

Aiea

AMERICAN CABINETRY, INC
98-820 Moanalu Road
Aiea, HI 96701

Honolulu

AMERICAN CABINETRY, INC.
Aina Haina Shopping Center
820 Hind Drive Shop # 114
Honolulu, HI 96821

DESIGN GUILD INC.
909 Kapahulu Avenue
Honolulu, HI 96816

DETAILS INTERNATIONAL
560 N Nimitz Highway
Suite 119B Mailbox 111
Honolulu, HI 96817

HOMEOWNERS DESIGN
CENTER
1030 Kohou Street #201
Honolulu, HI 96817

JOHN COOK ASSOCIATES INC
1020 Auahi Street Building #4
Honolulu, HI 96814

KITCHEN CONCEPTS PLUS
INC
770 Kapiolani Boulevard
Honolulu, HI 96813

KITCHENS BY ARTHUR
THOMSON
1210 Queen Street
Suite 12
Honolulu, HI 96814

MIDPAC LUMBER COMPANY
LTD
1001 Ahua Street
Honolulu, HI 96819

REMODELING SPECIALISTS
HAWAII
3160 Waialae Avenue
Honolulu, HI 96816

STUDIO BECKER KITCHENS
560 N. Nimita Highway
Suite 121A
Honolulu, HI 96817

Kailua

PACIFIC DYNAMICS
CONSTRUCTION
150 Hamakna Drive
Kailua, HI 96734-2846

Kailua Kona

KITCHEN CABINETS INC
74 5598 Luhia Street
Kailua Kona, HI 96740

Kailua-Kona

DURALITH PRODUCTS
PO Box 241 73-7776 Kandlani St
Kailua-Kona, HI 96745

ROY LAMBRECHT
WOODWORKER
73-5573 Kauhola Street
Kailua-Kona, HI 96740

IDAHO

Boise

ANITA PETERSON INTERIOR
DESIGN
445 Main Street
Boise, ID 83702

Nampa

TREASURE VALLEY
WOODWORKING INC
12783 Orchard Ave
Nampa, ID 83651

ILLINOIS

Antioch

THE BATH WORKS
902 Main Street
Antioch, IL 60002

Arlington Heights

DETAIL KITCHEN & BATH
COMPANY
11 W College Drive
Suite C
Arlington Heights, IL 60004

KITCHEN VILLAGE
1081 East Gulf Road
Arlington Heights, IL 60005

LAMICO DESIGNERS
1732 Algonquin Road
Arlington Heights, IL 60005

PAGEL & SON DESIGNED
KITCHENS
914 S Arthur Avenue
Arlington Heights, IL 60005

Barrington

BARRINGTON HOMEWORKS
KITCHEN CENTER
301 E Main Street
Barrington, IL 60010

INSIGNIA KITCHEN & BATH
DESIGN GROUP LTD
1435 South Barrington Road
Barrington, IL 60010

Belleville

SCHIFFERDECKER KITCHENS
& BATHS
747 E Main
Belleville, IL 62220

Berwyn

MARCELLES KITCHEN BATH
& TILE LTD
6519 W 26th Street
Berwyn, IL 60402

Bloomingdale

GREAT ROOMS INC
20070 N Rand Road
PO Box 6235
Bloomingdale, IL 60108-6235

Brookfield

LAMANTIA BUILDING &
SUPPLY CO INC
9100 Ogden
Brookfield, IL 60513

Buffalo Grove

ALAN L FOSS & ASSOCIATES
INC
160 Weidner Road
Buffalo Grove, IL 60089

Cary

KITCHEN WHOLESALERS INC
188 S Northwest Highway
Cary, IL 60013

Champaign

KITCHEN BATH & CABINET
COMPANY OF CHAMPAIGN
115 West Kirby
Champaign, IL 61820

Chicago

CHICAGO KITCHEN & BATH
INC
1521 N Sedgwick Street
Chicago, IL 60610

DESIGN CONCEPTS
INTERNATIONAL MERCHANISE
The Merchandise Mart Suite 1378
Chicago, IL 60654

G & S SUPPLY COMPANY
5801 S Halsted Street
Chicago, IL 60621

KITCHEN BATH CONCEPTS
1123 West Belmont
Chicago, IL 60657

KITCHENS & BATHS BY DON
JOHNSON
Suite 1375
Merchandise Mart
Chicago, IL 60654

LUCKY STRIKE CABINET
COMPANY
3350 N Milwaukee Avenue
Chicago, IL 60641

MAX GERBER INC
2293 N Milwaukee
Chicago, IL 60647

Chicago Ridge

MIKOFF CUSTOM KITCHEN &
BATH
10527 S Ridgeland Avenue
Chicago Ridge, IL 60415

Crestwood

M/R PLUMBING MART, INC.
14024 South Cicero
Crestwood, IL 60445

Danville

DANVILLE CASH & CARRY
LUMBER COMPANY
508 W Williams Street
Danville, IL 61832

Deerfield

DESIGNER KITCHENS &
BATHS INC.
768 Osterman Avenue
Deerfield, IL 60015

Des Plaines

A B C KITCHENS & BATHS
454 NW Highway
Des Plaines, IL 60016

GEISER-BERNER PLUMBING,
HEATING & AIR CONDITIONING
1484 East Rand Road
Des Plaines, IL 60016

Downers Grove

BRADFORD KENT BUILDERS
807 Ogden Avenue
Downers Grove, IL 60515

LARSON CABINETS INC
1310D 75th Street
Downers Grove, IL 60516

NORMANDY BUILDERS
734 Ogden Avenue
Downers Grove, IL 60515

STEPHENS PLUMBING &
HEATING INC
747 Ogden Avenue
Downers Grove, IL 60515

Dunlap

WOODSIDE CABINET AND
MILLWORK
1715 W Woodside Drive
Dunlap, IL 61525

Edwardsville

KITCHENLAND EDWARDSVILLE
LUMBER COMPANY
201 W High Street
Edwardsville, IL 62025

Elgin

KITCHEN & BATH MART BY
BLOEDE'S
877 Villa Street
Elgin, IL 60120

SEIGLES HOME & BUILDING
CENTER
1331 Davis Road
Elgin, IL 60123

Elmhurst

KITCHENS & BATHS BY
PORTER DESIGN
575 7 W Street
Charles Road
Elmhurst, IL 60126

Elmwood Park

ABRUZZO KITCHEN & BATH
STUDIO
7612 W North Avenue
Elmwood Park, IL 60635

SPROVIERI'S KITCHENS
7506 W Grand Avenue
Elmwood Park, IL 60635

Evanston

KARLSON KITCHENS
1815 Central Street
Evanston, IL 60201

Evergreen Park

DEL-MONT BUILDERS INC
3360 W 95th Street
Evergreen Park, IL 60642

Fairfield

B-WAY HOME CENTER
900 Leininger Road
PO Box 340
Fairfield, IL 62837

Forrest

KNAPP KITCHENS...AND
MORE
Corner Oak And Krack Streets
Forrest, IL 61741

Freeport

SUPERIOR KITCHEN AND
BATH INC.
1858 South West Avenue
Freeport, IL 61032

Galena

HOLLAND PLUMBING, INC.
4359 Industrial Park Drive
Galena, IL 61036

Geneva

FAYEBOBS CUSTOM
CABINETRY
302 E State Street
Geneva, IL 60134

PAST BASKET CABINETRY
200 S Third Street
Geneva, IL 60134

Glenview

DDK KITCHEN DESIGN
GROUP INC
600 Waukegan Road
Glenview, IL 60025

KITCHENS UNLIMITED INC
1232 Waukegan Road
Glenview, IL 60025

Highland Park

NUHAUS KITCHEN BATHS &
LIFESTYLE ENVIORONMENT
1665 Old Skokie Road
Highland Park, IL 60035

Huntley

J.H. PATTERSON COMPANY
36 W Main Street
Huntley, IL 60142

Itasca

DANIELLE'S KITCHEN AND
BATH/CRYSTAL A FINE
NAME IN CABINETS
206 W Irving Park Road
Itasca, IL 60143

La Grange Park

TEACHERS' REMODELING
INC
1101 N Beach
La Grange Park, IL 60525

Lacon

ALLEN LUMBER COMPANY
220 Fifth Street
Lacon, IL 61540

Lake Forest

COURTYARD CABINETRY &
DESIGN, INC.
516 N Western Avenue
Lake Forest, IL 60045

Lansing

MINK BROTHERS KITCHENS
18610 Burnham Avenue
Lansing, IL 60438

Lemont

LEMONT KITCHEN & BATH
106 Stephen Street Suite 101
Lemont, IL 60439

Libertyville

LIBERTY KITCHEN & BATH
627 North Second Street
Libertyville, IL 60048

ROYAL FABRICATORS INC
1920 Industrial Drive
Libertyville, IL 60048

Lincolnwood

AIROOM INC
6825 N Lincoln Avenue
Lincolnwood, IL 60646

Lockport

ROMAR CABINET AND TOP
COMPANY INC
3357 South State Street
Lockport, IL 60441

Marion

P.D.W. INC
603 S Court
Route 37 So
Marion, IL 62959

Moline

GREEN VALLEY CABINET
COMPANY
3907 16th St
Moline, IL 61265

Morris

DESIGN CLASSICS IN
CABINETRY SIMMS SUPPLY
1427 Division Street
Morris, IL 60450

Morton

CREATIVE KITCHENS INC OF
MORTON
2001 W Jackson Street
Morton, IL 61550

Murphysboro

J WRIGHT BUILDING CENTER
INC
Williams Street
Po Box 10
Murphysboro, IL 62966

Naperville

THE KITCHEN MASTER
600 Industrial Drive
Naperville, IL 60563

Niles

BETTER KITCHENS INC
7640 N Milwaukee Avenue
Niles, IL 60714-3133

VILLAGE PLUMBING &
SEWER SERVICE
9017 Milwaukee Avenue
Niles, IL 60714

Northbrook

BATHLINES
571 Waukegan Road
Northbrook, IL 60062

COMPLETE BATH &
KITCHEN
310 Melvin Drive #20
Northbrook, IL 60062

WILLIAM B PARK INC
812 Skokie Highway
Northbrook, IL 60062

Oak Brook

ARTISTIC KITCHEN DESIGNS
610 Enterprise Drive
Oak Brook, IL 60521

Oak Lawn

THE BATH HOUSE
4811 W 103rd Street
Oak Lawn, IL 60453

Oak Park

NEW ERA INDUSTRIES
1117 Chicago Avenue
Oak Park, IL 60302

THE KITCHEN STUDIO INC
115 S. Maple Avenue
Oak Park, IL 60302-2005

Palatine

CABINETS PLUS
706 E Northwest Highway
Palatine, IL 60067

Palos Hills

KITCH'N BATH SHOWCASE
7630 W 111th Street
Palos Hills, IL 60465

Park Ridge

KITCHENS & ADDITIONS INC
817 West Devon Avenue
Park Ridge, IL 60068

Quincy

JON'S HOME CENTER
30th & State
Quincy, IL 62301

River Grove

REYNOLDS ENTERPRISES
INC.
2936 North River Road
River Grove, IL 60171

Rockford

CITATION DISTRIBUTORS
INC
5245 27th Avenue
Rockford, IL 61109

DAHLGREN & JOHNSON INC
1000 Ninth Street
Rockford, IL 61104

HOME IMPROVEMENT
SYSTEMS INC
1125 5th Avenue
Rockford, IL 61104

KITCHEN DISTRIBUTORS OF
AMERICA INC
3224 S Alpine Road
Rockford, IL 61109

Saint Charles

KITCHEN & BATH DESIGN
CONCEPTS
1519 E Main Street
Saint Charles, IL 60174

Schaumburg

HANDY ANDY HOME
IMPROVEMENT CENTERS
INC
905 E Golf Road
Schaumburg, IL 60173

Skokie

TARLOS KITCHENS & BATH
INC
8808 Gross Point Road
Skokie, IL 60077-1809

South Elgin

SCHRECK KITCHENS
CORPORATION
194 N La Fox Street
South Elgin, IL 60177

Springfield

DISTINCTIVE DESIGNS FOR
KITCHENS & BATHS
226 Highland
Springfield, IL 62704

REARDEN KITCHENS INC
2743 S Veterans Parkway
317
Springfield, IL 62704-6402

Taylorville

BROWN & SONS INC
BROWN'S BARN
421 Springfield Road
Taylorville, IL 62568

Villa Park

DESIGNER'S SHOWCASE
135 W Saint Charles Road
Villa Park, IL 60181

Westmont

CUSTOMWOOD KITCHENS
17 E Chicago Avenue
Westmont, IL 60559

THE CABINETRY GALLERY
800 B Ogden Avenue
Westmont, IL 60559

Wheeling

HERROLD KITCHEN & BATH
COMPANY INC
102 E Dundee Road
Wheeling, IL 60090

Wilmette

DE GIULIO KITCHEN & BATH
DESIGN
1121 Central Avenue
Wilmette, IL 60093

KARL G KNOBEL INC
1218 Washington Avenue
Wilmette, IL 60091

KITCHEN CLASSICS INC
519 Fourth Street
Wilmette, IL 60091

Woodridge

CEREN DESIGNS LTD
6810 Route 53
Woodridge, IL 60517

Woodstock

JENSEN'S HOME IMPROVEMENT
CENTER
670 E Calhoun Street
Woodstock, IL 60098

INDIANA

Anderson

GENTRY'S CABINET INC
415 Main Street
PO Box 168
Anderson, IN 46015

Batesville

WALSMAN SUPPLY
COMPANY INC
1818 State Road 46 E
PO Box 225
Batesville, IN 47006

Bluffton

CLINE KITCHEN CENTER DIV
CLINE LUMBR
717 W Washington Street
Bluffton, IN 46714

Brownsburg

KITCHEN AND BATH HOUSE
847 North Green Street
Brownsburg, IN 46112

Carmel

CARMEL KITCHEN
SPECIALISTS INC
606 Station Drive
Carmel, IN 46032

METZGER LUMBER CO
9901 N Michigan Road
Carmel, IN 46032

Columbus

ALEXANDERS' CABINET &
APPLIANCE CENTER
1817 24th Street
Columbus, IN 47201

BRANDS INC
1425 California Street
PO Box 90
Columbus, IN 47201-0090

COLUMBUS CUSTOM
CABINETS
8750 North US # 31
Columbus, IN 47201

Crawsfordsville

TOWN & COUNTRY
HOMECENTER INC
401 E South Boulevard
Crawsfordsville, IN 47933

Demotte

KAPERS BUILDING
MATERIALS
Highway 231 & Begonia Street
PO Box 517
Demotte, IN 46310

Evansville

CABINETS BY DESIGN
4619 Lincoln Avenue
Evansville, IN 47714

FEHRENBACHER CABINETS
INC
8944 Highway 65
Evansville, IN 47720

KITCHEN INTERIORS
5545 Boonville Highway
Evansville, IN 47715

Fort Wayne

GIANT CUSTOM CABINETS
INC
7923 Lima Road
Fort Wayne, IN 46818

THE PANEL MART INC
4602 Lima Road
Fort Wayne, IN 46808

Goshen

DUTCH MILLS INC
P O Box 805
Goshen, IN 46527-0805

Greenwood

KITCHENS BY TEIPEN
586 S Street Road 135
Greenwood, IN 46142

Highland

THOMPSON NELSON
KITCHEN DESIGN CENTER
INC
9434 Indianapolis Boulevard
Highland, IN 46322

Indianapolis

BARBER CABINET COMPANY
INC
2957 S Collier Street
Indianapolis, IN 46241

CASEWORKS
9423 N Meridian Street
Indianapolis, IN 46260

DIAL ONE TREMAIN INC
9337 Castle Gate Drive
Indianapolis, IN 46256

HAWKINS CABINET
COMPANY INC
2125 S Keystone Avenue
Indianapolis, IN 46203

JIM JORDAN SHOWPLACE
KITCHENS
2206 Lafayette Road
Indianapolis, IN 46222

KITCHENS & BATHS OF
DISTINCTION
4842-4850 North College Avenue
Indianapolis, IN 46205

MILLER MAID CABINETS INC
4805 Hardegan
PO Box 27086
Indianapolis, IN 46227

STEWARD BOARMAN
KITCHENS INC
1627 Oliver Avenue
Indianapolis, IN 46221

Jasper

KITCHEN JEWELS INC
844 East 13th Street
Jasper, IN 47546

Kokomo

BUCKNER DISTRIBUTING INC
505 E Center Road
PO Box 2205
Kokomo, IN 46904-2205

Lafayette

J A ANDREW INC
1201 Sagamore Parkway N
Lafayette, IN 47905

Lebanon

KITCHENS BY MICHAEL
118 N Lebanon Street
PO Box 108
Lebanon, IN 46052

Liberty

MILES RICHMOND INC
PO Box 360
Liberty, IN 47353

Martinsville

EARL GRAY & SONS INC
398 State Road 37 N
Martinsville, IN 46151

Maxwell

KLINE WOODWORKING INC
Highway 9 PO Box 12
Greenfield
Maxwell, IN 46154

Michigan City

DESIGN CENTER INC
8474 W US 20
Michigan City, IN 46360

Mishawaka

METROPOLITAN HOME
PLUMBING SERVICE
4014 Fir Road
Mishawaka, IN 46545

Mount Vernon

KUEBER'S CABINET SHOP
2300 Highway 62W
Mount Vernon, IN 47620

Muncie

RICHARD'S KITCHEN & BATH
CENTER
4209 N Weeling Avenue
Muncie, IN 47304

UNITED HOME SUPPLY INC
1420 S Hoyt Avenue
Muncie, IN 47302

Nappanee

NAPPANEE WOOD
PRODUCTS
1205 E Lincoln Street
Nappanee, IN 46550

Newburgh

COMPLETE DESIGN
KITCHENS BY MITCHELL
4395 Highway 261
PO Box 396
Newburgh, IN 47629

LANCE CABINET SHOP
4222 Sharon Road
Newburgh, IN 47630

Noblesville

B & E CUSTOM CABINETS
INC
14000 State Road 32 E
Noblesville, IN 46060

Shelbyville

RISLEY'S KITCHEN
SPECIALISTS
212 E Broadway
Shelbyville, IN 46176

South Bend

LOUIE SEAGO & SONS
REMODELING SERVICE INC
2506 S Michigan Street
South Bend, IN 46614

Terre Haute

KITCHENS AND INTERIORS
INC
4414 South 7th Street Suite C
Terre Haute, IN 47802-4304

Valparaiso

GARY R. SCHMITT &
COMPANY LTD
1603 E Lincolnway
Suite A
Valparaiso, IN 46383

SPESCO INC
52 Marks Road
Valparaiso, IN 46383

Vincennes

GALLERY OF KITCHENS,
DIVISION OF WARREN
HOMES INC
1721 Washington Avenue
Vincennes, IN 47591

Warsaw

CABINET HOUSE INC
417 East Winona Avenue
Warsaw, IN 46580

IOWA

Ames

KITCHEN BATH & HOME
201 Main Street
Ames, IA 50010

KITCHENS BY DESIGN
429 S Duff Avenue
Ames, IA 50010

Burlington

FOX APPLIANCE AND
KITCHEN CENTER INC
705-711 Jefferson Street
Burlington, IA 52601

Cedar Rapids

BEST PLUMBING BEST BATH
DIVISION
5412 Center Point Road NE
Cedar Rapids, IA 52402

CEDAR RAPIDS LUMBER
COMPANY
902 2nd Street SW
Cedar Rapids, IA 52404

Denison

COLOR CENTER LTD
1711 E Highway 30
Denison, IA 51442

Fort Dodge

ATLAS KITCHEN & BATH
1903 1st Avenue S
Fort Dodge, IA 50501

Indianola

BORTS CUSTOM CABINETS
INC
1200 North 14th Street
Indianola, IA 50125

Iowa City

HAMM'S HEARTH & HOME
1134 S Gilbert Street
Iowa City, IA 52240

Manchester

TEGELER DESIGN CENTER
INC
953 E Main Street
Manchester, IA 52057

Marion

GREAT PLAINS SUPPLY INC
3115 7th Avenue
PO Box 347
Marion, IA 52302

Marshalltown

STEWART BUILDING CENTER
110 W Madison Street
Marshalltown, IA 50158

Menlo

SARGENT'S CUSTOM
CABINETS
506 Shermen
Menlo, IA 50164

Ottumwa

BROWN'S KITCHEN CENTER
206 South Iowa Avenue
Ottumwa, IA 52501

Sioux City

HANDY MAN REMODELING
CENTER
3460 Gordon Drive
Sioux City, IA 51106

HOUSE OF KITCHENS LTD
308 S Floyd Boulevard
Sioux City, IA 51101

Washington

WIDMER INTERIOR DESIGN
200 E. Polk Street
Washington, IA 52353-1140

West Des Moines

CITY DESIGN
208 4th Street
West Des Moines, IA 50265

KANSAS

Eskridge

COUNTERTOPS UNLIMITED
INC
212 Main
PO Box 206
Eskridge, KS 66423

Independence

WOODS LUMBER OF
INDEPENDENCE KS INC
915 N 8th
PO Box 528
Independence, KS 67301

Topeka

DILLON'S CUSTOM
KITCHENS INC
1507 S W 21st Street
Topeka, KS 66604

Wichita

STAR LUMBER & SUPPLY
COMPANY INC
PO Box 7712
Wichita, KS 67277

THE KITCHEN PLACE, INC
7732 E Central Ave #118
Wichita, KS 67206-2163

KENTUCKY

Bowling Green

SIGNATURE KITCHEN AND
BATH
979 Lovers Lane
Bowling Green, KY 42103

Cresent Springs

BUILDERS CABINET SUPPLY
2464 Anderson Road
Cresent Springs, KY 41017

Elizabethtown

WALTERS CABINETS INC.
1340 Middle Creek Road
Elizabethtown, KY 42701

Erlanger

O'BRYAN KITCHENS INC
3420 Dixie Highway
Erlanger, KY 41018

Florence

WESTERN KITCHEN & BATH
CENTER
4971 Houston Road
Florence, KY 41042

Jamestown

WILKERSON'S DO-IT CENTER
263 N Main Street
PO Box 30
Jamestown, KY 42629

Lexington

CREATIVE KITCHEN & BATH
1141 Industry Road
Lexington, KY 40505

DESIGNER KITCHENS INC
1269 Eastland Drive
Lexington, KY 40505

Louisville

KITCHEN CRAFTERS
111 Street Matthews Avenue
Louisville, KY 40207

MOUSER KITCHENS INC
12204 Shelbyville Road
Louisville, KY 40243

Owensboro

CABINETS BY DESIGN
3149 Commonwealth Court
Owensboro, KY 42301

Springfield

BARBER CABINET COMPANY
INC
215 Progress Avenue
PO Box 271
Springfield, KY 40069

LOUISIANA

Baton Rouge

ACADIAN HOUSE KITCHENS
& BATHS
1288 Jefferson Highway
Baton Rouge, LA 70816

Covington

POOLE LUMBER COMPANY
PO Box 1240
Covington, LA 70434

Gretna

CABINETS BY DESIGN
429 Wall Boulevard
Suite 1A
Gretna, LA 70056

Harahan

CAMPBELL CABINET
COMPANY INC
220 Hord St
PO Box 23884
Harahan, LA 70183

Lafayette

TOP'S WOODWORK &
SUPPLY
5826 Johnston Street
PO Drawer 31810
Lafayette, LA 70503

Metairie

MARCHAND INTERIOR
SPECIALTIES INC
3517 Division Street
Metairie, LA 70002

Monroe

KEY MILLWORK & SUPPLY
CO., INC.
4200 Jackson Street
Monroe, LA 71202

New Orleans

CAMERON KITCHEN & BATH
DESIGNS
8019 Palm Street
New Orleans, LA 70125

CLASSIC CUPBOARDS INC
4747 Earhart Blvd
New Orleans, LA 70125

LAGARDE INDUSTRIES, LTD.
4513 Eve Street
New Orleans, LA 70125

TOP'S WOODWORK &
SUPPLY INC
4344 Earhart Boulevard
New Orleans, LA 70125

Shreveport

DESIGNER KITCHENS &
FLOORS INC
6210-B Fairfield Avenue
Shreveport, LA 71106

MAINE

Alfred

ROUX'S KITCHEN & BATH
CENTER
Route 202
PO Box 337
Alfred, ME 04002

Belfast

COASTAL PLUMBING &
HEATING INC.
119 Northport Avenue
Route 1
Belfast, ME 04915

MATHEWS BROTHERS
COMPANY
Spring Street
Belfast, ME 04915

Boothbay

PROUTY PLUMBING INC
Back River Road
PO Box 257
Boothbay, ME 04537

Brunswick

BRUNSWICK COAL &
LUMBER
18 Spring Street
Brunswick, ME 04011

East Waterboro

SYLCO KITCHEN & BATH
Junction Route 202 & 5
PO Box 34
East Waterboro, ME 04030

Ellsworth

ELLSWORTH BUILDERS
SUPPLY INC
RR 4 Box 4 State Street
Ellsworth, ME 04605-0004

SUNRISE BUILDING CENTER
Bar Harbor Road
Ellsworth, ME 04605

Kittery

BOLD CABINETRY
162 State Road
Kittery, ME 03904

Lewiston

BELLEGARDE CUSTOM
KITCHENS
516 Sabattus Street
Lewiston, ME 04240

DICK'S PLUMBING &
HEATING
693 Sabattus Street
Lewiston, ME 04240

Moody

LAVALLEY LUMBER
PO Box 476
Route 1
Moody, ME 04054

Norway

KITCHEN & BATH DESIGNS
INC
106 Main Street
PO Box 717
Norway, ME 04268

Rangeley

RANGELEY LAKES BUILDERS
SUPPLY COMPANY
PO Box 549
Rangeley, ME 04970

Rockland

E C HART & SON INC
101 Maverick Street
Rockland, ME 04841

MATHEWS BROTHERS
COMPANY
25 Rankin Street
Rockland, ME 04841

Saco

HEARTWOOD DISTRIBUTORS
778 Portland Road
Saco, ME 04072

Sanford

LAVALLEY LUMBER
COMPANY
New Dam Road
PO Box P
Sanford, ME 04073

Van Buren

GAGNON'S HARDWARE &
FURNITURE INC
184 Main Street
Van Buren, ME 04785

Waterville

CREATIVE KITCHENS &
DESIGNS
16 Main Street
Waterville, ME 04901

MARYLAND

Baltimore

COX KITCHEN & BATH INC
6322 Falls Road
Baltimore, MD 21209

GREENBAUM AND
ASSOCIATES INC
1201 S Howard Street
Baltimore, MD 21230

KENWOOD KITCHENS INC
6231 Kenwood Avenue
Baltimore, MD 21237

NORTHFIELD SALES
COMPANY INC
6413 15 Harford Road
Baltimore, MD 21214

S D KITCHENS
1201 Greenwood Road
Baltimore, MD 21208

THOMSON REMODELING
COMPANY INC
505 W Coldspring Lane
Baltimore, MD 21210

WELSH CONSTRUCTION
REMODELING COMPANY
3901 E Monument Street
Baltimore, MD 21205

Bel Air

DON ROOS CONSTUCTION
COMPANY
227 Gateway Drive
Suite D
Bel Air, MD 21014

Beltsville

BRAY & SCARFF INC
11950 Baltimore Avenue
Beltsville, MD 20705

BUILDERS WHOLESALE FOR
KITCHENS & BATHS
10401 Tucker Street
Beltsville, MD 20705

TOWN & COUNTRY
BATHS/BATH & KITCHEN
REMODELING A DIVISION OF
EJ WHELAN & CO
6655 Mid Cities Avenue
Beltsville, MD 20705-1415

Bethesda

CASE DESIGN REMODELING
INC
4701 Sangamore Road
N Plaza Suite 40
Bethesda, MD 20816

NANCY THORNETT
ASSOCIATES
6701 Democracy Boulevard
Suite 809
Bethesda, MD 20817

California

BEAUTIFUL KITCHENS
2006 Wildewood Center
California, MD 20619

Chevy Chase

RICHARD M. TUNIS INC
7032 Wisconsin Avenue
Chevy Chase, MD 20815

THOMAS W. PERRY INC
8513 Connecticut Avenue
Chevy Chase, MD 20815

Clinton

CLINTON CUSTOM
KITCHENS INC
8904 Simpson Lane
Clinton, MD 20735

College Park

METROPOLITAN BATH &
TILE INC
9035 Baltimore Avenue
College Park, MD 20740

Ellicott City

DON ROOS CONSTRUCTION
COMPANY INC
10176 Baltimore National Pike
Ellicott City, MD 21042

KITCHEN GALLERY
10314-A Baltimore National Pike
Ellicott City, MD 21042

Frederick

DESIGNER KITCHENS &
BATHS INC
10 S Market Street
Frederick, MD 21701

Gaithersburg

BARRONS GAITHERSBURG
LUMBER
23 W Diamond Avenue
Gaithersburg, MD 20877

KWC INC
8154 Beechcraft Avenue
Gaithersburg, MD 20879

SANFORD'S BATH GALLERY
7600 D Lindbergh Drive
Gaithersburg, MD 20879

Glen Burnie

SUTTON CORPORATION
722 Hyde Park Drive
Glen Burnie, MD 21061-4834

Grantsville

CASSELMAN LUMBER
St. Rt. Box 32B
Grantsville, MD 21536

Hagerstown

GALLERY OF BATHS
101 East Baltimore Street
Hagerstown, MD 21740

HAGERSTOWN LUMBER
COMPANY INC
700 Frederick Street
Hagerstown, MD 21740

Hebron

RICKARDS CABINET INC
PO Box 520
Hebron, MD 21830

Hollywood

DEAN HOME CENTER
North On Route 235
Hollywood, MD 20636

Hughesville

COLONIAL WORKSHOP INC
PO Box 370
Hughesville, MD 20637

Jarrettsville

KITCHENS BY REQUEST
3802 Norrisville Road
PO Box 452
Jarrettsville, MD 21084

Kensington

CUSTOM CRAFTERS
4000 Howard Avenue
Kensington, MD 20895

Lutherville

KITCHEN & BATH CENTER
INC
1518 York Road
Lutherville, MD 21093

Millersville

KITCHEN DESIGN STUDIO
8213 Jumpers Hole Road
Millersville, MD 21108

North Bethesda

JACK ROSEN CUSTOM
KITCHEN INC
White Flint Mall Level 3
11301 Rockville Pike
North Bethesda, MD 20895

Pasadena

FAMILY KITCHENS, INC
8541 Ft Smallwood Road
Pasadena, MD 21122

STUART KITCHENS INC.
8031 Ritchie Highway
Pasadena, MD 21122

Phoenix

HAYES CONSTRUCTION
COMPANY
14307 Jarrettsville Pike
Phoenix, MD 21131

Pikesville

STUART KITCHENS INC.
1858 Reistertown Road
Pikesville, MD 21208

Rising Sun

CECIL COMMERCIAL
INTERIORS INC
38 Buckley Avenue
PO Box 648
Rising Sun, MD 21911

Rockville

BEAUTIFUL BATHS
11500 Schuylkill Road
Rockville, MD 20856

CABINET DESIGNS INC
712 E Gude Drive
Rockville, MD 20850

CREATIVE KITCHENS INC
1776 E Jefferson Street
Rockville, MD 20852

DESIGNS BY GILL
328 D North Stonestreet Avenue
Rockville, MD 20850

IDEAL INDUSTRIES
651 Southlawn Lane
Rockville, MD 20850

KITCHEN PLANNERS INC
12140-B Parklawn Drive
Rockville, MD 20852

KITCHEN TECHNIQ INC
12011 Nebel Street
Rockville, MD 20852

POTOMAC DESIGNS
6227 Executive Boulevard
Rockville, MD 20852

Salisbury

BUYERS MARKETING
SERVICE INC
PO Box 2593
Salisbury, MD 21802

Silver Spring

GILDAY COMPANY INC
9162 Brookville Road
Silver Spring, MD 20910

SHOWCASE KITCHENS INC
13824 Old Columbia Pike
Silver Spring, MD 20904

Temple Hills

ED'S KITCHEN AND CABINET
SHOP INC
7039 Allentown Road
Temple Hills, MD 20748

Westminster

SCHAEFFER LUMBER
COMPANY
27 Liberty Street
PO Box 865
Westminster, MD 21158

White Plains

BATH & KITCHEN CONCEPTS
BY WALDORF MARBLE, INC.
4317 Charles Crossing Drive
White Plains, MD 20695

MASSACHUSETTS

Agawam

KITCHENS BY HERZENBERG
INC
South End Bridge Circle
Agawam, MA 01001

Amesbury

EASTERN LUMBER KITCHEN
& BATH CENTER
65 Haverhill Road
Route 110
Amesbury, MA 01913

Andover

ANDOVER KITCHEN & BATH
CENTER INC
2 Stevens Street
Andover, MA 01810

Bedford

HOUSE OF CABINETS INC
119 Great Road
Bedford, MA 01730

Bellingham

CRYSTAL INDUSTRIES INC
95 Mechanic Street
PO Box 175
Bellingham, MA 02019

Beverly

MOYNIHAN LUMBER OF
BEVERLY INC
82 River Street
PO Box 509
Beverly, MA 01915

Boston

ALLMINO OF NEWBURY
STREET
39 Newbury Street
Boston, MA 02116

HARRISON SUPPLY
COMPANY
1011 Harrison Avenue
Boston, MA 02119

LEE KIMBALL KITCHENS INC
276 Friend Street
Boston, MA 02114-1801

Cambridge

ECONOMY HARDWARE
438 Massachusetts Ave
Cambridge, MA 02139

Concord

ACORN STRUCTURES
PO Box 1445
Concord, MA 01742

Dalton

L P ADAMS COMPANY INC
484 Housantonic Street
PO Box 256
Dalton, MA 01227

Danvers

BROWN'S KITCHEN & BATH
CENTER
56 North Putnam Street
Danvers, MA 01923

Dennisport

KITCHEN STUDIO DCM INC
66 Upper County Road
PO Box 1188
Dennisport, MA 02639

Duxbury

GOOD RICH KITCHEN
WORKS
85 Railroad Avenue
Duxbury, MA 02332

SOUTH SHORE CABINET
CENTER INC
PO Box 1608
122 Tremont Street
Duxbury, MA 02331

E Longmeadow

KITCHENS BY CHAPDELAINE
87 Shaker Road
E Longmeadow, MA 01028

Framingham

KITCHEN CENTER OF
FRAMINGHAM INC
697 Waverly Street
Framingham, MA 01701

Gloucester

BUILDING CENTER INC
1 Harbor Loop
PO Box 180
Gloucester, MA 01930

Greenfield

CLASSIC KITCHENS
6 French King Highway
Greenfield, MA 01301

RUGG LUMBER COMPANY
66 Newton Street
PO Box 507
Greenfield, MA 01302

Hudson

RS LAMSON & SONS INC
29 Lake Street
Hudson, MA 01749

Hyannis

CLASSIC KITCHEN DESIGN
INC
200 Thornton Drive
Hyannis, MA 02601

JOHN HINCKLEY & SON
COMPANY
49 Yarmouth Road
PO Box 2110
Hyannis, MA 02601

R.B. CORCORAN COMPANY
349 Iyannough Road
Route 28 PO Box 340
Hyannis, MA 02601

Lawrence

JACKSON LUMBER &
MILLWORK
215 Market Street
PO Box 449
Lawrence, MA 01842

Lexington

DRAKE CABINET &
REMODELING INC
401 Lowell Street (Rear)
Lexington, MA 02173

Lynn

STANDARD OF LYNN INC
400 Lynnway
PO Box 830
Lynn, MA 01903

Marblehead

NORTHSHORE KITCHENS
PLUS
183 Tedesco Street
Marblehead, MA 01945

Marlboro

HOLLAND WOODWORKING
INC
40 Florence Street
Marlboro, MA 01752

Mashpee

KITCHEN DESIGN CENTER
800 Falmouth Road (Route 28)
Mashpee, MA 02649

Mattapoisett

DESIGNER KITCHENS BY
ANGELA
92 North Street
PO Box 85
Mattapoisett, MA 02739

MAHONEY'S BUILDING
SUPPLY CENTER
One Industrial Drive
Mattapoisett, MA 02739

Maynard

THE FAUCETORIUM
161 Main Street
Maynard, MA 01754

Melrose

HEARTWOOD KITCHEN &
BATH CABINETRY
99 Washington Street
Melrose, MA 02176

Monson

B J KENNISON COMPANY
KITCHENS BATHS & MORE
200 Town Farm Road
Monson, MA 01057

Nantucket

MARINE HOME CENTER/
MARINE LUMBER CO
Lower Orange Street
Nantucket, MA 02554

Natick

KITCHEN INTERIORS
255 Worcester Road
Natick, MA 01760

New Bedford

KITCHENS & BATHS
54 Nauset Street
New Bedford, MA 02746

TAILORED KITCHENS &
BATH
100 Tarkiln Hill Road
PO Box 50004
New Bedford, MA 02745

Newton

MASTERPIECE KITCHEN &
BATH INC
381 Elliot Street
Newton, MA 02164

NATIONAL LUMBER
COMPANY
15 Needham Street
Newton, MA 02161

North Attleboro

INEL KITCHENS & BATHS INC
560 Kelley Boulevard
Route 152
North Attleboro, MA 02760

North Dartmouth

DARTMOUTH BUILDING
SUPPLY COMPANY INC
958 Reed Road
North Dartmouth, MA 02747

Northampton

RUGG LUMBER COMPANY
HAMPSHIRE DIV.
33 Hawley Street
P.O. Box 90
Northampton, MA 01061-0090

Norwell

KITCHEN CONCEPTS, INC.
159 Washington Street
Norwell, MA 02061

Norwood

REPUBLIC PLUMBING
SUPPLY CO. INC
890 Providence Highway
Norwood, MA 02062

Orleans

MID-CAPE HOME CENTER
NICKERSON LUMBER
15 Main Street
PO Box 99
Orleans, MA 02653

Osterville

BOTELLO LUMBER CO INC
PO Box V
Osterville, MA 02655

KITCHEN & BATH DESIGNS
UNLIMITED INC
5 Parker Road
Osterville, MA 02655

Pembroke

CLASSIC KITCHENS, INC.
345 Washington Street
Pembroke, MA 02359

Pittsfield

SHEDD INC
730 Tyler Street
Pittsfield, MA 01201

Plymouth

DESIGNER KICHENS INC.
116 Long Pond Road
Plymouth, MA 02360

THE CABINET CONNECTION
INC
27 Samoset Street
Plymouth, MA 02360

Salem

BERGERON BATH &
KITCHEN
47 Canal Street
Salem, MA 01970

Sandwich

KITCHEN TECH INC
374 Route 130
PO Box 1030
Sandwich, MA 02563

Saugus

KITCHENS BY HASTINGS INC
Box 1129
38 Broadway Rt 1
Saugus, MA 01906

Somerset

HORNER MILLWORK CORP
1255 G A R Highway
Route 6
Somerset, MA 02726

South Dartmouth

COSTA'S QUALITY KITCHENS
6 McCabe Street
South Dartmouth, MA 02748

South Walpole

THE KITCHEN AND
BATHROOM
175 Summer Street
South Walpole, MA 02071

Springfield

CUSTOM CABINET &
MILLWORK INC
784 Page Boulevard
Springfield, MA 01104

KITCHENS BY CURIO INC
1045 Boston Road
Springfield, MA 01119

Sterling

KITCHEN ASSOCIATES INC
76 Leominster Road
Route 12
Sterling, MA 01564

Stoneham

CLASSIC CABINETRY LTD
607 Main Street
Stoneham, MA 02180

Stoughton

RICHARD KUBLIN KITCHENS INC
489 Page Street
Stoughton, MA 02072

Stow

CREATIVE DESIGNS IN KITCHENS INC
132 Great 3Road
Route 117
Stow, MA 01775

Taunton

Kitchen Concepts, Inc. 451 Winthrop Street
Taunton, MA 02780

W Chatham

ARCHIBALD WOODWORKING
39 George Ryder Road
PO Box 282
W Chatham, MA 02669

Watertown

ARCHITECTURAL CABINET COMPANY
635 Main Street
Watertown, MA 02172

Wellesley

JARVIS APPLIANCE INC
958 Worcester Street
Wellesley, MA 02181

WESTON KITCHENS
868 Worcester Road
Wellesley, MA 02181

West Boylston

KITCHENS BY DESIGN, INC.
65 Central Street
West Boylston, MA 01583

Weymouth

J B KITCHENS AND BATHS
1471 Main Street
Rte 18
Weymouth, MA 02190

MICHIGAN

Alpena

HISER KITCHEN & BATH CENTER
3303 W Washington Avenue
Alpena, MI 49707

Ann Arbor

KITCHEN AND BATH GALLERY Division of D & C Supply
5161 Jackson Road
Ann Arbor, MI 48103

MARY CHRISTENSEN'S KITCHEN & BATH DESIGN CENTER
3921 Jackson Ave
Ann Arbor, MI 48103-1823

Athens

ATHENS HARDWARE, INC.
133 South Capital
Athens, MI 49011

Baroda

BARODA LUMBER COMPANY
PO Box 98
Baroda, MI 49101

Bay City

HEPPNER KITCHEN CENTER
3909 N Euclid
Bay City, MI 48706

Belleville

CRAFTMASTERS KITCHENS & BATHS
21620 Sumpter Road
Belleville, MI 48111

Big Rapids

BIG RAPIDS CASH & CARRY
130 South Third
Big Rapids, MI 49307

Birmingham

BLOOMFIELD CUSTOM KITCHENS INC
4068 West Maple
Birmingham, MI 48010

KITCHENS BY LENORE & RICHARDS INC
912 S Woodward Avenue
Birmingham, MI 48009

Bloomfield Hills

EUROSTYLE LTD
1030 N Hunter Boulevard
Bloomfield Hills, MI 48304

Brighton

CARE CRAFTED LTD
12619 E Grand River
Brighton, MI 48116

KSI KITCHEN SUPPLIERS INC
9325 Maltby Road
Brighton, MI 48116

Burton

RON'S KITCHENS/BATHS, INC
G-4437 S Saginaw Street
Burton, MI 48529

Cadillac

COUNTRYSIDE KITCHEN & BATH CENTER
7401 E 35 Mile Road
Cadillac, MI 49601

Canton

MANS KITCHEN & BATH
41900 Ford Road
Canton, MI 48187

Caro

GRAFF & SONS CABINET GALLERY
1539 E Caro Road
Caro, MI 48723

Centerville

MILL RACE DISTRIBUTING INC
240 W Main Street
PO Box 577
Centerville, MI 49032

Charlotte

CHARLOTTE KITCHEN CENTER
630 W Lawrence Avenue
Charlotte, MI 48813

Chassell

ANDERSON & JARVI LUMBER COMAPNY
U S 41
P O Box 439
Chassell, MI 49916

Clawson

WOODLAND KITCHEN & BATH
238 West 14 Mile Road
Clawson, MI 48017

Coldwater

H & S SUPPLY INC
317 N Fiske Road
Coldwater, MI 49036

Davisburg

DAVISBURG LUMBER COMPANY INC
13180 Andersonville Road
PO Box 16
Davisburg, MI 48350

Davison

KENNETH R. LAWRENCE & SON CONSTRUCTION INC
205 E Flint Street
Davison, MI 48423

E Grand Rapids

LIFESTYLE KITCHEN & BATH
2216 Wealthy SE
E Grand Rapids, MI 49506

East Lansing

MERIDIAN PLUMBING INC
2654 East Grand River
East Lansing, MI 48823

Farmington Hill

ARTISTIC KITCHENS INC
29586 Orchard Lake Road
Farmington Hill, MI 48334

Farmington Hills

CHESNEY BUILDING REPAIR & SERVICE COMPANY INC
28972 Orchard Lake Road
Farmington Hills, MI 48334

Flint

CASTLES BROTHERS KITCHENS
1471 W Bristol Road
Flint, MI 48507-5591

FLINT KITCHEN & BATH CENTER
G 3463 W Pierson Road
Flint, MI 48504

KEN'S KUSTOM KITCHENS & BATHS
2501 Clio Road
Flint, MI 48504

OK PLUMBING & HEATING COMPANY INC
5317 N Saginaw Street
Flint, MI 48505-2967

Flushing

STARLINE DISTRIBUTORS
G 5500 W Pierson
PO Box 158
Flushing, MI 48433

Fowlerville

FOWLERVILLE LUMBER
118 N Ann Street
PO Box 352
Fowlerville, MI 48836

Fraser

SHOWCASE KITCHEN & BATH INC
31435 Utica Road
Fraser, MI 48026

Grand Blanc

BLESSING COMPANY
122 East Grand Blanc Road
Grand Blanc, MI 48439

Grand Rapids

GALLERY OF KITCHENS INC
5243 Plainfield N E
Grand Rapids, MI 49505

KITCHENS BY A & B DISTRIBUTORS INC
5234 Plainfield N E
Grand Rapids, MI 49505

KITCHENS BY STEPHANIE
2880 Thornhills SE
Grand Rapids, MI 49546

STANDARD KITCHENS
1450 Kalamazoo SE
Grand Rapids, MI 49507

WOODLAND HOUSE OF KITCHENS INC
6619 S Division SW
Grand Rapids, MI 49548

Grandville

INTERIORS BY CHERI
3901 Chicago Drive
Suite 120
Grandville, MI 49418

Grosse Point Woods

MUTSCHLER KITCHENS INC
20227 Mack Avenue
Grosse Point Woods, MI 48236

Grosse Pointe Woods

RIVERSIDE KITCHEN & BATH
20956 Mack AVenue
Grosse Pointe Woods, MI 48236-1355

Hale

BERNARD BUILDING CENTER INC
395 South Washington
PO Box 190
Hale, MI 48739

Hillsdale

MC CALL HOME CENTER
123 E Carleton Road
PO Box 247
Hillsdale, MI 49242

Howell

OPIE'S CABINET & DESIGN CENTER INC
3220 E Grand River
Howell, MI 48843

Ithaca

INTERIORS BY NEVILLE
P.O. Box 15
712 E. Center Street #15
Ithaca, MI 48847

Jackson

ROYAL CABINET INC
3900 Francis Street
Jackson, MI 49203

THE KITCHEN SHOP INC
407 First Street
Jackson, MI 49201

Lansing

ACCENT KITCHEN BATH CENTER INC
615 S Waverly
Lansing, MI 48917

HEDLUND PLUMBING COMPANY
6323 W Saginaw
Lansing, MI 48917

THE KITCHEN SHOP
5320 South Pennsylvania Avenue
Lansing, MI 49811

Lincoln Park

UNIQUE KITCHENS & BATHS
3504 Fort Street
Lincoln Park, MI 48146

Livonia

KITCHENS PLUS
31815 W Eight Mile Road
Livonia, MI 48152

KURTIS KITCHEN & BATH CENTERS
12500 Merriman Road
Livonia, MI 48150-1923

Marquette

SCHWALBACH KITCHEN SPECIALISTS
500 N Third Street
Marquette, MI 49855

Marshall

TRIMBILT KITCHENS
519 S Kalamazoo Avenue
Marshall, MI 49068

Midland

OWENS CABINET
1928 Stark Road
Route 3
Midland, MI 48640

Monroe

MATTHES KITCHENS & BATH
2351 W Albain Road
Monroe, MI 48161

WEINLANDER KITCHENS & BATHS
310 N Telepgraph Road
Monroe, MI 48161

Mount Pleasant

JOE MCDONALD'S HOUSE OF CABINETS INC
5800 E Pickard
Mount Pleasant, MI 48858

Muskegon

STYLE TREND KITCHENS & BATHS
792 W Laketon Avenue
Muskegon, MI 49441

Northville

LONG PLUMBING COMPANY
190 E Main Street
Northville, MI 48167-1692

Novi

MANSFIELD CABINETS
45033 Grand River
Novi, MI 48375

Petoskey

PRESTON FEATHER BUILDING CENTER LIFESTYLES KITCHEN & BATH
896 Spring Street
Petoskey, MI 49770

PUFF'S OF PETOSKEY
1200 Bay View Road
PO Box 807
Petoskey, MI 49770

SWEET'S KITCHEN CENTER
2449 US 31 North
Petoskey, MI 49770

Pinconning

LLOYD'S CABINET SHOP INC
1947 North M 13
Pinconning, MI 48650

Plymouth

KITCHENS BY STELLA
747 S Main Street
Plymouth, MI 48170

Pontiac

ACORN KITCHEN & BATH DISTRIBUTORS
111 South Telegraph Road
Pontiac, MI 48341

Port Huron

CABINETS N COUNTERS
3300 Lapeer Road
Port Huron, MI 48060

Romulus

ISLAND CABINET TREE
27588 Dupre
Romulus, MI 48138

Royal Oak

ROYAL OAK KITCHENS INC
4518 N Woodward
Royal Oak, MI 48073

Saginaw

RADKA'S KITCHEN & BATH CENTER
5641 Bay Road
Saginaw, MI 48604-2509

REMER PLUMBING & HEATING INC
5565 State Street
Saginaw, MI 48603

SAGINAW KITCHEN & BATH CENTER
315 W Holland
Saginaw, MI 48602

Saint Clair Shores

WOODMASTER KITCHENS
26510 Harper
Saint Clair Shores, MI 48081

Saline

BRIDGEWATER LUMBER COMPANY
7895 E Michigan Avneue
Saline, MI 48176

Sault Ste Marie

ERICKSON APPLIANCE & FURNITURE CENTER
2405 Ashmun Street
Sault Ste Marie, MI 49783

Spring Arbor

SPRING ARBOR APPLIANCE & TV KITCHEN & BATH
7650 Spring Arbor Road
Spring Arbor, MI 49283

Sterling Heights

STERLING IMPROVEMENTS & DESIGN
11445 15 Mile Road
Sterling Heights, MI 48312

Sturgis

DE RAND KITCHENS INC
315 S Clay Street
PO Box 397
Sturgis, MI 49091

Swartz Creek

THE KITCHEN SHOP OF HAGER FOX
5376 Miller Road
Swartz Creek, MI 48473

Three Oaks

HARBOR COUNTRY KITCHENS & BATHS
8E Maple Street
Three Oaks, MI 49128

Traverse City

BROWN LUMBER & SUPPLY COMPANY VISIONS KITCHEN & BATH
1701 S Airport Road
Traverse City, MI 49684

CABINETS BY ROBERT
2774 Garfield
Traverse City, MI 49684

CREATIVE KITCHEN
747 Woodmerelace
Traverse City, MI 49684

NORTHWOOD KITCHENS INC
10240 Cherry Bend Road
Traverse City, MI 49684

Trenton

CAREFREE KITCHENS INC.
1625 West Road
Trenton, MI 48183

MANS KITCHEN AND BATH TRENTON
3300 West Jefferson
Trenton, MI 48183

Troy

ALTIMA KITCHENS
2821 Rochester Road
Troy, MI 48083

MADISON DESIGN GROUP
INC
1700 Stutz Drive
Suite 27
Troy, MI 48084

Utica

NU-WAY SUPPLY CO., INC.
PO Box 189004
Utica, MI 48318-9004

Vassar

WEBER LUMBER &
MILLWORK INC
8586 W Sanilac Road
Vassar, MI 48768

Walled Lake

NEWMYER INC
3081 Haggerty Road
Suite 1
Walled Lake, MI 48390

Waterford

ACCURATE WOODWORKING,
INC
7675 Highland Road
Waterford, MI 48327

Woodhaven

GRAHL'S KITCHEN & BATH
DESIGN CENTER
21111 Allen Road
Woodhaven, MI 48183

MINNESOTA

Albert Lea

JIM & DUDES PLUMBING &
HEATING INC
724 West Clark Street
Albert Lea, MN 56007

Anoka

HIRSCH INC CABINETS BY
DESIGN
357 McKinley Street N W
Anoka, MN 55303

HUTTON AND ROWE INC.
THE PLUMBERY
2126 2nd Avenue N
Anoka, MN 55303

Austin

CLASSIC KITCHENS/DC
CONSTRUCTION
704 West Oakland Avenue
Austin, MN 55912

Belle Plaine

PIONEER KITCHENS & BATHS
113 North Meridian
Belle Plaine, MN 56011

Chanhassen

CHANHASSEN KITCHEN &
BATH
530 West 79th Street
PO Box 6
Chanhassen, MN 55317

Crookston

RED RIVER CABINETS
101 S. Broadway
Crookston, MN 56716

Crystal

JP MILLWORK & DESIGN INC
5525 34th Avenue N
Crystal, MN 55422

Duluth

CONTARDO LINDQUIST &
COMPANY
926 East 4th Street
Duluth, MN 55805

HANNA INTERIORS INC
106 East Superior Street
Duluth, MN 55802

SUPREME KITCHEN & BATHS
4877 Miller Trunk Highway #1
Duluth, MN 55811

Edina

NORTH STAR SERVICES
4402 France Avenue S
Edina, MN 55410

THE WOODSHOP OF AVON
3918 Sunnyside Road
Edina, MN 55424

Ely

W N PLUMBING & HEATING
203 E Conan Street
Ely, MN 55731

Freeborn

FREEBORN LUMBER
COMPANY
PO Box 173
Freeborn, MN 56032

Fridley

PREFERRED KITCHENS INC
7221 University Avenue N E
Fridley, MN 55432

Golden Valley

CRYSTAL KITCHEN CENTER
668 North Highway 169
Golden Valley, MN 55427

International Falls

SHANNON'S BATH GALLERY
2612 Crescent Drive
International Falls, MN 56649

Marshall

MINNESOTA CABINETS INC
202 Oconnell Street
Marshall, MN 56258

Mendota Heights

ACCENT DESIGN STUDIO
1408 Northland Drive
Suite 305
Mendota Heights, MN 55120

Minneapolis

BUILDERS GALLERY, INC.
3001 Hennepin Avenue South
Minneapolis, MN 55408

KITCHENS BY PHOENIX INC
5435 Lyndale Avenue S
Minneapolis, MN 55419

PARTNERS 4 DESIGN INC
275 Market Street
Suite 109
Minneapolis, MN 55405

SAWHILL CUSTOM KITCHENS
& DESIGN INC
275 Market Street
Suite 157
Minneapolis, MN 55405

VALLEY INTERIOR
PRODUCTS INC
4626 Lyndale Avenue N
Minneapolis, MN 55412

Minnetonka

BUDGET POWER
12201 Minnetonka Boulevard
Minnetonka, MN 55343

New Ulm

PUHLMANN LUMBER
COMPANY
301 1st Street South
New Ulm, MN 56073

Osseo

GREAT IDEAS (KITCHENS &
BEYOND)
8686 Jefferson Highway
Osseo, MN 55369

Plato

PLATO HOME CENTER
119 E Main Street
PO Box 68
Plato, MN 55370

Prior Lake

MINNESOTA WOODS AND
INTERIORS INC
6867 Boudin Street N E
Prior Lake, MN 55372-1433

Robbinsdale

SAWHORSE DESIGNERS AND
BUILDERS
4740 42nd Avenue North
Robbinsdale, MN 55422

Rochester

KITCHENS OF DISTINCTION
1115 7th Street N W
Rochester, MN 55901

THE KRUSE CO.
111 7th Street North East
Rochester, MN 55906

UNITED BUILDING CENTERS
2751 7Th Street
Nw Box 6066
Rochester, MN 55903

Saint Louis Park

ANDERSEN CABINETS
5814 Excelsior Boulevard
Saint Louis Park, MN 55416

Saint Paul

ANDERSEN CABINET INC
2500 N Charles
Saint Paul, MN 55109

CLASSIC KITCHENS BY
LANCE FORMERLY SAINT
CHARLES OF MN
1146 Grand Avenue
Saint Paul, MN 55105

KITCHENS BY KRENGEL INC
1688 Grand Avenue
Saint Paul, MN 55105

Waile Park

SIMONSON LUMBER WEST
900 W Division
Waile Park, MN 56387

Wayzata

UNIQUE KITCHENS
3420 Highway 101 South
Minnehaven Square
Wayzata, MN 55391

White Bear Lake

WHITE BEAR CARPENTRY
2222 Seventh Street
At Hwy 61
White Bear Lake, MN 55110

Willmar

KITCHEN FAIR
313 W 5th Street
Willmar, MN 56201

MISSISSIPPI

Greenwood

CUSTOM KITCHENS AND
DESIGN SPECIALTIES INC.
PO Box 488
Greenwood, MS 38930

Gulfport

BAILEY LUMBER & HOME
CENTER
813 Pass Road
Gulfport, MS 39507

BUILDERS SPECIALTY
SUPPLY CO
1312 31st Avenue
PO Box 403-39502
Gulfport, MS 39501

Jackson

CREATIVE DESIGNS
5001 Highway 80 W
Jackson, MS 39209

FRIERSON BUILDING SUPPLY
4525 Lynch Street Extension
PO Box 10817
Jackson, MS 39289

KITCHEN KREATORS
LIMITED
1513 B Lakeland Drive
Jackson, MS 39216

McComb

CITY PAINT & GLASS INC
334 - 25th Street
McComb, MS 39648

MISSOURI

Bridgeton

DECORATIVE KITCHEN
SALES INC
11820 Saint Charles Rock Road
Bridgeton, MO 63044

Camdenton

DESIGNED KITCHENS &
INTERIORS
Highway 5 N Ryland Center
Route 76 Box 830
Camdenton, MO 65020

Columbia

DESIGNER KITCHENS AND
BATHS
1729 West Broadway
Columbia, MO 65203

Des Peres

BUELER CUSTOM KITCHEN &
CONSTRUCTION INC.
13314 Manchester Road
Des Peres, MO 63131

CUTTER'S CUSTOM
KITCHENS & BATHS INC
12878 Manchester Road
Des Peres, MO 63131

Florissant

EHRLICH'S KITCHEN AND
BATH
3236 Parker Road
Florissant, MO 63033

LASTING IMPRESSIONS HOME
REMODEL CENTER
2168 North Waterford
Florissant, MO 63033

PHIL L. MILLER PLUMBING
COMPANY
661 Sreet Ferdinand Street
Florissant, MO 63031

Jefferson City

CAPITAL SUPPLY COMPANY
418 W Elm Street
PO Box 455
Jefferson City, MO 65102

Kirkwood

BAYGENTS COMPANY
117 West Argonne
Kirkwood, MO 63122

SCHUMACHER KITCHEN &
BATH STUDIO
10030 Big Bend Boulevard
Kirkwood, MO 63122

Manchester

ROY E DUENKE CABINET
COMPANY
14436 Manchester Road
Manchester, MO 63011

Poplar Bluff

ARNDT CABINET COMPANY
INC
Route 1 Box 476
Poplar Bluff, MO 63901

Rockhill

WILLIAM A ROSE KITCHEN &
REMODELING CENTER INC
9807 Manchester Road
Rockhill, MO 63119

Rolla

POWELL'S LUMBER & HOME
CENTER
6th and Rolla Streets
PO Box 1039
Rolla, MO 65401

Saint Charles

CALLIER'S CUSTOM
KITCHENS & BATHS
INCORPORATED
4524 Parktowne Drive
Saint Charles, MO 63304

Saint Louis

CALLIER'S CUSTOM
KITCHENS
2570 South Brentwood Boulevard
Saint Louis, MO 63144

GLEN ALSPAUGH COMPANY
9808 Clayton Road
Saint Louis, MO 63124

INNOVATIONS FOR KITCHEN
& BATH
2025 S Big Bend
Saint Louis, MO 63117

KARR-BICK KITCHENS &
BATHS
2715 Mercantile Drive
Saint Louis, MO 63144

KITCHEN & BATH RESOURCE
STUDIO
2901 Olive Street
Saint Louis, MO 63103

MODERN KITCHENS & BATHS
INC
3122 S Kings Highway
Saint Louis, MO 63139

MORGAN WIGHTMAN
SUPPLY COMPANY
5668 Anglum
Main PO Box 1
Saint Louis, MO 63166

THOMPSON'S HOUSE OF KIT
& BATHS IN. INC.
5452 Southfield Center
Saint Louis, MO 63123

THOMPSON'S HOUSE OF
KITCHENS & BATHS INC
11718 Manchester Road
Saint Louis, MO 63131

Troy

ACTIVE PLUMBING SUPPLY
HOUSE BATHS SHOWROOM
684 S Lincoln Drive PO Box 355
Troy, MO 63379

Webster Groves

NATIONAL KITCHEN & BATH
INC
280 East Kirkham
Webster Groves, MO 63119

MONTANA

Billings

AMERICAN APPLIANCE
COMPANY
2121 First Avenue South
PO Box 1937
Billings, MT 59103

KITCHENS PLUS INC
2225 King Avenue W
Billings, MT 59102

Bozeman

BOZEMAN TV & APPLIANCE
INC
34 North Bozeman
Bozeman, MT 59715

MCPHIE CABINETRY
435 E Main
Bozeman, MT 59715

Great Falls

THE CABINET COMPANY
801 9th Street S
Great Falls, MT 59405

Missoula

THURMANS KITCHEN &
BATH
3020 Reserve
Missoula, MT 59801

Polson

WEST SHORE CABINET
474 Rocky Point Road
PO Box 77
Polson, MT 59860

NEBRASKA

Grand Island

THE KITCHEN GALLERY INC
2808 Old Fair Road
Suite G
Grand Island, NE 68803

Hastings

SHOWCASE
347 W 2nd
Hastings, NE 68901

Humboldt

MERRITTS DISCOUNT
CABINETS
801 3rd Street
Box 43
Humboldt, NE 68376

Kearney

BABL COMPANY
1209 Avenue A
PO Box 280
Kearney, NE 68848

Lincoln

CAMPBELL'S KITCHEN
CABINETS, INC.
1210 Nance Avenue
Lincoln, NE 68521

CROWL'S KITCHENS &
BATHS
137 S 9th Street
Lincoln, NE 68508

CS KITCHEN & BATH STUDIO
4708 Prescott Avenue
Lincoln, NE 68506

GREEN FURNACE &
PLUMBING COMPANY INC
2747 N 48th
PO Box 4556
Lincoln, NE 68504

HANDY MAN HOME
REMODELING CENTER
501 W Gate Boulevard
Lincoln, NE 68528

HYLAND BROTHERS INC
1060 N 33Rd Street
Lincoln, NE 68503

LINCOLN CABINET
624 K Street
Lincoln, NE 68508

MCEWEN/ODBERT
CONSTRUCTION & CABINET
COMPANY
5034 Old Cheney Road
Lincoln, NE 68516

PAULEY LUMBER
945 South 27th Street
Lincoln, NE 68510

REYNOLDS KITCHEN DESIGN
INC
2406 J
Lincoln, NE 68510

WAYNE GIEBELHAUS
PLUMBING & HEATING
2231 Winthrop Road
Lincoln, NE 68502

McCook

CORKY'S MODERN
INTERIORS
214 Norris Avenue
McCook, NE 69001

Omaha

ARLON MILLER COMPANY
CUSTOM KITCHENS &
INTERIORS
3909 Farnam Street
Omaha, NE 68131

EUROWOOD CUSTOM
CABINETS INC
4327 S 90th
Omaha, NE 68127

KITCHENS BY DESIGN
1263 South 120
Omaha, NE 68144

LARSON CUSTOM KITCHENS
629 North 98 Street
Omaha, NE 68114

MILLARD LUMBER INC
5005 South 135th Street
Omaha, NE 68137

NEBRASKA CUSTOM
KITCHENS
4601 Dodge Street
Omaha, NE 68132

TRETIAK'S
15th & Davenport Street
Omaha, NE 68102

WARD'S KITCHENS & BATHS
10908 Elm Street
Omaha, NE 68144

NEVADA

Incline Village

WESTERN STATES SALES
PO Box 4640
847 Tanager #4
Incline Village, NV 89450

Las Vegas

EUROPEAN BATH &
KITCHEN
4850 W Flamingo Road 36
Las Vegas, NV 89103

KITCHEN STUDIO INC
610 1/2 E Sahara Avenue
Las Vegas, NV 89104

Reno

CABINET & LIGHTING
SUPPLY
6970 S Virginia Street
Reno, NV 89511

CLASSIC KITCHENS &
DESIGNS
605 Chance Lane
Reno, NV 89511

KITCHENS & BATHS BY
LOUISE GILMARTIN
245 Vine Street
Suite B
Reno, NV 89503

NEW HAMPSHIRE

Amherst

CURRIER KITCHENS
101 Route 101A
Amherst, NH 03031

R-HOUSE KITCHENS & BATHS
71 Route 101A Windmere Place
Amherst, NH 03031

Bedford

MUIR'S KITCHEN STORE
63 S River Road
Bedford, NH 03102

Claremont

LAVALLEY'S CLAREMONT
BUILDING SUPPLY
Pleasant & Mulberry Streets
Claremont, NH 03743

Concord

KITCHEN FASHIONS
Lamplighter Plaza # 8
133 Loudon Rd.
Concord, NH 03301

Jaffrey

MASTER DECORATING
Park Place
Jaffrey, NH 03452

Keene

GRASHOW'S
147 Winchester Street
Keene, NH 03431

HAMSHAW LUMBER INC
3 Bradco Street
Keene, NH 03431

Manchester

NOT JUST KITCHENS
39 Hamel Drive
Manchester, NH 03104-2139

SUNDEEN'S BUILDING
CENTER
271 Mamoth Road
Manchester, NH 03103

Nashua

DREAM KITCHENS
139 Daniel Webster Highway
Nashua, NH 03060

Newington

ADAPTATIONS UNLIMITED
INC.
2001 Woodbury Avenue
Newington, NH 03801

Newport

LA VALLEY BUILDING
SUPPLY INC
Box 267 Guild Road
Newport, NH 03773

North Conway

CHICK HOME BUILDING
CENTER
PO BOX 3060
Mtn. Valley Mall Blvd.
North Conway, NH 03860

R.L. MEAD INC
PO Box 560
East Conway Road
North Conway, NH 03860

Peterborough

UPCOUNTRY KITCHENS &
BATHS
PO Box 367
23 Elm Street
Peterborough, NH 03458

Portsmouth

AREA KITCHEN CENTRE
105 Bartlett Street
Portsmouth, NH 03801

STANDARD PLUMBING
& HEATING SUPPLY
CORPORATION
430 W Road PO Box 1267
Portsmouth, NH 03801

Stratham

THE CABINETWORKS
62 Portsmouth Avenue
Stratham, NH 03885

NEW JERSEY

Bayonne

ABBEY'S KITCHENS & BATHS
INC
685 Broadway
Bayonne, NJ 07002

Belle Mead

NASSAU KITCHEN AND BATH
COMPANY INC
1109 Route 206
Belle Mead, NJ 08502

Belleville

KITCHENS & BATHS BY
MODERN MILLWORK
624 Washington Avenue
Belleville, NJ 07109

Belmar

DU CRAFT INC
1919 Highway 71
Belmar, NJ 07719

Bergenfield

DOVETAIL DESIGNS INC
7 Irving Place
Bergenfield, NJ 07621

Bloomfield

BOYETTE KITCHENS &
BATHS
214 Montgomery Street
Bloomfield, NJ 07003

Bridgeton

MIKE KELLY'S KITCHENS
RD #8 Box 229
Landis Avenue
Bridgeton, NJ 08302

Butler

RICH'S KITCHENS INC
309 Hamburg Turnpike
Butler, NJ 07405

THE KITCHEN CORNER
Route 23 S & Boonton Avenue
Box 41
Butler, NJ 07405

Cherry Hill

APPLE KITCHENS INC
1334 Brace Road
Cherry Hill, NJ 08034

Chester

KITCHENS UNIQUE BY LOIS
INC
259 Main Street
Box 6899
Chester, NJ 07930

Cliffside Park

AMSTERDAM ASSOCIATES
INC
200 Winston Drive-3103
Cliffside Park, NJ 07010

Cliffwood Beach

FLO DAR INC
Highway 35
Cliffwood Beach, NJ 07735

Clifton

R & R REMODELERS INC
423 Hazel Street
Clifton, NJ 07011

Dover

LAKELAND INDUSTRIES
CABAINET CORNER
408 Route 46
Dover, NJ 07801

Dumont

NICK'S KITCHEN CENTER
71 New Milford Avenue
Dumont, NJ 07628

Elizabeth

CRINCOLI WOODWORK
COMPANY INC
160 Spring Street
Elizabeth, NJ 07201

Englishtown

KITCHENS BY TORRONE
PO Box 309
Englishtown, NJ 07726

Fair Lawn

KITCHEN TECHNIQUE INC
4-10 Fair Lawn Avenue
Fair Lawn, NJ 07410

Farmingdale

THE KITCHEN COLLECTION
GERALD SACCA
5105 Highway 33 34
Farmingdale, NJ 07727

Garwood

DUDICK & SON
40 North Avenue
Garwood, NJ 07027

Gibbsboro

ABSOLUTE KITCHENS, INC.
Route 561
Haddonfield Berlin Road
Gibbsboro, NJ 08026

Green Brook

BEAUTY CRAFT KITCHENS &
BATHS INC
283 US Highway 22
Green Brook, NJ 08812

FRESH IMPRESSIONS, INC
326 US Highway 22 West
Green Brook, NJ 08812-1713

Hackettstown

HACKETTSTOWN SUPPLY
COMPANY INC
47 Route 46
Hackettstown, NJ 07840

Haddonfield

HADDONFIELD KITCHENS
INC
423 Haddon Avenue
Haddonfield, NJ 08033

Hawthorne

HAWTHORNE KITCHENS INC
Fifth and Utter Avenues
Hawthorne, NJ 07506

HOME SUPPLY & LUMBER
CENTER KITCHEN DIVISION
160 Van Winkle Avenue
Hawthorne, NJ 07506

Hopewell

SAUMS INTERIORS INC
75 Princeton Avenue
Hopewell, NJ 08525

Kearny

AANENSEN'S
142 Midland Avenue
Kearny, NJ 07032

Lake Hiawatha

KITCHENS BATHS INTERIORS
58 N Beverwyck Road
Lake Hiawatha, NJ 07034

Lambertville

C.A. NIECE COMPANY
Elm Street
Lambertville, NJ 08530

Lebanon

CWI KITCHENS & BATHS INC
Route 22 PO Box 528
Lebanon, NJ 08833

Linden

ECONOMY KITCHENS
431 N Wood Avenue
PO Box 1352
Linden, NJ 07036

Little Silver

LITTLE SILVER KITCHEN &
BATH STUDIO INC
2 Fairview Avenue
Little Silver, NJ 07739

S D DESIGNS INC.
116 Oceanport Avenue
Little Silver, NJ 07739

Livingston

RAY RIVERS & ASSOCIATES
INC
34 E Northfield Road
Livingston, NJ 07039

Manalapan

CABITRON DISTRIBUTORS
INC
Home Fashion Center
520 Route 9 N
Manalapan, NJ 07726

Margate

DILLON CUSTOM KITCHENS
1 S Granville Avenue
Margate, NJ 08402

Marmora

A-1 CUSTOM KITCHENS &
BATHS
22 Norwood Road
PO Box 787
Marmora, NJ 08223

Middlesex

MICHAEL GEORGE
KITCHEN'S
679 Bound Brook Road
Middlesex, NJ 08846

Montvale

PASCACK SHOWCASE INC
PO Box 367
33 S Kinderkamack Road
Montvale, NJ 07645

Morristown

DISTINCTIVE KITCHENS
171 Ridgedale Avenue
Morristown, NJ 07960

N Plainfield

KITCHEN IDEAS INC
918 Route 22
N Plainfield, NJ 07060

New Providence

ROSAN CUSTOM KITCHENS
AND BATH
1294 Springfield Avenue
New Providence, NJ 07974

Newfield

KITCHENS N THINGS INC
Route 40
PO Box 346
Newfield, NJ 08344

Northfield

SOUTH JERSEY KITCHEN
DIST INC. KITCHEN AND
BATH DESIGN CENTER
1333 New Road Plaza 9
Northfield, NJ 08225

Norwood

NORWOOD KITCHENS, INC.
49 Oak Street
Norwood, NJ 07648

Ocean City

REBER MCLEAN KITCHENS
INC
628 West Avenue
Ocean City, NJ 08226

SHOEMAKER LUMBER
COMPANY INC
1200 W Avenue
PO Box 357
Ocean City, NJ 08226

Parsippany

R & S PLUMBING & HEATING
SUPPLIES, INC.
3460 Route 46 W
Parsippany, NJ 07054

Pequannock

THE KITCHEN SHOP INC
35 Newark Pompton Turnpike
Pequannock, NJ 07440

Perth Amboy

WHOLESALE KITCHEN
CABINET DISTRIBUTOR INC
533 Krochmally Avenue
Perth Amboy, NJ 08861

Piscataway

STELTON CABINET & SUPPLY
COMPANY
1358 Stelton Road
Piscataway, NJ 08854

Pleasantville

JOTI KITCHENS
413 S Main Street
Pleasantville, NJ 08232

Point Pleasant

IDEAL KITCHENS INC
407 Sea Avenue
Point Pleasant, NJ 08742

Pompton Lakes

HANS' KITCHENS & BATHS
INC
10 Colfax Avenue
Pompton Lakes, NJ 07442

LORANGER & SONS INC
324 Ringwood Avenue
Pompton Lakes, NJ 07442

Pompton Plains

JEFFREYS & LUTJEN INC
29 Evans Place
Pompton Plains, NJ 07444

Ramsey

BONDI'S WORLD OF
KITCHENS INC
455 Route 17 S
Ramsey, NJ 07446

Randolph

KITCHENS BY SPITALNY
425 State Route 10 East
Randolph, NJ 07869

Raritan

THE CABINET CENTER BY
FLEETWOOD
20 Route 206
Raritan, NJ 08869

Red Bank

CREATIVE KITCHENS
19 East Front Street
Red Bank, NJ 07701

THE KITCHEN GALLERY INC.
24 Mechanic Street
Red Bank, NJ 07701

Ridgewood

ULRICH INC
100 Chestnut Street
Ridgewood, NJ 07450

Roselle

PROVEN DESIGN INC
225 E First Avenue
Roselle, NJ 07203

Sea Girt

DESIGN LINE KITCHENS
2127 Highway 35
Sea Girt, NJ 08750

Shrewsbury

MONMOUTH BUILDING
CENTER
777 Shrewsbury Avenue
Shrewsbury, NJ 07702

Somerdale

THE PURPLE THUMB INC
6 South White Horse Pike
Somerdale, NJ 08083

Somerset

BATHS PLAIN & FANCY J.
DOLAN SONS PLUMBING &
HEATING
696 Franklin Boulevard
Somerset, NJ 08873

South Plainfield

JOANNE'S KITCHENS
2208 Hamilton Boulevard
PO Box 267
South Plainfield, NJ 07080

South Somerville

ROYAL CABINET COMPANY
INC
14 Park Avenue
South Somerville, NJ 08876

Sparta

SPARTA TRADES KITCHENS
& BATHS
580 Route 15
Sparta, NJ 07871

Spotswood

ALBECKER'S KITCHEN &
BATH
272 Main Street
Spotswood, NJ 08884

COMBINED CRAFTMEN INC
168 Manalapan Road
Spotswood, NJ 08884

Springfield

KURT'S CONCEPTS
615 Morris Avenue
Springfield, NJ 07081

Summit

BAZALA KITCHENS INC
37 Maple Street
Summit, NJ 07901

CABRI INC
323 Springfield Avenue
Summit, NJ 07901

DESIGNER KITCHENS &
BATHS INC
66 River Road
Summit, NJ 07901

Surf City

TLC SALES
200 North Boulevard Box 281
Surf City, NJ 08008

Sussex

KITCHENS & BATHS BY RAN
COMPANY INC
56 E Main Street
Sussex, NJ 07461

Teaneck

NATIVE WOOD
370 Queen Anne Road
Teaneck, NJ 07666

SUBURBAN CABINET CORP
1465 Palisade Avenue
Teaneck, NJ 07666

Totowa

REMY'S KITCHEN & BATH
STUDIO
394 Union Boulevard
Totowa, NJ 07512

Trenton

BOB LANG INCORPORATED
1842 S Broad Street
Trenton, NJ 08610

CAMELOT KITCHENS
1589 Reed Road
Trenton, NJ 08628

DREAMLINE KITCHENS &
BATHS
1439 Hamilton Ave
Trenton, NJ 08629

HAMILTON KITCHENS
4441 Nottingham Way
Hamiliton Square
Trenton, NJ 08690

KITCHEN QUEST INC
1453 Kuser Road
Trenton, NJ 08619

Union

JAEGER LUMBER
2322 Morris Avenue
PO Box 126
Union, NJ 07083

Vineland

REMODELING CONCEPTS
319 West Weymouth Road
Vineland, NJ 08360

Warren

CHUCK DETORRE, INC. AKA
KING GEORGE PLUMBING &
HEATING
20 Mountain Boulevard
Warren, NJ 07059

SUPERIOR CUSTOM
KITCHENS
126 Mount Bethel Road
Warren, NJ 07059

Washington

SCHNEIDER'S KITCHENS INC
426 Rt 31 N
Washington, NJ 07882

Whippany

ARROW CRAFTS INC
71 Route 10
Whippany, NJ 07981

SCHLEIFER CONSTRUCTION
INC
20 North Jefferson Road
Whippany, NJ 07981

Windsor

FORM TOPS LAMINATORS
Route 130 Box 389
Windsor, NJ 08561

Wyckoff

A & B KITCHENS & BATHS
INC
279 Franklin Avenue
Wyckoff, NJ 07481

THE HAMMER & NAIL INC.
232 Madison Avenue
Wyckoff, NJ 07481

NEW MEXICO

Albuquerque

AMERICAN BATH
REMODELING
1540 Juan Tabo NE
Albuquerque, NM 87112

CREATIVE KITCHENS INC
7923 Menaul NE
Albuquerque, NM 87110

DESIGN PROFESSIONALS
KITCHEN & BATH CENTER
1309 San Mateo N E
Albuquerque, NM 87110

Roswell

BUSH WOODWORKS AND
APPLIANCE INC
111 West Country Club Road
Roswell, NM 88201

Santa Fe

CREATIVE KITCHENS
1209 Cerrillos Road
Santa Fe, NM 87501

PITTMAN BROTHERS
WOODWORKS
1241 Siler Road
Santa Fe, NM 87501

STATEMENTS IN KITCHENS
821-C West San Mateo
Santa Fe, NM 87501

NEW YORK

Adams

LUNMAN FURNITURE &
APPLIANCE CENTER
70 North Main Street
Adams, NY 13605

Albany

KITCHEN & BATH WORLD
INC
345 New Karner Road
Albany, NY 12205

KNIGHT KITCHENS OF
ALBANY, INC.
1770 Central Avenue
Albany, NY 12205

MARCO'S SHOWCASE
1814 Central Avenue
Albany, NY 12205

Amherst

WEINHEIMERS INC.
PO Box 1888
Amherst, NY 14226

Auburn

QUIG ENTERPRISES
COMPLETE HOME CENTER
RD 6 Mutton Hill Road
Auburn, NY 13021

Ballston Spa

CURTIS LUMBER COMPANY
INC
885 Route 67
Ballston Spa, NY 12020

Batavia

GIAMBRONE APPLIANCE
SALES
634 E Main Street
Batavia, NY 14020

Bayside

KITCHEN AND BATHROOM
DESIGNS BY RIKK DAVIDSON
214-26 41st Avenue
Bayside, NY 11361

Bedford Hills

DESIGNER KITCHENS BY
PAMELA INC
61 Adams Street
Bedford Hills, NY 10507

WESTCHESTER ARCHITECTUAL
WOODWORKING INC.
385 Adams Street
Bedford Hills, NY 10507

Binghamton

CREATIVE KITCHENS &
BATHS
331 Main Street
Binghamton, NY 13905

MCGOWAN CORPORATION
368 Kattelville Road R D #9
Box 1
Binghamton, NY 13901

Brewster

DILLS BEST BUILDING
CENTER
2 All View Avenue
Brewster, NY 10509

Bridgehampton

BENCHMARK INC
Snake Hollow Road
PO Box 1252
Bridgehampton, NY 11932

Bronx

KITCHEN SOLUTIONS
1086 East Gun Hill Road
Bronx, NY 10469

Brooklyn

COUNTERTOPS INC GENESIC
CUSTOM CABINETRY
2125 Utica Avenue
Brooklyn, NY 11234

GOLD & REISS CORPORATION
312 McDonald Avenue
Brooklyn, NY 11218

REGENCY KITCHENS INC
4204-14 Avenue
Brooklyn, NY 11219

TIVOLI TILE & MARBLE
COMPANY INC
883 65th Street
Brooklyn, NY 11220

Buffalo

KEN TON FABRICATORS INC
2505 Main Street
Buffalo, NY 14214-2097

Carle Place

EURO KITCHEN PLUS
222 Glen Cove Road
Carle Place, NY 11514

Carmel

ALPINE KITCHENS INC
220 Brewster Avenue
Route 6
Carmel, NY 10512

Centereach

THERESE MARCEL'S INC
1456 Middle Country Road
Centereach, NY 11720

Claverack

THE COOK'S CORNER
Old Lane
Box 220
Claverack, NY 12513

Cleverdale

KAIDAS KITCHENS & BATHS
PO Box 268
Cleverdale, NY 12820-0268

Commack

CONSUMERS WAREHOUSE
CENTER INC
258 Commack Road
Commack, NY 11725

MICA ELEGANCE
196 Commack Road
Commack, NY 11725

Copiague

CONSUMERS WAREHOUSE
CENTER INC
1250 Sunrise Highway
Copiague, NY 11726

THE BATH FACTORY
1270 Sunrise Highway
Copiague, NY 11726

Corning

ADAMYS INC
PO Box 59
Corning, NY 14830

SULLIVAN KITCHEN & BATH
64 Denison Parkway E
Corning, NY 14830-2727

THE CORNING BUILDING
COMPANY INC
CBC Plaza Park Avenue
Corning, NY 14830

Cortland

BUILDERS BEST HOME
IMPROVEMENT CENTER
3798 Luker Road
Cortland, NY 13045

E Meadow

KITCHENS UNIQUE BY DELF
482 E Meadow Avenue
E Meadow, NY 11554

East Hampton

RIVERHEAD BUILDING
SUPPLY
15 Railroad Avenue
East Hampton, NY 11937

East Meadow

ALURE HOME IMPROVEMENTS
1999 Hempstead Turnpike
East Meadow, NY 11554

CONSUMERS WAREHOUSE
CENTER INC
2280 Hempstead Turnpike
East Meadow, NY 11554

JARRO BUILDING
INDUSTRIES CORP.
1796 Hempstead Turnpike
East Meadow, NY 11554

Elmira

KITCHEN & BATH GALLERY
1055 Walnut Street
Elmira, NY 14905

ROBINSON BUILDING
MATERIALS INC
PO Box 325
Elmira, NY 14902-0325

Endicott

M & M KITCHEN & BATH
243 Maple Lane
Endicott, NY 13760-8953

Fairport

KITCHEN CONCEPTS
1350 Fairport Road
Fairport, NY 14450

Farmingville

CANCOS TILE CORPORATION
1085 Portion Road
Farmingville, NY 11738

Floral Park

WINDHAM INTERIORS
146 Jericho Turnpike
Floral Park, NY 11001-2006

Flushing

ATLANTIS KITCHEN & HOME
IMPROVEMENT CENTER
40-37 162nd Street
Flushing, NY 11358

HOME IDEAL INC
171 10 39 Avenue
Flushing, NY 11358

Franklin Square

BATHROOMS & KITCHENS BY
ROYAL
958 Hempstead Turnpike
Franklin Square, NY 11010

CONSUMERS WAREHOUSE
CENTER INC
600 Franklin Avenue
Franklin Square, NY 11010

Fredonia

PATTON ELECTRIC
COMPANY
10378 Bennett Road
Fredonia, NY 14063

THE GALLERY
112 W Main Street
Fredonia, NY 14063

Freeport

KITCHEN EXCELLENCE INC
27A West Merrick Road
Freeport, NY 11520

Fulton

JOICE & BURCH
2 West First Street North
Fulton, NY 13069

Garden City

HERBERT P BISULK INC
KITCHEN OF DISTINCTION
BY MONTE
295 Nassau Boulevard S
Garden City, NY 11530

Geneva

L.A. JOHNSON'S KITCHENS &
BATHS
PO Box 129
Route 5 & 20
Geneva, NY 14456

Glendale

FREDERICK HOME
REMODELING CORPORATION
79-49 Myrtle Avenue.
Glendale, NY 11385

Goshen

MASTERWORK KITCHENS
134 West Main Street
Goshen, NY 10924

Granite Springs

JILCO WINDOW CORPORATION
PO Box 1 Mahopac Avenue
Granite Springs, NY 10527

Great Neck

D & M KITCHENS INC
400 Great Neck Road
Great Neck, NY 11021

Hauppauge

UNITED CERAMIC TILE
923 Motor Parkway
Hauppauge, NY 11788

Henrietta

CAVE'S CABINETRY
CONCEPTS
3081 E Henrietta Road
PO Box 268
Henrietta, NY 14467

Hewlett

KITCHEN WORKS
1157A Broadway
Hewlett, NY 11557-2321

Holbrook

CONSUMERS WAREHOUSE
CENTER INC
717 Broadway Avenue
Holbrook, NY 11741

Hornell

MAIN PLUMBING HEATING
KITCHENS INC
299 Main Street
Hornell, NY 14843

Huntington

ALAMODE DESIGN
CONCEPTS INC
595 W Jericho Turnpike
Huntington, NY 11743-6362

C.H. JONES FINE KITCHEN
AND BATH CABINETRY
220 East Main Street
Huntington, NY 11743

CUSTOM CONCEPTS INC
741-A W Jericho Turnpike
Huntington, NY 11743

EURO CONCEPTS OF
HUNTINGTON LTD
1802 E Jericho Turnpike
Huntington, NY 11743

Huntington Station

ARTHUR CHRISTENSEN INC.
CHRISTENSEN'S
545 East Jericho Turnpike
Huntington Station, NY 11746

HUNTINGTON KITCHEN AND
BATH INC
673 E Jericho Turnpike
Huntington Station, NY 11746

Ithaca

CAYUGA LUMBER INC
801 W State Street
Ithaca, NY 14850

Jay

WARD LUMBER COMPANY
INC
PO Box 154
Glen Road
Jay, NY 12941

Kenmore

ORVILLE D. WILSON INC.
PLUMBING & HEATING
845 Englewood Avenue
Kenmore, NY 14223

Lake Placid

HUNTER DESIGNS INC
Cascade Road
PO Box 244
Lake Placid, NY 12946

Larchmont

LAWRENCE R. LOFFREDO
INC
2406 Boston Post Rd
Larchmont, NY 10538-3403

Lathamide

THE KITCHEN & BATH CO
332 Old Loubon Road
Lathamide, NY 12110-2932

Liverpool

MIDSTATE WHOLESALE
CORPORATION
Morgan Place
PO Box 97
Liverpool, NY 13088

Lockport

L.J. FAERY CUSTOM
KITCHEN & BATH
6620 Lincoln Avenue
Lockport, NY 14094

Long Island City

DI FIORE & SONS CUSTOM
WOODWORKING
42 02 Astoria Boulevard
Long Island City, NY 11103

Malone

MALONE LUMBER & READY
MIX 1
259 Elm Street
Malone, NY 12953

Mamaroneck

BILOTTA HOME CENTER INC
564 Mamaroneck Avenue
Mamaroneck, NY 10543

FUHRMANN KITCHENS
253 Halstead Avenue
Mamaroneck, NY 10543

Massapequa

KITCHENS & BATHS BY MR.
D., INC.
4163 Merrick Road
Massapequa, NY 11758

Massapequa Park

ALADDIN REMODELERS INC
5020 Sunrise Highway
Massapequa Park, NY 11762

Medford

CREATIVE CABINET
CORPORATION OF AMERICA
3731 Horseblock Road
Medford, NY 11763

Merrick

CREATIVE KITCHENS &
BATHS INC
1829 Merrick Avenue
Merrick, NY 11566

GLENDALE KITCHENS &
BATHS LTD
20 Grundy Place
Merrick, NY 11566-2711

THE KITCHEN STORE INC
PO Box 341
Merrick, NY 11566

Middletown

KITCHENS BY MC CAREY
531 N Street
Middletown, NY 10940

ROWLEY KITCHEN SALES
INC
87 Wisner Avenue
Middletown, NY 10940

Mineola

ALAMODE KITCHEN CENTER
INC
206 E Jericho Turnpike
Mineola, NY 11501

MERILLON BATH AND
KITCHEN CENTER
550 Jericho Turnpike
Mineola, NY 11501

Mount Morris

MOUNT MORRIS KITCHEN
CENTER
86 Main Street
Mount Morris, NY 14510

Mt Kisco

BEDFORD TILE CORPORATION
510 Lexington Avenue
Mt Kisco, NY 10549

Nassau

MILLBROOK CUSTOM
KITCHENS INC
Route 20
Nassau, NY 12123

New Hartford

CHARM KITCHENS BY
SPETTS
100 Seneca Turnpike
Route 5
New Hartford, NY 13413

NEW HARTFORD PLUMBING
SUPPLY CORP
1103 Commercial Drive
New Hartford, NY 13413-9563

New Hyde Park

KITCHEN DESIGNS BY KEN
KELLY INC
2115 Hillside Avenue
New Hyde Park, NY 11040

New Rochelle

RIEMER KITCHENS INC
1327 N Avenue
New Rochelle, NY 10804

New York

ELGOT KITCHENS
937 Lexington Avenue
New York, NY 10021

HASTINGS KITCHEN STUDIO
230 Park Avenue S
New York, NY 10003

LEESAM KITCHEN & BATH
124 7th Avenue
New York, NY 10011

NEMO TILE COMPANY INC
48 E 21 Street
New York, NY 10010

QUINTESSENTIALS
525 Amsterdam Avenue
New York, NY 10024

SAINT CHARLES KITCHENS
OF NEW YORK
150 E 58th Street
New York, NY 10155

THE KITCHEN & BATH
EXPERTS
473 Amsterdam Avenue
New York, NY 10024

Newburgh

R. I. M. PLUMBING HEATING
28 Johnes Street
Newburgh, NY 12550

North Bangor

DWYERS HOME IMPROVEMENT
CENTER INC
PO Box 308 Depot Street
North Bangor, NY 12966

North Tarrytown

SLEEPY HOLLOW CUSTOM
KITCHENS
42 River Street
North Tarrytown, NY 10591

Northport

BRUCE CABINET
350 A Woodbine Avenue
Northport, NY 11768

Norwich

KUNTRISET KITCHENS
Road 2 Box 254
Norwich, NY 13815

Nunda

MODERN HOME CENTER
10 South State Street
PO Box 395
Nunda, NY 14517

Olean

GREEN STREET CUSTOM
KITCHEN & BATH
202 East Green Street
Olean, NY 16740

Oneonta

PICKETT BUILDING
MATERIAL
RD 2 Box 2066
Oneonta, NY 13820

Peekskill

ULTIMATE DESIGN
CONCEPTS
Crompond Road
Peekskill, NY 10566

Plattsburgh

GREGORY SUPPLY
COMPANY INC
Tom Miller Road
PO Box 70
Plattsburgh, NY 12901-0070

Pleasantville

ALPINE CONTRACTING
COMPANY INC
79 Grandview Avenue
Pleasantville, NY 10570

ARNOLD WILE & ASSOCIATES
34 Marble Avenue
Pleasantville, NY 10570

Pomona

SOUTH MOUNTAIN
WOODWORKING GROUP
161 Camp Hill Road
Pomona, NY 10970

Port Jefferson

CUSTOM CABINETS BY K & I
INC
617-2 Bicycle Path
Port Jefferson, NY 11776

Port Jervis

SMITH KITCHEN & BATH
GALLERY
66 Jersey Avenue
Port Jervis, NY 12771

Potsdam

D.L. THOMAS KITCHENS &
BATHS
Outer Market Street
PO Box 5046
Potsdam, NY 13676

Poughkeepsie

J.F. BAHRENBURG INC
35 Manchester Circle
Poughkeepsie, NY 12603

Red Hook

KITCHEN KREATIONS
9B Old Farm Road
Red Hook, NY 12571-1628

Rego Park

LINGOLD DESIGN &
CONSTRUCTION CORP
63-76 Woodhaven Boulevard
Rego Park, NY 11374

Rhinebeck

WILLIAMS LUMBER
Route 9 N
PO Box 31
Rhinebeck, NY 12572

Riverhead

CABINETS PLUS
1086 Route 58
Riverhead, NY 11901

RIVERHEAD BUILDING
SUPPLY CORPORATE
CABINET SHOWCASE
1295 Pulaski Street
Riverhead, NY 11901

Rochester

CHASE PITKIN
3131 Winton Road S
Rochester, NY 14623

DELL'S HOUSE OF KITCHENS
INC
3445 Winton Place
Rochester, NY 14623

MCKENNA'S ROCHESTER
KITCHEN & BATH CENTER
3401 Winton Road
Rochester, NY 14623

Rome

GENERAL LUMBER &
HARDWARE
529 Erie Boulevard West
Rome, NY 13440

Roslyn

BRANDT WOODCRAFT OF
ROSLYN INC
18 Lumber Road
Roslyn, NY 11576

CLASSIC KITCHEN & BATH
CENTER LTD
1062 Northern Boulevard
Roslyn, NY 11576

Saint James

NORTH COUNTRY KITCHEN
& BATH INC
437 N Country Road
Saint James, NY 11780

Saranac Lake

CASIER FURNITURE
10 Bloomingdale Avenue
Saranac Lake, NY 12983

Saratoga Spring

ALLERDICE BUILDING
SUPPLY
Division & Wallworth Street
Saratoga Spring, NY 12866

KITCHEN DIMENSIONS
2 Franklin Square
Saratoga Spring, NY 12866

Saugerties

HICKORY MEADOWS
CUSTOM KITCHENS
83 Lauren Tice Road
Saugerties, NY 12477

Scarsdale

GARTH CUSTOM KITCHENS
INC
24 Garth Road
Scarsdale, NY 10583

Schenectady

AMERICAN WOODWORK
THE YANKEE BUILDER
1702 Chrisler Avenue
Schenectady, NY 12303

BELLEVUE BUILDER'S
SUPPLY
500 Duanesburg Road
Schenectady, NY 12306

MARCO'S SUPPLY COMPANY
INC
315 Green Street
Schenectady, NY 12305-1442

YOUR KITCHEN & BATH INC
2245 Central Avenue
Schenectady, NY 12304

Scotia

CENTRAL PLUMBING &
HEATING SUPPLY COMPANY
INC.
141 Freemans Bridge Road
Scotia, NY 12302

HOMECREST KITCHENS INC
110 Freemans Br Road
Scotia, NY 12302

Setauket

THREE VILLAGE/SETAUKET
KITCHEN & BATH
278 Main Street
Setauket, NY 11733-2944

South Fallsburg

KAPLAN CABINET COMPANY
221 Main Street
PO Box 804
South Fallsburg, NY 12779

Southampton

E.T. CABINET CORP.
106 Mariner Drive
Southampton, NY 11968

Spencerport

PA FLORAMO'S HOME
IMPROVEMENT SHOWCASE
42 Nichols Street
Spencerport, NY 14559

Staten Island

ANDERSON KITCHENS
77 Lincoln Avenue
Staten Island, NY 10306

COPPOLA ENTERPRISES INC
53 New Dorp Plaza
Staten Island, NY 10306

DESIGN STUDIO
1572 Richmond Road
Staten Island, NY 10304

Syracuse

DISTINCTIVE INTERIORS
5891 Firestone Drive
Syracuse, NY 13206

Tallman

GEIGER LUMBER & SUPPLY
Route 59
Tallman, NY 10982

Tarrytown

ZAMBELLETTI'S CUSTOM
KITCHENS & BATHS
92 Central Avenue
Tarrytown, NY 10591

Valatie

DIECKELMANN HOME
CENTER
Rt 9
Valatie, NY 12184

Vista

RING'S END INC
386 Smith Ridge Road
Route 123
Vista, NY 10590

Wantagh

GOLD COAST KITCHENS &
BATHS INC
3004 Merrick Road
Wantagh, NY 11793

Wappinger Falls

EMPIRE KITCHEN &
WOODWORKING INC
862 South Road
Wappinger Falls, NY 12590

Waverly

RYNONE KITCHEN & BATH
410 Spaulding Street
Waverly, NY 14892

Webster

KITCHEN & BATH
EXPRESSIONS BY GARY
LARZZARO
1175 Ridge Road
Webster, NY 14580

West Babylon

CANCOS TILE CORPORATION
710 Montauk Highway
West Babylon, NY 11704

West Hempstead

ARTISAN CUSTOM
INTERIORS
163 Hempstead Turnpike
West Hempstead, NY 11552

Westbury

CANCOS TILE CORPORATION
801 Old Country Road
Westbury, NY 11590

White Plains

MAJESTIC KITCHENS
530 Tarrytown Road
White Plains, NY 10607

Whitestone

KITCHENS ETC
20-08 Utopia Parkway
Whitestone, NY 11357

Yonkers

QUAKER MAID KITCHENS OF
N.Y. INC.
1880 Central Park Avenue
Yonkers, NY 10710

Yorktown

BEST PLUMBING SUPPLY INC
BUILDING DESIGN CENTER
33331 Crompond Road
Yorktown, NY 10598

Yorktown Heights

YORKTOWN INTERIOR
WOODWORKING
1776 Front Street
Yorktown Heights, NY 10598

NORTH CAROLINA

Apex

BEAUTIFUL BATHZ INC
299 North Salem Street
Apex, NC 27502

Asheville

BALLARD APPLIANCE
& CABINET COMPANY
COMPANY INC
1238 Hendersonville Road
Asheville, NC 28803

COOPER HOUSE INC
479 Hendersonville Road
Asheville, NC 28803

NOVA KITCHEN & BATH
1257 Sweeten Creek Road
PO Box 5594
Asheville, NC 28813

Charlotte

AMERICAN KITCHENS INC
CUSTOM CABINETRY &
DESIGN
1123 McAlway Road
Charlotte, NC 28211

CLASSIC DOORS & KITCHENS
9315 Monroe Road Suite E
Charlotte, NC 28270

INTERSTATE KITCHEN &
BATH INC
8200 South Boulevard
Charlotte, NC 28273

THE MARBLE & STONE SHOP
INC
PO Box 32773
1001 West Morehead Street
Charlotte, NC 28208

Davidson

INTERNATIONAL KITCHEN &
BATH INC
18835 B Statesville Road
Davidson, NC 28036

Durham

ACME PLUMBING AND
HEATING CO. OF DURHAM,
INC
636 Foster Street PO Box 2288
Durham, NC 27702

ALASKA'S BEST
1405-A Old Oxford Highway
Durham, NC 27704

KITCHENS ET CETERA INC
2514 University Drive
Durham, NC 27707

THE KITCHEN SPECIALIST
3407 University Drive
Durham, NC 27707-2629

Elizabeth City

CARTER'S CABINETS
1400 West Church Street
Elizabeth City, NC 27909

Fayetteville

CAPE FEAR SUPPLY
1001 S Reilly Rd Industiral Pk
#561
PO Box 40408
Fayetteville, NC 28309

Greensboro

BATH & KITCHEN
MENAGERIE
4141 Spring Garden
Greensboro, NC 27407

DESIGNER CABINETS
2505 Carroll Street #C
Greensboro, NC 27408

HATCH CABINET DESIGNS
4604 West Market Street
Greensboro, NC 27407

KITCHEN WORKS & BATH
WORKS COMPAMY INC
3844 Battleground Avenue
Apt 36
Greensboro, NC 27410-9433

OLD MASTER KITCHENS
BURLINGTON DIST. CO., INC
1401 W Lee Street
Greensboro, NC 27403

Hendersonville

KITCHEN INTERIORS INC
1630 Asheville Highway
Hendersonville, NC 28739

Hickory

PIEDMONT DESIGNS OF
HICKORY
2250 Highway 70 South East
Suite 458
Hickory, NC 28602

High Point

SNOW LUMBER COMPANY
INC
PO Box 530
High Point, NC 27261

Kitty Hawk

COZY HOME CUSTOM
CABINETS INC
921 Kitty Hawk Road
Kitty Hawk, NC 27949

Mooresville

CARTER COMPANIES
PO Box 980
Mooresville, NC 28115

New Bern

KITCHEN ART INC.
1907 S Glenburnie Road
PO Box 12882
New Bern, NC 28561-2882

P & F CABINETS
Route 1
Box 200C
New Bern, NC 28560

Pinehurst

KITCHEN & BATH
SHOWPLACE
PO Box 3880
Pinehurst, NC 28374

Raleigh

HAMPTON KITCHENS OF
RALEIGH
5024 Old Wake Forest Road
Raleigh, NC 27609

TRIANGLE DESIGN
KITCHENS INC
5216 Holly Ridge Drive
Raleigh, NC 27612

Southern Pines

SANDAVIS CUSTOM
KITCHENS
515 F Midland Road
PO Box 1100
Southern Pines, NC 28387

Waynesville

HAYWOOD BUILDERS
SUPPLY
403 Chas Street
PO Box 187
Waynesville, NC 28786

Wilmington

CREATIVE KITCHEN & BATH
DESIGNS
1717 N 23rd Street
Wilmington, NC 28405

SUPERIOR MILLWORK INC
615 S 17th Street
Wilmington, NC 28401

THE BECKER BUILDERS
SUPPLY COMPANY
PO Box 1697
Wilmington, NC 28405

Winston Salem

AMARR CABINETS INC
1033 Burke Street
Winston Salem, NC 27101-2412

GREAT KITCHENS AND
BATHS
8001 A North Point Boulevard
Winston Salem, NC 27106

NORTH DAKOTA

Bismarck

THE DOOR STOP
1416 East Front Avenue
Bismarck, ND 58504

Fargo

BACHMAN INC
360 36th Street S
Fargo, ND 58103

BRAATEN CABINETS INC
25th & Main Avenue
PO Box 249
Fargo, ND 58107-0249

Minot

GREAT PLAINS SUPPLY
PO Box 1781
Minot, ND 58702

Wahpeton

KITCHENS UNLIMITED
PO Box 903
Wahpeton, ND 58074

New York

Clifton Park

JOMAR KITCHENS &
WINDOWS ETC.
1483 Route 9
Clifton Park, NY 12065

OHIO

Akron

BUILDER'S KITCHENS
1095 Home Avenue
Akron, OH 44310

LUMBERJACK'S INC
723 E Tallmadge Avenue
Akron, OH 44310

Barberton

WOOD PRO INC
27 4th Street NW
PO Box 29
Barberton, OH 44203

Bay Village

HERON BAY LIMITED INC
660 Dover Center Road
Bay Village, OH 44140

Beachwood

PURDY'S DESIGN STUDIO
2101 Richmond Road
Beachwood, OH 44122

Bedford Heights

SOMRAK KITCHENS INC
26201 Richmond Road
Bedford Heights, OH 44146

Brecksville

D A BRANCH INC
8921 Brecksville Road
Brecksville, OH 44141

Canfield

KITCHEN & BATH WORLD
INC
Route 224
Canfield, OH 44406

Canton

HOME CONCEPTS INC
3654 Harris Avnue NW
Canton, OH 44708-1027

Chardon

NORTHEASTERN KITCHEN &
BATH COMPANY
695 South Street
Suite #9
Chardon, OH 44024

Cincinnati

CITY-WIDE KITCHENS &
BATHS
6706 Montgomery Road
Cincinnati, OH 45236

DAYTON SHOWCASE
COMPANY CINCINNATI
11402 Reading Road
Cincinnati, OH 45241

ESQUIRE KITCHEN
SPECIALISTS
2280 Quebec Road
Cincinnati, OH 45214

KITCHEN CONCEPTS INC
6026 Ridge Avenue
Cincinnati, OH 45213

STANLEY DOE KITCHENS &
BATHS INC
5200 Beechmont Avenue
Cincinnati, OH 45230

THE DEVINE COMPANY
6916 Plainfield Road
Cincinnati, OH 45236

VALLEY FLOOR COVERING
BATH/KITCHEN SPECIALISTS
401 W Wyoming Avenue
Cincinnati, OH 45215

WESTERN HOME CENTER
INC
7600 Colerain Avenue
Cincinnati, OH 45239

Cleveland

ARTISAN CUSTOM-MAID INC
3321 W 140th Street
Cleveland, OH 44111

BREIT'S INC
5218 Detroit Avenue
Cleveland, OH 44102

BUILDER'S WORLD INC
4918 Neo Parkway
Cleveland, OH 44128

FOREST CITY/BABIN
COMPANY
5111 Richmond Road
Cleveland, OH 44146

Cleveland Heights

NATIONAL KITCHENS &
BATHS
3962 Mayfield Road
Cleveland Heights, OH 44121

Columbus

BIG 8 CO'S INC
2900 Ole Country Lane
Columbus, OH 43219

CABINET WAREHOUSE INC
2988 East 5th Avenue
Columbus, OH 43219

DAVE FOX CONTRACTING
INC
1151 Bethel Road
Columbus, OH 43220

ELLIS KITCHEN & BATH
STUDIO
477 S Front Street
Columbus, OH 43215

EUREKA INC
5156 Sinclair Road
Columbus, OH 43229

HAYWARD INC
909 W Fifth Avenue
Columbus, OH 43212

JAE COMPANY
955 W Fifth Avenue
Columbus, OH 43212

KINGSWOOD LUMBER
COMPANY
900 West Third Avenue
PO Box 12129
Columbus, OH 43212-0219

KITCHEN KRAFT INC
999 Goodale Boulevard
Columbus, OH 43212-3888

LONDON KITCHENS
1065 Dublin Road
Columbus, OH 43215

MASTER WOODWORKS
KITCHEN STUDIO
6323 Busch Boulevard
Columbus, OH 43229

THE BATH & BRASS
EMPORIUM
683 E Lincoln Avenue
Columbus, OH 43229

Dayton

A BETTER KITCHEN SUPPLY
3810 Dayton Xenia Road
Dayton, OH 45432

DAYTON SHOWCASE
COMPANY
2601 W Dorothy Lane
Dayton, OH 45439

DESIGN PRO REMODELING,
INC.
214/216 N Springboro Pike
Dayton, OH 45449

SHAWNEE SUPPLY INC.
43 Pierce Avenue
Dayton, OH 45449

SUPPLY ONE CORPORATION
210 Wayne Avenue
PO Box 636
Dayton, OH 45401

THE KITCHEN SHOPPE INC
5575 Far Hills Avenue
Dayton, OH 45429

East Liverpool

BIRCH SUPPLY COMPANY
INC
16477 Saint Clair Avenue
PO Box 9000
East Liverpool, OH 43920

Findlay

CAVINS KITCHEN VILLAGE
215 South Main Street
Findlay, OH 45840

Garfield Heights

BUILDERS WORLD INC
4918 NEO Parkway
Garfield Heights, OH 44128

Hartville

SCHUMACHER LUMBER
COMPANY
120 Mill Street
Hartville, OH 44632

Kettering

A D KISTLER KITCHEN&
BATH SPECIALIST
4638 Wilmington Pike
Kettering, OH 45440

La Grange

VIRGIL'S KITCHENS INC
100 Public Square
PO Box 625
La Grange, OH 44050

Lakewood

IMPERIAL HOME CENTER
INC
16000 Madison Avenue
Lakewood, OH 44107

Lancaster

KARSHNER SALES INC
735 N Slocum
Lancaster, OH 43130

Lima

LIMA BUILDING PRODUCTS
INC.
PO Box 1846
227 S Main Street
Lima, OH 45802

Loveland

SPECIALTY CABINETS
COMPANY
900 Loveland-Madeira Road
Loveland, OH 45140

Mantua

76 SUPPLY COMPANY INC
3384 Sr 82
Mantua, OH 44255

Marietta

MATERIAL DIFFERENCE
1408 Colegate Drive
Marietta, OH 45750

Marion

NU SUPPLY INC
1585 Harding Highway E
Marion, OH 43302

Mayfield Heights

CABINET EN-COUNTERS INC
6265 Mayfield Road
Mayfield Heights, OH 44124

Mentor

FASHION TREND KITCHENS
AND BATHS
7507 Tyler Boulevard
Mentor, OH 44060

MENTOR LUMBER COMPANY
7180 N Center Street
Mentor, OH 44060

MIKE ROSS CONSTRUCTION
INC
9309 Mercantile Drive
Mentor, OH 44060

Millersburg

MULLET CABINET INC
SR 241 7488
Millersburg, OH 44654

New Knoxville

HOGE LUMBER COMPANY
PO Box 159
New Knoxville, OH 45871

North Olmsted

BUILDERS WORLD INC
24355-57 Lorain Road
North Olmsted, OH 44070

North Ridgeville

BLANCHETTE'S A UNIQUE
KITCHEN & BATH CONCEPT
9425 Avon Belden Road SR 83
North Ridgeville, OH 44039

Painesville

LAKE COUNTY KITCHEN &
BATH CORP
1245 Mentor Ave
Painesville, OH 44077

Parma

FRIAR HOME IMPROVEMENT
3435 Brookpark Road
Parma, OH 44134

Parma Heights

LITT'S PLUMBING KITCHEN
& BATH GALLERY
6510 Pearl Road
Parma Heights, OH 44130

Plain City

THE MILLER CABINET
COMPANY INC
6217 Converse Huff Road
Plain City, OH 43064

Poland

E H DUNCAN THE BATH &
KITCHEN CENTER
108 S Main Street
Poland, OH 44514

Reynoldsburg

STOUT SALES INC
6320 E Main Street
Reynoldsburg, OH 43068

Rocky River

CLEVELAND TILE &
CABINET COMPANY
19560 Center Ridge Road
Rocky River, OH 44116

Salem

R H HOMEWORKS INC
850 W State Street
Salem, OH 44460

Steubenville

C B JOHNSON INC
621 Market Street
Steubenville, OH 43952

Tiffin

BUCKEYE PANEL PLY INC
2525 W Street Route 18 Box P
Tiffin, OH 44883

Toledo

ADVANCE KITCHEN & BATH,
INC
3520 Heatherdowns Boulevard
Toledo, OH 43614

DAVID HAHN FINE
KITCHENS
5345 Heatherdowns Boulevard
Toledo, OH 43614

KITCHENS BY JEROME INC
2138 N Reynolds Road
Toledo, OH 43615

LUMA BUILDING PRODUCTS
1607 Coining Drive
Toledo, OH 43612

MAINLINE KITCHEN & BATH
DESIGN CENTER
4730 W Bancroft Street
Toledo, OH 43615

VOLMAR'S KITCHEN & BATH
CENTER
45 W Alexis Road
Toledo, OH 43612

Uniontown

HOSTETLERS CUSTOM
KITCHENS
10233 Cleveland Avenue
Uniontown, OH 44685

Van Wert

KITCHENS INC
10098 W Ridge Road
Van Wert, OH 45891

Warren

MODERN HOME KITCHEN &
BATH CENTER INC
1002 W Market Street
Warren, OH 44481

Waverly

MILL'S PRIDE
423 Hopewell Road
Waverly, OH 45690

Westerville

DESIGNER KITCHENS &
BATHS INC
9020 Columbus Pike
US Route 23 N
Westerville, OH 43081

Willoughby Hills

FARALLI'S KITCHEN & BATH
DESIGN STUDIO
2804 S.O.M. Center Road
Willoughby Hills, OH 44094

Wooster

HORST CABINET & HOME
CENTER
840 E Milltown Road
Wooster, OH 44691

Zanesville

ZANESVILLE FABRICATORS
73 Shawnee Avenue
PO Box 1816
Zanesville, OH 43702-1816

OKLAHOMA

Bartlesville

JIM'S CUSTOM KITCHENS
720 NE Washington Boulevard
Bartlesville, OK 74006

Claremore

PIXLEY LUMBER COMPANY
715 West Will Rogers Boulevard
Box 308
Claremore, OK 74018

Oklahoma City

CLASSIC KITCHENS INC
548 E Memorial
Oklahoma City, OK 73114

KITCHEN SHOWCASE &
DESIGN CENTER
2761 N Country Club
Oklahoma City, OK 73116

Sand Springs

MORROW-GILL LUMBER
COMPANY
PO Box 666
Sand Springs, OK 74063

Tulsa

SILVER BATH & KITCHEN
SHOWROOM
6916 South Lewis
Tulsa, OK 74136

OREGON

Beaverton

NEIL KELLY DESIGNERS
REMODELERS
8101 S W Numbus Building 11
Beaverton, OR 97005

Bend

KITCHEN & BATH CONCEPTS
190 North East Irving Avenue
Bend, OR 97701

Central Point

THE KITCHEN AND BATH
CENTER
359 S Front
PO Box 3441
Central Point, OR 97502

Eugene

THE NEW KITCHEN
2817 Oak
Eugene, OR 97405

Hood River

HOODCRAFT CABINETMAKERS
INC
1450 Tucker Road
Hood River, OR 97031

Milwaukie

DICK BALLARD REMODELING
11923 SE McLoughlin Boulevard
Milwaukie, OR 97222

Portland

NEIL KELLY
804 N. Alberta
Portland, OR 97217

THE KITCHEN BROKER EAST
3354 S E Powell Boulevard
Portland, OR 97202

THE KITCHEN BROKER WEST
8685 S W Canyon Road
Portland, OR 97225

Salem

KITCHEN CENTER
3090 Lancaster Drive NE
Salem, OR 97305

Tigard

TOTAL BUILDING PRODUCTS
INC
PO Box 23337
Tigard, OR 97223

PENNSYLVANIA

Adamstown

MARTIN CUSTOM KITCHENS
PO Box 567
Adamstown, PA 19501

Allentown

BATHS WITH CLASS INC.
3101 Berger Street
Allentown, PA 18103

KITCHENS BY DESIGN INC
1802 Allen Street
Allentown, PA 18104

KITCHENS BY WIELAND INC
4210 Tilghman Street
Allentown, PA 18104

QUAKER MAID KITCHENS OF
ALLENTOWN
665 Union Boulevard
Allentown, PA 18103

Ambridge

DELUCA CABINET SHOP
998 Merchant Street
Ambridge, PA 15003

Annville

RM KITCHENS, INC.
Box #212-D, RD #1
Annville, PA 17003

Avonmore

DOVERSPIKE CUSTOM
KITCHEN
RD #1
Avonmore, PA 15618

Bala Cynwyd

MOSER CORPORATION
129 Montgomery Avenue
Bala Cynwyd, PA 19004

Bally

LONGACRE ELECTRICAL
SERVICE INC
602 Main Street
PO Box 159
Bally, PA 19503

Beaver Falls

KITCHEN CITY
415 7th Avenue
Beaver Falls, PA 15010

Bentleyville

SAN DELL KITCHENS INC
PO Box 613
Bentleyville, PA 15314

Beth Ayres

A A PERRY & SONS INC
2528 Huntingdon Pike
Beth Ayres, PA 19006

Bethel Park

BROOKSIDE LUMBER AND
SUPPLY COMPANY
500 Logan Road
PO Box 327
Bethel Park, PA 15102

CLARK CONSTRUCTION
COMPANY
3180 Industrial Boulevard
Bethel Park, PA 15102

Bethlehem

OBERHOLTZER KITCHENS
77 W Broad Street #1
Bethlehem, PA 18018

PHILIP J. STOFANAK INC
176 Nazareth Pike
Bethlehem, PA 18017

Bloomsburg

BOB JOHNSON COMPANY
1611 New Berwick Highway
Bloomsburg, PA 17815

Bristol

CAMEO KITCHENS
248 Mill Street
Bristol, PA 19007

DOMESTIC DESIGNS
2605 Durham Road
PO Box 702
Bristol, PA 19007

Broomall

MADSEN KITCHENS & BATHS
2901 Springfield Road
Broomall, PA 19008

REBER MC LEAN KITCHENS
2912 West Chester Pike
Broomall, PA 19008

Bryn Mawr

MAIN LINE CUSTOM
KITCHENS LTD
19 N Merion Avenue
Bryn Mawr, PA 19010

PETERSEN KITCHENS INC
592 Lancaster Avenue
Bryn Mawr, PA 19010

Buckingham

LIVING QUARTERS DESIGNS
INC
Routes 202 & 263
Buckingham Green POB 517
Buckingham, PA 18912

Butler

BOMBARA & SONS KITCHENS
INC
534 Fairground Hill
Butler, PA 16001

Camp Hill

LEGGETT INC.
1989 Hummel Avenue
Camp Hill, PA 17011

Canonsburg

ROBERT JOHNSTON KITCHEN
& BATH
156 Morganza Road
Canonsburg, PA 15317-1719

Carlisle

CARLISLE KITCHEN CENTER
1034 Harrisburg Pike
Carlisle, PA 17013

HOME FASHION CENTER INC
1150 Walnut Bottom Road
Carlisle, PA 17013

Carnegie

PATETE KITCHENS & BATHS
1105 Washington Avenue
Carnegie, PA 15106

Centre Hall

ASSOCIATED WOODCRAFT
RD 2 Box 9
Centre Hall, PA 16828

Chadds Ford

DESIGNER KITCHENS INC
P.O. Box 1335
Chadds Ford, PA 19317

Chambersburg

WADEL'S KITCHEN CENTER
1882 Wayne Road
Chambersburg, PA 17201

Chester

CHESTER WOODWORKING
INC
503 E 7th Street
Chester, PA 19013

Christiana

WINDING GLEN WOODCRAFT
INC
PO Box 40
28 South Bridge
Christiana, PA 17509

Clarks Summit

ABINGTON CABINETRY
PO Box 101
Clarks Summit, PA 18411

Conshohocken

TOWN & COUNTRY
KITCHENS & BATHS INC
123 West Ridge Pike
Po Box 309
Conshohocken, PA 19428

Corry

THE KITCHEN VILLAGE
12275 Route 6
Corry, PA 16407

Darby

JOSEPH J KELSO & SONS INC
1300 Main Street
Darby, PA 19023

Derry

GEORGE BUSH KITCHEN
CENTER INC
1309 West 4th Avenue
Derry, PA 15627

Doylestown

UNIQUE KITCHENS & BATHS
33 North Main Street
Doylestown, PA 18901

Dresher

D L POST INC
1400 Candlebrook Drive
Dresher, PA 19025

Drexel Hill

REGGIE'S CUSTOM
KITCHENS
3009 Garrett Road
Drexel Hill, PA 19026

Dunmore

TECHNIQUES IN WOOD
419 S Blakely Street
Dunmore, PA 18512-2234

Effort

EFFORT WOODCRAFT INC
Evergreen Hollow Road
PO Box 90
Effort, PA 18330

Ellwood City

DESIGNING INTERIORS
KITCHENS & BATH STUDIO
728 Lawrence Avenue
PO Box 810
Ellwood City, PA 16117

DOM'S HOME DESIGN
CENTER
739 Portersville Road
Ellwood City, PA 16117

Elysburg

KNOEBEL LUMBER-H.H.
KNOEBEL SONS INC
RD 1 Route 487
Elysburg, PA 17824

Erie

KITCHEN CONCEPTS BY
RICK CONSTANTINO
2402 State Street
Erie, PA 16503-1853

KITCHENS BY MEADE INC
2401 West 12th Street
Erie, PA 16505

ROBERTSON'S KITCHEN &
REMODELING SERVICE OF
ERIE
2630 W 12th Street PO Box 8112
Erie, PA 16505

Fairless Hills

HERITAGE DISTRIBUTORS
INC CUSTOM KITCHENS &
BATHS
413 Andover Road
Fairless Hills, PA 19030

Feasterville

WEILER'S APPLIANCE &
KITCHEN CENTER
350 Bustleton Pike
Feasterville, PA 19053

Frazer

COVENTRY KITCHENS INC
490 Lancaster Avenue
Frazer, PA 19355

Fredonia

BUCHANAN KITCHEN &
BATH BOUTIQUE
109 Second Street
Fredonia, PA 16124

Glen Rock

HALF PRICE BUILDING
SUPPLY
240 Main Street
Glen Rock, PA 17327

Glenolden

JOHN MURPHY'S BATH &
KITCHENS
327 North Chester Pike
Glenolden, PA 19036

Glenside

GAVALA KITCHENS & BATHS
233 Keswick Avenue
Glenside, PA 19038

Greensburg

MANOR HOUSE KITCHENS
INC
589 Rugh Street
Greensburg, PA 15601

PETERSONS CUSTOM
KITCHENS & BATH
BOUTIQUE
503 New Alexandria Road
Route 119N
Greensburg, PA 15601

QUALITY HOUSE INC
231 South Main Street
Office 211
Greensburg, PA 15601

Harleysville

I T LANDES & SON
INCORPORATION
247 Main Street
Harleysville, PA 19438

Harrisburg

KITCHEN & BATH
DISCOUNTERS
2424 East Bayberry Drive
Harrisburg, PA 17112

Hatfield

ESTATE OF GEORGE S
SNYDER
1700 Hatfield Valley Road
PO Box 130
Hatfield, PA 19440

Havertown

DESIGN CONCEPTS PLUS
CORP
18 E Eagle Road
Havertown, PA 19083

Hollidaysburg

HOLIDAY KITCHEN & BATH
INC
737 Logan Boulevard
Hollidaysburg, PA 16648

Holmes

MURPHY PLUMBING &
HEATING INC
2357 MacDade Boulevard
Holmes, PA 19043

Honesdale

DESIGNER KITCHENS BY
NARROWSBURG LUMBER CO.
RD 4 BOX 218
Honesdale, PA 18431

ROCHE SUPPLY
Route 191 S
PO Box 30
Honesdale, PA 18431

Huntingdon

ENDRES WOOD PLASTICS
INC
11th Susquehanna Avenue
Huntingdon, PA 16652

Jenkintown

CUSTER KITCHENS
204 Old York Road
Jenkintown, PA 19046

King of Prussia

QUEEN KITCHENS AND
BATHS
150 W DeKalb Pike
King of Prussia, PA 19406

THE CABINET WORKS
337 E De Kalb Pike
King of Prussia, PA 19406

Kingston

CABINET DESIGN
CONSULTANTS, INC.
44 Pierce Street
Kingston, PA 18704-4711

Kreamer

CHARLES ASSOCIATES INC
Route 522
Kreamer, PA 17833

Lancaster

BRUBAKER INC
1284 Rohrerstown Road
Lancaster, PA 17601

Lansdale

M W DONNELLY INC
37 W 2nd Street
Lansdale, PA 19446

Latrobe

MCBROOM'S HOME CENTER
RD 5 Route 30 E
Latrobe, PA 15650

THREE "K" CABINETS
125 Hillview Avenue
Latrobe, PA 15650

Lehigh Valley

MORRIS BLACK & SONS INC
984 Marcon Boulevard
PO Box 20570
Lehigh Valley, PA 18002

Lemoyne

ED LANK KITCHENS INC
313 Market Street
Lemoyne, PA 17043

EXCEL INTERIOR CONCEPTS
& CONSTRUCT
570 South 3rd Street
Lemoyne, PA 17043

Levittown

MC HALES KBA
2450 Trenton Road
Levittown, PA 19056

Lititz

MERVIN ZIMMERMAN INC
723 Rothsville Road
Lititz, PA 17543

Littlestown

KITCHENS BY TED RON
1480 White Hall Road
Littlestown, PA 17340

Lock Haven

HW RAYMOND COMPANY
INC
111 Woodward Avenue
PO Box 395
Lock Haven, PA 17745

Malvern

THE CREATIVE NOOK INC
Malvern Design Center
203 E King Street
Malvern, PA 19355

Mars

STIEHLER KITCHEN
CABINETS WINDOWS DOORS
PO Box 817 100 Irvine
Mars, PA 16046

Mc Murray

TOMORROW'S KITCHENS INC
1009 Waterdam Plaza Drive
Mc Murray, PA 15317

Mechanicsburg

ADVANCED KITCHENS &
BATHS
5222 E Trindle Road
Mechanicsburg, PA 17055

MOTHER HUBBARD'S
KITCHEN CENTER
5309 E Trindle Road
Mechanicsburg, PA 17055

Media

THE KITCHEN PEOPLE OF
CH MARSHALL INC
PO Box 196
Media, PA 19063

Mifflintown

JUNIATA KITCHENS INC
18 N Main Street
PO Box #131
Mifflintown, PA 17059

Milton

CLINGER LUMBER COMPANY
Arch Street at Locust Street
PO Box 315
Milton, PA 17847

Monaca

LUCCI KITCHEN CENTER
INC
1271 N Brodhead Road
Monaca, PA 15061

Mount Pleasant

VALLEY KITCHEN SALES &
SERVICE INC
555 Valley Lane
Mount Pleasant, PA 15666

N Huntingdon

CARUSO CABINET
MANUFACTURING INC
10809 Route 30
N Huntingdon, PA 15642

New Holland

HOMEWERKS
870 E Main Street
New Holland, PA 17557

QUALITY CUSTOM KITCHENS
125 Peters Road
PO Box 189
New Holland, PA 17557-0189

Olyphant

RIST CONSTRUCTION
KITCHEN & BATH DESIGN
GALLERY
1505 E Lackawana Avenue
Olyphant, PA 18447

Ottsville

BAUMHAUER'S KITCHEN-
BATH DESIGN CTR
Route 611 at 412
PO Box 100
Ottsville, PA 18942

Oxford

MARTIN W. SUMNER INC
121 S Third Street
Oxford, PA 19363

Paradise

PARADISE CUSTOM
KITCHENS
3333 Lincoln Highway E
PO Box 278
Paradise, PA 17562

Parkesburg

LANTZ CUSTOM KITCHENS
Lincoln Highway West
RD 1 Box 337 E
Parkesburg, PA 19365

Peckville

VALLEY CABINET CENTER
505 3rd Street
Peckville, PA 18452

Philadelphia

JOANNE HUDSON
ASSOCIATES LTD
2400 Market Street
Suite 310
Philadelphia, PA 19103

KULLA KITCHENS
7800 Rockwell Avenue
Philadelphia, PA 19111

MORTON BLOCK ASSOCIATES
DIVISION OF DESIGN
KITCHEN INC
2400 Market Street N S Suite 205
Philadelphia, PA 19103

OLDE TIME KITCHENS &
BATH RENOVATION
4333 Main Street
Philadelphia, PA 19127-1516

PLY GEMS KITCHEN AND
BATH CENTER
6948 Frankford Avenue
Philadelphia, PA 19135

Phoenixville

VALLEY FORGE KITCHEN &
BATH
1193 Valley Forge Road
Phoenixville, PA 19460

Pittsburgh

ANGELO ASSOCIATES INC
1125 Forest Way
Pittsburgh, PA 15236

BAXTER REMODELING
1345 Mc Laughlin Run Road
Pittsburgh, PA 15241

BILL GLIVIC KITCHENS
3845 Willow Avenue
Pittsburgh, PA 15234

EXCEL KITCHEN CENTER
1800 Fifth Avenue
Pittsburgh, PA 15219

KITCHEN & BATH CONCEPTS
OF PITTSBURGH
7901 Perry Highway N
Pittsburgh, PA 15237

KITCHEN DESIGNS OF
PITTSBURGH
2260 Babcock Boulevard
Pittsburgh, PA 15237

KITCHEN WORKS
1002 Greentree Road
Pittsburgh, PA 15220

MORRISON KITCHEN & BATH
INC
5121 Clairton Boulevard
Pittsburgh, PA 15236

RIVER CITY CONTRACTING
INC
390 Freeport Rd
Pittsburgh, PA 15238

STEIN'S CUSTOM KITCHENS
& BATHS
3559 Bigelow Boulevard
Pittsburgh, PA 15213

Quakertown

TRIANGLE BUILDING
CENTERS
472 California Road
Quakertown, PA 18951

Red Lion

KEENER KITCHEN
MANUFACTURING COMPANY
560 W Boundary Avenue
Red Lion, PA 17356

Robesonia

RICH CRAFT DESIGN
CENTER INC
157 W Penn Avenue
Robesonia, PA 19551

Sellersville

HICKS DISTRIBUTORS, INC.
1122 Old Route 309
Sellersville, PA 18960

Somerset

KITCHEN DESIGNS BY
MARSH
1024 N Center Avenue
Somerset, PA 15501

SDC BUILDING CENTER
S Edgewood Avenue
PO Box 755
Somerset, PA 15501

Southampton

SUBURBAN KITCHEN
COMPANY
650 Street Road
Southampton, PA 18966

Springfield

EASTERN KITCHENS INC
35 Baltimore Pike
Springfield, PA 19064

Springhouse

BLUE BELL KITCHENS
1104 Bethlehem Pike
Springhouse, PA 19477

State College

HOUSEWRIGHTS INC
2790 W College Avenue
Suite 1000
State College, PA 16801

Stockertown

PEOPLE'S BUILDING SUPPLY
COMPANY
201 East Center Street
Stockertown, PA 18083

Stroudsburg

BENNISON WOOD PRODUCTS
INC
RR 2 Box 2114
Stroudsburg, PA 18360

Tarrs

C & C BUILDING SUPPLIES
SUPERMARKET
PO Box C
Tarrs, PA 15688

Telford

CHELLEW KITCHENS INC
222 N Hamilton Street
Telford, PA 18969

Washington Crossing

KITCHEN CONCEPTS OF
WASHINGTON CROSSING
INCORPORATED
1107 Taylorsville Road
Washington Crossing, PA 18977

Wellsboro

PATTERSON LUMBER
COMPANY INC
41 45 Charleston Street
Wellsboro, PA 16901

West Chester

MUHLY KBA INC
7 North Five Points Road
West Chester, PA 19380

VANGUARD KITCHEN &
BATH DISTRIBUTOR
1105 W Chester Pike
West Chester, PA 19380

West Conshohocken

MAIN LINE DESIGN
539 Ford Steet
West Conshohocken, PA 19428

Wind Gap

KEEPSAKE KITCHENS INC
122 N Broadway
Wind Gap, PA 18091

York

BOB HARRY'S KITCHEN
CENTER INC
3602 E Market Street
York, PA 17402

THOMAS D. KLING INC
2474 N George Street
York, PA 17402

RHODE ISLAND

Barrington

BARRINGTON KITCHENS INC
496 Maple Avenue
Barrington, RI 02806

Cranston

COLE CABINET COMPANY
INC
530 Wellington Avenue
Cranston, RI 02910

East Greenwich

M & J KITCHEN SUPPLY CO.
INC.
461 Main Street
East Greenwich, RI 02818

East Providence

ALLMILMO DESIGN STUDIO
63 Warren Avenue
East Providence, RI 02914

Johnston

CREATIVE KITCHENS INC
2656 Hartford Avenue
Johnston, RI 02919

KITCHEN & BATH GALLERY
DIV OF AMERICAN BATH &
SUPPLY INC
1665 Hartford Avenue
Johnston, RI 02919

Pawtucket

DROLET KITCHEN CENTER
122 Benefit Street
Pawtucket, RI 02861

Smithfield

DOUGLAS LUMBER &
KITCHENS
Route 7 & Twin River Road
Smithfield, RI 02917

Tiverton

P D HUMPHREY COMPANY
590 Main Road
PO Box 39
Tiverton, RI 02878

Warwick

FERENDO KITCHEN & BATH
SUPPLY COMPANY
110 Jefferson Boulevard
Warwick, RI 02888-3854

GRENON KITCHENS BY
DESIGN
212 Greenwich Avenue
Warwick, RI 02886

West Warwick

RI KITCHEN & BATH INC
95 Manchester Street
West Warwick, RI 02893

Westerly

VIC MORGAN & SONS INC
42 Canal Street
Westerly, RI 02891

WESTERLY CABINET
COMPANY INC
95 Franklin Street
Westerly, RI 02891

Woonsocket

CABINET GALLERY LTD
520 Social Street
PO Box 336
Woonsocket, RI 02895

HOMESTEAD KITCHEN
CENTER
332 River Street
Woonsocket, RI 02895

SOUTH CAROLINA

Anderson

SMITH CABINET SHOP INC
817 Williamston Road
Anderson, SC 29621

Charleston

SIGNATURE KITCHENS
& BATHS OF CHARLE
CHARLESTON INC
1926 Savannah Highway
Charleston, SC 29407

Columbia

NORTHEAST KITCHEN AND
BATH
116 N Brickyard Road
Columbia, SC 29223

Florence

KITCHENS!
1811 Cherokee Road
Florence, SC 29501

Greenville

BUILDERWAY INC
PO Drawer 27107
Greenville, SC 29616

Greenwood

BATH & KITCHEN CENTER
1601 Calhoun Road
Greenwood, SC 29649

Mount Pleasant

KITCHEN CONCEPTS INC
1260 Ben Sawyer Boulevard
Mount Pleasant, SC 29464

KITCHENS BY DESIGN INC
Fairmount Shopping Center
1035 Johnnie Dodds Boulevard
Mount Pleasant, SC 29464

Mt Pleasant

JILCO CORP
1547-D Ben Sawyer Blvd
Mt Pleasant, SC 29464

Myrtle Beach

CAROLINA KITCHEN
DESIGNS
PO Box 3544
Myrtle Beach, SC 29578

KREATIVE KITCHENS INC
4923 Highway 17 South ByPass
Myrtle Beach, SC 29577

Sumter

REBECCA B. COMPTON
INTERIORS
227 Mason Croft Drive
PO Box 908
Sumter, SC 29151

West Columbia

CREGGER COMPANY INC
629 12th Street Ext
West Columbia, SC 29169

SOUTH DAKOTA

Sioux Falls

DEL'S QUALITYBUILT
CABINETS, INC.
RR2 Box 208
Sioux Falls, SD 57103

HANDY MAN SG SWENSON &
SONS
1103 South Cliff Avenue
PO Box 1201
Sioux Falls, SD 57105

Yankton

MIDWEST KITCHEN & BATH
200 Walnut
Yankton, SD 57078

TENNESSEE

Alcoa

WALKER'S SUPPLY
COMPANY
102 Lincoln Road
Alcoa, TN 37701

Chattanooga

ANA WOODWORKS
10 Meadow Street
Chattanooga, TN 37405

Columbia

R.D. VANN BATHS, KITCHEN
AND PLUMBING
1409 South Main Street
Columbia, TN 38401

Crossville

VILLAGE KITCHENS, BATHS
& INTERIORS
PO Box 1396
407 W Avenue S
Crossville, TN 38557

Johnson City

SUMMERS HARDWARE &
SUPPLY COMPANY
Buffalo & Ashe
PO Box 210
Johnson City, TN 37605

Knoxville

JOHN BERETTA TILE
COMPANY INC
2706 Sutherland Avenue
Knoxville, TN 37919

KITCHEN GALLERY
1034 Woodland Avenue
Knoxville, TN 37917

SIGNATURE KITCHENS &
BATHS INC
316 Nancy Lynn Lane
Suite 23B
Knoxville, TN 37919

STANDARD KITCHEN &
HEARTH
8003 Kingston Pike
Knoxville, TN 37919

Memphis

KEVIN WRIGHT INC
5690 Summer Avenue
Memphis, TN 38134

KITCHEN CONCEPTS INC
1725 Madison Avenue
Memphis, TN 38104

KITCHENS UNLIMITED INC
3550 Summer Avenue
Memphis, TN 38122

Nashville

DEAN'S KITCHEN CENTER
INC
1023-16th Avenue S
Nashville, TN 37212

HENRY KITCHENS & BATH
306 8th Avenue S
Nashville, TN 37203

HERMITAGE KITCHEN &
BATH GALLERY
531 Lafayette Street
Nashville, TN 37203

TONY HERRERA'S KITCHEN
AND BATH CONCEPTS, INC.
3307 Charlotte Avenue
Nashville, TN 37209

TEXAS

Amarillo

TROOK CABINETS INC
401 N Tyler
Amarillo, TX 79107

Austin

KITCHENS INC.
2712 Bee Cave Road Suite 122
Austin, TX 78746

THE URBAN KITCHEN INC
1617 W Koenig Lane
Austin, TX 78756

Corpus Christi

ADVANCE KITCHEN & BATH
4535 S Padre Island Drive
Corpus Christi, TX 78411

CABINET ALTERNATIVES INC
4341 S Alameda
Corpus Christi, TX 78412

Dallas

CABINETMASTERS INC
5400 E Mockingbird Lane
Suite # 115
Dallas, TX 75206

KITCHEN DESIGNS INC
14227 Inwood Road
Dallas, TX 75244

REDSTONE KITCHENS &
BATHS
9856 Plano Road
Suite 200
Dallas, TX 75238

El Paso

KITCHENS BY WILLIAMSON
& GELABERT
211 North Florence Street
El Paso, TX 79912

Fort Worth

DESIGN'S BY DROSTE
4818 Camp Bowie Boulevard
Fort Worth, TX 76107

KITCHEN PLANNERS
3300 Airport Freeway
Fort Worth, TX 76111-3930

Harlingen

PEACOCK'S CUSTOM
KITCHENS
801 E Grimes
PO Box 95
Harlingen, TX 78551

Houston

ALLMILMO DESIGN STUDIO
OF HOUSTON
1705 W Grey
Houston, TX 77019

FLECKWAY HOUSEWORKS
612 West Bough Lane
Houston, TX 77024

GAY FLY DESIGNER
KITCHENS AND BATHS
4200 Westheimer Suite 120
Houston, TX 77027

HALLMARK FASHION
KITCHENS INC
3413 E Greenridge Drive
Houston, TX 77057

KIRK CRAIG COMPANY, INC.
2431 Sunset Blvd.
Houston, TX 77005

KITCHEN & BATH CONCEPTS
2627 Westheimer
Houston, TX 77098

URBAN KITCHEN & BATHS
INC
3601 W Alabama
Houston, TX 77027

Humble

MEAD ASSOCIATES CUSTOM
KITCHENS & BATHS
203 N Houston Avenue
Humble, TX 77338

McAllen

DESIGN ALTERNATIVE
706 N McColl
PO Box 326
McAllen, TX 78505

San Angelo

S & P KITCHEN INTERIORS
3402 Arden Road
San Angelo, TX 76901

San Antonio

BELDON ROOFING &
REMODELING
PO Box 13380
San Antonio, TX 78213

CASA LINDA REMODELING
INC
4212 San Pedro
San Antonio, TX 78212-1836

Sherman

INSCAPE DESIGN STUDIO
2001 Skyline Dr Ste 165
Sherman, TX 75090-3165

Webster

BAY AREA KITCHENS &
BATHS
17306 Highway 3
Webster, TX 77598

UTAH

Draper

COTTONWOOD
12757 S State
Draper, UT 84020

Midvale

THE KITCHEN CENTER
7515 S State
Midvale, UT 84047

Salt Lake City

ARENDAL KITCHEN DESIGN
INC
1941 South 1100 East
Salt Lake City, UT 84106

CARLSON KITCHENS
2261 East 3300 South
Salt Lake City, UT 84109

CRAFTSMAN KITCHENS &
BATHS
2200 S Main
Salt Lake City, UT 84115

HALLMARK CABINETS INC
4851 Warehouse Road
Salt Lake City, UT 84118

THOMAS FRANK INTERIOR
DESIGNERS
3369 Highland Drive
Salt Lake City, UT 84106

West Jordon

WASATCH CABINET &
FURNITURE COMPANY INC
3412 West 8600 South
West Jordon, UT 84084

VERMONT

Barre

ALLEN LUMBER COMPANY
INC
502 N Main Street
Barre, VT 05641

CONCEPTS IN CABINETRY
393 N Main Street
Barre, VT 05641

Brattleboro

KITCHEN CONCEPTS
RFD 5 Box 228 Putney Road
Black Mountain Square
Brattleboro, VT 05301

Clarendon

KNIGHT CABINET DIVISION
NEW ENGLAND DESK CORP.
RR1 Box 231 1 N
Clarendon, VT 05759

Essex Junction

BOUCHARD PIERCE
127 Pearl Street
Essex Junction, VT 05452

WOOD STOCK KITCHENS &
BATHS
163 Pearl Street
Essex Junction, VT 05452

N Springfield

BIBENS HOME CENTER INC
PO Box 381
N Springfield, VT 05150

Rutland

MINTZER BROTHERS INC
247 West Street
PO Box 955
Rutland, VT 05702-0955

ROTELLA KITCHEN & BATH
DESIGN CENTER
325 W Street
PO Box 6309
Rutland, VT 05702

VIRGINIA

Annandale

REGENCY TILE & MARBLE
COMPANY
7106 Columbia Pike
Annandale, VA 22003

Arlington

CUSTOM CRAFTERS INC
6023 Wilson Boulevard
Arlington, VA 22205

VOELL CUSTOM KITCHENS
4788 Lee Highway
Arlington, VA 22207

Charlottesville

CRITZER'S CABINET
CREATIONS INC.
355 West Rio Road
Suite 104 Westpark Plaza
Charlottesville, VA 22901

Christiansburg

IDEAL CABINETS INC
103 N Franklin Street
PO Box 301
Christiansburg, VA 24073

Fairfax

COURTHOUSE KITCHENS &
BATHS DKB INC
9974 Main Street
Fairfax, VA 22031

RON WHEATON CUSTOM
KITCHENS INC
11244 Waples Mill Road
Suite J-2
Fairfax, VA 22030

Falls Church

CAMEO KITCHENS & BATHS,
INC.
7297 M Lee Highway
Falls Church, VA 22042

F A MCGONEGAL
1061 West Broad Street
Falls Church, VA 22046

Harrisonburg

COUNTRYSIDE KITCHENS
40 South Carlton Street
PO Box 1479
Harrisonburg, VA 22801-1479

INTERIORS R US
182-W 10 Neff Avenue
Harrisonburg, VA 22801

Lancaster

ABSOLUTE WOODWORKS,
LTD.
Rt. 3 Box 1200
Lancaster, VA 22503

Leesburg

J T HIRST & COMPANY INC
41 Catocin Circle S E
Leesburg, VA 22075

Lynchburg

TAYLOR BROTHERS INC
905 Graves Mill Road
PO Box 11198
Lynchburg, VA 24506

Manassas Park

CRAFTWOOD CABINET
COMPANY
9250 Venture Ct
Manassas Park, VA 22111-4804

McLean

KITCHEN GALLERY DESIGN
CENTER INC
6823A Tennyson Drive
McLean, VA 22101

Middleburg

MIDDLEBURG MILLWORK
INC
106 S Madison Street
PO Box 407
Middleburg, VA 22117

Midlothian

INNOVATIVE KITCHEN &
BATH INC
1119 Alverser Drive
Midlothian, VA 23113

Newington

B & F CERAMICS DESIGN
SHOWROOM INC
8900 Telegraph Road
PO Box 1544
Newington, VA 22122

PMC CONTRACTORS INC
7913 Kincannon Place
PO Box 1415
Newington, VA 22122

Newport News

VIRGINIA MAID KITCHENS
INC
737 Ble Crab Road
Suite 1A
Newport News, VA 23606

Norfolk

KITCHENS & BATHS
INTERNATIONAL INC
222 West 21st Street
Norfolk, VA 23517

Petersburg

DAVE'S CABINET SHOP INC
22504 Cox Road
Petersburg, VA 23803

Portsmouth

KITCHEN EMPORIUM
3411 High Street
Portsmouth, VA 23707

Radford

THE CABINET COMPANY
921 First Street
Radford, VA 24141

Richmond

CUSTOM KITCHENS INC
6412 Horsepen Road
Richmond, VA 23226

THE KITCHEN AND BATH
DESIGN SHOP LTD
2317 West Main Street
Richmond, VA 23220

Roanoke

CARTER'S CABINET SHOP OF
ROANOKE INC
2132 Shenandoah Valley
Roanoke, VA 24012

PERDUE CABINET SHOP INC
3806 Brambleton Avenue
Southwest
Roanoke, VA 24018

Springfield

COYLE & KLEPPINGER INC
7420 Fullerton Road
Suite 102
Springfield, VA 22153

Sterling

H & H CUSTOM CABINETS
22560 Glenn Drive
Suite 115
Sterling, VA 20164

Virginia Beach

DESIGNER KITCHENS &
BATHS INC
4143 Virginia Beach Boulevard
Virginia Beach, VA 23452

GREENWICH SUPPLY CORP
5789 Arrowhead Drive
PO Box 61737
Virginia Beach, VA 23462

WASHINGTON

Bellevue

INTERNATIONAL CABINETS
INC
13500 Bel Red Road # 7
Bellevue, WA 98005

RONNELLCO INC
1034 116th Avenue NE
Bellevue, WA 98005

Bellingham

SASH & DOOR
3801 Hannegan Road
Bellingham, WA 98226

Bremerton

BRISTOL KITCHENS
5889 State Highway 303 N E
Suite #101
Bremerton, WA 98310

Kennewick

BUILDERS LUMBER &
MILLWORK
3919 West Clearwater
Kennewick, WA 99336

Kirkland

KITCHENS FOR DREAM
HOMES
12024 Juanita Drive N E
Kirkland, WA 98034

THURMAN INDUSTRIES INC
PO Box 3359
Kirkland, WA 98083

Lynnwood

CREATIVE KITCHEN AND
BATH INC.
19503 56th Avenue West
Lynnwood, WA 98036

Oak Harbor

FINE WOOD CABINETS
645 W Oak Street
Oak Harbor, WA 98277

Olympia

CORNERSTONE KITCHEN &
BATH
3530 Martin Way
Unit 2
Olympia, WA 98506

LUMBERMEN'S BUILDING
CENTER
3773 Martin Way E
PO Box 3406
Olympia, WA 98503

Redmond

SHOWPLACE KITCHENS &
BATH
PO Box 955
Redmond, WA 98073

Seattle

KITCHEN & BATHS BY
BLODGETT
4515 44th SW
Seattle, WA 98116

KITCHEN DISTRIBUTING
COMPANY
PO Box 24979
Seattle, WA 98124

MORGAN ELECTRICAL &
PLUMBING SUPPLY
8055 15th NW
Seattle, WA 98117

NORTHWEST CABINETPAK
KITCHENS INC.
3809 Stoneway N
Seattle, WA 98103

O'NEILL PLUMBING
COMPANY
6056 California Avenue SW
Seattle, WA 98136

RAINER WOODWORKING OF
KING COMPANY INC
1011 NE 65th Street
Seattle, WA 98115

ROY RICKETTS INC
3417 1st Avenue S
Seattle, WA 98134

SEATTLE KITCHEN DESIGNS
10002 Holman Road NW
Seattle, WA 98177

Spokane

A-KITCHEN & BATH DESIGN
North 1202 Division
Spokane, WA 99202

Tacoma

CUSTOM DESIGN CABINETRY
INC
701 72nd Street E
Tacoma, WA 98404

DOUGLAS DESIGN CABINET
& REMODELING COMPANY
4804 Center Street
Tacoma, WA 98409

OLD TIME WOODWORK INC
2105 S
Tacoma, WA 98402

Vancouver

T SQUARE REMODELING
10600 N E 94th Avenue
Vancouver, WA 98662

Woodinville

BOLIG KITCHEN STUDIO
13110 N E 177th Place
Woodinville, WA 98072

WESTERN CABINET &
MILLWORK INC
PO Box 137
Woodinville, WA 98072

WEST VIRGINIA

Barboursville

WOODY'S KITCHENS BATHS
STUDIO
5841 Davis Creek Road
Barboursville, WV 25504

Bluefield

KITCHENS PLUS
1130 Bland Street
PO Box 1623
Bluefield, WV 24701

Clarksburg

MIKE'S KITCHEN & BATH
Rt. 3 Box 3A
Clarksburg, WV 26301

Huntington

CREATIVE KITCHENS PLUS
PO Box 2786
Huntington, WV 25727

Martinsburg

KITCHENS AND BATHS
UNLIMITED
2035 Shephardstown Road
Martinsburg, WV 25401

Morgantown

GENERAL GLASS COMPANY
INC
PO Box 618
Morgantown, WV 26507

Parkersburg

HARMON'S CABINET SHOP
1933 Ohio Avenue
Parkersburg, WV 26101

WISCONSIN

Appleton

KUSTOM KITCHENS & BATHS
741 W College Avenue
Appleton, WI 54914

STOCK LUMBER APPLETON
1924 W College Avenue
Appleton, WI 54914

Baraboo

THE MERCHANDISE CENTER
54066 Highway 12
Baraboo, WI 53913

Beloit

THE WITTE BARKER
SHOWROOM
419 E Grand Avenue
Beloit, WI 53511

Brookfield

S & K PUMP & PLUMBING
INC
20880 W Enterprise Avenue
Brookfield, WI 53045

THE KITCHEN CENTER
4060 N 128th Street
Brookfield, WI 53005

Burlington

COURTYARD CABINETRY
109 Dodge Street
Burlington, WI 53105

Cedarburg

CEDARBURG LUMBER
COMPANY INC
North 144 West 5800 Pioneer
Road
Cedarburg, WI 53012

Delavan

KUSTOM KITCHEN DESIGNS
1102 Ann Street
PO BOX 526
Delavan, WI 53115

Eau Claire

CHARLSON'S BUILDING &
DESIGNS
97 West Madison Street
Eau Claire, WI 54703

WIERSGALLA COMPANY, INC
1720 North Clairemont Avenue
Eau Claire, WI 54703

Fontana

VISNER BUILDERS INC.
223 Third Avenue
PO Box 327
Fontana, WI 53125

Franklin

KS REMODELERS INC
11113 W Forest Home Avenue
Franklin, WI 53132

Green Bay

SHOWCASE KITCHEN AND
BATH
2674 Packerland Drive
Green Bay, WI 54313

WILCO CABINET MAKERS
INC
1844 Sal Street
Green Bay, WI 54302

Janesville

J.C. BUILDERS, INC.
2505 Milton Avenue
Janesville, WI 53545

MARLING KITCHEN
DISTRIBUTOR
1236 Barberry Drive
Box 999
Janesville, WI 53547

Kenosha

NELSON MILLWORK &
SUPPLIES
6935 14th Avenue
Kenosha, WI 53143

Kohler

PAST BASKET
765 F Wood Lake Road
Kohler, WI 53044

Lacrosse

STOCK LUMBER
1735 Kramer Street
PO Box 2195
Lacrosse, WI 54603

Madison

KITCHENS OF DISTINCTION
6719 Seybold Road
Madison, WI 53719

MODERN KITCHEN SUPPLY
INC
3003 Kapec Road
P.O. Box 44189
Madison, WI 53744

THE LOST FINISH INC
6903 Mangrove Lane
Madison, WI 53713

Manitowoc

BRAUN BUILDING CENTER
3303 Menasha Avenue
Manitowoc, WI 54220

Marshfield

KABINET KONNECTION
1304 N Central
Marshfield, WI 54449

REIGEL PLUMBING &
HEATING INC
1701 S Galvin Avenue
Marshfield, WI 54449

THE CABINET STUDIO
107 North Central Avenue
Marshfield, WI 54449

Medford

CABINETRY BY DESIGN
N3452 Highway 13
Medford, WI 54451

Middleton

KITCHEN AND BATH
CONCEPTS
6333 University Avenue
Middleton, WI 53562

Milwaukee

A FILLINGER INC
6750 N 43rd Street
Milwaukee, WI 53209

BLAU BATH AND KITCHEN
INC
1320 S. 108th Street
Milwaukee, WI 53214-2437

BUILT-IN KITCHENS INC
7289 N Teutonia Avenue
Milwaukee, WI 53209

Mosinee

KITCHENS BY FEATHERSTONE
10606 Tesch Lane
Mosinee, WI 54455

Necedah

JAMES & JEAN SCHMIDT
W5175 Highway 21 E
Necedah, WI 54646

New Richmond

COUNTRYSIDE PLUMBING
AND HEATING INC
753 S Knowles Avenue
New Richmond, WI 54017

Oshkosh

FOX VALLEY KITCHEN
SPECIALISTS
2721 Oregon Street
Oshkosh, WI 54901

KITCHEN GALLERY
1804 Evans Street
Oshkosh, WI 54901

VAL CORPORATION OF
WISCONSIN/VALCO
2056 Dickinson Avenue
Oshkosh, WI 54904

Port Washington

THE STREFF SHOP INC
981 S Spring Street
Port Washington, WI 53074

Rhinelander

FRASIER'S SHOWPLACE
INTERIORS INC
130 North Brown Street
Rhinelander, WI 54501

Rio

SANDENWOOD PRODUCTS
W4265 Sampson Road
Rio, WI 53960

Saint Nazianz

REINDL PLUMBING &
HEATING INC
403 S Fourth Avenue
Saint Nazianz, WI 54232

Schofield

DE LISLE COMPANY INC
624 Moreland Avenue
Schofield, WI 54476

Sheboygan

CREATIVE KITCHEN
CONCEPTS
1504 Saint Clair Avenue
Sheboygan, WI 53081

K.B.A.E.R. DESIGN
SHOWROOM
1020 Michigan Avenue
Sheboygan, WI 53081

RICHARDSON LUMBER
COMPANY
822 North 14th Street
Sheboygan, WI 53081

THE KITCHEN AND THE
BATH BY KYM
1202 North 8th Street
Sheboygan, WI 53081

Slinger

HORSCH & MILLER INC
136 Kettle Moraine Drive North
Slinger, WI 53086

Stevens Point

CABINETS & MORE INC
2309 Division Street
Stevens Point, WI 54481

CHET'S PLUMBING &
HEATING INCORPORATION
5009 Coye Dr
Stevens Point, WI 54481

FALK CABINET SYSTEMS INC
2817 Post Road
Stevens Point, WI 54481

Stratford

STRATFORD BUILDING
SUPPLY INC
PO Box 146
Stratford, WI 54484

Twin Lakes

STAN'S LUMBER INC
PO Box 40
Twin Lakes, WI 53181

Waupaca

ARROW KITCHEN CABINET
COMPANY
N2331 Highway 22
Waupaca, WI 54981

Wauwatosa

KITCHEN DESIGN STUDIO
8932 W North Avenue
Wauwatosa, WI 53226

West Allis

CABINET WHOLESALERS OF
WISCONSIN INC
1013 S 108th
West Allis, WI 53214

DO IT YOURSELF
BATHROOM CENTER
6135 W Greenfield Avenue
West Allis, WI 53214

West Bend

COUNTRY CABINETRY OF
WEST BEND INC
2139 W Washington
West Bend, WI 53095

Wisconsin Rapid

QUALITY KITCHENS
1211 8th Street South
Wisconsin Rapid, WI 54494

WYOMING

Gillette

B & I SUPPLY INC
2808 Elder Avenue
Gillette, WY 82718

Kemmerer

BOB GREENE CABINETS
1434 7th W
Kemmerer, WY 83101

Bermuda

Hamilton

BERMUDA GLASS COMPANY
LTD
PO Box HM 1557
Hamilton, HMFX

EUROTILE BERMUDA
No 4 Mill's Creek Lane
Pembroke, HM 05
Hamilton,

British West Indies

Cayman Islands

MARBLE CRAFT LTD
Grand Cayman
PO Box 2155GT
Cayman Islands,

Canada

ALBERTA

Calgary

DENCA CABINETS
555-60 Avenue SE
Calgary, AB T2H 0R1

HEARTWOOD KITCHEN &
BATH DESIGN
1925 10th Avenue SW
Calgary, AB T3C 0K3

KITCHEN SHOWPLACE LTD
Bay 23 3220-5th Avenue NE
Calgary, AB T2A 5N1

THE KITCHEN CRAFT
CONNECTION
3404 25th Street NE
Calgary, AB T1Y 6C1

Edmonton

ARISTOCRAT KITCHENS
8716 51 Avenue
Edmonton, AB T6E 5E8

THE KITCHEN CRAFT
CONNECTION
2866 Calgary Trail South
Edmonton, AB T6J 6V7

THE KITCHEN STUDIO LTD.
4724 99 Street
Edmonton, AB T6E 4Y1

TOWNE & COUNTREE
KITCHENS LTD
17212-107 Avenue
Edmonton, AB T5S 1E9

Fort McMurray

MATT-N-AL WOODWORKING
(1986) LTD
215 MacDonald Crest
Fort McMurray, AB T9H 4B5

Sherwood Park

JEAN'S CUSTOM INTERIORS
AND DRAPERY
106 Redwood Court
Sherwood Park, AB T8A 1L1

BRITISH COLUMBIA

Aldergrove

KITCHEN KORNER
26929 Fraser Highway
Aldergrove, BC V4W 3E4

Burnaby

BURTINI DESIGNS
8533 Eastlake Drive
Burnaby, BC V5A 4T7

KITCHEN KORNER
106-3790 Canada Way
Burnaby, BC V5G 1G4

PREMIER INSTALLATIONS
LTD
4710 E Hastings Street
Burnaby, BC V5C 2K7

Courtenay

LIFETIME DESIGNS
#5 204 Island Highway
Courtenay, BC V9N 3P1

Kelowna

KELOWNA KITCHEN CENTRE
LTD
#30-2789 Highway 97N
Kelowna, BC V1X 4J8

Ladner

KINGSWOOD DESIGN
GALLERY
4989 Bridge Street
Ladner, BC V4K 2K3

Langley

LANGLEY WOODCRAFT LTD
5780-203 Street
Langley, BC V3A 1W3

N Vancouver

KSI (KITCHEN SPACE INC)
15 Chesterfield Place
N Vancouver, BC V7M 3K3

Nanaimo

KITCHENS UNLIMITED
2520 Bowen Road
Nanaimo, BC V9T 3L3

New Westminister

BAY DESIGN COMPANY INC
#7 720 6th Street
New Westminister, BC V3L 3C5

New Westminster

EUROPEAN KITCHEN
CABINETS LTD
143 E Columbia Street
New Westminster, BC V3L 3V9

North Vancouver

CO-ORDINATED KITCHENS
LTD
225 East First Street
North Vancouver, BC V7L 1B4

Richmond

SUNCREST CABINETS
12580 Vickers Way
Richmond, BC V6V 1H9

THUNDERBIRD HOME
CENTRES
2440 Viking Way
Richmond, BC V6V 1N2

Squamish

SUNCOAST KITCHEN & BATH
LTD.
#15-38918 Progress Way
Squamish, BC V0N 3G0

Terrace

TERRACE BUILDERS CENTRE
LTD
3207 Munroe Street
Terrace, BC V8G 3B3

Vancouver

CACHET KITCHEN
INTERIORS LTD
1080 Mainland Street
Suite 204
Vancouver, BC V6B 2T4

CONTOUR KITCHEN DESIGN
LTD
1128 Mainland Street
Vancouver, BC V6B 5L1

KINGS-WAY KITCHEN
CENTRE LTD
3195 Kingsway
Vancouver, BC V5R 5K2

LONETREE ENTERPRISES
LTD
2990 Artbutus Street
Vancouver, BC V6J 3Y9

PRESTIGE KITCHENS (1978)
LTD
6158 East Boulevard
Vancouver, BC V6M 3V6

SHOWCASE KITCHENS
1120 Mainland Street
Vancouver, BC V6B 2T9

Vernon

26TH STREET KITCHEN &
BATH LTD
5201 26th Street
Vernon, BC V1T 5G4

Victoria

ALPHA FINISHERS LTD
568 Alpha Street
Victoria, BC V8Z 1B2

ARTLINE KITCHENS LTD
1838 Oak Bay Avenue
Victoria, BC V8R 1C2

GRIFFIN DESIGN KITCHENS
714 View Street
Victoria, BC V8W 1J8

LAZLO ROSSINI DESIGN LTD
CENTRE
141 Skinner
Victoria, BC V9A 6X4

PACIFIC CABINETS LTD
3031 Jutland Road
Victoria, BC V8T 2T1

STARTEK BATHING SYSTEMS
LTD
491 A Burnside Road E
Victoria, BC V8T 2X3

West Vancouver

Y FRANKS APPLIANCES LTD
503 15th Street
West Vancouver, BC V7T 2S6

MANITOBA

Winnipeg

THE KITCHEN CRAFT
CONNECTION LTD
1500 Regent Avenue West
Winnipeg, MB R2C 3A8

NEW BRUNSWICK

Moncton

LAWSONS INC
194 Killam Drive
Moncton, NB E1C 3S4

ONTARIO

Barrie

BRADFORD PLANNED
KITCHENS
35 Cedar Pointe Drive
Barrie, ON L4N 5R7

Brampton

UNIQUE KITCHENS INC
25 Rutherford Road S
Brampton, ON L6W 3J3

Brockville

KITCHEN AND BATH
CENTRE R.V. SPRACKLIN &
SONS LTD
Highway 29 N
PO Box 1425
Brockville, ON K6V-5Y6

Burlington

GRAVELLE KITCHEN & BATH
STUDIO
4084 Fairview Street
Burlington, ON L7L 4Y8

O/B OPAL BATHS & DESIGN
4104 Fairview Street
Unit #3
Burlington, ON L7L 2A4

Cambridge

BECKERMANN KITCHEN
CONCEPTS
240 Holiday Inn Drive
Cambridge, ON N3C 3X4

Cornwall

MENARD RENOVATION
CENTER LTD
1100 Marleau Avenue
PO Box 38
Cornwall, ON K6H 5R9

Etobicoke

MARCON KITCHEN & BATH
STUDIO
4221 Dundas Street West
Etobicoke, ON M8X 1Y3

Gorrie

WATSON HOME HARDWARE
Highway 87
Gorrie, ON N0G 1X0

Hanover

HANOVER KITCHEN & BATH
GALLERY
655 10th Street
Hanover, ON M4N 1R9

Kingston

COUNTRYWIDE KITCHEN &
FLOORING INC
407 Counter
Suite 110
Kingston, ON K7K 6A9

WINSTON'S KITCHENS/A
DIVISION OF WINBET
MANAGEMENT CORP.
1469 Princess Street Unit 3A
Kingston, ON K7M 3E9

Kitchener

BECKERMANN EXQUISITE
KITCHENS
44 Otonabee Drive
Kitchener, ON N2C 1L6

GREAT CABINETS PLUS INC
1244 Victoria Street N
Kitchener, ON N2B 3C9

London

CARDINAL KITCHENS
LIMITED
215 Exeter Road
London, ON N6L 1A4

DEAN'S KITCHEN CENTRE
LTD
10 Techumseh Avenue West
Unit #3
London, ON N6J 1K6

Oakville

OAKVILLE KITCHEN CENTRE
599 Third Line
Oakville, ON L6L 4A8

Orillia

PENISTON INTERIORS (1980)
INC
300 West Street South
PO Box 186
Orillia, ON L3V 6J3

Oshawa

MILLWORK HOME CENTER
1279 Simcoe St. North
Oshawa, ON L1G 4X4

THE KITCHEN PLACE LTD
861 Simcoe Street South
Oshawa, ON L1H 4K8

Ottawa

DESIGN FIRST KITCHEN
INTERIORS
24 Clarence Street
Ottawa, ON K1N 5P3

MODULAR KITCHENS LTD
16 Pretoria
Ottawa, ON K1S 1W7

Owen Sound

BATH AND KITCHEN BY
ACTON'S
RR #5
Owen Sound, ON N4K SN7

Peterborough

BALL KITCHEN CENTRE INC
1135 Lansdowne Street W
Peterborough, ON K9J 7M2

WHITLER INDUSTRIES LTD
789 O'Brien Drive
PO Box 2018
Peterborough, ON K9J 7Y4

Pickering

BINNS DESIGNER KITCHENS
333 Kingston Road
Pickering, ON L1V 1A1

MONARCH KITCHEN
CENTRE DIVISION OF RJF
CUSTOM HOMES
1020 Brock Road Unit 6
Pickering, ON L1W 3H2

PROBILT KITCHENS LIMITED
1080 Brock Road Unit #8
Pickering, ON L1W 3H3

THE KITCHEN COURT
1755 Pickering Parkway
Unit 13
Pickering, ON L1V 6K5

Renfrew

DESLAURIER CUSTOM
CABINETS INC
405 Hall Avenue Unit 12
Renfrew, ON K7V 2S6

Sault Saint Marie

KITCHEN AND HOME
CENTRE
64 Industrial Park Crescent
Sault Saint Marie, ON P6B 5P2

Stittsville

BAILLARGEON CRAFTS &
CUSTOM WOODWORKING
LTD
1057 Carp Road
Stittsville, ON K2S 1B9

Stoneycreek

IMAGES KITCHEN & BATH
DESIGN INC
43 Teal Ave Unit 3
Stoneycreek, ON L8E 3B1

Thornhill

RAYWAL LTD
68 Green Lane
Thornhill, ON L3T 6K8

Toronto

DUNBAR & ROSS LIMITED
3425 Yonge Street
Toronto, ON M4N 2N1

KINGSWAY KITCHENS
4247 Dundas Street West
Toronto, ON M8X 1Y3

LAURENTIDE DESIGN LTD
945 Eglinton Avenue East
Toronto, ON M4G 4B5

THE ROBINSON GROUP
263 Davenport Road
Toronto, ON M5R 1J9

Waterloo

VANITY MART BATH &
KITCHEN CENTER
90 Frobisher Drive
Waterloo, ON N2V 2A1

Windsor

NAYLOR'S KITCHEN & BATH
3260 Jefferson Boulevard
Windsor, ON N8T 2W8

Woodstock

THE KITCHEN EMPORIUM
INC
54 Kent Street
Woodstock, ON N4S 6Y7

QUEBEC

Montreal

LES CUISINES INTERNATIONALES
G M B H
8100 Decarie
Montreal, PQ H4P 2S4

Costa Rica

San Jose

EUROMOBILIA SA
Apdo 7 1540
San Jose,

Dutch Caribbean

Aruba

PLUS TEN INC
162 Caya Betico Croes
Aruba,

APPROVED NKBA
CERTIFIED KITCHEN DESIGNER
and
CERTIFIED BATH DESIGNER
MEMBERS

ALABAMA

Ashland

Marie A Greeson CKD
WELLCRAFT CUSTOM
CABINETRY
PO Box 1090
Hwy 77S
Ashland, AL 36251

Birmingham

Robert F Gornati CKD
1833 Burning Tree Circle
Birmingham, AL 35226

Betsy Hedrick-Smith CKD
705 Morning Sun Drive
Birmingham, AL 35242

Charles R Lambert CKD
CABINET SYSTEMS SOUTH INC
410 Lorna Square
Birmingham, AL 35216

Mobile

Tracy M Hooper CKD
BY DESIGN
PO Box 8567
Mobile, AL 36689

Jeannine S McNeely CKD
5519 Richmond Road
Mobile, AL 36608

Wayne A Williams CKD
WILLIAMS & ASSOCIATES
PO Box 81486
Mobile, AL 36689-1486

Montgomery

Lorna Aho CKD
3557 Wareingwood Drive
Montgomery, AL 36109

Mary Dawson McCall CKD
REDLAND DESIGN
1067 B-1 Woodley Road
Montgomery, AL 36106

ALASKA

Anchorage

Elizabeth Breon CKD
REPALASKA
6345 Thurman Drive
Anchorage, AK 99502

Hollie M Ruocco CKD
7500 Beluga Circle
Anchorage, AK 99504

Hot Springs

Marion H Herman CKD
P.O. Box 1609
Hot Springs, AK 76102

ARIZONA

Catalina

Donald K Paugh CKD
P.O. Box 8521
Catalina, AZ 85738

Lake Havasu City

Barbara A Gialdini CKD
WOOD PRO
1980 San Juan Avenue
Lake Havasu City, AZ 86403

Duane M Leber CKD
CABINETS UNLIMITED INC
703 Enterprise Drive
Lake Havasu City, AZ 86403

Mesa

Rita L Phillips CKD
MASTERCRAFT KITCHENS
P.O. Box 40910
Mesa, AZ 85202

Tucson

Colleen B Langston CKD
ALBRITE BATH & KITCHEN
3640 E. Ft. Lowell
Tucson, AZ 85716

Jeffrey A. Miller CKD
DAVIS KITCHENS
3391 E Hemisphere Loop
Tucson, AZ 85706

Tamara S Newell CKD
ARIZONA DESIGNS KITCHENS
& BATHS
3444 North Dodge Boulevard
Tucson, AZ 85716-1456

Janice L O'Brien CKD
ARIZONA DESIGNS KITCHENS
& BATHS
3444 N Dodge Blvd.
Tucson, AZ 85716

Michael P O'Brien CKD
ARIZONA DESIGNS KITCHENS
& BATHS
3444 N Dodge Blvd.
Tucson, AZ 85716

ARKANSAS

Jonesboro

Vilas H Elder CKD
1304 Dupwe
Jonesboro, AR 72401

Little Rock

Kaye M Osburn CKD
LAING SALES & SERVICE INC
200 W Roosevelt Road
Little Rock, AR 72206

CALIFORNIA

Alameda

Andrea L Hite CKD
1047 Santa Clara Ave #2
Alameda, CA 94501

Richard B Stuart CKD
ALAMEDA DESIGN CENTER
2425 Clement Avenue
Alameda, CA 94501

Joy H Wilkins CKD
3000 Central Avenue
Alameda, CA 94501

Berkeley

Carolyn Sell CKD
1529 A Delaware Street
Berkeley, CA 94703

Bermuda Dunes

Mary Grace Satterfield CKD
CALIFORNIA CABINET
DISTRICT
42630 Maypen
Bermuda Dunes, CA 92201

Burbank

Barry Korn CKD
CALIFORNIA KITCHENS
2305 W Alameda Avenue
Burbank, CA 91506

Burlingame

Susan Bates CKD
SIGNATURE KITCHENS
344 Lorton Avenue
Burlingame, CA 94010

Camarillo

James E Franklin CKD
SHOWCASE KITCHENS &
BATHS
2650 Ventura Blvd. #101
Camarillo, CA 93010

Capitola

Marilyn A. Woods CKD
MARILYN A. WOODS DESIGN
ASSOCIATES
4650 Opal Street
Capitola, CA 95010-3129

Carmel

Barry Rowley CKD
SEGERS KITCHENS & BATH
26386 Carmel Rancho Lane
Carmel, CA 93923

CKD-Certified Kitchen Designer; CBD-Certified Bath Designer

Carmel Valley

Candace Ihlenfeldt CKD
15 Encina Dr.
Carmel Valley, CA 93924

Carpinteria

Holly G Thompson CKD
ARISTOKRAFT INC
5950 Via Real 1
Carpinteria, CA 93013

Cerriots

Donald R. Edgin CKD
EVANS KITCHEN & BATH
11304 South Street
Cerriots, CA 90701

Chowchilla

Sheron W Bailey CKD
DESIGN IDEAS
12390 Avenue 18 1/2 C
Chowchilla, CA 93610

City of Industry

Peter T Baccaro CKD
BACCARO KITCHEN & BATH
CENTRE
18605 E Gale Ave
Suite 110
City of Industry, CA 91748

Clovis

DeAnn Martin CKD
KITCHENS BY DEANN
77 Burgan Avenue
Clovis, CA 93611

Concord

Al Drachman CKD
1080 San Miguel
Concord, CA 94518

Costa Mesa

Cynthia Roberts McCue CKD
621 Shasta Lane
Costa Mesa, CA 92626

Shanda K Stephenson CKD
KITCHEN SPACES
2915 Redhill Avenue
Ste B105
Costa Mesa, CA 92626

El Cajon

Nancy Blandford CKD
BUILT IN DESIGN
475 Murray Drive
El Cajon, CA 92020

El Toro

Jerry E Hagler CKD
24701 Raymond Way, #111
El Toro, CA 92630

Encino

T C L Ginoux-Wemple CKD
KITCHEN SPECIALISTS OF
CALIFORNIA
5211 Yarmouth Avenue
Encino, CA 91316

David Lemkin CKD
5211 Yarmouth Avenue #15
Encino, CA 91316

Fair Oaks

Kathy A Maraglio CKD
ORIGINAL DESIGNS
10100 Fair Oaks Boulevard
Suite F
Fair Oaks, CA 95628

Foster City

Pamela Baird CKD
KB ASSOCIATES
1169 Chess Drive
Suite I
Foster City, CA 94404

Fountain Valley

Joan M Owen CKD
KITCHENS BY JONI
18384 Brookhurst
Fountain Valley, CA 92708

Fremont

William R Pease CKD
CUSTOM KITCHEN BATH
CENTER
40900 Fremont Boulevard
Fremont, CA 94538

Fresno

Louis A Hall CKD
RESIDENTIAL DESIGN
CONSULTANTS
363 W Stuart Avenue
Fresno, CA 93704

Fullerton

Carol E Lamkins CKD
3901 Madonna Drive
Fullerton, CA 92635

Glendora

Virginia Griffin CKD
KITCHENS ALPHA OMEGA
1247 E Sierra Madre Avenue
Glendora, CA 91740

Nellie Layne CKD
J.B. KITCHENS BATH DESIGN
631 E Arrow Highway Suite Q
Glendora, CA 91740

Grass Valley

Karen Austin CKD
CREATIVE KITCHENS AND
BATHS
13399 Capitol Drive
Grass Valley, CA 95945

Hayward

Patsy Zakian-Greenough CKD
P ZAKIAN-GREENOUGH
INTERIORS
513 Ethan Court
Hayward, CA 94544

Hillsborough

Stanley M Macey CKD
2031 Forest View Avenue
Hillsborough, CA 94010

Huntington Beach

Richard B Pulsifer CKD
8342 Munster
Huntington Beach, CA 92647

Irvine

G Townsend Bradner CKD
13831 Margene Circle
Irvine, CA 92720

Ernest Roger Sanchez CKD
31 Bear Paw #34D
Irvine, CA 92714

Shanda K Stephenson CKD
THE JM COMPANY KITCHEN
& BATH SHOWROOM
15333 Culver Drive
Suite 220
Irvine, CA 92714

La Jolla

Ellen M Becker CKD
DESIGN STUDIO WEST
7422-24 Girard Avenue
La Jolla, CA 92037

Leslie A Cohen CKD
DESIGN STUDIO WEST
7422-24 Girard Avenue
La Jolla, CA 92037

Jacquin D Kranz CKD
DESIGN STUDIO WEST
7422-24 Girard Avenue
La Jolla, CA 92037

Timothy L Woods CKD
DESIGN STUDIO WEST
7422-24 Girard Avenue
La Jolla, CA 92037

La Mesa

John DeLuca CKD
KITCHENS BY DELUCA
7872 LaMesa Boulevard
La Mesa, CA 91941

Gary D Heidman CKD
KITCHENS PLUS
7943 University Avenue
La Mesa, CA 91941

Laguna Beach

Karen S Costello CKD
SKYLINE KITCHENS & BATHS
31671 South Pacific Coast Highway
Laguna Beach, CA 92677

Lake Forest

Annabelle Marshall CKD
VALLEY KITCHENS
22541 Aspan Suite A
Lake Forest, CA 92630

Lawndale

John H Caveney CKD
JHC KITCHEN & BATH CO
4734 W 167th Street
Lawndale, CA 90260

Long Beach

Edythe I Rabon CKD
KITCHENS BY THE SEA
4403 Los Coyotes Diagonal
Long Beach, CA 90815

Loomis

James M Liston CKD
4965 Del Road
Loomis, CA 95650

Los Alamitos

George D Alemshah CKD
GEORGE ALEMSHAH CKD ISID
10900 Los Alamitos Boulevard
Suite 216
Los Alamitos, CA 90720

Los Altos

Ilona D Lindauer CKD
ILONA KITCHEN & BATH
385 Cherry Avenue
Los Altos, CA 94022

Los Angeles

Dennis J Avram CKD
JOHN W. AVRAM AND
ASSOCIATES
1328 South Santa Fe Avenue
Los Angeles, CA 90021

John W Avram CKD
JOHN W. AVRAM AND
ASSOCIATES
1328 South Santa Fe Avenue
Los Angeles, CA 90021

William T Boyle CKD
DESIGN STUDIO WEST
8656 Sunset Boulevard
Los Angeles, CA 90069

Neil R Cooper CKD
COOPER-PACIFIC KITCHENS
INC
8687 Melrose Avenue
Suite G #776
Los Angeles, CA 90069-5701

Laurence I Geisser CKD
CLEVELAND WRECKING
COMPANY
3170 E Washington Boulevard
Los Angeles, CA 90023

Michael Goldberg CKD
BRENTWOOD KITCHENS
2378 Westwood Boulevard
Los Angeles, CA 90064

Randall E. Langston CKD
JOHN W. AVRAM AND
ASSOCIATES
1328 South Santa Fe Avenue
Los Angeles, CA 90021

Todd L Mead CKD
THE KITCHEN SPECIALIST
10643 W Pico Boulevard
Los Angeles, CA 90064

John A Pace CKD
8700 Burton Way #103
Los Angeles, CA 90048

CKD-Certified Kitchen Designer; CBD-Certified Bath Designer

Donald E Silvers CKD
KITCHENS & OTHER
ENVIRONMENTS BY DES
155 S Orange Drive
Los Angeles, CA 90036

Rick A Skalak CKD
SHOWCASE KITCHENS
2317 Westwood Boulevard
Los Angeles, CA 90064

Los Gatos

Cheryl A Little CKD
CHERYL KITCHEN DESIGN
302 Almendra Avenue
Los Gatos, CA 95030

Menlo Park

Mary Jo Camp CKD
GREAT KITCHENS
842 Santa Cruz Avenue
Menlo Park, CA 94025

Iris F Harrell CKD
HARRELL REMODELING INC
108 Gilbert Avenue
Menlo Park, CA 94025

Mill Valley

Maureen Moulton-Kaye CKD
376 Marin Avenue
Mill Valley, CA 94941

Monterey

Nancy E Becker CKD
G.O. REMODEL STORE
1105 Del Monte Avenue
Monterey, CA 93940

Arthur M Brost CKD
M & S BUILDING SUPPLY
2456 Del Monte Avenue
Monterey, CA 93940

Newport Beach

Gary E White CKD
KITCHEN & BATH DESIGN
1000 Bristol Street N 21
Newport Beach, CA 92660

Oakland

Carlene Anderson CKD
KITCHEN DESIGN INC
5818 Balboa Drive
Oakland, CA 94611

Fred M Brasch CKD
SUPERIOR HOME REMODELING
4700 Telegraph Avenue
Oakland, CA 94609

Tim W Jollymore CKD
FINISH DESIGN
9120 Skyline Boulevard
Oakland, CA 94611

Maureen O'Brien-Morsch CKD
CUSTOM KITCHENS BY JOHN
WILKINS INC
6624 Telegraph Avenue
Oakland, CA 94609

Orange

James B Galloway CKD
CAREFREE KITCHENS INC
453 N Anaheim Boulevard
Orange, CA 92668

Theresa M Matusek CKD
KITCHENEERING
514 W. Katella Ave.
Orange, CA 92667

Orinda

Sharon R Buffa CKD
PREMIER KITCHENS
2 Theater Square 140
Orinda, CA 94563

Dagmar T Thiel CKD
KITCHEN AND BATH DESIGN
2 Theater Square
Suite 307
Orinda, CA 94563

Oxnard

Terry Breese CKD
235 Central Avenue
Oxnard Palm Desert, CA 93030

Palm Desert

Carrie Lynn Wallace CKD
KITCHENS BY LYNN
44-489 Town Center Way
S-D #254
Palm Desert, CA 92260

Leo H Kelsey CKD
44489 Town Center Way
Suite D-203
Palm Desert, CA 92260

Palo Alto

Kathleen Claudon CKD
KM DESIGNS
1220 Wilson Street
Palo Alto, CA 94301-7453

Steven C Mohr CKD
810 College Ave
Palo Alto, CA 94306

Michelle R Seabrook CKD
THE DESIGN STUDIO OF
MICHELE R. SEABROOK
3747 Ladonna Avenue
Palo Alto, CA 94306

Pasadena

Birgit Zempel CKD
KOKKEN-SCANDINAVIAN
KITCHEN DESIGN
54 W Green Street
Pasadena, CA 91105

Pinole

Gary A Taylor CKD
2810 Wright Avenue
Pinole, CA 94564

Pleasant Hill

Margie Little CKD
INDEPENDENT KITCHEN &
BATH DESIGNER
1432 Stonehedge Drive
Pleasant Hill , CA 94523

Patricia K Stenger CKD
STENGER DESIGN ASSOCIATES
443 Coleman Court
Pleasant Hill , CA 94523

Rancho Lacosta

Peter M Del Vecchio CKD
7720-B El Camino Real #178
Rancho Lacosta, CA 92009

Rancho Palos Verdes

Suzanne J Karbach CKD
KARBACH KITCHENS &
INTERIORS
5935 Flambeau Road
Rancho Palos Verdes, CA 90274

Redding

Shirley E Anderson CKD
KITCHENS & BATHS BY
SHIRLEY
1301 Court Street
Redding, CA 96001

Redondo Beach

Jacqueline Balint CKD
THE KITCHEN COLLECTION
241 Avenida Del Norte
Redondo Beach, CA 90277

S. San Francisco

Peggy Deras CKD
548 Theresa Drive
S. San Francisco, CA 94080

Ernest Weidner CKD
QUALITY KITCHEN CABINETS
INC
161 El Camino Real
S. San Francisco, CA 94080

Sacramento

Joseph W Aievoli CKD
2306 Loma Vista Drive
Sacramento, CA 95825

Mark Cohn CKD
KUSTOM KITCHENS DESIGN
CONSULTANT
1220 "X" Street
Sacramento, CA 95818

Molly J. Korb CKD
MK DESIGNS
PO Box 216295
Sacramento, CA 95821

San Diego

Dianne L Harsch CKD
EUROPEAN KITCHEN & BATH
6440 Lusk Boulevard
San Diego, CA 92121

Peter M. Lauterbach CKD
HOME DEPOT
6611 University Ave
San Diego, CA 92115

Cynthia L Radcliff CKD
RADCLIFF ASSOCIATES
PO Box 17332
San Diego, CA 92117

San Francisco

Karen L Brown CKD
MASCO CORP
1355 Market Street #236
San Francisco, CA 94103

Ernie J Giramonti CKD
235 Bayshore Drive
San Francisco, CA 94124

Carolyn S Mobley CKD
GILMAN SCREENS &
KITCHENS
228 Bayshore Boulevard
San Francisco, CA 94124

Kathleen A St. Clair CKD
KEN TOPPING HOME
IMPROVEMENTS
3101 Vicente Street
San Francisco, CA 94116

San Jose

Molly Anne Conroy CKD
CONROY & CONROY
1887 Lincoln Avenue
San Jose, CA 95125

San Leandro

Jennie Gisslow CKD
DESIGN SOURCE KITCHENS &
BATHS
1181 Begier Avenue
San Leandro, CA 94577

Brian Peck CKD
SOMERSET REMODELING INC
15255 Hesperian Boulevard
San Leandro, CA 94578

San Leonardo

Marilyn S Gray CKD
GRAY & GRAY
16608 Kildare Road
San Leonardo, CA 94578

San Rafaelo

Arthur Krikor Halajian CKD
KITCHENS & MORE
4178 Redwood Highway
San Rafaelo, CA 94903

Santa Barbara

Joseph E Madden CKD
SANTA BARBARA KITCHENS
710 N Milpas Street
Santa Barbara, CA 93103

Susan Thielmann-Bigelow CKD
THIELMANN'S KITCHENS AND
BATHS
208 Cottage Grove Avenue
Santa Barbara, CA 93103 93101

Santa Clara

Lila Levinson CKD
ACCENT ON DESIGN
2075 De La Cruz Blvd. #101
Santa Clara, CA 95050

CKD-Certified Kitchen Designer; CBD-Certified Bath Designer

Santa Monica

Paul C Bailly CKD
KITCHEN DESIGN STUDIO
1349 Franklin Street
Santa Monica, CA 90404

Michael B Baugus CKD
BAY CITIES KITCHENS/BATHS/
APPLIANCES
1412 14th Street
Santa Monica, CA 90404

William E. Peterson CKD
BAY CITIES KITCHENS/BATHS/
APPLIANCES
1412 14th Street
Santa Monica, CA 90404

Santa Paula

David Johnson CKD
933 Cliff Drive
Santa Paula, CA 93060

Santa Rosa

Nancy Lind Cooper CKD
COOPER KITCHENS INC
1133 Sunnyslope Drive
Santa Rosa, CA 95404

Santee

Michael S De Luca CKD
MICHAEL DE LUCA AND
ASSOCIATES
11355 Canyon Park Drive
Santee, CA 92071

Tustin

Ayeshah T Morin CKD
DESIGNER KITCHENS INC
17300 E 17th St Ste A
Tustin, CA 92680

Vacaville

Susan S Holbrook CKD
356 Shannon Drive
Vacaville, CA 95688

W Sacramento

John B Curtis CKD
CURTIS & COMPANY
1152 Fernwood Street
W Sacramento, CA 95691

Walnut Creek

Sharon L Hopkins CKD
DESIGN PRO
2400 Olympic Blvd. Suite 3-193
Walnut Creek, CA 94595

Yorba Linda

Patricia J Otto CKD
5081 West Knoll
Yorba Linda, CA 92686

Phillip H Stidham CKD
5570 Camino Dorado
Yorba Linda, CA 92687

COLORADO

Aurora

Angela S Lawrence CKD
FIRST CLASS KITCHENS AND
DESIGN
1917 Hanover Street
Aurora, CO 80010

Robert R Oxley CKD
ROBERT OXLEY TRAINING &
CONSULTING
401 S Kalispell Way
Suite #107
Aurora, CO 80017

Kenneth W. Smith CKD
NKBA TRAINING/CHAPTER
RELATIONS MGR
1671 Dunkirk Court
Aurora, CO 80011

Boulder

Karen Bryant CKD
KITCHEN PLANNERS
11627 28TH
Boulder, CO 80501

Diane M Ebeling CKD
THE THURSTON KITCHEN AND
BATH BY THURSTON, INC.
5785 Arapahoe Ave.
Boulder, CO 80303

Seth T Fordham CKD
5785 Arapahoe Drive
Boulder, CO 80303

Barbara J. Gibbons CKD
4619 Field Court
Boulder, CO 80301-3904

Kevin A Jean CKD
KITCHEN PLANNERS
1627 28th Street
Boulder, CO 80301

Colorado Springs

Ed Medran CKD
KITCHEN DESIGN SPECIALISTS
218 East Monument
Colorado Springs, CO 80903

Carl E Varley CKD
KITCHEN'S AT THE DEPOT
76 S Sierra Madre St #B
PO Box 489
Colorado Springs, CO 80901

Denver

Joan M Adducci CKD
BRADLEY DISTRIBUTORS, INC
3850 "A" Nome Street
Denver, CO 80239

Cynthia R Buechler CKD
ARTISTIC FABRICATIONS INC
2449 South Broadway
Denver, CO 80210

Joyce J Combs CKD
KITCHEN CONNECTION
639 Kalamath Street
Denver, CO 80204

Bonnie DeGabain CKD
THE THURSTON KITCHEN AND
BATH BY THURSTON, INC.
2920 E 6th Avenue
Denver, CO 80206

Catherine Dulacki CKD
WM OHS SHOWROOMS INC
2900 E 6th Avenue
Denver, CO 80226

Albert B Fink CKD
1021 Steele Street
Denver, CO 80206

Helen D Francis CKD
CARUSO KITCHEN DESIGN
3496 W. 32nd Ave
Denver, CO 80211

Edward Hanley CKD
EDWARD HANLEY & COMPANY
1448 Oneida Street
Denver, CO 80220

Thomas J Kesicki CKD
KITCHEN GALLERY LTD
66 S Logan Street
Denver, CO 80209

Cynthia Leonard CKD
THE THURSTON KITCHEN AND
BATH BY THURSTON, INC.
2920 E 6th Avenue
Denver, CO 80206

Pamela L Ludwig CKD
3060 W. 39th
Denver, CO 80211

Linda J McLean CKD
WM OHS SHOWROOMS INC
2900 E 6th Avenue
Denver, CO 80226

Lynne W McMurtry CKD
WM OHS SHOWROOMS INC
2900 E 6th Avenue
Denver, CO 80226

Julie A Mills CKD
TIMBERLINE KITCHEN & BATH
1842 South Broadway
Denver, CO 80210

Sharon Overstake CKD
WM OHS SHOWROOMS INC
2900 E 6th Avenue
Denver, CO 80226

Mary Lynn Rockwell CKD
WM OHS SHOWROOMS INC
2900 E 6th Avenue
Denver, CO 80226

Klaudia H Spivey Norlen CKD
DESIGN TIMES INC
3504 E. 12th Avenue
Denver, CO 80206

Erie

Dan R. Lunsford CKD
L SQUARED ENTERPRISES
PO Box 397
4121 Weld City RD 3
Erie, CO 80516

Estes Park

Kathryn A Moyse CKD
P.O. Box 5197
Estes Park, CO 80517-5197

Fraser

Lynne Hada Anderson CKD
LINTERIORS
Box 1019
Fraser, CO 80442

Glenwood Springs

Robin M Slattery CKD
MODERN KITCHEN CENTER
5050 Road 154
Glenwood Springs, CO 81602

Golden

Ed Winger CKD
25318 Foothills Drive, North
Golden, CO 80401-9171

Lafayette

Madelin Nelson CKD
TECHNI-KITCHEN & BATH
DESIGN
613 E Emma Street
Lafayette, CO 80026

Lakewood

Norman L Van Nattan CKD
KITCHENS FOR COLORADO INC
6381 W Alameda Avenue
Lakewood, CO 80226

Littleton

Beverly G Adams CKD
KITCHEN DISTRIBUTORS INC
1309 W Littleton Boulevard
Littleton, CO 80120

Mikel Altenhofen CKD
KITCHEN DISTRIBUTORS INC
1309 W Littleton Boulevard
Littleton, CO 80120

E.J. Jerry Forwood CKD
KITCHEN DISTRIBUTORS INC
1309 W Littleton Boulevard
Littleton, CO 80120

Esther M Hartman CKD
KITCHEN DISTRIBUTORS INC
1309 W Littleton Boulevard
Littleton, CO 80120

Thomas Hartman CKD
KITCHEN DISTRIBUTORS INC
1309 W Littleton Boulevard
Littleton, CO 80120

Diane D Johnson CKD
5504 South Hoyt Street
Littleton, CO 80123

Sharon Reznicek Lamb CKD
4691 W. Lake Circle, North
Littleton, CO 80123-6772

Jo Ann D Roach CKD
7449 S. Clarkson Circle
Littleton, CO 80122

Westminster

Charles Martin CKD
CHARLES MARTIN &
ASSOCIATES
7931 Bradburn Boulevard
Westminster, CO 80030

CONNECTICUT

Bloomfield

Peggy Stanwood CKD
21 Stuart Drive
Bloomfield, CT 06002

Bristol

Genard E Dolan CKD
A & L ASSOCIATES
10 Carpenter Avenue
Bristol, CT 06010

Brookfield

Mary Jo Peterson CKD
3 Sunset Cove
Brookfield, CT 06804

Cos Cob

Vincent Cappello CKD
PUTNAM KITCHENS INC
406 E Putnam Avenue
Cos Cob, CT 06807

Danbury

Terry Scarborough CKD
ETHAN ALLEN INC
Gallery Ethan Allen Drive
Danbury, CT 06811

Darien

Leona S Hess CKD
RING'S END INC
181 West Avenue
PO Box 1066
Darien, CT 06820

Farmington

Lorey A Cavanaugh CKD
KITCHEN & BATH DESIGN
CONSULTANTS
PO Box 894
Farmington, CT 06034

Harwinton

Cheryl Carpentier CKD
PO Box 71
Harwinton, CT 06791-0071

Huntington

Ramona Eldridge CKD
DESIGN CONCEPTS INC
314 Aspetuck Village
Huntington, CT 06484

Henry Jacoby CKD
DESIGN CONCEPTS INC
314 Aspetuck Village
Huntington, CT 06484

Jenett City

Kevin J Johnson CKD
A D TRIPP COMPANY
6 Mathewson Street
Jenett City, CT 06351

Madison

Laurie Eriksson CKD
KITCHENS BY GEDNEY INC
84 Bradley Road
Madison, CT 06443

Curtis D Gedney CKD
KITCHENS BY GEDNEY INC
84 Bradley Road
Madison, CT 06443

Richard R Gedney CKD
KITCHENS BY GEDNEY INC
84 Bradley Road
Madison, CT 06443

Richard R. Gedney CKD
KITCHENS BY GEDNEY INC
84 Bradley Road
Madison, CT 06443

Charles E Karas CKD
73 Soundview Avenue
Madison, CT 06443-2709

Manchester

Donald T Davis CKD
694 Keeney Street
Manchester, CT 06040

Monroe

Ingrid Becker CKD
204 Windgate Circle #F
Monroe, CT 06468

Mark A Rutter CKD
MARC DESIGN & REMODELING
PO Box 200
Monroe, CT 06488-0200

Morris

Robert L. Gelormino CKD
94 Alain White Road
Morris, CT 06763

New Canaan

Tom Bailey CKD
THE KITCHEN DESIGN STUDIO
21 South Avenue
New Canaan, CT 06840

New London

Douglas Getty CKD
GENERAL WOODCRAFT
531 Broad Street
New London, CT 06320

New Milford

Cynthia P Beck CKD
RINGS' END INC
140 Danbury Road
New Milford, CT 06776

Old Lyme

George D Crane CKD
PAUL DOLAN COMPANY INC
Old Lyme Shopping Center
P.O. Box 873
Old Lyme, CT 06371-0873

Old Saybrook

Sue McAlexander CKD
3 Wild Apple Lane
Old Saybrook, CT 06475

Prospect

Thomas D Biron CKD
CASEWORK DESIGNS
10 Roy Mountain Road
Prospect, CT 06712

Putnam

Frederick Kress CKD
KRESLINE KITCHENS
PO Box 389
Putnam, CT 06260

Sherman

Paul Levine CKD
4 Deer Hill
Sherman, CT 06784

Stamford

Sarah A Blank CKD
KITCHENS BY DEANE
1267 E Main Street
Stamford, CT 06902

Alice M Hayes CKD
KITCHENS BY DEANE
1267 E Main Street
Stamford, CT 06902

Wendy Johnson CKD
KITCHENS BY DEANE
1267 E Main Street
Stamford, CT 06902

Joanne M Stage CKD
KITCHENS BY DEANE
1267 E Main Street
Stamford, CT 06902

Kelly Loyd Stewart CKD
KITCHENS BY DEANE
1267 E Main Street
Stamford, CT 06902

Torrington

Charles W Olsen CKD
DUCCI KITCHENS
379 Goshen Road
Torrington, CT 06790

Gail Olsen CKD
DUCCI KITCHENS
379 Goshen Road
Torrington, CT 06790

Bruno Pasqualucci CKD
DUCCI KITCHENS
379 Goshen Road
Torrington, CT 06790

Peter F Roth CKD
DUCCI KITCHENS
379 Goshen Road
Torrington, CT 06790

W Hartford

James D Tate CKD
SIGNATURE INC
50 Ridgebrook Drive
W Hartford, CT 06107

Waterbury

Timothy J Bates CKD
LES-CARE KITCHENS INC
One Les-Care Drive
Waterbury, CT 06705

Susan D Drake CKD
176 Chipper Road
Waterbury, CT 06704-1101

West Hartford

Kenneth W Peterson CKD
64 High Farms Road
West Hartford, CT 06110

West Haven

Stephanie Martin CKD
SPEAR NEWMAN
55 Railroad Ave
West Haven, CT

Westbrook

Joseph B Ciccarello CKD
COVENANT KITCHENS &
BATHS
1871 Boston Post Road
Westbrook, CT 06498

DELAWARE

Seaford

Michael R Griffith CKD
CREATIVE KITCHENS AND
FLOORS INC
8 N Arch Street
Seaford, DE 19973

Wilmington

Steven J Campbell CKD
BATH/KITCHEN & TILE CENTER
P.O. Box 2680
103 Greenbank Road
Wilmington, DE 19808

Jeanette A Compton CKD
BATH KITCHEN & TILE CENTER
103 Greenbank Road
Wilmington, DE 19808

Pietro A. Giorgi CKD
GIORGI KITCHENS INC
218 Philadelphia Pike
Penny Hill
Wilmington, DE 19809

Lisa H Greene CKD
207 Potomac Road
Wilmington, DE 19803-3120

Mark J Pyle CKD
BATH KITCHEN & TILE CENTER
103 Greenbank Road
Wilmington, DE 19808

DISTRICT OF
COLUMBIA

Washington

Allan R Dresner CKD
A R DRESNER, CKD, MARKET-
ING CONSULT
7026 Wyndale Street N W
Washington, DC 20015-1429

Nancy R Meyer CKD
4545 Connecticut Avenue NW
Washington, DC 20008

Robert D Schafer CKD
THE KITCHEN GUILD
5027 Connecticut Avenue NW
Washington, DC 20008

FLORIDA

Alachua

Sharon R Diehl CKD
DESIGN CABINETS INC
PO Box 1108
Alachua, FL 32615

Altamonte Springs

Mark L Poole CKD
ADVANCED EURO INC
958 Explorer Cove
Altamonte Springs, FL 32701

Alva

Carl E Bergner CKD
MONTGOMERY CABINETRY
COMPANY INC
2191 Dixie Lane
Alva, FL 33920

Boca Raton

Robert O Geddes CKD
DYNAMIC KITCHEN DESIGNS
1120 Holland Drive
Suite 17
Boca Raton, FL 33487

Chuck Kingsland CKD
INNOVATIVE CABINETRY
6590 West Rogers Circle Studio 7
Boca Raton, FL 33487

Charlotte Harbor

Cyril F Schrage CKD
KITCHEN CLASSICS INC.
4265 K Tamiami Trail
Charlotte Harbor, FL 33980

Clearwater

Deborah C Vance CKD
HOME DEPOT
21870 U.S. Highway 19N
Clearwater, FL 34625

Charlotte Clark CKD
CHARLOTTE CLARK KITCHENS
PO Box 3039
Clearwater, FL 34630

Coral Gables

Beryl Armstrong CKD
LA ASSOCIATES
4200 Aurora Street
Suite B
Coral Gables, FL 33146

Fort Lauderdale

Charles Poole CKD
DESIGNER KITCHENS &
BATHS INC
2500 Wilton Drive
Fort Lauderdale, FL 33305

Robert L Welky CKD
DESIGNER KITCHENS &
BATHS INC
2500 Wilton Drive
Fort Lauderdale, FL 33305

Fort Pierce

Celeste C Bush CKD
DESIGN KITCHENS
412 Farmers Market Road
Fort Pierce, FL 34982

Fort Walton Beach
Richard V Nivens CKD
GULF SOUTH DISTRIBUTORS
INC
707 Anchors Street
Fort Pierce, FL 32548

Ft. Lauderdale

Carl R Aden CKD
ADEN CO
P.O. Box 100445
Ft. Lauderdale, FL 33310

Hialeah

Ivan Parron CKD
7990 W. 25th Avenue
Hialeah, FL 33016

Indian Lake Estates

William T. Langohr CKD
OMEGA CABINETS
907 Park Ave.
P.O. Box 7337
Indian Lake Estates, FL 33855

Jacksonville

Paul A Barton CKD
6001-27 Argyle Forest - Bl #235
Jacksonville, FL 32244

Melanie P Hastings CKD
KITCHENS ETC BY REGENCY
8321 Atlantic Boulevard
Jacksonville, FL 32211

William L Oxley CKD
6318 Mercer Circle E
Jacksonville, FL 32217

Lakeland

Glenn D Bridges CKD
FLORIDA KITCHEN DESIGNS
608 N Ingraham Avenue
Lakeland, FL 33801

Largo

Betty J Gold CKD
THE CABINET CORNER INC
426 W Bay Drive
Largo, FL 34640

Clarice E Terepka CKD
THE CABINET CORNER INC
426 W Bay Drive
Largo, FL 34640

Longwood

Sandra L Linn CKD
226 Cambridge Drive
Longwood, FL 32779

Miami

Nancy Ware CKD
TRIM LINE KITCHENS & BATHS
10001 S Dixie Highway
Miami, FL 33156

New Port Richey

Martin M Frank CKD
PANNEBAKER CABINET
COMPANY
5249 Saltamonte Drive
New Port Richey, FL 34655-1278

North Palm Beach

Dwayne Perry CKD
GALLEY CABINETS
212 US Highway One
North Palm Beach, FL 33408

Pensacola

James H Baldwin Jr CKD
4344 Langley Avenue - #G-242
Pensacola, FL 32504

Sharon F Holley CKD
KAY'S KITCHEN & BATH
DESIGN
2901 N "E" Street
Pensacola, FL 32501

Franklin D Kay CKD
KAY'S KITCHEN AND BATH
DESIGNS
2901 N "E" Street
Pensacola, FL 32501

Rachael L Muller CKD
KAY'S KITCHEN AND BATH
DESIGNS
2901 N "E" Street
Pensacola, FL 32501

Saint Petersburg

Sharon Armstrong CKD
KITCHEN & BATH IDEAS
7219 Central Avenue
Saint Petersburg, FL 33710

Sarasota

Larry E Compton CKD
6585 Tarawa Drive
Sarasota, FL 34241

Robert B Eckert CKD
5417 Chantilly
Sarasota, FL 34235-4629

Pricilla Lindsay CKD
THE CABINET MILL INC
2311 Whitfield Industrial Way
Sarasota, FL 34243

Sherry L Strebeck CKD
AQUI KITCHEN & BATH
613 North Washington Blvd
Sarasota, FL 34236

Tallahassee

Susan M Grabowski CKD
TALLAHASSEE KITCHEN
CENTER, INC.
634 E. Park Avenue
Tallahassee, FL 32301-2527

Vero Beach

Robert W Stoddard CKD
THE KITCHEN SCENE
89 Royal Palm Boulevard
Vero Beach, FL 32960

West Palm Beach

Gary E Blow CKD
BENCHMARK KITCHENS INC.
1860 Old Okeechobee Rd., Suite 101
West Palm Beach, FL 33409

Thomas G Burns CKD
RYNONE KITCHEN & BATH
CENTRE
7740 Byron Drive
West Palm Beach, FL 33404

Windermere

Mickey Riemondy CKD
MICKEY RIEMONDY DESIGNS
11308 Lake Butler Blvd.
Windermere, FL 34786

Winter Haven

Ray W Afflerbach CKD
RAY AFFLERBACH CKD
413 Greenfield Road
Winter Haven, FL 33884

GEORGIA

Alpharetta

Shirley J McFarlane CKD
5200 Skidaway Drive
Alpharetta, GA 30201

Jennifer D Reed CKD
11815 Leeward Walk Cir.
Alpharetta, GA 30202

Atlanta

Barbara E. Barton CKD
KITCHENSMITH INCORPORATED
1198 North Highland Avenue
Atlanta, GA 30306

Lee Woodall CKD
KITCHENSMITH INC
3098 Roswell Rd
Atlanta, GA 30305

Thomas A Caswell CKD
BROOKWOOD KITCHENS
2140 Peachtree Road NW
Suite 310
Atlanta, GA 30309

Carlene K Dockery CKD
2882 Ashford Road
Atlanta, GA 30319

Robert F Foltz CKD
ROBERT FOLTZ, CKD
1739 Cheshire Bridge Road NE
Atlanta, GA 30324

Stanley Kopkin CKD
THELEN KITCHEN & BATH
STUDIOS
5566 Chamblee Dunwoody Road
Atlanta, GA 30338

Jacqueline Naylor CKD
JACKIE NAYLOR INTERIORS
4287 Glengary Drive
Atlanta, GA 30342

Carla C Nitz CKD
50 Lakeland Drive C-1
Atlanta, GA 30305

Herbert H Schmidt CKD
KITCHENSMITH INCORPORATED
1198 North Highland Avenue
Atlanta, GA 30306

Cailin M Thelen CKD
THELEN KITCHEN & BATH
STUDIOS
5566 Chamblee Dunwoody Road
Atlanta, GA 30338

Kenneth J Thelen CKD
THELEN KITCHEN & BATH
STUDIOS
5566 Chamblee Dunwoody Road
Atlanta, GA 30338

Doraville

Simone O. Feldman CKD
3169 Wanda Woods Drive
Doraville, GA 30340

Duluth

Jere M Bowden CKD
TOWN & COUNTRY KITCHENS
MAGBEE CONTRACTORS
SUPPLY
2883 Pleasant Hill Road
PO Box 956967
Duluth, GA 30136

Gaithersburg

Robinette Lynch CKD
718 Beacon Hill Terrace
Gaithersburg, GA 20878

Lawrenceville

Elizabeth Jaye Moore CKD
1222 Grayland Lane
Lawrenceville, GA 30245

Marietta

Charlotte A Fisher CKD
3582 Clubland Drive
Marietta, GA 30068

Newnan

Claude G Cooper CKD
CLASSIC KITCHENS INC
PO Box 963
Newnan, GA 30264

Norcross

Jo Alese Bruce CKD
THE CARAPACE CORPORATION
3250 A Peachtree Corners Circle
Norcross, GA 30092

Roswell

Gertrude E McGinnis CKD
MCGINNIS GROUP
1350 Ridgefield Drive
Roswell, GA 30075

James P Meloy CKD
DIKAB INC
11444 Alpharetta Highway
Roswell, GA 30076

Hans Schuon CKD
SCHUON KITCHENS, INC.
108 Oak Street - Suite "C"
Roswell, GA 30075

Roswella

Patrick J Dunbar CKD
THE HOME DEPOT 9901
1425 Market Boulevard
Roswella, GA 30076

Saint Simons Island

Beverly M Wolfe CKD
BMW DESIGNER KITCHENS INC
508 E. Island Square Drive
Saint Simons Island, GA 31522-1640

Patricia B Burgess CKD
KITCHEN & BATH CONCEPTS
OF ST SIMONS INC
1627 Frederica Road
Suite 16
Saint Simons Island, GA 31522

HAWAII

Aiea

Wayne T. Bouille CKD
AMERICAN CABINETRY,INC
98-820 Moanalua Road
Aiea, HI 96701

Honolulu

Troy L Adams CKD
STUDIO BECKER KITCHENS
560 N. Nimita Highway
Suite 121A
Honolulu, HI 96817

Marie Blackburn CKD
KITCHEN SOURCE
758 Kapahulu Avenue
Suite 270
Honolulu, HI 96816

Judy Dawson CKD
DESIGNER KITCHENS AND
BATHS
3055 Maigret Street
Honolulu, HI 96816

Marcia Gleason CKD
DESIGN GUILD INC
909 Kapahula Avenue
Honolulu, HI 96816

Susan Palmer CKD
KITCHEN CONCEPTS PLUS INC
770 Kapiolani Boulevard
Honolulu, HI 96813

Michael L Smith CKD
KITCHEN CONCEPTS PLUS INC
770 Kapiolani Boulevard
Honolulu, HI 96813

Cheri Villberg CKD
KITCHEN & BATH
DESIGNWORKS
350 Ward Avenue #106
Honolulu, HI 96814

Deborah Walsh CKD
DEBORAH WALSH &
ASSOCIATES
909 Kapahula Ave
Honolulu, HI 96816

Pukalani

Sydney U Zimmerman CKD
MASTERWORK KITCHENS
2691 Keikilani Street
Pukalani, HI 96768

IDAHO

Boise

Lyndell Kline CKD
FREEDOM WOODCRAFT INC
448 South Maple Grove
Boise, ID 83709

Nampa

Dena Rae Jurries CKD
TREASURE VALLEY
WOODWORKING INC
12783 Orchard Ave
Nampa, ID 83651

Norman L Myers CKD
12787 Orchard Ave
Nampa, ID 83651

Tim B Myers CKD
TREASURE VALLEY
WOODWORKING INC
12783 Orchard Ave
Nampa, ID 83651

Rexburg

Shawna Strobel CKD
SHAWNA INTERIORS
444 Morgan Drive
Rexburg, ID 83440

ILLINOIS

Alsip

Bernice G Greenwald CKD
5024 West 122nd Street
Alsip, IL 60658

Apple River

Robert M Gee CKD
GEE AND ASSOCIATES INC
3-162 Gen Jackson Court
Apple River, IL 61001

Arthur

Cathy M Kopel CKD
O.E. SCHROCK INC.
107 S. Moses
Arthur, IL 61911

Aurora

Robert Best CKD
KITCHEN DISTRIBUTORS OF
AMERICA
4462 East New York
Aurora, IL 60504

Dean R Mamprisio CKD
KITCHEN DISTRIBUTORS OF
AMERICA
4462 East New York
Aurora, IL 60504

Norman J. Moret CKD
KITCHEN DISTRIBUTORS OF
AMERICA
4462 East New York
Aurora, IL 60504

Barrington

Julie Loehner CKD
INSIGNIA KITCHEN & BATH
DESIGN GROUP LTD
1435 South Barrington Road
Barrington, IL 60010

Helen Lundstrom CKD
KITCHENS & MORE
260 Center Timber Ridge
Barrington, IL 60010

James R Walker CKD
BARRINGTON HOMEWORKS
KITCHEN CENTER
301 E Main Street
Barrington, IL 60010

Batavia

Neal J Conde CKD
CONDE CREATIONS
210 N Washington Avenue
Batavia, IL 60510

Belleville

Verla M Stratton CKD
MARKUS CABINETS
7 N High
Belleville, IL 62220

Berwyn

Constance Rabias CKD
2123 South Harlem Avenue
Berwyn, IL 60402

Brookfield

Lynn Larsen CKD
LAMANTIA KITCHEN DESIGN
STUDIO
9100 Ogden
Brookfield, IL 60513

Chicago

Susan J Alderson CKD
2343 W McLean
Chicago, IL 60647

Karen E Conforti CKD
ARTISTIC KITCHEN DESIGNS
800 North Wells Street
Chicago, IL 60610

Ehab A Debdeb CKD
8201 W Addison Street
Chicago, IL 60634

Dale E Johnson CKD
KITCHENS & BATHS BY
DON JOHNSON
Merchandise Mart
Suite 1375
Chicago, IL 60654

Donald C Johnson CKD
KITCHENS & BATHS BY
DON JOHNSON
Merchandise Mart
Suite 1375
Chicago, IL 60654

Kenneth W Krengel CKD
KRENGEL & ASSOCIATES INC
13101 The Merchandise Mart
Chicago, IL 60654

Joan L Rabinowitz CKD
1913 N Cleveland Avenue
Chicago, IL 60614

Chicago Ridge

Michael J Mikoff CKD
MIKOFF CUSTOM KITCHEN &
BATH
10527 S Ridgeland Avenue
Chicago Ridge, IL 60415

Crystal Lake

Andrea L McCarthy CKD
ANDREA MC CARTHY
DESIGN INC.
1381 Lucerne Drive
Crystal Lake, IL 60014

Downers Grove

Charles W Bidgood CKD
BRADFORD KENT BUILDERS
807 Ogden Avenue
Downers Grove, IL 60515

Hugh Cook CKD
KITCHEN DISTRIBUTORS OF
AMERICA INC
1728 W Ogden Avenue
Downers Grove, IL 60515

Joseph A LaMantia CKD
LAMANTIA CONSTRUCTION
COMPANY
1227 Ogden Avenue
Downers Grove, IL 60515

Adrien M. Medow CKD
LAMAMTIA DESIGN
1227 Ogden Ave
Downers Grove, IL 60515

Dwight

Beverly A Hogan CKD
HOGAN DESIGNS
RR 1 Box 10
Dwight, IL 60420

Edwardsville

Robert J Davis CKD
EDWARDSVILLE LUMBER
COMPANY KITCHENLAND
201 W High
Edwardsville, IL 62025

Richard V Mueller CKD
EDWARDSVILLE LUMBER
201 W High Street
Edwardsville, IL 62025

Elmwood Park

Pamela J Polvere CKD
SPROVIERI'S KITCHENS
7506 W Grand Avenue
Elmwood Park, IL 60635

Evanston

David M Karlson CKD
KARLSON KITCHENS
1815 Central Street
Evanston, IL 60201

Fairview Heights

Richard E Schmitt CKD
8 Briarcliff
Fairview Heights, IL 62208

Glen Ellyn

Gail Drury CKD
DRURY DESIGNS
244 Exmoor Avenue
Glen Ellyn, IL 60137

Harrisburg

Harold Wilson CKD
101 Southwest Drive
Harrisburg, IL 62946

Jacksonville

Floyd R Taylor CKD
TAYLOR MADE KITCHENS
RR 3 Box 57
Jacksonville, IL 62650

Libertyville

Nancy E Snow CKD
LIBERTY KITCHEN & BATH
627 North Second Street
Libertyville, IL 60048

Lincolnwood

Thomas D. Graham CKD
AIROOM INC
6825 N Lincoln Avenue
Lincolnwood, IL 60646

Seymour Turner CKD
AIROOM INC
6825 N Lincoln Avenue
Lincolnwood, IL 60646

Lockport

William B Ellinger CKD
ROMAR CABINET AND TOP
COMPANY INC
3357 South State Street
Lockport, IL 60441

Lombard

Karen Walsh Roberts CKD
KITCHENS-BATHS & OTHER
LIVING SPACES
563 Edson Avenue
Lombard, IL 60148

Morton

Ronald L Smallenberger CKD
CREATIVE KITCHENS INC OF
MORTON
2001 W Jackson Street
Morton, IL 61550

Morton Grove

Wilma E Wendt CKD
W W DESIGNS INC
9112 Parkside
Morton Grove, IL 60053

Mount Prospect

Jules P Kastens CKD
210 East Lonnquist Boulevard
Mount Prospect, IL 60056

Naperville

Judith A Blanks CKD
KITCHEN & BATH DESIGNER
1032 N Loomis Street
Naperville, IL 60540

Niles

Edmund L Zielinski CKD
BETTER KITCHENS INC
7640 N Milwaukee Avenue
Niles, IL 60714-3133

Normal

Mary D Sandy CKD
121 S Orr Drive
Normal, IL 61761

Oak Park

Donna Norell CKD
THE KITCHEN STUDIO INC
115 S. Maple Avenue
Oak Park, IL 60302-2005

Laura Trujillo CKD
THE KITCHEN STUDIO INC
115 S. Maple Avenue
Oak Park, IL 60302-2005

Palatine

Mary Falkenberg CKD
KITCHEN & BATH MART
116 South Northwest Hwy.
Palatine, IL 60067

Park Ridge

Howard H Sersen CKD
1608 South Courtland Avenue
Park Ridge, IL 60068

Pawnee

Kathryn E Schultz CKD
89 Michele Drive
Pawnee, IL 62558

River Grove

Zenon D. Bojko CKD
REYNOLDS ENTERPRISES INC.
2936 North River Road
River Grove, IL 60171

Walter A Reynolds CKD
REYNOLDS ENTERPRISES INC.
2936 North River Road
River Grove, IL 60171

Rockford

Donald C Johnson CKD
DAHLGREN & JOHNSON INC
1000 Ninth Street
Rockford, IL 61104

Douglas S. Trussoni CKD
KITCHEN DISTRIBUTORS OF
AMERICA INC.
3224 S Alpine Road
Rockford, IL 61109

Skokie

Steven C Standard CKD
TARLOS KITCHEN & BATH INC
8808 Gross Point Road
Skokie, IL 60077-1809

Joe G Tarlos CKD
TARLOS KITCHEN & BATH INC
8808 Gross Point Road
Skokie, IL 60077-1809

Springfield

Darlene H Weaver CKD
DISTINCTIVE DESIGNS FOR
KITCHENS & BATHS
226 Highland Avenue
Springfield, IL 62704

St. Charles

Dennis M Regole CKD
41W119 Colson Dr.
St. Charles, IL 60175

Taylorville

Charles D Brown CKD
BROWN & SONS INC
BROWN'S BARN
421 Springfield Road
Taylorville, IL 62568

Wauconda

Star Norini CKD
DISTINCTIVE KITCHEN
DESIGNS INC
203 S Main Street
Wauconda, IL 60084

Wheaton

Claudia Penna CKD
KITCHEN & BATH SOURCE
611 West Roosevelt Road
Wheaton, IL 60187

Wilmette

Maggie F Burke CKD
NORTH SHORE KITCHEN &
BATH CENTER
3207 West Lake Avenue
Wilmette, IL 60091

Michael De Giulio CKD
DE GIULIO KITCHEN DESIGN
INC
1121 Central
Wilmette, IL 60091

Daniel J DeGiulio CKD
DEGIULIO KITCHEN DESIGN
INC
1121 Central Avenue
Wilmette, IL 60091

K Peter Knobel CKD
KARL G KNOBEL INC
1218 Washington Avenue
Wilmette, IL 60091

Paul R Knobel CKD
KARL G KNOBEL INC
1218 Washington Avenue
Wilmette, IL 60091

INDIANA

Batesville

Thomas P Walsman CKD
WALSMAN SUPPLY COMPANY
INC
1818 State Road 46 E
PO Box 225
Batesville, IN 47006

Bloomington

Larry G Routen CKD
ROUTEN DESIGN ASSOCIATES
3915 Sugar Lane E
Bloomington, IN 47404

Bremen

Robert A Waters CKD
BREMTOWN KITCHENS
1456 State Road 331 N
PO Box 409
Bremen, IN 46506

Clarksville

Kurt R Grant CKD
HOME QUARTERS WAREHOUSE
1416 Blackiston Mill Rd.
Clarksville, IN 47129

Columbus

Larry W Alexander CKD
ALEXANDERS' CABINET &
APPLIANCE CENTER
1817 24th Street
Columbus, IN 47201

Evansville

Jimmy D Mitchell CKD
MITCHELL'S KITCHEN
CENTER INC
PO Box 5749
5611 Boonville Highway
Evansville, IN 47715

Lynda M Wilhelmus CKD
CABINETS BY DESIGN
A DIVISION OF LENSING
WHOLESALE
4619 Lincoln Avenue
Evansville, IN 47714

Fishers

David D Darnell CKD
DARNELL'S INTERIORS
11986 Parkview Lane
Fishers, IN 46038

Fort Wayne

W. D Rupel CKD
WD BILL RUPEL CKD
10128 Arbor Trail
Fort Wayne, IN 46804-4602

Goshin

Carl Kelly Hunsberger CKD
65775 CR #7
Goshin, IN 46526

Greenwood

Michael F Teipen CKD
KITCHENS BY TEIPEN
586 S State Road 135
Greenwood, IN 46142-1426

Indianapolis

Bridget Bonham CKD
CASEWORKS
9423 N Meridian Street
Indianapolis, IN 46260

Chester Gray CKD
INDIANA CABINET DIS-
TRIBUTING COMPANY
6857 Hawthorn Park Drive
Indianapolis, IN 46220

James S Jordan CKD
JIM JORDAN SHOWPLACE
KITCHENS
2206 Lafayette Road
Indianapolis, IN 46222

Brenda J Merritt CKD
CASEWORKS
9423 N Meridian Street
Indianapolis, IN 46260

La Porte

Tom McPherson CKD
DYE PLUMBING & HEATING
PO BOX 96
712 Madison St
La Porte, IN 46350

Muncie

Greg R Rawson CKD
RICHARD'S KITCHEN & BATH
CENTER
4209 N Wheeling Avenue
Muncie, IN 47304

Richard Rawson CKD
RICHARD'S KITCHEN & BATH
CENTER
4209 N Wheeling Avenue
Muncie, IN 47304

Nappanee

Donald P Guckenberger CKD
NAPPANEE WOOD PRODUCTS
1205 E Lincoln Avenue
Nappanee, IN 46550

Schererville

Vernon A Wietbrock CKD
KOREMEN LTD
2146 US 41
Schererville, IN 46375

Shelbyville

Joe L Risley CKD
RISLEY'S KITCHEN
SPECIALISTS
212 E Broadway
Shelbyville, IN 46176

South Bend

Louis M Seago CKD
LOUIE SEAGO AND SONS INC
2506 S Michigan Street
South Bend, IN 46614

Syracuse

William M Beemer CKD
BEEMER ENTERPRISES INC
PO Box 5
Syracuse, IN 46567

Vincennes

Douglas G Warren CKD
40 Meier Circle
Vincennes, IN 47591

Westfield

Carol L Demaree CKD
WICKES LUMBER COMPANY
#372
16708 U S 31 N
Westfield, IN 46074

IOWA

Ames

Kathleen K Cupp CKD
KITCHENS BY DESIGN
429 Duff Avenue
Ames, IA 50010

Burlington

Walter C Fox CKD
FOX APPLIANCE AND
KITCHEN CENTER INC
709-711 Jefferson Street
Burlington, IA 52601

Cedar Rapids

Richard J Felter CKD
AR-JAY BUILDING PRODUCTS
1515 Blairs Ferry Road N E
PO Box 10017
Cedar Rapids, IA 52410-0017

Joanne L Just CKD
AR-JAY BUILDING PRODUCTS
1515 Blairs Ferry Road N E
PO Box 10017
Cedar Rapids, IA 52410-0017

Richard W Moritz CKD
P H I DISTRIBUTORS
1570 42nd Street NE
Cedar Rapids, IA 52402

Don L Novak CKD
NOVAK CONSTRUCTION
COMPANY
10400 Club Road S W
Cedar Rapids, IA 52404

Ralph H. Palmer CKD
AR-JAY BUILDING PRODUCTS
1515 Blairs Ferry Road N E
PO Box 10017
Cedar Rapids, IA 52410-0017

Jodi L Schultz CKD
AR-JAY BUILDING PRODUCTS
1515 Blairs Ferry Road N E
PO Box 10017
Cedar Rapids, IA 52410-0017

Denison

Loren Schultz CKD
Color Center
Denison, IA 51442

Des Moines

Valerie Cunningham CKD
3817 Tiffin Avenue
Des Moines, IA 50317

Fort Dodge

Phil D Stephenson CKD
ATLAS KITCHEN & BATH
1903 1st Avenue S
Fort Dodge, IA 50501

Iowa City

Ernst Redeker CKD
777 Keswick Drive
Iowa City, IA 52246

Marshalltown

Steven L Fritz CKD
SWANCO ENTERPRISES INC
815 N 3rd Avenue
Box 1030
Marshalltown, IA 50158

Northwood

Sarah L Reep CKD
FIELDSTONE CABINETRY INC
PO Box 109
Highway 105 E
Northwood, IA 50459

Washington

Richard J Widmer CKD
WIDMER INTERIOR DESIGN
200 E. Polk Street
Washington, IA 52353-1140

Waterloo

Lucie C Van Metre CKD
2237 Edgemont #10
Waterloo, IA 50702

KANSAS

Lenexa

Nancy McLeod CKD
SHAWNEE MISSION PLUMBING
HEATING COOLING
11306 West 89 Street
Lenexa, KS 66214

Salina

Robert J Duffield CKD
700 Victoria Heights Terrace
Salina, KS 67401

Richard J Greene CKD
CRESTWOOD INC
353 E Avenue A
Salina, KS 67401

Carl A Long CKD
CRESTWOOD INC
353 E Avenue A
Salina, KS 67401

Wichita

Joe Gordon CKD
GORDON'S HOUSE OF
CABINETRY
1206 E First Street
Wichita, KS 67214

Jan E Parker CKD
KITCHENS BY DESIGN
1824 E Douglas Avenue
Wichita, KS 67214

KENTUCKY

Campbellsville

Pamela Munson CKD
COX CABINET COMPANY
PO Box 148
950 Campbellsville Bypass
Campbellsville, KY 42719

Fort Mitchell

RB Davis CKD
SIGNATURE KITCHENS
18 Pleasant Ridge Avenue
Fort Mitchell, KY 41017

Lexington

Nancy C Braamse CKD
CREATIVE KITCHEN & BATH
1141 Industry Drive
Lexington, KY 40503

Mike Butcher CKD
DESIGNER KITCHENS INC
1269 Eastland Drive
Lexington, KY 40505

Louisville

Peggy R Edlin CKD
MOUSER KITCHENS
12204 Shelbyville Road
Louisville, KY 40243

Louise A Sachs CKD
504 Ledgeview Court
Louisville, KY 40206

Kathleen M Thomas CKD
MOUSER KITCHENS
12204 Shelbyville Road
Louisville, KY 40243

Prospect

C Jean Mattingly CKD
CJM DESIGNS INC G E
PO Box 708
Prospect, KY 40059

Henry A Schmidt CKD
6905 Bridgepointe Boulevard
Prospect, KY 40059

Marvin F Stich CKD
MARVIN F STICH &
ASSOCIATES
5552 Forest Lake Drive
Prospect, KY 40059

LOUISIANA

Baton Rouge

David W Johnston CKD
ACADIAN HOUSE KITCHEN &
BATH STUDIO
12888 Jefferson Highway
Baton Rouge, LA 70816

Covington

Charles J Wheeler CKD
1216 W. Presidents Drive
Covington, LA 70433

Lafayette

Marlon D Duhon CKD
TOP'S WOODWORK &
SUPPLY INC
5826 Johnston Street
PO Drawer 31810
Lafayette, LA 70503

Mandeville

Nancy L Gladen CKD
CAMPBELL CABINET
COMPANY INC
4040 Hwy 59
Mandeville, LA 70448

New Orleans

Belva M Johnson CKD
CAMERON KITCHEN & BATH
DESIGNS
8019 Palm Street
New Orleans, LA 70125

Gerald C Johnson CKD
CAMERON KITCHEN & BATH
DESIGNS
8019 Palm Street
New Orleans, LA 70125

Stewart J. Lagarde CKD
CLASSIC CUPBOARDS INC
4747 Earhart Blvd
New Orleans, LA 70125

Henry P Simon CKD
CAMERON KITCHEN & BATH
DESIGNS
8019 Palm Street
New Orleans, LA 70125

Shreveport

William J Patten CKD
DESIGNER KITCHENS &
FLOORS INC
6210-B Fairfield Avenue
Shreveport, LA 71106

MAINE

Alfred

Daniel L Roux CKD
ROUX'S KITCHEN & BATH
CENTER
Route 202
PO Box 337
Alfred, ME 04002

Brunswick

Carol E Bartlett CKD
BRUNSWICK COAL & LUMBER
18 Spring Street
Brunswick, ME 04011

Edgecomb

Elaine C Murdoch CKD
R.R. 1, Box 773
Edgecomb, ME 04556

Ellsworth

Gwen M Dewitt CKD
ELLSWORTH BUILDERS
SUPPLY INC
State Street
Ellsworth, ME 04605

Kittery

Charles E Bold CKD
BOLD CABINETRY
162 State Road
Kittery, ME 03904

Pamela P Bold CKD
BOLD CABINETRY
162 State Road
Kittery, ME 03904

Lewiston

Joanne D. Baribault CKD
DION DISTRIBUTORS
PO Box 1668
Lewiston, ME 04241-1668

Charles Bellegarde CKD
CHARLES BELLEGARDE &
SON INC
23 Columbia Avenue
Lewiston, ME 04240

Peter Clifford CKD
BELLEGARDE CUSTOM
KITCHENS
516 Sabattus Street
Lewiston, ME 04240

Robert O Dion CKD
DION DISTRIBUTORS
PO Box 1668
Lewiston, ME 04241-1668

Norway

Jerald M Foster CKD
PO Box 717
Norway, ME 04268

Sanford

DeTopsham
Marjorie Otis CKD
RR 1 114D Middlesex Road
Sanford, ME 04086

Van Buren

Cynthia M Dufour CKD
GAGNON'S HARDWARE &
FURNITURE INC
184 Main Street
Van Buren, ME 04785

MARYLAND

Accident

Richard L Alexander CKD
PO Box 103
Accident, MD 21520

Annapolis

Mark T White CKD
DESIGN SOLUTIONS
582 B Bellerive Drive
Annapolis, MD 21401

Joan E Zimmerman CKD
DESIGN SOLUTIONS
582 B Bellerive Drive
Annapolis, MD 21401

Baltimore

Lynne M Abrams CKD
DETAILS INC.
69 Greenwich Place
Baltimore, MD 21208

Stuart D Bunyea CKD
STUART KITCHENS INC
1858 Reisterstown Road
Baltimore, MD 21208

Alan L Caplan CKD
STUART KITCHENS INC
1858 Reisterstown Road
Baltimore, MD 21208

Jodi Connolly CKD
STUART KITCHENS INC
1858 Reisterstown Road
Baltimore, MD 21208

Robert F Cox CKD
BOB COX TRAINING SCHOOLS
616 E 33rd Street
Baltimore, MD 21218

Gordon H Davis CKD
JOHN H MORGAN &
ASSOCIATES
3800 Timber View Way
Baltimore, MD 21136

Stu Dettelbach CKD
SD KITCHENS
1201 Greenwood Road
Baltimore, MD 21208

Joan M Eisenberg CKD
JME CONSULTING INC
2106 Burdock Road
Baltimore, MD 21209

Robert L Gibbs CKD
COX KITCHEN & BATH INC
6322 Falls Road
Baltimore, MD 21209

Stanley Klein CKD
6800 Westridge Road
Baltimore, MD 21207

James Lichty CKD
STUART KITCHENS INC
1858 Reisterstown Road
Baltimore, MD 21208

Maxine D Lowy CKD
SD KITCHENS
1201 Greenwood Road
Baltimore, MD 21208

James J Mittelkamp CKD
4546 Ambermill Road
Baltimore, MD 21236

John H Morgan CKD
JOHN H MORGAN &
ASSOCIATES
3800 Timber View Way
Baltimore, MD 21136

Ilene Silberg CKD
SD KITCHENS
1201 Greenwood Road
Baltimore, MD 21208

Gary Wedeking CKD
STUART KITCHENS INC
1858 Reisterstown Road
Baltimore, MD 21208

Victor P Williams CKD
STUART KITCHENS INC
1858 Reisterstown Road
Baltimore, MD 21208

Beltsville

Deborah J Miller CKD
BRAY & SCARFF INC
11950 Baltimore Avenue
Beltsville, MD 20705

Rebecca Phillips CKD
BRAY & SCARFF INC
11950 Baltimore Avenue
Beltsville, MD 20705

Debra L Saling CKD
KITCHEN KONNECTION, INC.
10801 Tucker Street
Beltsville, MD 20705

Kara L Sibley CKD
BRAY & SCARFF INC
11950 Baltimore Avenue
Beltsville, MD 20705

Mark A Yost CKD
CONTRACT KITCHEN
DISTRIBUTORS INC
12002 Old Baltimore Pike
Beltsville, MD 20705

Bethesda

Polly W Evans CKD
4701 Sangamore Rd. #P-40
Bethesda, MD 20815-2508

William C Hurley CKD
SEARS ROEBUCK & COMPANY
7103 Democracy Boulevard
Bethesda, MD 20817

Randi J Place CKD
NANCY THORNETT
ASSOCIATES
6701 Democracy Boulevard
Suite 809
Bethesda, MD 20817

Bowie

Francine B Blumenfeld CKD
2818 Stoneybrook Drive
Bowie, MD 20715

Chevy Chase

James W Bingnear CKD
RICHARD M. TUNIS INC
7032 Wisconsin Avenue
Chevy Chase, MD 20815

Donna L Cunningham CKD
RICHARD M. TUNIS INC
7032 Wisconsin Avenue
Chevy Chase, MD 20815

Nancy M Elliott CKD
NANCY ELLIOTT &
ASSOCIATES
37 W Irving Street
Chevy Chase, MD 20815

Harriet Finder CKD
RICHARD M. TUNIS INC
7032 Wisconsin Avenue
Chevy Chase, MD 20815

Jennifer L Gilmer CKD
KITCHEN AND BATH
STUDIO'S INC
7001 Wisconsin Avenue
Chevy Chase, MD 20815

Jerry R Weed CKD
KITCHEN AND BATH
STUDIO'S INC
7001 Wisconsin Avenue
Chevy Chase, MD 20815

Clinton

D Lynne Labanowski CKD
CLINTON CUSTOM
KITCHENS INC
8904 Simpson Lane
Clinton, MD 20735

Gaithersburg

Mary K Quinn CKD
LOWES
205 Kentlands Blvd
Gaithersburg, MD 20878

Kenneth L Watkins CKD
KWC INC
8154 Beechcraft Avenue
Gaithersburg, MD 20879

Carol A Will CKD
9908 Shrewsbury Court
Gaithersburg, MD 20879

Germantown

Steven D Edwards CKD
12830 Kitchen House Way
Germantown, MD 20874

Glenn Dale

Jeffrey R Beynon CKD
11335 Daisey Lane
Glenn Dale, MD 20769

Jarrettsville

Nova Counts CKD
NOVA DESIGNS
3607 North Furnace Rd.
Jarrettsville, MD 21084

Linthicum

William E Murphy CKD
459 Mary Kay Court
Linthicum, MD 21090

Lutherville

John M. Christopher CKD
KITCHEN & BATH CENTER INC.
1518 York Road
Lutherville, MD 21093

Robert J Townsend CKD
KITCHEN & BATH CENTER INC.
1518 York Road
Lutherville, MD 21093

Owings Mills

Edward E. Charest CKD
DURKEE KITCHENS
10220 South Dolfield Roar
Owings Mills, MD 21117

Pasadena

Beverly Alig CKD
STUART KITCHENS INC.
8031 Ritchie Highway
Pasadena, MD 21122

Joseph C Birner CKD
STUART KITCHENS INC.
8031 Ritchie Highway
Pasadena, MD 21122

Phoenix

David P Rackl CKD
RACKI-GILBERT ASSOCIATES
INC
4004 Sweet Air Road
Phoenix, MD 21131

Potomac

Robert B Cutler CKD
8715 Postoak Road
Potomac, MD 20854

Rockville

Sharon A. Cotta CKD
KITCHEN TECHNIQ INC
12011 Nebel Street
Rockville, MD 20852

Jay Dobbs CKD
CREATIVE KITCHENS INC
1776 E Jefferson Street
Rockville, MD 20852

Gwyneth L Hand CKD
TRAVIRAH SQUARE KITCHEN
BATH
10070 Darnestown Road
Rockville, MD 20905

Melvin Keller CKD
BEAUTIFUL BATHS
11500 Schuylkill Road
Rockville, MD 20856

Harry C Schuder CKD
BRAY & SCARFF
142 Halpine Road
Rockville, MD 20852

John William Smith CKD
BEAUTIFUL BATHS
11500 Schuylkill Road
Rockville, MD 20856

Severna Park

Carol S Goldring CKD
BAY KITCHENS LTD
688 Ritchie Highway
Severna Park, MD 21146

Donna K Sisson CKD
BAY KITCHENS LTD
688 Ritchie Highway
Severna Park, MD 21146

Robin S Wallace CKD
BAY KITCHENS LTD
688 Ritchie Highway
Severna Park, MD 21146

Shady Side

Walt Fadeley CKD
FADELEY ASSOCIATES INC
PO Box 807
Shady Side, MD 20764

Silver Spring

Linda L Settle CKD
SETTLE CUSTOM CARPENTRY
13421 Locksley Lane
Silver Spring, MD 20904

Timonium

Ken A Freebairn CKD
STUART KITCHENS INC
2221 Greenspring Drive
Timonium, MD 21093

Waldorf

Holmes E Fowler CKD
WALDORF SUPPLY INC
PO Box 578
Waldorf, MD 20604

Helen J. LaValley CKD
AFFORDABLE KITCHENS, INC.
Bldg. 3 Unit P, J P Morgan Ct.
Waldorf, MD 20602

White Plains

Robert Garner CKD
BATH & KITCHEN CONCEPTS
BY WALDORF MARBLE, INC.
4317 Charles Crossing Drive
White Plains, MD 20695

MASSACHUSETTS

Acton

Geleta F Fenton CKD
57 Maple Street
Acton, MA 01720

Agawam

Jerry Herzenberg CKD
KITCHENS BY HERZENBERG
INC
South End Bridge Circle
Agawam, MA 01001

Susan M Orena CKD
KITCHENS BY HERZENBERG
INC
South End Bridge Circle
Agawam, MA 01001

Andover

Jill A Kehoe CKD
ANDOVER KITCHEN & BATH
CENTER INC
2 Stevens Street
Andover, MA 01810

Deborah McQuesten CKD
ANDOVER KITCHEN & BATH
CENTER INC
2 Stevens Street
Andover, MA 01810

Auburn

Robert M Chesley CKD
AGREN APPLIANCE KITCHEN
& BATH
40 Minot Avenue
Auburn, MA 04210

Barre

Majorie E Tabor CKD
33 Sheldon Rd., RFD 1 Box 132
01005

Bellingham

Gary W Sandford CKD
SCANDIA KITCHENS INC
PO Box 456
Bellingham, MA 02019

CKD-Certified Kitchen Designer; CBD-Certified Bath Designer

Boston

Leon K Johnson CKD
LEE KIMBALL KITCHENS INC
276 Friend Street
Boston, MA 02114

Chelmsford

Suzanne M. L'Hussier CKD
3 Virginia Lane
Chelmsford, MA 01824

Concord

Claire Miller CKD
SPECIALTY CRAFTSMEN OF
CONCORD
9 Milldam Lane
Concord, MA 01742

Rhoda E Miller CKD
53 Monument Street
Concord, MA 01742

Danvers

Stanley F Brown CKD
BROWN'S KITCHEN & BATH
CENTER
56 North Putnam Street
Danvers, MA 01923

Dana E Mortensen CKD
THE HOME DEPOT #2663
92 Newbury St.
Danvers, MA 01923

Dennisport

Daniel F Stepnik CKD
KITCHEN STUDIO DCM INC
66 Upper County Road
PO Box 1188
Dennisport, MA 02639

Gloucester

Joseph Parisi CKD
BUILDING CENTER INC
1 Harbor Loop
Gloucester, MA 01930

Gt. Barrington

Sandra F Beebe CKD
95 West Avenue
Gt. Barrington, MA 01230

Harwich

LeAnn Daniels CKD
MID CAPE HOME CENTERS
10 Haskell Lane
Harwich, MA 02645

Janet M Rice Rustin CKD
HACKBERRY & CHATHAM
506 Depot Street
Harwich, MA 02645

Hull

Donna Wilfert CKD
D'LYN DESIGN
11 E Street
Hull, MA 02045

Hyannis

Ronald A Durgin CKD
JOHN HINCKLEY & SON
COMPANY
49 Yarmouth Road
PO Box 2110
Hyannis, MA 02601

Lexington

Frank Drake CKD
DRAKE CABINET &
REMODELING INC
401 Lowell Street (Rear)
Lexington, MA 02173

Magnolia

Helen Hagenlocher CKD
DESIGNER KITCHENS
4 Flume Road
Magnolia, MA 01930

Marblehead

Thomas Kelly CKD
NORTHSHORE KITCHENS PLUS
183 Tedesco Street
Marblehead, MA 01945

Mashpee

Patricia A Clement CKD
KITCHEN DESIGN CENTER
800 Falmouth Road (Route 28)
Mashpee, MA 02649

Mattapoisett

Wayne Walega CKD
WALEGA ASSOCIATES
92 North Street
PO Box 496
Mattapoisett, MA 02739

Needham

Susan R Brisk CKD
CHARLES RIVER KITCHENS
837 Highland Avenue
Needham, MA 02194

New Bedford

Normand E Robitaille CKD
TAILORED KITCHENS & BATH
100 Tarkiln Hill Road
PO Box 50004
New Bedford, MA 02745

Newbury Port

Lisa M. Lane CKD
CABINETRY BY LANE
WOODWORKS
22 Pleasant Street
Newbury Port, MA 01950-2610

Newton

Steven M. Levine CKD
EURO-PLUS DESIGN
29 Crafts Street
Suite 510
Newton, MA 02160

George Magyar CKD
SPLASH
244 Needham Street
Newton, MA 02164

North Andover

Maeve M Cullen CKD
605 Osgood Street
North Andover, MA 01845

Northampton

Robert F Barnes CKD
RUGG LUMBER COMPANY
HAMPSHIRE DIVISION
33 Hawley Street
P.O. Box 90
Northampton, MA 01061-0090

Northboro

Melissa A Flahive CKD
128 Northgate Road
Northboro, MA 01532

Norwell

Mark L Karas CKD
KITCHEN CONCEPTS, INC.
159 Washington Street
Norwell, MA 02061

Cameron M Snyder CKD
KITCHEN CONCEPTS, INC.
159 Washington Street
Norwell, MA 02061

Osterville

Thomas F Leckstrom CKD
KITCHEN & BATH DESIGNS
UNLIMITED INC
5 Parker Road
Osterville, MA 02655

Paxton

Heather Pond-Lombardi CKD
366 Pleasant Street
Paxton, MA 01612

Plymouth

John F Corcoran CKD
THE CABINET CONNECTION
27 Samoset Street
Plymouth, MA 02360

Eric A Kavanagh CKD
DZIGNS
57 West Pond Road
Plymouth, MA 02360

Phillip M Rothschild CKD
THE CABINET CONNECTION
27 Samoset Street
Plymouth, MA 02360

Alan M Sharp CKD
DESIGNER KITCHENS INC
116 Long Pond Road 6
Plymouth, MA 02360

S Dennis

Rebecca H Brown CKD
16 Sawyer Circle
S Dennis, MA 02660

Shrewsbury

Kristina L Cullen CKD
MODULAR KITCHENS INC
33 Boston Turnpike
Route 9
Shrewsbury, MA 01545

Peter J Lawton CKD
27 Edgemere Blvd.
Shrewsbury, MA 01545

South Dartmouth

Gilbert W Costa CKD
COSTA'S QUALITY KITCHENS
6 McCabe Street
South Dartmouth, MA 02748

Springfield

Curio Nataloni CKD
KITCHENS & BATHS BY CURIO
INC
1045 Boston Road
Springfield, MA 01119

Francis E Nataloni CKD
KITCHENS & BATHS BY
CURIO INC
1045 Boston Road
Springfield, MA 01119

Sterling

Robert E Sponenberg CKD
KITCHEN ASSOCIATES
76 Leominster Road
Route 12
Sterling, MA 01564

Stoughton

Richard Kublin CKD
RICHARD KUBLIN KITCHENS
INC
489 Page Street
Stoughton, MA 02072

West Barnstable

Amy E O'Haire CKD
HILL-O'HAIRE INTERIOR
DESIGN
Box 821
W Barnstable, MA 02668

West Bridgewater

Daniel C Patchett CKD
WOOD-HU INC
343 Manley Street
W Bridgewater, MA 02379

West Hatfield

Barbara V. Henderson CKD
DANCO KITCHENS INC
10 West Street
W Hatfield, MA 01088

Ware

Denise A. Lucier CKD
86 Beaver Lake Rd.
Ware, MA 01082

Wellesley

Payson T Lowell CKD
17 Durant Road
Wellesley, MA 02181-2325

Wellesley Hills

Donna S Dami CKD
3 Roberts Road
Wellesley Hills, MA 02181

CKD-Certified Kitchen Designer; CBD-Certified Bath Designer

West Boylston

Francis V Garofoli CKD
KITCHENS BY DESIGN, INC.
65 Central St.
West Boylston, MA 01583

Westwood

Dianne P Landry CKD
METROPOLITAN CABINET
DISTRIBUTORS
345 University Avenue
Westwood, MA 02090

Catherine Pratt CKD
PRATT & SON INC
91 Alder Road
Westwood, MA 02090

MICHIGAN

Adrian

Richard A Seifrid CKD
MERILLAT INDUSTRIES INC
5353 W US Route 223
Adrian, MI 49221

Ann Arbor

Richard L Tarantowski CKD
MARY CHRISTENSEN'S
KITCHEN & BATH DESIGN
CENTER
3921 Jackson Ave
Ann Arbor, MI 48103-1823

Birmingham

Phyllis R. Andreae CKD
PHYLLIS ANDREAE DESIGNS
288 E. Maple Road
Suite 163
Birmingham, MI 48009

Eric Richards CKD
KITCHENS BY LENORE &
RICHARDS INC
912 S Woodward Avenue
Birmingham, MI 48009

Thomas A Richards CKD
KITCHENS BY LENORE &
RICHARDS INC
912 S Woodward Avenue
Birmingham, MI 48009

Brighton

Scott A Bowyer CKD
STERLING CABINET SALES
4985 Langdon
Brighton, MI 48116

Dean Buckley CKD
5139 Milroy Lane
Brighton, MI 48116

Stanley D Kowal CKD
KITCHEN SUPPLIERS INC
9325 Maltby Rd.
Brighton, MI 48116

Burton

Stephen E Allen CKD
RON'S KITCHENS/BATHS INC.
G-4437 S Saginaw Street
Burton, MI 48529

Canton

Michael A Glaser CKD
48315 Ford Road
Canton, MI 48187

Centerville

Joseph Wayne Hittler CKD
MILL RACE DISTRIBUTING INC
240 W Main Street
PO Box 577
Centerville, MI 49032

Chesaning

Murray Cox CKD
COX/GREGORY AGENCY
16160 Briggs Road
Chesaning, MI 48616

Climax

Daryl Ann Letts CKD
SHOWCASE KITCHENS &
INTERIORS
12717 P Avenue East
Climax, MI 49034

Clinton Township

Christine Kosmalski CKD
18428 Manorwood E
Clinton Township, MI 48038

Coldwater

Donald N Streets CKD
H & S SUPPLY INC
317 N Fiske Road
Coldwater, MI 49036

Davison

Royce R Lawrence CKD
LAWRENCE'S KITCHEN &
BATH THEATER
205 E Flint Street
Davison, MI 48423

E Grand Rapids

Susan L Bloss CKD
LIFESTYLE KITCHEN & BATH
2216 Wealthy SE
E Grand Rapids, MI 49506

Marilyn A Nagelkirk CKD
LIFESTYLE KITCHEN & BATH
2216 Wealthy SE
E Grand Rapids, MI 49506

Flint

Richard Harris CKD
5405 Don Shenk Drive
Flint, MI 48473

Flushing

Bernard J Maday CKD
STARLINE DISTRIBUTORS, INC
65500 W. Pierson Rd.
Flushing, MI 48433

Fraser

John Paul Krause CKD
SHOWCASE KITCHEN & BATH
31435 Utica Road
Fraser, MI 48026

Cesar Rastelli CKD
SHOWCASE KITCHEN & BATH
31435 Utica Road
Fraser, MI 48026

Grand Rapids

Jack M Damstra CKD
GALLERY OF KITCHENS INC
5243 Plainfield N E
Grand Rapids, MI 49505

David L Offringa CKD
WOODLAND HOUSE OF
KITCHENS INC
6619 S Division SW
Grand Rapids, MI 49548

Stephanie Witt CKD
KITCHENS BY STEPHANIE
2880 Thornhills SE
Grand Rapids, MI 49546

Grosse Ile

Sally Gilbert CKD
8356 Rucker Road
Grosse Ile, MI 48138

Grosse Pointe Woods

James W Morris CKD
MUTSCHLER KITCHENS INC
20227 Mack Avenue
Grosse Pointe Woods, MI 48236

Jackson

Kathy L Kemler CKD
ROYAL CABINET INC
3900 Francis Street
Jackson, MI 49203

Lansing

Mark J Voss CKD
THE KITCHEN SHOP
5320 South Pennsylvania Avenue
Lansing, MI 49811

Mason

Tad E Muscott CKD
MUSCOTT & ASSOCIATES
930 West South Street
Mason, MI 48854-2017

Midland

Sally Fisher CKD
OWENS CABINET
1928 Stark Road
Route 3
Midland, MI 48640

Okemos

Dave E Hagerman CKD
HAGERMAN DESIGN GROUP
2331 Jolly Road
Okemos, MI 48864

Judith A Heinowski CKD
KITCHENS & BRASS
1875 W Grand River Avenue
Okemos, MI 48864

Robert B Vandervoort CKD
HAGER FOX KITCHEN SHOP
MICH KIT DIST
2331 Shawnee Trail
Okemos, MI 48864

Petoskey

Elizabeth Firebaugh CKD
KITCHEN & COMPANY
319 Bay Street
PO Box 2450
Petoskey, MI 49770

Robin N Hissong CKD
LIFESTYLES KITCHEN & BATH
Preston Feather Building Center
900 Spring Street
Petoskey, MI 49770

Cheri L Knaffle CKD
PUFF'S OF PETOSKEY
1200 Bayview Road
Petoskey, MI 49770

Jennier S Page CKD
KITCHEN & COMPANY
319 Bay Street
PO Box 2450
Petoskey, MI 49770

K Stephen Sweet CKD
SWEET'S KITCHEN CENTER
2449 US 31 North
Petoskey, MI 49770

Plymouth

Jeffrey S Stella CKD
KITCHENS BY STELLA
747 S Main Street
Plymouth, MI 48170

Royal Oak

Joan I. Charles CKD
ROYAL OAK KITCHENS INC
4518 N Woodward
Royal Oak, MI 48073

Cheryl A Feit CKD
ROYAL OAK KITCHENS INC
4518 N Woodward
Royal Oak, MI 48073

Chris R Holton CKD
ROYAL OAK KITCHENS INC
4518 N Woodward
Royal Oak, MI 48073

Rex E Holton CKD
ROYAL OAK KITCHENS INC
4518 N Woodward
Royal Oak, MI 48073

Timothy J. Holton CKD
ROYAL OAK KITCHENS INC
4518 N Woodward
Royal Oak, MI 48073

Sylvan Lake

Scott Grandis CKD
LIVING SPACES INC.
2678 Orchard Lake Road
Sylvan Lake, MI 48320

Kimberly A Saffel CKD
LIVING SPACES INC.
2678 Orchard Lake Road
Sylvan Lake, MI 48320

Traverse City

Barbara B Eager CKD
P.O. Box 85
Traverse City, MI 49685

CKD-Certified Kitchen Designer; CBD-Certified Bath Designer

Trenton

Janet A Logan CKD
MANS KITCHEN & BATH
TRENTON
3300 West Jefferson
Trenton, MI 48183

Troy

Gary Lloyd Fried CKD
1920 Coolridge #207
Troy, MI 48084

Walled Lake

Mary Furr CKD
THE FURR CONNECTION INC
8905 Lyniss Dr
Walled Lake, MI 48390

West Bloomfield

James R Allcorn CKD
BLOOMFIELD CUSTOM
KITCHENS INC
2170 Locklin Lane
West Bloomfield, MI 48324

Linda L Roth CKD
DESIGNS UNLIMITED
3160 Haggerty Road
West Bloomfield, MI 48323

Wixom

Douglas C Goodhue CKD
E W KITCHEN DISTRIBUTORS
29750 Anthony Drive
Wixom, MI 48393

J D House CKD
E W KITCHEN DISTRIBUTORS
29750 Anthony Drive
Wixom, MI 48393

Woodhaven

Frederick Flock CKD
GRAHL'S KITCHEN & BATH
DESIGN CENTER
21111 Allen Road
Woodhaven, MI 48183

MINNESOTA

Anoka

Barbara Hirschfeld CKD
HIRSCH INC. CABINETS BY
DESIGN
357 McKinley Street N W
Anoka, MN 55303

Apple Valley

Donald T Carman CKD
12785 Ethelton Way
Apple Valley, MN 55124

Brooklyn Center

Steven Ptaszek CKD
PREMIUM CRAFT, INC
1600 Freeway Blvd
Brooklyn Center, MN 55430

Duluth

Rebecca G Lindquist CKD
CONTARDO, LINDQUIST &
COMPANY
926 East 4th Street
Duluth, MN 55805

Eagan

Susan A Turner CKD
WOODMASTERS INC
990 Lone Oak Road #150
Eagan, MN 55121

Edina

Gary N Conner CKD
NORTH STAR SERVICES
4402 France Avenue S
Edina, MN 55410

Michelle C Rooney CKD
NORTH STAR SERVICES
4402 France Avenue S
Edina, MN 55410

John Sacarelos CKD
NORTH STAR SERVICES
4402 France Avenue S
Edina, MN 55410

Elk River

Marletta M Cairns CKD
BRAD CAIRNS
19171 Zebulon Street
Elk River, MN 55330

Goldlen Valley

Jolynn R Johnson CKD
CRYSTAL KITCHEN CENTER
668 North Highway 169
Goldlen Valley, MN 55427

Raymond N Pasch CKD
CRYSTAL KITCHEN CENTER
668 North Highway 169
Goldlen Valley, MN 55427

Howard Lake

Glen O Peterson CKD
DURA SUPREME INC
300 Dura Drive
Howard Lake, MN 55349

Lino Lakes

Richard E Petroske CKD
ENDLESS IDEAS KIT & BATHS
332 Main Street
Lino Lakes, MN 55014

Minneapolis

Timothy J Aden CKD
SAWHILL CUSTOM KITCHENS
& DESIGN INC
275 Market Street
Suite 157
Minneapolis, MN 55405

Charles R Geerdes CKD
NORTH STAR SURFACES
275 Market Street
#156
Minneapolis, MN 55405

Connie L Gustafson CKD
SAWHILL CUSTOM KITCHENS
& DESIGN INC
275 Market Street
Suite 157
Minneapolis, MN 55405

Karen K Lehmann CKD
PARTNERS 4 DESIGN INC
275 Market Street
Suite 109
Minneapolis, MN 55405

Valerie Stuessi CKD
PARTNERS 4 DESIGN
275 Market Street
Suite 109
Minneapolis, MN 55405

Minnetonka

Peter Dukinfield CKD
6085 Rowland Road #206
Minnetonka, MN 55343

New Ulm

Eugene J Altmann CKD
426 South Jefferson
New Ulm, MN 56073

Owings Mill

Margaret Szalecki CKD
KITCHEN & BATH WORLD
10435 Reisterstown Road
Owings Mill, MN 21117

Plato

Olive Pinske CKD
PLATO HOME CENTER
119 E Main Street
PO Box 68
Plato, MN 55370

Plymouth

Zee Gee Franzen CKD
1885 Black Oaks Lane
Plymouth, MN 55447

Princeton

Thomas H. Adams CKD
CRYSTAL CABINET WORKS
INC.
1100 Crystal Drive
Princeton, MN 55371

Ramsey

N Tim Brown CKD
BENCHMARK ENTERPRISES
14326 Waco Street N W
Ramsey, MN 55303

Saint Paul

James W Krengel CKD
KITCHENS BY KRENGEL INC
1688 Grand Avenue
Saint Paul, MN 55105

Stephen A Lyons CKD
MERLE'S CONSTRUCTION
COMPANY
860 Randolph Avenue
Saint Paul, MN 55102

Richard Miner CKD
KITCHENS BY KRENGEL INC
1688 Grand Avenue
Saint Paul, MN 55105

Michael J Palkowitsch CKD
KITCHENS BY KRENGEL INC
1688 Grand Avenue
Saint Paul, MN 55105

Mark S Peterson CKD
ANDERSEN CABINET INC
2500 N Charles
Saint Paul, MN 55109

Shoreview

Diana L Berndt CKD
THE KITCHENPLAN COMPANY
811 Tanglewood Drive
Shoreview, MN 55126

St. Paul

Donald G Gustason CKD
NORTH STAR SERVICES
688 Hague Ave.
St. Paul, MN 55104

Matthew H Piepkorn CKD
NORTH STAR SERVICES
688 Hague Ave.
St. Paul, MN 55104

Vadnais Heights

Barbara J. Bircher CKD
4363 Bramblewood Avenue
Vadnais Heights, MN 55127

Willmar

Bruce L Dexter CKD
KITCHEN FAIR
313 W 5th Street
Willmar, MN 56201

MISSISSIPPI

Gulfport

Sandra B Meadows CKD
BUILDERS SPECIALTY
SUPPLY CO
1312 31st Avenue
PO Box 403-39502
Gulfport, MS 39501

Jackson

Jerry Burns CKD
5409 Wayneland Drive
Jackson, MS 39211-4044

Raymond A Sanders CKD
1850 Eastover Drive
Jackson, MS 39211

MISSOURI

Columbia

Trudy Cornelison CKD
DESIGNER KITCHENS &
BATHS
1729 W. Broadway
Columbia, MO 65203

Garry Spotts CKD
KERRY BRAMON REMODELING
AND DESIGN
1204 Rogers, Suite G
Columbia, MO 65201

Crestwood

Paul H Stratton CKD
SEARS ROEBUCK & COMPANY
HIPS DIVISION
15 Crestwood Plaza
Crestwood, MO 62216

Des Peres

Fred L Bueler CKD
BUELER INC.
13314 Manchester Road
Des Peres, MO 63131

Ellisville

Susan J Schumacher CKD
808 Surrey Meadows Court
Ellisville, MO 63021

Florissant

Neil E Clark CKD
595 Carrico
Florissant, MO 63034

Barbara J Miller CKD
PHIL L MILLER PLUMBING &
HEATING
661 Street Ferdinand
Florissant, MO 63031

Four Seasons

Howard Schrock CKD
H & S SALES INC
3 Acacia Court
Four Seasons, MO 65049

Grover

James R Schmidt CKD
2470 Eatherton Road
Grover, MO 63040

Kirkwood

Howard A Baygents CKD
BAYGENTS COMPANY
117 West Argonne
Kirkwood, MO 63122

James A Baygents CKD
BAYGENTS COMPANY
117 West Argonne
Kirkwood, MO 63122

Charles R Schumacher CKD
10030 Big Bend Blvd.
Kirkwood, MO 63122

Scott A Schumacher CKD
SCHUMACHER KITCHEN &
BATH STUDIO
10030 Big Bend Boulevard
Kirkwood, MO 63122

Dana E Sheets CKD
BAYGENTS COMPANY
117 West Argonne
Kirkwood, MO 63122

Manchester

Roy E Duenke CKD
ROY E DUENKE CABINET
COMPANY
14436 Manchester Road
Manchester, MO 63011

Saint Charles

Jerry E Weaver CKD
KITCHENS BY WEAVER INC
2281 First Capitol Drive
Saint Charles, MO 63301

Saint Louis

Arlene M Allmeyer CKD
RSI DISTRIBUTING INC
8110 Eager Road
Saint Louis, MO 63144

Joyce Bishop CKD
CUTTER'S CUSTOM KITCHENS
& BATHS INC
12878 Manchester Road
Saint Louis, MO 63131

Gerald L Cutter CKD
CUTTER'S CUSTOM KITCHENS
& BATHS INC
12878 Manchester Road
Saint Louis, MO 63131

Pat Duffy CKD
KARR-BICK KITCHENS &
BATHS
2715 Mercantile Drive
Saint Louis, MO 63144

Linda D Gordon CKD
KARR-BICK KITCHENS &
BATHS
2715 Mercantile Drive
Saint Louis, MO 63144

David W Laurence CKD
THOMPSON'S HOUSE OF
KITCHENS & BATHS
11718 Manchester Road
Saint Louis, MO 63131

James A Lodderhose CKD
THOMPSON'S HOUSE OF
KITCHENS & BATHS
11718 Manchester Road
Saint Louis, MO 63131

Thompson C Price CKD
THOMPSON'S HOUSE OF
KITCHENS & BATHS
11718 Manchester Road
Saint Louis, MO 63131

St. Louis

Jean Baum CKD
ALBERT BAUM ASSOCIATES
9973 Coddington Way
St. Louis, MO 63132

C J Polley CKD
HQ WAREHOUSE
6303 Lindberg W Blvd
St. Louis, MO 63128

Webster Groves

Douglas C Chapman CKD
NATIONAL KITCHEN &
BATH INC
280 East Kirkham
Webster Groves, MO 63119

Matthew L Chapman CKD
NATIONAL KITCHEN &
BATH INC
280 East Kirkham
Webster Groves, MO 63119

MONTANA

Bozeman

Mary K. Cichosz CKD
P.O. Box 1824
Bozeman, MT 59715

Kristie McPhie CKD
MCPHIE CABINETRY
435 E Main Street
Bozeman, MT 59715

Columbia Falls

Maureen R Cordoza CKD
296 Wishart Road
Columbia Falls, MT 59912

Great Falls

Arnie Owen CKD
THE CABINET COMPANY INC
801 9th Street S
Great Falls, MT 59405

Helena

Christine M Kershaw CKD
PO Box 9735
Helena, MT 59604

Kalispell

Carol J. Nelson CKD
CAROL NELSON DESIGN
115 W Nevada
Kalispell, MT 59901

NEBRASKA

Axtell

Leo H Soderquist CKD
SODERQUIST CUSTOM
CABINET COMPANY
407 N Main
PO Box 326
Axtell, NE 68924

Kearney

Kenneth E Anderson CKD
TASK LIGHTING CORPORATION
910 E 25th Street
PO Box 1090
Kearney, NE 68848-1090

Todd Halbert CKD
HALBERT & ASSOCIATES
524 W 23rd Street
Kearney, NE 68847

Lincoln

Gary R Crowl CKD
CROWL'S KITCHENS & BATHS
137 S 9th Street
Lincoln, NE 68508

Robert E Crowl CKD
3939 South 58th Street
Lincoln, NE 68506

Anda R Schmaltz CKD
HYLAND BROS LUMBER
33 & Y Street
Lincoln, NE 68503

Mc Cook

Corky D Krizek CKD
CORKY'S MODERN INTERIORS
214 Norris Avenue
Mc Cook, NE 69001

Omaha

Bard Goedeker CKD
NEBRASKA CUSTOM
KITCHENS
4601 Dodge Street
Omaha, NE 68132

NEVADA

Las Vegas

Sidney B Wechter CKD
KITCHEN STUDIO INC
610 1/2 E Sahara Avenue
Las Vegas, NV 89104

NEW HAMPSHIRE

Amherst

Patricia A Currier CKD
CURRIER KITCHENS
Route 101A
Amherst, NH 03031

Concord

Norman D Mabie CKD
KITCHEN FASHIONS
133 Louden Road
Lamplighter Plaza #8
Concord, NH 03301

Epsom

William G Magan CKD
BBD ENTERPRISES
RFD #1 Box 42
New Orchard Road
Epsom, NH 03234

Greenland

Linda Clough CKD
LIFESTYLE COLLECTIONS
KITCHENS & BATHS
Breakfast Hill Crossing
Greenland, NH 03840

Hampton

Cathy H. Stathopoulos CKD
95 Dunvegan Woods Dr.
Hampton, NH 03842

Hillsboro

Trisha Sauve CKD
EAGLE ASSOCIATES
Route 9
PO Box 1429
Hillsboro, NH 03244

Hooksett

Earl Mabie CKD
MABIE ENTERPRISES
60 Sherwood Drive
Hooksett, NH 03106

Keene

Gary M Grashow CKD
GRASHOW CORPORATION
147 Winchester Street
Keene, NH 03431

Barbarann Mainzer-Burger CKD
HAMSHAW LUMBER INC
3 Bradco Street
Keene, NH 03431

Manchester

Carole J Neely CKD
NOT JUST KITCHENS
39 Hamel Drive
Manchester, NH 03104-2139

Meredith

Stacy A Morel CKD
MEREDITH BAY CABINETRY
31 Main St.
Meredith, NH 03253

Milford

Norman S Fay CKD
7 Foster Road
Milford, NH 03055-3610

Nashua

Paul L Hackel CKD
DREAM KITCHENS INC
139 Daniel Webster Highway
Nashua, NH 03060

Newbury

Patricia M Ross CKD
65 Old Post Road
Newbury, NH 03255

Newington

Kathlyn G Box CKD
ADAPTATIONS UNLIMITED INC.
2001 Woodbury Avenue
Newington, NH 03801

Mary E DeCoster CKD
ADAPTATIONS UNLIMITED INC.
2001 Woodbury Avenue
Newington, NH 03801

Maryterese Russo CKD
ADAPTATIONS UNLIMITED INC.
2001 Woodbury Avenue
Newington, NH 03801

Peterborough

James F Russell CKD
UPCOUNTRY KITCHENS &
BATHS
PO Box 367
23 Elm Street
Peterborough, NH 03458

Plaistow

Denyne M Bonin CKD
HOME TRANSFORMATIONS LTD
147 Plaistow Rd.
P.O. Box 1151
Plaistow, NH 03865

Portsmouth

Scott D Purswell CKD
AREA KITCHEN CENTRE
105 Bartlett Street
Portsmouth, NH 03801

Rye

Walter C Teufel CKD
116 Central Road
Rye, NH 03870

Stratham

Anita Colby CKD
THE CABINETWORKS
62 Portsmouth Avenue
Stratham, NH 03885

NEW JERSEY

Bayonne

Daniel P. Pietruska CKD
14 Hartley Place
Bayonne, NJ 07002

John F Pietruszka CKD
109 Garretson Avenue
Bayonne, NJ 07002

Rudy S Santos CKD
133 West 30th Street
Bayonne, NJ 07002

Belleville

Andrew F Colannino CKD
KITCHENS & BATHS BY
MODERN MILLWORK
624 Washington Avenue
Belleville, NJ 07109

Bergenfield

Mark Cobucci CKD
DOVETAIL DESIGNS INC
7 Irving Place
Bergenfield, NJ 07621

Bloomfield

Michael J Boyette CKD
BOYETTE KITCHENS & BATHS
214 Montgomery Street
Bloomfield, NJ 07003

Bridgeton

Michael R Kelly CKD
MIKE KELLY'S KITCHENS
RR #8 Box 229
Landis Avenue
Bridgeton, NJ 08302

Anne B Miller CKD
MIKE KELLY'S KITCHENS
RR #8 Box 229
Landis Avenue
Bridgeton, NJ 08302

Cherry Hill

Michelle Fleming CKD
APPLE KITCHENS INC
1334 Brace Road
Cherry Hill, NJ 08034

Chester

Stephen A Kinon CKD
KITCHENS UNIQUE BY LOIS
259 Main Street
Chester, NJ 07930

Clifton

Ralph F Zielinski CKD
R & R REMODELERS INC
423 Hazel Street
Clifton, NJ 07011

Dumont

Nicholas F D'Aloisio CKD
NICK'S KITCHEN CENTER
71 New Milford Avenue
Dumont, NJ 07628

Egg Harbor Township

Judith M Schaeffer CKD
DIAMOND KITCHENS
3112-A Fire Road
Egg Harbor Township, NJ 08232

Fair Lawn

Joseph F Major CKD
KITCHEN TECHNIQUE INC
4-10 Fair Lawn Avenue
Fair Lawn, NJ 07410

Fairfield

Lothar C Birkenfeld CKD
ALLMILMO CORPORATION
70 Clinton Road
Fairfield, NJ 07004

Far Hills

Davie Peer CKD
EUROPEAN COUNTRY
KITCHENS
Mall at Far Hills
Rt 202
Far Hills, NJ 07931-0125

Farmingdale

Jerry Sacca CKD
KITCHEN COLLECTION INC
5105 Highway 34
Farmingdale, NJ 07727

Franklin Lakes

Michael B. Laido CKD
LAIDO DESIGNS
PO Box 457
Franklin Lakes, NJ 07417

Garwood

M Edward Dudick CKD
DUDICK & SON
40 North Avenue
Garwood, NJ 07027

David N Lugara CKD
DUDICK & SON
40 North Avenue
Garwood, NJ 07027

Green Brook

Christopher Brovich CKD
FRESH IMPRESSIONS, INC
326 US Highway 22 West
Green Brook, NJ 08812-1713

Jeffrey Kennedy CKD
FRESH IMPRESSIONS, INC
326 US Highway 22 West
Green Brook, NJ 08812-1713

Hackettstown

Joseph T Potvin CKD
IAMNIVTOP INC
PO Box 789
Hackettstown, NJ 07840

Annette M DePaepe CKD
NKBA
687 Willow Grove Street
Hackettstown, NJ 07840

Nicholas J Geragi CKD
12 Canada Goose Drive
Hackettstown, NJ 07840

Roseann Mai Potvin CKD
IAMNIVTOP INC
P.O. Box 789
Hackettstown, NJ 07840

Ellen Sarra Haspel CKD
HACKETTSTOWN SUPPLY
COMPANY INC
47 Route 46
Hackettstown, NJ 07840

Hawthorne

Theodore J Bogusta CKD
TED BOGUSTA DESIGNS
19 Tenth Avenue
Hawthorne, NJ 07506

James Kershaw CKD
JAMES KERSHAW ASSOCIATES
120 7th Avenue
Hawthorne, NJ 07506

Lake Hiawatha

Ronald G Goldsworth CKD
84 A Mara Road
Lake Hiawatha, NJ 07034

Lakewood

Lynda C Eber CKD
HOME DEPOT STORE #902
1900 Shorrock Road & Rte. 70
Lakewood, NJ 08701

Marc R Eber CKD
MARC R EBER & ASSOCIATES
1200 Cross Street
Lakewood, NJ 08701-4009

Lambertville

Neil MacDonald CKD
MACDONALD THOMPSON
ASSOCIATES
71 N Main Street
Lambertville, NJ 08530

Livingston

Natalie D Raskin CKD
RAY RIVERS & ASSOCIATES
INC
34 E Northfield Road
Livingston, NJ 07039

Marlton

Conrad A Hidalgo CKD
304 Berkshire Way
Marlton, NJ 08053-4223

Medford

Carol J Cherry CKD
CHERRY'S DESIGNS INC
560 Stokes Rd.
Ironstone Village #9
Medford, NJ 08055

Raymond E Mayer CKD
560 Stokes Road
Suite 23 306
Medford, NJ 08055

Montvale

Jane P Gummere CKD
PASCACK SHOWCASE
33 S Kinderkamack Road
Montvale, NJ 37645

New Providence

Mary M Banas CKD
ROSAN CUSTOM KITCHENS &
BATHS
1294 Springfield Avenue
New Providence, NJ 07974

North Haledon

William F Earnshaw CKD
18 Hillside Drive
North Haledon, NJ 07508

Nutley

John P Castronova CKD
PARAMOUNT KITCHENS
291 Bloomfield Avenue
Nutley, NJ 07110

Ocean City

Sandra Aromando CKD
EURO LINE DESIGNE INC
809 Seacliff Road
Ocean City, NJ 08226

Oxford

Francis Jones CKD
496 Valley Road
Oxford, NJ 07863

Perth Ambo

Robert P Kirsten CKD
WHOLESALE KITCHEN
CABINET
DISTRIBUTOR INC
533 Krochmally Avneue
Perth Ambo, NJ 08861

Pompton Plains

David L Kennedy CKD
JEFFREYS & LUTJEN INC
29 Evans Place
Pompton Plains, NJ 07444

Theodore E Lutjen CKD
JEFFREYS & LUTJEN INC
29 Evans Place
Pompton Plains, NJ 07444

Ramsey

Bonnie Hufnagel CKD
BONDI'S WORLD OF
KITCHENS INC
455 Route 17 S
Ramsey, NJ 07446

Raritan

Catherine Reed CKD
THE CABINET CENTER BY
FLEETWOOD
20 Route 206
Raritan, NJ 08869

Richard Van Fleet CKD
THE CABINET CENTER BY
FLEETWOOD
20 Route 206
Raritan, NJ 08869

Ridgewood

Alan S Asarnow CKD
ULRICH INC
100 Chestnut Street
Ridgewood, NJ 07450

Philip W Fluhr CKD
ULRICH INC
100 Chestnut Street
Ridgewood, NJ 07450

Sharon L Sherman CKD
ULRICH INC
100 Chestnut Street
Ridgewood, NJ 07450

J David Ulrich CKD
ULRICH INC
100 Chestnut Street
Ridgewood, NJ 07450

Roselle

Darryl Scott Horvath CKD
PROVEN DESIGN INC
225 First Avenue E
Roselle, NJ 07203

Glenn C Horvath CKD
PROVEN DESIGN INC
225 First Avenue E
Roselle, NJ 07203

Saddle Brook

Peter Salerno CKD
SALERNO'S KITCHEN
CABINETS INC
599 Midland Avenue
Saddle Brook, NJ 07662

Somerdale

Cheryl A Cronce CKD
INDEPENDENT DESIGN
SERVICES
103 Holyoke Avenue
Somerdale, NJ 08083

Somerville

Paul Milea CKD
57-1B Taurus Drive
Somerville, NJ 08876

South Somerville

Susanita M Levy CKD
ROYAL CABINET COMPANY
INC
14 Park Avenue
South Somerville, NJ 08876

Sparta

Chester Basher CKD
SPARTA TRADES KITCHENS &
BATHS
580 Route 15
P.O. Box 963
Sparta, NJ 07871

Dennis Daniels CKD
SPARTA TRADES KITCHENS &
BATHS
580 Route 15
P.O. Box 963
Sparta, NJ 07871

Spotswood

John H Albecker CKD
ALBECKER'S KITCHENS &
BATHS
272 Main Street
Spotswood, NJ 08884

Eileen G Jaedicke CKD
ALBECKER'S KITCHENS &
BATHS
272 Main Street
Spotswood, NJ 08884

Summit

Maria Brisco CKD
CABRI INC
323 Springfield Avenue
Summit, NJ 07901

Matt Ezmat CKD
CABRI INC
323 Springfield Avenue
Summit, NJ 07901

Trenton

Charles Eardley CKD
HAMILTON KITCHENS
Hamilton Sqaure
4441 Nottingham Way
Trenton, NJ 08690

Judith A Vernon CKD
VERNON'S PENN SUPPLY
514 Hamilton Avenue
Trenton, NJ 08609

Turnersville

Leen Van Bergen CKD
KITCHEN & BATHWORKS
980 Blackhorse Pike
Turnersville, NJ 08012

Verona

Leo Lemchen CKD
STRUCTURAL & INTERIOR
DESIGN
2 Claridge Drive 9DW
Verona, NJ 07044-3051

W Belmar

Barry R Tunbridge CKD
DU CRAFT INC
1919 Route 71
W Belmar, NJ 07719

West Paterson

Albert Castrucci CKD
CASTRUCCI CABINET
17 Pompton Avenue
West Paterson, NJ 07424

Wyckoff

Herman Brandes CKD
A & B KITCHENS & BATHS INC
279 Franklin Avenue
Wyckoff, NJ 07481

Randy J Brandes CKD
A & B KITCHENS & BATHS INC
279 Franklin Avenue
Wyckoff, NJ 07481

Virginia R Loretto CKD
A & B KITCHENS & BATHS INC
279 Franklin Avenue
Wyckoff, NJ 07481

Karen L Moyers CKD
HEART OF THE HOME
350 Dartmouth Street
Wyckoff, NJ 07481

NEW MEXICO

Albuquerque

Michelle A Carr CKD
DESIGN PROFESSIONALS
KITCHEN & BATH CENTER
1309 San Mateo N E
Albuquerque, NM 87110

Robert C Carr CKD
DESIGN PROFESSIONALS
KITCHEN & BATH CENTER
1309 San Mateo N E
Albuquerque, NM 87110

Diane Wandmaker CKD
CREATIVE KITCHENS
7923 B Menaul NE
Albuquerque, NM 87110

Santa Fe

Robert M Baker CKD
PITTMAN BROTHERS
WOODWORKS
1241 Siler Road
Santa Fe, NM 87501

Andrea M Cypress CKD
620 West San Francisco Street
Santa Fe, NM 87501

Diane Fish CKD
DAHL PLUMBING
1000 Siler Park Lane
Santa Fe, NM 87501

Peter G Merrill CKD
CREATIVE KITCHENS
1209 Cerrillos Road
Santa Fe, NM 87501

Joan Viele CKD
KITCHEN DIMENSIONS, INC
611 Old Santa Fe Trail
Santa Fe, NM 87501

CKD-Certified Kitchen Designer; CBD-Certified Bath Designer

NEW YORK

Albany

Clifford M Peterson CKD
122 Hackett Boulevard
Albany, NY 12209

Altamont

Geoffrey Martin CKD
Box 775
Altamont, NY 12009

Amsterdam

John J Miller CKD
996 Co Route 126
Amsterdam, NY 12010

Auburn

Robert Quigley CKD
QUIG ENTERPRISES
Mutton HIll Road
Route 6
Auburn, NY 13021

Baldwin

Howard Gainsburg CKD
BALDWIN SALES
CORPORATION
795 Merrick Road
Baldwin, NY 11510

Beacon

Patrick R. Walsh CKD
13 Helen Ct.
Beacon, NY 12508

Bellmore

Joyce R Wyman CKD
WYMAN BUILDING
INDUSTRIES INC
1786 Newbirdge Road
Bellmore, NY 11710

Central Valley

David A Forshay CKD
P.O. Box 55
Central Valley, NY 10917

Clarence

Douglas Holt CKD
D.W. HOLT AND COMPANY
5195 Donnington Road
Clarence, NY 14031

Philip J Zakrzewski CKD
D.W. HOLT AND COMPANY
5195 Donnington Road
Clarence, NY 14031

Cortland

David G. Brown CKD
BUILDERS BEST HOME
IMPROVEMENTCENTER
3798 Luker Road
Cortland, NY 13045

E Meadow

Stephen H. Rubenstein CKD
KITCHENS UNIQUE BY DELF
482 E Meadow Avenue
E Meadow, NY 11554

E Northport

Meri Pontell CKD
UNITED CERAMIC TILE CORP
1992 E Jericho Tpke
E Northport, NY 11731

East Hampton

Robert P Wolfram CKD
RIVERHEAD BUILDING SUPPLY
"CABINET SHOWCASE"
15 Railroad Avenue
East Hampton, NY 11937

Elmira

Tammy J Gray CKD
KITCHEN & BATH GALLERY
1055 Walnut Street
Elmira, NY 14905

Fredonia

Stanley C Gilfoyle CKD
PATTON ELECTRIC
10378 Bennett Road
Fredonia, NY 14063

Fulton

Jill M Stoughton CKD
JOICE & BURCH INC
2 West First Street
Fulton, NY 13069

Garden City

Monte G Berkoff CKD
HERBERT P BISULK INC
KITCHEN OF DISTINCTION BY
MONTE
295 Nassau Boulevard S
Garden City, NY 11530

Goshen

Joseph M Matta CKD
MASTERWORK KITCHENS
134 West Main Street
Goshen, NY 10924

Great Neck

Chris Mustello CKD
D & M KITCHENS INC
400 Great Neck Road
Great Neck, NY 11021

Henrietta

Deborah M Ellison CKD
CAVES CABINETRY CONCEPTS
3081 E Henrietta Road
PO Box 268
Henrietta, NY 14467

Howard Beach

Michael K Storms CKD
28 Russel Street
Howard Beach, NY 11414

Huntington

Merle Cook CKD
MERLE COOK INTERIORS
289 West Neck Road
Huntington, NY 11743

Joseph C Ferrara CKD
CUSTOM CONCEPTS INC
741 A W Jericho Turnpike
Huntington, NY 11743

Louise Ferrara CKD
CUSTOM CONCEPTS INC
741 A W Jericho Turnpike
Huntington, NY 11743

Theodore M Frank CKD
DESIGN CONCEPTS TMF, INC.
595 W Jericho Turnpike
Huntington, NY 11743-6362

Patricia A Monaghan CKD
C.H. JONES
Fine Kitchen and Bath Cabinetry
220 East Main Street
Huntington, NY 11743

Huntington Station

Frank Diliberto CKD
HUNTINGTON KITCHEN &
BATH
673 E. Jericho Turnpike
Huntington Station, NY 11746

Ithaca

Andrew M Foster CKD
216 Wood Street
Ithaca, NY 14850

Roxanne Repper Simmons CKD
CREATIVE KITCHENS BY
ROXANNE
23 Cinema Drive
Ithaca, NY 14850

Kew Gardens

Ann M Morris CKD
ANN MORRIS INTERIORS
84-50 Austin Street
Kew Gardens, NY 11415

Lake George

Delos H Dunbar CKD
DEL DUNBAR AND ASSOCIATES
Route 3, Bloody Pond Road
Box 3425
Lake George, NY 12845

Lake Placid

David W Hunter CKD
HUNTER DESIGNS INC
Cascade Road
PO Box 244
Lake Placid, NY 12946

Latham

Robert W Wiltsie CKD
HOME QUARTERS WARE-
HOUSE INC
579 Troy-Schenectady Road
Latham, NY 12110

Liverpool

Edward G Tracey CKD
MIDSTATE WHOLESALE CORP.
P.O. Box 97
Liverpool, NY 13088

Malverne

Tino Passaro CKD
176 Rider Avenue
Malverne, NY 11565

Mamaroneck

Greg W Weiss CKD
D I Y KITCHEN CENTER
300 Waverly Avenue
Mamaroneck, NY 10543

Massapequa

Jo Ann Campo CKD
KITCHENS & BATHS BY
MR. D., INC.
4163 Merrick Road
Massapequa, NY 11758

Massapequa Park

Michael Graziano CKD
ALADDIN REMODELERS INC
5020 Sunrise Highway
Massapequa Park, NY 11762

William T Luther CKD
NO QUEST INC
228 Oak Street
Massapequa Park, NY 11762

Middletown

John R Decker CKD
ROWLEY KITCHEN SALES INC
DIVISION OF ROWLEY
BUILDING PRODUCTS
87 Wisner Avenue
Middletown, NY 10940

Michael F Garr CKD
62 Mulberry Street
Middletown, NY 10940

David S McCarey CKD
531 North Street
Middletown, NY 10940

Randy B O'Kane CKD
ROWLEY KITCHEN SALES INC
DIVISION OF ROWLEY
BUILDING PRODUCTS
87 Wisner Avenue
Middletown, NY 10940

Mineola

Felix M Frank CKD
ALAMODE KITCHEN CENTER
INC
206 E Jericho Turnpike
Mineola, NY 11501

Montgomery

Jack L Clouser CKD
CLOUSER SALES INC
136 Bracken Road
Montgomery, NY 12549

N Syracuse

Ruth M Lenweaver CKD
COUNTRY GENTLEMEN
KITCHEN & BATH CENTER
720 N Main Street
N Syracuse, NY 13212

Nassau

Robert W Baum CKD
MILLBROOK KITCHENS INC
Box 21 Route 20
Nassau, NY 12123

New Hartford

Carmen R Spetts CKD
CHARM KITCHENS BY SPETTS
100 Seneca Turnpike Route 5
New Hartford, NY 13413

New Hyde Park

James T Kelly CKD
KITCHEN DESIGNS BY
KEN KELLY INC
2115 Hillside Avenue
New Hyde Park, NY 11040

Kenneth G. Kelly CKD
KITCHEN DESIGNS BY
KEN KELLY INC
2115 Hillside Avenue
New Hyde Park, NY 11040

New York

Charles F Adams CKD
SAINT CHARLES KITCHENS OF
NEW YORK
150 E 58th Street
New York, NY 10155

Debrah M. Adams CKD
ALLMILMO NEW YORK INC
150 E 58th Street
8th Floor
New York, NY 10155

Edward C Collier CKD
SAINT CHARLES OF
NEW YORK INC
150 E 58th Street
New York, NY 10155

Neal W Deleo CKD
T O GRONLUND COMPANY INC
200 Lexington Avenue
New York, NY 10016

Theodore B Gronlund CKD
T O GRONLUND COMPANY INC
200 Lexington Avenue
New York, NY 10016

Florence Perchuk CKD
DESIGNS BY FLORENCE
PERCHUK
127 E 59th Street
Suite 201
New York, NY 10022

Mark L Rosenhaus CKD
321 Avenue C
New York, NY 10009

Michelle F Salinard CKD
MICHELLE SALINARD
DESIGNS
60 Gramercy Park N
New York, NY 10010

Lee P Wanaselja CKD
ALLMILMO NEW YORK INC
150 E 58th Street
8th Floor
New York, NY 10155

North Tarrytown

Joseph S Bracchitta CKD
SLEEPY HOLLOW CUSTOM
KITCHENS
42 River Street
North Tarrytown, NY 10591

Northport

Susan Serra CKD
SUSAN SERRA ASSOCIATES INC
15 Starlit Drive
Northport, NY 11768

Norwich

Michael C Stockin CKD
KUNTRISET KITCHENS
RD 2 Box 254
Norwich, NY 13815

Orangeburg

Laurie M Kaplan CKD
Blue Hill Commons - #15L
Orangeburg, NY 10962

Peekskill

Thomas Baione CKD
ULTIMATE DESIGN CONCEPTS
3795 Crompton Road
Peekskill, NY 10566

Plattsburgh

John P. Mayette CKD
LEE APPLIANCE COMPANY
Route 3
Plattsburgh, NY 12901

Pomona

Kingsley N Van Wagner CKD
SOUTH MOUNTAIN
WOODWORKING CORP.
161 Camp Hill Road
Pomona, NY 10970

Potsdam

Durward L Thomas CKD
D.L. THOMAS KITCHENS &
BATHS
Outer Market Street
PO Box 5046
Potsdam, NY 13676

Poughkeepsie

Dorretta Waite CKD
37 Circular Road
Poughkeepsie, NY 12601

Remsenburg

Mary Jane Longo CKD
BALDWIN SALES
CORPORATION
White Birch Lane
Remsenburg, NY 11960

Rhinebeck

George V Krom CKD
WILLIAMS LUMBER & HOME
CENTER
Route 9 N
P.O. BOX 31
Rhinebeck, NY 12572

Riverhead

Joseph S Dowling CKD
RIVERHEAD BUILDING SUPPLY
1295 Pulaski Street
Riverhead, NY 11901

Frank Tommasini CKD
KITCHEN AND BATH INC
1179 Route 58
Riverhead, NY 11901

Rochester

Samuel L Ayres CKD
122 Saranac Street
Rochester, NY 14621

Thomas W. Hussar CKD
HUSSAR KITCHENS
66 Moorland Road
Rochester, NY 14612

Roslyn

Don Boico CKD
CLASSIC KITCHEN & BATH
CENTER LTD
1062 Northern Boulevard
Roslyn, NY 11576

Poul Brandt CKD
BRANDT WOODCRAFT OF
ROSLYN INC
18 Lumber Road
Roslyn, NY 11576

Sag Harbor

Anthony J De Pinto CKD
KITCHEN FAIR INC
79 Bay View Drive
Sag Harbor, NY 11963

Saint James

Richard J Rizzi CKD
NORTH COUNTRY KITCHEN
AND BATH INC
437 N. Country Road
Route 25A
Saint James, NY 11780

Saratoga Spring

Patricia French CKD
KITCHEN DIMENSIONS
2 Franklin Square
Saratoga Spring, NY 12866

Saugerties

Richard M Downey CKD
HICKORY MEADOWS CUSTOM
KITCHENS
83 Lauren Tice Road
Saugerties, NY 12477

Schenectady

Lawrence H Miller CKD
AMERICAN WOODWORK THE
YANKEE BUILDER INC
1702 Chrisler Avenue
Schenectady, NY 12303

Scotia

John M Torelli CKD
CENTRAL PLUMBING &
HEATING SUPPLY COMPANY
INC.
141 Freemans Bridge Road
Scotia, NY 12302

Seneca Falls

Jane Ann Ross CKD
2919 Route 89
Seneca Falls, NY 13148

South Salem

Naomi Dempsey CKD
Ring's End of Lewisburo
386 Smith Ridge Road., Rt. 123
South Salem, NY 10509

St James

Thomas Vecchio CKD
6 White Avenue
St James, NY 11780

Staten Island

Thomas J Kehoe CKD
99 Acorn Street
Staten Island, NY 10306

Syracuse

Ann M Davis CKD
CASE INDUSTRIAL SUPPLY
COMPANY
PO Box 1032
109 Wyoming Street
Syracuse, NY 13201

Anthony P Iannettone CKD
CASE INDUSTRAIL SUPPLY
COMPANY
601 W Fayette Street
PO Box 1032
Syracuse, NY 13204

Paul D Thompson CKD
CASE SUPPLY
601 West Fayette Street
P.O. Box 1032
Syracuse, NY 13201

Vestal

Arthur H Andrews CKD
4508 West Marshall Drive
Vestal, NY 13850

Victor

Sue Smith CKD
DAVID K SMITH ASSOCIATES
INC/NORTH EAST MARKETING
6796 Spring Creek Drive
Victor, NY 14564

Wappinger Falls

Frank O Algier CKD
EMPIRE KITCHEN &
WOODWORKING INC
862 South Road
Wappinger Falls, NY 12590

William H Algier CKD
862 South Road
Wappinger Falls, NY 12590

Randall A Thoms CKD
EMPIRE KITCHENS &
WOODWORKING INC
862 South Road
Wappinger Falls, NY 12590

Warwick

Marisa Panecki CKD
BATHS KITCHENS & BEYOND
13 Main Street
Warwick, NY 10990

Water Mill

Betsy Meyer CKD
BETSY MEYER ASSOCIATES, INC.
Box 1179
Water Mill, NY 11976

Watkins Glen

Karen R Edwards CKD
KAREN EDWARDS DESIGN
PO Box 230
Watkins Glen, NY 14891

Webster

Jacob J Horvat CKD
CHASE PITKIN HOME & GARDEN
900 Holt Road
Webster, NY 14580

West Babylon

Barbara Brunette CKD
27 Farber Drive
West Babylon, NY 11704

Yonkers

Daniel J Lowen CKD
QUAKER MAID KITCHENS OF
NEW YORK INC
1880 Central Park Avenue
Yonkers, NY 10710

Yorktown Heights

Frank R Massello CKD
HOME DESIGNS INC
BUILDING & DESIGN CENTER
3333 Crompound Road
Yorktown Heights, NY 10598

NORTH CAROLINA

Apex

Thomas A Cambron CKD
BEAUTIFUL BATHZ INC
229 North Salem Street
Apex, NC 27502

Asheville

Rex E Ballard CKD
BALLARD APPLIANCE & CABI-
NET COMPANY
1238 Hendersonville Road
Asheville, NC 28803

Robert R Cooper CKD
COOPER HOUSE INC
479 Hendersonville Road
Asheville, NC 28803

Chapel Hill

Janine Jordan CKD
J J INTERIORS,KITCHEN &
BATH DESIGN BY JANINE
PO Box 5130
Chapel Hill, NC 27514

Charlotte

Elizabeth Brunnemer CKD
KITCHEN LOGIC
809 South Edgehill Road
Charlotte, NC 28207

Al Herold CKD
AMERICAN KITCHENS INC
CUSTOM CABINETRY &
DESIGN
1123 McAlway Road
Charlotte, NC 28211

Wyona Fay Hodges CKD
DEALER SUPPLY
2032 Gateway Blvd.
Charlotte, NC 28208

David A Prunczik CKD
INTEXT DIVERSIFIED SALES
INC
11660 Old Surry Lane
Charlotte, NC 28277

Margaret Vogt CKD
SIEMATIC
1419 East Blvd Suite I
Charlotte, NC 28203

Durham

Mary Liebhold CKD
THE KITCHEN SPECIALIST
3407 University Dr.
Durham, NC 27707-2629

Leon E Meyers CKD
LE MEYERS BUILDERS
4528 Hillsborough Road
Durham, NC 27705

Fayetteville

Sherman E Holt CKD
KITCHEN KREATIONS
165 Westwood Shopping Center
Fayetteville, NC 28304

Greensboro

Robert T Koehler CKD
OLD MASTER KITCHENS
1401 W Lee Street
PO Drawer 5486
Greensboro, NC 27403

Joseph P Mitchell CKD
OLD MASTER KITCHENS
1401 W Lee Street
PO Drawer 5486
Greensboro, NC 27403

Jon H White CKD
J & J CUSTOM KITCHENS
3404 A W Wendover Avenue
Greensboro, NC 27407

Greenville

Marjorie Inman CKD
210 Fairlane
Greenville, NC 27834

Kitty Hawk

Susan M. Kirkwood CKD
COZY HOME CUSTOM
CABINETS INC
DBA/ COZY KITCHENS
921 Kitty Hawk Road
Kitty Hawk, NC 27949

Raleigh

William J. Camp CKD
TRIANGLE DESIGN KITCHENS
INC
5216 Holly Ridge Drive
Raleigh, NC 27612

Max G Isley CKD
HAMPTON KITCHENS OF
RALEIGH
5024 Old Wake Forest Road
Raleigh, NC 27609

Waxhaw

Arthur L Wyse CKD
7123 McCaslan Lane
Waxhaw, NC 28173

Wilmington

Theodore L Frank CKD
SUPERIOR MILLWORK INC
615 S Seventeenth Street
Wilmington, NC 28401

Cynthia Sporre CKD
KITCHEN BLUEPRINTS INC
4231 D Princess Place Drive
Wilmington, NC 28405

Winston Salem

Bruce R. Holliday CKD
THE CABINET STUDIO
1033 Burke Street
Winston Salem, NC 27101-2412

Sandra B Jones CKD
THE CABINET STUDIO
1033 Burke Street
Winston Salem, NC 27101-2412

NORTH DAKOTA

Bismarck

Ryland J Larimer CKD
DESIGNS ON BROADWAY
2304 East Broadway
Bismarck, ND 58501

Fargo

William Tweten CKD
THE FLOOR TO CEILING STORE
360 36th Street S
Fargo, ND 58103

OHIO

Bedford Heights

Darlene J. Hackbart-Somrak CKD
SOMRAK KITCHENS INC
26201 Richmond Road
Bedford Heights, OH 44146

Canfield

Gene Renz CKD
KITCHEN & BATH WORLD
Route 224
Canfield, OH 44406

Chagrin Falls

Alan G Luzius CKD
STONE GATE ASSOCIATES
7181 Chagrin Road, Ste. 200
Chagrin Falls, OH 44023

Chesterland

Drenda L Lunka CKD
THE WOODLAND DESIGN STU-
DIO INC
8389 Mayfield Road
Chesterland, OH 44026

Cincinnati

Sandra L Daye CKD
HOWARD'S SUPPLY
4200 Plainville Road
PO Box 27165
Cincinnati, OH 45227

Terry L Hupp CKD
DAYTON SHOWCASE
COMPANY CINCINNATI
11402 Reading Road
Cincinnati, OH 45241

Scott A Kronour CKD
DAYTON SHOWCASE
COMPANY CINCINNATI
11402 Reading Road
Cincinnati, OH 45241

Patti A Lawson CKD
DAYTON SHOWCASE
COMPANY CINCINNATI
11402 Reading Road
Cincinnati, OH 45241

John F Rugh CKD
VALLEY FLOOR &
BATH/KITCHEN SPECIAISTS
401 W Wyoming Avenue
Cincinnati, OH 45215

Patrick H Ryan CKD
KITCHEN CONCEPTS INC
6026 Ridge Ave.
Cincinnati, OH 45213

Cleveland Heights

Arthur C Zigerelli CKD
NATIONAL KITCHENS &
BATHS
3962 Mayfield Road
Cleveland Heights, OH 44121

Columbus

David L Fox CKD
DAVE FOX CONTRACTING INC
1151 Bethel Road
Columbus, OH 43220

Michael A Noble CKD
LONDON KITCHENS
1065 Dublin Road
Columbus, OH 43215

Frank W Wright CKD
WRIGHT CONSTRUCTION
COMPANY
3001 Asbury Drive
Columbus, OH 43221

Dayton

Caroline C. Adamo CKD
SUPPLY ONE CORPORATION
210 Wayne Avenue
PO Box 636
Dayton, OH 45401

Luellen A Brown CKD
DAYTON SHOWCASE
COMPANY
2601 W Dorothy Lane
Dayton, OH 45439

William Paul Kemna CKD
DAYTON SHOWCASE
COMPANY
2601 W Dorothy Lane
Dayton, OH 45439

Dublin

Joseph F Fehn CKD
113 Longview Drive
Dublin, OH 43017

East Liverpool

Cynthia K Birch CKD
BIRCH SUPPLY COMPANY INC
16477 Saint Clair Avenue
PO Box 9000
East Liverpool, OH 43920

Fairfield

Connie M Hampton CKD
HAMPTON CUSTOM KITCHENS
4838 Dixie Highway
Fairfield, OH 45014

Findlay

Bryan V Cavins CKD
CAVINS KITCHEN VILLAGE
215 South Main Street
Findlay, OH 45840

Fort Recovery

Daniel J Schoen CKD
HOME IDEA CENTER INC
111 W Butler Street
Fort Recovery, OH 45846

Maineville

Susan E Chenault CKD
CABINETRY CONCEPTS &
DESIGNS INC
7487 Kings Mills Road
Maineville, OH 45039-9786

Mayfield Heights

Alan Abrams CKD
CABINET EN-COUNTERS INC
6868 Wildwood Trail
Mayfield Heights, OH 44143

Mayfield Hts.

Lisa M Perfetto CKD
BUILDER'S WORLD, INC.
5885 Mayfield Rd.
Mayfield Hts., OH 44124

New Knoxville

Evelyn A Flock CKD
HOGE LUMBER COMPANY
PO Box 159
New Knoxville, OH 45871

Oliver H Hoge CKD
HOGE LUMBER COMPANY
PO Box 159
New Knoxville, OH 45871

North Olmsted

Fred M Helyes CKD
BUILDER'S WORLD INC
14355 Lorain Road
North Olmsted, OH 44070

Parma Heights

Samuel L Besunder CKD
LITT'S PLUMBING KITCHEN &
BATH GALLERY
6510 Pearl Road
Parma Heights, OH 44130

Plain City

Katherine Miller CKD
THE MILLER CABINET
COMPANY INC
6217 Converse Huff Road
Plain City, OH 43064

Rocky River

Christi S Bechtold CKD
CLEVELAND TILE & CABINET
COMPANY
19560 Center Ridge Road
Rocky River, OH 44116

Steubenville

Ronald A Johnson CKD
C B JOHNSON INC
621 Market Street
Steubenville, OH 43952

Ricky T Patterson CKD
C B JOHNSON INC
621 Market Street
Steubenville, OH 43952

Toledo

Richard A Mc Kimmy CKD
RAM MARKETING
5250 Renwyck Drive #C
Toledo, OH 43615

Jerome B Waxman CKD
KITCHENS BY JEROME INC
2138 N Reynolds Road
Toledo, OH 43615

Twinsburg

Royce V Hogue CKD
2226 Heather Lane
Twinsburg, OH 44087

Willoughby Hill

John F Hall CKD
STUDIO FARALLI
2804 S O M Center
Willoughby Hill, OH 44094

Youngstown

Ralph M Watson CKD
DON WALTER KITCHEN
DISTR INC
260 Victoria Road
Youngstown, OH 44515

OKLAHOMA

Duncan

Billie Latham CKD
LATHAM'S INCORPORATION
702 Willow
Duncan, OK 73533

Oklahoma City

Karen K Black-Roberts CKD
KITCHEN SHOWCASE &
DESIGN CENTER
2761 North Country Club Drive
Oklahoma City, OK 73116

Donald G Dobbs CKD
KITCHEN SHOWCASE &
DESIGN CENTER
2761 North Country Club Drive
Oklahoma City, OK 73116

Zachary Taylor CKD
CLASSIC KITCHENS INC
548 E Memorial
Oklahoma City, OK 73114

Stephen Wells CKD
CLASSIC KITCHENS INC
548 E Memorial
Oklahoma City, OK 73114

Tulsa

Ralph Lackner CKD
JAY RAMBO COMPANY
8401 E 41st
Tulsa, OK 74145

Beverly Nicely CKD
BEVERLY K. NICELY
8219 South College Avenue
Tulsa, OK 74137

OREGON

Aloha

Ralph D Baumgardner CKD
BAUMGARDNER
CONSTRUCTION
18110 SW Madeline
Aloha, OR 97007

Beaverton

Michelle Heaton Rolens CKD
NEIL KELLY DESIGNERS
REMODELERS
8101 S W Nimbus
Beaverton, OR 97005

Martha Kerr CKD
NEIL KELLY DESIGNERS
REMODELERS
8101 S W Nimbus
Beaverton, OR 97005

Amalia B Parecki CKD
10645 SW 135th Avenue
Beaverton, OR 97005

Karen Richmond CKD
NEIL KELLY DESIGNERS
REMODELERS
8101 S W Nimbus
Beaverton, OR 97005

Brookings

Hazel L. Wilcher CKD
INSIDE IMAGE
PO Box 895
Brookings, OR 97415

Corvallis

Brian P Egan CKD
CORVALLIS CUSTOM
KITCHENS
459 SW Madison
Corvallis, OR 97333

Hillsboro

Loren E Wright CKD
DIAMOND CABINETS
PO Box 547
Hillsboro, OR 97123

Oregon City

J Lynette Black CKD
LR BLACK DESIGNS
16299 South Eaden Road
Oregon City, OR 97045

Portland

Faye Cornelison CKD
NEIL KELLY DESIGNERS
REMODELERS
804 N Alberta
Portland, OR 97217

Kathleen F Donohue CKD
NEIL KELLY DESIGNERS
REMODELERS
804 N. Alberta St.
Portland, OR 97217

Victor R Greb CKD
J GREB & SON INC
5027 N E 42nd Avenue
Portland, OR 97218

Richard C Hallberg CKD
HALLBERG REMODELING
COMPANY
1710 N E 82nd Avenue
Portland, OR 97220

Mert Meeker CKD
NEIL KELLY DESIGNERS
804 North Alberta
Portland, OR 97217

Rhonda A Reed CKD
NEIL KELLY DESIGNERS
REMODELERS
804 N Alberta
Portland, OR 97217

Julia B Spence CKD
NEIL KELLY DESIGNERS
REMODELERS
804 N Alberta
Portland, OR 97217

Kenneth P Stanley CKD
NEIL KELLY DESIGNERS
REMODELERS
804 N Alberta
Portland, OR 97217

Salem

Richard L Pizzuti CKD
SCHULER CORPORATION
560 21st Stree S.E.
Salem, OR 97309

Tigard

Bob Cone CKD
TOTAL BUILDING PRODUCTS
INC
PO Box 23337
Tigard, OR 97223

Wendi Conover Hawley CKD
HAWLEY CONSTRUCTION
14790 S W 79th Ave
Tigard, OR 97224

PENNSYLVANIA

Adamstown

Irvin L Martin CKD
MARTIN CUSTOM KITCHENS
Box 567
Adamstown, PA 19501

Aliquippa

Richard Lucci CKD
303 Baker Drive
Aliquippa, PA 15001

Allentown

Russell W Platek CKD
KITCHENS BY DESIGN
1802 Allen St.
Allentown, PA 18104

Lynn E. Salash CKD
KITCHENS BY WIELAND INC
4210 Tilghman Street
Allentown, PA 18104

Robert L Wieland CKD
KITCHENS BY WIELAND INC
4210 Tilghman Street
Allentown, PA 18104

Altoona

William Sandrus CKD
YOUR BUILDING CENTER INC
2607 Beale Avenue
Altoona, PA 16603

Annville

Lee E. Bachman CKD
RM KITCHENS, INC
RD 1, Box 212-D
Annville, PA 17003

Robert H. Hossler CKD
RM KITCHENS, INC
RD 1 Box 212-D
Annville, PA 17003

Bala Cynwyd

Ted R Moser CKD
MOSER CORPORATION
129 Montgomery Avenue
Bala Cynwyd, PA 19004-2828

Andrew R Stein CKD
DESIGN MANIFEST INC
PO Box 254
5 Maple Avenue
Bala Cynwyd, PA 19004

Bethayres

Arthur A Perry CKD
A A PERRY & SONS INC
2528 Huntington Pike
Bethayres, PA 19006

Bethlehem

Daniel J Lenner CKD
MORRIS BLACK & SON
984 Marcon Boulevard
Bethlehem, PA 18001

Dennis R Oberholtzer CKD
OBERHOLTZER KITCHENS
77 W Broad St #1
Bethlehem, PA 18018-5722

Bird In Hand

Sylvia Terry CKD
TERRY'S ENTERPRISES
PO Box 279
Bird In Hand, PA 17505

Bristol

Joseph D'Emidio CKD
CAMEO KITCHENS
212 East Circle
Bristol, PA 19007

Canonsburg

Tracy M Johnston Caruso CKD
ROBERT JOHNSTON KITCHEN
& BATH
156 Morganza Road
Canonsburg, PA 15317

Carlisle

Harold B Gibb CKD
CARLISLE KITCHEN CENTER
1034 Harrisburg Pike
Carlisle, PA 17013

James F Goodman CKD
154 West Middlesex Drive
Carlisle, PA 17013

Carnegie

Steven M Erenrich CKD
PATETE KITCHEN & BATH
1105 Washington Avenue
Box 669
Carnegie, PA 15106

Chambersburg

Glenn Wadel CKD
WADEL'S KITCHEN CENTER
1882 Wayne Road
Chambersburg, PA 17201

Chester

James H Stefanide CKD
CHESTER WOODWORKING INC
812 R Crum Creek Road
Chester, PA 19013

John C Stefanide CKD
CHESTER WOODWORKING INC
503 E 7th Street
Chester, PA 19013

Clarks Summit

A Wayne Trivelpiece CKD
ABINGTON CABINETRY
PO Box 101
Clarks Summit, PA 18411

Corry

Raymond A Anderson CKD
THE KITCHEN VILLAGE
12275 Route 6
Corry, PA 16407

Downingtown

Thomas A Ingle CKD
MIDLANTIC KITCHENS
P.O. Box 309
Downingtown, PA 19335

Duncansville

Jill S Shaw CKD
SHOWCASE KITCHENS INC
921 3rd Avenue
PO Box 713
Duncansville, PA 16635

Dunmore

Fred N Schank CKD
P.O. Box 617
Dunmore, PA 18512-0617

Ellwood City

Joseph R DeOtto CKD
DESIGNING INTERIORS
KITCHEN & BATH STUDIO
502 Glen Ave
PO Box 810
Ellwood City, PA 16117

Erie

Paulette H Hessinger CKD
DESIGNS FOR LIVING
3244 Willis Street
Erie, PA 16506

James J Robertson CKD
ROBERTSON KITCHENS INC
2630 West 12th Street
PO Box 8112
Erie, PA 16505

Fredonia

Richard L Buchanan CKD
BUCHANAN KITCHEN & BATH
BOUTIQUE
109 Second Street
Fredonia, PA 16124

Glenmoore

Sheila P Gallagher CKD
AMARANTH INTERIORS, INC.
89 Indian Springs Drive, West
Glenmoore, PA 19343

Goodville

Barbara R Herr CKD
RUTT CUSTOM CABINETRY
1564 Main Street
PO Box 129
Goodville, PA 17528

Ruth Ann Stoltzfus CKD
RUTT CUSTOM CABINETRY
PO Box 129
1564 Main Street
Goodville, PA 17528

Greensburg

Wendell Peterson CKD
PETERSON'S CUSTOM
KITCHEN BATH BOUTIQUE
503 New Alexandria Road
Greensburg, PA 15601

Havertown

Merrie A Fredericks CKD
DESIGN CONCEPTS PLUS INC
18 East Eagle Road
Havertown, PA 19083

Hellam

Jesse Dagenhardt CKD
SUSQUEHANNA CABINETS INC
361 West Market Street
Hellam, PA 17406

Hermitage

C.H. "Bud" Miller CKD
BUD MILLER'S KITCHEN &
BATH DIST INC
3005 E State Street
Hermitage, PA 16148

Huntingdon

Richard J Endres CKD
ENDRES WOOD-PLASTICS INC
760 Bryant Street
Huntingdon, PA 16652

Johnstown

Carmen A Formica CKD
PATSY FORMICA'S KITCHEN
DESIGNS
734 Railroad Street
Johnstown, PA 15901

Kennett Square

Douglas R Small CKD
KITCHENS ETC WATERBURG
714 E Baltimore Pike
Kennett Square, PA 19350

Kimberton

Carol Crane CKD
Box 126
Kimberton, PA 19442

Kreamer

Joseph E. Callender CKD
BATTRAM COMPANY INC
Route 522
Box 582
Kreamer, PA 17833

Lawrence J Tempel CKD
WOOD-MODE INC
#1 Second Street
Kreamer, PA 17833

Lancaster

Michael R Bowers CKD
51 Deer Ford Drive
Lancaster, PA 17601

Stephen M Brown CKD
107 Spring Ridge Ct
Lancaster, PA 17601-1759

Elizabeth Dodds CKD
154 Knollwood Drive
Lancaster, PA 17601-5661

Mark F Ehrsam CKD
22 Parkside Avenue
Lancaster, PA 17602-3244

Kathy Schmick CKD
BRUBAKER KITCHENS INC
1121 Manheim Pike
Lancaster, PA 17601

Landisville

Valerie Kissinger CKD
405 Holly Ann Drive
Landisville, PA 17538

Langhorne

Gary R Ulanowski CKD
SIEMATIC CORPORATION
886 Town Center Drive
Langhorne, PA 19047

Lehigh Valley

Donna Lyman Snover CKD
MORRIS BLACK & SONS INC
984 Marcon Boulevard
PO Box 20570
Lehigh Valley, PA 18002

Lemoyne

Roland Stock CKD
ED LANK KITCHENS INC
313 Market Street
Lemoyne, PA 17043

Ligonier

James A Frey CKD
1261 Griffith Road
Ligonier, PA 15658

Littestown

Ronald Hedges CKD
KITCHENS BY TED RON
1480 White Hall Road
Littestown, PA 17340

Malvern

Alex R Hall CKD
THE CREATIVE NOOK INC
MALVERN DESIGN CENTER
203 E King Street
Malvern, PA 19355

Mechanicsburg

Sharon Brown CKD
UNUSUAL SOLUTIONS
502-4 E. Elmwood Avenue
Mechanicsburg, PA 17055-4214

Roy McLain CKD
ADVANCED KITCHENS &
BATHS
5222 E Trindle Road
Mechanicsburg, PA 17055

John A Petrie CKD
MOTHER HUBBARD'S
KITCHEN CENTER
5309 E Trindle Road
Mechanicsburg, PA 17055

Les Petrie CKD
MOTHER HUBBARD'S
KITCHEN CENTER
5309 E Trindle Road
Mechanicsburg, PA 17055

Mohnton

Jerry Long CKD
157 Boulder Hill Road
Mohnton, PA 19540

Monaca

Guy D Lucci CKD
LUCCI KITCHEN CENTER INC.
1271 North Brodhead Road
Monaca, PA 15061

Richard J Lucci CKD
LUCCI KITCHEN CENTER INC.
1271 North Brodhead Road
Monaca, PA 15061

Monroeville

Ida M McConnell CKD
860 MacBeth Dr., Apt. #21
Monroeville, PA 15146

Frank A Sevcik CKD
CONCEPTS II BY C & C
BUILDERS SUPPLY
4526 Broadway Boulevard
Haymaker Village
Monroeville, PA 15146

Mt. Joy

Sandra L Steiner Houck CKD
313 S. Market Avenue
Mt. Joy, PA 17552

Munhall

M Paul Cook CKD
OMNI RENOVATION
114 East James Street
Munhall, PA 15120

N Huntingdon

Dennis S Caruso CKD
CARUSO CABINET
MANUFACTURING INC
10809 Route 30
N Huntingdon, PA 15642

Narvon

Michael E White CKD
CONESTOGA VALLEY CUS-
TOM KITCHENS INC
2042 Turkey Hill Road
Narvon, PA 17555

New Holland

Ellen M Cheever CKD
HERITAGE CUSTOM KITCHENS
215 Diller Avenue
New Holland, PA 17557

Joe D'Aloisio CKD
HERITAGE CUSTOM KITCHENS
215 Diller Avenue
New Holland, PA 17557

Wilmer Esbenshade CKD
HERITAGE CUSTOM KITCHENS
215 Diller Avenue
New Holland, PA 17557

Garry L Lydic CKD
HERITAGE CUSTOM KITCHENS
215 Diller Avenue
New Holland, PA 17557

Elmer R Martin CKD
HERITAGE CUSTOM KITCHENS
215 Diller Avenue
New Holland, PA 17557

New Kensington

Frank R Boyd CKD
STYLE-RITE KITCHENS
1306 Greensburg Road
New Kensington, PA 15068

Newmanstown

Dolores J Hurst CKD
KOUNTRY KRAFT KITCHENS
RD #2 Box 570
Newmanstown, PA 17073

Old Forge

Arlene Hawker CKD
MARIOTTI BUILDING PROD-
UCTS
1 Louis Industrial Drive
Old Forge, PA 18518

Philadelphia

Marc W Block CKD
MORTON BLOCK ASSOCIATES
DIVISION OF DESIGN KITCHEN
INC
2400 Market Street N S
Suite 205
Philadelphia, PA 19103

Morton M Block CKD
MORTON BLOCK ASSOCIATES
DIVISION OF DESIGN KITCHEN
INC
2400 Market Street N S
Suite 205
Philadelphia, PA 19103

Bud Fleet CKD
COGAN & GORDON INC
2200 N American Street
Philadelphia, PA 19133

Sidney Haifetz CKD
COGAN & GORDON INC
2200 N American Street
Philadelphia, PA 19133

James S Kaufer CKD
810 Susquehanna Road
Philadelphia, PA 19111

Samuel Kulla CKD
KULLA KITCHENS
7800 Rockwell Avenue
Philadelphia, PA 19111

Linda Pera CKD
TODAYS KITCHENS AND
BATHS
8830 Frankford Avenue
Philadelphia, PA 19136

Harvey Steiner CKD
KULLA KITCHENS
7800 Rockwell Avenue
Philadelphia, PA 19111

Pittsburgh

Oscar R Acevedo CKD
MASTERKRAFT KUSTOM
KITCHEN DIVISON OF
MASTERKRAFT CONSTRUCTION
100 A Street
Pittsburgh, PA 15235

Thomas E Backus CKD
BACKUS CABINET COMPANY
307 Timber Ct.
Pittsburgh, PA 15238-2437

Charles Buchsbaum CKD
MASTERKRAFT KUSTOM
KITCHEN DIVISON OF
MASTERKRAFT CONSTRUCTION
100 A Street
Pittsburgh, PA 15235

Robert P Butt CKD
KITCHEN WORKS INC
1002 Greentree Road
Pittsburgh, PA 15220

Alan Ehrensberger CKD
EXCEL KITCHEN CENTER
1800 Fifth Avenue
Pittsburgh, PA 15219

Raymond C Franke CKD
FRANKE'S CABINET SHOP
641 Butler Street
Pittsburgh, PA 15223

William J Glivic CKD
BILL GLIVIC KITCHENS
3845 Willow Avenue
Pittsburgh, PA 15234

August R Lang CKD
EXCEL KITCHEN CENTER
1800 Fifth Avenue
Pittsburgh, PA 15219

Victoria Liscinsky CKD
EXCEL KITCHEN CENTER
1800 Fifth Avenue
Pittsburgh, PA 15219

Chester Mandella CKD
800 E. Monroe Circle
Pittsburgh, PA 15229

W Kenneth Niklaus CKD
7005 Ohio River Blvd
Pittsburgh, PA 15202

Kenneth R Rogg CKD
STRAIGHT LINE CABINET
CORP
101 S Main Street
PO Box 7883
Pittsburgh, PA 15215

Joseph H Safyan CKD
2118 Beechwood Blvd.
Pittsburgh, PA 15217

CKD-Certified Kitchen Designer; CBD-Certified Bath Designer

Abe Sambol CKD
STEIN'S CUSTOM KITCHENS
& BATHS
3559 Bigelow Boulevard
Pittsburgh, PA 15213

Jerry A Sambol CKD
STEIN'S CUSTOM KITCHENS
& BATHS
3559 Bigelow Boulevard
Pittsburgh, PA 15213

William E Takacs CKD
MASTERKRAFT KUSTOM
KITCHENS
100 A Street
Pittsburgh, PA 15235

Thomas D Trzcinski CKD
KITCHEN & BATH CONCEPTS
OF PITTSBURGH
7901 Perry Highway N
Pittsburgh, PA 15237

Regina A Williams CKD
W T LEGGETT COMPANY INC
40th & Butler Streets
Pittsburgh, PA 15201

Red Lion

Stephen Keener CKD
KEENER KITCHEN
MANUFACTURING COMPANY
560 W Boundary Avenue
Red Lion, PA 17356

Shaefferstown
Joe F Edwards CKD
Box 302
Red Lion, PA 17088

Sharon

Barry E Kirby CKD
267 Case Avenue
Sharon, PA 16146

Slippery Rock

Julia A Lorentz CKD
306 Normal Avenue
Slippery Rock, PA 16057

Somerset

Marshall A Trigona CKD
KITCHEN DESIGNS BY MARSH
1024 N Center Avenue
Somerset, PA 15501

Southampton

Alvin J Moeser CKD
SUBURBAN KITCHEN COMPANY
650 Street Road
Southampton, PA 18966

Springfield

Edmund W McGarvey CKD
MCGARVEY & COMPANY
512 Baltimore Pike
Springfield, PA 19064

Tarrs

Jospeh M Barrick CKD
C & C LUMBER BUILDING
SUPPLIESSUPERMARKET
PO Box C
Off Route 31
Tarrs, PA 15688

Telford

Gretchen L Edwards CKD
INTERIOR DESIGN SERVICES
276 N Third Street
Telford, PA 18969

Upper Darby

Charles J Walsh CKD
WALL & WALSH INC
8320 W Chester Pike
Upper Darby, PA 19082

W Chester

Conrad E Muhly III CKD
MUHLY KBA INC
7 N Five Point Road
W Chester, PA 19380

Warren

Susan A Reinke CKD
SUE REINKE KITCHENS &
BATHS
514 Beech Street
Warren, PA 16365

Washington Cross

Lynne D Mercantane CKD
KITCHEN CONCEPTS OF
WASHINGTON
1107 Taylorville Road
Washington Cross, PA 18977

Washington Crossing

Michael A. Mercatante CKD
KITCHEN CONCEPTS OF
WASHINGTON
1107 Taylorsville Road
Washington Crossing, PA 18977

West Chester

H Richard Hurlbrink CKD
HURLBRINK KITCHENS
701 Old Westtown Road
West Chester, PA 19382

West Lawn

Daphne D Frownfelter CKD
2333 Highland Street
West Lawn, PA 19609

West Reading

Jerald G Heffleger CKD
J & J HEFFLEGER CUSTOM
KITCHENS INC
600 Penn Avenue
West Reading, PA 19611

White Oak

Ronald R Massung CKD
KITCHEN DESIGNS OF
PITTSBURGH
3026 Stewartsville Road
White Oak, PA 15131-2704

Wind Gap

Larry C Hess CKD
KEEPSAKE KITCHENS INC
122 N Broadway
Wind Gap, PA 18091

Ruth S. Schoeneberger CKD
KEEPSAKE KITCHENS INC
122 N Broadway
Wind Gap, PA 18091

York

Thomas D Kling CKD
THOMAS D KLING INC
2474 N George Street
York, PA 17402

RHODE ISLAND

Barrington

Robert W Chew CKD
BARRINGTON KITCHENS INC
496 Maple Avenue
Barrington, RI 02806

East Greenwich

Gene M Parise CKD
M & J KITCHEN SUPPLY CO. INC.
461 Main Street
East Greenwich, RI 02818

Greenville

Richard L Manocchia CKD
14 Kimberly Ann Drive
Greenville, RI 02828

Johnston

Ronald J Finacchiaro CKD
CREATIVE KITCHENS INC
2656 Hartford Avenue
Johnston, RI 02919

Middletown

Manuel E Mendes CKD
DISTINCTIVE DESIGNS
153 Meadow Lane
Middletown, RI 02840

Warwick

Frank J Ferendo CKD
FERENDO KITCHEN & BATH
SUPPLYCOMPANY
110 Jefferson Boulevard
Warwick, RI 02888-3854

Wyoming

Elisabeth McHenry CKD
P.O. Box 67
Wyoming, RI 02898

SOUTH CAROLINA

Beaufort

Raymond C Clausen CKD
77 Dolphin Point Drive
Beaufort, SC 29902

Charleston

Ann E. Chittum CKD
SIGNATURE KITCHENS &
BATHS OF CHARLESTON INC.
1926 Savannah Highway
Charleston, SC 29407

James R McLain CKD
SIGNATURE KITCHENS &
BATHS OF CHARLESTON INC.
1926 Savannah Highway
Charleston, SC 29407

Linda McLain CKD
SIGNATURE KITCHENS &
BATHS OF CHARLESTON INC.
1926 Savannah Highway
Charleston, SC 29407

Claudette Pimm CKD
SIGNATURE KITCHENS &
BATHS OF CHARLESTON INC.
1926 Savannah Highway
Charleston, SC 29407

Allison Ryan CKD
SOUTHEAST KITCHEN
FURNITURE
480 E Bay Street
Charleston, SC 29403

Columbia

W Hampton Oliver CKD
HAMPTON KITCHENS
2205 N Main Street
PO Box 7273
Columbia, SC 29201

Florence

Agnes H Willcox CKD
KITCHENS!
1811 Cherokee Road
Florence, SC29501

Hilton Head Island

Norman H Armstrong CKD
CRYSTAL CABINETS OF
HILTON HEAD
Northside Park
PO Box 21993
Hilton Head Island, SC 29925

Mount Pleasant

Duval B Acker CKD
KITCHENS BY DESIGN INC
Fairmount Shopping Center
1035 Johnnie Dodds Boulevard
Mount Pleasant, SC 29464-6154

Malcolm C Bogan CKD
KITCHEN CONCEPTS INC
1260 Ben Sawyer Boulevard
Mount Pleasant, SC 29464

Myrtle Beach

Lloyd C Rice CKD
KREATIVE KITCHENS INC
4923 Highway 17 South Bypass
Myrtle Beach, SC 29577

Piedmont

Steven T Maddox CKD
1226 Westwood Drive
Piedmont, SC 29637-8408

Rock Hill

William T McPherson CKD
1226 Twin Lakes Road
Rock Hill, SC 29730

Summerville

Jill Absher Patton CKD
CREATIVE KITCHEN DESIGNS
622 Old Trolley Road
Suite 126
Summerville, SC 29485

SOUTH DAKOTA

Rapid City

Darlene L Davignon CKD
DARLENE'S KITCHEN
GALLERY
3275 Pioneer Drive
Rapid City, SD 57701

TENNESSEE

Chattanooga

Charles Kessel CKD
KESSEL AND ASSOCIATES
100 Woodland Avenue
PO Box 4647
Chattanooga, TN 37405

Kathy D Massey CKD
FERGUSON ENTERPRISES
4100 Amnicola Highway
Chattanooga, TN 37406

Katharine G Powell CKD
POWELL & ASSOCIATES
1124 Dana Avenue
Chattanooga, TN 37443

Crossville

Lorie K. Smith CKD
VILLAGE KITCHENS BATHS
INTERIORS
407 W Avenue S
PO Box 1396
Crossville, TN 38557

Germantown

Georgia L Kilpatrick CKD
KITCHENS BY KILPATRICK
2025 Woodgate Drive
Germantown, TN 38138

Knoxville

David H Newton CKD
DAVID NEWTON AND
ASSOCIATES
6903 Sheffield Drive
PO Box 51706
Knoxville, TN 37950

Mitchell L Robinson CKD
MODERN SUPPLY COMPANY
525 Lovell Road
PO Box 22997
Knoxville, TN 37932

Memphis

Charles A Tracy CKD
231 Lorece Lane
Memphis, TN 38117

Nashville

Terry A. Burton CKD
HERMITAGE ELECTRIC
SUPPLY CORP.
DBA/HERMITAGE KITCHEN &
BATH GALLERY
531 Lafayette Street
Nashville, TN 37203

Vicki T Edwards CKD
5141 Hilson Road
Nashville, TN 37211

Gerald Fleischer CKD
HERMITAGE ELECTRIC
SUPPLY CORP.
DBA/HERMITAGE KITCHEN &
BATH GALLERY
531 Lafayette Street
Nashville, TN 37203

James R Henry CKD
HENRY KITCHENS & BATH
306-8th Avenue S
Nashville, TN 37203-3744

Tony Herrera CKD
TONY HERRERA'S KITCHEN
AND BATH CONCEPTS, INC.
3307 Charlotte Avenue
Nashville, TN 37209

Caroline A Weismueller CKD
HENRY KITCHENS & BATH INC
306 8th Avenue S
Nashville, TN 37203

TEXAS

Amarillo

Julie K Sutton CKD
TSTI
PO Box 11038
Amarillo, TX 79111

Arlington

Georgie L Skover CKD
KITCHENS BY DESIGN INC
2905 Greenbrook Drive
Arlington, TX 76016

Mark A Wessels CKD
HERMAN JOHNS & ASSOCIATES
652 Lincoln Square
Arlington, TX 76011

Austin

R Kent Barnes CKD
KITCHENS INC.
2712 Bee Cave Road
Suite 122
Austin, TX 78746

Bryan

Alice F. Price CKD
PRICE DESIGN STUDIO
4110 Laura Lane
Bryan, TX 77803

Carrollton

William Bradford CKD
THE HOME DEPOT
1441 W Trinity Mills Road
Carrollton, TX

Corpus Christi

Edward L Bokamper CKD
4918 Calallen Drive
Corpus Christi, TX 78410

Lynna L Simpson CKD
LL SIMPSON SELECT DESIGNS
1822 Holly Road
110
Corpus Christi, TX 78417

Dallas

Denise M Dick CKD
HOME DEPOT
Dallas, TX 75244

Sharon L. Flatley CKD
INTERIOR ELEGANCE
13650 Spring Grove Avenue
Dallas, TX 75240

Brad Pence CKD
BRAD PENCE COMPANY
4508 Lovers Lane
Dallas, TX 75225

Carl G Soderstrom CKD
KITCHEN DESIGNS INC
14227 Inwood Road
Dallas, TX 75244

Fort Worth

Walter J Chambless CKD
KITCHEN PLANNERS
3300 Airport Freeway
Fort Worth, TX 76111-3930

Sally Pack CKD
GEARHEART CONSTRUCTION
COMPANY INC
3221 Hulen
Suite E
Fort Worth, TX 76107

Beth M Stribling CKD
KITCHEN PLANNERS
3300 Airport Freeway
Fort Worth, TX 76111

James L. West CKD
DESIGNS BY DROSTE
4818 Camp Bowie Boulevard
Fort Worth, TX 76133

Garland

Richard D Walden CKD
SEARS HOME IMPROVEMENT
4118 Miller Park Dr.
Garland, TX 75042

Houston

Cherye Burns CKD
KITCHEN & BATH
CONCEPTS/SIEMATIC
5120 Woodway, #119
Houston, TX 77056

Dorel P Carter CKD
DOREL CARTER KITCHEN
DESIGNS
3655 Wickersham
Houston, TX 77027

Virgil L Church CKD
FURROWS BUILDING
MATERIALS
14051 Bellaire Boulevard
Houston, TX 77083

Kirk Craig CKD
KIRK CRAIG COMPANY
2431 Sunset Boulevard
Houston, TX 77005

Robert E Crellen CKD
CABINETS & DESIGNS INC
3637 W Alabama #380
Houston, TX 77027

Theodore B Currier CKD
KITCHEN & BATH CONCEPTS
2627 Westheimer
Houston, TX 77098

Aurolyn M Devine CKD
332 Litchfield Ln.
Houston, TX 77024

Richard S. Difazzio CKD
KITCHENS OF HOUSTON INC
12819 Tennis Drive
Houston, TX 77099-2927

W Donald Fleck CKD
FLECKWAY HOUSEWORKS INC
612 W Bough Lane
Houston, TX 77024

Gay Fly CKD
GAY FLY DESIGNER
KITCHENS & BATHS
4200 Westheimer
Suite 120
Houston, TX 77027

Margaret J Granc CKD
12850 Whittington Drive
Houston, TX 77077

Collin T Hahn CKD
HALLMARK FASHION
KITCHENS INC
3413 E Greenridge Drive
Houston, TX 77057

Ines Lombardi CKD
KITCHEN & BATH CONCEPTS
2627 Westheimer
Houston, TX 77098

Micqui L McGowen CKD
KITCHEN & BATH CONCEPTS
2627 Westheimer
Houston, TX 77098

Peggy McGowen CKD
KITCHEN & BATH CONCEPTS
2627 Westheimer
Houston, TX 77098

Jane S Putman CKD
ACCENT CABINET INC
1953 Ridgemore
Houston, TX 77055

Zena C Wong CKD
URBAN KITCHEN & BATHS INC
3601 W Alabama 380
Houston, TX 77027

Humble

Jacqueline Mead CKD
MEAD ASSOCIATES
203 N Houston Avenue
Humble, TX 77338

New Braunfels

Linda Whitworth CKD
KITCHEN DESIGN
318 Clemens Avenue
New Braunfels, TX 78130

San Antonio

Diana H Hawkins CKD
CABINETRY DESIGNS
10618 Gulfdale Street
San Antonio, TX 78216

Robert G Thompson CKD
KITCHENS BY BELDON
BELDON ROOF REMOD
5039 W Avenue
San Antonio, TX 78249

Spring

Laura H Scott CKD
SCOTT DESIGNS
6503 Inway Drive
Spring, TX 77389

The Woodlands

Catherine Locetta CKD
15 Raintree Crossing
The Woodlands, TX 77381

UTAH

Salt Lake City

Larry A Carlson CKD
CARLSON KITCHENS
2261 East 3300 South
Salt Lake City, UT 84109

Sandra M Fassett CKD
KITCHENETICS
396 E Woodlake Avenue #396
Salt Lake City, UT 84107

Gary N Sheffield CKD
HALLMARK CABINETS
6205 Rodeo Lane
Salt Lake City, UT 84121

West Jordon

Howard H Tullis CKD
WASATCH CABINET &
FURNITURE COMPANY INC
3412 West 8600 South
West Jordon, UT 84084

VERMONT

Barre

Richard E Fournier CKD
INTERIOR CREATIONS
92 S Main Street
Barre, VT 05641

Roy D. Kilburn CKD
CONCEPTS IN CABINETRY
393 N Main Street
Barre, VT 05641

Ludlow

Lois A Harken CKD
10 Bridge Street
Ludlow, VT 05149

North Clarendon

George A Ritter CKD
KNIGHT CABINETS
Route 7 B
RR 1 Box 231 1
North Clarendon, VT 05759

VIRGINIA

Alexandria

Alvin E Dennis CKD
ALMAR DESIGNER KITCHENS
5930 Tilbury Road
Alexandria, VA 22310

Annandale

Peggy Fisher CKD
FISHER BUILDING & DESIGN
4108 Chatelain Road
Annandale, VA 22003

Arlington

Dee David CKD
KITCHEN CLASSICS BY CUS-
TOM CRAFTERS
6023 Wilson Boulevard
Arlington, VA 22205

Louis E Schucker CKD
VOELL CUSTOM KITCHENS
4788 Lee Highway
Arlington, VA 22207

Ann R Stokes CKD
1901 N Harvard Street
Arlington, VA 22201

Fairfax

Robert W Clements CKD
9405 Larkdale Terrace
Fairfax, VA 22039

Lisa M Foley CKD
3929 Tedrich Boulevard
Fairfax, VA 22031

Ann Unal CKD
3205 Wynford Drive
Fairfax, VA 22031

Carolyn K Willingham CKD
COURTHOUSE KITCHENS &
BATHS DKB INC
9974 Main Street
Fairfax, VA 22031

Falls Church

Nabil A Abdul-Aal CKD
F A MCGONEGAL
1061 West Broad Street
Falls Church, VA 22046

Nick Bianco CKD
3304 Brandy Court
Falls Church, VA 22042

Louise E Perini CKD
PWEINI DESIGNS KITCHENS
3008 Cedarwood Lane
Falls Church, VA 22042

Inga K Willner CKD
F A MCGONEGAL
1061 W Broad Street
Falls Church, VA 22046

Herndon

Judith R Bracht CKD
2707 Viking Drive
Herndon, VA 22071

McLean

Donna Dougherty CKD
1215 Old Stable Road
McLean, VA 22102

Diane H Small CKD
DIANE H SMALL INC
1969 Massachusetts Avenue
McLean, VA 22101

John C Spitz CKD
DIANE H SMALL INC
1969 Massachusetts Avenue
McLean, VA 22101

Newington

Patrick H Padberg CKD
PMC CONTRACTORS INC
7913 Kincannon Place
PO Box 1415
Newington, VA 22122

Newport News

Don R Ligon CKD
VIRGINIA MAID KITCHENS INC
737 Blue Crab Road
Suite 1A
Newport News, VA 23606

Hugh H Parker CKD
VIRGINIA MAID KITCHEN INC
737 Blue Crab Road
Newport News, VA 23606

Marguerite Staley CKD
29 Westover Rd.
Newport News, VA 23601

John D Willis CKD
SEARS-TIDEWATER DISTRICT
SALES OFFIC
PO Box 5500
Newport News, VA 23605

Norfolk

Ann Hux Johnson CKD
421 Peace Haven Drive
Norfolk, VA 23502

Petersburg

David J Roane CKD
DAVE'S CABINET SHOP INC
22504 Cox Road
Petersburg, VA 23803

Richmond

Morris E Gunn CKD
CUSTOM KITCHENS INC
6412 Horsepen Road
Richmond, VA 23226

Deborah Harry Sneeder CKD
CUSTOM KITCHENS INC
6412 Horsepen Road
Richmond, VA 23226

David A Hendrick CKD
CUSTOM KITCHENS INC
6412 Horsepen Road
Richmond, VA 23226

Richard F Hendrick CKD
CUSTOM KITCHENS INC
6412 Horsepen Road
Richmond, VA 23226

Dayton Leadbetter CKD
KITCHEN ART INC
2337 West Broad Street
Richmond, VA 23220

Douglas B Leake CKD
CUSTOM KITCHENS INC
6412 Horsepen Road
Richmond, VA 23226

Rena Lipkind CKD
RICHMOND CABINETS INC
6305 Hull Street Road
Richmond, VA 23224

W Brian Pilgrim CKD
CUSTOM KITCHENS INC
6412 Horsepen Road
Richmond, VA 23226

Katheryn W Robertson CKD
KATHERYN ROBERTSON &
ASSOCIATES, LTD
CUSTOM KITCHENS & BATHS
2225 Hanover Ave
Richmond, VA 23220-3401

Marie S Schlief CKD
CUSTOM KITCHENS INC
6412 Horsepen Road
Richmond, VA 23226

Roanoke

Brownie S Carter CKD
CARTER'S CABINET SHOP OF
ROANOKE INC
2132 Shenandoah Valley Avenue NE
Roanoke, VA 24022

Springfield

Richard H Coyle CKD
COYLE & KLEPPINGER INC
7420 Fullerton Road
Suite 102
Springfield, VA 22153

Sterling

Becky Phillips CKD
HARVEY'S KITCHENS & BATHS
22560 Glenn Drive
Suite 115
Sterling, VA 20164

Lisa M Robey CKD
HARVEY'S KITCHENS & BATHS
22560 Glenn Drive
Suite 115
Sterling, VA 20164

Vienna

Janis M Magnuson CKD
394 Park Street, S.E.
Vienna, VA 22180

Virginia Beach

Ray Boggs CKD
4903 Ocean View Avenue
Virginia Beach, VA 23455

Benton Flax CKD
2827 Charlemagne Drive
Virginia Beach, VA 23451

Clark J Janssen CKD
PRESTIGE KITCHENS OF
VIRGINIA INC
2798 "A" Dean Drive
Virginia Beach, VA 23452

Michael L Lawless CKD
GREENWICH'S KITCHEN
CENTER
5789 Arrowhead Drive
Virginia Beach, VA 23462

Winchester

Connie Edwards CKD
AMERICAN WOODMARK
CORPORATION
3102 Shawnee Drive
Winchester, VA 22601

WASHINGTON

Bellevue

Lynn Lloyd Conner CKD
LYNN LLOYD CONNER
KITCHEN & BATH DESIGN
12819 SE 38th Street
Suite 394
Bellevue, WA 98006

Kathrine E. Finley CKD
CABINETS BY SCHNELL
1034-116th Ave N.E
Bellevue, WA 98005

Jitka M Urban CKD
DESIGNS BY JITKA
14590 NE 35TH STREET #D204
Bellevue, WA 98007

Bellingham

Monica P Oppel CKD
CABINET & FLOORING
SUPPLY INC.
5980 Meridian
Bellingham, WA 98226

Bothell

Martha Kildall CKD
MARTHA KILDALL DESIGNS
7338 NE 140th Place
Bothell, WA 98011

Robert D Mac Donald CKD
21809-35th Avenue, S.E.
Bothell, WA 98021

Bremerton

Ronald L Edmondson CKD
BRISTOL KITCHENS
5889 State Highway 303 N E Suite 101
PO Box 2279
Bremerton, WA 98310-0302

Kirkland

Jerald D Hilzinger CKD
KITCHENS FOR DREAM HOMES
12024 Juanita Drive N E
Kirkland, WA 98034

Lynnwood

Lynn D Sheffield CKD
SHEFFIELD DESIGNS
4320 196th Street SW B750
Lynnwood, WA 98036

Moxee

Kelly S Petty CKD
P.O. Box 308
Moxee, WA 98936

Oak Harbor

Barbara R Hertzler CKD
FINE WOOD CABINETS
645 W Oak Street
Oak Harbor, WA 98277

Puyallu

Margaret R Stephens CKD
6714 92nd Street, East
Puyallu, WA 98371

Redmond

Delores L Hyden CKD
SHOWPLACE KITCHENS &
BATHS
8710 Willows Road
PO Box 955
Redmond, WA 98073

Bruce R Kelleran CKD
SHOWPLACE KITCHENS &
BATH
8710 Willows Road
PO Box 955
Redmond, WA 98073

Diana K Valentine CKD
SHOWPLACE KITCHENS &
BATH
8710 Willows Road
PO Box 955
Redmond, WA 98073

Seattle

Charles S Blodgett CKD
KITCHEN & BATHS BY
BLODGETT
4515 44th S W
Seattle, WA 98116

John W Brush CKD
KITCHEN DISTRIBUTING
COMPANY
2246 1st Ave. S.
Seattle, WA 98134

Judith E Gates CKD
2300 Elliott Ave #510
Seattle, WA 98121

Jackie A Goedde CKD
J G DESIGN
3338 Hunter Boulevard S
Seattle, WA 98144

Kimithy H Nagel CKD
KITCHENS & BATHS BY
BLODGETT
4515 44th Avenue SW
Seattle, WA 98116

Douglas C. Reymore CKD
CASCADE CONSTRUCTION INC
4801 Aurora Avenue N
Seattle, WA 98103

Barbara S Wahler CKD
ROY RICKETTS INC
3417 1st Avenue S
Seattle, WA 98134

Shelton

Donna L Brinati CKD
LUMBERMEN'S
1st & Pine
PO Box 700
Shelton, WA 98584

Spokane

David Schenk CKD
EAGLE HARDWARE & GARDEN
N 6902 Division
Spokane, WA 99208

Tacoma

Mary Ellen Jackl CKD
ABC CABINET
3865 Center Street
Tacoma, WA 98409

Jere L Johnson CKD
CUSTOM DESIGN CABINETRY
INC
701 72nd Street E
Tacoma, WA 98404

R. Kim Kramer CKD
OLD TIME WOODWORK INC
2105 S "C" Street
Tacoma, WA 98402

Robert J Miller CKD
CUSTOM DESIGN CABINETRY
INC
701 72nd Street E
Tacoma, WA 98404

Michael K. Northover CKD
OLD TIME WOODWORK INC
2105 S "C" Street
Tacoma, WA 98402

Douglas E Off CKD
DOUGLAS DESIGN CABINET &
REMODELING COMPANY
4804 Center Street
Tacoma, WA 98409

Shiela M Off CKD
DOUGLAS DESIGN CABINET &
REMODELING COMPANY
4804 Center Street
Tacoma, WA 98409

Tukwila

Kenneth E Peterson CKD
CLASSIC AMERICAN HOMES
6000 Southcenter Boulevard
Suite 70
Tukwila, WA 98188

Wenatchee

Jan L Harmon CKD
CONCEPTS KITCHEN & BATH
DESIGNS
14 Kittitas Street
Wenatchee, WA 98801

Woodinville

Ane K. Brusendorff CKD
J. STEPHEN PETERSON AIA &
ASSOC.
18209 NE 175th Place
Woodinville, WA 98072

Jeannine T Laitres CKD
CONTAINER HOME SUPPLY INC
7627 W Bostain Road
Woodinville, WA 98072

Susan M Larsen CKD
BOLIG KITCHEN STUDIO
13110 N E 177th Place
Woodinville, WA 98072

Catherine Larsen-Jepson CKD
BOLIG KITCHEN STUDIO
13110 N E 177th Place
Woodinville, WA 98072

WEST VIRGINIAV

Barboursville

Beverly Renee Pauken CKD
WOODY'S KITCHENS BATHS
DECORATE STUDIO
5841 Davis Creek Road
Barboursville, WV 25504

Charleston

James D Maddox CKD
3612-A Staunton Ave., S.E.
Charleston, WV 25304

Huntington

Robert E Stepp CKD
CREATIVE KITCHENS INC
1242 Fifth Avenue
PO Box 2786
Huntington, WV 25701

Morgantown

J Keith Carr CKD
GENERAL GLASS COMPANY INC
PO Box 618
Morgantown, WV 26507

Prosperity

Lesia B Campbell CKD
INTERIOR CONCEPTS
PO Box 8
Prosperity, WV 25909

S Charleston

Charles A Arey CKD
WARDEN'S INC
5621 MacCorkle Avenue S W
S Charleston, WV 25309

Vienna

Wayne L Brown CKD
MOORE'S
1502 Grand Central Avenue
Vienna, WV 26105

Williamson

Jennifer A Rowe CKD
310 Slater Street
Williamson, WV 25661

WISCONSIN

Appleton

Beth A Marsden CKD
2700 W. College Ave. #108
Appleton, WI 54914

Dennis L Schwersenka CKD
KUSTOM KITCHENS & BATHS
741 W College Avenue
Appleton, WI 54914

Blue Mounds

Debra Doud CKD
2566 Highway 7
Blue Mounds, WI 53517

Brookfield

Kathie Kroening CKD
THE KITCHEN CENTER
4060 N 128th Street
Brookfield, WI 53005

Germantown

Leonard E Riebau CKD
RIEBAU'S CABINETS LTD
W186 N11676 Morse Drive
PO Box 458
Germantown, WI 53022

Greendale

Timothy J Benkowski CKD
CUSTOM DESIGN ASSOCIATES
INC
5101 West Loomis Road
Greendale, WI 53129

JanesvilleMarie E Garot CKD
CABINET COUNTRY LTD
1515 Newport Avenue
Greendale, WI 53545

Kohler

Peter D Cameron CKD
KOHLER COMPANY
444 Highland Drive
Kohler, WI 53044

James R Dase CKD
KOHLER COMPANY
444 Highland Drive
MSN 002
Kohler, WI 53044

Madison

Steven P Emerson CKD
KITCHENS OF DISTINCTION
6719 Seybold Road
Madison, WI 53719

Barbara Englund CKD
WISCONSIN SUPPLY
CORPORATION
6800 Gisholt Drive
PO Box 8124
Madison, WI 53708

James R Luck CKD
J R LUCK & ASSOCIATES INC
1118 Saybrook Road
Madison, WI 53711

Marshfield

David A Burger CKD
THE CABINET STUDIO
107 North Central Avenue
Marshfield, WI 54449

Milwaukee

Cheryl A Bokelman CKD
BLAU BATH AND KITCHEN INC
1320 S. 108th Street
Milwaukee, WI 53214-2437

William M Feradi CKD
BUILT-IN KITCHENS INC
7289 N Teutonia Avenue
Milwaukee, WI 53209

Cindi M. Matt CKD
BLAU BATH AND KITCHEN INC
1320 S. 108th Street
Milwaukee, WI 53214-2437

New Berlin

Brent Baker CKD
MORGAN-WIGHTMAN
16405 W. Lincoln Avenue
New Berlin, WI 53151

Oshkosh

John A Lieske CKD
KITCHEN SPECIALISTS LTD
2721 Oregon Street
Oshkosh, WI 54901

Portage

Bernard J Lessner CKD
North 4544 Allan Road
Portage, WI 53901-9651

Rhinelander

Larry E Frasier CKD
FRASIER'S SHOWPLACE
INTERIORS INC
130 North Brown Street
Rhinelander, WI 54501

Schofield

Thomas E De Lisle CKD
DE LISLE COMPANY INC
624 Moreland Avenue
Schofield, WI 54476

Sheboygan Falls

Barbara J Blasing CKD
RICHARDSON LUMBER
904 Monroe
Box 904
Sheboygan Falls, WI 53085

Ivan Nagode CKD
RICHARDSON LUMBER
904 Monroe
Box 904
Sheboygan Falls, WI 53085

Stevens Point

Ronald J Nowacki CKD
2309 Division Street
Stevens Point, WI 54481

Sun Prairie

Harry Guy Haynes CKD
1811 Oakland Avenue
Sun Prairie, WI 53590

Wautoma

Steven A Weiss CKD
MID STATE SUPPLY COMPANY
Highway 21 E
PO Box 510
Wautoma, WI 54982

Wauwatosa

Jane A. Altenbach CKD
2729 Mayfair Court
Wauwatosa, WI 53222

Eugene L Delfosse CKD
KITCHEN DESIGN STUDIO INC
8932 W North Avenue
Wauwatosa, WI 53226

Wisconsin Rapids

Debra DeCaluwe CKD
QUALITY KITCHENS
1211 8th Street S
Wisconsin Rapids, WI 54494

CKD-Certified Kitchen Designer; CBD-Certified Bath Designer